W9-BUL-938

Beyond Appearance

Beyond Appearance

A New Look at Adolescent Girls

EDITED BY

Norine G. Johnson
Michael C. Roberts
Judith Worell

AMERICAN PSYCHOLOGICAL ASSOCIATION
WASHINGTON, DC

Published by
American Psychological Association
750 First Street, NE
Washington, DC 20002

Copies may be ordered from
APA Order Department
P.O. Box 92984
Washington, DC 20090-2984

In the U.K., Europe, Africa, and the Middle East, copies may be ordered from
American Psychological Association
3 Henrietta Street
Covent Garden, London
WC2E 8LU England

Typeset in Goudy by EPS Group Inc., Easton, MD

Printer: Braun-Brumfield, Inc., Ann Arbor, MI
Cover Designer: Berg Design, Albany, NY
Technical/Production Editor: Anne Woodworth

Library of Congress Cataloging-in-Publication Data
Beyond appearance : a new look at adolescent girls / edited by Norine
    G. Johnson, Michael C. Roberts, Judith Worell.—1st ed.
        p.   cm.
    Includes bibliographical references.
    ISBN 1-55798-582-0
    1. Teenage girls—United States—Social conditions.   2. Teenage
girls—United States—Psychology.   I. Johnson, Norine G.
II. Roberts, Michael C.   III. Worell, Judith, 1928–   .
HQ798.B43   1999
305.235—dc21   99-14475
                                                                        CIP

British Library Cataloguing-in-Publication Data
A CIP record is available from the British Library.

Printed in the United States of America
First Edition

CONTENTS

v

97086

CONTRIBUTORS

Bonnie Barber received her PhD in developmental psychology from the University of Michigan. She is currently an associate professor in family studies at the University of Arizona, Tucson. Her interests range from adolescent development to divorce.

Susan A. Basow is Charles A. Dana professor and head of the Psychology Department at Lafayette College in Easton, Pennsylvania. A licensed psychologist, she is the author of many chapters, articles, and books on women and gender.

Geraldine Kearse Brookins is a vice president of programs at the W. K. Kellogg Foundation. She is currently on leave from the University of Minnesota as the Gamble-Skogmo professor of child welfare and youth policy. Her research interests include relationships between African American girls and women.

Lyn Mikel Brown is associate professor and chair of the Education and Human Development Program at Colby College. She is the author of *Meeting at the Crossroads: Women's Psychology and Girls Development* (with Carol Gilligan) and *Raising Their Voices: The Politics of Girls' Anger.*

Fary M. Cachelin is assistant professor of psychology at California State University, Los Angeles. Her research includes the study of disordered eating in women of minority groups, particularly Asian American and Hispanic women. She received her doctorate in psychology from Harvard University in 1996.

Joanne E. Callan is a professor at the California School of Professional Psychology and a clinical professor at the University of California, San

Diego. She maintains an independent practice and was formerly the director of the Education Directorate of the American Psychological Association (APA).

Dorothy W. Cantor is a psychologist in private practice in Westfield, New Jersey and a former president of the APA. She is also the author of *Divorced Parents and Their Children, The Psychology of Today's Woman*, and *Women in Power: The Secrets of Leadership*.

Jessica Henderson Daniel is assistant professor of psychology in the Department of Psychiatry at Harvard Medical School. She is codirector of training in psychology at the Children's Hospital and the Judge Baker Children's Center, and an associate director of leadership education in adolescent health in the Division of Adolescent Medicine at Children's Hospital.

Elizabeth Debold is a consultant and director of evaluation for the Ms. Foundation for Women's Healthy Girls/Healthy Women Collaborative Fund. She is author of *Mother–Daughter Revolution: From Betrayal to Power* (with Marie Wilson and Idelisse Malave). One of her interests includes developing participatory research practices.

Cynthia de las Fuentes is an assistant professor of psychology at Our Lady of the Lake University in San Antonio, Texas. Her research, publications, and presentations have focused primarily on multiculturalism and diversity, especially Latinos and Latinas, women and gender, and ethics.

Florence L. Denmark is Robert Scott Pace distinguished professor and chair of the Psychology Department at Pace University in New York and a former president of the APA. She has received numerous national awards for her scholarship.

Denise M. DeZolt is a member of the school psychology faculty in the Department of Educational and Counseling Psychology at the University at Albany, State University of New York. She is committed to issues of social justice. She is also a partner, a mother, and a storyteller.

Denise M. Dougherty is Child Health Coordinator for the Agency for Health Care Policy and Research, Office of Policy Analysis of the U.S. Department of Health and Human Services. She wrote the departmental report to Congress, *Pediatric Outcomes Research*.

Julia L. Duff is currently a research scientist at the American Institutes for Research in Palo Alto, California. Her research interests include adolescent friendship, gender identities, and the role of friendship in moral life.

Jacquelynne S. Eccles is the Wilber McKeachie collegiate professor of psychology, women's studies and education; a research scientist at the Institute for Social Research, University of Michigan; and the chair of the combined program in education and psychology at the University of Michigan. She has extensive research experience.

Michele Harway is director of research and core faculty at the Phillips Graduate Institute. She is also a consulting faculty member at the Fielding Institute and maintains a part-time private practice in which she specializes in working with trauma survivors.

Mary Henning-Stout is a professor in the counseling psychology program at Lewis and Clark College in Portland, Oregon, where she coordinates the graduate program in school psychology and directs the Girls' Leadership Center; she is also a mother, a feminist, an activist, and an observer.

Norine G. Johnson is an independent practitioner and clinical assistant professor at Boston University Medical School. She is coeditor with Judith Worell of the book *Shaping the Future of Feminist Psychology: Education, Research, and Practice* and is cochair with Karen Zager of APA's Presidential Task Force on Adolescent Girls.

Deborah Jozefowicz is an advanced graduate student in the joint program in social work and psychology at the University of Michigan. Her interests include gendered development, high school dropouts, and prevention/intervention programs.

Marsha Liss has a PhD in developmental psychology (State University of New York at Stony Brook) and a JD (University of California, Los Angeles). She is an attorney in the Child Exploitation and Obscenity Section of the Criminal Division of the U.S. Department of Justice.

Oksana Malenchuk, senior research associate at the Institute for Social Research, received both her BA and PhD (social psychology) degrees at the University of Michigan. Her major interests are in social identity and self-esteem.

Bonnie Y. Ohye is clinical associate in the Department of Psychiatry, Massachusetts General Hospital and clinical instructor in psychiatry (psychology), Harvard Medical School.

Michael C. Roberts is professor and director of the Clinical Child Psychology Program at the University of Kansas. His previous books include *Handbook of Clinical Child Psychology, Handbook of Pediatric Psychology*, and *Managing Managed Care*.

Lisa R. Rubin is a doctoral student in clinical psychology at Arizona State University whose interests include girls' and women's body image and feminist identity development. She previously worked as a research assistant at Columbia University.

Ruth H. Striegel-Moore is professor and chair of psychology at Wesleyan University. She has published extensively on the etiology, treatment, and prevention of eating disorders. Her current research focuses on risk factors for binge eating disorder in African American and White adolescent girls and young women.

Deborah L. Tolman is senior research scientist and director of the adolescent sexuality project at the Center for Research on Women, Wellesley College. Her forthcoming book, *Dilemma of Desire*, explores adolescent girls' experiences with their own sexuality.

Melba J. T. Vasquez is a psychologist in independent practice in Austin, Texas. She has published in the areas of ethics, ethnic minority psychology, psychology of women, and supervision and training. She has served in various professional leadership positions, including as president of the APA Division 35, Psychology of Women.

Mina Vida is a research associate at the Institute for Social Research at the University of Michigan. She received her MA in 1975 from Washington State University. Her research interests focus on adolescent psychological issues and social supports and their effects on achievement, mental health, and career choices.

Niobe Way is assistant professor in applied psychology at New York University. She is author of *Everyday Courage: The Lives and Stories of Urban Teenagers*, and her research interests include urban adolescent development and the sociocultural and ecological factors influencing human development.

Susan Weseen is a Ms. Foundation for Women scholar on the Collaborative Fund for Healthy Girls/Healthy Women Evaluation. [The mother of a remarkable daughter] She is currently exploring women's experiences of being mothers as well as relational and programmatic contexts that support strength and resilience.

Brian L. Wilcox is a professor of psychology at the University of Nebraska and director of the Center on Children, Family, and Law. He previously served as public policy officer for the APA.

Judith Worell is a professor of child clinical psychology at the University of Kentucky. She is the author or coauthor of six prior books, a past editor of *Psychology of Women Quarterly*, and past president of APA's Division of the Psychology of Women.

FOREWORD

Approaching my term as President of the American Psychological Association (APA) in 1994, I realized that I had a wonderful opportunity to move an agenda critical to women. This was important to me not solely because of my gender, but because I was only the eighth woman in the history of the APA to hold that office, and the first in a decade! To help me formulate the agenda, I convened an unusual meeting at the annual convention, a "cabinet" meeting attended by 35 outstanding women who were currently active or who had a long history of involvement in the APA.

We spent nearly two hours together brainstorming and sharing ideas. The energy and excitement in the room were palpable. From the myriad suggestions, we were able to achieve consensus. The major issue on which we would focus was the development of girls during adolescence.

We decried the image of adolescent girls as eating disordered, pregnant, or drug abusing. We recognized that the psychological research focused on pathology. We wanted to turn the lens onto healthy girls, their strengths, and their resiliency.

Therefore, as one of my Presidential Initiatives, I formed the Task Force on Adolescent Girls: Strengths and Stresses. I asked Norine G. Johnson, who had first proposed the idea, and Karen Zager, who had also been part of the historic "cabinet" meeting, to cochair, which, thankfully, they agreed to do. Both had long histories of research and clinical practice with adolescent girls. They assembled a remarkable group of diverse, but like-minded, dedicated colleagues to serve with them. Jessica Henderson Daniel, Denise M. DeZolt, Lyn Mikel Brown, Michael C. Roberts, Alice Rubenstein, and Judith Worell have worked and continue to work to realize the mission of the Task Force:

> to integrate current knowledge regarding adolescent girls to identify strengths, challenges, and choices of adolescent girls today. The Task

Force will also identify gaps and inconsistencies in research, education, practice, and public policy. In this endeavor, the Task Force is committed to the inclusion of the voices and lives of a range of adolescent girls in terms of age, racial and ethnic diversity, socioeconomic status, geographic area, and sexual orientation. The Task Force will work to raise public and professional consciousness in regard to adolescent girls, with a particular focus on those who affect their lives, including parents, educators, health care professionals, and policymakers. Through its activities, the Task Force will chart directions into the new frontiers of the next century through a critical examination of the policy issues, current knowledge, and research approaches to understanding adolescent girls.

The Task Force had the good fortune to work with exceptional members of the APA staff—Judy Strassburger and Liz Kaplinski of the Central Office, with able help from Mayella Valero and Kelly Kennai during the first year and later by Mary Campbell of the Public Interest Directorate, whose energies and dedication contributed vastly to the work—and to have the active participation of Gary VandenBos, Susan Bedford, Julia Frank-McNeil, and Judy Nemes of APA Books. Gwen Keita and Henry Tomes have supported the efforts from the outset, and Rhea Farberman added her knowledge to facilitate involvement with the media and to increase the Task Force's sophistication in delivering their message.

This volume, *Beyond Appearance: A New Look at Adolescent Girls*, fills a vast gap in the professional literature and should be a major resource for educators and clinicians alike. Our goal is healthy girls who grow into strong, competent women, able to contribute to society in the home, the workplace, the halls of government, and everywhere that their lives take them.

Dorothy W. Cantor
Westfield, NJ

Beyond Appearance

1

PASSAGE ON THE WILD RIVER OF ADOLESCENCE: ARRIVING SAFELY

NORINE G. JOHNSON AND MICHAEL C. ROBERTS

A sixth-grade student in the Boston public schools wrote an essay about courage. Her essay is but one example among many of the strengths and diversity of adolescent girls today, twin themes of this book.

> To me, courage means standing up to someone or something you don't like. Once, I showed courage by standing up to someone. . . . I saw an old friend being humiliated. These guys were trying to make her do something that she did not want to do. One of them was going to punch her. . . . I got in the middle of it. The guy said it was none of my business. I answered back that I was making it my business. If he was going to punch my friend, he was going to have to punch me first. He put his hands up, but when he saw I didn't back off, he left us alone. . . . I learned to stand up to something I thought was wrong.

If one envisions the teen years as an adventure on an unexplored, sometimes wild, river, the boarding dock might be the safety of childhood and the landing dock the unknown region of adulthood. In between, imagine boiling rapids, pleasant calm places, narrow chutes, wide bends, swirling eddies, huge boulders, and occasional shore-lined havens that remind one of the safety of childhood. If one were a teen girl about to set out on this

3

voyage, whom and what might she take along? What would be the skills one might need? Who might be one's companions on the trip? What would be on the banks of the river as her voyage passes by? What should her community put in the water and the air through which she passes? This book is a compendium of what is known and what needs to be known about girls on their developmental journey. All too often, the passage of adolescent girls is viewed as inevitably problematic. All too often, media and societal attention have focused on how girls look or their presumed self-absorption with appearances. We intend for this book to provide a new look at adolescent girls, one that looks beyond appearances. As will become evident, we chose the title of this book with care for communicating our belief that girls' sociopsychological development is complex, rich, and enriching, meaningful at multiple levels.

A NEW LOOK AT ADOLESCENT GIRLS

This book provides a new look at adolescent girls. The sections and chapters reveal the strengths and positive assets of adolescent girls, their relationships, and their communities. We take a new look at the strengths and successes of adolescents within the context of their race, ethnicity, class, self, sexual orientation, relationships, and community. Focusing on strengths, we take a unique look at factors of resilience and propose models to support adolescent girls in their transitional development, such as the concept of "hardiness" that Elizabeth Debold and others explore in their chapter.

It is all too tempting to categorize adolescents in general, and adolescent girls in particular, by listing the multiple problems facing them and assuming that these form accurate images or themes. Although we do want to note some current-day stresses and problem behaviors, we do not want to dwell on them as if they should take precedence in a discussion of adolescent girls. This book shares the concern of Kagawa-Singer, Katz, Taylor, and Vanderryn (1996) that in the absence of knowledge, blame will be assigned to the individual and the group. Consequently, in this book, we focus on developmental trends and diversity while sharing with educators, health providers, policymakers, researchers, parents, and others who need to know what may help adolescent girls. We focus on what others have found to work, what needs to be done, and what needs to be known—instead of just what is wrong. As we go beyond the appearance of adolescent girls into their competencies, their relationships, and their communities, we see opportunities to enhance their voyage and ways to ease their passage. We see girls today creating a new and different definition of strength. As Norine G. Johnson (1995) proposed a change in women's concepts of being strong, including enacting upon their lives as well as the more traditional value of enduring, so too the vision of this book is to encourage changing perceptions and expectations of adolescent girls to include a look at their strengths, their contributions, and their actions upon their world. We see this new generation of adolescent girls as strong and as looking to find new ways to be women.

Cross-Cutting Themes

There are four significant themes in this volume that cut across all chapters. These include (a) an emphasis on considering the strengths of adolescent girls, (b) the developmental perspective, (c) a valuing of diversity, and (d) a reliance on research for guiding discussions.

Looking at Strengths

Looking at strengths rather than deficits, opportunities rather than risks, assets rather than liabilities is slowly becoming an increasing presence in the psychotherapy, education, and parenting literature. Worell and Danner (1989) stressed the cognitive competencies in adolescents by focusing their book on the decision-making aspects of adolescent development. They called for a refocusing of the psychology of adolescence to include helping students learn from positive experiences. A decade ago, researchers began to challenge the accuracy of the stereotype of an inevitable, problematic adolescence (e.g., Offer, Ostrov, Howard, & Atkinson, 1988). Martin Seligman's *The Optimistic Child* (1995) presented an approach to working with children that built on his research with depression. His basic premise was that there is an epidemic of pessimism in the United States and that the prevalence of depression today is a result of that pessimism. He then provided an approachable method for parents, educators, and therapists to help children learn an adaptive, optimistic way of thinking about themselves and about problem solving.

In the National Longitudinal Study on Adolescent Health, Resnick et al. (1997) were interested in identifying the key protective variables to adolescent health. The report of this study stated the following:

> Some children who are at high risk for health-compromising behaviors successfully negotiate adolescence, avoiding the behaviors that predispose them to negative health outcomes; while others, relatively advantaged socially and economically, sustain significant morbidity as a consequence of their behaviors. These issues of vulnerability and resilience have stimulated an interest in the identification of protective factors in the lives of young people—factors that, if present diminish the likelihood of negative health and social outcomes. (Resnick et al., 1997, p. 823)

Joy Dryfoos (1998), in her new book *Safe Passage: Making it Through Adolescence in a Risky Society*, emphasized the theme of optimism to show that teens can be helped. Her book contains innumerable examples of effective programs, and she calls for public policy to recognize and fund what is possible to assist adolescents today. The present volume emphasizes this theme of looking at strengths of adolescent girls.

Developmental Perspective

By taking a developmental perspective as one cross-cutting theme for this book, we are expressing a value that change in adolescent girls is inevitable and desirable. The age range that we defined as adolescence was from 10 to 18 years, and this book looks at the different stresses and strengths that girls might experience at the different times in development: from preadolescence to middle adolescence to late adolescence. The complex and interacting changes contain stresses and challenges to the physical and psychological functioning of each girl uniquely, but with some commonality and predictability. These physiological changes for the teen girl include the onset of menses, the ability to procreate, and the alterations in her body and are concurrent with psychological changes in perceptions of body image and development of personal identity, interest in herself as a sexual being, and an increasing ability to think abstractly and to experience increasingly complex emotions. Thus, concomitant changes include cognitive, social, and emotional development.

Valuing Diversity

Diversity is similarly a major cross-cutting theme in this book. Throughout the chapters, race, ethnicity, class, gender, sexual orientation, and physical disability are seen as necessary lenses through which one can see and understand the complexity of girls' lives. Many psychologists have espoused a similar value to Millstein and Igra (1995) where they note, "There are significant age, gender, and racial–ethnic variations in the rates and causes of morbidity and mortality during the decade we define as adolescence" (p. 52), and any research needs to value this.

The adolescent girl's race and ethnicity affect her personal identity as well as influence others' views of her and behavior toward her. Race, ethnicity, gender, class, and sexual identity all shape and define opportunities in America and need to be acknowledged for both the strengths and the stresses they bring into girls' lives. According to Brooks-Gunn and Duncan (1997), 12 to 14 million children live in families with incomes below the official poverty threshold, and too little is known of these children's lives. In a series of studies and publications, these authors have alerted us to the damages that poverty does to children and how it affects well-being in all spheres: physical and emotional health, cognitive ability, and school achievement. For example, in one study, Duncan, Yeung, Brooks-Gunn, and Smith (in press) examined the outcome of poverty across the first 15 to 18 years of life. These investigators have reported that to understand the effects of poverty and class, researchers cannot just look at the current economic class of an adolescent; the adolescent must be understood through the context of her various family conditions. Duncan et al. found that if researchers or policymakers look only at an adolescent's family income status while he or she is in high school, the important connection between early poverty and not graduating will be missed. Because of this importance to a complete understanding of adolescents, the authors examine the range of diversity issues.

Research on Adolescent Girls

Another cross-cutting theme is the importance of research in understanding adolescent girls. This book is based on a review of the research on adolescent girls, with an emphasis on the last 10 years. The research from a variety of disciplines, approaches, and orientations was reviewed, with a view to assist psychological knowledge and discussion. All the authors demonstrate how psychological research has been slow to acknowledge the effects of race, ethnicity, social class, and sexual orientation on adolescent girls. This book attempts to add more voices to gain a comprehensive overview of the issues of adolescent girls. It cautions readers of the research and literature on adolescent girls, whether it is quantitative or qualitative, peer reviewed or not, before accepting the findings, to consider the representativeness of the sample in terms of race, ethnicity, class, and gender and to look at the results and conclusions with the diversity of the sample in mind.

The research philosophy adopted by the editors of this book is consistent with the conclusions about feminist research espoused by Grossman et al. (1997): Feminist research is purposeful and has two primary tenets:

1. It illuminates the lives of women and girls, gives voice to marginalized women, develops a critique of the discipline of psychology, reflects feminist values.
2. All methods of inquiry can be used to produce feminist knowledge. (p. 89)

A complete picture of the world of adolescent girls will be a mosaic, with each piece containing some information about certain situations, using a particular research strategy. The variety of research approaches, the different pieces of glass and ceramics, will give the reader the information necessary to visualize the overall picture as well as to perceive the shading and color that enrich the mosaic. Thus, the research into the topics involving adolescent girls should be valued for the contributions of information from a variety of approaches, whether qualitative or quantitative, large-scale epidemiological or small-scale intensive interviews, applied behavior analysis or psychodynamic, N of one or surveys. Not one single approach provides the complete picture; together they form a mosaic.

STRESSES, PROBLEMS, AND RISKS OF ADOLESCENT GIRLS

Although one of the main focuses of this book is the development of strengths, resiliency, and health in adolescent girls, any discussion of teens obviously must include the stresses, problems, and risks of adolescence. The authors in this volume include the stresses and risks inherent in the topic they are discussing; each chapter varies in its emphasis and focus on the stresses.

The period of adolescence has long been characterized as a time of "storm and stress" deriving from the "Sturm und Drang" concepts of G. Stanley Hall in the early 1900s and later adapted by Anna Freud to define the emotional state of persons in this age period. These notions of turmoil in adolescence continue to dominate thinking today. The seeming difficulties of teens' tasks in adolescence are now combined with the new risks of drugs and alcohol, depression, eating disorders, sexual diseases, an economy that does not need untrained workers, families struggling, and many other stressors. Mary Pipher (1994), in the preface to her best-selling book *Reviving Ophelia*, wrote as follows:

> But girls today are much more oppressed. They are coming of age in a more dangerous, sexualized and media-saturated culture. They face incredible pressures to be beautiful and sophisticated, which in junior high means using chemicals and being sexual. As they navigate a more dangerous world, girls are less protected. (p. 12)

The researchers of the National Longitudinal Study on Adolescent Health (Resnick et al., 1997) analyzed the risk behaviors of the following: emotional distress, suicidality, violence perpetration, cigarette smoking, alcohol consumption, sex and pregnancy history, and use of marijuana. Easy access to alcohol, guns, tobacco, and illicit substances as well as having extended work hours and feeling "out of sync" with one's peers were related to adolescents' health problems.

What follows is a very brief review of some of the risks adolescent girls face and the negative effect of the stresses present in the culture in their day-to-day lives. Each risk and stress is discussed in this volume, although not each risk has its own chapter. No list of risks is exhaustive, and today's scholars have considerable overlap in their categories of risk. Joy Dryfoos (1990), in an influential book *Adolescents at Risk*, selected delinquency and acting out, substance abuse, adolescent pregnancy, school failure, and dropping out as salient categories. In a comprehensive book edited by DiClemente, Hansen, and Ponton (1996), adolescent health risk behaviors included the following: tobacco, drug, and alcohol use; disordered eating; suicide and suicidal behavior; unintentional injuries; delinquency; adolescent violence; adolescent pregnancy; sexually transmitted diseases; runaway and homeless youth; and academic underachievement and school refusal. Chronicling the risks may not tell parents and professionals how to help, but it may help arouse the resources of this country to join with these girls in their passage and it provides one context to view the strengths and resiliency girls need to thrive in today's culture.

Violence

Several chapters discuss the real presence of violence in the lives of adolescent girls, just as it is in the lives of women, and one of the purposes of this book is to inform with an intent of influencing public policy. Throughout the literature on girls, alarming statistics are often cited. Psychologists interested in public policy have been concerned about such statistics as that contained in the Commonwealth Fund Survey of 3,532 high school girls and boys in which over 20% of the girls said they had been physically or sexually abused (Commonwealth Fund, 1997). Several authors alert the reader that to know what adolescent girls must deal with today is to know and accept the reality of the extent of violence in their day-to-day lives wherever they live, whoever they are.

Suicide and Depression

Suicide and depression are attended to in this book as well as addressing methods for helping girls develop resiliency to these risks. Several of the chapters document how adolescent girls are experiencing feelings of depression at record rates. Some of the areas covered in these discussions are (a) the public's, parents', and professionals' increasing awareness of the mental health issues faced by adolescent girls; (b) research findings similar to that of the Commonwealth Fund (1997), which found that 23% of the girls in their survey of the Health of Adolescent Girls reported depressive symptoms in the previous 2 weeks and 10% reported severe depressive symptoms; and (c) ethnic differences that indicate important differences in the type and intensity of eating disorders among Hispanic, Asian American, African American, and European American girls.

Eating Disorders

There are many psychologists who look to the effects of the culture on adolescent girls' body image. Psychological researchers have concluded that media portrayals help teens define what it means to be a girl and later a woman. The way girls and women are portrayed in the media, including how they look, what they do, what motivates them, and their goals has been seen by Signorelli (1993) as having a major influence on how adolescent girls form ideas about their own lives. These and other psychologists hypothesize a strong connection between the images of girls and women portrayed by the media and the increase in eating disorders among young women of all races and ethnic groups. One chapter in this book discusses eating disorders and their effects on girls today. Other chapters in the book also relate to this topic by integrating it in with a particular context and by emphasizing strengths to combat eating disorders.

Sexual Behaviors

The reader has many occasions in this book to enter the discussion about a changing perspective on girls' sexuality. Several of the authors cite research that highlights the strengths of girls' owning their sexuality. Other chapters discuss areas such as prostitution and the implications of public policy on funding for research on adolescent girls. Statistics such as those contained in *The Girls' Power Backgrounder* (1997) indicate the connections between sexual behavior risks and abuse and are part of the discussion. This book goes beyond looking at girls as victims and recommends changes in all areas of discussion about girls' sexuality: research, public policy, and therapeutic interventions.

Alternative Views of "Risky Behavior"

Millstein and Igra (1995) argued against assertions that there is a "syndrome" of risk-taking behaviors inherent in adolescence. They stated that exploration is "essential for growth" and that "characterizing all 'risky behaviors' as negative" is antithetical to healthy adolescent development.

> There is a need to distinguish healthy, exploratory activity from behaviors that carry significant potential for loss of health and life. In this latter category, we would include behaviors such as vehicle use while under the influence of alcohol or other substances, as well as the early onset of substance use or sexual intercourse. These behaviors, while risky at age 12, are normative by age 18. Clearly, the construct of risk-taking behavior needs not only to be better defined, but also defined within a developmental context. (p. 65)

In framing the lenses of this book, the task force members decided that the categorization of adolescents through lists of stresses, problems, and risky behaviors, however essential for delineating the challenges facing adolescents, does not capture the positive essence of girls in adolescence and their multiple facets. This book attempts to integrate the reality of the stresses and risks of adolescence with a new understanding of adolescent girls and the contexts that shape their development.

ADOLESCENT GIRLS' IDENTITIES AS MULTIPLE SELVES

The reader will find many chapters that approach identity formation for adolescent girls from the framework of Valerie Walkerdine's (1984) work, as cited in Michelle Fine and Pat Macpherson's (1992) reiteration that young women must negotiate their multiple selves.

If we expand the questions usually raised in discussions of identity, we begin to focus on the implications of the experience of multiple selves and the importance of context. Questions such as "Who am I?" become "Who am I when I'm with my friends?" "Who am I when I'm with my family?" "Who am I when I'm participating in sports?" "Who am I in class?" "Who am I when I'm with White girls?" "Who am I when I'm with Black girls?" "Who am I when I'm alone?" and so on. Contexts, of course, are not just settings or doings or relationships; contexts are within the self and outside the self. These questions may rarely be asked directly to oneself but portray some of the searching for a sense of oneself.

Theories of adolescent identity formation have undergone many re-iterations since Erik Erikson (1963) articulated a psychosocial developmental stage theory that presented each stage as a crisis to be resolved. For the stage corresponding to adolescence, Erikson theorized the crisis of identity versus role confusion. However, this traditional developmental theory has been challenged by a closer examination of girls' development that expanded the historical overemphasis on boys' development. Of course, traditional developmentalists also recognized that changes can and do occur in a person's identity concepts over time, in different contexts, and with various experiences; the differences lie primarily with the newer approaches' emphasis on the importance of diversity in understanding adolescent development. Each one of the contexts briefly described below is infused within this book and is covered in more depth in a separate chapter.

Context of Families

Adolescents gain much of their values and ideas from various reference groups, such as families, peers, teachers, ethnic culture, spiritual structures, and so on. Although strains may emerge in the relationship of the teen with her family, family dynamics and interaction, including parenting style, remain major influences in an adolescent's development of identities. In the Resnick et al. (1997) National Longitudinal Study on Adolescent Health referred to earlier, one of the primary findings was that key protective variables to adolescent health were parent–family connectivity and perceived school connectivity. Thus the context of family is important for understanding adolescent girls. Throughout this book, *family* will be used in the broad sense to include the diversity of family structures in the United States today.

Context of Ethnicity, Culture, and Race

The authors in this volume elaborate on and respect the importance of *ethnic identity*, which generally refers to adolescents' awareness and acceptance of their membership in an ethnic, racial, or cultural group. For youth, developing a consciousness and acceptance of the values and perspectives of their culture aids their development of a personal identity. Phinney (1990) and Phinney and Rosenthal (1992) found evidence that African American, Asian American, and Mexican American teens who were searching for or had attained an ethnic identity had higher self-esteem than those who had not examined their ethnic identity. In addition, such ethnic and cultural identity can assist the adolescent in buffering the negative impact of racism and stereotypes perpetrated by the majority culture.

Context of Gender and Sexuality

Sexual identity is defined as awareness and acceptance of the sexual orientation, such as bisexual, gay or lesbian, or heterosexual. Starting in early adolescence, the influence of gender intensifies as both internal and external demands require adjustments to changing circumstances. Conceptions about gender roles and gender identity move into new focus. The female adolescent's awareness and acceptance of her biological characteristics are given impetus by the physiological changes manifested in this period. The reader will find references in the text to the importance of sexual identity, gender identity, and sex role identity. The terms *gender identity* and *sex role identity* are generally used by developmental psychologists to denote the adolescent's perceptions of him- or herself as "masculine" or "feminine" (Eccles & Hoffman, 1984). There is a significant focus in this book on gender identity. These gender roles and societal expectations are changing and so, too, are adolescents in their sex role identity.

Context of Peers

Another context is a teen's peer group. For all teens, the peer group is a major source of emotional support and ideas and a social forum for testing and learning. In Eleanor Maccoby's (1990) review of gender and development, she concluded that styles of gendered interaction begin early in a child's development and continue to the teens and through adulthood and that it is in observing peer groups that one may see the differing styles. Therefore, an important element of self-development occurs within the context of peer relationships. An underlying premise of this book is that the socialization process with peers plays an increasingly important role with adolescents. Julia Harris's (1995) group socialization theory is one framework for considering the importance of peer groups. However, this book asserts that it is necessary to attend to all contexts as important continuing influences in teens' development rather than overvaluing one, such as peers, or minimizing others, such as ethnicity, parents, "other mothers," and so on.

Context of Schools

No look at adolescence would be complete without including the importance of the school environment and learning opportunities for teens, and this important context is discussed in a chapter in this book and is referred to in several others. Among the landmarks in the study of the effect of schools on adolescent girls and the awakening of the public to the needs of girls were the 1991 and 1992 American Association of University Women (AAUW) studies. These findings suggested that as girls moved into early adolescence, their performances in school and their self-esteem decreased significantly compared with boys. The authors of this book move beyond the AAUW studies' emphasis on global self-esteem in a manner similar to the movement beyond early discussions of identity. The general frame of the authors is that schools frequently are the arena in which many of the aspects of a girl's self, relationships, community, and societal influences come together. Therefore, it would be expected that each girl both brings into school the multiple aspects of her emerging self and takes from the complexity of the school's contexts. Therefore, what needs to be explored is the synergy of girls and schools.

Editors and Authors

The volume editors and section editors of this book, as members of the Adolescent Girls' Task Force, have completed a journey of their own—individually and collectively. The richness of gained understanding should be evident throughout this book. We hope the enduring impact will be reflected in influencing future discussion and research. The authors of this book are experts in the field and represent the diversity of thought and approaches to topics related to adolescent girls. The authors provide each chapter with cutting-edge, in-depth contributions of salient issues rather than a broad surface sweep of adolescence. These experts have engaged in original research from their own framework. The expertise of the editors and authors has been augmented by other members of the task force and by an advisory committee of psychologists with national reputations in the multiple facets of adolescent psychology.

THE FIVE SECTIONS OF *BEYOND APPEARANCE*

To provide a sense of the coverage and integrative organization of this book, we will review briefly here the sections and chapters of this book. Each section editor has written an overview of her or his section that describes the themes and purpose of the section and the chapters within it.

Section I

Developing the Woman in Myself, edited by Judith Worell, considers the development of self in the context of sociocultural expectations for the gendered self, the competent self, and the physical self. In "Gender Influences on Adolescent Development," Susan A. Basow and Lisa R. Rubin examine the research on female gender role from a developmental perspective, with a particular emphasis on its effect on adolescent girls' development. The authors conclude this chapter with an informative section on what factors the research suggests may aid girls to resist negative cultural messages.

In the chapter "Self-Evaluations of Competence, Task Values, and Self-Esteem," Jacquelynne Eccles, Bonnie Barber, Deborah Jozefowicz, Oksana Malenchuk, and Mina Vida reinterpret the data on declines in girls' achievement and expectancies for success; the authors also explore protective factors and strengths to help build and preserve self-esteem during the teen years.

Ruth H. Striegel-Moore and Fary M. Cachelin, in "Body Image Concerns and Disordered Eating in Adolescent Girls: Risks and Protective Factors," review the salient literature and present an innovative model for assessing risks and strengths in dealing with adolescent girls' eating disorders.

Section II

Adolescent Girls of Color: Declaring Their Place and Voice, edited by Jessica Henderson Daniel, both underscores the critical importance of understanding the role of ethnicity, culture, and race in any discussion of adolescent girls and provides data about the implications of the neglect in the psychological research of attention to diversity. In their chapter "The 'Other' Adolescent Girls: Who Are They?" Bonnie Y. Ohye and Jessica Henderson Daniel describe the diversity of race, ethnicity, and culture for the over 6 million girls who are Black, Hispanic, Asian/Pacific Islander, Native American, Eskimo, or Aleut. They provide an in-depth look at the absence of adequate research data on these girls. Cynthia de las Fuentes and Melba J. T. Vasquez, in their chapters "Immigrant Adolescent Girls of Color: Facing American Challenges" and "American-Born Asian, African, Latina, and American Indian Adolescent Girls: Challenges and Strengths," have written a cutting-edge discussion of the role of immigration in the United States. The first chapter provides the reader with a brief history of people of color in the United States and lays out some of the effects of oppression. The second chapter effectively fulfills its purpose "to address the unique experience of adolescent immigrant, Asian, Black, and Latina girls." In both chapters, the authors infuse the discussion with information about sources of resiliency and strength that exist for these girls and their families.

Section III

To the Heart of the Matter: The Relational Lives of Adolescent Girls, edited by Lyn Mikel Brown, provides complex lenses for looking at and thinking about adolescent girls' relationships. In their chapter "Cultivating Hardiness Zones for Adolescent Girls: A Reconceptualization of Resilience in Relationships With Caring Adults," Elizabeth Debold, Lyn Mikel Brown, Susan Weseen, and Geraldine Kearse Brookins consider the questions arising out of the dichotomy of middle-class values that seem to pit success and a family's cultural values against each other. The authors preview and critique the literature on resilience and end with a conceptual framework for how adults may foster teens' health and strength through relationships and appropriate contexts. Lyn Mikel Brown, Niobe Way, and Julia L. Duff, in "The Others in My I: Adolescent Girls' Friendships and Peer Relations," review a breadth of research on girls' friendships and peer relationships, with an emphasis on contextual forces. In their consideration of the impact of power relations on girls' friendships, the authors highlight the restrictive lenses of current research methodologies and advocate for methodology that incorporates listening to the girls "in their own terms." In "Female Adolescent Sexuality in Relational Context: Beyond Sexual Decision Making," Deborah L. Tolman moves away from the traditional review of the problems of female adolescent sexuality and advocates for acknowledging girls' sexual desire and the desirability of examining their sexuality in terms of interpersonal relationships.

Section IV

Coping, Negotiating, and Problem Solving in Community Contexts, edited by Denise M. DeZolt, covers three critical areas for adolescent girls:

the schools, the health system, and the courts. Denise M. DeZolt and Mary Henning-Stout, in "Adolescent Girls' Experiences in School and Community Settings," enter the debate about the role and effect of schools on adolescent girls. They take on issues such as single-sex classes or schools and present a project designed to enhance leadership skills in adolescent girls. Michele Harway and Marsha Liss, in "Dating Violence and Teen Prostitution: Adolescent Girls in the Justice System," consider adolescent girls' interface with the legal–justice system both as victims and as offenders and offer recommendations regarding the types of interventions needed. They provide the reader with statistics about the occurrence and effects of partner or dating violence and teen prostitution on girls from diverse ethnic cultures. In "Health Care for Adolescent Girls," Denise M. Dougherty describes the range of adolescent girls' health problems and provides an overview of the health care system in the United States as it exists for these girls. She organizes the discussion around eight focused areas and includes recommendations for improving the system.

Section V

Implications and Future Trends, edited by Michael C. Roberts, appropriately ends the discussion on adolescent girls with its offerings on public policy, education and training, and clinical practice. The section concludes with a summary view of past discussions on adolescent girls and what might be their future. Brian L. Wilcox, in "Sexual Obsessions: Public Policy and Adolescent Girls," warns readers that "the United States lacks a coherent youth policy" (p. 333). He traces the history of public policy for adolescent girls with a focus on sexuality-related policies and argues for a public policy approach that would pursue enhancing adolescents' sexual health. In "Practice and Education Issues Related to Adolescent Girls," Joanne E. Callan undertakes the formidable task of reviewing current clinical practice issues and approaches ranging the continuum from one-to-one psychotherapy to prevention programs. She concludes by describing the models of current graduate programs in psychology and how some programs self-define their training in working with adolescent girls. This book concludes with "Enhancing the Development of Adolescent Girls" by Florence L. Denmark, who outlines the present conditions of adolescent girls and envisions interventions to promote an optimistic future in three areas: education, families, and leadership.

We sincerely expect that Beyond Appearance: A New Look at Adolescent Girls will add a new dimension to scholarly discourse. And we hope that you, the reader, experience as much excitement and fulfillment and challenge in reading this book as we did in preparing it.

REFERENCES

American Association of University Women. (1991). *Shortchanging girls, short-changing America.* Washington, DC: American Association of University Women Educational Foundation.

American Association of University Women. (1992). *How schools shortchange girls: Study of major findings on girls and education.* Washington, DC: American Association of University Women Educational Foundation.

Brooks-Gunn, J., & Duncan, G. J. (1997). The effects of poverty on children. *The future of children, 7,* 55–71.

Commonwealth Fund. (1997). *Survey of the health of adolescent girls.* New York: Author.

DiClemente, R. J., Hansen, W. B., & Ponton, L. E. (Eds.). (1996). *Handbook of adolescent health risk behavior.* New York: Plenum.

Dryfoos, J. G. (1990). *Adolescents at risk: Prevalence and prevention.* New York: Oxford University Press.

Dryfoos, J. G. (1998). *Safe passage: Making it through adolescence in a risky society.* New York: Oxford University Press.

Duncan, G. J., Yeung, W., Brooks-Gunn, J., & Smith, J. R. (in press). Does childhood poverty affect the life chances of children? *American Sociological Review.*

Eccles, J. S., & Hoffman, L. W. (1984). Sex roles, socialization, and occupational behavior. In H. W. Stevenson & A. E. Siegel (Eds.), *Child development research and social policy* (pp. 367–420). Chicago: University of Chicago Press.

Erikson, E. H. (1963). *Childhood and society* (2nd ed.). New York: Norton.

Fine, M., & Macpherson, P. (1992). Over dinner: Feminism and adolescent female bodies. In M. Fine (Ed.), *Disruptive voices: The possibilities of feminist research* (p. 196). Albany: State University of New York Press.

Girl Power! Campaign. (1997). *Girls' power backgrounder.* Washington, DC: U.S. Federal Government.

Grossman, F. K., Gilbert, L. A., Genero, N. P., Hawes, S. E., Hyde, J. D., & Marecek, J., with Johnson, L. (1997). Feminist research: Practice and problems. In J. Worell & N. G. Johnson (Eds.), *Shaping the future of feminist psychology: Education, research, and practice* (pp. 73–91). Washington, DC: American Psychological Association.

Harris, J. R. (1995). Where is the child's environment? A group socialization theory of development. *Psychological Review, 102,* 458–489.

Johnson, N. G. (1995, August). *Feminist frames of women's strength: Visions for the future.* Presidential address to the Division of the Psychology of Women presented at the annual convention of the American Psychological Association, New York.

Kagawa-Singer, M., Katz, P. A., Taylor, D. A., & Vanderryn, J. H. M. (1996). *Health issues in minority adolescents.* Lincoln: University of Nebraska Press.

Maccoby, E. E. (1990). Gender and relationships: A developmental account. *American Psychologist, 45*, 513–520.

Millstein, S. G., & Igra, V. (1995). Theoretical models of adolescent risk-taking behavior. In J. L. Wallander & L. J. Siegel (Eds.), *Adolescent health problems: Behavioral perspectives* (pp. 52–71). New York: Guilford Press.

Offer, D., Ostrov, E., Howard, K. I., & Atkinson, R. (1988). *The teenager: Adolescents' self image in ten countries.* New York: Plenum Medical Book Company.

Phinney, J. S. (1990). Ethnic identity in adolescents and adults: Review of research. *Psychological Bulletin, 108*, 449–514.

Phinney, J. S., & Rosenthal, D. A. (1992). Ethnic identity in adolescence: Process, context, and outcome. In G. R. Adams, T. P. Gullotta, & R. Montemayor (Eds.), *Adolescent identity formation* (pp. 145–172). Newbury Park, CA: Sage.

Pipher, M. (1994). *Reviving Ophelia: Saving the selves of adolescent girls.* New York: Ballantine Books.

Resnick, M. D., Bearman, P. S., Blum, R. W., Bauman, K. E., Harris, K. M., Jones, J., Tabor, J., Beuhring, T., Sieving, R. E., Shew, M., Ireland, M., Bearinger, L. H., & Udry, J. R. (1997). Protecting adolescents from harm: Findings from the National Longitudinal Study on Adolescent Health. *Journal of the American Medical Association, 278*, 823–832.

Seligman, M. E. (1995). *The optimistic child.* New York: Houghton Mifflin.

Signorielli, N. (1993). Television, the portrayal of women and children's attitudes. In G. L. Berry & J. K. Asamen (Eds.), *Children and television: Images in a changing sociocultural world* (pp. 229–239). Newbury Park, CA: Sage.

Worell, J., & Danner, F. (1989). Adolescents in contemporary context. In J. Worell & F. Danner (Eds.), *The adolescent as decision-maker* (pp. 3–12). San Diego, CA: Academic Press.

I

DEVELOPING THE WOMAN
IN MYSELF

INTRODUCTION

JUDITH WORELL

If you ask any adolescent girl to describe herself, you will probably obtain a range of responses. She may say "I am a girl, I'm 15, I'm African (Japanese, Latina) American, I'm a high school junior, a soccer player, a choir singer, a friend." She may also describe herself as short, chubby, and dark haired. She thinks of herself as kind, responsible, and a good listener but at times feels sad, lonely, and confused. These typical aspects of self-awareness and self-definition incorporate characteristics of both personal and social identity (Reid & Deaux, 1996). The answers to "Who am I?" here contain some personal qualities as well as extended connections to others. Self-awareness thus reflects an interdependence of personal identity and the broader community and cultural contexts within which each person is embedded (Marcus & Kitayama, 1994).

In this section, we consider the developing adolescent in the context of sociocultural expectations for the gendered self, the competent self, and the physical self. From the interaction between her individual and her community experiences, each girl moves toward womanhood with an amalgam of the unique and the collective, forging her identity and her distinctive self. The three chapters here illuminate the personal–social interconnections with research that documents both similarities and differences across girls from diverse communities.

In considering "Gender Influences on Adolescent Development," Susan A. Basow and Lisa R. Rubin (chap. 2) point to the increasing pressures on adolescent girls to conform to female gender role prescriptions. Starting in early adolescence, the influence of gender intensifies as both internal and external demands require adjustments to changing circumstances. Processes of sociocultural gendering will influence the formation of self-esteem, self-competency, and perceptions of the physical, sexual, and social self. These gendered expectations may foster increased stress, leading to lowered self-regard and efforts to reconstruct the self as well as to resistance and resilience. These authors suggest that important sources of resistance to cultural messages for conformity to restrictive gender roles include a strong ethnic identity and verbal assertiveness as well as "athletics, strong female role models, feminist beliefs, and nontraditional attitudes" (p. 40). Areas of needed research include exploring the experiences of resilient girls and how they are able to resist negative cultural messages about women. More research is also indicated to better understand the intersection of gender with the experiences of racial, ethnic, religious, and sexual minorities as well as with socioeconomic status and level of acculturation.

In chapter 3, "Self-Evaluations of Competence, Task Values, and Self-Esteem," Jacquelynne Eccles and her colleagues review extensive data on girls' and boys' achievement strivings and sense of competence across the adolescent years. Although during the primary years, girls achieve at a level equal to or better than boys in most academic areas, by early adolescence they begin to doubt their abilities. This decline occurs especially in math and science, but for some girls it cuts across domains. Of particular interest are the reports from three longitudinal studies with large mixed sex and ethnic samples. The authors point out that the documented changes are not as dramatic as portrayed by the media. They find more variation in gendered self-concepts of ability and self-esteem across groups of girls than between girls and boys.

However, some changes during adolescence are gender typed: Boys are more confident of their future success in physical science and engineering fields and girls more confident about their future success in health-related fields such as medicine. In contrast, there were no differences between girls and boys in their confidence of success in business, law, leadership, independence, intellectual ability, or computer skills. These authors also explore the drop in self-esteem that occurs for both girls and boys during adolescence, examining factors that may protect girls from low self-regard during this period. Among these protective factors are ethnicity, family support, and personal coping strategies such as perceived competence in social, athletic, and academic arenas and, especially for girls, their physical appearance. Overall, most girls appear to possess more strengths than liabilities as they move toward adulthood. The sources of these strengths across differing groups of girls are still not well understood and are in need of further research.

In targeting concerns about physical appearance as a significant risk factor for girls, Ruth H. Striegel-Moore and Fary M. Cachelin contend that disordered eating patterns present a major health hazard. In chapter 4, "Body Image Concerns and Disordered Eating in Adolescent Girls: Risk and Protective Factors," Striegel-Moore and Cachelin present a detailed model of the multiple factors that may prevent or promote negative self- and body image and disordered patterns of dieting and binge eating. The model includes four domains that provide hypotheses for future research: social and cultural factors, family environment, personal characteristics, and life events. The overrepresentation of girls with body image concerns and eating disorders reflects the gendered cultural requirements for "femininity" and pressures for female physical attractiveness. Despite the significance of early adolescence for signaling the onset of eating disorders, little research has addressed questions regarding etiology and appearance at this stage. As well, there is a dearth of research on protective factors contributing to girls' resistance to unhealthy dieting and disordered eating. The chapter explores a range of developmental factors that contribute to resistance to destructive social stereotypes, such as self-awareness, self-esteem, independence, and cognitive flexibility. Group identity, as in the African American community, may also contribute to resistance through promoting a positive self- and body image. The authors call for increased research that further identifies both the risk and the protective factors involved in the development of high self-esteem, positive body image, and healthy patterns of living.

Across these three chapters, the influence of gender and gender stereotypes becomes apparent. All three chapters emphasize the major risk factor for adolescent girls in adhering to traditional or inflexible stereotypes that restrict their range of options. As well, there is considerable agreement that resistance and resilience in the face of restrictive gender messages contribute to girls' self-esteem and healthy development of the self.

REFERENCES

Marcus, H. R., & Kitayama, S. (1994). A collective fear of the collective: Implications for selves and theories of the self. *Personality and Social Psychology Bulletin, 20,* 568–579.

Reid, A., & Deaux, K. (1996). Relationship between social and personal identities: Segregation or integration? *Journal of Personality and Social Psychology, 71,* 1084–1091.

2

GENDER INFLUENCES ON ADOLESCENT DEVELOPMENT

SUSAN A. BASOW AND LISA R. RUBIN

Adolescence is a period in which girls are increasingly confronted with expectations to conform to female gender role prescriptions. The predominant tone of the literature describing girls' development during this age generally has been bleak. Research has noted the risks girls face as they are suddenly confronted with the conflicting expectations that embody our society's current female gender role, and has emphasized the negative outcomes that often result as girls attempt to fulfill these expectations. However, these findings do not apply to all adolescent girls, in part, because research has not sufficiently accounted for the diversity of experiences encountered by girls of varying racial, ethnic, and socioeconomic backgrounds. Girls outside of the dominant culture are often confronted with gender role expectations that differ from the dominant culture. Such expectations may foster greater resilience in minority girls than in girls of European descent. In this chapter, we examine the female gender role, girls' developing awareness of this role, and the impact such awareness has on adolescent girls' development. We end this chapter with an examination of girls' strategies of resistance and research implications.

Gender is a psychological and cultural term that refers to the meaning attached to being female or male in a particular culture. It is distinct from sex, which refers to the biological aspects of being female or male. Gender roles are based on societal evaluations of behaviors as either masculine or feminine; these gender expectations vary from one society to another. Gender identity refers to one's subjective feelings of maleness or femaleness. Thus, gender role identity (sometimes called sex typing) describes the degree to which an individual identifies with the definitions of masculinity or femininity constructed by a given society.

Societal definitions of gender influence stereotypic beliefs about men and women. For the most part, in the United States, men are expected to be strong in agentic qualities, such as competency, instrumentality, and activity, whereas women are expected to be strong in communal qualities, such as warmth, expressiveness, and nurturance. These masculine and feminine sets of personal traits are assumed to be not only different from but also opposite from each other. That is, women are assumed to possess the feminine traits but not the masculine ones and vice versa. Research has demonstrated considerable cultural agreement regarding the general agentic–communal distinction between males and females, regardless of the age, the sex, the religion, the educational level, or the marital status of respondents (Basow, 1992). Cultural variations exist in the specific traits assigned to each sex and are discussed below.

Despite strong consensus regarding the meanings of femininity and masculinity, research has suggested that most females and males are not solely feminine or masculine, respectively. Although males, on the average, have more assertive traits than do females and females, on the average, have more nurturant traits than do males (Feingold, 1994), most females have some agentic traits and most males have some communal traits. In fact, the two sets of traits are not opposite each other at all. People can be strong in one set or the other, or they can be strong in both (androgynous) or in neither (undifferentiated; Bem, 1974; Spence & Helmreich, 1978). Among White middle-class college students, only about 40% of men and women are traditionally sex-typed; about 30% fall in the androgynous category, 20% fall in the undifferentiated category, and 10% are cross-sex-typed (i.e., they possess the traits associated with the other sex; Bem, 1981a). By midlife, even more people seem to fall into the androgynous category (Sinott, 1987).

Most men and women do not conform to the cultural stereotypes of masculinity and femininity, yet these cultural expectations still serve as standards against which people judge themselves and others. At no time are these expectations more salient than at the start of adolescence. It is at this time that girls and boys are most concerned with learning what is expected of them as adults. One of the most salient expectations is that women and men will differ in terms of personality and abilities, and these assumed personality and competency differences will equip men and women for different roles in society.

The roles assigned to women generally are ones that require a communal orientation, such as homemaker, nurse, teacher, or service worker. These activities tend to be low status and poorly paid. In contrast, the roles assigned to men generally require a more agentic orientation, such as breadwinner, manual laborer, professional, or executive. Relative to women's roles, these activities tend to be associated with higher status and better pay.

One school of thought, the evolutionary perspective, suggests that sexual selection operates to create these gender differences in personality, academic ability, and occupational interests (e.g., Geary, 1998). In contrast, *social role theory* (Eagly, 1987) suggests that our expectations of females and males *result* from the different roles they have held in society. Engaging in different tasks frequently means developing different skills and beliefs. If such differences develop, they then would be due to the roles women and men have been assigned, not to some innate differences between the sexes. For example, when women are described as full-time employees and men are described as full-time homemakers, beliefs about their traits and abilities are reversed—full-time working women are viewed as having low communal and high agentic characteristics, whereas the converse is true for men (Eagly & Steffen, 1986). Thus, social role theory suggests that stereotypic beliefs result from the division of labor. Such a division occurs in nearly all societies and appears based, at least originally, on the degree of compatibility of societal tasks (such as hunting and gathering) with childbearing and nursing (Blumberg, 1984). Assumptions about agentic and communal trait differences developed from such divisions of tasks and roles, a split still with us today. Such assumptions and the existence of sex-differentiated roles further encourage young women and men to pursue sex-typed interests and careers.

CULTURAL VARIATIONS IN GENDER STEREOTYPES AND ROLES

Because the traits assumed to describe females and males are attached to the social roles assigned to each sex, it is not surprising that there are cultural variations in the gender role expectations and gender stereotypes of individuals of different racial, ethnic, socioeconomic, and sexual orientations. For example, a study of sex typing and sex role attitudes in 175 young adult White and African American women found that African American women were twice as likely as White women to describe themselves as androgynous (i.e., with strong active–instrumental traits and strong nurturant–expressive traits), although White women held more liberal attitudes toward the female role in the family (Binion, 1990). These findings may be due, in part, to the fact that racist and economic conditions have required most African American women to engage in both nurturing–communal and independent–agentic roles in the family and in the workforce. Consequently, stereotypes of African Americans depict males and females as more similar to each other in terms of expressiveness and competence than do the stereotypes of Anglo American males and females (Milham & Smith, 1981; P. A. Smith & Midlarsky, 1985).

Other ethnic groups differ in gender roles and stereotypes as well. In Hispanic culture, expectations of females are influenced by the traditional cultural values of *marianismo*, which honors self-sacrifice and nurturance. For Hispanic men, *machismo*, which honors courage and protection, appears to be important. Hispanic women tend to be viewed as more feminine than White women in terms of submissiveness and dependence (Vasquez-Nuttall, Romero-Garcia, & De Leon, 1987). Traditional gender role expectations also are pronounced for Asian American women, who are expected to be particularly passive and subservient (Homma-True, 1990; Uba, 1994). Stereotyped images of Native Americans often portray Native American women as squaws or princesses. Such stereotypes are probably the result of non-native, male-centered research biases that have underestimated the diverse and egalitarian roles traditionally held by Native American women (LaFromboise, Heyle, & Ozer, 1990).

Many minority children grow up in two worlds, that of their native culture and that of the dominant culture. Their socialization experiences frequently require them to accommodate bicultural expectations. That is, not only do some children grow up in homes in which a language other than English is spoken but they also grow up in homes in which the world view, foods, lifestyles, and traditions are different from mainstream culture. Such children generally learn to live in and navigate their way through both cultures, something particularly challenging for first- and second-generation adolescent girls (Allen, Denner, Yoshikawa, Seidman, & Aber, 1996). Although different cultural expectations may cause conflict within the girl, they also may provide a refuge from the negative gender messages of the dominant culture.

Aside from racial and ethnic differences, gender stereotypes exist for women and men of different social classes and sexual orientations. For example, working-class women are stereotyped as more hostile, confused, inconsiderate, and irresponsible than middle-class women (Landrine, 1985). Male homosexuals are stereotyped as possessing predominantly feminine traits, whereas lesbians are viewed as possessing predominantly masculine traits (Kite & Deaux, 1987). These variations in gender stereotypes and expectations mean that girls growing up in different cultural and social contexts have different views and face different pressures regarding their developing womanhood.

GENDER DEVELOPMENT

Most of the theories of gender development emphasize the first 6 or 7 years as critical in the establishment of an individual's gender identity. Feminist psychodynamic theorists, such as Nancy Chodorow (1978, 1990), have suggested that the first 2 years of development are particularly crucial. These theorists posit that being raised primarily by a mother or another female figure leads to the development of different cognitive orientations and personalities in girls and boys. Girls develop their sense of self in the context of a similar "other," and they continue to identify with the female socializer, developing a more personal and embedded style of being—a self-in-relation identity. Boys, in contrast, develop their sense of self with a dissimilar "other." They must reject this "other" and identify with male figures who are often more distant and diffuse, and in the process, develop a more abstract and impersonal style of being.

Cognitive developmental theorists (Bem, 1981b; Kohlberg, 1966) recognized the importance of the individual's changing mental capacities in dealing with conceptions of gender. For example, Kohlberg proposed that just as children cannot understand physical constancy until about age 7, they cannot maintain constancy of their gender until then either. During late preschool and early school years, children begin to understand the permanence of one's biological sex, despite situational changes, and they then begin to strive for conformity with gender-stereotyped roles. As part of this gender identification process, young children start preferring same-sex playgroups (American Association of University Women [AAUW], 1992).

During middle childhood, ages 8 to 11, girls become more androgynous as their identification with feminine characteristics declines. L. M. Brown and Gilligan (1992) and others (Dorney, 1995) have found that girls during this age period tend to be strong, self-confident, and outspoken. They trust their feelings and their knowledge and are not afraid to say what they think. They play sports, music, or games with little concern about the activity's gender-stereotyped "appropriateness." The social world also tends to support preadolescent girls' adventurousness and flexible gender role behaviors.

A reorganization of gender identity and gender conceptions occurs around age 11, the threshold of adolescence. The increased flexibility of early childhood diminishes, and both boys and girls adopt more rigid conceptions of gender roles, a process described as gender intensification (Hill & Lynch, 1983; Richards & Larson, 1989). These changes can be understood in terms of the physiological, psychological, and social changes that adolescence brings. When children begin developing secondary sex characteristics and experiencing surges in hormones, their attention becomes focused on their sexual selves and their attraction to others as well as their own sexual attractiveness. Girls become more concerned with how women are "supposed" to behave at the same time that others, especially males, start reacting to them in markedly gendered ways. Other social agents, especially parents, also begin pressuring girls to conform to their gender role (e.g., by encouraging girls to take more of an interest in their appearance). One result of these converging influences is to make girls more anxious about themselves, as evidenced by increased depression, lower self-esteem, more dissatisfaction with their body, and diminished academic achievement (Hill & Lynch, 1983). Such concerns frequently lead girls to revert to the security of stricter gender norms. Thus, adolescent girls typically appear more gender stereotyped in behaviors and attitudes and more rigid with respect to gender conceptions compared with their preteen years, although the timing of puberty may be an important factor in this process (Galambos, Almeida, & Petersen, 1990; Ge, Conger, & Elder, 1996; Urberg, 1979; Worell, 1989).

Cognitive changes also occur at the threshold of adolescence, as children become capable of abstract reasoning during the Piagetian stage of formal operations. Although such cognitive development is related to maturing ego processes in both girls and boys, the type of cognitive process involved differs. Girls' maturity is much more related to their level of interpersonal reasoning than is boys', supporting the idea that girls develop a more relational self than do boys (Hurtig, Petersen, Richards, & Gitelson, 1985).

Changes in gendered traits, behaviors, and attitudes are neither purely biological nor purely cognitive in origin, however. There appears to be an interaction among physiological, cognitive, and social factors with respect to gender-related attitudes and behaviors. Although more research is needed in this area, the findings of Alfieri, Ruble, and Higgins (1996) suggest that social factors actually may be the most important with regard to changing gender conceptions.

Alfieri et al. (1996) examined stereotypes in children of two different school districts in Grades 4 through 11, using a cross-sectional, longitudinal research design. Students in District 1 began junior high school in seventh grade, whereas those in District 2 began in eighth grade. Students were presented with 12 trait-related terms, half of which were masculine and half of which were feminine. Participants were asked to indicate whether the items described males, females, or both, with the "both" option indicating gender role flexibility. The researchers found that gender role flexibility increased as children entered adolescence, peaking in the seventh grade for students in District 1, and in eighth grade for those in District

2—the first year of junior high school in the respective districts. Gender flexibility became significantly lower after 1 year of junior high education, and this trend continued through high school. Boys tended to have lower gender flexibility than girls, particularly with regard to the flexibility of masculine traits.

Thus, early adolescence is marked by gender role rigidity, although the Alfieri et al. (1996) study does not indicate whether such rigidity is modified by racial, ethnic, or socioeconomic factors. This is an important area for future research. It should also be kept in mind that although girls become more rigid with respect to gender roles and traits during this period relative to their earlier years, they remain more flexible than their male peers. This has been found in a variety of cultural groups with respect to attitudes toward women's roles as well (e.g., Gibbons, Stiles, & Shkodriani, 1991). That is, relative to boys, adolescent girls hold more liberal attitudes about the rights and roles of women.

As adolescence proceeds, each sex strives to develop a secure personal gender identity in a social context, which may be extremely difficult in a society in which gender roles appear to be in flux (Katz, 1986). Issues of sexuality, labor force participation, and relationships must be confronted. As gender identity becomes more secure by late adolescence, more gender flexibility is again visible. With adulthood, life choices continue the process of socializing women and men with respect to gender. Those who marry and those who have children add another component to their gender identity, that of wife–husband or mother–father. The assumption of different social roles (such as homemaker, secretary, or lawyer) encourages people to develop different traits and behaviors that may be gender conforming or gender nonconforming, depending on the roles themselves. After middle age, many men and women evidence considerable gender flexibility (Levinson, 1978; Mitchell & Helson, 1990).

THE ADOLESCENT CROSSROADS—A CRITICAL PERIOD

How do expectations imposed by the female gender role affect girls' development? Research has indicated that for girls, early adolescence is an age characterized by developmental risks. It is the time when girls attempt to negotiate between staying in touch with themselves and their thoughts and feelings and meeting the gender role expectations imposed by others. This developmental age has been termed a *crossroads* in which girls, who during middle childhood are trusting of themselves and comfortable bringing their knowledge into their relationships, are confronted with heightened expectations to conform to the more restricted female role (Brown & Gilligan, 1992). What is the adult female role in our culture? For the dominant group, it is a role focused on being attractive to and serving the needs of men specifically and other people in general (Basow, 1992). It is a role in which women's true feelings are considered less important than the feelings of others. Examining the different voices of men and women, Brown and Gilligan found that whereas men spoke as if they lived autonomously, free to speak and move as they pleased, women described themselves as living in relation to others, subduing their voices and self-interests to maintain relationships and be "good women."

As the roles girls are encouraged to develop often are devalued in our society, girls, especially those in the dominant culture, come to discredit their own feelings and experience increased self-doubt and conflict (Hill & Lynch, 1983). Societal expectations of autonomy and independence, considered part of "growing up" for European Americans, often conflict with the development and maintenance of relationships. For girls whose identity thus far has developed in relation to others, attempts to pursue these qualities of autonomy and independence may have harsh consequences, often leading to problems such as eating disorders and body dissatisfaction, low self-esteem, depression, and restricted achievement strivings. For example, by age 15, girls are twice as likely as boys to be depressed, a ratio that remains through adulthood (Nolen-Hoeksema & Girgus, 1994). A plausible explanation for this gender disparity is the greater risk factors for depression that girls bring to the adolescent experience (such as sexual abuse) plus the greater challenges girls face during early adolescence. In addition to the conflict between connection and autonomy, adolescent girls also experience mixed messages regarding dating and sexuality. These pressures can create additional problems for girls' development. We examine some of these potential problem areas briefly before examining the strengths and resistance strategies girls bring to this stage of their development.

Dating and Sexuality

With the onset of puberty, the sexual component of gender roles brings sexual attraction and attractiveness into focus. For girls, a great deal of emphasis is placed on conforming to conventional standards of physical attractiveness (typically an unrealistically thin, perfectly featured ideal). During early adolescence, girls may spend a great deal of time learning the "female arts" of makeup, hair and skin care, and body adornment. Being sexually attractive typically means being sexually attractive to males. Indeed, early dating and going steady appear to be positively related to self-esteem in high school girls, perhaps because having an exclusive relationship validates young girls' sense of attractiveness (McDonald & McKinney, 1994). However, continuous involvement with the same boy, at least into 10th grade, is associated with lower self-esteem. Perhaps going steady during middle adolescence is more a sign of insecurity than of attractiveness.

Or perhaps maintaining a steady partner means suppressing one's own achievement strivings. It certainly is the case that men and boys tend to hold more traditional attitudes toward women than do girls (Gibbons et al., 1991). The relationship between dating and self-esteem for girls is an area in which more research is needed, especially with different cultural and ethnic groups.

Messages about female sexuality are contradictory: Females are supposed to be sexy and attract males' sexual interest, but sexually active females often are viewed negatively, especially among Whites, Hispanics, and Asian Americans. Perhaps this is why early maturing White girls have higher levels of psychological distress (such as anxiety and depression) than girls who mature on time or even late (Ge et al., 1996). Such distress may be due to the greater pressure on early maturing girls to behave sexually. Girls learn about sexuality in the context of reproduction and relationships, not in terms of their own sexual pleasure (Fine, 1988; Tolman, 1994). The most common reason teens (both female and male) engage in sexual intercourse is peer pressure ("Teen Sex," 1989). For girls, that pressure comes both from other girls and from boys. By age 18, 60% of Black girls and more than 50% of White girls have had sexual intercourse at least once (Brooks-Gunn & Furstenberg, 1989).

Teen pregnancy is a major concern, particularly for poor urban adolescent girls who may lack a sense of social or sexual entitlement and who hold traditional notions of what it means to be female (Fine, 1988). Teen girls who devalue their abilities, or whose perception of their economic and social situations becomes the basis for hopelessness, may be more likely to yearn for or accept pregnancy and motherhood as a means toward satisfaction and achievement than do other girls. Research indicates that pregnant teens have more traditional views of gender than do girls who use birth control (Blum & Resnick, 1982). Socioeconomic status is particularly important in understanding teen pregnancy, as low-income girls may see few options for identity development beyond motherhood. Indeed, the lowest fertility rates occur among Black and White adolescents who have the best alternatives to motherhood, including education, employment, and economic independence (McBride Murray, 1996). Cultural variations in these alternatives to motherhood may account for the findings that White non-Hispanic teens under age 20 have the lowest pregnancy rates (4%), Blacks the highest (22%), and Hispanics have intermediate rates (11%; U.S. National Center for Health Statistics, 1992).

The transition to adolescence also can be understood as a period of entry into the institution of compulsory heterosexuality (Thorne, 1993). Assumptions of heterosexual interest and activity can create confusion and discomfort for girls whose feelings may run counter to mainstream expectations, especially in our homophobic and heterosexist culture. A heterosexual interest is considered normative, as are a feminine appearance and personality and a female gender identity. Girls who do not fit these norms, whether because they feel transgendered, or masculine or androgynous in personality, or bisexual or lesbian in their sexual orientation, find adolescence a painful time. Additional confusion results from the cultural misunderstanding of three different aspects of gender: gender identity (female, male, or transgendered), sex typing (feminine, masculine, androgynous, or undifferentiated), and sexual orientation (same sex, other sex, or both sexes). These three aspects actually are independent of each other (Bem, 1993). That is, masculine females can be heterosexual, and lesbians can have a female gender identity and feminine personality traits (Brown, 1995; Patterson, 1995). The view that deviations from gender norms is pathological combined with the view that if one does deviate, it should be in a prescribed way, may make many young lesbians and female bisexuals feel alienated and confused (Savin-Williams, 1995).

Although developmental research of lesbian identities is virtually nonexistent, in retrospective accounts, lesbians often claim to have felt different even before adolescence and indicate that these feelings were compounded in adolescence when they became increasingly aware of their same-sex sexual interests (Bailey & Zucker, 1995; Savin-Williams, 1995). Lesbian and bisexual adolescents may deny their homosexuality, often attempting to fulfill heterosexual expectations. Most lesbian adolescents engage in heterosexual and homosexual experimentation before "coming out" and declaring their sexual identity. The adjustment problems faced by gay teens are exemplified in their high rates of depression, academic problems, and alarmingly high suicide rates (Herdt, 1989). Coming out, although quite difficult and frightening for most, is associated with feelings of self-worth, particularly for lesbian youth. In fact, girls who know they are "queer" at an early age may have particularly high self-esteem according to Savin-Williams.

Overall, dealing with sexual feelings, whether heterosexual or homosexual, is a challenge for young people, particularly girls, who encounter a range of mixed cultural messages on the topic. The conflict of experiencing sexual desire in a culture that is alternately silent and disapproving about such feelings in girls makes dealing with those feelings a struggle for many (Tolman, 1994). Much more research is needed in this area: For example, longitudinal studies of sexual orientation; cross-cultural variations in messages regarding sexuality and their effects; the relationships among sex typing, gender identity, and sexual orientation; and the effects of early versus late maturing on dating, sexual activity, and coming out.

Body Image and Eating Disorders

In recent years, increased attention has been given to negative body image and eating disorders, particularly in adolescent girls (Striegel-Moore, chap. 4). Although there has been widespread criticism of the new "heroin chic" look for women—an image of a weak woman who does not carry enough body fat to maintain her secondary sex characteristics—this look still is promoted by media and advertisements. Adolescent girls trying to make their developing body accommodate this image may be putting themselves at risk for eating disorders and its related complications (e.g., amenorrhea and depression). During puberty, the body goes through enormous changes leading to the development of secondary sex characteristics in preparation for motherhood (breasts, pubic and axillary hair, and menstruation). The hips widen, fat stores increase, and a girl's shape generally changes from straight lines to curves. The timing and scope of these changes are a function of nutrition, genes, and hormones. Yet the dominant culture presents a certain female image as the ideal through advertising, and all girls are encouraged to aspire to it (and buy products to attain it). Whether this image is the thin yet full-breasted ideal represented in *Playboy* and other male-oriented magazines or the "heroin chic" look of the 1990s supermodels, these forms are virtually unattainable for most females without extreme dieting or cosmetic surgery.

The manner in which conflictual gender expectations affect a girl's body image is exemplified in a study by Catherine Steiner-Adair (1990). In this investigation, 32 White girls, aged 14 to 18 years, were interviewed to explore their perceptions of cultural values and cultural and individual images of women. Three weeks after the interviews were conducted, girls completed the Eating Attitudes Test (EAT) to assess eating disordered behavior. Interpretation of the interviews revealed two patterns of responses: the wise woman pattern and the superwoman pattern. Sixty-percent of the girls fell into the wise woman response pattern, indicating an awareness of the cultural expectations and values of a woman's autonomy and independent achievement in career and appearance, yet differentiating their own ideal from this societal image. Forty-percent of the girls responded with a superwoman response pattern, identifying the independent and autonomous superwoman as the societal as well as their own ideal. All of the wise women scored in the noneating disorder range of the EAT, whereas 11 of the 12 superwomen scored in the eating disorder range. Thus, those girls who uncritically accept a societal image that conflicts with their developmental history are at a greater risk for developing eating disorders.

Researchers have suggested that dieting may be a strategy some females use to increase self-esteem (Root, 1990). For middle- and upper-class White girls and women, thinness may be a way to accommodate conflicting gender role prescriptions—to communicate control and to attain power and respect while simultaneously appearing soft, fragile, and dependent. For girls and women in different racial and ethnic groups, however, female beauty standards may differ from the mainstream culture. Thus, minority girls and women may not view the attainment of extreme thinness as a way to convey femininity, beauty, autonomy, and independence. Indeed, White girls and women do report greater levels of disordered eating and dieting and greater body dissatisfaction than do African American and Asian American girls and women (Akan & Grilo, 1995). African American and Hispanic culture's appreciation of a healthy body size and its own distinct beauty standards may provide some degree of protection against the development of eating disorders, although such disorders do affect minority girls and women as well (Root, 1990). Indeed, it may be those minority girls and women who are most acculturated who are most vulnerable to eating disorders (Pumariega, 1986).

Another group of girls who may be less affected by the unnatural female physical ideal presented in the media are lesbians. There is some evidence that among adults, women who are sexually attracted to other women have less dissatisfaction with their bodies than do heterosexual women, perhaps because the thin ideal is viewed as attractive mainly to men (Siever, 1994). Whether this pattern holds true among adolescents is unclear. More research is needed to identify what helps girls resist the cultural message to be dissatisfied with their bodies.

Self-Esteem

The conflicting expectations imposed by "the crossroads" not only influences adolescent girls' body esteem but also may have an impact on more global measures of self-esteem. Although research indicates that self-esteem decreases for both sexes after elementary school, the drop in White girls' self-esteem is the most dramatic. The AAUW (1992) found that among elementary school girls, 55% of White girls, 65% of Black girls, and 68% of Hispanic girls reported being "happy as I am." In high school, agreement with this statement dropped to 22% among White girls, 58% among Black girls, and 30% among Hispanic girls. The drop in self-esteem for White girls appeared to start in middle school (around Grade 7), whereas the drop among Hispanic girls started in high school. Although the methodology of this study has been criticized because only the most extreme ratings were examined, the findings regarding African American girls are consistent with those of the Rosenberg and Simmons (1971) classic study, in which they found that a higher proportion of Blacks than Whites of the same age (from ages 8 to 19) reported feelings of high self-esteem. Unfortunately, Rosenberg and Simmons did not break their data down by gender, but a more recent study did so. Dukes and Martinez (1994) found that Black adolescent girls had higher self-esteem levels than did their Hispanic, White, Native American, or Asian classmates.

It may be that the gender role expectations for White girls interfere with their self-acceptance and self-regard. Adolescent White girls who hold traditional attitudes toward women's roles tend to have lower self-esteem than do girls who hold more liberal attitudes (Galambos, Petersen, Richards, & Gitelson, 1985). The contradictory and restrictive messages—about being attractive but not too vain, about being sexy but not too sexual, about being an individual but pleasing others, about developing one's abilities but not being too achievement oriented, and so on—primarily affect girls of the dominant culture, in which White women still are trying to find a place for themselves. In many minority cultures, the roles of women frequently are less ambivalent. Among African Americans, for example, adult women are respected in their community for being strong, outspoken, and achievement focused as well as for being nurturant and caring. Dealing with racism may teach Black girls more ways of resisting dominant cultural messages. We look at some of these strategies in the next section.

Research on self-esteem in Asian American girls has been sparse; most studies often fail to distinguish between boys and girls. In general, the results of this research have been mixed. Among college students, those with Asian backgrounds had lower overall self-esteem and more depression than did both White and Black students, although it is possible that Asian Americans may have a response set to present themselves in a modest and self-effacing light (Crocker, Luhtanen, Blaine, & Broadnax, 1994). Unfortunately, this study did not report on gender differences, although the results are consistent with research indicating that Asian American women who are traditional with respect to sex typing have lower self-esteem and maintain lower occupational statuses than do nontraditional Asian women (Uba, 1994). The Dukes and Martinez (1994) study of five ethnic groups in junior high and high school confirmed that Asian girls had the lowest self-esteem of all groups.

Overall, a strong ethnic identity appears to be significantly related to self-esteem among minority group girls, especially among Blacks and Hispanics (Phinney & Alipuria, 1990; Phinney & Chavira, 1992). The picture is less clear for Asian American girls, perhaps because of the variety of Asian subcultures and the various levels of acculturation. In any case, a strong ethnic identity may serve as a buffer against the damaging effects of the dominant cultural messages regarding femininity on girls at adolescence. More research is needed to elucidate which factors can help all girls maintain high self-esteem throughout adolescence.

Achievement

Adolescence is also a time when gender differences in certain subject areas and in career aspirations become more visible. The labeling of certain academic areas (such as math and science) and occupations as masculine influences girls' exposure to these fields and affects their level of interest and confidence. By 11th grade, most girls believe they would be better at female-dominated than male-dominated occupations (Gorrell & Shaw, 1988). Such beliefs appear independent of demonstrated ability. For example, even when there is no actual difference in math performance, girls tend to be less confident of their math abilities than do boys (Hyde, Fennema, Ryan, Frost, & Hopp, 1990). Although gender discrepancies in academic performance have been reduced for most fields of study, differences in science achievement increased from 1978 to 1986 (AAUW, 1992). Using data of 24,500 students from the National Educational Longitudinal Study of 1988, Catsambis (1995) found that girls received better grades in science than their male counterparts during middle school. However, boys were more likely to express interest in science and engage in science-related extracurricular activities. By eighth grade, twice as many boys as girls were interested in pursuing a science-related career.

Although research has begun to examine gender differences in academic motivation and achievement, the effects of racial, ethnic, and socioeconomic differences have been relatively neglected. The research that does exist frequently is inconsistent. For example, contrary to reports that African American girls do not have high levels of self-esteem in academic areas, Richman, Clark, and Brown (1985) found that African American girls had greater school self-esteem than White girls and Black boys and that Black girls' scores were virtually no different than those of White boys. However, the academic self-esteem of Black girls does seem to decline over the adolescent years (AAUW, 1992). Furthermore, the actual educational attainment of Black girls, although higher than that for Black boys, tends to be lower than that for White female and male adolescents (E. J. Smith, 1982). Thus, although African American girls start off with a high level of academic self-esteem, they lose some of their confidence over time and tend to achieve less academically than do their White counterparts. This may be the result of a lack of validation in the school system and of limited career planning because of factors related to class boundaries and racism as well as teenage pregnancy.

Socioeconomic status seems to be the best predictor of educational outcomes. In fact, racial differences in achievement and aspirations are reduced considerably when comparing students within the same socioeconomic group. Vonnie McLoyd and Debra Hernandez Jozefowicz (1996) examined the future expectations of 115 seventh- and eighth-grade African American female students and their mothers living in an urban Midwestern city. They found that mothers experiencing economic hardship are more pessimistic about the future of their daughters than are mothers who are not experiencing such difficulties. Daughters who experience such parental expectations, combined with their own sense of socioeconomic disadvantage, show reduced occupational aspirations and expectations and restricted knowledge about various occupations and their necessary training.

Traditional attitudes toward gender roles, coupled with limited opportunities and job discrimination, may hinder young women from lower socioeconomic groups from pursuing nontraditional occupations. In fact, traditional views of gender roles are strongly correlated with lower socioeconomic status (AAUW, 1992). Unfortunately, vocational training programs tend to encourage non-college-bound girls, usually from lower socioeconomic status groups, to pursue traditional occupations, which tend to be low status and low paying (AAUW, 1992). Still, active involvement in vocational training increases the likelihood of contraceptive use and decreases the likelihood of repeat pregnancies (Polit, Kahn, & Stevens, 1985, as cited in Fine, 1988). The latter point is of particular importance, as rapid repeated childbearing is the single greatest impediment to success in education, employment, and parenting (Apfel & Seitz, 1996). It may be that encouraging women to be self-sufficient, even through traditional employment, instills girls with greater feelings of control over their future.

Gender roles affect most girls' future plans, regardless of socioeconomic status. For example, high school girls with exceptional math and science abilities still are far less likely than their male counterparts to pursue majors in science or engineering due, in large part, to gender-related expectations (AAUW, 1992). If adolescent girls believe that occupational success and raising a family are mutually exclusive goals, girls' career expectations will be minimized. During the last 2 years of high school, the proportion of girls in gifted programs drops (Read, 1991). When girls were asked why they dropped out, they cited pressures from parents, peers, and counselors. Even top-achieving girls appear to experience conflicts regarding achievement that are related to gender role. A longitudinal study followed up high school valedictorians over a 10-year period, through college and into the workforce (Arnold & Denny, 1985, as cited in Berk, 1994). By sophomore year in college, women as a group showed a decline in estimates of their intelligence, whereas men showed no decline. Women also shifted their expectations to less demanding careers because of concerns of motherhood and unresolved questions about their ability. It is important to note that although the influence of gender role expectations on academic and occupational achievement still is considerable, increased gender role flexibility over the last 20 years (along with the passing and enforcement of nondiscriminatory laws and reduced societal barriers) has led to an increase in the number of women entering nontraditional occupations.

Overall, adolescent girls must grapple with what it means to be a woman. Because the meaning of womanhood is highly contested, especially in the dominant culture, it is no wonder that many girls experience conflicts or problems around such areas as sexuality, body image, self-esteem, and achievement strivings. Yet not all girls experience such problems. It is helpful to look at the strategies girls use to resist negative gender messages and the strengths they bring to this developmental period.

What factors influence the way in which adolescent girls from diverse backgrounds interpret the obstacles and opportunities posed by their gender? Research has begun to examine how girls of different racial, ethnic, and socioeconomic backgrounds negotiate their "crossroads." It is useful to look at minority girls first because many seem to be less negatively affected than White middle-class girls are by contradictory gender pressures. Indeed, a strong ethnic identity and speaking one's mind appear to be important sources of resistance to negative cultural messages regarding femininity. Other important sources of resistance for all girls are athletics, strong female role models, and feminist beliefs and nontraditional attitudes.

Ethnic Identity

The socialization practices used by different racial, ethnic, and socioeconomic groups influence how girls understand and deal with pressures to conform to idealized standards of femininity. As noted previously, a well-developed ethnic identity is related to high self-esteem in minority girls. This is particularly the case among African American girls. Racism and poverty, which have all too often characterized the African American experience, have required that Black women engage in the labor force while simultaneously serving as head of the household. Thus, as the Eurocentric female ideal of full-time homemaking has not been the reality for a majority of Black women, young Black girls are socialized to expect that they will have to support themselves and, perhaps, a family (Greene, 1990). Furthermore, African American mothers must communicate to their daughter messages to resist the dominant culture's standard of beauty, as these standards are based on White women and Black features are considered unattractive (Greene, 1990; hooks, 1993). Overall, Black mothers must prepare their daughters to confront racism as well as sexism and learn not to internalize the culture's negative views of them. Liberating truth telling and strong connections to the larger African American community are two ways Black mothers train their daughters to resist (Ward, 1996).

Tracy Robinson and Janie Victoria Ward (1991) have outlined two means through which African American girls attempt to deal with and resist the dominant culture's devaluation of Black women: survival strategies and liberation strategies. Although both strategies are means through which girls negotiate obstacles to their development, not all strategies serve the best interest of the individual or the community. Survival strategies are the "quick fix" resistance strategies that serve the short-term interests of individual survival in a hostile and oppressive environment. Survival strategies are used when girls do not challenge the standards and expectations created by the dominant culture. These strategies can manifest in a variety of ways, including self-denigration because of internalization of negative self images, excessive autonomy at the expense of connectedness with one's community, as well as unplanned pregnancies and school dropout. For example, Signithia Fordham (1991) found that African American girls who voice their opinions, attitudes, or objections in the classroom frequently receive negative feedback for doing so from their (predominantly White) teachers. As a result, many African American girls view success in the academy as dependent on their invisibility and silencing and a rejection or denial of their place in the Black community. If they subdue their voices, they risk distancing themselves from the Black community and thereby becoming more susceptible to internalizing negative images of Blackness. If they refuse to subdue their voices, however, the only other way they may be able to maintain strong self-esteem is by rejecting academic achievement, thereby contributing to the high school dropout rate of African American girls.

In contrast to survival strategies, liberation strategies are those resistance strategies in which Black girls and women acknowledge the problems and demands for change in an environment that oppresses or demeans them. They do this by learning positive messages about themselves and their community and by trusting themselves as sources of knowledge. Although resistance for liberation strategies may be difficult to foster in an antagonistic environment, racial socialization may cultivate adaptive resistance. *Racial socialization* refers to what is communicated to Black children about what it means to be Black in America, what they may expect from Black and White people and how to cope with it, and whether the disparaging messages of the broader culture are true. A failure to openly confront these issues can foster maladaptive adjustment (Greene, 1990).

"Truth Telling"

As we have seen, one important component of racial socialization is "truth telling" or "speaking one's mind" (Ward, 1996). Although Robinson and Ward (1991) developed their resistance model based on the experiences of African American women, this model can be effectively applied to other racial or ethnic minorities dealing with the complexities of biculturality. For example, the Harvard Project on Women's Psychology and Girls' Development recently completed the Understanding Adolescence Study, a 3-year longitudinal study examining the experiences, voices, and resistance of 26 adolescents attending a large urban high school in the Northeast (Taylor, Gilligan, & Sullivan, 1995). The girls in the study represented diverse backgrounds: 8 were African American or Caribbean, 4 were Latina, 8 were Portuguese, and 6 were Irish or Italian American. In listening for resistance, or the process through which girls consciously or unconsciously resist psychological and relational disconnection, the study examined the challenges girls face and the capacities they use in coming to terms with the cultural conventions of femininity and womanhood. Through the interviews, the investigation found that "there is little evidence that the majority of these girls experience pressure to conform to the idealized standards of femininity so prominent in the dominant culture" (Taylor et al., 1995, p. 40). For example, the girls in the investigation did not express a need to suppress their anger to protect their relationships. Being forthright, however, may not be valued by high school teachers and administrators, as Fordham (1991) suggested. Not coincidentally, then, these same girls were identified by their high school as at risk for dropping out.

Niobe Way (1995) also found that speaking one's mind is a major resistance strategy of the twelve 15- and 16-year-old poor and working-class urban girls, from a diversity of ethnic backgrounds, that she interviewed. The girls in this study, like those in the Harvard study, felt that expressing themselves—their opinions and their anger—was important, in fact, necessary to maintain their relationships. Their experiences differ from those of middle-class White adolescent girls, who frequently feel that they must silence themselves for the sake of their relationships (Brown & Gilligan, 1992).

Speaking one's mind is thus a strong aspect of resistance, especially for minority girls. For African Americans, in particular, the culture appears to emphasize truth telling, strong female role models, deep connections to the broader community, and an androgynous female ideal—aspects that appear to empower girls. Latino culture, however, does not encourage the more androgynous female sex role that has come to characterize African American women and girls. For bicultural Latina girls, the crossroads requires coming to terms with a double dose of the "tyranny of femininity" —the idealized female in the dominant culture as well as their own culture's idealized female—one who is defined by her goodness, suffering, and nurturance and who must endure a marked sexual double standard (Taylor, 1996). For such girls, a major source of resistance is developing a positive ethnic identity, one in which they feel empowered despite strong gender role conformity. The same process may occur through a strong religious identity. Another major source of resistance is close connection to a nuclear and extended family that supports a girl's achievements (De Leon, 1996). More research is needed into the ways ethnic minority girls can learn to resist the negative effects of the female gender role.

Resistance strategies are not exclusively the domain of racial and ethnic minorities. Adolescent girls of all races and ethnicities must come to terms with their relationship to the devalued female gender role. Just as racial and ethnic minorities often distance themselves from their communitiy as a "survival strategy" of resistance, adolescent girls may devalue and distance themselves from other girls or women. *Gender passing* refers to the way in which women "act male" to be taken seriously and to avoid the negative images associated with being female. Investigating girls' attitudes toward themselves and women in general, Macpherson and Fine (1995) conducted exploratory discussions with 4 girls, ages 14 to 17 years. The researchers found that the girls they interviewed had internalized negative female images and prefer to be considered "just one of the guys" than one of the girls. The authors warn of the danger for girls when they confront sexism through choosing to distance themselves from other girls instead of deconstructing and evaluating the negative images of women.

Although some girls do prefer to be "one of the guys," many adolescent girls are engaging in liberation strategies and are challenging negative images of girls and women presented in the media and promoted through society. *Truth telling*, the style of directly confronting negative cultural messages (e.g., ones on gender roles), appears to benefit all girls, although it is not particularly encouraged among majority-group girls. More research is needed on the effects of speaking one's mind on self-esteem and resisting negative gender messages. Two additional factors that may aid in girls' resistance to negative messages regarding the female role are athletic participation and feminist attitudes and role models.

Athletic Participation

Activities that involve challenge, effort, and concentration, such as sports, appear to be very beneficial for girls' self-image and for developing nontraditional gender role traits. An investigation of self-esteem and sex roles among female and male high school students found that girls who are more physically active were characterized by greater self-esteem and greater positive masculine and positive feminine traits than those who were less physically active (Delaney & Lee, 1995). Athletic activities seem to be a prime way for girls, especially low socioeconomic ones, to feel good about themselves (Erkut, Fields, Sing, & Marx, 1996). Sports and physical activity may be beneficial, in part, because they provide girls and boys with a positive identity (i.e., "I am a soccer player."). This may be similar to the value of a strong ethnic identity.

Another benefit of athletics for girls may be the opportunity to challenge traditional expectations. In an investigation of 10th-grade girls and boys, Susan Shaw, Douglas Kleiber, and Linda Caldwell (1995) found that, for girls only, sports and physical activity are associated with psychological maturity and identity development on the basis of a psychosocial development scale measuring one's sense of self as an independent and autonomous individual. Other research supports the finding that girls who engage in athletics tend to be androgynous in terms of sex-typing and to have more active–instrumental personality traits than do female nonathletes (Butcher, 1989; Marsh & Jackson, 1986).

In addition to improved self-esteem and development, athletics may provide girls with a buffer against negative feelings toward their body shape—girls learn to appreciate the body for what it can do rather than what they must do to change it. Female athletes generally have more positive self-concepts concerning their physical appearance and body image than do female nonathletes (Miller & Levy, 1996). However, girls who participate in physical activities in which body shape pressure is magnified (e.g., dance and gymnastics) evidence higher rates of anorexia and bulimia (Stice, 1994). Thus, physical activities that magnify sociocultural expectations for a slender female form may reflect, rather than challenge, traditional expectations. Physical activities that emphasize strength, speed, and proficiency may have the opposite effect. That is, such activities may promote the model of a strong, competent, and active girl—one who is valued for her abilities rather than her appearance.

Given the positive value of girls' athletic participation, it is noteworthy that the percentage of girls participating in sports continues to increase. Whereas in 1972, only 1 in 27 girls played high school varsity sports, that number in 1996 was 1 in 3 (Hilliard, 1996).

Feminism

As evident in the literature on minority girls, having strong female models and androgynous traits seems to help girls resist negative cultural messages regarding women. For majority girls as well, having an employed mother, especially one who is in a nontraditional profession, is associated with a more liberal sex role orientation and liberal attitudes toward sexuality among daughters (Fingerman, 1989; Gardner & LaBrecque, 1986).

Strong nontraditional mothers appear to serve as important role models for daughters, who learn from them either directly or indirectly how to resist the traditional and restrictive female roles. We have already seen that for minority girls, it is particularly important to receive training in viewing negative cultural messages as political and not personal. This is a key way by which the negative effects of racism and sexism can be buffered. In general, girls who hold liberal attitudes toward women's rights and roles also tend to have high self-esteem (Galambos et al., 1985). In her interviews with 50 women who were daughters of feminists, Rose Glickman (1993) found that almost all held egalitarian sex role beliefs and were challenging traditions in the workplace, the home, and the world at large, even if they didn't embrace the term *feminist* themselves.

But many teens are, in fact, embracing the term *feminist*. Teachers and researchers describe an increasing interest in feminism among young women (Henneberger, 1994). Girls are confronting women's issues by forming their own groups and by joining established groups. For example, there are high school National Organization for Women chapters in 12 states.

Among other concerns, these groups are targeting issues such as sexual harassment and media representations of women. There are several programs aimed at educating high school teachers, especially women teachers, so that they will be better able to work with their female students on how to resist the many cultural messages that silence girls and women (e.g., Dorney, 1995). What seems critically important is for girls of all ethnicities to learn not only about discrimination but also about activist strategies to confront conditions of injustice (Pastor, McCormick, & Fine, 1996).

The "grrrls movement" is another way in which adolescent girls are challenging expectations of the female role. This movement puts the anger ("grrr") into "girls"—anger at male domination and traditional expectations of femininity (Spencer, 1993). Riot Grrrls are an aggressive group of vegetarian-inclined, drug-free, punk-styled girls whose feminism is more implicit than explicit. Riot Grrrls seek to create mediums of expression for girls outside of male-dominated culture: grrrl's music, grrrl's "zines" (underground magazines, frequently on the Internet), grrrl's conventions, and grrrl's solidarity.

Thus, many girls do not feel confined to the traditional female role. Important resistance strategies are strong female role models, feminist ideas, androgynous sex-typing, athletic participation, a positive racial identity, and an emphasis on using one's "voice" to facilitate relationships. Among White girls as well as ethnic minority girls, these factors appear important in resisting the negative aspects of the female gender role. Psychologists need to understand more about how these resistance strategies develop and how they can be fostered in more girls.

CONCLUSION AND RESEARCH GAPS

There are many areas psychologists know little about with respect to gender influences on adolescent girls. We know that puberty marks the start of enormous changes for girls in terms of their own gender-related attitudes and behaviors. Although physiological and cognitive developments contribute to these changes, sociocultural factors appear most critical. In particular, the conflicting and often negative views of adult women, especially in the dominant White Christian culture, make early adolescence difficult for many girls. Areas that are particularly challenging because of gender roles relate to dating and sexuality, body image and eating disorders, self-esteem, and achievement. Yet not all girls succumb to negative gender messages, and indeed the gender messages themselves may vary for girls from different ethnic groups. Certainly, appropriate roles for adult women is a hotly contested topic. Factors that foster resistance include a strong ethnic identity, assertive female role models, feminist ideas, and nontraditional sex typing.

More research is needed to understand the ways in which gender-related biological, psychological, and cultural factors interact during the adolescent period. We also must examine how all these factors may vary as a function of minority group status. The minority experience includes not only ethnic and racial minority girls but also religious minorities (Jews, Muslims, and others) and sexual minorities (lesbians, bisexuals, and transgendered girls). We also need more information on gender development among different socioeconomic classes and how social class might interact with minority status. More attention must be paid to level of acculturation; issues related to gender development appear to be different for first- and second-generation girls than among those girls who are more acculturated.

More research needs to be done on teens' specific attitudes on a range of issues related to women's roles in society and relationships. The issue of sexual desire for girls also is something psychologists need to understand better, including the experience of incipient lesbians. The various resistance strategies girls use in mediating negative culture messages about women need to be explored. And most of all, we need to learn how to inculcate effective resistance strategies in all girls so that they have a chance to develop fully rather than being constrained to fit into the traditional and narrow female role.

REFERENCES

Akan, G. E., & Grilo, C. M. (1995). Sociocultural influences on eating attitudes and behaviors, body image, and psychological functioning: A comparison of African-American, Asian-American, and Caucasian college women. *International Journal of Eating Disorders, 18*, 181–187.

Alfieri, T., Ruble, D. N., & Higgins, E. T. (1996). Gender stereotypes during adolescence: Developmental changes and the transition to junior high school. *Developmental Psychology, 32*, 1129–1137.

Allen, L., Denner, J., Yoshikawa, H., Seidman, E., & Aber, J. L. (1996). Acculturation and depression among Latina urban girls. In B. J. Ross Leadbeater & N. Way (Eds.), *Urban girls: Resisting stereotypes, creating identities* (pp. 337–352). New York: New York University Press.

American Association of University Women. (1992). *The AAUW report: How schools shortchange girls.* Washington, DC: Author.

Apfel, N., & Seitz, V. (1996). African American adolescent mothers, their families, and their daughters: A longitudinal perspective over twelve years. In B. J. Ross Leadbeater & N. Way (Eds.), *Urban girls: Resisting stereotypes, creating identities* (pp. 149–172). New York: New York University Press.

Bailey, J. M., & Zucker, K. J. (1995). Childhood sex-typed behavior and sexual orientation: A conceptual analysis and quantitative review. *Developmental Psychology, 31*, 43–55.

Basow, S. A. (1992). *Gender stereotypes and roles* (3rd ed.). Pacific Grove, CA: Brooks/Cole.

Bem, S. L. (1974). The measurement of psychological androgyny. *Journal of Consulting and Clinical Psychology, 42,* 155–162.

Bem, S. L. (1981a). *Bem Sex-Role Inventory, professional manual.* Palo Alto, CA: Consulting Psychologists Press.

Bem, S. L. (1981b). Gender schema theory: A cognitive account of sex typing. *Psychological Review, 88,* 354–364.

Bem, S. L. (1993). *The lenses of gender: Transforming the debate on sexual inequality.* New Haven, CT: Yale University Press.

Berk, L. E. (1994). *Child development* (3rd ed.). Boston: Allyn & Bacon.

Binion, V. J. (1990). Psychological androgyny: A Black female perspective. *Sex Roles, 22,* 487–507.

Blum, R. W., & Resnick, M. D. (1982). Adolescent sexual decision-making: Contraception, pregnancy, abortion, and motherhood. *Pediatric Annals, 11,* 797–805.

Blumberg, R. L. (1984). A general theory of gender stratification. In R. Collins (Ed.), *Sociological theory* (pp. 23–101). San Francisco: Jossey-Bass.

Brooks-Gunn, J., & Furstenberg, F. F., Jr. (1989). Adolescent sexual behavior. *American Psychologist, 44,* 249–257.

Brown, L. S. (1995). Lesbian identities: Concepts and issues. In A. R. D'Augelli & C. J. Patterson (Eds.), *Lesbian, gay, and bisexual identities over the lifespan: Psychological perspectives* (pp. 3–23). New York: Oxford University Press.

Brown, L. M., & Gilligan, C. (1992). *Meeting at the crossroads: Women's psychology and girl's development.* Cambridge, MA: Harvard University Press.

Butcher, J. E. (1989). Adolescent girls' sex role development: Relationship with sports participation, self-esteem and age at menarche. *Sex Roles, 20,* 575–593.

Catsambis, S. (1995). Gender, race, ethnicity, and science education in the middle school grades. *Journal of Research in Science Teaching, 32,* 243–257.

Chodorow, N. (1978). *The reproduction of mothering: Psychoanalysis and the sociology of gender.* Berkeley: University of California Press.

Chodorow, N. (1990). *Feminism and the psychoanalytic theory.* New Haven, CT: Yale University Press.

Crocker, J., Luhtanen, R., Blaine, B., & Broadnax, S. (1994). Collective self-esteem and psychological well-being among White, Black, and Asian college students. *Personality and Social Psychology Bulletin, 20,* 503–513.

Delaney, W., & Lee, C. (1995). Self esteem and sex roles among male and female high school students: Their relationship to physical activity. *Australian Psychologist, 30,* 84–87.

De Leon, B. (1996). Career development of Hispanic adolescent girls. In B. J. Ross Leadbeater & N. Way (Eds.), *Urban girls: Resisting stereotypes, creating identities* (pp. 380–398). New York: New York University Press.

Dorney, J. (1995). Educating towards resistance: A task for women teaching girls. *Youth & Society, 27,* 55–72.

Dukes, R. L., & Martinez, R. (1994). The impact of ethgender on self-esteem among adolescents. *Adolescence, 29*, 105–115.

Eagly, A. H. (1987). *Sex differences in social behavior: A social role interpretation.* Hillsdale, NJ: Erlbaum.

Eagly, A. H., & Steffen, V. J. (1986). Gender stereotypes, occupational roles, and beliefs about part-time employees. *Psychology of Women Quarterly, 10,* 252–262.

Erkut, S., Fields, J. P., Sing, R., & Marx, F. (1996). Diversity in girls' experiences: Feeling good about who you are. In B. J. Ross Leadbeater & N. Way (Eds.), *Urban girls: Resisting stereotypes, creating identities* (pp. 53–64). New York: New York University Press.

Feingold, A. (1994). Gender differences in personality: A meta-analysis. *Psychological Bulletin, 116,* 429–456.

Fine, M. (1988). Sexuality, schooling, and adolescent females: The missing discourse of desire. *Harvard Educational Review, 58,* 29–53.

Fingerman, K. L. (1989). Sex and the working mother: Adolescent sexuality, sex role typing and family background. *Adolescence, 24,* 1–18.

Fordham, S. (1991). "Those loud Black girls": (Black) women silence, and gender "passing" in the academy. *Anthropology and Education Quarterly, 24,* 3–32.

Galambos, N. L., Almeida, D. M., & Petersen, A. C. (1990). Masculinity, femininity, and sex role attitudes in early adolescence: Exploring gender intensification. *Child Development, 61,* 1905–1914.

Galambos, N. L., Petersen, A. C., Richards, M. H., & Gitelson, I. B. (1985). The Attitudes Toward Women Scale for Adolescents (AWSA): A study of reliability and validity. *Sex Roles, 13,* 343–356.

Gardner, K. E., & LaBrecque, S. V. (1986). Effects of maternal employment on sex role orientation of adolescents. *Journal of Adolescence, 21,* 875–885.

Ge, X., Conger, R. D., & Elder, G. H., Jr. (1996). Coming of age too early: Pubertal influences on girls' vulnerability to psychological distress. *Child Development, 67,* 3385–3400.

Geary, D. C. (1998). *Male, female: The evolution of human sex differences.* Washington, DC: American Psychological Association.

Gibbons, J. L., Stiles, D. A., & Shkodriani, G. M. (1991). Adolescents' attitudes toward family and gender roles: An international comparison. *Sex Roles, 25,* 625–643.

Glickman, R. (1993). *Daughters of feminists.* New York: St. Martin's Press.

Gorrell, J., & Shaw, E. L., Jr. (1988). Upper elementary and high school students' attitudes toward gender-typed occupations. *Journal of Adolescent Research, 3,* 189–199.

Greene, B. (1990). Sturdy bridges: The role of African American mothers in the socialization of African American children. *Women and Therapy, 10,* 205–225.

Henneberger, M. (1994, April 27). In the young, signs that feminism lives. *The New York Times*, p. B1ff.

Herdt, G. (1989). Introduction: Gay and lesbian youth, emergent identities, and cultural scenes at home and abroad. *Journal of Homosexuality, 17*, 1–42.

Hill, J. P., & Lynch, M. E. (1983). The intensification of gender-related role expectations during early adolescence. In J. Brooks-Gunn & A. C. Peterson (Eds.), *Girls at puberty: Biological and psychological perspectives* (pp. 201–230). New York: Plenum.

Hilliard, W. (1996, October). Leveling the field: The trickle-down effect. *Women's Sports & Fitness*, 55.

Homma-True, R. (1990). Psychotherapeutic issues with Asian American women. *Sex Roles, 22*, 477–486.

hooks, b. (1993). *Sisters of the Yam: Black women and self recovery*. Boston: South End Press.

Hurtig, A. L., Petersen, A. C., Richards, M. H., & Gitelson, I. B. (1985). Cognitive mediators of ego functioning in adolescence. *Journal of Youth and Adolescence, 14*, 435–450.

Hyde, J. S., Fennema, E., Ryan, M. Frost, L. A., & Hopp, C. (1990). Gender comparisons of mathematics attitudes and affect: A meta-analysis. *Psychology of Women Quarterly, 14*, 299–324.

Katz, P.A. (1986). Gender identity: Development and consequences. In R. D. Ashmore & F. K. DelBoca (Eds.), *The psychology of female–male relations: A critical analysis of central concepts* (pp. 21–67). New York: Academic Press.

Kite, M. F., & Deaux, K. (1987). Gender belief systems: Homosexuality and the implicit inversion theory. *Psychology of Women Quarterly, 11*, 83–96.

Kohlberg, L. (1966). A cognitive-developmental analysis of children's sex-role concepts and attitudes. In E. E. Maccoby (Ed.), *The development of sex differences* (pp. 82–173). Stanford, CA: Stanford University Press.

LaFromboise, T. D., Heyle, A. M., & Ozer, E. (1990). Changing and diverse roles of women in American Indian cultures. *Sex Roles, 22*, 455–476.

Landrine, H. (1985). Race × class stereotypes of women. *Sex Roles, 13*, 65–75.

Levinson, D. (1978). *The seasons of a man's life*. New York: Knopf.

Macpherson, P., & Fine, M. (1995). Hungry for an us: Adolescent girls and women negotiating territories of race, gender, and class difference. *Feminism and Psychology, 5*, 181–200.

Marsh, H. W., & Jackson, S. A. (1986). Multidimensional self-concepts, masculinity, and femininity as a function of women's involvement in athletics. *Sex Roles, 15*, 391–415.

McBride Murray, V. (1996). Inner-city girls of color: Unmarried, sexually active nonmothers. In B. J. Ross Leadbeater & N. Way (Eds.), *Urban girls: Resisting stereotypes, creating identities* (pp. 272–290). New York: New York University Press.

McDonald, D. L., & McKinney, J. P. (1994). Steady dating and self-esteem in high school students. *Journal of Adolescence, 17,* 557–564.

McLoyd, V. C., & Hernandez Jozefowicz, D. M. (1996). Sizing up the future: Predictors of African American adolescent females' expectancies about their economic fortunes and family life courses. In B. J. Ross Leadbeater & N. Way (Eds.), *Urban girls: Resisting stereotypes, creating identities* (pp. 355–379). New York: New York University Press.

Milham, J., & Smith, L. E. (1981). Sex-role differentiation among Black and White Americans: A comparative study. *Journal of Black Psychology, 7,* 77–90.

Miller, J. L., & Levy, G. D. (1996). Gender role conflict, gender-typed characteristics, self-concepts, and sport socialization in female athletes and nonathletes. *Sex Roles, 35,* 111–122.

Mitchell, V., & Helson, R. (1990). Women's prime of life: Is it the 50s? *Psychology of Women Quarterly, 14,* 451–470.

Nolen-Hoeksema, S., & Girgus, J. S. (1994). The emergence of gender differences in depression during adolescence. *Psychological Bulletin, 115,* 424–443.

Pastor, J., McCormick, J., & Fine, M. (1996). Makin' homes: An urban girl thing. In B. J. Ross Leadbeater & N. Way (Eds.), *Urban girls: Resisting stereotypes, creating identities* (pp. 15–34). New York: New York University Press.

Patterson, C. J. (1995). Sexual orientation and human development: An overview. *Developmental Psychology, 31,* 3–11.

Phinney, J. S., & Alipuria, L. L. (1990). Ethnic identity in college students from four ethnic groups. *Journal of Adolescence, 13,* 171–183.

Phinney, J. S., & Chavira, V. (1992). Ethnic identity and self-esteem: An exploratory longitudinal study. *Journal of Adolescence, 15,* 271–281.

Pumariega, A. J. (1986). Acculturation and eating attitudes in adolescent girls: A comparative and correlational study. *Journal of the American Academy of Child Psychiatry, 25,* 276–279.

Read, C. R. (1991). Achievement and career choices: Comparisons of males and females. *Roeper Review, 13,* 188–193.

Richards, M. H., & Larson, R. (1989). The life space and socialization of the self: Sex differences in the young adolescent. *Journal of Youth and Adolescence, 18,* 617–626.

Richman, C. L., Clark, M. L., & Brown, K. P. (1985). General and specific self-esteem in late adolescent students: Race × gender × SES effects. *Adolescence, 79,* 555–566.

Robinson, T., & Ward, J. V. (1991). "A belief in self far greater than anyone's disbelief": Culitivating resistance among African American female adolescents. *Women and Therapy, 11,* 87–103.

Root, M. P. P. (1990). Disordered eating in women of color. *Sex Roles, 22,* 525–536.

Rosenberg, M., & Simmons, R. (1971). *Black and White self esteem: The urban school child.* Washington, DC: American Sociological Association.

Savin-Williams, R. C. (1995). Lesbian, gay male, and bisexual adolescents. In A. R. D'Augelli & C. J. Patterson (Eds.), *Lesbian, gay, and bisexual identities over the lifespan: Psychological perspectives* (pp. 167–189). New York: Oxford University Press.

Shaw, S. M., Kleiber, D. A., & Caldwell, L. L. (1995). Leisure and identity formation in male and female adolescents: A preliminary investigation. *Journal of Leisure Research, 27,* 245–263.

Siever, M. D. (1994). Sexual orientation and gender as factors in socioculturally acquired vulnerability to body dissatisfaction and eating disorders. *Journal of Consulting and Clinical Psychology, 62,* 252–260.

Sinott, J. D. (1987). Sex roles in adulthood and old age. In B. Carter (Ed.), *Current conceptions of sex roles and sex typing: Theory and research* (pp. 155–177). New York: Praeger.

Smith, E. J. (1982). The Black female adolescent: A review of the educational, career and psychological literature. *Psychology of Women Quarterly, 6,* 261–288.

Smith, P. A., & Midlarsky, E. (1985). Empirically derived conceptions of femaleness and maleness: A current view. *Sex Roles, 12,* 313–328.

Spence, J. T., & Helmreich, R. (1978). *Masculinity and femininity: The psychological dimensions, correlates, and antecedents.* Austin: University of Texas Press.

Spencer, L. (1993, January 3). Grrrls only. *The Washington Post,* p. C1ff.

Steiner-Adair, C. (1990). The body politic: Normal female adolescent development and the development of eating disorders. In C. Gilligan, N. P. Lyons, & T. J. Hanmer (Eds.), *Making connections: The relational worlds of adolescent girls at the Emma Willard School* (pp. 162–182). Cambridge, MA: Harvard University Press.

Stice, E. (1994). Review of the evidence for a sociocultural model of bulimia nervosa and an exploration of the mechanisms of action. *Clinical Psychology Review, 14,* 633–661.

Taylor, J. M. (1996). Cultural stories: Latina and Portuguese daughters and mothers. In B. J. Ross Leadbeater & N. Way (Eds.), *Urban girls: Resisting stereotypes, creating identities* (pp. 117–131). New York: New York University Press.

Taylor, J. M., Gilligan, C., & Sullivan, A. M. (1995). *Between voice and silence: Women and girls, race and relationship.* Cambridge, MA: Harvard University Press.

Teen sex: Not for sale. (1989, May). *Psychology Today,* 10, 12.

Thorne, B. (1993). *Gender play: Girls and boys in school.* New Brunswick, NJ: Rutgers University Press.

Tolman, D. L. (1994). Doing desire: Adolescent girls' struggles for/with sexuality. *Gender & Society, 8,* 324–342.

Uba, L. (1994). *Asian Americans: Personality patterns, identity, and mental health.* New York: Hillsdale Press.

Urberg, K. A. (1979). Sex role conceptualizations in adolescents and adults. *Developmental Psychology, 15,* 90–92.

U.S. National Center for Health Statistics. (1992). *Monthly vital statistics, 43*(12).

Vasquez-Nuttal, E., Romero-Garcia, I., & De Leon, B. (1987). Sex roles and perceptions of femininity and masculinity of Hispanic women: A review of the literature. *Psychology of Women Quarterly, 11,* 409–425.

Ward, J. V. (1996). Raising resisters: The role of truth telling in the psychological development of African American girls. In B. J. Ross Leadbeater & N. Way (Eds.), *Urban girls: Resisting stereotypes, creating identities* (pp. 85–99). New York: New York University Press.

Way, N. (1995). "Can't you see the courage, the strength that I have?": Listening to urban adolescent girls speak about their relationships. *Psychology of Women Quarterly, 19,* 107–128.

Worell, J. (1989). Sex roles in transition. In J. Worell & F. Danner (Eds.), *The adolescent as decision-maker: Applications to development and education* (pp. 245–280). San Diego, CA: Academic Press.

3

SELF-EVALUATIONS OF COMPETENCE, TASK VALUES, AND SELF-ESTEEM

JACQUELYNNE ECCLES, BONNIE BARBER, DEBORAH JOZEFOWICZ, OKSANA MALENCHUK, AND MINA VIDA

Over the last 10 years, there have been extensive discussions in media and academic publication outlets regarding the costs of adolescence for females in terms of mental health, self-esteem, and identity. For example, the American Association of University Women (AAUW; 1990) reported marked declines in girls' self-confidence during the early adolescent years. Similarly, Carol Gilligan (1990) has reported that girls lose confidence in their ability to express their needs and opinions as they move into the early adolescent years; she referred to this process as "losing one's voice." Finally, Mary Pipher (1994), in her very popular book *Reviving Ophelia*, outlined a variety of ways in which young female adolescents lose confidence in themselves and become depressed.

We wish to thank all of our colleagues and former students who have worked with us in developing the studies summarized in this chapter: Diane Early, Elaine Belansky, Karen McCarthy, Arnold Sameroff, Linda Kuhn, Carol Midgley, David Reumen, Allan Wigfield, Janis Jacobs, and Kim Updegraff. This chapter was supported by grants from the National Institute of Mental Health, the National Institute on Child Health and Human Development, the National Science Foundation, and the MacArthur Research Network on Successful Pathways for Adolescents Living in High-Risk Settings.

Although these patterns do exist, evidence from other sources suggests that the developmental changes may not be large or as general as portrayed in the popular media. For example, although Simmons and Blyth (1987) found that girls who made the junior high school transition experienced a dramatic decline in their self-esteem during early adolescence, girls in kindergarten through eighth grade (elementary school) did not experience this decline. Similarly, although the girls in Eccles et al.'s (1989) study had lower levels of self-esteem at all time points than did the boys, the girls' and boys' self-esteem dropped about the same amount following the junior high school transition. Both of these studies suggest that the drop in girls' self-esteem is not universal and often not substantially different from the drop in boys' self-esteem.

In addition, many of the reports of the costs of adolescence for females focus on only one or two aspects of development (e.g., self-esteem, confidence in one's academic abilities, "voice," or depression) and then report only the negative changes, failing to note that many aspects of girls' self-perceptions and mental health do not decline and that the variations within girls, even on those indicators that do show average declines, are much larger than the average differences in the mean levels for girls and boys. For example, Simmons and Blyth (1987) found in their sample far less marked declines among African American girls than among European American girls.

Other researchers, for example Gilligan and her colleagues (e.g., Gilligan, 1990), did not include boys in their samples and yet concluded that the changes in girls' self-perceptions were linked to gender role identity development rather than to a more general process linked to adolescent development in both girls and boys. Like any developmental period, adolescence poses both challenges and opportunities to all young people. Unless one looks at the pattern of change for both girls and boys, one may incorrectly attribute the changes in girls' self-perceptions and mental health to gender-related issues rather than to these more general developmental issues linked to adolescence.

In this chapter, we review changes in both girls' and boys' confidence, ability self-concepts, task values, and self-esteem. We pay particular attention to variations in the pattern of change across (a) different arenas of both girls' and boys' adolescent lives and (b) different female subpopulations in the United States. In addition, we pay particular attention to the work we have been doing on these topics over the past 25 years. During this time, we have investigated developmental changes in domain-specific ability self-concepts, expectations for future success, and values–motivation across several domains significant to adolescents' lives (e.g., math, English, physical science, sports, peer-related social skills, popularity, and physical attractiveness). We also investigated developmental changes in indicators of more general self-esteem. Although we found developmental changes on many of these indicators, these patterns of change do not consistently favor males. Instead, the patterns of change in our data reflect increasing congruence with gender role stereotypes: With increasing age, the girls come to hold more female gender role stereotypic views of their abilities and interests, and the boys come to hold more male gender role stereotypic views of their abilities and interests. The changes on indicators of mental health reflect a similar pattern: An increasing number of girls reported symptoms of low self-esteem and depression, and an increasing number of boys reported either being victimized or engaging in aggressive and physically risky behaviors. These types of changes suggest that adolescence provides both opportunities and risk for both girls and boys—some of which are linked to gender roles and some to more general processes, which in turn are linked to the types of demands American society places on early adolescent children. It is important to include findings for both girls and boys to distinguish between these two types of influences. We summarize such patterns in the following sections.

COMPETENCE AND EXPECTANCY-RELATED SELF-PERCEPTIONS

As noted earlier, there has been considerable public attention focused on the issue of girls' declining confidence in their academic abilities. In addition, researchers and policymakers interested in young women's educational and occupational choices have stressed the potential role that such declining confidences might play in undermining young women's educational and vocational aspirations, particularly in the technical fields related to math and physical science (Bell, 1989; Betz & Fitzgerald, 1987; Eccles, 1987, 1994; Farmer, 1985; Hollinger, 1983; Kerr, 1985; National Science Foundation, 1996; Updegraff, Eccles, Barber, & O'Brien, 1996). For example, these researchers have suggested that girls may drop out of math and physical science because they lose confidence in their math abilities as they move into and through adolescence—leading to the fact that females are less likely to pursue these types of careers than are males (e.g., Betz & Fitzgerald, 1987; Eccles [Parsons] et al., 1983). Similarly, these researchers have suggested that gender differences in confidence in one's abilities in other areas underlie gender differences across the board in educational and occupational choices. But even more important for this chapter, Eccles and her colleagues have suggested that the individual differences among females in educational and occupational choices also are related to variations among females in their confidence in their abilities in different domains.

But do females and males differ on measures commonly linked to expectations for success, particularly with regard to their academic subjects and various future occupations? Are females more confident of their abilities in female gender role stereotyped domains? In most but not all studies, the answer to both these questions is yes. For example, both Terman (1926) and Strauss and Subotnik (1991) found that gifted girls were more likely to underestimate their intellectual skills and their relative class standing than were gifted boys—who were more likely to overestimate theirs. Strauss and Subotnik also found that gifted high school girls reported more test anxiety than their gifted male peers. Similarly, girls enrolled in a special gifted elementary school program rated their test anxiety higher than did their male peers (Eccles & Harold, 1992). Gender differences in the competence beliefs of more typical samples also are often reported, particularly in gender role stereotyped domains and on novel tasks. Often these differences favor males. For example, high-achieving females are more likely than their male peers to underestimate both their ability level and their class standing; in contrast, their male peers are more likely than these females to overestimate their likely performance (Crandall, 1969; Frome & Eccles, 1995; Strauss & Subotnik, 1991; Terman, 1926).

In other studies, the difference depends on the gender role stereotyping of the activity. For example, boys hold higher competence beliefs than girls for math and sports, even after all relevant skill-level differences are controlled. In contrast, girls have higher competence beliefs than boys for reading and social skills, and the magnitude of these differences often increases following puberty (e.g., Eccles, 1984; Eccles et al., 1989; Harter, 1982; Huston, 1983; Wigfield, Eccles, Mac Iver, Reuman, & Midgley, 1991). Furthermore, in each of these studies, the young women on average had greater confidence in their abilities in reading and social skills than they did in their abilities in math, physical science, and athletics.

Works By Eccles and Colleagues

We have focused our work directly on both gender differences and individual differences within females in competence-related beliefs. Over the last 15 years, we have conducted three longitudinal studies of the ontogeny of children's and adolescents' ability-related self-perceptions and values in an effort to understand individual differences in achievement-related task choice, engagement, and performance. The role of gender has been one of our primary concerns. Because we present findings from each of these studies throughout this chapter, we now provide a brief summary of each study. The first study, the Michigan Study of Adolescent Life Transitions (MSALT), began in 1982 with a sample of approximately 3,000 sixth graders in 12 different school districts in southeastern Michigan. These districts served primarily European American working-class and middle-class, small city communities. Although the sample is predominantly European American, it does include about 150 African American adolescents. We have now followed approximately 2,000 of these adolescents well into their early adulthood years, using standard survey-type methods. The second study, Childhood and Beyond, began in 1985 with a sample of approximately 800 European American early elementary school children in three middle-class school districts in southeastern Michigan. We have now followed this sample through elementary and secondary school using standard survey-type methods. The third study, Maryland Adolescent Growth in Context (MAGIC), began in 1990 with approximately 1,000 seventh graders attending 23 different junior high schools in one public school district in Maryland. This sample is 65% African American and 30% European American. We are following these adolescents through the end of high school, again using standard survey-type methods.

In each of these studies, we found consistent evidence of gender differences in expectations for success and confidence in one's abilities for mathematics, English, athletics, and peer-related social skills, especially among junior and senior high school students (e.g., Eccles, 1984, 1989; Eccles & Harold, 1991; Eccles et al., 1989; Eccles [Parsons], Adler, & Meece, 1984; Wigfield et al., 1991). However, the direction of the difference depends on the gender typing of the domain, and the differences are always quite small. For example, during the first four waves of data collection in the MSALT (when the adolescents were in the sixth and seventh grades), boys rated their math and sports ability higher than did the girls; in contrast, the girls rated their English and social abilities higher than did the boys (Wigfield et al., 1991).

But even more important for this chapter, female and male adolescents rank ordered these skill areas differently. The girls rated themselves as most competent in English and social activities and as least competent in sports. The boys rated themselves as most competent, by a substantial margin, in sports, followed by math and then social activities; the boys rated themselves as least competent in English. Such within-sex, rank order comparisons are critically important for understanding differences in life choices. In our follow-up studies of these same adolescents, we were able to predict individual differences among the young women in their occupational goals with the pattern of their confidences across subject domains (Jozefowicz, Barber, & Eccles, 1993). The young women who wanted to go into occupations requiring a lot of writing, for example, had high confidence in their artistic and writing abilities and relatively lower confidence in their math and science abilities. In contrast, the young women who wanted to go into science and advanced health-related fields (e.g., a physician) had very high confidence in their math and science abilities.

We asked about these same academic self-concepts as these adolescents moved through high school. Figure 3.1 illustrates the findings for math, English, and sports. One can see the association of gender stereotypes and the developmental patterns in these adolescents' responses. Somewhat contrary to the media portrayal of the gender differences related to mathe-

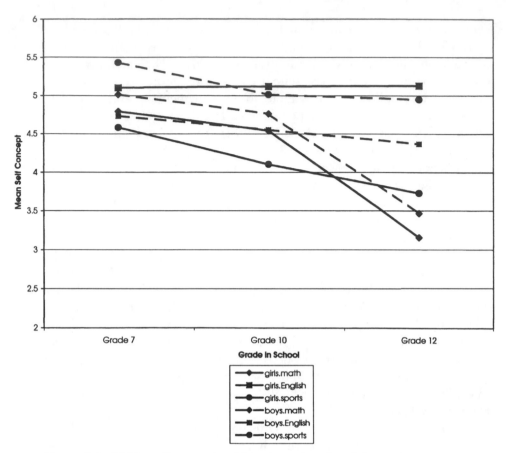

Figure 3.1. Ability self-concepts of female and male adolescents.

matics, the size of this sample's gender difference for math is much smaller than the gender difference, favoring females, in these adolescents' ratings of their English ability. Furthermore, the gender difference for math is the largest in Grade 12—exactly the time when high-performing girls begin to drop out of challenging high school math courses (Updegraff et al., 1996). Most striking about this figure is the extent to which boys' confidence in their athletic ability exceeds their confidence in their academic abilities. When one averages across math and English, boys have lower confidence than do girls in their academic abilities in general. This could be one explanation for the fact that the boys in this sample—as in the nation more generally—are more likely to drop out of high school than are the girls.

Given the media attention to the girls' supposed lack of confidence in their math skills, it is important to note that our findings are not anomalous. Mathematics has never been one of the most strongly gender role stereotyped subject areas. For example, in her early work, Aletha Stein (aka Huston) found that girls and boys rated math as neither especially feminine nor masculine (see Huston, 1983). Furthermore, the proportion of bachelor's degree awarded to women in mathematics in the United States has matched the proportion of women enrolled in college since 1950. Instead, physics and engineering are seen as male-typed subject areas, and many college students enrolled in college math courses are actually majoring in these other fields. In addition, the gender difference favoring males for physical science and engineering is much greater than the gender difference favoring older male adolescents for mathematics (National Science Foundation, 1996).

Ability Self-Concepts

One of the most interesting findings from the studies of academic self-confidence is that the gender differences in self-perceptions are usually much larger than one would expect, given objective measures of actual performance and competence. First, consider mathematics: With the exception of performance on the most anxiety-provoking standardized test, girls do as well as boys on all measures of math competence throughout primary, secondary, and tertiary education. Furthermore, the few gender differences that do exist have been decreasing in magnitude over the last 20 years and do not appear with great regularity until late in the primary school years (National Science Foundation, 1996). Similarly, the gender difference in perceived sports competence is much larger (accounting for 9% of the variance in one study; see Eccles & Harold, 1991) than the gender difference in the measures of actual sport-related skills (which accounted for between 1% and 3% of the variance on these indicators).

Causal Attributions and Locus of Control

So why do girls rate their math and sports competence so much lower than boys and so much lower than they rate their English ability and social skills? Some theorists have suggested that girls and boys may interpret variations in their performance in various academic subjects and leisure activities in a gender role stereotyped manner. For example, girls might be more likely to attribute their math and sports successes to hard work and effort than would boys; in contrast, boys might be more likely than girls to attribute their successes to natural talent. Similarly, girls more so than boys might be more likely to attribute their English and social successes to natural ability and their math and sports successes to hard work and luck (and vice versa for boys). Such differences in interpretation would lead to both the gender differences and the within-gender differences in confidence levels reported above. Unfortunately, there is very little research on the within-gender differences in attributional patterns across domains. More empirical work has been conducted on gender differences; although the empirical evidence of such gender differences in interpretative style is mixed, the general patterns are worth considering.

Some researchers (e.g., Dweck & Licht, 1980; Stipek & Hoffman, 1980) have found that girls are less likely than boys to attribute success to ability and more likely to attribute failure to a lack of ability. Others have found that this pattern depends on the kind of task used, occurring more with unfamiliar tasks or stereotypically masculine achievement task (see Eccles [Parsons] et al., 1984; Eccles [Parsons] et al., 1983; Yee & Eccles, 1988). The most consistent difference occurs for attributions of success to ability versus effort: Girls are less likely than boys to stress the relevance of their own ability as a cause of their successes. Instead, girls tend to rate effort and hard work as a more important determinant of their success than ability; it is interesting to note that so do their parents (Yee & Eccles, 1988). There is nothing inherently wrong with attributing one's successes to hard work. In fact, Stevenson and his colleagues (e.g., Stevenson, Chen, & Uttal, 1990) stressed that this attributional pattern is a major advantage Japanese students have over American students. Nonetheless, it appears that within the United States, this attributional pattern undermines students' confidence in their ability to master increasingly more difficult material—perhaps leading girls to stop taking math courses prematurely (Eccles, 1994).

Both gender and age differences favoring males are also sometimes reported in the locus of control literature. For example, in Crandall, Katkovsky, and Crandall's (1965) study using the Individual Achievement Responsibility Scale, girls had higher internal locus of responsibility scores than did boys for both positive and negative events. But even more important, high school girls had higher internality for negative events than did younger girls; this developmental difference resulted in the older girls accepting more blame for negative events than both the older boys and the younger girls—a pattern consistent with earlier reports of declining confidence among girls in their academic abilities during the adolescent years (see also Dweck & Licht, 1980; Dweck & Repucci, 1973).

This greater propensity for older adolescent girls to take personal responsibility for their failures, coupled with their more frequent attribution of failure to a lack of ability (a stable, uncontrollable cause), has been interpreted as evidence of greater learned helplessness in females (see Dweck & Licht, 1980). However, evidence for gender differences on behavioral indicators of learned helplessness is quite weak (see Eccles [Parsons] et al., 1984). In fact, in most studies of academic underachievers, boys outnumber girls 2 to 1 (see McCall, Evahn, & Kratzer, 1992). Similarly, boys are more likely than girls to be referred by their teachers for motivational problems and are more likely to drop out before completing high school (Eccles, Wigfield, & Schiefele, 1998). Instead, the evidence is stronger that females, compared with males, select easier laboratory tasks, are more likely to avoid challenging and competitive situations, lower their expectations more following failure, shift more quickly to a different college major when their grades begin to drop, and perform more poorly than they are capable of on difficult, timed tests (see Dweck & Licht, 1980; Parsons & Ruble, 1977; Ruble & Martin, 1997; Spencer & Steele, 1995). In addition, the age differences on these types of indicators of confidence support the hypothesis that females on average lose confidence in their academic abilities during the adolescent years.

Gendered Stereotypes

Furthermore, the extent to which female adolescents endorse the cultural stereotypes regarding which sex is likely to be most talented in each domain predicts the extent to which girls distort their ability self-concepts and expectations in the gender stereotypic direction (Early, Belansky, & Eccles, 1992; Eccles & Harold, 1991). Spencer and Steele (1995) suggested a related mechanism linking culturally gendered stereotypes to competence: *stereotype vulnerability*. They hypothesized that members of social groups (e.g., females) who are stereotyped as being less competent in a particular subject area (e.g., math) will become anxious when asked to do difficult problems because they are afraid the stereotype may be true of them. This vulnerability is also likely to increase girls' vulnerability to failure feedback on male-stereotyped tasks, leading to a lowering of their expectations and their confidence in their ability to succeed for these types of tasks. To test these hypotheses, Spencer and Steele gave college students a difficult math test under two conditions: being told that males typically do better on this test or that males and females typically do about the same. The women scored lower than the males only in the first condition. Furthermore, the manipulation's effect was mediated by variations across condition in reported anxiety. Apparently, knowing that one is taking a test on which males typically do better than females increases young women's anxiety, which in turn undermines their performance. This study also suggests that changing this dynamic is relatively easy if one can change the women's perception of the test's sex typing.

Anxiety

Gender differences have also emerged fairly regularly in other studies of anxiety (e.g., Douglas & Rice, 1979; Hill & Sarason, 1966; Manley & Rosemier, 1972; Meece, Wigfield, & Eccles, 1990). However, Hill and Sarason (1966) suggested that boys may be more defensive than girls about admitting anxiety on questionnaires. In support of this suggestion, Lord, Eccles, and McCarthy (1994) found that test anxiety was a more significant predictor of poor adjustment to junior high school for boys, even though the girls reported higher mean levels of anxiety. Thus, even though the girls reported higher levels of test anxiety, the negative consequences of test anxiety seemed much more marked for girls. As reported later, concerns about their physical appearance emerged as a much more salient and detrimental anxiety among the girls.

Summary

In summary, when either gender differences or within-gender individual differences emerge on competence-related measures for academic subjects and other important skill areas, they are consistent with gender role stereotypes. These differences have also been found to be important mediators of both gender differences and within-gender individual differences in various types of achievement-related behaviors and choices. Such gendered patterns are theoretically important because they point to the power of gender role socialization processes as the key to understanding both girls' and boys' confidence in their various abilities (see Eccles, Jacobs, et al., 1993; Huston, 1983; and Ruble & Martin, 1997, for a full discussion of these processes). In addition, to the extent that gender role socialization is key, it is important to study how and why females differ in the extent to which they either are exposed to these socialization pressures or resist them when they are so exposed.

It should be noted, however, that gendered patterns do not occur in all studies. For example, in several studies of gifted adolescents, researchers found no gender differences on measures of general self-concept, locus of control, general self-confidence and assertiveness, and general self-esteem (Dauber & Benbow, 1990; Tidwell, 1980; Tomlinson-Keasey & Smith-Winberry, 1983). Furthermore, although the girls in our study of gifted elementary school children reported higher estimates for their reading ability than did the boys, the boys and girls reported equivalent confidence in their mathematical ability (Eccles & Harold, 1992). Similarly, Benbow and Stanley (1982) found no substantial gender difference in gifted students' estimates of their math and science competence. Although the gifted students in the Terman (1926) study did prefer courses that they thought were easier for them, the boys and girls did not differ in their perceptions of the ease of mathematics. Schunk and Lilly (1982) also found no gender difference in gifted children's expectations for success on a laboratory math task. Finally, in our longitudinal study of intellectually capable students, gender differences in expectations for success in future math courses did not mediate the gender differences in math course enrollment; the perceived value of the math course did (Eccles [Parsons] et al., 1984). Furthermore, in all of our studies, the individual differences among the young women in both confidence and task values were very powerful predictors of individual differences in educational and occupational choices.

It should also be noted that most of the studies documenting the stereotypic gender differences relied exclusively on European American, middle-class samples. We know very little about the generalizability of these findings to other populations both within the United States and across the world. As we discuss later, this is a major problem because evidence for the debilitating effects of gender stereotypic biases on females is much weaker in the few studies of African Americans (see the later discussion for more details).

Given this mixed set of results for intellectually able and gifted adolescents and the limited range of populations studied, it is not clear that girls in general are less confident than boys either of their intellectual abilities in general or of their mathematical ability in particular. Although the differences when they are found do support this conclusion, these differences are always small and often not found. It is also not clear whether this difference, even when it is found, is the primary mediator of gender differences in the educational and occupational decisions. Gender differences in task value may be just as important. These differences are discussed in a later section.

But even more important, in all of the relevant studies researchers have documented extensive variation within each sex. Females vary a great deal among themselves in their intellectual confidence for various academic domains. They also vary considerably in their test anxiety, attributional styles, and locus of control. Variation on these characteristics predict variation in females' educational and occupational choices (Betz & Fitzgerald, 1987; Eccles, 1987; Eccles, Barber, & Jozekowicz, 1998; Farmer, 1985; Kerr, 1985): Female adolescents who aspire to careers in math and science and take advanced courses in math and physical science have greater confidence in their math and science abilities than those that do not. They also have just as much, if not more, confidence in their math and science abilities as they do in their English abilities.

Occupational Ability Self-Concepts

We extended the work on academic, social, and athletic self-concepts by looking at adolescents' competence ratings for skills more directly linked to adult occupational choice. As the MSALT sample moved into and through high school, we asked them a series of questions directly related to future job choices. First, we asked them to rate how good they were compared with other students at each of several job-related skills. Second, we asked them to rate the probability that they would succeed at each of a series of standard careers. The results for their responses when they were seniors are summarized in Table 3.1. On the one hand, the results are quite

TABLE 3.1
Gender Differences in Values, Expectations, and Perceived Ability

Measure	Females		Males	
	M	SD	M	SD
Expected efficacy in jobs				
1. Health related[b]	4.2	1.9	3.7	1.7*
2. Science related[a]	3.5	1.6	4.1	1.7*
3. Skilled labor (male)/protective services[a]	2.4	1.0	4.2	1.2*
4. Skilled labor (female)/human services[b]	4.5	1.2	3.3	1.2*
5. Business and law[b]	4.6	1.4	4.9	1.4
6. Artist[a]	3.5	1.9	3.3	1.7
Self-perception of skills				
1. Working with others[b]	5.5	0.9	4.8	1.0*
2. Leadership[a]	5.3	1.1	5.3	1.0
3. Independence[a]	5.2	1.1	5.3	1.0
4. Intellectual[a]	5.1	1.2	5.3	1.0
5. Mechanical[a]	2.3	1.4	4.2	1.7*
6. Computers[a]	4.0	1.7	4.2	1.6
Lifestyle values				
1. High status/competitive[a]	4.4	1.4	4.8	1.4*
2. Risk taking[a]	4.7	1.1	5.1	1.0*
3. Careerism[a]	5.7	1.0	5.5	1.0
4. Family and friends before work[b]	4.5	1.0	4.0	1.1*
5. Material wealth[a]	4.7	1.2	5.1	1.1*
Valued job characteristics				
1. Flexibility to meet family obligations[a]	5.5	1.1	5.4	1.0
2. People/society oriented[b]	5.7	1.0	5.1	1.1*
3. Prestige/responsibility[a]	5.4	1.1	5.6	0.9
4. Creative/educational[a]	5.7	1.2	5.8	1.1
5. Machinery/manual work[a]	3.0	1.2	3.9	1.6*
6. Math/computer work[a]	3.9	1.5	4.2	1.5*

Note. Both multivariate analyses of variance (MANOVAs) were significant at the $p < .001$ level. Significant relationships in the table are based on univariate tests of significance.
[a]First MANOVA set.   [b]Second MANOVA set.
*$p < .001$.

gender role stereotyped: The female students were less confident of success than were the male students in science-related professions and in male-typed skilled labor occupations. In contrast, the male students were less confident of their success than were the female students in health-related professions and female-typed skilled labor occupations (Jozefowicz et al., 1993). On the other hand, there were no gender differences in these seniors' ratings of either their confidence of success in business and law or their leadership, independence, intellectual, and computer skills. Furthermore, although the male students were more confident of success in physical science and engineering fields, the female students were more confident than the males of success in health-related fields, which involve extensive scientific training.

The within-gender patterns are equally interesting. On average, these young women saw themselves as quite competent in traditionally female-typed jobs and skills related to human service, particularly in comparison to their confidence for science-related jobs and mechanical skills. It is interesting to note that these young women also saw themselves as quite competent in terms of leadership, intellectual skills, and independence.

Clearly, these young women see themselves as quite efficacious in terms of possible occupational pathways. Which particular pathway they select or end up on likely has as much, if not more, to do with their values as their sense of efficacy. In the next section, we review the gendered findings related to achievement-related values.

GENDER AND ACHIEVEMENT VALUES

Do females and males make gender role stereotypic life choices because they have gender role stereotypic values? We addressed this question in each of our studies, and the answer is yes. Gender role stereotypic patterns in adolescents' valuing of sports, social activities, and English emerged consistently in our studies (e.g., Eccles et al., 1989; Wigfield et al., 1991). It is interesting to note that the gendered pattern associated with the value of math does not emerge until high school (Eccles, 1984). Finally, the gendered pattern of valuing math and computer skills emerged as the key predictors of both gender differences and individual differences among female students in their plans to enter math-related scientific and engineering fields (Eccles, Barber, & Jozefowicz, 1998; Jozefowicz et al., 1993).

We also found clear evidence of gendered patterns of task value for various school subjects and activities in our study of elementary school children (see Eccles & Harold, 1992; Eccles, Wigfield, et al., 1993; Wigfield et al., 1997). Although there was no gender difference in expectations for success in mathematics, these girls reported liking both math and sports less than the boys did. In contrast, the girls reported liking reading and social activities more than the boys did. Finally, the girls reported liking reading and social activities more than athletic activities. Math fell in the middle and had very high variability. A substantial portion of the girls liked math better than reading; however, an equally substantial portion of the girls liked math much less than reading.

Other studies yielded similar findings. When asked to name their favorite school subjects, gifted girls rated English, foreign languages, composition, music, and drama higher than physical sciences, physical training, and U.S. history (George & Denham, 1976; Terman, 1926). Once again, math yielded a variable pattern among the girls, and there was little evidence of gender differences in interest in mathematics. In contrast, evidence for both stereotypic gender differences in interest in physics and applied mathematical fields, like engineering, and the relatively low rating of interest in these fields compared with other subject areas by girls was quite consistent (Benbow, 1988; Benbow & Minor, 1986). Similarly, when asked their occupational interests and anticipated college major, gifted girls rated domestic, secretarial, artistic, biological science, and both medical and social service occupations and training higher than both higher status and business-related occupations in general and physical sciences, engineering, and the military in particular; boys showed the opposite pattern (Fox, Pasternak, & Peiser, 1976; Terman, 1926). Finally, when gifted males and females were asked their leisure time activities and hobbies, similar gendered patterns of interest emerge. At all ages, gifted females both liked and reported spending more time on reading, writing, and participating in a variety of activities related to arts and crafts, domestic skills, and drama than on sports, working with machines and tools, and involved with scientific, math-related, and electronic hobbies. Males showed the opposite pattern (Dauber & Benbow, 1990; Fox, 1976; McGinn, 1976; Terman, 1926; Terman & Oden, 1947).

It is important to note that these gendered patterns have decreased over time. Young women today are more likely to aspire to the male-stereotyped fields of medicine, law, and business than their mothers and grandmothers. Although the numbers are not nearly as large, young women today are also much more likely to seek out occupations related to engineering and physical science (National Science Foundation, 1996). Young women today are also much more involved in athletic activities than their mothers and grandmothers (see Eccles & Harold, 1991).

Because of our interest in understanding career choice, we extended this work in MSALT to include a series of measures of more general life and occupational values. When they were seniors, we asked the participants to rate how important each of a series of job-related and life-related values and of job characteristics were to them. The results are summarized in Table 3.1. As was true for the job-related skills, we found evidence of gender role stereotypic differences and transcendence. In keeping with traditional stereotypes, the female students rated family and friends as more important to them than did the male students; the female students also were more likely than the male students to want jobs that were people oriented. In contrast but also consistent with traditional stereotypes, the male students placed a higher value on high-risk and competitive activities and wealth; they also were more interested in jobs that allowed for work with machinery, math, or computers. However, counter to traditional stereotypes, there were no gender differences in careerism (focus on career as a critical part of one's identity), and the female and male students were equally likely to want jobs that allowed them flexibility to meet family obligations, entailed prestige and responsibility, and provided opportunities for creative and intellectual work.

Evidence of both gender role typing and transcendence was also evident in the within-gender patterns. Although these young women still, on average, attached most importance to having a job with sufficient flexibility to meet family obligations and with the opportunity to help people, they also placed great importance on the role of their career for personal identity (careerism) and on both prestige–responsibility and creativity as key components of their future occupations.

We next used the values and ability self-concepts to predict these young women's occupational aspirations. The results for the ability self-concepts were summarized earlier. As predicted by the expectancy-value model of achievement-related choices (see Eccles, 1994; and Eccles [Parsons] et al., 1983), the lifestyle and valued job characteristics did an excellent job of discriminating between these young women's occupational plans. Perhaps most interesting was the value placed on helping other people that predicted which women aspired to advanced level health-related professions (e.g., a physician) and which women aspired to PhD-level science careers. Both of these groups of women had very high confidence in their math and science abilities. In contrast, they differed dramatically in the value they placed on helping others: The women aspiring to the health-related fields placed more importance on this dimension than any other value dimension. In contrast, the women aspiring to PhD-level science careers placed less importance on this dimension than any other dimension, particularly the value of being able to work with math and computers (Jozefowicz et al., 1993).

In summary, there is still strong evidence of gendered patterns in the valuing of different academic subject areas and activities. Although it is encouraging that girls value math during elementary school, the fact that adolescent girls have less positive views of both their math ability and the value of math is problematic because these differences lead girls to be less likely than boys to take optional advanced level math courses and physical science (see Eccles, 1987, 1994; and Eccles [Parsons] et al., 1984).

Psychological Processes Related to These Gendered Patterns

Gendered patterns of responses have also been found on many of the psychological processes proposed by Eccles and her colleagues to underlie these differences in values. For example, Eccles [Parsons] et al. (1983) predicted that the attainment value of particular tasks would be linked to (a) conceptions of one's personality and capabilities, (b) long-range goals and plans, (c) schema regarding the proper roles of men and women, (d) instrumental and terminal values (Rokeach, 1973), (e) ideal images of what one should be like, and (f) social scripts regarding proper behavior in a variety of situations. If gender role socialization leads males and females to differ on these core self- and role-related beliefs, then related activities will have differential value for males and females. Similarly, young women who hold traditional gender role stereotyped beliefs and values should be more likely than other young women to aspire to female-stereotyped occupations and life roles. For example, in a study of the link between personal values and college major, Dunteman, Wisenbaker, and Taylor (1978) identified two sets of values that both predicted major and differentiated the sexes: The first set (labeled *thing orientation*) reflected an interest in manipulating objects and understanding the physical world; the second set (labeled *person orientation*) reflected an interest in understanding human social interaction and a concern with helping people. Students with high thing orientation and low person orientation were more likely than other students to select a math or science major. Not surprising, female students were more likely than male students to major in something other than math or science because of their higher person-oriented values. Similarly, the young women in Jozefowicz, Eccles, and Barber's (1993) study placed more value than the young men on a variety of career-related skills and interests, such as doing work that directly helps people and meshes well with child-rearing responsibilities. As noted earlier, these values along with ability self-concepts predicted the career plans of both males and females.

Finally, the role of conflict between gender roles and achievement in gifted girls' lives is well illustrated by an ethnographic study of a group of gifted elementary school girls by Bell (1989). She interviewed a multiethnic group of third- to sixth-grade gifted girls in an urban elementary school regarding the barriers they perceived to their personal achievement in school. Five gender role-related themes emerged with great regularity: (a) concern about hurting someone else's feeling by winning in achievement contests, (b) concern about seeming to be a braggart if one expressed pride in one's accomplishments, (c) concern over the reaction to nonsuccess experiences (apparently not being the very best is very painful to these girls), (d) concern over their physical appearance and what it takes to be beautiful, and (e) concern with being overly aggressive in terms of getting the teacher's attention. In each case, the gifted girls felt caught between doing their best and either appearing feminine or doing the caring thing.

Disidentification

Drawing on the writings of William James (1892/1963), we suggest that adolescents will lower the value they attach to particular activities or subject areas if they lack confidence in these areas to maintain their self-esteem (see also Harter, 1990). Spencer and Steele (1995) suggested a similar phenomenon related to stereotype vulnerability. They hypothesized that women will disidentify with those subject areas in which women are stereotyped as less competent than men. By disidentifying with these areas, women will not only lower the value they attach to these subject areas, but they will also be less likely to experience pride and positive affect when they are doing well in these subjects. Consequently, these subjects will become irrelevant to their self-esteem. Although these hypotheses remain to be tested directly, our findings are certainly consistent with them. In the next section, we discuss self-esteem in more detail.

SELF-ESTEEM

An AAUW (1990) report concludes that girls' self-esteem falls dramatically during early adolescence. Similar findings have emerged in several studies (e.g., Gilligan, 1990; Orenstein, 1994; Pipher, 1994). For example, Simmons and Blyth (1987) found that girls' self-esteem is more likely than boys' to drop between sixth and seventh grade. But this was only true for European American early adolescents who made a transition from elementary school to junior high school at the same time that they moved from sixth to seventh grade, suggesting that both school structure and ethnic culture play an important role in this developmental change. Drawing on cumulative stress theory, Simmons and Blyth suggested that gender differences in the rate of decline in self-esteem among European American adolescents result from the fact that girls making the transition to junior high school at the end of Grade 6 are more likely than boys to be coping with two major transitions (both pubertal and school changes) at the same time. Because coping with multiple transitions is more difficult than coping with only one, these young women should be at greater risk of negative outcomes than adolescents who have to cope with only one transition (either school or pubertal changes) during this developmental period. As seen later, the fact that this effect emerged only among European American adolescents suggests that pubertal changes may be more stressful for European American girls than for African American girls.

Our own data from MSALT yield a similar junior high school transition effect. However, in our study, the unadjusted mean levels of boys' and girls' self-esteem dropped at about the same rate. Nonetheless, the boys had higher self-esteem than did the girls in both sixth and seventh grade, and this gender difference increased in magnitude as these adolescents moved through junior high school and into high school.

Thus, across these three studies, there is clear evidence of lower self-esteem in girls, as compared with boys, during adolescence. Furthermore, there is fairly consistent evidence that this gender difference increases in some populations during this developmental period primarily because the girls' self-esteem drops to a greater extent than does the boys'.

In the next section, we explore some possible reasons for this drop in some girls' self-esteem. We begin with a brief summary of our findings regarding race differences in self-concepts and self-esteem because this work makes clear how variable the magnitude of this decline is across different groups of female adolescents.

Race–Ethnic Differences in Girls' Self-Concepts and Self-Esteem

We compared African American and European American girls' self-perceptions in both our MSALT and MAGIC study. First, in both studies, the general pattern of gender differences was much weaker, if significant at all, among the African American girls. Second, the African American girls had higher self-esteem than both the European American girls and the African American boys. Third, significant race differences in these girls' self-perceptions could explain the race differences in their self-esteem: African American girls had either similar or higher academic ability self-concepts than European American girls. African American girls also had higher athletic and social self-concepts and were more satisfied with their physical attractiveness (Winston, Eccles, & Senior, 1997). For example, in the MSALT, the African American students rated themselves higher than did European American students with regard to math ability ($F = 24.16$, $p < .001$), English ability ($F = 26.05$, $p < .001$), sports ability ($F = 45.35$, $p < .001$), and peer–social relations ($F = 54.36$, $p < .001$). Finally, unlike the evidence for European American girls, there was no evidence of a decline in African American girls' self-esteem during the early adolescent years. Similar comparative studies on other ethnic groups are badly needed.

Predicting Self-Esteem

Neither the processes underlying individual differences nor the processes underlying developmental changes in self-esteem are well understood. Some researchers have pointed to the critical role of the family, particularly during the early years of life, to explain individual differences in self-esteem (see Harter, 1997). Other researchers have focused on changes in the school environment as one important influence on the age-related changes over time (see Eccles, Midgley, et al., 1993; Simmons & Blyth, 1987). Similarly, some researchers have suggested that changes in the nature of one's familial relationships during adolescence could contribute to the developmental declines in self-esteem during early adolescence (Eccles, Midgley, et al, 1993). Finally, the variations in the patterns of self-concepts and values discussed earlier are also likely to be relevant. All of these explanations could account for differences in self-esteem equally among females and males. They tell us less about the unique characteristics of being female that seem to put some females at greater risk for a decline in self-esteem during the adolescent years.

Several researchers have offered possible explanations for females' increased risk for declining self-esteem (e.g., Simmons & Blyth, 1987). Before presenting and discussing these explanations, we examine the ethnic group differences summarized above. African American female adolescents do not appear to be at greater risk than their male peers for declines in self-esteem.

Consequently, any viable explanations must account for both the gender and race–ethnic group patterns. We return to this point later.

The processes or mechanisms explaining the declines in European American girls' self-esteem in early adolescence are not well understood. Drawing on cumulative stress theory, Simmons and Blyth (1987) suggested this increased vulnerability results from these girls being more likely than boys to be exposed to two major life transitions at once during their early adolescent years: the physical changes associated with puberty and the transition from elementary school to junior high school. Because boys go through the physical changes associated with puberty about 18 months later than do girls, they are more likely to experience these changes after they have made the junior high school transition. Although this explanation might be useful for understanding the different pattern of change in European American girls and boys, it is not very useful for understanding the ethnic group differences in the girls' vulnerability to this school transition. That is, it is not clear why African American girls would not be vulnerable to this same dynamic.

The different patterns of social role changes associated with pubertal development for girls and boys may also have a differential impact on boys' and girls' self-esteem. For example, the social role changes in characteristics associated with heterosocial–peer relationships in European American populations may lead pubertal girls to become excessively sensitive to their physical appearance (see Buchanan, Eccles, & Becker, 1992; Eccles, Midgley, et al., 1993; Simmons & Blyth, 1987). In fact, several researchers have found that early maturation among European American girls is associated with less self-confidence, lower self-esteem, and more depressive affect (see Stattin & Magnusson, 1990; similar findings have also been found for Swedish girls).

In an attempt to investigate several possible influences at once, Lord et al. (1994) looked at several predictors of self-esteem change across the junior high school transition using the MSALT data. They based their selection of predictors on psychological models of risk and protective factors. Several investigators have suggested that personal coping resources are the key protective influences on individuals' adjustment to stressful situations, such as school transitions. Personal coping resources include relatively stable personality, attitudinal, and cognitive dispositions that promote effective adaptation, thereby reducing the potentially harmful effects of stress (Fenzel, 1991). Lord et al. proposed that a sense of autonomy, a sense of personal efficacy, and confidence in one's most salient abilities were the personal coping resources most likely to buffer against the detrimental effects of a stressful school transition (see Bandura, 1986; Harter, 1990). Of these, Lord et al. assumed that perceptions of one's abilities would be especially relevant. Several studies support a connection between these self-relevant beliefs. For example, Bohrnstedt and Felson (1983) showed that perceived academic and athletic competence is positively predictive of self-esteem among adolescents. Similarly, Harter has shown that perceived competence in academic, social, athletic, and physical appearance domains is positively related to self-esteem, with confidence in one's physical appearance and social competence having the strongest relations, particularly among girls.

Other studies focus on the protective role that actual abilities may play as an adolescent makes the junior high transition. This work demonstrates that success in academic and social domains in the sixth grade is positively related to increases in self-esteem following the junior high school transition (e.g., Simmons & Blyth, 1987). These studies suggest that both ability self-concepts and actual achievement levels are related to the adolescents' overall self-esteem and to their adjustment to the junior high school transition. Finally, Lord et al. (1994) assumed that family factors would be important protective factors. Specifically, they focused on the opportunities provided within the family for democratic decision making and the quality of the emotional relationship between the adolescent and her or his parents.

In terms of risk factors, achievement-related worries and self-consciousness seemed the most likely candidates. For example, Elkind and Bowen (1979) have shown that self-consciousness is negatively related to self-esteem. Similarly, several studies indicate that anxiety about one's performance in the academic and social domains is negatively related to an adolescent's school performance (e.g., Willig, Harnisch, Hill, & Maehr, 1983). Eccles and her colleagues have suggested that both anxiety and self-consciousness may be particularly detrimental as the early adolescent is forced to adjust to a new school environment characterized by increased rigor in grading, less variety in evaluation techniques, and an increase in social comparison among students (e.g., Eccles, Midgley, et al., 1993). These detrimental effects are likely to be especially salient during early adolescence because this developmental period is characterized by increased self-focus and self-consciousness (see Eccles, Midgley, et al., 1993). These effects are also likely to be especially detrimental for European American girls because the standards of beauty within this cultural group are so at odds with the basic nature of pubertal changes associated with the developing female body (Orbach, 1994; Wolf, 1991).

The results of the Lord et al. (1994) analyses support these predictions. As predicted, controlling for sixth-grade self-esteem and academic ability, the psychological protective factors—positive self-concepts of one's ability in both academic and nonacademic domains—were associated with positive change in self-esteem over this school transition. As a set, students' ratings of their abilities in academic, athletic, and peer social domains and of their physical attractiveness all predicted gains in self-esteem at both waves. In competition with each other as predictors, ratings of one's physical attractiveness, math ability, and peer social ability yielded the strongest coefficients for both girls and boys. The only major gender difference in these predictive relations occurred for physical attractiveness: Confidence in one's physical attractiveness was a much stronger predictor among the young women than among the young men.

Finally as hypothesized, the psychological risk factors—worries and self-consciousness related to math, school deadlines, and social acceptance—were associated with declines in self-esteem during the junior high school transition for both girls and boys. In competition with the other predictors, only social and academic self-consciousness yielded significant negative coefficients. In addition, academic anxieties and worries were a much stronger predictor of declines in self-esteem among the boys than among the girls, despite the fact that girls reported higher mean levels on these measures.

That confidence in one's peer-related social skills and physical attractiveness emerged as such salient contributors to adolescents' adjustment to junior high school probably reflects the impact of changing pressures on adolescents at this particular period of life. Several investigators have suggested that there is an increased emphasis at this time, from both peers and families, on physical appearance, social presentation, and popularity with the opposite sex (Higgins & Eccles [Parsons], 1983; Hill & Lynch, 1983). Coupled with the new and much larger social environment of the junior high setting, confidence in one's competence in peer–social relationships and one's physical attractiveness may be particularly important protective factors.

The salience of physical appearance for the stability of these young women's self-esteem across the transition to junior high is troubling. Given that both individual differences in physical appearance and the exact nature of pubertal changes in different individuals' bodies are substantially biologically determined and thus is somewhat out of the individual's control, a focus on physical attractiveness for people who are not or do not feel attractive enough is likely to undermine some young women's self-esteem. It is also likely to push some young women toward extreme efforts to try to change their bodies to meet both real and perceived peer and societal standards. It follows that girls at this age who have a negative perception of their appearance may be at risk for developing symptoms that reflect their diminished self-esteem, such as eating disorders. In fact, in the MAGIC data, lack of confidence in one's physical appearance was one of the primary significant predictors of bulimia-related eating behaviors.

Finally, Lord et al. (1994) looked specifically at the extent to which gender itself was a significant predictor of self-esteem change after all of the other predictors were controlled. Even though gender was weakly related in a predictable pattern to several of the predictor variables as well as to self-esteem, gender added very little to the predictive power of the regression equation when it was added at the final step of the regression model for self-esteem measured in the fall of the seventh-grade year. In contrast, being a female adolescent predicted greater than expected declines in self-esteem measured in the spring of the seventh-grade year. Thus, consistent with the findings of Simmons and Blyth (1987) and a report by the AAUW (1990), these results suggest that being a female adolescent is a risk factor for decline in self-esteem during this developmental period. However, it should be noted that this effect was quite small, and the vast majority of the young women did not experience a loss in their self-esteem across this transition—most either remained the same or experienced an increase (Eccles, Lord, et al., 1997).

Race–Ethnic Group Differences in Self-Esteem

As we noted earlier, African American girls had higher self-esteem and ability self-concepts than did European American girls in the MSALT. Next, we reran separately the regression analyses reported above for European American and African American girls. Most interesting in these analyses is the fact that none of the ability self-concepts or anxieties significantly predicted the African American girls' self-esteem. This result is consistent with Spencer and Steele's (1995) hypothesis that African American girls disidentify with the criteria that European American adolescents use to evaluate their self-worth. The Lord et al. (1994) model was based on empirical work conducted with and by European Americans. The predictors chosen likely reflect the values of this cultural group. Consequently, it should not come as a surprise that these constructs did not predict African American girls' self-esteem. But the number of African Americans in the MSALT was relatively small (73 girls).

We explored this ethnic group difference in more detail in the MAGIC study. This study's 1,100 adolescents live in a racially mixed, African American majority county in Maryland. We administered many of the same measures to this sample as were administered in the MSALT. The results reported here come from the first wave of data collection in the MAGIC study when the adolescents were in seventh grade (junior high school).

As was true for the MSALT, the African American girls in the MAGIC study had higher self-esteem than did the European American girls. We wanted to investigate why this might be the case. Given the findings in MSALT, we also wanted to expand the range of predictors to capture other aspects of adolescents' lives that might be relevant to both ethnic groups.

For the first set of these analyses, we used the following predictors: confidence in one's femininity, confidence in one's physical strength and assertiveness (which we labeled *masculine skills*), worries about one's weight, school-related worries and test anxiety, social self-consciousness, confidence in one's physical attractiveness, confidence in one's academic and athletic abilities, confidence in one's popularity, and the difference between one's educational aspirations and actual educational expectations (how much education one would like vs. how much education one actually expects to get).

African American girls were higher than European American girls on each of the following predictors: confidence in their femininity ($R^2 = 10\%$), confidence in their masculine skills ($R^2 = 5\%$), confidence in their physical attractiveness ($R^2 = 16\%$), confidence in their popularity ($R^2 = 13\%$), and the difference between their educational aspirations and actual expectations ($R^2 = 1\%$). The European American girls were higher on worrying about their weight ($R^2 = 3\%$) and social self-consciousness ($R^2 = 5\%$). Clearly, the African American girls in this sample had a more positive view of themselves across the board than did the European American girls.

But do these differences explain the ethnic group difference in self-esteem? To answer this question, we ran a path analysis using simultaneous regression analyses to estimate the parameters. First, we regressed the set of proposed mediators on ethnic group to estimate the size of the relations between ethnic group membership and each mediator. Next, we regressed self-esteem on the full set of proposed mediators and an ethnic group. If the relation between ethnic group and self-esteem is no longer significant, then we can conclude that the ethnic group differences on the proposed mediators explain the ethnic group difference in self-esteem. All significant paths are summarized in Figure 3.2. As predicted, the ethnic group differences in the mediators fully explained the ethnic group difference in self-esteem (see Figure 3.2).

In addition, to parallel the analyses conducted for the MSALT, we ran regression analyses separately for each ethnic group. In these analyses,

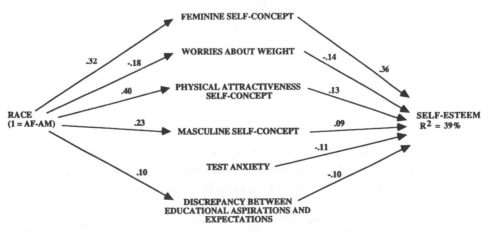

Figure 3.2. Predicting young women's self-esteem. AF-AM = African American.

we included indicators of academic and athletic self-concepts and anxieties as well as the set of predictors yielding ethnic group differences (i.e., those displayed in Figure 3.2). For both groups of girls, self-esteem was predicted most strongly by confidence in their femininity and physical attractiveness and by a lack of worry about their weight. In addition, for European American girls, confidence in their masculine skills and low levels of general anxiety predicted high self-esteem; for African American girls, low levels of social self-consciousness was an important predictor.

Equally important, when forced to compete for variance with a broader range of predictors, academic and athletic self-concepts did not predict self-esteem in either group. Apparently, these academic self-concepts are not as important for young women's self-esteem as other work using a more limited set of predictors suggests. Instead, constructs more directly linked to either the physical changes associated with pubertal change or physical attractiveness more generally are more salient for these young women. Whether this remains the case as these young women move through adolescence still needs to be tested. But clearly African American girls have a more positive view of themselves on all of these dimensions than European American girls.

These results suggest that the debilitating processes linked to pubertal development in European American girls may be much less pervasive among African American girls. African American girls did not show the classic declines in confidence in their physical attractiveness and increases in concerns about their popularity and their weight reported by these European American girls (and by European American girls in most other studies of adolescent development). In addition, these advantages protected their self-esteem.

To investigate this possibility further, we separated each ethnic group into early and on-time maturers (Michael, 1996, 1997). Only the European American girls' self-esteem and mental health were related to their maturational rate—with early maturing girls reporting lower self-esteem and mental health and higher rates of bulimic eating patterns. Maturational rate had no relation to these outcomes among African American girls. Again, these results suggest that pubertal development is not the same kind of risk factor for African American girls that it is for some European American girls.

The reasons for this difference need to be explored because (a) we need to understand the sources of resilience in African American girls, (b) understanding these differences will help us understand the nature of cultural differences between these two ethnic groups, and (c) they will offer insights into the kinds of preventive interventions that might help bolster European American girls' self-esteem during this critical transitional period. It seems likely that cultural differences in the standards of feminine beauty are one piece of this difference, but this hypothesis has not been studied

Other possible influences include variations in the meaning of sexual maturity and in the response of both adults and peers to signs of pubertal development.

CONCLUSION

If we learned nothing else from the work reported in this chapter, we learned that gendered self-concepts and self-esteem vary across domains and ethnic groups. We also learned that there is much more variation within groups than between groups. It is not the case that females, in general, are less confident of their abilities than males. Nor is it the case that females, in general, have less self-esteem than males. Some do but many do not. And in some domains, females in general have more confidence in their abilities than males, even during the early pubertal period of development when European American girls appear to be most at risk. The data discussed in this chapter make it clear that most females have many strengths that serve them well as they move through adolescence and into young adulthood. They express confidence in their abilities in many domains, particularly female gender role stereotyped domains. For example, they are more confident than males in their general academic abilities (averaged across subject areas) and general social skills. Both of these strengths serve them well in adjusting to school and in finding a meaningful place for themselves in this context. Consequently, it should not come as a surprise that female students are less likely to drop out of school and to get into trouble at school than are male students.

Our analyses of individual differences among females also suggest that females use their ability self-concepts and values in predictable ways to make sensible educational and occupational choices for themselves—just as sensible as their male peers. In fact, if anything our data suggest that young women place less weight in these decisions than do young men on such extrinsic job characteristics as money and status. These strengths help the majority of young women make wise choices about their educational and occupational trajectories.

Nonetheless, the results discussed in this chapter point to three problem areas for young women. First, evidence from several lines of research suggests that girls are more negatively affected by failure experiences and by anticipated failures than are boys. This sensitivity likely limits their willingness to take risks for higher rewards or more demanding opportunities. Second, many young women still believe that there is an inherent conflict between feminine goals–values and highly competitive achievement activities. Belief in this conflict creates added ambivalence and anxiety when these young women find themselves in competitive achievement settings. Third, the physical changes associated with pubertal development are problematic for many European American young women. Several authors have discussed the negative consequences of European American society's unrealistic and narrow standards of women's beauty (Wolf, 1991). The findings reported in this chapter both reinforce these conclusions and illustrate how culturally centered these effects are. The data suggest that African American girls are not as susceptible to these debilitating influences. They react much more positively to the physical changes associated with pubertal development. These results (the findings for African American girls) make it clear that the declines in self-esteem experienced by many European American girls are not an inevitable consequence of either pubertal development or school transitions. Instead, it is likely that these declines are firmly grounded in the unrealistic European American culture of feminine beauty.

REFERENCES

American Association of University Women. (1990). *Shortchanging girls, shortchanging America: Full data report.* Washington, DC: Author.

Bandura, A. (1986). *Social foundations of thought and action: A social cognitive theory.* Englewood Cliffs, NJ: Prentice-Hall.

Bell, L. A. (1989). Something's wrong here and it's not me: Challenging the dilemmas that block girls' success. *Journal for the Education of the Gifted, 12,* 118–130.

Benbow, C. P. (1988). Sex differences in mathematical reasoning ability in intellectually talented preadolescents: Their nature, effects, and possible causes. *Behavioral and Brain Sciences, 11,* 169–183.

Benbow, C. P., & Minor, L. L. (1986). Mathematically talented males and females and achievement in the high school sciences. *American Educational Research Journal, 23,* 425–436.

Benbow, C. P., & Stanley, J. C. (1982). Consequences in high school and college of sex differences in mathematical reasoning ability: A longitudinal perspective. *American Educational Research Journal, 19,* 598–622.

Betz, N. E., & Fitzgerald, L. F. (1987). *The career psychology of women.* Orlando, FL: Academic Press.

Bohrnstedt, G., & Felson, R. (1983). Explaining the relations among children's actual and perceived performances and self-esteem: A comparison of several causal models. *Journal of Personality and Social Psychology, 45,* 43–56.

Buchanan, C. M., Eccles, J. S., & Becker, J. (1992). Changes in hormones, moods, and behavior in adolescence. *Psychological Bulletin, 111,* 62–107

Crandall, V. C. (1969). Sex differences in expectancy of intellectual and academic reinforcement. In C. P. Smith (Ed.), *Achievement-related behaviors in children* (pp. 11–45). New York: Russell Sage Foundation.

Crandall, V. C., Katkovsky, W., & Crandall, V. J. (1965). Children's beliefs in their own control of reinforcements in intellectual-academic achievement situations. *Child Development, 36,* 91–109.

Dauber, S. L., & Benbow, C. P. (1990). Aspects of personality and peer relations of extremely talented adolescents. *Gifted Child Quarterly, 34,* 10–15.

Douglas, J. D., & Rice, K. M. (1979). Sex differences in children's anxiety and defensiveness measures. *Developmental Psychology, 15,* 223–224.

Dunteman, G. H., Wisenbaker, J., & Taylor M. E. (1978). *Race and sex differences in college science program participation.* Research Triangle Park, NC: National Science Foundation.

Dweck, C. S., & Licht, B. G. (1980). Learned helplessness and intellectual achievement. In J. Garber & M. E. P. Seligman (Eds.), *Human helplessness: Theory and applications* New York: Academic Press.

Dweck, C. S., & Repucci, N. D. (1973). Learned helplessness and reinforcement responsibility in children. *Journal of Personality and Social Psychology, 25,* 109–116.

Early, D. M., Belansky, E., & Eccles, J. S. (1992, March). *The impact of gender stereotypes on perceived ability and attributions for success.* Poster session presented at the biennial meeting of the Society for Research on Adolescence, Washington, DC.

Eccles, J. S. (1984). Sex differences in achievement patterns. In T. Sonderegger (Ed.), *Nebraska Symposium on Motivation* (Vol. 32, pp. 97–132). Lincoln: University of Nebraska Press.

Eccles, J. S. (1987). Gender roles and women's achievement-related decisions. *Psychology of Women Quarterly, 11,* 135–172.

Eccles, J. S. (1989). Bringing young women to math and science. In M. Crawford & M. Gentry (Eds.), *Gender and thought: Psychological perspectives* (pp. 36–57). New York: Springer-Verlag.

Eccles, J. S. (1994). Understanding women's educational and occupational choices: Applying the Eccles et al. model of achievement-related choices. *Psychology of Women Quarterly, 18,* 585–609.

Eccles, J. S., Barber, B. L., & Jozefowicz, D. (1998). Linking gender to educational, occupational, and recreational choices: Applying the Eccles et al. model of achievement-related choices. In W. B. Swann, Jr., L. H. Langlois, & L. A. Gilbert (Eds.), *Sexism and stereotypes in modern society: The gender science of Janet Taylor Spence* (pp. 153–185). Washington, DC: American Psychological Association.

Eccles, J. S., & Harold, R. D. (1991). Gender differences in sport involvement: Applying the Eccles' expectancy-value model. *Journal of Applied Sport Psychology, 3,* 7–35.

Eccles, J. S., & Harold, R. D. (1992). Gender differences in educational and occupational patterns among the gifted. In N. Colangelo, S. G. Assouline, & D. L. Ambroson (Eds.), *Talent development: Proceedings from the 1991 Henry B. and Jocelyn Wallace National Research Symposium on Talent Development* (pp. 3–29). Unionville, NY: Trillium Press.

Eccles, J. S., Jacobs, J., Harold, R. D., Yoon, K. S., Arbreton, A. J. A., & Freedman-Doan, C. (1993). Parents and gender role socialization. In S. Oskamp & M. Costanzo (Eds.), *Claremont Symposium on Applied Social Psychology, 1992: Gender and social psychology* (pp. 59–84). Thousand Oaks, CA: Sage.

Eccles, J. S., Lord, S. E., Roeser, R. W., Barber, B. L., & Jozefowicz, D. M. H. (1997). The association of school transitions in early adolescence with developmental trajectories through high school. In J. Schulenberg, J. Maggs, & K. Hurrelmann (Eds.), *Health risks and developmental transitions during adolescence* (pp. 283–320). New York: Cambridge University Press.

Eccles, J. S., Midgley, C., Buchanan, C. M., Wigfield, A., Reuman, D. A., & Mac Iver, D. (1993). Developmental during adolescence: The impact of stage–environment fit. *American Psychologist, 48*, 90–101.

Eccles, J. S., Wigfield, A., Flanagan, C. A., Miller, C., Reuman, D. A., & Yee, D. (1989). Self-concepts, domain values, and self-esteem: Relations and changes at early adolescence. *Journal of Personality, 57*, 283–310.

Eccles, J. S., Wigfield, A., Harold, R. D., & Blumenfeld, P. C. (1993). Ontogeny of children's self-perceptions and subjective task values across activity domains during the early elementary school years. *Child Development, 64*, 830–847.

Eccles, J. S., Wigfield, A., & Schiefele, U. (1998). Motivation. In W. Damon (Series Ed.) & N. Eisenberg (Vol. Ed.), *Handbook of child psychology: Vol. 3. Social, emotional, and personality development* (5th ed., pp. 1017–1094). New York: Wiley.

Eccles (Parsons), J. S., Adler, T. F., Futterman, R., Goff, S. B., Kaczala, C. M., Meece, J. L., & Midgley, C. M. (1983). Expectations, values and academic behaviors. In J. T. Spence (Ed.), *Perspectives on achievement and achievement motivation* (pp. 75–146). San Francisco: Freeman.

Eccles (Parsons), J. S., Adler, T., & Meece, J. L. (1984). Sex differences in achievement: A test of alternate theories. *Journal of Personality and Social Psychology, 46*, 26–43.

Elkind, D., & Bowen, R. (1979). Imaginary audience behavior in children and adolescents. *Developmental Psychology, 15*, 38–44.

Farmer, H. S. (1985). A model of career and achievement motivation for women and men. *Journal of Counseling Psychology, 32*, 363–390.

Fenzel, L. M. (1991, April). *A prospective study of the relationships among role strain, self-esteem, competence, and social support in early adolescence.* Paper presented at the biennial meeting of the Society for Research in Child Development, Seattle, WA.

Fox, L. H. (1976). Sex differences in mathematical precocity: Bridging the gap. In D. P. Keating (Ed.), *Intellectual talent: Research and development* (pp. 183–214). Baltimore: Johns Hopkins University Press.

Fox, L. H., Pasternak, S. R., & Peiser, N. L. (1976). Career-related interests of adolescent boys and girls. In D. P. Keating (Ed.), *Intellectual talent: Research and development* (pp. 242–261). Baltimore: Johns Hopkins University Press.

Frome, P., & Eccles, J. S. (1995, April). *Underestimation of academic ability in the middle school years.* Poster session presented at the meeting of the Society for Research in Child Development, Indianapolis, IN.

George, W. C., & Denham, S. A. (1976). Curriculum experimentation for the mathematically talented. In D. P. Keating (Ed.), *Intellectual talent: Research and development* (pp. 103–131). Baltimore: Johns Hopkins University Press.

Gilligan, C. (1990). *Making connections: The relational world of adolescent girls at the Emma Willard School.* Cambridge, MA: Harvard University Press.

Harter, S. (1982). The Perceived Competence Scale for Children. *Child Development, 53,* 87–97.

Harter, S. (1990). Causes, correlates and the functional role of global self-worth: A life-span perspective. In J. Kolligian & R. Sternberg (Eds.), *Perceptions of competence and incompetence across the life-span* (pp. 67–98). New Haven, CT: Yale University Press.

Harter, S. (1997). The development of self-representation. In W. Damon Eisenberg (Vol. Ed.), *Handbook of child psychology: Vol. 3. Social, emotional, and personality development* (pp. 553–618). New York: Wiley.

Higgins, E. T., & Eccles (Parsons), J. (1983). Social cognition and the social life of the child: Stages as subcultures. In E. T. Higgins, D. N. Ruble, & W. W. Hartup (Eds.), *Social cognition and social behavior: Developmental issues* (pp. 15–62). New York: Cambridge University Press.

Hill, J. P., & Lynch, M. E. (1983). The intensification of gender-related role expectations during early adolescence. In J. Brooks-Gunn & A. C. Peterson (Eds.), *Girls at puberty: Biological and psychological perspectives* (pp. 201–228). New York: Plenum Press.

Hill, K. T., & Sarason, S. B. (1966). The relation of test anxiety and defensiveness to test and school performance over the elementary school years: A further longitudinal study. *Monographs for the Society for Research in Child Development, 31*(2, Serial No. 104).

Hollinger, C. L. (1983). Self-perception and the career aspirations of mathematically talented female adolescents. *Journal of Vocational Behavior, 22,* 49–62.

Huston, A. C. (1983). Sex-typing. In P. Mussen & E. M. Hetherington (Eds.), *Handbook of child psychology* (Vol. 4, pp. 387–467). New York: Wiley.

James, W. (1963). *Psychology.* New York: Fawcett. (Original work published 1892)

Jozefowicz, D. M. H., Barber, B. L., & Eccles, J. S. (1993, March). *Adolescent work-related values and beliefs: Gender differences and relation to occupational aspirations.* Paper presented at biennial meeting of the Society for Research on Child Development, New Orleans, LA.

Kerr, B. A. (1985). *Smart girls, gifted women.* Dayton: Ohio Psychology.

Lord, S., Eccles, J. S., & McCarthy, K. (1994). Risk and protective factors in the transition to junior high school. *Journal of Early Adolescence, 14,* 162–199.

Manley, J. J., & Rosemier, R. A. (1972). Developmental trends in general and test anxiety among junior high and senior high school students. *Journal of Genetic Psychology, 12,* 119–126.

McCall, R. B., Evahn, C., & Kratzer, L. (1992). *High school underachievers: What do they achieve as adults?* Newbury Park, CA: Sage.

McGinn, P. V. (1976). Verbally gifted youth: Selection and description. In D. P. Keating (Ed.), *Intellectual talent: Research and development* (pp. 160–184). Baltimore: Johns Hopkins University Press.

Meece, J. L., Wigfield, A., & Eccles, J. S. (1990). Predictors of math anxiety and its consequences for young adolescents' course enrollment intentions and performances in mathematics. *Journal of Educational Psychology, 82,* 60–70.

Michael, A. (1996, March). *Pubertal maturation: Relations to adolescent mental health in two ethnic groups.* Poster session presented at the biennial meetings of the Society for Research in Adolescence, Boston.

Michael, A. (1997, April). *Family relations during puberty: Parent and adolescent perspectives.* Poster session presented at the biennial meetings of the Society for Research in Child Development, Washington, DC.

National Science Foundation. (1996). *Women, minorities and persons with physical disabilities in science and engineering.* Washington, DC: Author.

Orbach, S. (1994). *Fat is a feminist issue.* New York: Berkley Books.

Orenstein, P. (1994). *Schoolgirls: Young women, self-esteem, and the confidence gap.* New York: Anchor Books.

Parsons, J. E., & Ruble, D. N. (1977). The development of achievement-related expectancies. *Child Development, 48,* 1075–1079.

Pipher, M. (1994). *Reviving Ophelia.* New York: Ballantine Books.

Rokeach, M. (1973). *The nature of human values.* New York: Free Press.

Ruble, D. N., & Martin, C. L. (1997). Gender development. In W. Damon Eisenberg (Vol. Eds.), *Handbook of child psychology: Vol. 3. Social, emotional, and personality development.* New York: Wiley.

Schunk, D. H., & Lilly, M. W. (1982, April). *Attributional and expectancy change in gifted adolescents.* Paper presented at the annual meeting of the American Educational Research Association, New York.

Simmons, R. G., & Blyth, D. A. (1987). *Moving into adolescence: The impact of pubertal change and school context.* Hawthorn, NY: Aldine de Gruyter.

Spencer, S., & Steele, C. M. (1995). *Under suspicion of inability: Stereotype vulnerability and women's math performance.* Unpublished manuscript, Stanford University, Stanford, CA.

Stattin, H., & Magnusson, D. (1990). *Pubertal maturation in female development.* Hillsdale, NJ: Erlbaum.

Stevenson, H. W., Chen, C., & Uttal, D. H. (1990). Beliefs and achievement: A study of Black, White, and Hispanic children. *Child Development, 61,* 508–523.

Stipek, D. J., & Hoffman, J. M. (1980). Children's achievement-related expectancies as a function of academic performance histories and sex. *Journal of Educational Psychology, 72,* 861–865.

Strauss, S., & Subotnik, R. F. (1991). *Gender differences in classroom participation and achievement: An experiment involving advanced placement calculus classes.* (Part 1). Unpublished manuscript, Hunter College, City University of New York.

Terman, L. M. (1926). *Genetic studies of genius* (Vol. 1). Stanford, CA: Stanford University Press.

Terman, L. M., & Oden, M. H. (1947). *Genetic studies of genius. Vol. 4: The gifted child grows up.* Stanford, CA: Stanford University Press.

Tidwell, R. (1980). Gifted students' self-images as a function of identification procedure, race, and sex. *Journal of Pediatric Psychology, 5,* 57–69.

Tomlinson-Keasey, C., & Smith-Winberry, C. (1983). Educational strategies and personality outcomes of gifted and nongifted college students. *Gifted Child Quarterly, 27,* 35–41.

Updegraff, K. A., Eccles, J. S., Barber, B. L., & O'Brien, K. M. (1996). Course enrollment as self-regulatory behavior: Who takes optional high school math courses. *Learning and Individual Differences, 8,* 239–259.

Wigfield, A., Eccles, J. S., Mac Iver, D., Reuman, D. A., & Midgley, C. M. (1991). Transitions at early adolescence: Changes in children's domain-specific self-perceptions and general self-esteem across the transition to junior high school. *Developmental Psychology, 27,* 552–565.

Wigfield, A., Eccles, J. S., Yoon, K. S., Harold, R. D., Arbreton, A. J. A., Freedman-Doan, C. R., & Blumenfeld, P. C. (1997). Change in children's competence beliefs and subjective task values in and across the elementary school years. *Journal of Educational Psychology, 89,* 145–469.

Willig, A. C., Harnish, D. L., Hill, K. T., & Maehr, M. L. (1983). Sociocultural and educational correlates of success–failure attributions and evaluation anxiety in the school setting for Black, Hispanic, and Anglo Children. *American Educational Research Journal, 20,* 385–410.

Winston, C., Eccles, J. S., & Senior, A. M. (1997). The utility of an expectancy/value model of achievement for understanding academic performance and self-esteem in African-American and European-American adolescents. *Zeitschrift fur Padagogische Psychologie, 11,* 177–186.

Wolf, N. (1991). *The beauty myth.* New York: Anchor Books.

Yee, D., & Eccles, J. S. (1988). Parent perceptions and attributions for children's math achievement. *Sex Roles, 19,* 317–333.

4

BODY IMAGE CONCERNS AND DISORDERED EATING IN ADOLESCENT GIRLS: RISK AND PROTECTIVE FACTORS

RUTH H. STRIEGEL-MOORE AND FARY M. CACHELIN

A major developmental challenge for adolescent girls in Western industrialized countries is to come to terms with the biological changes accompanying pubertal development. Puberty is associated with considerable weight gain, and this physical change occurs in a cultural context that upholds a female beauty ideal of extreme thinness. Hence, the physical changes of puberty are at odds with the cultural norms of female beauty. As described in detail by Striegel-Moore (1993), the tension between the cultural ideal of female beauty and the physical reality of the female body is magnified by two aspects of female gender role expectations. One, female identity is defined in relational terms, and two, beauty is a core aspect of female identity. Girls are expected to be interpersonally oriented, to care about others' feelings, needs, and interests, and, as a result, girls are more vulnerable than boys to others' opinions of them and behaviors toward them (Kaplan, 1986).

In our culture, physical attractiveness contributes significantly to interpersonal success (for review, see Rodin, Silberstein, & Striegel-Moore, 1985); hence, adolescent girls' pursuit of beauty to ensure popularity and respect makes sense (Hatfield & Sprecher, 1985; Lakoff & Scherr, 1984). Moreover, physically attractive girls or women are perceived as more feminine than less attractive girls or women (Mazur, 1986), and women who challenge traditional views of femininity because of their political views (e.g., feminists) or because of their sexual orientation (e.g., lesbians) are often stereotyped as physically unattractive (e.g., Klentz, Beaman, Mapelli, & Ullrich, 1987). By being concerned with her appearance and making efforts to achieve our culture's beauty ideal, a girl affirms for herself and for others that she is "feminine" (Striegel-Moore, 1993). The combination of the cultural prescript for girls to care about others' opinions and to define themselves through their physical appearance, and the particular beauty ideal of extreme thinness, creates a powerful motivational force for girls to pursue thinness.

Confronted with the weight gain associated with puberty and the intensification of gender role expectations, it is normative for adolescent girls to experience intense body image dissatisfaction (Attie & Brooks-Gunn, 1989). For many girls, adolescent concerns about their physical appearance become all consuming and eclipse concerns about other life goals. For a subset of girls, negative feelings about their body and the behavioral efforts to achieve or maintain a thin body contribute to the development of an eating disorder. Indeed, eating disorders represent a major health concern for adolescent girls. It is estimated that 1% to 3% of adolescent girls meet diagnostic criteria for either anorexia nervosa or bulimia nervosa (Hoek, 1991; Lewinsohn, Hops, Roberts, Seeley, & Andrews, 1993). Anorexia nervosa is characterized by the refusal to maintain a minimal average body weight, body image disturbance (e.g., feeling fat even when emaciated), and, in female adolescents and women, amenorrhea. The core clinical features of bulimia nervosa include recurrent episodes of binge eating, recurrent efforts to compensate for the eating binges by means of drastic weight control behaviors (e.g., fasting or purging), and body image disturbance (e.g., overvaluation of weight for one's sense of self-worth). In addition, a larger number of adolescent girls engage in eating patterns (such as extremely restrictive dieting, laxative abuse, vomiting, or binge eating) that, although not severe enough to meet diagnostic criteria of anorexia nervosa or bulimia nervosa, represent clinically significant symptoms of eating disorders (Rogers, Resnick, Mitchell, & Blum, 1997). Some experts have raised concerns about the narrow definition of eating disorders in the third and fourth editions of the *Diagnostic and Statistical Manual of Mental Disorders* (DSM–III and DSM–IV; American Psychiatric Association, 1980, 1994) because the current diagnostic criteria do not apply to a large number of girls or women who evidence clinically significant symptoms of disordered eating (e.g., recurrent binge eating) but do not meet all criteria required for a diagnosis of anorexia or bulimia nervosa (for review, see Striegel-Moore & Marcus, 1995).

Typically, eating disorders begin during adolescence; the first symptoms usually emerge during early adolescence, and in most cases, the full syndrome is evident by the late teen years (Woodside & Garfinkel, 1992). Although body image dissatisfaction and dieting are normative concerns for adolescent girls, only a minority of girls develop a clinical syndrome of anorexia nervosa or bulimia nervosa (Striegel-Moore, Silberstein, & Rodin, 1986). The growing literature of research on the etiology of eating disorders focuses on the question of which risk factors explain why some girls but not others are at risk for developing an eating disorder (for reviews, see Striegel-Moore, 1993). Although many experts describe eating disorders as the result of one's failing to adapt to the challenges of adolescence, surprisingly little research has studied risk and protective factors for eating disorders from a developmental perspective (Smolak, Levine, & Striegel-Moore, 1996). To date, etiologic research has been limited almost exclusively to adult samples and, with few exceptions, has studied risk with designs such as case control studies. These designs do not lend themselves easily to exploring the interplay of normative challenges and the unique vulnerabilities and stressors that might explain why eating disorders begin during adolescence.

As is true for other disorders of childhood and adolescence, however, factors that contribute to resilience against eating disorders have not yet been investigated in detail. Indeed, there is little discussion in the field of eating disorders of what factors might protect girls from developing an eating disorder. For example, only one research team has studied different developmental patterns related to eating concerns. Graber and colleagues (Graber, Brooks-Gunn, Paikoff, & Warren, 1994) identified three groups of girls on the basis of the presence or absence of disordered eating over time: girls with chronic eating problems, girls whose eating concerns were transient, and girls who did not experience disordered eating. Girls who reported chronic eating problems were heavier, had an earlier onset of menarche, and experienced greater levels of depression than girls whose eating problems were transient or girls who did not experience any eating concerns. There was some indication that positive family relations contributed to protection against developing eating disorder symptoms, but the generalizability of this study was limited by a small sample size and the select nature of the sample (private high school students). Understanding the combination of factors that lead to a positive body image and healthy eating is important for developing prevention efforts in the area of eating disorders. Moreover, understanding protective factors may contribute to the development of more effective therapeutic intervention.

In this chapter, we explore the risk and protective factors for the development of body image concerns and eating disorders in adolescent girls. The risk factor literature has described two types of risk factors: general risk factors (i.e., risk factors that explain the development of psychopathology in general) and specific risk factors (i.e., risk factors that explain the development of an eating disorder in particular). To date, in the eating disorder literature, researchers have been basically silent on the question of how to conceptualize protective factors. Protective factors can be conceived of as variables that contribute to a child's resilience against eating disorders as the opposite or "flip side" of general and specific risk factors. This line of argument directs attention to what is known about risk for developing an eating disorder. For example, if low self-esteem is a general risk factor for developing an eating disorder, then high self-esteem can be conceived of as a general protective factor. Similarly, if obesity is a specific risk factor for developing an eating disorder, then having a thin body build may represent a specific protective factor against the development of an eating disorder. Research on other mental disorders has shown that for some variables, the opposite end of a risk factor is not necessarily a protective factor. For example, whereas experiencing poor peer relationships constitutes a risk factor for depression in early adolescence, having good peer relationships at this age does not seem to be a protective influence (Peterson, Sarigiani, & Kennedy, 1991). Not yet explored at all is the question of whether there are protective factors that do not lie on the same continuum (i.e., that do not represent the opposite) of a risk factor.

We begin by introducing a model of risk and protective factors for eating disorders. Next, we summarize research on protective factors for healthy adolescent development in general and consider how these factors might raise resilience against eating disorders. We then review the research on risk factors for eating disorders. We conclude with suggestions for further research.

A MODEL OF RISK AND PROTECTIVE FACTORS FOR THE DEVELOPMENT OF EATING DISORDERS

Research on the etiology of eating disorders is not as advanced as research on other mental disorders (e.g., depression; Petersen et al., 1993), in that it has been focused so far on identifying risk *variables* rather than on testing risk *models*.[1] Moreover, few experts have conceptualized risk for eating disorders as derived from multiple pathways (for exceptions, see Striegel-Moore, 1993; Stice, 1994), yet clinical experience and preliminary empirical evidence suggest that eating disorders do not result from one single pathway. We propose that the etiology of eating disorders is multifactorial, involving the complex interplay of social, familial, personal, and

---

[1]This is beginning to change, however; for example, Stice and colleagues (e.g., Stice, 1998) have attempted to test a dual pathway model of risk for bulimia, but their work is limited to nonclinical samples whose diagnostic state is not verified.

biological variables. In Figure 4.1, we present a model of risk and protective factors that has not yet been tested as a full model. Rather, some of the variables depicted in this model have been investigated empirically, whereas the role of other variables as risk or protective factors is still speculative. We believe that risk and protective factors can be organized along two, often interrelated, pathways: the "restraint pathway" and the "interpersonal vulnerability pathway." Although, in some cases, risk may arise solely from variables that characterize one pathway, in other cases, risk factors may cumulate from both pathways (Striegel-Moore, 1993).

In brief, the restraint pathway involves a progression from a girl's internalizing societal ideals about beauty and femininity to her recognition of a discrepancy between her desired body size and her actual body size, to dietary restraints in an effort to attain the body ideal, or to binge eating as a response to the cognitive and affective consequences of dietary restraint. The restraint pathway describes mostly specific risk factors (i.e., variables that contribute specifically to the development of eating disorders).

The restraint model has been developed on the basis of clinical observations and empirical studies of Caucasian women. A growing literature of body image concern and eating problems among Black women suggests that the restraint model does not account well for the high rates of binge eating reported in this population (Striegel-Moore & Smolak, in press). Specifically, even though Black women experience significantly less body image dissatisfaction and fewer dieting attempts than Caucasian women, they still appear to be as likely as Caucasian women to engage in recurrent binge eating (for review, see Striegel-Moore & Smolak, 1996). Moreover, for a subset of women, regardless of race, dieting does not appear to play a role in the development of their binge eating behavior. These findings suggest the need for an alternative explanation for the development of eating disorders in which recurrent binge eating is a core feature.

In sum, the restraint model suggests that protective factors involve variables that buffer against the societal or social pressures to achieve thinness and to define oneself in terms of one's physical appearance. In addition, it suggests that variables that improve positive body esteem and that reduce the likelihood of initiation of restrictive dieting or related unhealthy weight control efforts may contribute as well to resilience against the development of eating disorders.

The interpersonal vulnerability pathway describes a developmental sequence beginning with inadequate interactions with child-care providers, leading to insecure attachment and to disturbance in self-image and social functioning that, in turn, promote the development of the affective (e.g., body image dissatisfaction) and behavioral symptoms of anorexia nervosa and bulimia nervosa (restrictive eating and binge eating). Interpersonal theory posits that an individual's self-image is constructed on the basis of

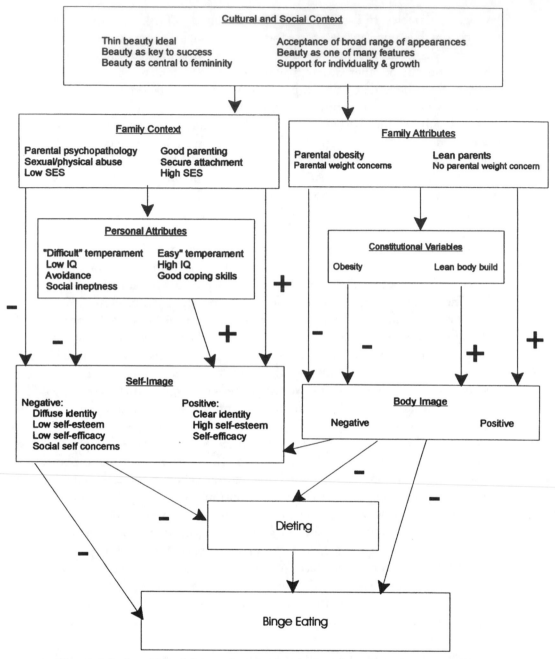

Figure 4.1. A model of risk and protective factors for eating disorders. (SES = socioeconomic status.)

and reflects his or her interpersonal experiences. Relationships provide the regulatory context in which behavior, affect, and cognition are organized (Rosenstein & Horowitz, 1996). A child whose early interactions have been marked by hostility or neglect internalizes a view of herself as needy, helpless, and unworthy of care, while learning to be interpersonally sensitive, socially anxious, and distrustful of others. These children learn to satisfy their relational needs through alternative strategies (Kobak & Sceery, 1988). Women's greater risk for developing eating disorders derives from the heavy emphasis placed in our culture on interpersonal orientation for women combined with girls' socialization toward "internalizing" their distress rather than expressing it overtly. Because of its soothing effect, eating becomes a strategy of coping with the aversive emotional states created by this "internalizing" style. Similarly, dieting and related cognitions and behaviors (e.g., counting calories, planning meals, or relentless exercising) may distract one's attention away from negative feeling states and may provide a sense of control. According to this interpersonal vulnerability pathway model of eating disorders, the core psychopathology of eating disorders is a disturbance of the self as it relates to others (social self) and to itself (self-esteem; see, e.g., Striegel-Moore, Silberstein, & Rodin, 1993).

The interpersonal vulnerability pathway describes mostly general risk factors, that is, variables that raise vulnerability for a number of psychiatric problems common among girls or women. Resilience against eating disorders, according to the interpersonal vulnerability model, derives from factors that buffer against the negative impact of events or experiences that threaten secure attachment (e.g., incest and physical abuse) and from factors that strengthen self-concept and enhance skills related to affect regulation and interpersonal skills.

Our cumulative model of risk and protective factors describes four major domains: (a) the societal and social context, (b) the familial context, (c) personal characteristics (including constitutional variables), and (d) life events. Because most of the negative life events associated with risk for eating disorders originate within the family, in the interest of keeping the model parsimonious, negative life events are captured under the familial context. We recognize that the particular organization of risk and protective factors within the domains of cultural or social context, familial context, and personal characteristics is somewhat arbitrary. (Certain adverse life events, e.g., may be seen as part of the cultural context.) We hope that the model displayed in Figure 4.1 is of heuristic value in organizing the research findings of etiologic studies and in pointing toward new topics of investigation.

Next, we describe what is known about resilience against childhood psychopathology in general and consider how this literature might apply to protection against the development of eating disorders in particular.

FACTORS THAT CONTRIBUTE TO CHILDHOOD RESILIENCE IN GENERAL

It is generally agreed that three broad sets of variables operate as protective factors, contributing to children's and adolescents' resilience against developing psychopathology: (a) personal characteristics, including high intelligence or IQ, a strong self-concept or sense of identity, high self-esteem and feelings of self-efficacy, an "easy" (versus a "difficult") temperament, and good coping skills; (b) familial context variables, including material and financial resources (typically measured in terms of socioeconomic status [SES]), a positive family environment, a close relationship with one's parent or primary caregiver, or both; and (c) social context factors, such as opportunities for change and growth and social support (see reviews by Kimchi & Schaffner, 1990; Wicks-Nelson & Israel, 1997). Each of these variables and its relation to eating disorders are discussed in turn. Although currently there are little data in terms of resilience available, the information provided suggests areas for further investigation.

Familial Context

Social Class

High social class is widely believed to act as a protective factor for children (Garmezy, Masten, & Tellegen, 1984; Rolf, Crowther, Teri, & Bond, 1984; Seifer & Sameroff, 1987). The relationship of social class and eating disorders, however, is not clear. The long-standing belief has been that eating disorders primarily affect girls from the middle to upper class, a belief that originates in the early descriptions of anorexia nervosa as a disease of Victorian girls from affluent bourgeois families (Brumberg, 1988). Recent empirical studies have produced conflicting findings, however, regarding the association of SES and eating disorders (for review, see Gard & Freeman, 1996). For example, Walters and Kendler (1995) found a greater prevalence of anorexic symptoms among women from higher socioeconomic classes, whereas anorexic symptoms were found to be unrelated with parental SES in a study of adolescent girls (Whitaker et al., 1989). Other studies indicate that clinical eating disorders cross socioeconomic class and have a higher rate of occurrence in lower SES groups than previously reported (Rogers et al., 1997). For example, the risk for bulimia nervosa was found to be equal across the SES spectrum in a community-based sample of adult women (Kendler et al., 1991). Further research is needed to clarify whether the level of SES is related to the increased risks for certain categories of eating disorders (e.g., anorexia nervosa), whether SES raises the risk for eating disorders in the context of additional risk variables, or both. The extant literature does, however, suggest that high SES does *not* serve as a buffer against the development of eating disorders in the same way that it does for most other childhood and adolescent disorders.

Personal Characteristics

Intelligence

Research in developmental psychopathology has identified intelligence as one of the most important personal attributes minimizing the impact of risk (Wicks-Nelson & Israel, 1997). The relationship of intelligence to eating disorders has not yet been studied. Because eating disorders are widespread among college populations (Hesse-Biber & Marino, 1991), it can be assumed that average to above-average intelligence does *not* serve as a protective factor against the development of eating pathology. However, the role of IQ in eating disorders has not been directly examined. Questions regarding differences in IQ warrant inquiry, such as the following: Within college populations, are those individuals with a higher IQ more resilient, and conversely, those with lower IQ more at risk for developing disordered eating? More information on the role of IQ and resilience to eating pathology is needed in terms of the role IQ may play in prevention. It has been shown, for example, that self-understanding and the ability to independently think and act protect adolescents from the negative effects of their parents' illness (Beardslee & Podorefsky, 1988). In a similar way, an adolescent girl's ability to think flexibly and to act independently may protect her against developing a negative body image by enabling her to resist cultural, peer, or family pressures toward thinness.

The ability to resist social stereotypes may be viewed as a component of *emotional intelligence*, which has been defined as including self-awareness, impulse control, persistence, zeal, self-motivation, empathy, and social deftness (Goleman, 1995). Goleman has proposed that low emotional intelligence might put children at risk for developing problems such as eating disorders. Lack of self-awareness, poor impulse control, and social deficiencies are generally believed to be characteristics of girls with clinical eating disorders (Striegel-Moore, Silberstein, & Rodin, 1993). High emotional intelligence as a protective factor against the development of problems with body image or eating may be a line of inquiry that warrants future investigation. Certain components of emotional intelligence (e.g., self-awareness, impulse control, and social skills) have been studied in terms of the risk for eating pathology and are discussed in the sections to follow. Those whose research involves understanding resilience might benefit from conceptualizing those features as part of one construct (i.e., emotional intelligence) and, in this way, integrate various findings. It is important that emotional intelligence may be more open to intervention than structural models of intelligence (such as IQ) that emphasize stability and hence provide little room for positive intervention or change.

Sense of Self and Positive Self-Regard

Children and adolescents' self-esteem and sense of self are important protective factors against psychopathology (Rutter, 1987). The most consistent finding in terms of resilience against eating disorders has concerned self-esteem. Although higher levels of disordered eating are associated with lower self-esteem, individuals with higher self-esteem seem to be less likely to develop disordered eating (Beren & Chrisler, 1990; Petrie, 1993). The association between low self-esteem and disordered eating is apparent across different racial groups (Abrams, Allen, & Gray, 1993). In one of the few prospective studies, Buton and colleagues (Button, Sonuga-Barke, Davies, & Thompson, 1996) found that girls with low self-esteem at age 11 to 12 were at significantly greater risk of developing the more severe signs of eating disorders by the age of 15 to 16. Similarly, girls who reported low levels of depression at study entry (age 14 years) were less likely to report eating disorder symptoms during the course of an 8-year study (Graber et al., 1994). Hence, as with other disorders of childhood, high self-esteem or positive self-regard appears to be a protective factor in eating disorders.

Similarly, a strong sense of identity is likely to reduce the risk for eating disorder pathology (Striegel-Moore et al., 1993). In terms of resilience, there is some evidence that the incidence of eating problems is lower in groups of women or girls who have strong racial identities (Pumariega, Gustavson, Gustavson, Stone-Motes, & Ayers, 1994). In their study, Erkut, Marx, Fields, Sing, and Ward (1997) found that African American girls' judgment of self-worth and positive self-regard was most highly related to academic competence, whereas for Caucasian girls, self-worth was most highly related to (attractive) physical appearance. Conversely, acculturation and assimilation—that is, weakening of one's sense of racial or ethnic identity—appears to be associated with an increased risk of developing an eating disorder (Abrams et al., 1993; Pumariega et al., 1994).

Coping Skills and Self-Efficacy

Healthy psychological development results from the capacity to master the developmental tasks and challenges of adolescence (Rutter, 1987). To date, the role of coping skills in eating disorders has been addressed primarily in the context of treatment or as a risk factor. Women with disordered eating have been described as having maladaptive coping skills; eating pathology is related to avoidant coping (Neckowitz & Morrison, 1991; Paxton & Diggens, 1997; Troop, Holbrey, Trowler, & Treasure, 1994), wishful thinking, and failure to seek social support (Troop et al., 1994). Correspondingly, treatment approaches such as cognitive-behavior therapy have focused on modifying and improving coping strategies in patients, resulting in some success (Hsu, Santhouse, & Chesler, 1991; Wilson

& Fairburn, 1993). Similarly, young women with eating concerns express feelings of ineffectiveness regarding not only eating and weight but also other aspects of their personal lives (Cachelin, Striegel-Moore, & Paget, 1997). Although strong coping skills and self-efficacy are believed to act as protective factors against psychopathology in general, and are considered to be essential components of the successful treatment of eating disorders, their contribution to resilience against the development of an eating disorder has not been studied.

Social Context

Social Support and Opportunity for Change

Resilient adolescents are sociable and able to seek and garner social support (Kimchi & Schaffner, 1990). By contrast, individuals suffering from eating pathology report a sense of social isolation (Grisset & Norvell, 1992; Wilson, Nonas, & Rosenblum, 1993), social anxiety, impoverished relationships (Fairburn et al., 1990; Striegel-Moore et al., 1993; Tobin, Johnson, Steinberg, Staats, & Enright, 1991), public self-consciousness (Striegel-Moore et al., 1993), and failure to seek social support (Troop et al., 1994). Indeed, having good social support from friends and family predicts recovery from eating disorders (Keller, Herzog, Lavori, & Bradburn, 1992; Sohlberg, Norring, & Rosmark, 1992), suggesting that these factors could contribute as well to a young woman's resilience.

In addition, through social support can come opportunities for change and adaptive growth. Change, personal development, and connection with others are integral aspects of the road to recovery from bulimia nervosa (Peters & Fallon, 1994), just as they are essential for recovery from and protection against other disorders of childhood and adolescence.

RISK AND PROTECTIVE FACTORS FOR EATING DISORDERS

Illustrated in Figure 4.1 are variables that have been shown in empirical studies to be associated with risk for developing anorexia nervosa or bulimia nervosa. We have added a number of protective variables of yet-to-be-determined empirical validity.

The Cultural and Social Context

The role of cultural factors in the etiology of eating disorders has been reviewed extensively elsewhere (Gilbert & Thompson, 1996; Stice, 1994; Striegel-Moore, Silberstein, & Rodin, 1986). At the sociocultural level, risk is hypothesized to derive from Western culture's social values and norms regarding female physical appearance and definitions of femininity.

Participation in cultures or subcultures that do not emphasize thinness as an important aspect of female beauty appears to protect one against developing body image concerns and to reduce the likelihood that a girl initiates dieting to lose weight. For example, Black girls report less social pressure to be thin, endorse a slightly larger body ideal, and have a more positive body image than White girls. Similarly, Black girls are less likely than White girls to diet to lose weight (for review, see Striegel-Moore & Smolak, 1996). However, the importance of social factors in developing eating pathology is illustrated in the fact that those Black girls who report being exposed to social pressure (e.g., peer pressure) are as likely as White girls to feel dissatisfied with their weight and to try to lose weight by dieting (Schreiber et al., 1996).

Even though a growing number of studies have attempted to show that femininity and disordered eating are correlated (e.g., Brown, Cross, & Nelson, 1990), significant methodological problems characterize this literature and results obtained to date have been inconsistent. Although some indication exists that identifying with masculine attributes may be an effective strategy for achieving a positive self-concept and for indirectly reducing the risk of disordered eating (Klingenspor, 1994), other studies have found no relationship between femininity or gender role identification and disordered eating (Striegel-Moore, Tucker, & Hsu, 1990; Timko, Striegel-Moore, Silberstein, & Rodin, 1987). Research to date has not properly tested the hypothesized link between femininity and eating disorders. Hence, it remains unclear whether subcultures that promote nontraditional gender roles protect against the development of disordered eating.

Although researchers can speculate about social contexts that raise resiliency, we are not aware of any studies that have examined certain cultural or peer contexts and their role in promoting resiliency to eating disorders. Typically, the role of culture or of various social contexts is explored indirectly through measuring how much a girl has internalized various cultural norms (e.g., beauty ideal, femininity, and acculturation) and the impact of these internalized values on risk for developing an eating disorder. Moreover, the literature is based largely on cross-sectional data, thus making it impossible to determine whether the observed correlations reflect a causal relationship or merely correlates of the current symptoms of an eating disorder.

Our model suggests that environments that enhance girls' sense of themselves, allowing them to develop positive self- (and body) image and that protect them from exposure to or reduce the impact of risk factors (e.g., incest and physical abuse), will raise resiliency to eating disorders.

The Familial Context

Two broad classes of risk factors originate from the familial context: factors that transmit or amplify culturally mandated concerns with weight and appearance and factors that interfere with secure attachment.

Parental Weight Concerns and Disordered Eating

Parents who are themselves overweight and concerned with their own weight are more likely to be concerned about their children's physical appearance and to instruct their children or model for their children how to diet to lose weight (Pike, 1995; Striegel-Moore & Kearney-Cooke, 1994). Consistently, research has shown that eating disorders "aggregate" in families: having a female family member with an eating disorder significantly increases the risk for an eating disorder in girls (for review, see Lilienfeld & Kaye, 1998). For example, one family study found that female relatives of probands with anorexia nervosa had a nearly tenfold increased risk for an eating disorder, compared with the family members of probands with an affective disorder (Strober, Lampert, Morrell, Burroughs, & Jacobs, 1990). Similarly, familial aggregation has been shown for bulimia nervosa (Kassett et al., 1989; Kendler et al., 1991). Although some are quick to take these studies as supportive of a genetic model of eating disorders, research on the genetic epidemiology of eating disorders has been inconclusive about the mechanisms of transmission (Kendler et al., 1991; Walters & Kendler, 1995). Studies of parenting behavior of women with an eating disorder indicate that these mothers are highly likely to have profound difficulties with properly feeding their children (Chatoor, Egan, Getson, Menvielle, & O'Donnell, 1988; Stein & Fairburn, 1989), thus suggesting a specific risk factor for eating disorders that has to do with learned skills related to appetite and satiety regulation. Moreover, as discussed below, a parent experiencing a major form of psychopathology may be impaired more generally in her or his ability to parent a child, thus contributing to the child's risk for developing a mental disorder. These variables related to parental concerns about weight, shape, and eating and parental pressure directed at the child to control her weight and shape have been shown to be specific risk factors for the development of eating disorders. In other words, these familial variables uniquely contribute to the development of eating disorders and are not associated with the development of other forms of psychopathology in women (e.g., Fairburn et al., 1997).

Eating disorders aggregate in families, and transmission occurs primarily among female relatives. Therefore, studying those daughters and sisters of women with eating disorders who themselves do not evidence an eating disorder may provide important clues about resilience.

Inadequate Parenting

Several studies have shown that familial factors or life events that potentially threaten the development of a secure attachment are associated with eating disorders. Prolonged parent–child separation, unempathic parenting style, lack of family cohesion, and parental psychopathology have been found to be more common among women with an eating disorder than among healthy women (Fairburn et al., 1997; Garfinkel et al., 1995; Holden, 1991; Kendler et al., 1991; Leon, Fulkerson, Perry, & Cudeck, 1993; Leon, Fulkerson, Perry, & Early-Zald, 1995). For example, recent large community-based studies have reported elevated rates of parental psychopathology (especially mood disorders and substance use disorders) among the parents of women with bulimia nervosa and subthreshold bulimia nervosa (defined as meeting all but one diagnostic criteria; Fairburn et al., 1997; Garfinkel et al., 1995, 1996).

It is a well-established finding that women with eating disorders have higher rates of childhood physical and sexual abuse than women who do not experience an eating disorder (for review, see Kearney-Cooke & Striegel-Moore, 1994). Inadequate or abusive parenting and sexual abuse are not specific risk factors for the development of eating disorders; rather, these variables have been shown to raise the risk for psychopathology in general (Fergusson, Horwood, & Lynskey, 1994). Why these factors contribute to eating disorders in some women and result in other forms of psychopathology (e.g., depression, post-traumatic stress disorder, substance use disorder, or anxiety disorders) in other women requires further exploration; perhaps food and eating become, for some women, salient mechanisms of self-soothing. Nevertheless, abusive or inadequate parenting is a powerful risk factor for the development of eating disorders, and the mere absence of this factor may protect one in terms of the development of an eating disorder.

Personal Vulnerability Factors

Several personal factors have been described that are thought to make a child more vulnerable to the cultural, social, and familial influences implicated in the risk for an eating disorder. These include obesity, timing of menarche, and perfectionism. For example, an overweight child may be particularly likely to develop body image concerns because of her experience of being different from the cultural beauty ideal. A child who experiences a strong sense of perfectionism may be particularly eager to meet cultural or parental or peer expectations to be thin. Some personal vulnerability factors may increase risk because they promote disordered eating through a "stress-induced eating link." For example, girls who experience negative affect as highly aversive may use self-starvation or binge eating to distract or soothe themselves (Heatherton & Baumeister, 1991).

Childhood Obesity and Timing of Menarche

Childhood obesity has been found to be a specific constitutional risk factor for bulimia nervosa (Fairburn et al., 1997), whereas its role in the etiology of anorexia nervosa is less clear. Obesity may increase the risk for eating disorders because of its negative impact on body image.

Timing of sexual maturation, a variable closely linked with adiposity, has long been considered an important variable in understanding adjustment problems experienced by adolescent girls. A comprehensive review found extensive empirical support for the hypothesis that girls who are ahead of their peer group in the onset and pace of sexual maturation are at risk for a wide range of behavioral and affective problems, including disordered eating, smoking, and symptoms of depression and anxiety (Stattin & Magnusson, 1990). Early sexual maturation has been proposed to increase the risk for an eating disorder because early maturation is associated with elevated adiposity that, in turn, is related to negative body image. Indeed, Attie and Brooks-Gunn (1989) have argued that the single biggest impact of early sexual maturation on adjustment is body image dissatisfaction. Early maturation was found to be a highly significant and specific risk factor for bulimia nervosa in one case control study (Fairburn et al., 1997); it is unclear, however, whether differences in weight status were taken into account. A prospective study following adolescent girls over 8 years found that early sexual maturation predicted "chronic eating problems," but the effect of timing was no longer significant when the percentage of body fat was added to the prediction model (Graber et al., 1994). Similarly, a 3-year prospective study of adolescent girls did not find that early onset menarche predicted a risk for disordered eating above and beyond the significant risk conferred by elevated adiposity (Leon et al., 1995). Hence, early maturation may increase the risk for eating disorders indirectly by contributing to the development of adiposity.

Moreover, early timing of sexual maturation may increase the risk for eating disorders because it forces the girls to confront developmental tasks before having acquired the emotional and intellectual maturity necessary for successful coping with these tasks. Compared with on-time or late-maturing peers, early developing girls have a greater number of older friends rather than same-age friends, initiate dating and sexual behavior earlier, report a greater decline in the quality of the parent–child relationship, and evidence lower self-esteem than their peers (for review, see Striegel-Moore, 1993). Hence, early maturation is associated with a wide range of interpersonal stresses that, in turn, may promote binge eating. Fear of adult sexuality has been considered an important risk factor for eating disorders (especially anorexia nervosa), yet empirical support is based solely on correlational data (Leon, Lucas, Colligan, Ferdinande, & Kamp, 1985). Researchers need to determine whether timing of sexual maturation is associated with maturity fears. We are intrigued by a recent report that pregnancy at a young age was a specific risk factor for bulimia nervosa (Fairburn et al., 1997). We speculate that getting pregnant at a young age may reflect difficulties in negotiating developmental challenges regarding sexuality.

Consistent with this view, recent studies have found that menarcheal status is a variable that moderates the relationship between dieting or disordered eating and girls' heterosexual activities (e.g., Cauffman & Steinberg, 1996). Girls who are dating are more likely to be engaged in dieting, and menarcheal status is predictive of whether girls are dating. This line of research further suggests that the timing of menarche, menarcheal status, and dating are not merely additive but may have interactive effects on dieting (see also Smolak, Levine, & Gralen, 1993). Early intervention, then, may be particularly necessary for girls who reach puberty at a relatively young age.

These studies of obesity and timing of menarche suggest that preventing obesity and prolonging the prepubertal stage may protect one against the development of eating disorders. This is a complicated charge: Advocates for the prevention of eating disorders have been outspoken against efforts to prevent obesity because the latter efforts may, inadvertently, reinforce risk factors for developing body image concerns and thus eating disorders. For example, there is considerable evidence indicating that dieting or food restriction may directly lead to the development of binge eating (see Polivy & Herman, 1993).

Perfectionism

Hilde Bruch (1978) considered perfectionism a risk factor for all eating disorders. On the basis of cross-sectional and retrospective studies, there is extensive support for an association between perfectionism and eating disorders (Fairburn et al., 1997; Garner & Olmsted, 1984; *Eating Disorders Inventory Manual*). However, most of these findings are based on retrospective reports; preliminary results of a 10-year longitudinal prospective study, comparing Black and White girls, raise questions about the role of childhood perfectionism as a risk factor for eating disorders (Striegel-Moore, 1999). If perfectionism is indeed shown to be a risk factor for the development of disordered eating, then intervention efforts should be aimed at educating girls with this characteristic about the detrimental effects of excessive focus on weight while, at the same time, emphasizing other more positive avenues of accomplishment.

CONCLUSION

Although resilience in eating disorders has not been directly examined, by combining risk factor research and research from general developmental psychopathology, a clearer picture emerges of strength and resilience against the development of eating disorders. Considerable theoretical information is available that can set the foundation for future investigations. To summarize, it seems likely that a cultural and social context that promotes the acceptance of a broad range of appearances, provides support for individuality and growth regardless of appearance, and protects girls from abusive experiences would play an instrumental role in protecting a young girl against the development of eating and weight-related concerns. At the level of the family, general factors such as good parenting and secure attachment to one caregiver and specific factors such as absence of parental weight problems or concern are likely to contribute to girls' resilience. Constitutional variables such as lean body build (and later-onset menarche) and personal attributes including strong social and coping skills and positive temperamental disposition can be protective factors by producing positive body and self-image. Positive self-image and body image, in turn, substantially decrease the likelihood of dieting, binge eating, and other pathological weight-related behaviors.

Although only a minority of adolescent girls develop clinical eating disorders, a large majority undertake dieting and suffer from subclinical eating concerns, body dissatisfaction, and what has been termed "a normal discontent" (Rodin et al., 1985). These subclinical behaviors represent a risk for other forms of psychopathology such as depression (e.g., Nolen-Hoeksema & Girgus, 1994). Hence, intervention studies are clearly needed that are based on models of risk and resilience in the area of disordered eating. Such prevention investigations can be initiated by first targeting specific variables or levels within models of risk and resilience, such as the one presented in this chapter. For instance, a girl who is constitutionally overweight can possibly be protected from developing pathological eating behaviors by an intervention that aims at educating her parents about the detrimental consequences of negative focus on weight and promoting positive focus on other sources of self-esteem, such as academic accomplishment. Future studies are needed that systematically examine such hypotheses.

In addition, future investigations should expand the focus of risk factor research. It is generally agreed that risk is multifactorial, with numerous variables from various domains contributing to vulnerability. Likewise, resilience is most probably multifactorial as well. However, with few exceptions, research on risk has tended to focus on each domain separately, without integrating information from various domains. Furthermore, although it has been shown that the risk for an eating disorder is cumulative (Fairburn et al., 1997; Killen et al., 1994; Pike, 1995), the precise nature of the relationship between risk variables has not been studied. The relationship between factors contributing to risk, and similarly resilience, could be additive, interactive, or both. Another consideration is that the degree of impact of a risk or a protective factor is likely to be influenced by the developmental stage of the individual; for example, parental weight concern may have less of an impact for younger children or older adolescents. Yet, such a complex approach to understanding risk for eating disorders has not yet been taken.

Finally, one has to wonder why the literature to date has been largely silent regarding factors that protect against development of disordered eating and negative body image. Could it be that societal attitudes and beliefs about "femininity" and "beauty" are so strongly and deeply entrenched that as a field, psychologists fail to look beyond them to characteristics that can make a young girl resilient and unyielding against societal pressure? Are we afraid that prevention efforts will produce attitudes which go against the "grain" of society and thus, at some level, be culturally undesirable (see, e.g., Striegel-Moore & Steiner-Adair, 1998)? Clearly eating disorders in girls are intimately connected with other disorders of adolescence such as depression and anxiety, and so any interventions that increase general protective factors such as self-esteem would not only decrease the likelihood of disordered eating but would also promote general mental health in this population.

REFERENCES

Abrams, K. K., Allen, L. R., & Gray, J. J. (1993). Disordered eating attitudes and behaviors, psychological adjustment, and ethnic identity: A comparison of Black and White female college students. *International Journal of Eating Disorders, 14*, 49–47.

American Psychiatric Association. (1980). *Diagnostic and statistical manual of mental disorders* (3rd ed.). Washington, DC: Author.

American Psychiatric Association. (1994). *Diagnostic and statistical manual of mental disorders* (4th ed.). Washington, DC: Author.

Attie, I., & Brooks-Gunn, J. (1989). Development of eating problems in adolescent girls: A longitudinal study. *Developmental Psychology, 25*, 70–79.

Beardslee, W. R., & Podorefsky, D. (1988). Resilient adolescents whose parents have serious affective and other psychiatric disorders: Importance of self-understanding and relationships. *American Journal of Psychiatry, 145*, 63–69.

Beren, S. E., & Chrisler, J. C. (1990). Gender role, need for approval, childishness, and self-esteem: Markers of disordered eating? *Research Communications in Psychology, Psychiatry and Behavior, 15*, 183–198.

Brown, J. A., Cross, H. J., & Nelson, J. M. (1990). Sex-role identity and sex-role ideology in college women with bulimic behavior. *International Journal of Eating Disorders, 9*, 571–575.

Bruch, H. (1978). *The golden cage: The enigma of anorexia nervosa.* Cambridge, MA: Harvard University Press.

Brumberg, J. J. (1988). *Fasting girls*. Cambridge, MA: Harvard University Press.

Button, E. J., Sonuga-Barke, E. J. S., Davies, J., & Thompson, M. (1996). A prospective study of self-esteem in the prediction of eating problems in adolescent schoolgirls: Questionnaire findings. *British Journal of Clinical Psychology, 35*, 193–203.

Cachelin, F. M., Striegel-Moore, R. H., & Paget, W. B. (1997). Comparison of women with various levels of dietary restraint on body image, personality and family environment. *Eating Disorders: The Journal of Treatment and Prevention, 5*, 205–215.

Cauffman, E., & Steinberg, L. (1996). Interactive effects of menarcheal status and dating on dieting and disordered eating among adolescent girls. *Developmental Psychology, 32*, 631–635.

Chatoor, I., Egan, J., Getson, P., Menvielle, E., & O'Donnell, R. (1988). Mother–infant interactions in infantile anorexia nervosa. *Journal of the American Academy of Child and Adolescent Psychiatry, 27*, 535–540.

Erkut, S., Marx, F., Fields, J. P., Sing, R., & Ward, J. (1997, August). *Raising competent girls*. Symposium presented at the 105th Annual Convention of the American Psychological Association, Chicago.

Fairburn, C. G., Jones, R., Peveler, R. C., Carr, S. J., Solomon, R. A., O'Connor, M. E., Burton, J., & Hope, R. A. (1990). Three psychological treatments for bulimia nervosa: A comparative trial. *Archives of General Psychiatry, 48*, 463–469.

Fairburn, C. G., Welch, S. L., Doll, H. A., Davies, B. A., & O'Connor, M. E. (1997). Risk factors for bulimia nervosa: A community-based case-control study. *Archives of General Psychiatry 54*, 509 517.

Fergusson, D. M., Horwood, L. J., & Lynsky, M. T. (1994). The comorbidities of adolescent problem behaviors: A latent class model. *Journal of Abnormal Child Psychology, 22*, 339–354.

Gard, M. C. E., & Freeman, C. P. (1996). The dismantling of a myth: A review of eating disorders and socioeconomic status. *International Journal of Eating Disorders, 20*, 1–12.

Garfinkel, P. E., Lin, E., Goering, P., Spegg, C., Goldbloom, D., Kennedy, S., Kaplan, A. S., & Woodside, D. B. (1995). Bulimia nervosa in a Canadian community sample: Prevalence and comparison of subgroups. *American Journal of Psychiatry, 152*, 1052–1058.

Garfinkel, P. E., Lin, E., Goering, P., Spegg, C., Goldbloom, D., Kennedy, S., Kaplan, A. S., & Woodside, D. B. (1996). Should amenorrhea be necessary for the diagnosis of anorexia nervosa? *British Journal of Psychiatry, 168*, 500–506.

Garmezy, N., Masten, A. S., & Tellegen, A. (1984). The study of stress and competence in children: A building block for developmental psychopathology. *Child Development, 55*, 97–111.

Garner, D. M., & Olmsted, M. P. (1984). *The Eating Disorders Inventory manual*. Odena, FL: Psychological Assessment Resources.

Gilbert, S., & Thompson, K. (1996). Feminist explanations of the development of eating disorders: Common themes, research findings, and methodological issues. *Clinical Psychology: Science and Practice, 3*, 183–202.

Goleman, D. (1995). *Emotional intelligence*. New York: Bantam Books.

Graber, J. A., Brooks-Gunn, J., Paikoff, R. L., & Warren, M. P. (1994). Prediction of eating problems: An 8-year study of adolescent girls. *Developmental Psychology, 30*, 823–834.

Grisset, N. I., & Norvell, N. K. (1992). Perceived social support, social skills, and quality of relationships in bulimic women. *Journal of Consulting and Clinical Psychology, 60*, 293–299.

Hatfield, E., & Sprecher, S. (1985). *Mirror, mirror: The importance of looks in everyday life*. New York: State University of New York Press.

Heatherton, T. F., & Baumeister, R. F. (1991). Binge eating as escape from self-awareness. *Psychological Bulletin, 110*, 86–108.

Hesse-Biber, S., & Marino, M. (1991). From high school to college: Changes in women's self-concept and its relationship to eating problems. *Journal of Psychology, 125*, 199–216.

Hoek, H. W. (1991). The incidence and prevalence of anorexia nervosa and bulimia nervosa in primary care. *Psychological Medicine, 21*, 455–460.

Holden, N. L. (1991). Adoption and eating disorders: A high-risk group? *British Journal of Psychiatry, 158*, 829–833.

Hsu, L. G., Santhouse, R., & Chesler, B. E. (1991). Individual cognitive behavioral therapy for bulimia nervosa: The description of a program. *International Journal of Eating Disorders, 10*, 273–283.

Kaplan, A. G. (1986). The "self-in-relation": Implications for depression in women. *Psychotherapy: Theory, Research and Practice, 23*, 234–242.

Kassett, J. A., Gershon, E. S., Maxwell, M. E., Guroff, J. J., Kazuba, D. M., Smith, A. L., Brandt, H. R., & Jimerson, D. C. (1989). Psychiatric disorders in the first-degree relatives of probands with bulimia nervosa. *American Journal of Psychiatry, 146*, 1468–1471.

Kearney-Cooke, A., & Striegel-Moore, R. H. (1994). Treatment of childhood sexual abuse in anorexia nervosa and bulimia nervosa: A feminist psychodynamic approach. *International Journal of Eating Disorders, 15*, 305–319.

Keller, M. B., Herzog, D. B., Lavori, P. W., & Bradburn, I. S. (1992). The naturalistic history of bulimia nervosa: Extraordinarily high rates of chronicity, relapse, recurrence, and psychosocial morbidity. *International Journal of Eating Disorders, 12*, 1–9

Kendler, K. S., MacLean, C., Neale, M., Kessler, R. C., Heath, A., & Eaves, L. (1991). The genetic epidemiology of bulimia nervosa. *International Journal of Eating Disorders, 10*, 679–687.

Killen, J. D., Taylor, C. B., Hayward, C., Wilson, D. M., Hammer, L. D., Robinson, T. N., Litt, I. F., Simmonds, B. A., Haydel, F., Varady, A., & Kramer, H. (1994). The pursuit of thinness and onset of eating disorder symptoms in a community sample of adolescent girls: A three year prospective analysis. *International Journal of Eating Disorders, 16,* 227–238.

Kimchi, J., & Schaffner, B. (1990). Childhood protective factors and stress risk. In L. E. Arnold (Ed.), *Childhood stress* (pp. 475–500). New York: Wiley.

Klentz, B., Beaman, A. L., Mapelli, S. D., & Ullrich, J. R. (1987). Perceived physical attractiveness of supporters and nonsupporters of the women's movement: An attitude-similarity-mediated error. *Personality and Social Psychology Bulletin, 13,* 513–523.

Klingenspor, B. (1994). Gender identity and bulimic eating behavior. *Sex Roles, 31,* 407–431.

Kobak, R. R., & Sceery, A. (1988). Attachment in late adolescence: Working models, affect regulation, and representation of self and other. *Child Development, 59,* 135–146.

Lakoff, R. T., & Scherr, R. L. (1984). *Face value: The politics of beauty.* Boston: Routledge & Kegan Paul.

Leon, G. R., Fulkerson, J. A., Perry, C. L., & Cudeck, R. (1993). Personality and behavioral vulnerabilities associated with risk status for eating disorders in adolescent girls. *Journal of Abnormal Psychology, 102,* 438–444.

Leon, G. R., Fulkerson, J. A., Perry, C. L., & Early-Zald, M. B. (1995). Prospective analysis of personality and behavioral vulnerabilities and gender influences in the later development of disordered eating. *Journal of Abnormal Psychology, 104,* 140–149.

Leon, G. R., Lucas, A. R., Colligan, R. C., Ferdinande, R. J., & Kamp, J. (1985). Sexual, body-image, and personality attitudes in anorexia nervosa. *Journal of Abnormal Child Psychology, 13,* 245–258.

Lewinsohn, P. M., Hops, H., Roberts, R. E., Seeley, J. R., & Andrews, J. A. (1993). Adolescent psychopathology: I. Prevalence and incidence of depression and other *DSM–III–R* disorders in high school students. *Journal of Abnormal Psychology, 102,* 133–144.

Lilienfeld, L. R., & Kaye, W. H. (1998). Genetic studies of anorexia nervosa and bulimia nervosa. In H. W. Hoek, J. L. Treasure, & M. A. Katzman (Eds.), *Neurobiology in the treatment of eating disorders* (pp. 169–194). New York: Wiley.

Mazur, A. (1986). U.S. trends in feminine beauty and overadaptation. *Journal of Sex Research, 22,* 281–303.

Neckowitz, P., & Morrison, T. L. (1991). Interactional coping strategies of normal weight bulimic women in intimate and nonintimate stressful situations. *Psychological Reports, 69,* 1167–1175.

Nolen-Hoeksema, S., & Girgus, J. S. (1994). The emergence of gender differences in depression during adolescence. *Psychological Bulletin, 115,* 424–443.

Paxton, S. J., & Diggens, J. (1997). Avoidance coping, binge eating, and depression: An examination of the escape theory of binge eating. *International Journal of Eating Disorders, 22,* 83–87.

Peters, L., & Fallon, P. (1994). The journey of recovery: Dimensions of change.

In P. Fallon, M. A. Katzman, & S. C. Wooley (Eds.), *Feminist perspectives on eating disorders* (pp. 339–354). New York: Guilford Press.

Petersen, A. C., Compas, B. E., Brooks-Gunn, J., Stemmler, M., Ely, S., & Grant, K. E. (1993). Depression in adolescence. *American Psychologist, 48,* 155–168.

Petersen, A. C., Sarigiani, P. A., & Kennedy, R. E. (1991). Adolescent depression: Why more girls? *Journal of Youth and Adolescence, 20,* 247–271.

Petrie, T. A. (1993). Disordered eating in female collegiate gymnasts: Prevalence and personality/attitudinal correlates. *Journal of Sport and Exercise Psychology, 15,* 424–436.

Pike, K. M. (1995). Bulimic symptomatology in high school girls: Toward a model of cumulative risk. *Psychology of Women Quarterly, 19,* 373–396.

Piran, N., & Levine, M. (1996). Introduction. *Eating Disorders: The Journal of Treatment and Prevention, 4,* 291–293.

Polivy, J., & Herman, C. P. (1993). Etiology of binge eating: Psychological mechanisms. In C. G. Fairburn & G. T. Wilson (Eds.), *Binge eating: Nature, assessment, and treatment* (pp. 173–205). New York: Guilford Press.

Pumariega, A. J., Gustavson, C. R., Gustavson, J. C., Stone-Motes, P., & Ayers, S. (1994). Eating attitudes in African-American women: The *Essence* eating disorders survey. *Eating Disorders: The Journal of Treatment and Prevention, 2,* 5–16.

Rodin, J., Silberstein, L. R., & Striegel-Moore, R. H. (1985). Women and weight: A normative discontent. In T. B. Sonderegger (Ed.), *Nebraska Symposium on Motivation: Vol. 32. Psychology and gender* (pp. 267–308). Lincoln: University of Nebraska Press.

Rogers, L., Resnick, M. D., Mitchell, J. E., & Blum, R. W. (1997). The relationship between socioeconomic status and eating-disordered behaviors in a community sample of adolescent girls. *International Journal of Eating Disorders, 22,* 15–23.

Rolf, J. E., Crowther, L., Teri, L., & Bond, L. (1984). Contrasting developmental risks in preschool children of psychiatrically hospitalized parents. In N. F. Watt, E. J. Anthony, L. C. Wynne, & J. E. Rolf (Eds.), *Children at risk for schizophrenia: A longitudinal perspective* (pp. 23–31). London: Cambridge University Press.

Rosenstein, D. S., & Horowitz, H. A. (1996). Adolescent attachment and psychopathology. *Journal of Consulting and Clinical Psychology, 64,* 244–253.

Rutter, M. (1987). Psychosocial resilience and protective mechanisms. *American Journal of Orthopsychiatry, 57,* 316–331.

Schreiber, G. B., Robins, M., Striegel-Moore, R. H., Obarzanek, E., Morrison, J. A., & Wright, D. J. (1996). Weight modification efforts reported by black and white preadolescent girls. *Pediatrics, 98,* 63–70.

Seifer, R., & Sameroff, A. J. (1987). Multiple determinants of risk and invulnerability. In E. J. Anthony & B. J. Cohler (Eds.), *The invulnerable child* (pp. 51–69). New York: Guilford Press.

Smolak, L., Levine, M. P., & Gralen, S. (1993). The impact of puberty and dating on eating problems among middle-school girls. *Journal of Youth and Adolescence, 22*, 355–368.

Smolak, L., Levine, M. P., & Striegel-Moore, R. H. (1996). Developmental perspectives on eating disorders. In L. Smolak, M. P. Levine, & R. H. Striegel-Moore (Eds.), *The developmental psychopathology of eating disorders* (pp. 1–7). Mahwah, NJ: Erlbaum.

Sohlberg, S. S., Norring, C. E. A., & Rosmark, B. E. (1992). Prediction of the course of anorexia nervosa/bulimia nervosa over three years. *International Journal of Eating Disorders, 12*, 121–131.

Stattin, H., & Magnusson, D. (1990). *Pubertal maturation in female development.* Hillsdale, NJ: Erlbaum.

Stein, A., & Fairburn, C. G. (1989). Children of mothers with bulimia nervosa. *British Medical Journal, 299*, 777–778.

Stice, E. (1994). Review of the evidence for a sociocultural model of bulimia nervosa and an exploration of the mechanisms of action. *Clinical Psychology Review, 14*, 633–661.

Stice, E. (1998). Relations of restraint and negative affect to bulimic pathology: A longitudinal test of three competing models. *International Journal of Eating Disorders, 23*, 243–260.

Striegel-Moore, R. H. (1993). Etiology of binge eating: A developmental perspective. In C. G. Fairburn & G. T. Wilson (Eds.), *Binge eating: Nature, assessment, and treatment* (pp. 144–172). New York: Guilford Press.

Striegel-Moore, R. H. (1997). Risk factors for eating disorders. In M. S. Jacobson, N. H. Golden, & C. E. Irwin (Eds.), *Adolescent nutritional disorders: Prevention and treatment* (pp. 98–109). New York: New York Academy of Sciences.

Striegel-Moore, R. H. (1999). *Risk factors for the development of eating disorders: The NHLBI growth and health study.* Unpublished report, Wesleyan University, Middletown, CT.

Striegel-Moore, R. H., & Kearney-Cooke, A. (1994). Exploring determinants and consequences of parents' attitudes about their children's physical appearance. *International Journal of Eating Disorders, 15*, 377–385.

Striegel-Moore, R. H., & Marcus, M. (1995). Eating disorders in women: Current issues and debates. In A. Stanton & S. Gallant (Eds.), *Psychology of women's health* (pp. 445–487). Washington, DC: American Psychological Association.

Striegel-Moore, R. H., Silberstein, L. R., & Rodin, J. (1986). Toward an understanding of risk factors for bulimia. *American Psychologist, 41*, 246–263.

Striegel-Moore, R. H., Silberstein, L. R., & Rodin, J. (1993). The social self in bulimia nervosa: Public self-consciousness, social anxiety, and perceived fraudulence. *Journal of Abnormal Psychology, 102*, 297–303.

Striegel-Moore, R. H., & Smolak, L. (1996). The role of race in the development of eating disorders. In L. Smolak, M. Levine, & R. H. Striegel-Moore (Eds.), *The developmental psychopathology of eating disorders* (pp. 259–284). Mahwah, NJ: Erlbaum.

Striegel-Moore, R. H., & Smolak, L. (in press). The influence of ethnicity on eating disorders in women. In R. M. Eisler & M. Hersen (Eds.), *Handbook of gender, culture, and health*. Mahwah, NJ: Erlbaum.

Striegel-Moore, R. H., & Steiner-Adair, C. (1998). Primary prevention of eating disorders: Further considerations from a feminist perspective. In W. Vandereycken & G. Noordenbos (Eds.), *The prevention of eating disorders* (pp. 1–22). London: Athlone Press.

Striegel-Moore, R. H., Tucker, N., & Hsu, J. (1990). Body image dissatisfaction and disordered eating in lesbian college students. *International Journal of Eating Disorders, 9*, 493–500.

Strober, M., Lampert, C., Morell, W., Burroughs, J., & Jacobs, C. (1990). A controlled family study of anorexia nervosa: Evidence of familial aggregation and lack of shared transmission with affective disorders. *International Journal of Eating Disorders, 9*, 239–253.

Timko, C., Striegel-Moore, R. H., Silberstein, L. R., & Rodin, J. (1987). Femininity/masculinity and disordered eating in women: How are they related? *International Journal of Eating Disorders, 6*, 701–712.

Tobin, D., Johnson, C., Steinberg, S., Staats, M., & Enright, A. B. (1991). Multifactorial assessment of bulimia nervosa. *Journal of Abnormal Psychology, 100*, 14–21.

Troop, N. A., Holbrey, A., Trowler, R., & Treasure, J. L. (1994). Ways of coping in women with eating disorders. *Journal of Nervous and Mental Disease, 182*, 535–540.

Walters, E. E., & Kendler, K. S. (1995). Anorexia nervosa and anorexic-like syndromes in a population-based female twin sample. *American Journal of Psychiatry, 152*(1), 64–71.

Whitaker, A., Davies, M., Shaffer, D., Johnson, J., Abrams, S., Walsh, T., & Kalikow, K. (1989). The struggle to be thin: A survey of anorexic and bulimic symptoms in a non-referred adolescent population. *Psychological Medicine, 19*, 143–163.

Wicks-Nelson, R., & Israel, A. C. (1997). *Behavior disorders of childhood* (3rd ed.). Upper Saddle River, NJ: Prentice Hall.

Wilson, G. T., & Fairburn, C. G. (1993). Cognitive treatments for eating disorders [Special Section: Recent developments in cognitive and constructivist psychotherapies]. *Journal of Consulting and Clinical Psychology, 61*, 261–269.

Wilson, G. T., Nonas, C. A., & Rosenblum, G. D. (1993). Assessment of binge eating in obese patients. *International Journal of Eating Disorders, 13*, 25–33.

Woodside, D. B., & Garfinkel, P. E. (1992). Age of onset in eating disorders. *International Journal of Eating Disorders, 12*, 31–36.

II

ADOLESCENT GIRLS OF COLOR: DECLARING THEIR PLACE AND VOICE

INTRODUCTION

JESSICA HENDERSON DANIEL

The emblematic American girl is White. Although diversity and inclusion are now common terms in the United States, the reality is that adolescent girls of color are invisible, used as tokens in organization photographs that misrepresent their presence, and they are segregated and marginalized into the negative "other" (e.g., pregnant girl, gang member, or academic failure). As a consequence, most "general" discussions about adolescent girls are really about White girls and are experienced as irrelevant by girls of color. The implied message is that all adolescent girls are the same and that social problems among adolescent girls are largely restricted to certain groups—primarily girls of color and poor girls.

The goals for this section on adolescent girls of color are to increase the level of visibility, to understand the role of context in their lives, to present the current research and practice literature, and to advocate for research and practice that are grounded in the life texts of the girls. The adolescent girls of color in the 1990s update the words of Sojourner Truth and declare "Look, I am a girl!"

In "The 'Other' Adolescent Girls: Who Are They?" Bonnie Y. Ohye and Jessica Henderson Daniel (chap. 5) present the watercolored canvas of adolescent girls instead of the traditional charcoal sketches. For many years, race in this country has been seen as Black and White. Times have changed, and with this change has come increased acknowledgment and the real presence of persons of color who are Asian, Latino, and Native American. Even Black people are not all African Americans. Such global racial categories mask the diversity (i.e., geography, color, class, and ethnic origins) within these groups. Widening the scope of lenses to include many different groups is a current challenge.

To provide a context for the readers, authors in this section have presented census data that place adolescent girls of color and their families in the general U.S. population. The numbers validate their presence, and the predictions address anticipated growth patterns. The projection is that the percentage of people of color in the United States will increase over the years.

Although identity development is at the core of understanding adolescent girls, the major psychology journals have few articles on this topic that include adolescent girls of color. The smaller number of adolescent girls of color means the use of less powerful statistical procedures for data analyses. The following is the hard truth: The less powerful the analyses, the less likely is publication in the prestigious journals. The result is that many researchers may opt to exclude girls of color or to collect data on girls of color but exclude them from the data analyses. The combination of inclusion (usually for funding purposes) and exclusion (for the purpose of increased likelihood of acceptance in a prestigious journal) still results in the absence of information about adolescent girls of color. A strong recommendation to journal editors would be for them to reconsider the criteria for publication of journal articles that include girls of color.

In "Immigrant Adolescent Girls of Color: Challenges and Resilience" (chap. 6), Cynthia de las Fuentes and Melba J. T. Vasquez provide a general history of immigration to the United States. The reasons for immigration are delineated as well as the presence and impact of violence on immigrants.

The multiple factors that influence the rate and degree of acculturation, including age, socioeconomic level, education, and fluency in English are identified along with how they influence the lives of adolescent girls of color. In particular, the focus is on both parent–child relationships and identity formation for the adolescent girls of color and their families. As in the chapter that follows, the authors present coping strategies that immigrant families have used in an attempt to promote resiliency.

Melba J. T. Vasquez and Cynthia de las Fuentes's "American-Born Asian, African, Latina, and American Indian Adolescent Girls: Challenges and Strengths" (chap. 7) places these girls and their families in historical and contemporaneous contexts. They remind or inform readers that at one time, all of the groups of color had been immigrants except for American Indians and some Mexicans. The distinctly different immigrant pasts of persons of African descent are highlighted as well as history matters for people of color in general and adolescent girls of color in particular.

Both family and community often provide the psychosocial foundations and buffers in the lives of the adolescent girls of color as they work through the issues of this developmental period. Specific examples are provided to reflect the range of issues among the various groups. The rationale for placing research findings in a psychosocial–cultural context is presented as a way to enrich one's understanding of the lives of these girls.

Adolescent girls of color are confronted with the realities of gender and race in their lives. Similarities and differences among the groups are presented. The authors also describe one unique culturally evolved project that may contribute to the identity development of the girls in terms of their gender and race.

All three chapters document the need for research that uses new models of thinking, that is, an emphasis on health rather than on pathology, respect for the role of race and ethnicity in adolescent girls' lives, and an awareness of differences among and within the groups. The inclusion of adolescent girls of color in all aspects of science, practice, instruction, and public policy is not just a political issue. It is intellectually honest. It contributes to our knowledge base and will make possible a more effective preparation of service providers, the evolution of a science without blinders, and the development of public policy that recognizes the full diversity of adolescent girls.

5

THE "OTHER" ADOLESCENT GIRLS: WHO ARE THEY?

BONNIE Y. OHYE AND JESSICA HENDERSON DANIEL

I know I once longed to be white.
How? you ask
Let me tell you the ways. . . .

when I was growing up, I read magazines
and saw movies, blonde movie stars, white skin,
sensuous lips and to be elevated, to become
a woman, a desirable woman, I began to wear
imaginary pale skin. . . .

> —Nellie Wong
> Excerpt from "When I Was Growing Up"

THREE WAVES OF FEMINISM

In her recent social history of the feminist movement, Sheila Tobias (1997) identified three waves of feminism in the United States. The first was the 19th-century women's suffrage movement, culminating in women's right to vote in 1919. The second was marked by the publication of Betty Friedan's (1963) *The Feminine Mystique* and was a time in which long-standing cultural myths, stereotypes, and prejudices about women were challenged, most notably "biology as destiny" and women's "biological inferiority" to men. In the third and most recent wave of feminism, the assertion of women's equality with men is less prominent, and in its place has evolved an effort to explore women's capacities and experiences in their own right.

The authors wish to acknowledge with appreciation the research assistance of Deborah Offner and Judy S. Ohye.

Women Psychologists' Contributions

In both the second and third phases of the feminist movement, psychology and women psychologists, in particular, have figured significantly in reformulating the popular culture's images and conceptions of women and of womanhood. Through rigorously documenting the absence of a difference in intellectual competence between men and women, feminist scholars in psychology such as Maccoby and Jacklin (1974) provided a crucial impetus in this revision. Many, notably Gilligan (1977), Brown and Gilligan (1992), Belenky, Clinchy, Goldberger, and Tarule (1986), and scholars at the Stone Center (Miller, 1976; Jordan, Kaplan, Miller, Stiver, & Surrey, 1991) have eloquently underscored women's epistemology and psychology as distinct from that of men. These collective efforts have established and legitimized the psychological study of women and girls and have created an intellectual climate in which it is now commonplace to conceptualize gender as a social construction of enormous influence in individual psychology and female self-definition.

Symbolic Annihilation

Less well-known in our knowledge of the struggle to free women from the constraints of cultural myth have been the contributions of feminist women of color. For example, the participation of Black women in the suffrage movement occupies a minimal role in our common understanding of the right-to-vote movement (Giddings, 1984). Similarly, the participation of Black women in the second wave of feminist history is blurred by its historical overlap with the Civil Rights movement. Black feminist theoreticians presented an analysis of domination along three axes—race, gender, and class—expanding the dominant discourse by speaking about all three factors as they affect the majority of Black women. This analysis is in stark contrast to the arguments of the recognized founding feminists, who were White, middle or upper class, and privileged, which had focused exclusively on gender. Black feminists spoke to create knowledge about themselves. Their voices and writings were the tools to challenge domination and to fuel resistance to constructions of Black women that contributed to their oppression in society at large and in the feminist movement itself (Collins, 1990; Comas-Diaz & Greene, 1994; hooks, 1984; Lorde, 1984). Theorists in the field of cultural and media studies have spoken of this tendency to ignore certain groups in cultural representations and discourse or only to represent them in ways congruent with our socially rooted conceptions of them as *symbolic annihilation* (Dines & Humez, 1995).

LIMITATIONS OF METHODOLOGIES FOR UNDERSTANDING ADOLESCENT GIRLS

At heart, this chapter is about the phenomenon of symbolic annihilation with respect to the adolescent girl. It is concerned with the process of eliding some girls but not others and of placing some racial and ethnic groups in the background and others in the foreground of our culture's defining perceptions of the female adolescent. Just as psychology now more readily accepts the notion that males and females differ in their development toward self-definition, it must similarly continue to work toward fuller recognition of the contribution of race, ethnicity, culture, class, and sexual orientation to development in general (Greene et al., 1997; Zahn-Waxler, 1996) and to our understanding and study of adolescence in particular.[1]

Six Million Girls Silenced

Six million girls pass to womanhood without adequate representation in our understanding of their developmental and psychological transitions. According to the 1990 census, approximately one third of the 18.5 million girls between the ages of 10 and 18 living in the United States today are Black, Hispanic, Asian/Pacific Islander, Native American, Eskimo, or Aleut. Their psychological diversity and the culture-linked sources of resilience, strength, and self-definition remain unrecognized and unarticulated by our discipline. They are muted and invisible.

Psychologists' efforts to address their absence should not be limited to creating "more room" for girls of color in our discussions of adolescent teens in America today or to highlighting "minority" cultural attitudes and practices as legitimate phenomena for scientific study. Rather, it is necessary to examine the manner in which the assumptions underlying our traditional research methodologies restrict our capacity to capture and fully represent the diversity in adolescent female psychologies. Here, we draw attention to one particular assumption that we believe sustains less inclusive approaches to the study of adolescent girls, namely, "There are not enough of them to *count*." We use the word *count* very deliberately to suggest two meanings that we believe are mutually reinforcing: "the total number of units involved" and "to esteem; to have value or significance" (*Webster's Seventh New Collegiate Dictionary*, 1976).

---

[1] We regret the scope of this chapter is insufficient to address the significant issues of socioeconomic circumstance or of bisexual or homosexual orientation and, even more complexly, the interaction of race, family financial socioeconomic status, and sexuality as sources of influence and variation within the adolescent experience. We refer the reader to Brooks-Gunn, Duncan, and Maritato (1997), Duncan and Brooks-Gunn (1997), D'Augelli (1996), Mallon (in press), and Savin-Williams (1995) for more adequate treatment of these pressing and often concomitant aspects of adolescent female psychology.

We found this principle at work throughout our efforts to gather information and data for this chapter. We were repeatedly struck by the uneven racial and ethnic representation available from sources as widely cited as the official report on the status of children issued by the U.S. Bureau of the Census (U.S. Department of Commerce, Economics and Statistics Division, U.S. Bureau of the Census, 1993) *We the American Children*, the Association of American University Women (AAUW; 1995) report *How Schools Shortchange Girls*, and a large-scale survey of adolescent girls and the media funded jointly by the Kaiser Family Foundation and Children Now (1997) *Reflections of Girls in the Media.*

This chapter illustrates how methodologies that rely on large numbers of participants result in overgeneralization for some and symbolic annihilation for others. Two domains in which traditional research methodologies appear to restrict our understanding of American adolescent girls are presented. The first is the demographic characterization of our national population as prepared by the U.S. Bureau of the Census. The second is that of our own discipline of psychology, specifically as reflected in a selected review of the empirical literature (1991–1996) on adolescent identity development. We close with some thoughts about the place of multiple methodologies in our efforts to articulate the diversity within the transition from girlhood to womanhood in the United States today.

VIEW ONE—THE 1990 CENSUS

According to the 1990 U.S. Census, there are approximately 18,651,402 American girls between the ages 10 and 18. On the basis of the race and ethnicity categories currently recognized by the U.S. government, of these 18.5 million girls, approximately two thirds, or 12.5 million, are White but not of Hispanic origin.

White Girls

The statistically average American teen girl is White (67%). She lives with two parents, a father who is employed outside the home full time and a mother who is employed outside the home part time. However, one in five White adolescent girls lives either with one parent or with neither of her parents. If she is living in a single-parent household, that parent is overwhelmingly likely to be her mother, and there is a 50% chance her family is a "low-income" household.

Non-Hispanic Black, Hispanic, Asian/Pacific Islander or Native American, Eskimo, or Aleut

The remaining third of all American adolescents girls are considered to fall into one of four groups: (a) non-Hispanic Black, (b) Hispanic, (c) Asian/Pacific Islander, or (d) Native American, Eskimo, or Aleut, with more specific designations based on country of origin available in the categories of Asian/Pacific Islander and Hispanic (see Figure 5.1).

Black Girls

Black girls comprise the largest non-White group (15% or 2,870,000). Most of these young women (63%) live in a mother-headed household in which the mother works full time or part time outside the home. The family income in nearly 7 out of 10 of these families (69%) is "low," or less than $25,000 per year. Therefore, if you are an "average" Black teen girl in America today, you are more likely to be experiencing economic hardship than not, and to live only with your mother rather than with two parents.

Hispanic Girls

Girls of Hispanic ancestry accounted for 12% of all adolescent girls in the United States today: approximately 2.3 million girls. On average, if you are a Hispanic teen girl, you live with both of your parents (64%), have a mother who either does not work outside the home or works only

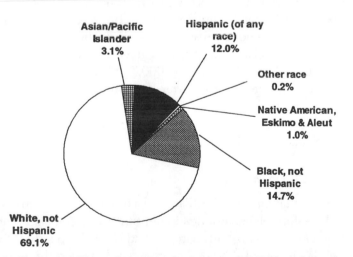

Figure 5.1. Race and Hispanic origin of adolescent females under 18 years of age. Data are from U.S. Department of Commerce, Bureau of the Census, 1993.

part time outside the home, and come from a family whose income is equally likely to be "low" or "comfortable or prosperous." If you live with one parent only, like most adolescent girls living in single-parent households, you are probably living with your mother. If you are living with your mother as the only wage earner in the home, you have a 70% chance of being a low-income family.

Asian/Pacific Islander and Native American, Eskimo, and Aleut Girls

Over three-quarters of a million teen girls are of Asian/Pacific Islander descent (3.1%), and nearly a quarter of a million, approximately 222,000, are Native American, Eskimo, or Aleut (1%). Although the Census Bureau gathers income data on these 1 million households, its official publication on the status of children, We, the American Children (U.S. Department of Commerce, Economics and Statistics Division, Bureau of the Census, 1993) does not report them. Information is presented on the three most populous groups only: White, Black, and Hispanic. This seems a striking oversight and an illustration of how a purely quantitative criterion systematically excludes certain girls of color from public and scientific view and subtly suggests that only certain children of color living in the country "count."

To obtain information on family economic status of Asian/Pacific Islander and Native American, Eskimo, and Aleut adolescent girls that is comparable to those published in We, the American Children, it was necessary to examine the data reported in Census Table 4B, Income in 1989 of Households, Families, and Persons by Race and Hispanic Origin: 1990. There are some limitations in turning to this supplementary source, however. For example, the total numbers of households reported in each racial category in Table 4B do not correspond exactly to the percentages reported in We, the American Children. Income categories are broken down into quantitative ranges (e.g., "less than $5,000," "$10,000 to $14,999") in the former document, whereas in the latter they are qualitative ("low," "comfortable"). Bearing these restrictions to direct comparability in mind, we do find that distinct characterizations of Asian/Pacific Islander and Native American, Eskimo, and Aleut families emerge.

Asian and Pacific/Islander Girls

It appears that most Asian/Pacific Islander girls live in traditional familial and comfortable economic circumstances. Five of six Asian/Pacific Islander teen girls live with both parents, and there is a nearly 50% chance that her family's income is $50,000 or more. If, however, she is among the one in six Asian/Pacific Islander girls who lives with her mother only, it is most likely (53%) that the yearly household income is less than

$25,000. The median annual income for "female-headed" Asian/Pacific Islander households is reported as $15,791.

Native American, Eskimo, and Aleut Girls

According to the Census figures, one in two Native American, Eskimo, and Aleut girls lives in two-parent families. More than half (53%) of these are families in which the yearly income is less than $25,000; this figure is 24% for White two-parent families, 34% for Black two-parent families, 23% for Asian/Pacific Islander two-parent families, and 40% for two-parent Hispanic families. If a Native American, Eskimo, or Aleut girl lives with a single wage-earning mother, for 84% of these young women the annual family income is less than $25,000, with the median family income reported as $8,692.[2]

Impact of Limitations of the Data

These data reaffirm for us that young women today live in a multiplicity of domestic circumstances. This means there is not one invariant set of demographic and socioeconomic parameters in which teens negotiate the developmental challenges of adolescence. For most young White women, these years of transition take place with the guidance of two parents living together and under comfortable economic circumstances. The young Black woman is most likely to face the stresses and opportunities of her adolescence as she lives with her mother only and under economic hardship. There are two equally likely family circumstances for the Hispanic adolescent: She lives with two parents and her family struggles economically or she lives with two parents and her family is of comfortable financial means. The Asian/Pacific Islander adolescent girl is most likely to grow up in a two-parent family with comfortable economic resources available to her. By contrast, the "average" Native American, Eskimo, and Aleut teen girl is making her way toward adulthood under conditions of significant economic strain.

If an adolescent girl, whether White, Black, Hispanic, Asian/Pacific Islander, or Native American, Alaskan, or Aleut is living only with her single wage-earning mother, she is overwhelmingly likely to be dealing with her adolescence in the context of severely limited economic resources. This is a factor of critical significance, given the strong tendency to misattribute problems in academic, social, and emotional functioning to racial and cul-

---

[2]An even more dire economic picture for mother-headed Native American families is presented by LaFromboise, Choney, James, and Running Wolf (1995). They reported that 45% of Native American households are headed by women, and the percentage living below the poverty line, currently defined as $13,000 gross income annually, may be as high as 47% (Navajo Indian Health Service).

tural factors rather than to the often monumental limitations associated with poverty.

These data illustrate further that if you are a teen girl of Asian/Pacific Islander or Native American, Eskimo, or Aleut descent, it is more difficult to obtain information about the characteristics of the family in which you are living than about your Black and Hispanic age-mates. These groups, representing only 4.1% of the population of adolescent girls, appear not to be large enough to warrant inclusion in surveys of girls of color. This was evident in the Bureau of the Census publication mentioned above as well as in two other widely cited reports on the status of adolescent girls: *How Schools Shortchange Girls* (AAUW, 1995) and the report on gender and the media prepared by the Kaiser Family Foundation and Children Now (1997), *Reflections of Girls in the Media*. This is symbolic annihilation at work.

A similarly startling disparity arises as psychologists examine the trend toward more differentiated race categories available for self-identification in the Census population count. For example, two thirds of Hispanic families identify their country of origin as Mexico; the remaining third report their national origins in Puerto Rico, Cuba, El Salvador, Colombia, Guatemala, Nicaragua, Ecuador, Peru, Honduras, or other Central and South American countries. Although the three major groups—Mexican Americans, Puerto Ricans, and Cubans—share a common legacy in Spain's colonization of the New World, the social, economic, and political characteristics of these countries of origin as well as the social, political, and economic precipitants to immigration to the United States vary enormously. These groups are, to say the least, highly heterogeneous. Yet, they are routinely represented as the single category "Hispanic." The absence of descriptive data presented according to the more specific country of origin subcategories only serves to promote the impression that there is a single, monolithic Hispanic culture. Similarly, although it is now possible for Asian/Pacific Islander families to indicate their national origin (e.g., Chinese, Filipino, Japanese, Asian Indian, Korean, Vietnamese, Laotian, Cambodian, Thai, or Hmong), information on these groups is often reported under the category "Other Races." The category "Other Races" also frequently subsumes the 557 separate tribal groups with their marked differences in lifestyle and language that make up the Native American, Eskimo, and Aleut people.

VIEW TWO—PSYCHOLOGY'S STUDY OF IDENTITY DEVELOPMENT

We chose to review the literature on identity development because of its wide acceptance as one of the most significant developmental tasks of adolescence (Adams, Gullotta, & Montemayor, 1992; Baumeister, 1986; Erikson, 1968; Waterman, 1985). According to Baumeister, this self-definition, which includes social roles and personality traits, is the basis from which adolescents (a) make choices and clarify values and priorities, (b) grapple with identifying their abilities and potential, and (c) gain an understanding of themselves in relationship to society.

Selected Journal Articles Between 1992 and 1996

A search was conducted of the psychological literature on adolescent identity development published in the 5-year period between 1992 and 1996 in four prominent, widely circulated academic journals on childhood and adolescence in psychology and related disciplines. Articles addressing this issue were selected on the basis of title and abstract review from the experimental articles that appeared in *Adolescence*, *Child Development*, the *Journal of Research on Adolescence*, and the *Journal of Youth and Adolescence*. A total of 40 empirical studies were identified and reviewed. Of the 40 studies, 6 were eliminated from this review because participants were from countries other than the United States. Almost all of the remaining studies included male and female adolescents in approximately equal proportions; two investigations used all-female samples; none of the samples were all male.

Race and Ethnicity as Variables

Approximately one third (13 of 34 or 38%) of these articles did not provide any information regarding the ethnic racial background of the participants studied. Slightly less than another third (10 of 34 or 29%) described their samples as 80% to 100% Caucasian, often without describing the backgrounds of the non-Caucasian participants. Thus, two thirds (23 of 34) of these published studies did not mention ethnic minority groups or discuss the limitations of their findings due to the racial–ethnic characteristics of their samples.

Of those 11 studies that did include U.S. ethnic minority group members in their samples, 4 were concerned with a specific ethnic minority group for study. One compared members of minority and majority religious groups in a particular region of the United States, and 3 specifically addressed the issue of cultural variation in identity development. One included several Asian American groups, one was exclusively concerned with adolescent African American girls and boys, and one with Latinas. Of the remaining 7 studies, 3 did not include ethnicity in the data analysis as an independent variable, whereas 4 did analyze the impact of ethnicity on the outcome variable or variables (see Table 5.1).

TABLE 5.1
Numbers of Empirical Articles Including U.S. Racial–Ethnic Minority Girls in Their Samples in *Child Development, Adolescence, Journal of Youth and Adolescence,* and *Journal of Research on Adolescence* (1992–1996)

Participant information	Child Develop-ment	Adoles-cence	Journal of Youth and Ado-lescence	Journal of Research on Ado-lescence	Total
Ethnicity not provided	1	4	6	2	13
Majority White/White only	2	1	4	3	10
Only ethnic minority	0	2	1	1	4
Mixed ethnicities, in-clusive of minority group(s)	4	1	1	1	7
Non-U.S. sample	0	1	3	2	6
Total	7	9	15	9	40

Gender Analysis

Twenty-three of the 34 studies (68%) conducted analyses by gender. This finding that one third of the articles failed to address the issue of potential gender variation in the mechanisms of self-definition was contrary to our expectation that all the published reports would take this variable into account in their analyses.

The greatest number of these studies (10 of 34) concerned themselves with traditional sources of adolescent socialization such as parents and peers, whereas others examined relationships between intraindividual constructs such as identity, self, and personality (Clancy & Dollinger, 1993); self-understanding, social judgment, and prosocial behavior (Hart & Fegley, 1995); and cognitive development, identity, and epistemic doubt (Boyes & Chandler, 1992). Another subset of these studies examined the relationship between identity and behaviors or choices in social contexts such as identity and dating commitment (Matula, Huston, Grotevant, & Zamur, 1992), career aspirations (Wallace-Broscious, Serafica, & Osipow, 1994), and community service (Yates & Youniss, 1996). Others were reports on the developmental course of identity and self-esteem (Block & Robins, 1993; Mullis, Mullis, & Normandin, 1992; Streitmatter, 1993).

It appears that less than 10% of the investigations published during the 5-year period under review examined both gender and race or ethnicity in relationship to the processes of adolescent self-definition. Two studies examined race or ethnicity and gender as only possible sources of confound in the data. Only one was expressly designed to explore the interaction of race or ethnicity and gender, introducing the term *ethgender* to convey their presumed interrelationship (Dukes & Martinez, 1994).

We found the results from our review troubling. It seems that as an empirical discipline, we have yet to grant full recognition to the influence of gender and race or ethnicity in the fundamental psychological process of identity development. This strikes us as a situation defined in part by a conflict between our moral commitments and our experimental methodology. Because the number of independent variables specified by the experimental design dictates the number of participants required for valid data analysis, we were not surprised to find that the three studies that addressed both gender and race or ethnicity in design and data analyses used over 100 participants, with two reporting samples well over this number: 3,781 participants in one and 18,612 in the other. These are large numbers by anyone's definition.

When an experimenter attempts to increase the representativeness of a study, and therefore the generalizability of its findings, he or she is faced with a much greater burden in recruiting participants. The inclusion of race or ethnicity and gender as independent variables means not only increasing the absolute number of participants but also ensuring an adequate number of participants—in this case, men and women—within each ethnic and racial group (Kerlinger, 1986). This is often difficult to accomplish because of economic resources available to the researcher or of limitations imposed by the racial and ethnic characteristics of the geographic region in which the investigation is being conducted. Race and ethnicity are frequently treated as extraneous variables that must be controlled or, in other words, eliminated.

As two psychologists of color, we were intrigued that the three studies with nonmajority samples were among the reports that did not address gender as a relevant variable. We wondered whether this might be a response of researchers exploring ethnic and cultural variation to the marginalization of their work within mainstream academic psychology. Perhaps the challenge of bringing greater attention to the role of race and ethnicity in psychological processes evokes a reactive narrowing of focus and an unintended exclusion of other powerful sources of variation such as gender or class. We wondered whether this might not be another, more subtle, effect of symbolic annihilation—at work this time not in the lives of those we study, but in our own as scientists.

VIEW THREE—OURS

We believe that psychology can represent an active, transforming voice in our society; we believe it must do so on behalf of all, not just some, of us. To achieve this end, it seems to us essential to examine the manner in which our traditional research sensibility and methodology work against the objective of expanding the range of experiences represented in our understanding of development across the life span, including female adolescence. It is imperative that as a discipline psychologists embrace a wider range of methods of inquiry, granting equal scientific value to these as we grant to those currently most familiar to us. This is a shift in value orientation that must take place not only at the level of the individual investigator but also within the larger institutional contexts and funding systems in which the science of psychology is embedded.

This is not a new argument. The place of alternative conceptions of knowledge and alternate methodologies to those traditionally used in psychology has been argued in the feminist literature in psychology (e.g., Morawski & Bayer, 1995), culture psychology (e.g., Gergen, Gulerce, Lock, & Misra, 1996), and the psychological community at large (e.g., Schneider, 1998). Our review has persuaded us that if we are to make our understanding of female adolescent development inclusive of the experience of young women of color, we must bring "alternative" methodologies into the mainstream of our scientific theorizing and practice. Qualitative–descriptive research approaches (e.g., Monteiro & Dollinger, 1998; Spencer, 1996) bring forth compelling and valuable insights that are frequently obscured in traditional research designs and methods of data analysis and, as important, do not require large numbers of participants.

We opened this chapter with a poetic image. For us, it is a chilling statement of the effects of a single dominant image of womanhood on young women of color. It suggests that those who fail to see themselves reflected in the culture's representations of "woman" are at risk of achieving their sense of femininity through a process of psychological effacement. The challenge to resist unitary constructions of womanhood and femininity is indeed great. It is, however, critical if all girls are to be afforded the fullest freedoms to fulfill their potential and achieve a satisfying life. It is our greatest hope that the science of psychology will explicate the multiple, varied experiences of adolescence rather than perpetuate as singular, exclusive, and therefore ultimately impoverished, our image and understanding of who the adolescent woman in America is today.

REFERENCES

Adams, G. R., Gullotta, T. P., & Montemayor, R. (Eds.). (1992). *Advances in adolescent development: Vol. 4. Adolescent identity formation.* Newbury Park, CA: Sage.

Association of American University Women. (1995). *How schools shortchange girls.* New York: Marlowe.

Baumeister, R. F. (1986). *Identity: Cultural change and the struggle for self.* New York: Oxford University Press.

Belenky, M. F., Clinchy, B. M., Goldberger, N. R., & Tarule, J. M. (1986). *Women's ways of knowing: The development of self, voice and mind.* New York: Basic Books.

Block, J., & Robins, R. W. (1993). A longitudinal study of consistency and change in self-esteem from early adolescence to early adulthood. *Child Development, 64,* 909–923.

Boyes, M. C., & Chandler, M. (1992). Cognitive development, epistemic doubt, and identity formation in adolescence. *Journal of Youth and Adolescence, 21,* 277–304.

Brooks-Gunn, J., Duncan, G. J., & Maritato, N. (1997). Poor families, poor outcomes: The well-being of children and youth. In J. Brooks-Gunn & G. Duncan (Eds.), *Consequences of growing up poor* (pp. 1–17). New York: Russell Sage Foundation.

Brown, L. M., & Gilligan, C. (1992). *Meeting at the crossroads: Women's psychology and girls' development.* New York: Ballantine Books.

Clancy, S. M., & Dollinger, S. J. (1993). Identity, self and personality: I. Identity status and the five-factor model of personality. *Journal of Research on Adolescence, 3,* 227–245.

Collins, P. H. (1990). *Black feminist thought: Knowledge, thought, and the politics of empowerment.* New York: Routledge.

Comas-Diaz, L., & Greene, B. (Eds.). (1994). *Women of color: Integrating ethnic and gender identities in psychotherapy.* New York: Guilford Press.

D'Augelli, A. R. (1996). Lesbian, gay, and bisexual development during adolescence and young adulthood. In R. P. Cabaj & T. S. Stein (Eds.), *Textbook of homosexuality and mental health* (pp. 167–288). Washington, DC: American Psychiatric Press.

Dines, G., & Humez, J. M. (Eds.). (1995). *Gender, race and class in media: A textreader.* Thousand Oaks, CA: Sage.

Dukes, R. L., & Martinez, R. (1994). The impact of ethgender on self-esteem among adolescents. *Adolescence, 29,* 105–115.

Duncan, G. J., & Brooks-Gunn, J. (1997). Income effects across the life span: Integration and interpretation. In G. J. Duncan & J. Brooks-Gunn (Eds.), *Consequences of growing up poor* (pp. 596–610). New York: Russell Sage Foundation.

Erikson, E. H. (1968). *Identity: Youth and crisis.* New York: Norton.

Friedan, B. (1963). *The feminine mystique.* New York: Norton.

Gergen, K. J., Gulerce, A., Lock, A., & Misra, G. (1996). Psychological science in cultural context. *American Psychologist, 51,* 496–503.

Giddings, P. (1984). *When and where I enter: The impact of Black women on race and sex in America.* New York: William Morrow.

Gilligan, C. (1977). In a different voice: Women's conceptions of self and of morality. *Harvard Educational Review, 47,* 481–517.

Greene, B., Sanches-Hucles, J., Banks, M., Civish, G., Contratto, S., Griffith, J., Hinderly, H. H., Jenkins, Y., & Roberson, M. (1997). Diversity: Advancing an inclusive feminist psychology. In J. Worell & N. Johnson (Eds.), *Feminist visions: New directions in education and training for feminist psychology practice* (pp. 173–202). Washington, DC: American Psychological Association.

Hart, D., & Fegley, S. (1995). Prosocial behavior and caring in adolescence: Relations to self-understanding and social judgment. *Child Development, 66,* 1346–1359.

hooks, b. (1984). *Feminist theory from margin to center.* Boston: South End Press.

Jordan, J., Kaplan, A. G., Miller, J. B., Stiver, I., & Surrey, J. (1991). *Women's growth in connection.* New York: Guilford Press.

Kaiser Family Foundation and Children Now. (1997). *Reflections of girls in the media.* Menlo Park and Oakland, CA: Authors.

Kerlinger, F. (1986). *Foundations of behavioral research* (3rd ed.). New York: Holt, Rinehart & Winston.

LaFromboise, T. D., Choney, S. B., James, A., & Running Wolf, P. R. (1995). American Indian women and psychology. In H. Landrine (Ed.), *Bringing cultural diversity to feminist psychology: Theory, research, and practice* (pp. 197–239). Washington, DC: American Psychological Association.

Landrine, H. (1995). Cultural diversity, contextualism, and feminist psychology. In H. Landrine (Ed.), *Bringing cultural diversity to feminist psychology: Theory, research, and practice* (pp. 1–20). Washington, DC: American Psychological Association.

Lorde, A. (1984). *Sister outsider.* Freedom, CA: Crossing Press.

Maccoby, E. E., & Jacklin, C. (1974). *The psychology of sex differences.* Stanford, CA: Stanford University Press.

Mallon, G. P. (in press). Gay, lesbian and bisexual childhood and adolescent development: An ecological perspective. In G. Appleby & J. Anastas (Eds.), *Not just a passing phase: Social work with gay, lesbian and bisexual persons.* New York: Columbia University Press.

Matula, K. E., Huston, T. L., Grotevant, H. D., & Zamur, A. (1992). Identity and dating commitment among women and men in college. *Journal of Youth and Adolescence, 21,* 339–356.

Miller, J. B. (1976). *Toward a new psychology of women.* Boston: Beacon Press.

Monteiro, J. M. C., & Dollinger, S. J. (1998). An autophotographic study of poverty, collective orientation, and identity among street children. *Journal of Social Psychology, 138,* 403–406.

Morawski, J. G., & Bayer, B. M. (1995). Stirring trouble and making theory. In H. Landrine (Ed.), *Bringing cultural diversity to feminist psychology* (pp. 113–137). Washington, DC: American Psychological Association.

Mullis, A. K., Mullis, R. L., & Normandin, D. (1992). Cross-sectional and longitudinal comparisons of adolescent self-esteem. *Adolescence, 27,* 51–61.

Savin-Williams, R. C. (1995). Lesbian, gay male and bisexual adolescents. In A. R. D'Augelli & C. J. Patterson (Eds.), *Lesbian, gay and bisexual identities over the lifespan: Psychological perspectives* (pp. 165–189). New York: Oxford University Press.

Schneider, K. J. (1998). Toward a science of the heart: Romanticism and the revival of psychology. *American Psychologist, 53,* 277–289.

Spencer, M. B. (1996). Old issues and new theorizing about African American youth: A phenomenological variant of ecological systems theory. In R. L. Taylor (Ed.), *Black youth: Perspectives on their status in the United States* (pp. 37–69). Westport, CT: Praeger.

Streitmatter, J. (1993). Gender differences in identity development: An examination of longitudinal data. *Adolescence, 28,* 55–66.

Tobias, S. (1997). *Faces of feminism: An activist's reflections on the women's movement.* Boulder, CO: Westview Press.

U.S. Department of Commerce, Economics and Statistics Division, Bureau of the Census. (1993). *We, the American children.* Washington, DC: Author.

Wallace-Broscious, A., Serafica, F. C., & Osipow, S. H. (1994). Adolescent career development: Relationship to self-concept and identity status. *Journal of Research on Adolescence, 4,* 127–149.

Waterman, A. S. (Ed.). (1985). *New directions for child development: Vol. 30. Identity in adolescence: Processes and contents.* San Francisco: Jossey-Bass.

Webster's Seventh New Collegiate Dictionary. (1976). Springfield, MA: Merriam-Webster.

Wong, N. (1981). When I was growing up. In C. Moraga & G. Anzaldua (Eds.), *This bridge called my back: Writings by radical women of color* (p. 7). Boston: Persephone Press.

Yates, J., & Youniss, J. (1996). Community service and political–moral identity in adolescents. *Journal of Research on Adolescence, 6,* 271–284.

Zahn Waxler, C. (1996). Environment, biology, and culture. Implications for adolescent development. *Developmental Psychology, 32,* 571–573.

6

IMMIGRANT ADOLESCENT GIRLS OF COLOR: FACING AMERICAN CHALLENGES

CYNTHIA DE LAS FUENTES AND MELBA J. T. VASQUEZ

A major task of adolescence is the development of a personal identity; events and experiences occurring during that period have enormous power in shaping the developing identity. Adolescents' relative receptivity to the impact of social events, filtered through their families, is mediated by their life stage and has an impact on their individual personality development, including their values, expectations about the world, and themselves (Stewart & Healy, 1989). Ethnic heritage is another powerful influence in determining one's identity, as it is an important factor in developing a sense of belonging (McGoldrick & Giordano, 1996) as well as contributing to issues of inclusion and exclusion. These are major challenges for all adolescent girls, but in particular for immigrant adolescent girls of color who risk rejection and isolation because of discrimination.

One purpose of this chapter is to address the unique experiences of adolescent immigrant Asian, Black, and Latina girls, as those experiences contribute to and ultimately influence their identities and development. The framework for this chapter first includes providing a backdrop for the issues specifically involving immigrant adolescent girls of color. Thus, we first discuss general demographic and background information related to immigration. Later, we discuss common experiences and problems for these immigrant families, including specific issues experienced by immigrant adolescent girls of color in the United States. Finally, we make recommendations for research and practice in light of the current climate for immigrants in the United States. Interwoven in these discussions is the exploration of resilience and of sources of strength in these girls and their families as they navigate their way through a new culture.

It is impossible to accurately convey the unique experiences of each immigrant group. Although not all immigrants come in families, most adolescents do; those who come alone usually do so for educational purposes or under conditions of duress. There is a large variation among individuals' and groups' experiences; unfortunately, the interaction of this uniqueness with cultures, histories, and psychosocial experiences in this society is left largely unrealized in this chapter. Nevertheless, we try to identify themes and issues that may be common for immigrant adolescent girls of color and their families.

IMMIGRANTS AND IMMIGRATION: CHALLENGES AND ADJUSTMENTS

To understand the psychological impact of immigration on adolescence and, in particular, on adolescent girls of color, one may find it helpful to understand the process and experiences of the family who migrates. Even when willingly chosen, immigration results in a variety of experiences with significant consequences for the individual. Immigration usually involves major changes in the physical, cultural, and social settings in which families function and develop (Strier, 1996). Transitions result in a variety of feelings, including loss and loneliness from a lack of shared experiences with peers, strain and fatigue from the effort to adapt to and cope with cultural differences, feelings of rejection from the new culture that may affect self-esteem, confusion in terms of role expectations, values, and identity, and a sense of impotency resulting from an inability to function as effectively in the new culture as one did in the home culture (Espin, 1997).

For adolescents, the adjustment presents particular challenges because they have lost peers and a familiar culture that would have served in the development of identity (Espin, 1997). Because adolescent identities are not yet consolidated, it may be easier for them than their parents to adjust to the new way of life. However, changes to, or the surrendering of, the traditional culture often create stress and conflict with parents, who may not transition as quickly or who may even resist changes in values. Parents are often confronted with different child-rearing practices and beliefs held by the socializing agents of the host culture, such as schools, churches, and communities (Strier, 1996), at times resulting in challenges and risks to the authority of the parents in the family. In addition, parental loss of power and capability to function as effectively in the new society may leave adolescents feeling unsafe and unable to rely on their parents for protection (Espin, 1997).

The contextualization of the immigration experience is of utmost importance to researchers and providers of psychological services in understanding the historical and sociopolitical nature of immigration to the United States and its effects on the adolescent girl of color. It is important to know, for example, that most immigrants do not come to the United States seeking a land of milk and honey; many are fleeing war, torture, poverty, and political persecution, and in their flight, they must leave behind their home, country, language, cultures, and members of their families.

Immigration Statistics in the United States

Between 1980 and 1990, immigration contributed a full 39% of the population growth of the country (Portes, 1994). The pace of legal immigration doubled from about a quarter million annually during the 1950s to roughly a half million annually in recent decades (U.S. Immigration and Naturalization Service, 1991). Also, the percentage arriving from Asian and Latin American countries increased from about 30% of all immigrants during the 1950s to about 85% today, according to the U.S. Immigration and Naturalization Service.

Immigrants began to arrive in the United States in sizable numbers after the U.S. Immigration Act of 1965 was passed. This act ended the national origins quota system and opened the doors for individuals and their families to enter the United States as immigrants under various categories. It also allowed naturalized citizens to be able to sponsor the immigration of their siblings and parents (Ramisetty-Mikler, 1993).

The percentage of White immigrants declined from 88% of all immigrants arriving before 1960 to 38% in the 1980s. From pre-1960s to the 1980s, Black immigrants increased from 2% to over 8%; Asians, from 5% to 31%; and other ethnoracial groups, from 5% to 23%. It is significant that immigrants from the Americas have been the most racially diverse, with fewer than 45% self-reporting as White, 13% as Black, and 41% as other (predominantly mixed populations of mestizos and mulattos; Rumbaut, 1994).

In terms of national origins, for the first time in the history of the United States, in 1990, Latin American and Caribbean peoples surpassed Europeans as the largest immigrant population in the country by a wide margin, and those immigrants born in Asia also surpassed the total number of immigrants born in Europe (Rumbaut, 1994). Over half of these non-European immigrants arrived during the 1980s alone. Mexicans accounted for just over one quarter of all immigrants arriving since 1970, and Filipinos ranked second, with close to 1 million immigrants, as Rumbaut indicated. As a result, Mexicans and Filipinos comprise the largest Hispanic and Asian immigrant groups in the United States today.

Motives for Immigration

The reasons for immigration are as varied as the populations themselves. Some come to the United States seeking hopeful futures, whereas others are fleeing miserable conditions in their countries. For example, a large percentage of Asian Indian immigrants are professionals, such as doctors, engineers, scientists, academicians, and students seeking professional degrees in American universities (Ramisetty-Mikler, 1993). Therefore, career advancement seems to be an important motivation for those immigrating from India.

However, such is not the case for many other Asian immigrants. For example, since 1980, roughly 150,000 Cambodians have resettled in the United States, following the enormous destruction of that country by the Khmer Rouge from 1975 to 1979 (Clarke, Sack, & Goff, 1993). In addition, as in the case of Vietnamese, many Asians were hastily, and without adequate preparation, forced out of their homeland, without much control over their final destination, because of the threat of political persecution (Zhou & Bankston, 1994). Political persecution is also a problem in the Americas. Half of the victims of war in Guatemala and El Salvador during the early 1980s were children, thousands of whom immigrated with their families to North America during the last decade alone (Ronstrom, 1989).

Motives for immigration are complex; they may be positive or negative; most likely, they are both. These complex motives may affect adjustment and coping strategies (Strier, 1996). For example, if the reasons for immigration were positive—that is, a desire to improve one's socioeconomic situation or to achieve ideological fulfillment—then immigrants will be more likely to have optimistic perspectives and to be open to what they perceive as positive aspects of the host culture. If reasons for migration were negative—that is, if migration was forced to escape from physical danger or political oppression, for example—then attitudes may start out more distressed, and families may tend to see themselves as needing to protect and preserve their traditions from any outside systems that may negatively influence their children, as Strier pointed out. An example of negative motivation for migration has been illustrated with the widely publicized situation of Fauziya Kasinga, a 19-year-old woman from Africa who sought asylum in the United States after she fled her home in Togo 4 years ago to avoid genital mutilation (Shiner, 1996). Although one does not as yet know of Ms. Kasinga's adjustment to immigration, one does know that to spare herself from mutilation and the chronic pain that would have been her future, she has fled her homeland, her family, and the only sources of culture and support she knew. The picture for her future adjustment is precarious; yet, she does have supporters and advocates and the internal resources required to stand up against a culture and history that has for centuries kept her maternal lineage subjugated.

CHALLENGES FOR IMMIGRANT ADOLESCENTS AND THEIR FAMILIES

Violence and Loss

Since the 1970s, there has been a large increase of Southeast Asian refugee immigrants to the United States (Chung & Okazaki, 1990). The environment they fled was ravaged by atrocities, including personal and political violence, torture, and murder. Some Southeast Asians escaped to the United States with members of their fragmented families, but many adolescents arrived alone. Although educational opportunities motivated some of the adolescent and family separations (Mortland & Egan, 1987), in most cases, youths were sent to the United States by parents out of fear for personal and family safety (Bemak & Greenberg, 1994). The obvious loss of their primary support groups and disintegration of their families caused a deterioration of social support networks that created subsequent isolation, the legacy of which seemed to generalize to peer groups in the United States (Fry, 1984; Harding & Looney, 1977; Kroll et al., 1990). Similarly, the results from the Bemak and Greenberg study of 301 unaccompanied adolescent Southeast Asian refugees indicated that the experiences of these adolescents were punctuated by family loss, separation, difficulties of refugee camp experience, and generalized trauma. These adolescents felt a profound degree of isolation and depression. Language differences created communication barriers further impeding acculturation and effectively perpetuating the desolate cycle of alienation and loneliness.

In a study on war trauma, Clarke, Sack, and Goff (1993) found that Cambodian participants in their study experienced horrifying events during the time of the Khmer Rouge, as its leader, Pol Pot, attempted to transform their country of Cambodia into a primitive form of Marxist communism. As a result, genocide occurred in which a quarter of the population died of executions, starvation, or disease (Hawk, 1982). Many of the children in their study witnessed atrocities, including seeing their own family members executed, according to Clarke et al. Malnutrition was widespread. Death by execution for stealing food or by starvation was a daily threat in work camps. Children were separated from their families; some were taught to spy on their elders, and others were forced to commit atrocities themselves.

Unfortunately, the flight from war and torture often does not stop the violence. For example, a large proportion of Central American refugees, who were themselves victims of war and torture, endured further traumatic victimization during the journey to North America, including robberies, rapes, and beatings, mostly in Mexico but also upon their arrival to the United States (Rodriguez & Urrutia-Rojas, 1990, as cited in McCloskey, Southwick, Fernandez-Esquer, & Locke, 1995), where they encountered violent border patrol agents and death squads who pursued them.

The psychological sequelae of immigration because of political persecution have left their imprints on the lives of these children and adolescents. Studies of posttraumatic war effects on children show that psychosocial adjustment, as evidenced by group bonding and support, typically buffers children in crisis, but when these support systems are lost (as in the cases of children separated from parents and siblings), symptomatology and maladjustment may occur (Kopala, Esquivel, & Baptiste, 1994). For example, Lee (1983) described incidences of developmental arrests and transitional psychoses experienced by Vietnamese and Cambodian children during or soon after the migration process. In both clinical and research settings, adolescent and adult refugees from Cambodia exhibited primarily symptoms and diagnoses of post-traumatic stress disorder (PTSD) and depression (Kinzie & Sack, 1991; Kroll et al., 1990). These refugees reported considerable amounts of both war trauma and resettlement stress, a form of chronic strain (Clarke, Sack, & Goff, 1993). The contributions of both war trauma and resettlement strain to symptoms of PTSD is in keeping with the clinical perspective that having been severely traumatized by war leaves the individual more vulnerable to the variety of resettlement issues (Beiser & Fleming, 1986; Boehnlein & Kinzie, 1985; Kinzie, 1986).

In a comparative study on immigrant Latino children who have been exposed to violence in the home or because of war, McCloskey et al. (1995) found that children exposed to violence, in general, were much more likely to have higher PTSD symptoms than children who had no such exposure. Specifically, those children who lost fathers to the violence in their countries of origin were additionally more vulnerable to PTSD. Father absence, not because of death or violence, had no effect on the mental health status of the children, perhaps because of the strength and support of their mothers and extended families. It is interesting that the overall effects of political violence in this study were mitigated by maternal mental health, suggesting that the risk to children's mental health from war is mediated by positive bonding with and protection by their mothers. The finding also indicates that the effects of political violence on children are secondary to the problems resulting from poor parental mental health, according to McCloskey et al.

Language Fluency

Once in the United States, immigrant adolescent girls and their families are faced with unique challenges. Of immediate importance to these families are economic and educational survival. Some immigrants arrive in the United States with low English fluency and are subsequently at a disadvantage in the job market and in educational settings. Others, however, are exceptionally prepared. Increased contact with the host culture often facilitates accommodation and highlights impressive adaptive skills in immigrant families. Sometimes, however, especially for families with children and adolescents, this increased contact can also create a stress because of differing rates of acculturation and resulting emerging identities.

Few immigrant families know any English, and many have poor educational preparation. Fully one quarter of all second-generation children live in households in which English is spoken "not well" or "not at all." Not surprising, the children of more recent immigrants and foreign-born children are more likely to be found within "linguistically isolated" households (Jensen & Chitose, 1994).

Socioeconomic Status

The children of immigrants often confront the same barriers to economic prosperity that affect all racial and ethnic minorities in the United States, namely, racist and discriminatory practices (Jensen, 1990, as cited in Waters, 1994; Passel & Edmonston, 1992, as cited in Portes, 1994). For mostly non-White and poor second-generation youth, the ability to succeed economically, however, depends decisively on the resources of their families and ethnic communities, according to Portes.

In terms of class, immigrants of the last two decades include the most educated groups and the least educated groups in American society, as well as the groups with the lowest poverty rates and the highest (Rumbaut, 1994). This phenomenon reflects an immigration policy that continues to give priority to prospective immigrants with exceptional scientific, professional, or artistic credentials. For example, most Asian Indians in the United States are fluent in English and have had some exposure to Western values, a factor that facilitates entry into American society (Leonard-Spark & Saran, 1980). Because of their high educational levels and their professional training, most Indian immigrants have been able to establish themselves professionally in American society and have, therefore, been somewhat buffered to the overt class-related discrimination and oppression experienced by other ethnic minorities and Asian immigrant groups (Segal, 1991).

Oftentimes, regardless of their middle-class status prior to immigration, many immigrants, especially refugees, start their American lives in poverty (Zhou & Bankston, 1994). Although the poverty rate for domestic U.S. children was 17%, for children of immigrants it was closer to 22%, whereas for foreign-born children of recent arrivals, the poverty rate was near 38% (Jensen & Chitose, 1994). Central American immigrant families have the highest unemployment and lowest level occupational status (Mc-Closkey et al., 1995) because most are without working papers, relegating them to the exploitation of employers who pay under-the-table for low-wage service jobs, often in domestic, garment, and construction industries.

Acculturation

There is no uniform process to *acculturation* among children and adolescents (Kopala et al., 1994). Acculturation is the process whereby the attitudes and behaviors of persons from one culture are modified as a result of contact with a different culture. The process may result in a bicultural or a monocultural orientation. Studies have indicated that positive coping to the stresses of acculturation is enhanced by the development of ethnic social support networks (cf. Moyerman & Forman, 1992).

Certain predisposing variables such as age, language fluency, education, previous contact (Chiswick, 1977), family structure, and cultural similarity (Hirschman, 1982) influence acculturation. Children who are older than 14 years of age or who have had prolonged separation from their parents seem to have more problems in the process of acculturation (Bagley, 1972). In addition, the entrance of a family into poverty has been found to affect adolescents more adversely than young children; so for those whose economic conditions worsen by immigration, adolescents may be particularly at risk (Elder, Liker, & Cross, 1984). The reasons that prompt individuals to immigrate also influence the nature of acculturation (Wong-Reiger & Quintana, 1987). For example, children whose parents immigrated for educational or economic reasons acculturate easier, whereas those who fled to avoid political persecution have difficulty.

On the basis of their study of upper-middle-class White girls, Rogers and Gilligan (1988) have suggested that American society provides conflicted expectations of girls, including that they be sexy and attractive. What impact does this aspect of acculturation have on the traditions of immigrant girls of color? It is interesting that a study of the high levels of adolescent pregnancy among Latinas found that a high level of acculturation was related to high levels of sexual activity and to low usage of contraceptive devices. That is, the more acculturated Mexican American adolescents are at higher risk for unwanted pregnancies than are those less acculturated (Padilla, Salgado de Snyder, Cervantes, & Baezconde-Garbanati, 1987). More research is needed to determine the factors that contributed to increased sexual behavior without contraceptive devices and safer sex practices on the part of the more acculturated adolescents. Perhaps increased exposure to ads and media, which promote sexual images of women, is a factor. In any case, developing prevention efforts that focus on healthy choices regarding sexuality, the use of contraceptives, and the practice of safer sex is an important goal.

CHALLENGES TO TRADITIONS: COMMON EXPERIENCES OF IMMIGRANT FAMILIES WITH ADOLESCENT GIRLS

Parent–Child Relationships

Although most immigrant families try to maintain their traditions and rituals, their situation in a new culture, in which they are in a minority, necessarily changes their attitudes (Gupta & Gupta, 1985). For example, changes in traditional role expectations are inevitable in Asian Indian families, as couples become more egalitarian by sharing labor, responsibilities, and decision-making processes, and children enjoy more freedom and independence (Sinha, 1985). Studies investigating the changes in Asian Indian immigrant parent–child relationships have found that children were encouraged to take more initiative, persuasion was a commonly used form of guidance, and praise was used as a reward (Kurian & Ghosh, 1978; Siddique, 1977). In addition, immigrant parents granted more freedom to their children in their decision making.

However, research has indicated that children of immigrants often assimilate into the Western culture more and faster than their parents, and acculturative stress results as these two generations face conflicts in issues such as sex roles, peer relations with the other sex, dating, and marriage (Wakil, Siddique, & Wakil, 1981). In addition, acculturative stresses are considered to be key factors triggering adjustment problems and other psychosocial problems, including disordered eating patterns among immigrants and refugees (DiNicola, 1990; Mumford, Whitehouse, & Platts, 1991), lower self-esteem and higher depression (Rumbaut, 1994), and parent–child conflicts (Rumbaut, 1994; Sue, 1981; Wakil et al., 1981; Yau & Smetana, 1993).

It is estimated that nearly 30% of all Jamaicans now live in the United States, exacting a tremendous toll on the family members, including children, who are often left behind in Jamaica, in their parents' efforts to find a better life (Black, 1996). These immigrants often undergo months or years as undocumented workers until they get their green cards and are finally able to sponsor their children's immigration. The children they leave behind grow up with a sense of abandonment, according to Black, whereas the parents worry about the uncertainty of how their children are being raised and miss the joy of watching their children grow (Larmer & Moses,

1996). This pattern of separation is common for many African Caribbean families.

As Latino families acculturate to the dominant White culture in the United States, issues between first-generation adolescents, especially girls, and their parents emerge. One of these issues is the loss of the preeminence of the patriarchal hierarchy because of the fact that children tend to learn the English language at a faster rate and often become the family's "culture brokers; parents become dependent on their children to negotiate with the outside world" (Hernandez, 1996, p. 221). Among children, daughters struggle the most during the acculturation process as they begin to challenge their parents' traditional values and restrictions on their behaviors in their attempts to develop new identities in accordance to their new American peer group. This is particularly hard on Latino parents because of the beliefs they hold for proper and appropriate behaviors for girls. This challenge may be perceived as a loss of culture, indeed, a loss of family.

In a large multiethnic study of over 5,000 second-generation students, Rumbaut (1994) found that the strongest predictor associated with lower self-esteem and higher depression in second-generation adolescents was parent–child conflict, which significantly affected adolescent girls disproportionately, a finding consistent with other studies of adolescent girls (Phinney, 1990; Rosenberg, 1979). The fact that the daughters of immigrant parents are more likely than sons to be involved in parent–child conflict possibly reflects the contrast between traditional parental attitudes about sex roles and dating, against the adolescents' developmental identity crisis synergizing with assimilation to the American culture. These parent–daughter conflicts are more likely to occur in families in which the mother is less educated and the economic situation of the family has perceptively worsened (Rumbaut, 1994). Conflict with parents significantly increased when the adolescent preferred to speak in English, had a poor command of the parental native language, spent a greater number of hours watching television, spent fewer hours on homework, attained a lower academic grade point average (GPA), and maintained lower educational aspirations, according to Rumbaut.

The issue of discrimination is also associated strongly with parent–child conflict: The more the adolescent perceived anticipatory discrimination (the expectation that one will be discriminated against), the more conflict there appeared to be (Rumbaut, 1994). These findings are supported by another study that suggests that for domestic Latino adolescents, language conflicts, perceived discrimination, and perceptions of a closed society were associated with behavior problems, as reported by teachers (Vega, Khoury, Zimmerman, Gil, & Warheit, 1995). Conversely, parent–child conflict is significantly reduced in families in which both natural parents and siblings are relied on as main sources of support as Rumbaut indicated.

Identity Development

A fundamental task of development during this time of adolescence is the formation of a healthy sense of identity, when the self-concept is most influenced by environmental and personal factors (Phinney, 1990; Rosenberg, 1979). However, for children of immigrants, identity development can be complicated by experiences of intense acculturative and intergenerational conflicts as they strive to adapt in social contexts that may be racially, sexually, and culturally dissonant from their parents' culture of origin.

For example, recent research has noted that conflicts between immigrant Chinese parents and their Chinese American children occurred primarily because of conflicting values (Yew, 1987). Immigrant parents expect their children to be passive and obedient, whereas American culture encourages children to develop identities that emphasize active, independent, aggressive, and self-sufficient traits. Chinese parents, in particular, constantly emphasize the cultural tradition of their children's primary obligations to the family (Suc, 1981), whereas American culture emphasizes individuation from family.

The adolescent's perception that their family's economic situation had worsened compared with 5 years before is also significantly related with decreased self-esteem as well as increased depression and parent–child conflict (Rumbaut, 1994). A specific feature of this finding is that paternal unemployment and low education and, even more so, the absence of the father from the home are related to higher depression and lower self-esteem. Both depression and self-esteem worsened when adolescents had no one at home or elsewhere to help with school work, when they felt embarrassed by their parents, according to Rumbaut.

Among immigrant groups of children, only the Vietnamese and especially the Filipino adolescents showed significantly lower self-esteem scores regardless of other variables (Rumbaut, 1994), suggesting that in comparison to other immigrant groups, certain psychosocial vulnerabilities (e.g., experiences of war trauma) or dynamics may be linked to their diminished sense of self-worth.

English language proficiency and educational success were found to be significantly and positively related to self-esteem and psychological well-being. Specifically, the better the adolescent English fluency, the higher the academic GPA, the higher the self-esteem, and the lower the depression score (Rumbaut, 1994). The psychological importance of linguistic acculturation for children of immigrants in American social contexts is underscored by these data. The detrimental effects of racism and discrimination are evident in that having been discriminated against resulted in significantly elevated depressive symptoms, and anticipated discrimination was significantly associated with both increased depression and decreased self-esteem, as Rumbaut pointed out.

Goodenow and Espin (1993) elaborated on three different influences on the identity development of immigrant female adolescents. The first issue results from the very nature of the immigrant status and all that it encompasses. Second, the acculturative stress created from the divergence of female sex role traditions in American culture and the culture of origin influences identity. Last, the interaction between the nature of the immigrant status and the sex role conflicts also influences identity development in immigrant female adolescents.

Adolescent girls may also be influenced by the roles their mother models in the United States. For example, Mexican immigrant women who work outside of the home experience role expansion (adding the role of wage earner to her roles as mother and wife), which strongly influences conjugal relations in the direction of more mutuality (Guendelman, 1987). In addition, married working couples develop resiliency by establishing cooperative roles; they are drawn closer by working in the same place (often in the fields), sharing similar work hours, pooling incomes, and jointly deciding how the money would be spent. Activities related to child care, laundry, and household tasks are other areas of cooperation. Guendelman also indicated that these joint activities bridge the traditional gender distance and balance power relationships within the family (Guendelman, 1987).

Researchers, as well as those who provide service delivery, must carefully assess the unique experiences and implications for adolescent immigrant girls because both may vary according to culture and histories in the countries of origin. What is true for the Mexican group described above may not be generalizable to other immigrant groups.

Because adolescent identity development is a period of heightened psychological risk for girls, researchers have begun exploring the dimensions and the links to experiences of trauma (Brown & Gilligan, 1992). White girls at this period are observed to lose their vitality, resilience, immunity to depression, sense of themselves, and character. Research to determine whether these processes occur for immigrant girls in the same way as those in the Brown and Gilligan study has not been explored, and the complex factors that influence the experience of immigrant girls and their identities must be assessed in the research and service delivery processes.

Cultural Identities

Portes (1994) maintained that the second-generation children of immigrant parents are the ones who either will maintain the cultural identities of their parents or will augment the American ethnic and racial identities. Although the cultural and immigration experiences of different immigrant groups vary with regard to their exposure as victims of discrimination, injustice, and oppression, their experience of acculturation in terms of value adjustment and orientation of family life tends to be similar (Segal, 1991). Sue (1979) has suggested that children of immigrant parents identify the following themes in their explorations of cultural identity: (a) sense of belonging versus alienation, (b) identification with their adopted country's cultural values, and (c) familial and peer relations. To the extent that these are congruent, children develop an ego-syntonic identity that is accompanied by an increased self-esteem.

In addition, ethnic self-identification is a gendered process (Rumbaut, 1994); girls are much more likely than boys to choose additive or "hyphenated identities" (such as *Chinese American*) as well as panethnic labels (e.g., Asian American). However, adolescent identities are significantly influenced by the experience of being discriminated against, and those adolescents who have personally experienced racism or discrimination were less likely to identify themselves as American and were more likely to maintain their parents' national-origin identity, especially their mother's, according to Rumbaut.

In studying the identities among second-generation African Caribbeans, Waters (1994) found three types: a Black American identity, an ethnic or hyphenated national origin identity, and an immigrant identity. These three identities were also found to be associated with different perceptions and understandings of race relations and of opportunities in the United States. For example, those adolescents who identified themselves as Black Americans perceived more racial discrimination and barriers to opportunities. Those who identified themselves as ethnic West Indians saw more opportunities and rewards for the individual with "bootstrap" perspectives. Assimilation to America for the second-generation Black immigrant is convoluted by the intersection of race and class, with higher aspiring second-generation adolescents maintaining ethnic identities to their parents' national origins, whereas their peers, who felt less efficacious, assimilated to the Black American peer culture of their environment (Waters, 1994).

One of the most effective antidotes against what Fernandez-Kelly and Schaufler (1994) described as "downward mobility" is a sense of membership in a group with an "undamaged collective identity" (p. 682). The immigrant adolescents in this study saw themselves as maintaining their parents' ethnic identity, and that identity protected them from negative stereotypes and incorporation into more mainstream American ethnic and racial minorities. Supporting this finding is a study by Zhou and Bankston (1994) on second-generation Vietnamese adolescents. They stated the following:

We have found that students who have strong adherence to traditional family values, strong commitment to a work ethic, and a high degree of personal involvement in the ethnic community tend disproportionately to receive high grades, to have definite college plans, and to score high on academic orientation measures. (p. 821)

Strengths and Resiliencies for Families of Immigrant Adolescent Girls

A relatively new focus in the study of families, including immigrant families, has been on resiliency and healthy adaptation. Most models propose that whereas the individual and family are stressed by immigration, a systemic view of resilience takes into account the strengths and support of the family as well as the environment, resulting in "hardiness" for weathering changes and uncertainties (Hawley & DeHaan, 1996; Strier, 1996; Walsh, 1996).

Some models observe families that choose a traditional, "unicultural" strategy that serves as an important protective factor, with a focus on the traditions followed in their culture of origin. Ultraorthodox immigrant families, for example, experience low levels of acculturative stress because they manage to maintain cohesion (Strier, 1996). However, the adolescent who is exposed to the values of the host culture may experience conflict and may be ostracized if diverted from their parents' ways. Other families promote the development of a bicultural identity, partly out of the need to not feel different as well as to develop values and skills to succeed in the host culture, while maintaining aspects of their traditional culture of origin (Ramirez, 1991; Strier, 1996).

For many immigrant families, the family itself often serves as an important protective factor for resilient adolescents, especially those families able to convey warmth, affection, emotional support, and clear-cut, reasonable structure and limits. Relationships with older siblings, grandparents, and extended family as well as friends, neighbors, teachers, coaches, clergy, and mentors can provide that support as well (Walsh, 1996). A close connection to one's cultural roots seems to be a positive mediating factor as well as an opportunity to experience mastery in some area in which individuals can believe that their individual or group efforts and actions can work.

A long-range study of children of immigrants found that they performed better and had lower dropout rates in public schools than did American-born students (Rumbault, as cited in "School Success of Immigrants' Children Tracked," 1997). The study depicted children of immigrants as learning English quickly, and their grades were higher than those of the district's 133,000 students as a whole. For example, in the 12th grade, 46% of all students had at least a "B" average, whereas 50% of immigrant children performed that well. More impressively, less than 6% of the immigrants' children dropped out of school, compared with 16% districtwide. Unfortunately, the study also found marked dissimilarity in career aspirations among various ethnic groups (Rumbault, as cited in "School Success of Immigrants' Children Tracked," 1997). Only 22% of Laotians and 24% of Mexicans said they would like to earn an advanced degree, compared with 63% of Asians, 52% of non-Mexican Hispanics, and 47% of Vietnamese. The study also suggested that American culture may erode the work ethic of immigrants' children because the longer they lived in the United States, the less time they spent on homework.

CLIMATE FOR IMMIGRANTS IN THE 1990s: DISCUSSION AND RECOMMENDATIONS

The political, economic, social, and racial climates can contribute to or can negatively affect adjustment and resilience. The availability of community resources is essential; those who blame undersupported, low-income families for their problems fail to appreciate the oppressive power of discrimination and poverty (Aponte, 1994; Walsh, 1996). Societal strategies to promote optimism and hope are essential elements in a socially responsible society.

Although immigrants made up barely 8% of the total 1990 U.S. population, of the 19.8 million foreign-born persons counted in the 1990 census, fully 5 million—25% of the total—resided in the Los Angeles and New York metropolitan areas alone (Rumbaut, 1994), intensifying fervent public debate about the costs and benefits of immigration.

A recent report published by the National Academy of Sciences (Smith & Edmonston, 1997) indicated that immigration produces substantial economic benefits for the United States as a whole, although only slightly reducing the wages and job opportunities of low-skilled American workers, especially high school dropouts. In 15 or 20 years, immigrants produce fiscal benefits as they finish school, start working, and begin paying income and payroll taxes.

The political and social climate, nonetheless, has resulted in U.S. immigration laws in a number of states that crack down on illegal immigration and changes in welfare laws that cut welfare benefits to those who are in the United States legally. This climate can have deleterious, rejecting effects on immigrants, including adolescents, as the experience of an increased threat and a lack of access to benefits that Americans are entitled to can affect some immigrant families' feeling of safety.

As has been demonstrated, immigration presents many challenges to individuals and families. Families and communities that are able to minimize the disruptive impact of the stresses associated with immigration protect adolescent girls. Because adolescent girls tend to be vulnerable to conflicts with parents, discrimination from the social environment, and other challenges to the identity and sense of well-being, it is important for researchers and practitioners to note the wide variability in adaptation over time. The ability to deal with the losses and the incredible changes involved in immigration involves multiple, recurring processes over time. Resilience may be more evident at one point in the development of an adolescents' experience and not so at another.

In this chapter, we have looked at some specific issues of immigrant adolescent girls of color and the experiences they have encountered because of their membership in particular ethnic groups, as contextualized in a larger sociopolitical culture of White America. This chapter has focused on key parameters for understanding these unique experiences for the identity development of the immigrant adolescent girl of color: (a) the historical and political nature of their communities' involvement with the United States through immigration patterns and sociopolitical policies and laws and (b) challenges due to economic stresses, acculturative challenges to traditions, consequences on the parent–child relationship, and challenges to identity and cultural development. Women and girls of color necessarily have multiple sources of identity, and adolescence is a critical juncture in the development of those identities; the key parameters illustrated above are crucial to understanding these populations.

Future investigations must consider the complex contextualism for understanding the effects of culture, ethnicity, gender, and class, as these factors represent critical influences on socialization, and omission of these in the study of gender socialization must be corrected. Research trends should continue to identify varieties of coping strategies that families develop for dealing with the challenges and risks of immigration. In conducting research and providing services for adolescent immigrant girls, it is important to note the wide variability in adaptation over time. Of particular importance in these future investigations is the need to focus on the growth and adaptation of the second generations. In addition, there is a dearth of information on those immigrant adolescent girls of color who are poor, lesbian, or disabled, and future researchers should keep these populations in mind.

REFERENCES

Aponte, H. (1994). *Bread and spirit: Therapy with the new poor.* New York: Norton.

Bagley, C. (1972). Deviant behavior in English and West Indian school children. *Research in Education, 8,* 47–55.

Beiser, M., & Fleming, J. A. (1986). Measuring psychiatric disorder among Southeast Asian refugees. *Psychological Medicine, 16,* 627–639.

Bemak, F., & Greenberg, B. (1994). Southeast Asian refugee adolescents: Implications for counseling. *Journal of Multicultural Counseling and Development, 22,* 115–124.

Black, L. (1996). Families of African origin: An overview. In M. McGoldrick, J. Giordano, & J. K. Pearce (Eds.), *Ethnicity and family therapy* (2nd ed., pp. 57–65). New York: Guilford Press.

Boehnlein, J., & Kinzie, J. D. (1985). A one-year followup study of post traumatic stress disorder among survivors of Cambodian concentration camps. *American Journal of Psychiatry, 142,* 956–959.

Brown, L. M., & Gilligan, C. (1992). *Meeting at the crossroads: Women's psychology and girls' development.* New York: Ballantine Books.

Chiswick, B. (1977). Sons of immigrants: Are they at an earnings disadvantage? *American Economic Review, Papers and Proceedings, 67,* 376–380.

Chung, R., & Okazaki, S. (1990). Counseling Americans of Southeast Asian descent. In C. Lee & B. Richardson (Eds.), *Multicultural issues in counseling: New directions to diversity* (pp. 107–126). Alexandria, VA: American Association for Counseling and Development.

Clarke, G., Sack, W. H., & Goff, B. (1993). Three forms of stress in Cambodian adolescent refugees. *Journal of Abnormal Child Psychology, 21*(1), 65–77.

DiNicola, V. F. (1990). Anorexia multiforme: Self-starvation in historical and cultural context. Part II: Anorexia nervosa as a culture-reactive syndrome. *Transcultural Psychiatric Research Review, 27,* 245–286.

Elder, G. H., Jr., Liker, J. K., & Cross, C. E. (1984). Parent–child behavior in the great depression: Life course and intergenerational influences. *Life Span Development and Behavior, 6,* 109–158.

Espin, O. M. (1997). Crossing borders and boundaries: The life narratives of immigrant lesbians. In B. Greene (Ed.), *Ethnic and cultural diversity among lesbians and gay men* (pp. 191–215). Thousand Oaks, CA: Sage.

Fernandez-Kelly, M. P., & Schaufler, R. (1994). Divided fates: Immigrant children in a restructured U.S. economy. *International Migration Review, 28,* 662–689.

Fry, P. S. (1984). Stress ideations of Vietnamese youth in North America. *Journal for Social Psychology, 125,* 35–43.

Goodenow, C., & Espin, O. M. (1993). Identity choices in immigrant adolescent females. *Adolescence, 28*(109), 171–184.

Guendelman, S. (1987). The incorporation of Mexican women in seasonal migration: A study of gender differences. *Hispanic Journal of Behavioral Sciences, 9,* 245–264.

Gupta, O. K., & Gupta, S. O. (1985). A study of the influence of American culture on the child-rearing of Indian mothers. *Indian Journal of Social Work, 46*(1), 5–104.

Harding, R. K., & Looney, J. G. (1977). Problems of Southeast Asian children in a refugee camp. *American Journal of Psychiatry, 134,* 407–411.

Hawk, D. (1982). The killing of Cambodia. *New Republic, 187,* 17–21.

Hawley, D. R., & DeHaan, L. (1996). Toward a definition of family resilience: Integrating life span and family perspectives. *Family Process, 35,* 283–298.

Hernandez, M. (1996). Central American families. In M. McGoldrick, J. Giordano, & J. K. Pearce (Eds.), *Ethnicity and family therapy* (2nd ed., pp. 214–224). New York: Guilford Press.

Hirschman, C. (1982). Immigrants and minorities: Old questions for new directions in research. *International Migration Review, 16,* 474–490.

Jensen, L., & Chitose, Y. (1994). Today's second generation: Evidence from the 1990 U.S. census. *International Migration Review, 28,* 714–735.

Kinzie, J. D. (1986). Severe post traumatic stress syndromes among Cambodian refugees. In J. H. Shore (Ed.), *Disaster stress studies: New methods and findings.* Washington, DC: American Psychiatric Press.

Kinzie, J. D., & Sack, W. H. (1991). Severely traumatized Cambodian children: Research findings and clinical implications. In F. L. Ahearn Jr. & J. Athey (Eds.), *Refugee children: Theory, research, and services* (pp. 92–105). Baltimore: Johns Hopkins University Press.

Kopala, M., Esquivel, G., & Baptiste, L. (1994). Counseling approaches for immigrant children: Facilitating the acculturative process. *The School Counselor, 41,* 352–359.

Kroll, J., Habenicht, M., Mackenzie, T., Yang, M., Chan, S., Vang, C., Nguyen, T., Ly, M., Phommasonvanh, B., Nguyen, H., Vang, Y., Souvannasoth, L., & Cabrugao, R. (1990). Depression and post traumatic stress disorder in Southeast Asian refugees. *American Journal of Psychiatry, 146,* 1592–1597.

Kurian, G., & Ghosh, R. (1978). Changing authority within the context of socialization in Indian families. *Social Science, 53*(1), 24–32.

Larmer, B., & Moses, K. (1996, February 19). The barrel children. *Newsweek,* 45.

Lee, D. D. (1983). Mental health in Vietnamese children. In G. F. Powell (Ed.), *The psychosocial development of minority group children* (pp. 373–384). New York: Brunner/Mazel.

Leonard-Spark, P. J., & Saran, P. (1980). The Indian immigrant in America: A demographic profile. In E. Eames & P. Saran (Eds.), *The new ethnics* (pp. 136–162). New York: Praeger.

McCloskey, L. A., Southwick, K., Fernandez-Esquer, M. E., & Locke, C. (1995). The psychological effects of political and domestic violence on Central American and Mexican immigrant mothers and children. *Journal of Community Psychology, 23,* 95–116.

McGoldrick, M., & Giordano, J. (1996). Overview: Ethnicity and family therapy. In M. McGoldrick, J. Giordano, & J. K. Pearce (Eds.), *Ethnicity and family therapy* (2nd ed., pp. 1–30). New York: Guilford Press.

Mortland, C. A., & Egan, M. G. (1987). Vietnamese youth in American foster care. *Social Work, 32,* 240–245.

Moyerman, D. R., & Forman, B. D. (1992). Acculturation and adjustment: A meta-analytic study. *Hispanic Journal of Behavioral Sciences, 14,* 163–200.

Mumford, D. B., Whitehouse, A. M., & Platts, M. (1991). Sociocultural correlates of eating disorders among Asian schoolgirls in Bradford. *British Journal of Psychiatry, 158*, 222–228.

Padilla, A. M., Salgado de Snyder, N., Cervantes, R. C., & Baezconde-Garbanati, L. (1987, Summer). Self-regulation and risk-taking behavior: A Hispanic perspective. *Research Bulletin*, 1–5.

Phinney, J. S. (1990). Ethnic identity in adolescents and adults: Review of research. *Psychological Bulletin, 108*, 499–514.

Portes, A. (1994). Introduction: Immigration and its aftermath. *International Migration Review, 28*, 632–639.

Ramirez, M. R., III. (1991). *Psychotherapy and counseling with minorities: A cognitive approach to individual and cultural differences.* New York: Pergamon Press.

Ramisetty-Mikler, S. (1993). Asian Indian immigrants in America and sociocultural issues in counseling. *Journal of Multicultural Counseling and Development, 21*, 36–49.

Rogers, A., & Gilligan, C. (1988). *Translating the language of adolescent girls: Themes of moral voice and stages of ego development* (Monograph No. 6). Cambridge, MA: Harvard University, Center for the Study of Gender, Education, and Human Development.

Ronstrom, A. (1989). Children in Central America: Victims of war. *Child Welfare, 68*, 145–153.

Rosenberg, M. (1979). *Conceiving the self.* New York: Basic Books.

Rumbaut, R. G. (1994). The crucible within: Ethnic identity, self-esteem, and segmented assimilation among children of immigrants. *International Migration Review, 28*, 748–794.

School success of immigrants' children tracked. (1997, June 16). *Los Angeles Times*, p. A-1.

Segal, U. A. (1991). Cultural variables in Asian Indian families. *Families in Society: The Journal of Contemporary Human Services, 72*, 233–241.

Shiner, C. (1996, July 3). Persecution by circumcision. *The Washington Post*, p. A1.

Siddique, C. M. (1977). Structural separation and family change: An exploratory study of the immigrant Indian and Pakistani community of Saskatoon, Canada. *International Review of Modern Sociology, 7*, 13–34.

Sinha, S. R. (1985). Maternal strategies for regulating children's behavior. *Journal of Cross-Cultural Psychology, 16*(1), 27–40.

Smith, J. P., & Edmonston, B. (Eds.). (1997). *The new Americans: Economic, demographic, and fiscal effects of immigration.* Washington, DC: National Academy Press.

Stewart, A. J., & Healy, J. M. (1989). Linking individual development and social changes. *American Psychologist, 44*, 30–42.

Strier, D. R. (1996). Coping strategies of immigrant parents: Directions for family therapy. *Family Process, 35*, 363–376.

Sue, D. W. (1979). Eliminating cultural oppression in counseling. *Journal of Counseling Psychology, 23*, 419–428.

Sue, D. W. (1981). *Counseling the culturally different: Theory and practice.* New York: Wiley.

U.S. Immigration and Naturalization Service. (1991). *Statistical yearbook of the Immigration and Naturalization Service, 1990.* Washington, DC: U.S. Government Printing Office.

Vega, W. A., Khoury, E. L., Zimmerman, R. S., Gil, A. G., & Warheit, G. J. (1995). Cultural conflicts and problem behaviors of Latino adolescents in home and school environments. *Journal of Community Psychology, 23*, 167–179.

Wakil, S. P., Siddique, C. M., & Wakil, F. A. (1981). Between two cultures: A study in socialization of children of immigrants. *Journal of Marriage and the Family, 43*, 929–940.

Walsh, F. (1996). The concept of family resilience: Crisis and challenge. *Family Process, 35*, 261–281.

Waters, M. C. (1994). Ethnic and racial identities of second-generation Black immigrants in New York City. *International Migration Review, 28*, 795–820.

Wong-Reiger, D., & Quintana, D. (1987). Comparative acculturation of Southeast Asian and Hispanic immigrants and sojourners. *Journal of Cross-Cultural Psychology, 18*, 455–462.

Yau, J., & Smetana, J. G. (1993). Chinese-American adolescents' reasoning about cultural conflicts. *Journal of Adolescent Research, 8*, 419–438.

Yew, W. (1987). Immigrant families. *Challenger, 26*, 1–3.

Zhou, M., & Bankston, C. L., III. (1994). Social capital and the adaptation of the second generation: The case of Vietnamese youth in New Orleans. *International Migration Review, 28*, 821–845.

7

AMERICAN-BORN ASIAN, AFRICAN, LATINA, AND AMERICAN INDIAN ADOLESCENT GIRLS: CHALLENGES AND STRENGTHS

MELBA J. T. VASQUEZ AND CYNTHIA DE LAS FUENTES

Adolescence is a critical juncture in the development of the identity of individuals. It is a particularly challenging time for girls. Research on gender and achievement, for example, demonstrated that gender expectations and career stereotypes resulted in lowered educational aspirations for girls, which begin to be evident by the period of adolescence (American Association of University Women [AAUW], 1992; Gilligan, 1982; Hare-Mustin & Marecek, 1990; Rogers & Gilligan, 1988).

Very little research has been conducted on the unique lives of adolescent girls of color. Yet, when research on ethnic differences is noted, often it is reported without predicting the nature and direction of those differences and without presenting a theoretical explanation of why such differences should or would exist (Landrine, 1995). When researchers have examined gender socialization of adolescents, they rarely include girls of color or girls from different social classes (Reid, Haritos, Kelly, & Holland, 1995). Environmental factors, such as poverty and class, in addition to gender and ethnicity, should be considered, especially when comparing such differences as cognitive styles and standardized achievement scores. At times, the crushing effects of poverty have more to do with test score results than do factors such as gender, race, and ethnicity (Halpern, 1995). For example, in examining variables that predicted grades, test scores, student performance, and career plans, the AAUW (1992) report confirmed what has been known for many years: Although ethnicity and gender were important variables, socioeconomic status, more than any other variable, predicts educational outcomes.

The AAUW (1992) report revealed sharp differences in self-esteem among girls from different racial and ethnic groups. Among elementary school girls, 55% of White girls, 65% of Black girls, and 68% of Hispanic girls reported being "happy as I am." But by high school, agreement with the statement came from only 22% of the White girls and 30% of the Hispanic girls (the biggest percentage drop), compared with 58% of the Black girls (the lowest percentage drop). Although the Black girls reflected the lowest percentage drop in self-esteem, these Black girls particularly suffered from low levels of self-esteem in areas related to school. More research is needed to determine why Hispanic girls experience the biggest drop, after starting with the highest levels of self-esteem, and why Black girls reflect the lowest percentage drop, except in areas related to school.

The general assumptions about what happens to girls include that adolescence is a period when girls begin to notice what society expects of them, which includes prioritizing attractiveness and being nonthreatening to boys. It is possible that Hispanic adolescent girls see themselves as even further from the ideals of beauty in American society; for many, adolescence is also a time when ethnic differences become barriers to socializing. Yet, African American adolescent girls are apparently not similarly affected by those challenges. Explanations for differences such as these must consider the complex contextualism for understanding the effects of culture, ethnicity, gender, and class (Landrine, 1995; Reid, Haritos, Kelly, & Holland, 1995).

A summary of a new report released by the AAUW Educational Foundation (Washington, DC, October 1998) entitled *Gender Gaps: Where Schools Still Fail Our Children* (AAUW, 1998; Cain, 1999) indicated that some improvements have been made. For example, girls are taking more math and science classes, enrolling in higher level honors and advanced placement classes, and playing more sports. However, issues that interfere with students' ability to learn—such as pregnancy, violence, and sexual harassment—are still prevalent. These risk factors are often more problematic for ethnic minority adolescents. For example, although the teen pregnancy rate has dropped for African American and non-Hispanic White teens, there is no decline for Hispanic adolescents. Dropout rates are especially high as well; 30% of Hispanic young women ages 16 to 24 years had dropped out of school in 1995 and had not yet passed a high school equivalency test.

Unfortunately, the AAUW (1992) report did not investigate issues in Asian American or American Indian adolescent girls, and one questions whether these students may also experience events that lead to comparable drops in self-esteem and confidence. Some authors question the generalizability of the research on the topic of socialization and gender and suggest that the factors of ethnicity and social class represent critical influences on socialization and that the omission of these in the study of gender socialization must be corrected (Reid, Haritos, Kelly, & Holland, 1995). Given the unique challenges and experiences of ethnic minorities in this country, one can assume that ethnic minority adolescent girls are differentially affected by the socialization process in this society.

A major focus of this chapter is to explore the distinct themes in the lives of American adolescent girls of Asian, African, Latino, and American Indian heritages. In addition, we will also focus on the strengths and resilience that these young women develop to cope with the daily challenges they face. These challenges and successful adaptations influence the identity development of the adolescent girl. An adolescent girl's ethnicity can have an intense influence on the development of her identity, as it can affect her sense of belonging in a world that often determines inclusion and exclusion on the basis of skin color (McGoldrick & Giordano, 1996). An individual's impressionability by certain social and historical events is mediated by her family and her life stage; it shapes her personality, values, expectations about the world, and self-perceptions (Stewart & Healy, 1989). In our exploration of these themes, we have found it helpful to understand the backdrop of social and historical events because they affect the experiences of contemporary adolescent girls of color.

Generally, children raised in periods of stability and prosperity in families that are secure and economically "comfortable" tend to develop fairly positive and optimistic views of the world and social institutions, expecting that basic needs can and will be met (Stewart & Healy, 1989). Secure children tend to value opportunities for personal development and interpersonal relationships. However, children raised in hard times, especially if their own families suffer, develop more pessimistic views and assume that life may indeed be a struggle for subsistence. The impact is not all negative, however. Those raised in hard times may come to value independence, hard work, and security. In other words, they may develop resilience out of challenges. It is important to emphasize that although this resilience evolves by way of numerous avenues, perhaps one of the most prominent paths is the access to at least one supportive caretaker in the adolescent's nuclear or extended family or in her social world (Walsh, 1996).

In keeping a developmental perspective with regard to understanding the effects of challenges, Walsh (1996) suggested that psychosocial stresses are not simply short term and single stimulus but are a complex set of changing conditions with a past history and future course. Likewise, no single coping response is invariably most successful. At each developmental stage, any individual or family will shift in their abilities to deal with stressful events. At times, this repertoire of responses may involve more vulnerable reactions, whereas at other times, it may enhance resilience. In addition, adaptation is influenced by the meaning of experience, which is socially constructed. To understand and encourage psychosocial resilience and coping mechanisms, psychologists must "attend to the interplay between what occurs within families and what occurs in the political, economic, social and racial climates in which individuals perish or thrive" (Walsh, 1996, p. 266).

The goals of this chapter include the identification of overarching commonalities as well as some of the complexities and variability among and within adolescent girls' groups of color. We explore challenges that they face through the lenses of systems—multicultural and feminist perspectives—and focus on the resilience and ability that adolescent girls of color develop to thrive through crises and adversities. Lamentably, in our attempts to identify and describe themes and issues that may be common for domestic adolescent girls of color, we remain unable to justly describe the unique experiences of all individuals and the groups to which they belong.

The first main section of the chapter describes the adolescent's experience in the context of the historical legacy of American-born adolescent girls of color and provides a brief history of American Indian, Latino, African American, and Asian American peoples. That section is followed by descriptions of the role of family as a source of strength and resilience for all ethnic groups. Finally, we describe the challenge of identity formation—a major developmental task for adolescents—for ethnic minority adolescent girls in the face of oppression and discrimination.

AMERICAN-BORN ADOLESCENT GIRLS OF COLOR: DOCUMENTING THEIR EXPERIENCE

Adolescents girls who are ethnic minorities in this society are exposed to a wide range of experiences and display a variety of strengths. One of the biggest challenges in determining the effects of these experiences on a person of color in this society involves the interplay of race, ethnicity, gender, sexual orientation, and economic class. Sexism, racism, homophobia, and classism are all challenging experiences, and it is difficult to partial out the effects of those experiences on the adolescent girl of color. To understand those experiences, it is also important to assess the interplay of what occurs within families and what occurs in the political, economic, social, and racial climates in which these young girls are challenged (Walsh, 1996). Unfortunately, very little research has been conducted with adolescent ethnic minority girls, so much of the work is extrapolated from studies related to families. Many of our conclusions are in the form of tentative hypotheses, with need for further research.

It is vital to note that there is a dynamic interrelationship between immigration and ethnicity: Many of today's ethnic minorities were the immigrants of the past, and present immigrants are already conceiving tomorrow's ethnic identities (Fernandez-Kelly & Schaufler, 1994). This dynamic process is most clearly seen in the ethnic identity development of the second generation.

Unfortunately, the growth and adaptation of these second generations have not been investigated by researchers; they have remained focused on adult immigrants, who are more visible and therefore more easily studied (Portes, 1994). The data collection processes on this phenomenon of the second generation have melded its very character.

The sections that follow briefly describe the historical and contemporary experiences of American-born adolescent girls of Asian, Latino, American Indian, and African heritages. These experiences are complex and evolving. Yet it is vital to try to identify and validate the sociopolitical and historical differences and the unique strengths among and within groups. Although we cannot possibly cover the salient issues for all groups, we try to identify the major themes and issues that are particularly relevant to the experiences of the major visible ethnic minority groups in American society.

A BRIEF HISTORY OF PEOPLE OF COLOR IN THE UNITED STATES

Psychohistorical analyses of people of color are helpful in that major historical changes have significant implications regarding influences on self-identification, changes in value systems involving family members, and learned methods of coping in a prejudicial society (Padilla, 1976). Historical processes can shape an individual as well as a people's collective past.

Multicultural experts (Bernal, 1997) have suggested that the more recent historical legacy shared by people of color is one of oppression, exploitation, and conquest. The ideology of manifest destiny, the "divine right" to conquer and rule other people, unfortunately may have provided the roots of racism, colonialism, and imperialism that justified the genocide unleashed against American Indians and supported the slavery of Africans, the conquest of Mexico, and later the invasion of Cuba and Puerto Rico

(Bernal, 1997, p. 5), and the treatment of Asian workers culminating in the internment of Japanese Americans (Sue, 1981).

The history of people of color in the United States begins with the native peoples of the continent. Today, an estimated 2 million American Indians and Alaskan natives live in the United States. Their median age is 26 years 8 months and in the last decade, their population grew by 538,834 people (U.S. Bureau of the Census, 1991). In 1990, 60% of American Indians lived in urban areas and 22% lived in reservations (Snipp, 1996). Women are the heads of households in 45% of the families, and 42% of these women had their first child as a teen (Snipp & Aytac, 1990). American Indians account for about 1% of the total U.S. population (Hodgkinson, 1990, as cited in Garrett, 1995).

Multicultural experts perceive that American Indians have been subjected to oppressive treatment that has included massacres by the U.S. Army (over 90% of the American Indian population was decimated during the first 200 years of colonization), illegal seizure of their homelands, and systematic destruction of the social, political, and economic well-being of people living in these cultural groups (D'Andrea, 1994). Whereas the annihilation of American Indians may not operate in the same way as it has in the past, "cultural genocide continues to rear its ugly head in the form of institutionalized racism" (Atkinson, Morten, & Sue, 1993, p. 119).

An example of this institutionalized racism lies with the legacy of Richard H. Pratt, founder of one of the first American Indian boarding schools, who proposed his appalling slogan "Kill the Indian and save the man!" (as cited in Oswalt, 1978, p. 528) and started what would become "one of the most ruthless and inhumane methods of assimilation available to the U.S. government" (Tafoya & Del Vecchio, 1996, p. 50). The goals of the boarding school were to remove the children from their families and traditions and to immerse them in Western culture, thought, and beliefs. This boarding school system remained in effect for almost a century. As a result, Tafoya and Del Vecchio (1996) stated that several generations of American Indians were raised without family; these authors feared that children failed to thrive and hypothesized, from their observations, that a variety of negative survival skills have been adopted.

As a result of all these factors, acculturation has been a challenge for American Indian women because more than half live in urban areas (U.S. Bureau of Census, 1991), undermining the strength of their communities and tribal affiliations (LaFromboise, Berman, & Sohi, 1994). Acculturative challenges are implicated in the problems illustrated in the following data: a total unemployment rate of 14% for American Indians 16 years of age and older, which is almost three times the rate for unemployed White people of the same age (U.S. Bureau of the Census, 1990); high school dropout rates exceeding 60% on many reservations (Gade, Hurlbut, & Fuqua, 1986); a 3% college graduation rate (U.S. Bureau of the Census,

1990); and an alcoholism and drug abuse rate that is double the national average (LaFromboise, 1988).

The history of Latinos is as varied as the heterogeneity within the Latino culture. In Mexico, the history of native people's contact with the Europeans involved a conquest by the Spanish and French, from whom they eventually gained independence. However, much of the territory now known as the southwestern United States was owned by Mexico and was taken by the United States through several wars. The war fought in the Texas area in the 1840s, for example, generated a bitterness that many believe contributed to a discriminatory attitude that remains prevalent in that region (Melville, 1980).

Although many Mexican Americans have lived in the part of the world now owned by the United States long before the Mayflower arrived to the New World (Shorris, 1992), most Latinos have migrated to the United States after World War II as a result of economic depressions and political revolutions in their countries of origin. Latinos who migrate are intellectuals persecuted for their politics, the wealthy with resources, and the poor seeking economic respite.

Latinos come from islands as well. Puerto Rico, which was a colony of Spain for 400 years, is now a colony of the United States. All Puerto Ricans were made citizens of the United States in 1917 by an act of Congress. Puerto Ricans remain deeply divided in regard to three political options: statehood (or annexation), commonwealth (colonial status), and independence (Bernal, 1997). Approximately 3.5 million Puerto Ricans live on the island of Puerto Rico, whereas another 2.5 million live in the United States. As an island neighbor, Cuba is the closest communist country to the United States. A massive migration of over a million Cubans beginning in the early 1960s was stimulated by a national revolutionary movement that culminated in 1959. Today, continued migration has been perceived to result from interference by the U.S. government's policies attempting to destabilize the revolutionary government (Bernal, 1997).

Today, Latinas represent a rapidly growing number of women of color whose ethnic heritages have origins in Mexico, Puerto Rico, Cuba, the Caribbean, Central America, and South America. According to the 1990 U.S. Census Bureau, there are over 22 million Latinos living in the United States today. This figure does not reflect the numbers of undocumented immigrants who have come into this country. Most Latinos in the United States are below the age of 30 and tend to have large families, thus accounting for the fact that this ethnic population is one of the fastest growing in the United States. Latinos maintain a strong cultural heritage that is reinforced by a constant infusion of language and tradition due to the back-and-forth flow of families across the borders.

Unlike most other immigrants, the ancestors of most people of African heritage living in the United States and the Caribbean basin came to the Americas under horrific conditions, as a result of the slave trade that brought approximately 15 million Africans to the New World during the 15th through the 19th centuries (Black, 1996). African Americans consist of about 12% of all Americans living in the United States today. Not long ago, the vast majority lived in the South; however, between 1940 and 1970, over 1.5 million African Americans migrated mostly to the North and sometimes to the West. Now, over 84% live in urban areas (Henderson, 1994). This migration, largely motivated by employment opportunities, resulted in many African Americans rising to the middle class. For example, in the 1980s, 1 in 7 African American families earned $50,000 or more compared with 1 in 17 in 1967; the percentage of African Americans living below the poverty level decreased by 10.5% for 18- to 24-year-olds and 6.5% overall (Hines & Boyd-Franklin, 1996; Tidwell, 1994).

Any attempts to understand the experiences of American adolescent girls of African descent should begin with the unique nature of their African heritage and the history of slavery and its legacy of contemporary racism, discrimination, and institutional oppression (Boyd-Franklin, 1989; Pinderhughes, 1982). This historical context has been described by some as having obstructed the Black person's development of a strong ethnic identity, familial cohesion, and direction necessary for the success for development of viable communities (Wilson & Smith, 1993). Historical evidence suggests that to adapt to pressures of slavery and discrimination, Black families maintained ingenious resiliency and have persevered, organized, and succeeded despite odds. Black Americans continue to view their families as the source of most satisfaction in their lives. Hence, "traditional family life remains the one viable option for Black Americans on all socioeconomic strata because it is less subject to the vagaries of race than any other institution in American life" (Staples, 1985, p. 1011).

Asian American groups, including Chinese, Japanese, Koreans, Filipinos, East Indians, Southeast Asians, and Pacific Islanders (including peoples of Micronesia, Melanesia, Polynesia, and the U.S. Hawaiian Islands), differ in terms of migration history, population, language, religion, education level, occupation, income, degree of acculturation, preferred residential location, and political involvement (Lee, 1996).

The history of Asians in the United States includes a history bound to the economic needs and interests of this country. The high demand for cheap labor (the discovery of gold in California and the building of the transcontinental railroad), coupled with political unrest and overpopulation in certain provinces of China, for example, brought a large steady stream of Chinese male immigrants in the 1840s. When a series of business recessions coupled with the completion of the railroad made job competition fierce, labor began to agitate against the Chinese, which some feel developed an ideology of White supremacy and Asian inferiority compatible with American racism (Sue, 1981). The Japanese were the next large Asian group to migrate, and the pattern of violence and harassment was also channeled toward the Japanese. Perhaps the most blatant discrimination was evident in the World War II incarceration of Japanese Americans into concentration camps. The humiliating effects of this atrocity and psychological sequelae are evident today in the suspiciousness that many Asians have for the American mainstream, according to Sue. Filipinos and Koreans have fared no better than their Chinese and Japanese counterparts, and more recent refugees have struggled with similar attitudes and treatments.

It is difficult to determine the direct effects of the oppressive and exploitative historical legacy on the identities, values, and attitudes of girls of color. The degree to which parents have inoculated themselves and their children with positive messages of culture and heritage despite a history of poor treatment is promoted as a coping strategy. The intensive study of one's culture, traditions, literature, music, and roots can be a helpful strategy in making one feel whole. For example, a Latina in her early twenties, who minored in Mexican American studies, reported that she felt intellectually validated for the first time in her life as a direct result of her studies about her roots and heritage. Her poverty status growing up, in combination with exposure to traditional high school presentation of the history of the Southwest, resulted in low self-esteem in regard to her heritage. It is reasonable to assume that mistreatment of one's group has a serious and potentially negative transgenerational impact on the identities of a people.

Public national presidential apologies for historical atrocities, such as to the men and the families of the Tuskegee experiment, and reparations such as those by the U.S. Congress for the Japanese families of World War II internment can contribute to the healing, as does the passage of time, and changes in conditions. Societal attitudes about concern for past, current, and future tolerance and valuing of diversity also help deter the negative impact of oppression. The degree to which healing occurs in groups, communities, and families would have a positive impact on adolescent girls of color.

THE FAMILY

Perhaps the most resilient factor common to all ethnic minority groups is the identification with family and community. The bonding and sharing of values for families of people of color can provide strength and resources for adolescent girls of color struggling with the challenges of uncertainties, conflicting expectations, and rejection based on color, language, and class. Unfortunately, there is a severe imbalance in the social science literature in favor of studies that focus on pathology; more helpful research literature would focus on resiliency, effective adaptations and coping, and stories of survival. The most egregious omissions are in studies on American Indian families (LaFromboise, 1996).

In the American Indian world, in which extended family is an integral part of life, poverty is described as being without relatives (LaFromboise et al., 1994). Family kinship often includes various households consisting of relatives representing multiple generations, all of whom are expected to share in child-rearing responsibilities. In most Indian families, generations are very descriptive of the roles in the family in which members of the grandparents' generation are all called grandmother or grandfather and cousins are referred to as brothers and sisters (Tafoya, 1982).

Variations in family structure can be seen across tribes. For example, the Hopi practice matrilineal descent and matrilocal residence. Daughters live close to their mother's home after marriage, and children belong to the woman's clan (LaFromboise et al., 1994). The opposite is true for the Havasupai woman, who lives with her husband's relatives (Sutton & Broken Nose, 1996). The transition from childhood to adulthood in many Indian communities takes place through gender-specific rites of passage rather than through adolescent development over time (French, 1989). In the past, pubescent girls were segregated from the rest of the tribe and were prepared for their responsibilities as women. Today, public and private ceremonies mark the American Indian girl's change to womanhood (LaFromboise et al., 1994).

Large extended families have also been a source of strength and resilience for Latinas, and close friends are often considered part of this extended family network (Ginorio, Gutiérrez, Cauce, & Acosta, 1995). A strong, persistent familistic orientation is a source of strength and resiliency for Latinas, and White Western values of independence, individuality, and competition may not be as valid for Latinas (Vasquez, 1994). Several studies, for example, have indicated that Mexican American children develop stronger group enhancement and altruism motives (in completing a number of games) than do Anglo American children, who develop stronger competitive motives (Kagan, 1977). Research has identified the mechanisms, socialization, and children's ethnic identity by which children's ethnic behaviors are socialized; such studies continue to confirm that the ethnic identity of the Mexican American children, instilled by their mothers' teaching about the Mexican culture, is related to the more cooperative and less competitive preferences compared with samples of Anglo American children (Knight, Cota, & Bernal, 1993).

Respecto is an important concept among Latinos, especially respect for authority and elders, because they are sources of guidance, wisdom, and vital information. Support of adolescents from elder generations is considered a strength by those concerned about adolescents in the popular press, such as in Mary Pipher's *Reviving Ophelia* (Pipher, 1994) and Hillary Rodham Clinton's *It Takes a Village* (Clinton, 1995). The term *malcriado* (ill-bred) implies criticism of those who have reared a child who exhibits disrespect to authority figures (Castaneda, 1977). Thus, if someone were motivated to teach assertiveness to Latina adolescents from traditional backgrounds, it would be important to teach those skills in the context of respect for others. Trainers and therapists must appreciate the importance of incorporating in an acceptable manner a cultural component of respect for others, especially elders, into the assertiveness training and other empowerment strategies with Latina women (Comas-Diaz, 1987).

Among Asian Americans, common traditional characteristics also include a high value of the family unit, which is reinforced by rituals and customs such as ancestor worship, family celebrations, funeral rites, and genealogy records (Lee, 1996). Obligations and shame are the mechanisms that traditionally help to reinforce societal expectations and proper behavior, with an emphasis on harmonious interpersonal relationships, interdependence, and mutual obligations or loyalty.

Although there is limited information specifically on Asian American adolescent girls, we may extrapolate that Asian American adolescents experience a variety of messages from families, the community, and society about their expectations to achieve and to maintain cultural values. Differences in personal values and lifestyles of second- and third-generation Asian American women can contribute to substantial family discord when the more traditional parents and grandparents are disappointed by their daughter's departure from traditional expectations (Bradshaw, 1994).

For the Asian American family who resettles in America, adolescence is often a harsh reality, especially for families with first-generation daughters. Particularly for Southeast Asian refugee families, the American value of individuation in adolescence is often accompanied by the issue of cultural loss because separation and loss are at the core of the parents' immigration experience (Nguyen, 1992). Under the real or perceived threat of abandonment by their adolescent daughter (to college, to spending more time outside the home, or to involvement in romantic relationships), some Asian parents are reminded of having to leave behind their own families, their own villages, and their ancestors' tombs (Nguyen, 1992). As a result, many of these families implore their children to maintain the traditions of the culture, inadvertently creating an intergenerational conflict.

As an illustration, when de las Fuentes (second author) was working in a university counseling center in southern California, she had the occasion to treat a young woman Li[1] whose parents immigrated to the United States in the 1970s under stress of war. Li was born in America to older parents who were still suffering the psychological sequelae of the ravages

---

[1]Although this case is based on actual experience, the name used is not.

of war and the loss of their entire family, including all of their children. Her father, a physician in Cambodia, became a "root doctor" in the United States. After a few years, they built a small home with few windows in an isolated part of a southeastern state. Although the whole family of three would venture together to the grocery store or a fabric store, with the exception of school, these were Li's only ventures out of the home. During her senior year of high school, Li was offered a full scholarship to a prestigious New England university. Her parents forbade her attendance, stating that she was needed at home to care for them and to work in their small business (growing and selling medicinal herbs). A year later, Li ran away from home. Without her parents' knowledge, she had secured another scholarship and traveled alone to southern California. At the time that she was seen in the counseling center, she had lived in a dormitory on campus for three months, had not spoken to her parents, and had been referred by a resident assistant who was concerned that she was at risk for suicide.

Although much of the literature describes difficulties in acculturation, as the above extreme case shows, some evidence is emerging that acculturation does not necessarily erode familism. For example, Sabogal, Marin, Otero-Sabogal, Marin, and Perez-Stable (1987) identified dimensions of familism, including family obligations, perceived support from family, and family as referents, and found that perceived support from the family seemed to be the most stable dimension of familism and did not decrease significantly with acculturation. Although the other two dimensions decreased with acculturation, even highly acculturated Latinos were more familistic than Whites on dimensions of family obligations, support from family, and family as referents. Thus, identity of the family and support of family are major resilient factors for Latinos, and probably for most ethnic groups.

African American culture and family, which is also often defined as an extended kinship network, serve as crucial barriers against the racism of the dominant culture (Boyd-Franklin, 1989; Greene, 1994). Children are viewed as part of a communal network that extends beyond a child's natural parents, which provide them with alternative role models (Boyd-Franklin, 1989). In addition, although much of the literature on African American women and men has focused on their failure to conform to existing White gender norms—such as high rates of absence of a male head of household and matriarchal family structures—and on the existence of extended family networks (Reid et al., 1995), the very nature of the difference between African American and White households provides the greatest strengths and resiliency to African American adolescent girls. For example, the inclusiveness of the extended family network provides support in many ways and on various levels, including child rearing, lending money in times of need, and assistance in negotiating through the labyrinth of larger systems that newly arrived family members will encounter, whether they are from another state or another country (Black, 1996, p. 60).

The AAUW (1992) report previously described revealed the smallest overall drop in self-esteem among Black girls. Sixty-five percent reported being "happy as I am" in elementary school, compared with 58% in high school. We may extrapolate that the community and extended family network in which these young women live foster the maintenance of a relatively stronger sense of selves. However, although the Black girls reflected the lowest percentage drop in self-esteem, these Black girls suffered particularly from low levels of self-esteem in areas related to school (AAUW, 1992). Therefore, concerns about the intersection between African American adolescent girls and the educational environment should be a focus of concern and study.

In summary, the family tends to be the basis of identification for ethnic minorities. In general, this seems to serve as a strength for adolescent girls of color. Extended families, strong family values, and family unity have been a source of strength and resilience for adolescents of color, and close friends are often considered part of this extended family network. A strong, persistent familistic and community orientation is a source of strength and resiliency for adolescents and may provide "inoculation" against the ravages of ethnic and gender discrimination, particularly for African American adolescents.

Changes and acculturation processes of adolescents can serve as threats to parents' traditional values and restrictions on their behaviors. Evolving differences in personal values and lifestyles of adolescent girls can contribute to substantial family discord when the more traditional parents and grandparents are disappointed by their daughter's departure from traditional expectations.

More research is needed to determine which aspects and to what degree familism serves as a source of strength and support as well as how adolescent acculturation creates stress in the family. Psychologists involved in family therapy interventions can focus on identifying the strengths of the family unity and can facilitate strategies for dealing with that potential discord that adolescents may introduce.

GENDER AND RACIAL IDENTITIES: THE CHALLENGE OF OPPRESSION AND DISCRIMINATION

One of the most important, difficult, and challenging tasks for adolescent girls of color is the development of a sense of racial and cultural pride as an aspect of their identities. The ability to do so indicates resiliency. Because both gender and racial factors are the core of adolescent girls' identities, racism and sexism in both U.S. society, as well as in the culture of origin, can complicate the process. Other forms of discrimination based on sexual orientation, weight size and attractiveness, color, and disabilities can complicate the identity development of the adolescent girl of color who struggles with those challenges as well.

In terms of implications for gender roles and expectations, Chinese Americans tend to be more conservative in their sexual values and in their attitudes toward the role of women (Reid et al., 1995), and Asian American women have the highest labor force participation rate of any group of women. One must remember that values and belief systems are constantly in flux and that groups may be adaptable and flexible about holding to some aspects of gender role expectations when family needs are involved. For example, Asian American men earn less than do White men (Chan, 1985) and may account in part for the relatively higher numbers of women in workforce participation. Still, the women's movement within the Asian American community has had an impact. Asian American women are less defined by the men in their lives compared with only 20 years ago (Root, 1995). Notwithstanding these gains, although Asian American women completed college twice as often as White women, their average group income earnings are only slightly greater (Root, 1995).

We do know that many Asian American adolescents struggle with issues of self-esteem and identity based largely on issues of attractiveness, which Root (1995) believes are sometimes inseparable for women. Racism and sexism contribute to negative feelings that many Asian American women have internalized about their own racial features, such as common phenotypic characteristics: eye and nose shape, skin color, straight hair, and short stature (Chan, 1985; Root, 1995).

For all women, gender role socialization begins at the time of birth, and for Latinas, this includes traditionally stringent rules for behaviors, attitudes, and beliefs in attempts to shape girls and women in socially "respectable" ways. For example, the ultimate role for a Latina is best explained through the traditional concept of *marianismo*, following the ways of the Virgin Mary. Women who are marianistas are considered to be morally and spiritually superior to men and, therefore, are more able to tolerate any hardship. Implicit in this concept is the complete conquering of sexual desire so that when a woman or girl marries, sex is considered an act of obligation, resulting solely as a function of the sacrament of marriage for the purpose of procreation and as a sacrifice for the base pleasure of her husband. The explicit message girls hear is that if a woman engages in sexual behavior with a man prior to marriage or that if she enjoys sexuality once she is married, she is then a whore. This polarity between the Madonna–whore continuum leaves no room for balance between the two positions and is used in attempts to protect the family from dishonor and shame and to enhance the girls' marital prospects.

"African American women face a range of cultural imperatives and psychological realities that may challenge, facilitate, or undermine their development and adaptive functioning" (Greene, 1994, pp. 11–12). Challenges include the historical denigration and exploitation of African peoples as well as the chronic stressors due to the daily exposure to racism, sexism, and institutional oppression. African American women and girls contend with pervasive and devaluing stereotypes regarding lack of emotional control, impulsivity, lack of sexual restraint, and lower intelligence.

The developmental process of identity development during adolescence can be complicated by these experiences of intense acculturative stress as these girls attempt to adapt in social contexts that are racially, sexually, and culturally dissonant. A young African American woman comments on her experience in the following:

> I knew my high school experience was just very weird, just by the way the whites treated me. But my self-esteem has gone down the toilet since I've been here [in college] ... being made to feel that you're never quite good enough, never quite pretty enough, never quite smart enough, or even if you're all of those things, just being made to feel that you're different, something's not quite right. (Tatum, 1997, p. 97)

At this critical time of development, the African American adolescent girl is acutely receptive to strong societal messages that her own body image and sexuality are unacceptable (Tatum, 1997). Tatum described the racial identity development of one young Black woman who shares her experience of a White friend's succumbing to peer pressure to conform to racist attitudes. The young girl stated the following:

> It eventually got very difficult for him to deal. And so it was easier for him to call me a nigger and tell me, "Your lips are too big. I don't want to see you. I won't be your friend anymore." than to say like he used to, "Oh, you're so pretty." (p. 96)

The availability of "marriageable" African American men is also reduced by higher rates of incarceration, murder, mental and physical disabilities, drug and alcohol abuse, and deaths associated with poor health and with jobs involving a high degree of danger or health hazards. Thus, African American women, aware that they outnumber African American men, either are choosing to marry less-educated lower status men out of their race (Whites, Latinos, or Asians) or are remaining single (Hines & Boyd-Franklin, 1996). Many African American women are also choosing to become single parents.

Although few empirical data exist, observers note that African American women are assertive, independent, self-confident, and sexually confident (Reid et al., 1995). A self-defined, articulated Black feminist viewpoint has been described as the source of Black women's ability to resist the controlling images of the dominant society, which has depicted them as mammies, matriarchs, whores, welfare recipients, and unwed mothers

(Collins, 1990). One hopes that these Black feminist perspectives and behaviors are pervasive enough in the community to contribute to the positive socialization of African American girls. However, it is also noted that research conducted specifically on gender socialization of African American girls has been difficult to identify and that investigations focusing on the differences that exist between African American girls and boys are rare (Reid et al., 1995).

Adolescent American Indian girls are an especially vulnerable population to unwanted teen pregnancy, sexual abuse, alcohol and drug abuse, depression, and eating disorders (LaFromboise, Choney, James, & Running Wolf, 1995). Indeed, a 1989 Indian Adolescent Health Survey report found that young American Indian girls in boarding schools are more prone to depression and that 20% of all American Indian girls have attempted suicide (LaFromboise et al., 1995). Furthermore, as many as 76% of women using the Indian Health Service (IHS) for mental health purposes are suffering from depression (LaFromboise et al., 1994). Other studies have found that American Indian women have a much higher alcoholism rate than women in general and that the death rate due to alcohol and drug abuse among American Indian women 15 to 24 years of age exceeds that of American Indian men by 40% (IHS, 1991, as cited in LaFromboise et al., 1994).

A study that supports the above data involved surveying 148 Lakota children and youth (mean age 14 years 7 months) and revealed that girls reported significantly greater concern than boys about the possibility of sexual abuse and assault, the death of a parent, domestic violence, school-related concerns, and social and moral concerns about societal drug and alcohol abuse, violence, homelessness, and hunger in society (D'Andrea, 1994). More research will hopefully shed light on the strengths and survivorship of various ethnic groups, despite various challenges.

A 1992 report of a study conducted in California, for example, indicated that despite enduring poverty-level income, Latinos exhibit values and behaviors that included a strong belief in marriage and family, a vigorous work ethic, and a desire for education (Hayes-Bautista, 1992). The state's fast-growing Hispanic population also had a historically low rate of welfare dependency, a high rate of participation in the labor force, good life expectancy rates, and a high percentage of healthy babies. In fact, according to the Texas Department of Health's Bureau of Vital Statistics ("Hispanic girls' life expectancy," 1996), Hispanic baby girls born in 1995 will have the highest life expectancy of any racial or gender group; they are expected to live an average of 80 years 4 months. Because extended families provide emotional support, Hispanic women are less likely to live alone, are less likely to be smokers or drinkers, may have a better diet, and have a lower infant mortality rate than other groups.

Although we have focused on the strengths and challenges to the cultures and families of adolescent girls of color, there are also other sources for strength. Support for adolescent girls of color is provided by friends and peers, neighbors, teachers, coaches, clergy, or mentors (Walsh, 1996). These sources of support may buffer the challenges from discrimination as well as challenges of sexual abuse, depression, the risks of adolescent pregnancy, and other related risks during adolescence.

Unique projects for girls of color are also sources of support and provide opportunities to develop a positive identity. One young Latina who had been involved in a community ballet folklorico expressed that although she was not able to be involved in cheerleader or pep squad activities at school, she was able to dance ballet folklorico at various functions on a regular basis. These community experiences provide alternative opportunities for experiences that promote positive identities.

Political participation is another avenue for the development of resiliency. In a study of political participation among Black and White women, Cole and Stewart (1996) reported that Black women who had been involved with student activism continued political activity into midlife much more frequently than White women. Furthermore, political participation was associated with social responsibility. Political activism, insofar as it is a form of empowerment, can help individuals and groups diminish the effects of discrimination and prejudice.

SUMMARY AND RECOMMENDATIONS

Adolescence is a period when girls begin to notice what society expects of them. For ethnic minority adolescent girls, the combination of a troubled historical legacy with the challenges of current oppression and discrimination due to sexism, racism, and classism can be barriers to the development of a positive identity. We have attempted to identify unique challenges that all girls of color face (history of oppression and current discrimination and prejudice based on ethnicity, gender, class, race, and color). In addition, because there is a paucity of research on other possible challenges (such as sexual orientation, disability, weight, size, and attractiveness) and the interaction of these challenges with the sociohistorical–political ones already described, we can only speculate that we have touched the tip of an iceberg. The AAUW (1992) report revealed sharp differences in self-esteem among girls from different racial and ethnic groups. More research is needed to determine why Hispanic girls experience the biggest drop, after starting with the highest levels of self-esteem, and why Black girls reflect the lowest percentage drop, except in areas related to school. In addition, more research as well as programmatic efforts must be developed to decrease teen pregnancy and other risk factors in ethnic minority adolescent girls' ability to learn (Cain, 1999).

We have also striven to identify sources of strength for adolescent girls of color, including the values related to identities based on family. In our attempt to identify the aspects of familism that serve as strengths, one must remember that no single coping response is invariably most successful. At each developmental stage, any individual or family will shift in their abilities to deal with stressful events. At times, this repertoire of responses may involve more vulnerable reactions, whereas at other times, it may enhance resilience. Nevertheless, a basic assumption is that cultural practices associated with community and family bonding generally protect from and "inoculate" against some of the insidious effects of discrimination and prejudice. At other times, parental and extended family expectations may clash with those of the acculturating adolescent and may introduce other sources of stress and challenge.

Adaptation is influenced by the meaning of experience, which is socially constructed. To understand and encourage psychosocial resilience and coping mechanisms, psychologists must "attend to the interplay between what occurs within families and what occurs in the political, economic, social, and racial climates in which individuals perish or thrive" (Walsh, 1996, p. 266). At any point in time, the cultural milieu may demonstrate support, tolerance, and valuing of diversity. At other times, the backlash identified by Faludi (1991), and illustrated by such events as the dismantling of affirmative action and other policies designed to promote equity and fairness, can have a very discouraging and negative insidious effect on the developing identities of adolescent girls.

Diversity has been a historic fact in this country's foundation and development. As the population continues to become more diverse (ethnic minorities currently comprise 25% of the population, will soon comprise one third of the population, and are predicted to be the numerical majority by the year 2050), American society will be challenged to integrate a stronger appreciation of diversity. Ensuring the success and achievement of all its population is, at best, in the self-interest of the population as whole. Psychological preventive interventions in schools, communities, churches, and families must focus on valuing diversity and promoting strengths and skills in helping girls make healthy choices. Multicultural, or bicultural, skill training must be provided in the context of the cultural values, such as in the promotion of "respectful assertive skills" for Latinas and Asian adolescent girls.

Psychological research should continue to focus on diversity, especially the intersection of gender and ethnicity. Those who plan, read, and interpret research must attend to the recommendations such as those by Halpern (1995) and Reid et al. (1995) to ensure that the psychology students and researchers study is genuinely a psychology of all people. Topics such as achievement, gender expectations, career aspirations as well as parental influence, media effects, and school influences are particularly important factors to be studied to understand the socialization of adolescent girls of color. Furthermore, the strengths and resiliences of the many who cope and adapt successfully is a neglected area of study.

REFERENCES

American Association of University Women. (1992). *How schools shortchange girls: A study of major findings on girls and education.* New York: Marlowe.

American Association of University Women. (1998). *Gender gaps: Where schools still fail our children.* Washington, DC: American Association of University Women Educational Foundation.

Atkinson, D. R., Morten, G., & Sue, D. W. (1993). *Counseling American minorities: A cross-cultural perspective* (4th ed.). Madison, WI: Brown & Benchmark.

Bernal, G. (1997, Summer). *Reflections on the legacy of 1898 and ethnic minorities: Variability.* Washington, DC: American Psychological Association Minority Fellowship Program.

Black, L. (1996). Families of African origin: An overview. In M. McGoldrick, J. Giordano, & J. K. Pearce (Eds.), *Ethnicity and family therapy* (2nd ed., pp. 57–65). New York: Guilford Press.

Boyd-Franklin, N. (1989). *Black families in therapy: A multisystems approach.* New York: Guilford Press.

Bradshaw, C. K. (1994). Asian and Asian American Women: Historical and political considerations in psychotherapy. In L. Comas-Diaz & B. Greene (Eds.), *Women of color: Integrating ethnic and gender identities in psychotherapy* (pp. 72–113). New York: Guilford Press.

Cain, L. (1999, Winter). Are girls still playing catch-up in education? *Outlook, 92,* 12–13.

Castaneda, A. (1977). Traditionalism, modernism, and ethnicity. In J. L. Martinez, Jr. (Ed.), *Chicano psychology* (pp. 343–354). New York: Academic Press.

Chan, C. S. (1985). Self-esteem and body image of Asian American adolescent girls. *Journal of the Asian American Psychological Association, 4,* 24–25.

Clinton, H. R. (1995). *It takes a village.* New York: Simon & Schuster.

Cole, E. R., & Stewart, A. J. (1996). Meanings of political participation among Black and White women: Political identity and social responsibility. *Journal of Personality and Social Psychology, 71,* 130–140.

Collins, P. H. (1990). *Black feminist thought: Knowledge, consciousness, and the politics of empowerment.* New York: Routledge.

Comas-Diaz, L. (1987). Feminist therapy with mainland Puerto Rican women. *Psychology of Women Quarterly, 11,* 461–474.

D'Andrea, M. (1994). The concerns of Native American youth. *Journal of Multicultural Counseling and Development, 22,* 173–181.

Faludi, S. (1991). *Backlash: The undeclared war against American women*. New York: Crown.

Fernandez-Kelly, M. P., & Schaufler, R. (1994). Divided fates: Immigrant children in a restructured U.S. economy. *International Migration Review, 28*, 662–689.

French, L. A. (1989). Native American alcoholism: A transcultural counseling perspective. *Counseling Psychology Quarterly, 2*, 153–166.

Gade, E., Hurlbut, G., & Fuqua, D. (1986). Study habits and attitudes of American Indian students: Implications for counselors. *The School Counselor, 34*, 135–139.

Garrett, M. W. (1995). Between two worlds: Cultural discontinuity in the dropout of Native American youth. *The School Counselor, 42*, 186–195.

Gilligan, C. (1982). *In a different voice: Psychological theory and women's development*. Cambridge: MA: Harvard University Press.

Ginorio, A. G., Gutiérrez, L. Cauce, A. M., & Acosta, M. (1995). Psychological issues for Latinas. In H. Landrine (Ed.), *Bringing cultural diversity to feminist psychology: Theory, research and practice* (pp. 241–264). Washington, DC: American Psychological Association.

Greene, B. (1994). African American women. In L. Comas-Diaz & B. Greene (Eds.), *Women of color: Integrating ethnic and gender identities in psychotherapy*. New York: Guilford Press.

Halpern, D. F. (1995). Cognitive gender differences: Why diversity is a critical research issue. In H. Landrine (Ed.), *Bringing cultural diversity to feminist psychology: Theory, research and practice* (pp. 77–92). Washington, DC: American Psychological Association.

Hare-Mustin, R. T., & Marecek, J. (1990). Gender and the meaning of difference. In R. T. Hare-Mustin & J. Marecek (Eds.), *Making a difference: Psychology and the construction of gender* (pp. 22–64). New Haven, CT: Yale University Press.

Hayes-Bautista, D. (1992). *No longer a minority: Latinos and social policy in California*. Los Angeles: University of California, Los Angeles, Chicano Studies Research Center.

Henderson, L. (1994). African Americans in the urban milieu: Conditions, trends, and development needs. In B. Tidwell (Ed.), *The state of Black America* (pp. 11–26). New York: National Urban League.

Hines, P. M., & Boyd-Franklin, N. (1996). African American families. In M. McGoldrick, J. Giordano, & J. K. Pearce (Eds.), *Ethnicity and family therapy* (2nd ed., pp. 66–84). New York: Guilford Press.

Hispanic girls' life expectancy longest. (1996, December 11). *Austin American Statesman*, pp. B4–B5.

Kagan, S. (1977). Social motives and behaviors of Mexican-American and Anglo-American children. In J. L. Martinez, Jr. (Ed.), *Chicano psychology* (pp. 45–86). New York: Academic Press.

Knight, G. P., Cota, M. K., & Bernal, M. E. (1993). The socialization of cooperative, competitive, and individualistic preferences among Mexican American children: The mediating role of ethnic identity. *Hispanic Journal of Behavioral Sciences, 15,* 291–309.

LaFromboise, T. D. (1988). American Indian mental health policy. *American Psychologist, 43,* 628–654.

LaFromboise, T. D. (1996). American Indian mental health policy. In D. Atkinson, S. Morten, & D. Sue (Eds.), *Counseling American minorities: A cross-cultural perspective* (5th ed., pp. 137–158). Madison, WI: Brown & Benchmark.

LaFromboise, T. D., Berman, J. S., & Sohi, B. K. (1994). American Indian women. In L. Comas-Diaz & B. Greene (Eds.), *Women of color: Integrative ethnic and gender identities in psychotherapy* (pp. 30–71). New York: Guilford Press.

LaFromboise, T. D., Choney, S. B., James, A., & Running Wolf, P. R. (1995). American Indian women and psychology. In H. Landrine (Ed.), *Bringing cultural diversity to feminist psychology: Theory, research, and practice* (pp. 197–240). Washington, DC: American Psychological Association.

Landrine, H. (1995). Introduction: Cultural diversity, contextualism, and feminist psychology. In H. Landrine (Ed.), *Bringing cultural diversity to feminist psychology: Theory, research, and practice* (pp. 1–20). Washington, DC: American Psychological Association.

Lee, E. (1996). Asian American families: An overview. In M. McGoldrick, J. Giordano, & J. K. Pearce (Eds.), *Ethnicity and family therapy* (2nd ed., pp. 227–248). New York: Guilford Press.

McGoldrick, M., & Giordano, J. (1996). Overview: Ethnicity and family therapy. In M. McGoldrick, J. Giordano, & J. K. Pearce (Eds.), *Ethnicity and family therapy* (2nd ed., pp. 1–30). New York: Guilford Press.

Melville, M. B. (1980). Introduction. In M. B. Melville (Ed.), *Twice a minority: Mexican American women* (pp. 1–16). St. Louis, MO: Mosby.

Nguyen, N. A. (1992). Living between two cultures: Treating first generation Asian Americans. In L. A. Vargas & J. D. Koss-Chioino (Eds.), *Working with culture: Psychotherapeutic interventions with ethnic minority children and adolescents* (pp. 204–222). San Francisco: Jossey-Bass.

Oswalt, W. H. (1978). *This land was theirs: A study of North American Indians.* New York: Wiley.

Padilla, A. M. (1976). A set of categories for combining psychology and history in the study of culture. In J. W. Wilkie, M. C. Meyer, & E. Monzon de Wilkie (Eds.), *Contemporary Mexico: Papers of the IV International Congress of Mexican History.* Berkeley: University of California Press.

Pipher, M. (1994). *Reviving Ophelia: Saving the selves of adolescent girls.* New York: Ballantine Books.

Pinderhughes, E. (1982). Afro American families and the victim system. In M. McGoldrick, J. K. Pearce, & J. Giordano (Eds.), *Ethnicity and family therapy* (pp. 108–122). New York: Guilford Press.

Portes, A. (1994). Introduction: Immigration and its aftermath. *International Migration Review, 28,* 632–639.

Reid, P. T., Haritos, C., Kelly, E., & Holland, N. E. (1995). Socialization of girls:

Issues of ethnicity in gender development. In H. Landrine (Ed.), *Bringing cultural diversity to feminist psychology: Theory, research, and practice* (pp. 93–111). Washington, DC: American Psychological Association.

Rogers, A., & Gilligan, C. (1988). *Translating girls' voices: Two languages of development.* Cambridge, MA: Harvard University Graduate School of Education, Harvard Project on the Psychology of Women and the Development of Girls.

Root, M. P. P. (1995). The psychology of Asian American women. In H. Landrine (Ed.), *Bringing cultural diversity to feminist psychology: Theory, research, and practice* (pp. 265–301). Washington, DC: American Psychological Association.

Sabogal, F., Marin, G., Otero-Sabogal, R., Marin, B. V., & Perez-Stable, E. J. (1987). Hispanic familism and acculturation: What changes and what doesn't? *Hispanic Journal of Behavioral Sciences, 9,* 397–412.

Shorris, E. (1992). *Latinos: A biography of the people.* New York: Norton.

Snipp, C. M. (1996). The size and distribution of the American Indian population: Fertility, mortality, residence, and migration. In G. Sandefur, R. Rondfuss, & B. Cohen (Eds.), *Changing numbers, changing needs: American Indian demography and public health* (pp. 17–52). Washington, DC: National Academy Press.

Snipp, C. M., & Aytac, I. A. (1990). The labor force participation of American Indian women. *Research in Human Capital and Development, 6,* 189–211.

Staples, R. (1985). Changes in Black family structure: The conflict between family ideology and structural conditions. *Journal of Marriage and the Family, 47,* 1005–1013.

Stewart, A. J., & Healy, J. M. (1989). Linking individual development and social changes. *American Psychologist, 44,* 30–42.

Sue, D. W. (1981). *Counseling the culturally different: Theory and practice.* New York: Wiley.

Sutton, C., & Broken Nose, M. A. (1996). American Indian families: An overview. In M. McGoldrick, J. Giordano, & J. K. Pearce (Eds.), *Ethnicity and family therapy* (2nd ed., pp. 31–44). New York: Guilford Press.

Tafoya, T. (1982). Coyote's eyes: Native cognition styles. *Journal of American Indian Education* [Special Issue], *21,* 29–40.

Tafoya, N., & Del Vecchio, A. (1996). Back to the future: An examination of the Native American holocaust experience. In M. McGoldrick, J. Giordano, & J. K. Pearce (Eds.), *Ethnicity and family therapy* (2nd ed., pp. 45–54). New York: Guilford Press.

Tatum, B. D. (1997). Racial identity development and relational theory: The case of Black women in White communities. In J. V. Jordan (Ed.), *Women's growth in diversity: More writings from the Stone Center* (pp. 91–106). New York: Guilford Press.

Thomason, J. E. (1991). Counseling Native Americans: An introduction for non-Native American counselors. *Journal of Counseling and Development, 69,* 321–327.

Tidwell, B. (Ed.). (1994). *The state of Black America.* New York: National Urban League.

U.S. Bureau of the Census. (1990). *The 1990 census of population and housing.* Washington, DC: U.S. Government Printing Office.

U.S. Bureau of the Census. (1991). *1990 census count of American Indians, Eskimos, or Aleuts and American Indian and Alaska areas.* Washington, DC: Author.

Vasquez, M. J. T. (1994). Latinas. In L. Comas-Diaz & B. Greene (Eds.), *Women of color: Integrating ethnic and gender identities in psychotherapy* (pp. 114–138). New York: Guilford Press.

Walsh, F. (1996). The concept of family resilience: Crisis and challenge. *Family Process, 35,* 261–281.

Wilson, L. L., & Smith, S. M. (1993). Culturally sensitive therapy with Black clients. In D. R. Atkinson, G. Morten, & D. W. Sue (Eds.), *Counseling American minorities: A cross-cultural perspective* (4th ed., pp. 101–111). Madison, WI: Brown & Benchmark.

III

TO THE HEART
OF THE MATTER:
THE RELATIONAL LIVES
OF ADOLESCENT GIRLS

INTRODUCTION

LYN MIKEL BROWN

Among the many claims psychological theorists have made about human development, arguably the most enduring and widely accepted is the belief in an adolescent struggle for separation, individuation, and autonomy. Indeed, adolescence has become synonymous with the arduous struggle for an independent selfhood or for an autonomous sense of self. Perhaps it is not surprising, then, that the discourse of what Peter Blos (1967) termed "the second individuation process" is indistinguishable from the prevailing discourse of masculinity, that is, that of "the restless, searching teen; the Hamlet figure; the sower of wild oats and tester of growing powers" (Hudson, 1984, p. 35).

Research on girls and women of many colors and different social, material, and cultural locations offers an invaluable corrective to such discourse, revealing the relational and dialogic processes at the heart of identity development and rendering visible the political, historical, and systemic forces that have an impact on one's sense of self and relationships with others. Each of the chapters in this section contribute to this corrective and, more specifically, to an ever deepening understanding and appreciation of adolescent girls' development. In so doing, the authors heed Signithia Fordham's (1993) critique of efforts to suppress the diversity of gender constructions and embrace her assertion that "in a socially, culturally, and racially stratified society like the United States, culturally specific routes to womanhood are inevitable" (p. 8).

As the chapter authors in this section point out, it is difficult to navigate the complicated, layered, often uneven terrain of adolescent girls' relationships, drawing from a psychology that has typically attended to the qualities of individuals and to gender comparisons and that has only recently begun to address the significance of social class, race and ethnicity, sexual orientation, differing abilities and needs, geographic location, immigrant status, and cultural context on the nature and characteristics of adolescent girls' relationships. There is much work to be done if psychologists are to fully understand the rich diversity of adolescent girls' psychological and relational development.

Beginning with a critique of the resiliency literature, Debold, Brown, Weseen, and Brookins, in "Cultivating Hardiness Zones for Adolescent Girls: A Reconceptualization of Resilience in Relationships With Caring Adults" (chap. 8), suggest that girls' struggles at adolescence are, fundamentally, a response to loss of power and can best be understood within the relational and sociopolitical contexts of girls' lives. They introduce the notion of hardiness as an alternative to resilience and consider positive relationships with significant adults in girls' lives as potential hardiness zones, that is, spaces of real engagement and opportunities for girls to experience control, commitment, and challenge. Such hardiness zones move the focus from the individual girl to the network of relationships that create girls' social worlds and environments, allowing girls access to skills, relationships, and possibilities that enable them to experience power and meaning. What would it mean, the authors ask, if psychology functioned as a hardiness zone for adolescent girls?

After briefly reviewing the psychological literature on adolescent girls' friendships and peer relations, Brown, Way, and Duff, in "The Others in My I: Adolescent Girls' Friendships and Peer Relations" (chap. 9), consider how current power relations in the United States, made visible and concrete in daily discourse, social interactions, and school practices, are incorporated and played out, struggled with and resisted, in the contexts of adolescent girls' relationships, primarily with other girls. Such a theoretical framework invites an exploration of the varied ways that girls struggle with dominant cultural constructions of appropriate behavior and speech and reveals the limits of explaining girls' relational struggles in purely psychological terms. Attending to interdisciplinary reports of peer relations and friendship patterns, the authors address the social and systemic forces that underlie adolescent girls' relational struggles: forces that bring issues of loyalty and trust to the surface of girls' friendships as they threaten to divide girls and make it difficult for them to seek one another out for collective action against injustice or hurt.

Unlike the research on girls' friendships or relationships with adults, in chapter 10, "Female Sexuality in Relational Context: Beyond Sexual Decision Making," Deborah L. Tolman finds that "the understanding that girls' sexuality is contextualized in relationships has not been so much ignored or passed over as not even conceptualized" (personal communication, December 1997). As a result, they argue, adolescent girls are likely to be positioned as "rogue agents" whose sexual decisions seem more "a function of individual personality and demographic characteristics." When relationships are emphasized, they tend to be cast in a negative light, posited as predictors of negative outcomes, undermining a girl's ability to make "good" sexual decisions. Studies that explore girls' relational experiences and subjective understandings of sexuality, braiding the positive and pleasurable aspects of sexuality and the potential dangers and risks of unprotected sex, she argues, hold the promise of empowering girls to develop knowledgeable and responsible sexual subjectivities.

Collectively, these three chapters reconconceptualize the ways psychologists think about relationships and what they offer adolescent girls; read together, they complicate our view of what goes on among girls and between girls and those who care for and about them. Researchers are pushed to look and listen more closely, to scrutinize the effects of relational and political context, to pay more vigilant attention to the social and material locations of the girls we study, and to consider the complicated ways in which relationships can be possible sites of both psychological resilience and psychological stress, sources of both pleasure and danger. Acknowledging that power relations—both power over others and power to move another—are at the heart of girls' emerging subjectivities, the authors call for relational theories drawn from and reflective of the lives of girls from a range of experiences, lifestyles, and backgrounds, through which we can imagine new studies and interpret new findings.

REFERENCES

Blos, P. (1967). The second individuation process of adolescence. *Psychoanalytic Study of the Child, 22,* 162–186.

Fordham, S. (1993). "Those loud black girls": (Black) women, silence and gender "passing" in the academy. *Anthropology and Education Quarterly, 24,* 3–32.

Hudson, B. (1984). Femininity and adolescence. In A. McRobbie & M. Nava (Eds.), *Gender and generation* (pp. 31–51). London: Macmillan.

8

CULTIVATING HARDINESS ZONES FOR ADOLESCENT GIRLS: A RECONCEPTUALIZATION OF RESILIENCE IN RELATIONSHIPS WITH CARING ADULTS

ELIZABETH DEBOLD, LYN MIKEL BROWN, SUSAN WESEEN, AND
GERALDINE KEARSE BROOKINS

> This soil is bad for certain kinds of flowers. Certain seeds it will not
> nurture, certain fruit it will not bear, and when the land kills of its
> own volition, we acquiesce and say the victim had no right to live.
> —Toni Morrison, *The Bluest Eye*

In each of 3 years of a longitudinal study of poor and working-class urban adolescent girls, Anita,[1] an African American girl, speaks with clarity and passion about her hopes for the future and her connections in the present. In 8th, 9th, and 10th grades, Anita asserts that she wants to be a lawyer and that "kids, kids, kids," as she says in 8th grade, are the only thing that might get in her way. In 9th grade, she determines that "I ain't going to let nothing get in the way. The only thing that could probably

---

[1]Anita, a pseudonym, is 1 of 26 girls who were designated as "at-risk" for pregnancy and dropout by their urban school in the northeastern United States. She participated in a 3-year study, "Understanding adolescents: A study of urban teens considered to be at risk," directed by Jill McLean Taylor and Deborah L. Tolman; Carol Gilligan was the principal investigator. The quotations from Anita are drawn from interview excerpts that appear in a report to the Boston Foundation (Gilligan et al., 1992; Taylor, Gilligan, & Sullivan, 1995).

happen is a baby." Her strong statement echoes with bravado, however, when juxtaposed with her observation that getting pregnant "could probably happen." In the 10th grade, she wants to be a lawyer "because we need some Black lawyers up there" and is taking an elective for students interested in law. A powerful critique of race and class motivates her to "want to achieve in life." She observes that "there's a lot of people that I know that don't want a Black kid to be somebody." This same year, her response to the interviewer's question about what might get in her way is less forceful: "If I ever got pregnant." Anita also tells her interviewer that she has been sexually active without using contraceptives.

Perhaps Anita's sense that a baby "could probably happen" to her comes from being the daughter of a woman who had children in her teens. Her mother, she explains in another part of her first interview, "is part of me and I'm a part of my mother." Passionately, Anita explains how she and her mother "have trust in each other and we rely on each other," which comes from her mother's tendency to be "very open" with Anita, even open "about sex and boys and stuff." She concludes very powerfully that "we are not that different, . . . and we do the same because I follow behind her footsteps and sometimes she will follow behind mine." Anita is proud of her connection with her mother and the mutuality and reciprocity within their relationship. A baby does happen to Anita; she follows in her mother's footsteps. She's pregnant by the fall of 11th grade, when she drops out of school.

If resilience, that is, strength and stress resistance, has been assessed in developmental psychology as "defying expectations" (Luthar & Zigler, 1991), then Anita's decision to become a mother at 16 years of age certainly does not defy media-cultivated expectations of poor African American adolescent girls and therefore would not be construed as resilient. Through these images, it is often difficult to remember that Anita, as a teen mother, is a statistical minority in her own community. Even so, what does it mean for Anita that her "resilience," when it is assessed by her capacity to carry out her expectation-defying dreams, may also depend on a certain disconnection from her mother and the community through which she has come to know herself? And, indeed, perhaps a disconnection from mothering itself. Girls' psychological strength derives from their connections with significant others (Blum, 1997; Brown & Gilligan, 1992; Debold, Wilson, & Malavé, 1994; Gilligan, 1991; Harris, Blum, & Resnick, 1991; Minnesota Women's Fund, 1990; Robinson & Ward, 1991; Taylor et al., 1995; Ward, 1996). Anita's decision to have a baby places her in closer connection with her mother as it moves her away from the dreams for a better life that she, and her mother, shared.

This places Anita's story at the heart of a dilemma facing those who want to foster girls' strengths as they negotiate the stresses of adolescence: How can girls be encouraged to take positive risks that can lead to increased options for economic viability and well-being, when taking those risks runs the danger of disconnection with significant adults in their lives? If, for psychologists and social scientists, "strength" for adolescent girls implies the capacity to stay mentally and physically whole while being able to achieve, or maintain, middle-class (or better) economic status, then the question of how girls negotiate their relationships with the significant adults in their lives, and what girls need from these adults as well as from their communities and the institutions in their lives, becomes particularly urgent. Yet this is no simple or straightforward negotiation. Connection with adults and community is essential to girls' mental health and well-being. Those connections are often strained when girls embark on life paths different from the adults closest to them who, ironically and poignantly, often encourage these disconnections through their hopes for better lives for them. This lays the groundwork for a psychological mine field: On the one hand, "success" in middle-class terms too often means a betrayal of cultural and familial connections and the terror of isolation, whereas, on the other hand, not achieving such success can mean betraying one's own and one's parents' or community's hopes, economic marginalization, and restrictive notions of identity and social position.[2]

In this chapter, we address this fundamental issue by presenting a review and critique of the literature on resilience, particularly as it relates to girls' development and relationships with significant adults. We develop a conceptual framework for understanding how adults can provide relationships and contexts that can best foster girls' health and strength. In so doing, we hope to depathologize and destigmatize poor girls within resiliency research: Poor girls, including girls who become pregnant like Anita, do not make stupid choices; they make the best of tough situations in which they are faced, with few real options for psychological growth and long-term well-being. By exploring the critical importance of relationships within girls' lives, we intend to shift the focus from girls' alleged failures to the relational and environmental contexts that too often cannot fully support them in ways that have been considered to be health promoting.

---

[2]*Middle class* is an extremely complex concept in the United States. At least since the Reagan years, it has become iconic with most Americans identifying themselves as middle class and meaning a certain level of consumption of luxury consumer goods and an experience of desire or connection with a sociopolitical framework that includes ideology, economic privilege, and educational level. Central to the middle-class ideology is a fundamental priority given to individual achievement over and above the development or integrity of the collective (family, community, culture), an emphasis on education as the means to professional work in which one controls the labor of others, and a sense of entitlement to access pathways to recognized forms of authority within the dominant culture. Within this framework, human development is deeply linked to societally approved indices of achievement.

At the 1994 Ms. Foundation Research Roundtable on promoting girls' health and resilience, developmental psychologist Pamela T. Reid responded to the claim in the resilience literature that children need "one caring adult" (Resnick, Harris, & Blum, 1993; Rutter, 1979) in their lives by observing that such a statement "can fit not only girls but puppies! In other words, all young developing organisms need support and attention" (Debold, 1995, p. 18). Furthermore, such a simplistic statement insults parents, teachers, and those who care for and guide children through the complexity and struggles of day-to-day living. Without knowledge of the assumptions and the relational perspective that the work on resilience attempted to address, the slogan "one caring adult" makes no sense. As policy or theory, it is a disaster. Reid's statement points to the banality of reducing the complexity of diverse lives into "one-size-fits-all" and the difficulty that psychology, with its metric of individual differences, has in addressing the relational and environmental contexts through which individual selves emerge (see also Reid, 1993).

Identifying "odds-defying" children or children who "defy expectations" has been core to the construct of resilience (Cowen & Work, 1988; Luthar & Zigler, 1991). Resilient individuals are those who "adapt" in the direction of societal approval in the face of such risk factors. Resilience, as David Bartelt (1994) observed, "is never directly observed—it is always imputed" (p. 101) by the researcher and may be understood as "an artifact of the investigator's model of achievement" (p. 102). Researchers have defined adaptation as the presence of individual competencies frequently, and too conveniently, measured in relation to school, such as grades (Felner, Aber, Primavera, & Cauce, 1985; Luthar, 1991; Masten et al., 1988; Weist, Freedman, Paskewitz, Proescher, & Flaherty, 1995), school attendance (Resnick et al., 1993), and teacher ratings of children (Garmezy, 1987). The use of school as a primary arena for assessing competence most likely reflects its importance and familiarity to researchers as a context for adaptation for middle-class children (Weseen, 1998). As Anne Masten (1994) noted, investigation into adaptation is necessarily based on middle- and upper-middle-class life trajectories of normative development. Erkut and colleagues (Erkut, Fields, Sing, & Marx, 1996) also noted that "[n]otions of 'resilience' and 'protective factors' . . . often reflect white, middle-class cultural models" (p. 55).

The problem with linking successful adaptation to aspects of school performance or socialization is particularly evident when considering the relationship between poor girls of color and schools. Michelle Fine's (1991) study of school dropout in a comprehensive urban high school in New York City provocatively indicates that the brightest African American girls left school, whereas the ones remaining were depressed. As John U. Ogbu

(1981) demonstrated and Signithia Fordham's (1993, 1996) analysis makes even more painfully clear, the meaning of schooling, and the pathways to what is considered as "success," can be very different for poor African American girls. Burton, Obeidallah, and Allison (1996) noted that poor children often need to take on adult responsibilities at a very young age and may find the paternalism of the school setting annoyingly infantilizing. Their observation is in accord with Fine's finding that adolescent Latinas cite family responsibilities as the primary reason for dropping out of school. African American girls often struggle to be heard within schools where their voices, carrying as they often do a powerful critique, are considered "too loud," too disruptive, and thus unwelcome (Fordham, 1993, 1996; see also Taylor et al., 1995). Small wonder, then, that African American girls maintain a personal sense of self-worth but tend to disconnect from school and teachers as a source of relevant information about themselves (American Association of University Women [AAUW], 1991). This may explain the intriguing findings that intelligence and resilience are not related (White, Moffitt, & Silva, 1989) and that intelligence may actually interfere with the development of resilience (Luthar, 1991; Masten, 1986)—suggesting serious flaws in conception and measurement. Intelligence, in the absence of meaningful support, may hinder success as defined by societally approved standards.

The conceptual emphasis on "odds-defying" keeps the focus on the individual in ways that, as Norman Garmezy (1987) noted, lead to the "politicization of protection factors" (p. 171). Poor, urban adolescent girls who do not fit media-cultivated public images of "the school dropout, the teenage welfare mother, the drug addict, and the victim of domestic violence or of AIDS" are seen as "heroic or resilient individuals" (Leadbeater & Way, 1996, p. 5). The methodological emphasis on the individual as the unit of analysis in the search for factors that protect children and lead to resilient outcomes has led a number of researchers to raise serious concerns (Bartelt, 1994; Cowen & Work, 1988; Farber & Egeland, 1989; Garmezy, 1985, 1987; Leadbeater & Way, 1996; Weseen, 1998). As Weseen (1998) noted, "the push to discover what makes some children able to swim rather than sink in the turbulent waters of racism and poverty threatens to obscure the dynamics of social and economic injustice" (p. 16). The implication and endpoint of such individually based conceptualization and measurement becomes the search for a "cure" to apply to children suffering from the extreme stress generated by a profound lack of resources rather than for ways of addressing those inequities more directly.

Leo Rigsby (1994) has argued that resilience is a "quintessentially U.S. concept" (p. 85) because the agency of the individual is magnified to such a degree that anything other than middle-class achievement and success are considered virtually pathological. The power of the concept of resilience on the American imagination may well lie in its congruence with the myth of the self-determined individual as well as its convenience as a distraction from systemic problems of poverty and inequity. However, we are also suggesting that the methods that have more recently been brought to bear on this complex construct have necessitated oversimplification and have continued the emphasis on individual solutions to structural problems. In the ways that resilience has been studied, the rich relational contexts that support development are barely visible.

READING BETWEEN THE LINES

The research on resilience and protective factors appears remarkably one dimensional in the face of girls' struggles. For a complex set of reasons, many to do with the politics and nature of traditional psychological inquiry, most of what psychology knows about girls focuses on problems or pathology and on individuals compared with other individuals. Within this paradigm, research has consistently demonstrated that for girls, early adolescence is a time of particular vulnerability to stress and distress (Brooks-Gunn, 1991; Colten & Gore, 1991; Werner & Smith, 1992). Epidemiological research shows that compared with boys of the same age, adolescent girls are more stressed (Gore & Colten, 1991; Minnesota Women's Fund, 1990); are more likely to be depressed (Gjerde, Block, & Block, 1988; Gore & Colten, 1991; Kessler et al., 1994; Nolen-Hoeksema & Girgus, 1994); suffer from greater numbers of eating disorders, including obesity (Robinson & Ward, 1991; Steiner-Adair, 1986; Wooley & Wooley, 1980); experience greater distress over their looks (Brumberg, 1997; Fabian & Thompson, 1989; Minnesota Women's Fund, 1990); engage in abusive dieting behavior (Story et al., 1991); and attempt suicide more frequently (Cole, 1991).

If one assumes that the girls who exhibit these problems and pathologies are not fundamentally different from girls who are engaging in the "normative" developmental tasks of adolescence, then we can read between the lines of the research to discover what girls struggle with in the different contexts in which they are becoming young adults. In other words, we can learn much about what kinds of support and care girls need to negotiate their struggles to develop identities, to take on adult roles, and to integrate sexuality into their sense of self from those who succumb to depression, attempt suicide, drop out of school, engage in risky sexual behaviors, experience lowered self-worth, self-mutilate, or abuse themselves through food.

Physical and cognitive development during adolescence brings girls into a radically different relationship with themselves, their families, their peers, and the world around them. Exploring the greater prevalence of depression in adolescent girls led Nolen-Hoeksema and Girgus (1994) to observe that "many of the new biological and social challenges that emerge in early adolescence are, in fact, much greater for girls than for boys" (p. 438). The source of this difference does not appear to be directly related to the biological changes of puberty but to the social and psychological impact of such changes on girls (Brooks-Gunn, 1991; Brooks-Gunn & Petersen, 1983; Caspi & Moffit, 1991). Simmons and Blyth (1987) observed that the transition from the structure of grade school, with its emphasis on consistent relationships, to the abruptly changing structure of junior high had a particularly negative impact on girls. Within a newly chaotic school environment, their childhood social worlds that focused primarily on girls and women are replaced by competition for male protection and attention and by boys' assessment and rules for social engagement. Thus, the rules of relationships that they once understood are transformed by their entrance into a social world dominated by heterosexual dating (see Maccoby, 1990). With their newfound cognitive awareness, girls often find themselves increasingly stressed by what they perceive as the responsibilities of relationships (Gore & Colten, 1991) and their growing awareness of the systems of power in which they are embedded (Debold et al., 1994; Pastor, 1993). The result of this pattern of stress and distress can be seen in the increase in girls' substance abuse, gang activity, and smoking as well as in school dropout and teen pregnancy.

Thus, although in normative terms adolescence is considered to be a time of broadening horizons and efficacy, the sphere on which girls most often exert power and control to play out the conflict they are expected to negotiate is on or with themselves and their bodies. Deborah Tolman's (1992) research on diverse girls' experiences of sexuality indicates how fraught is girls' psychosexual development: Sexuality was typically experienced as a physical, psychological, or social danger (see also Thompson, 1995; Tolman, chap. 10, this volume). Rates of sexual abuse increase remarkably for girls between the ages of 10 and 14 years (Russell, 1984). Michael Males's (1993, 1994) research documents the fact that the youngest teen mothers were made pregnant by men who were, on average, 10 years their senior. The realization that their bodies are a site of temptation and conquest provides many girls with a profound sense of anxiety for their own safety and some girls, in addition, with an illusory sense of power that too often backfires. Girls' real powerlessness in their lives and worlds is implied by the constrained sphere of action—their bodies—on which they typically act. Their higher rates of depression may actually make sense, given that persons who are depressed are more realistic than those who are not (e.g., Petersen & Craighead, 1986).

The voices of girls in qualitative studies urge us to attend to the risky contexts in which they develop. Girls in these studies often make, enact, or embody a strong critique of the sociopolitical dimensions of their lives. Robinson and Ward (1991) described African American girls' struggles to develop a positive identity within a culture that devalues them. They noted the self-limiting strategies of "resistance for survival" that girls engage in within a hostile and demeaning dominant culture: "self-denigration due to the internalization of negative self images, excessive autonomy and individualism at the expense of connection to the collective, and 'quick fixes' such as early and unplanned pregnancies, substance abuse, school drop out and food addictions" (p. 89). Fordham's (1993, 1996; Fordham & Ogbu, 1986) research reveals that high-achieving African American girls were ostracized by their peers for "acting White," whereas the low-achieving girls were shut up and shut out of learning because their disruptive comments about the realities of school life fell on deaf ears and landed them in trouble. Jennifer Pastor (1993) observed that the Latina and African American girls in her study who appeared depressed and had the lowest sense of possibility for their own lives also had the most acute understanding of racism, sexism, and classism. Poor girls of color seem to notice systemic oppression very early in their lives. In contrast, Brown and Gilligan (1992) heard a critique emerge most powerfully from White middle-class girls in late childhood or early adolescence as they came to see the dominant cultural framework as if for the first time. Girls with eating disorders speak with their bodies of a powerful conflict between the excessive and competitive individualism of American culture and their desire for connection (Steiner-Adair, 1986). Contexts shaped by gender, ethnicity, race, and class, such as community and school, provide the content for development that, in turn, divides adolescents from aspects of themselves and from others.

For girls struggling with the effects of poverty, racism, homophobia, immigrant or refugee status, and disabilities, the promise of education and opportunities for life choices different from their families or communities often presents a particular conflict and a division of loyalties. In creating identities and making life choices, poor girls experience a forced choice between a middle-class American individualistic sense of well-being and success and their cultural well-being and familial connections (see, e.g., Chen, 1997; Fordham, 1996; Lee, 1996). Fine (1991) found that the best predictor for girls of school dropout, after social class, was number of siblings: The cultural expectation, and financial necessity, of girls' care taking, particularly among Latinas, pulled them out of school. Judith Musick (1993) noted that teen mothers' needs for connection to their families and communities often led them away from interventions designed to provide them with life options that would take them away from the relational worlds that they knew. For girls within refugee or immigrant communities, crossing the boundary of love, language, and shared struggle to embody other ways of being may be a tightrope walk across an emotional abyss (see Espin, 1997).

For girls, the changes in mind and body at adolescence mark a time of acute conflict over connection, control, and power. Although "girls," or even "poor girls," are not a monolithic group, across race, ethnicity, and class, adolescent girls share vulnerability to teen pregnancy, sexism, low expectations, and violence and abuse (particularly in intimate relationships). Research documents that poor girls often do poorly in relation to expected middle-class paths. However, we know very little that is positive about these girls, their strengths, and how they understand their lives (for notable exceptions, see Brown, 1998; Leadbeater & Way, 1996). There has been no systematic effort to determine what contextually relevant developmental goals might be, how they relate to mainstream goals, and how health might be assessed by taking into account the layers of context in which adolescents find themselves (Burton et al., 1996). We do know that girls report that there are few who are willing to listen, let alone join them in their critique (see Taylor et al., 1995). Girls have few safe opportunities to explore or experience their own possibility or potency in the world around them (Ms. Foundation for Women, 1993; Pastor, McCormick, & Fine, 1996).

FROM RESILIENCE TO HARDINESS ZONES

The research on resilience and protective factors suggests that connection to parents, significant adults, school, and, perhaps, some greater sense of purpose or perspective (as evidenced by the protective effect of both humor and spirituality but not religiosity) fosters resilience (Blum, 1997; Resnick et al., 1997). A dilemma of connection, a forced choice between competing loyalties, is often precisely what girls face. Girls' struggles are rooted in systemic problems, such as poverty, racism, and sexism, that require a collective rather than an individual response. What connection means for a girl is far more complex than providing her with a mentor (see Sullivan, 1996). In understanding the struggles and strengths of girls within the communities and contexts in which they live, our notions of health and the units of analysis need to change. This suggests a need for a new concept of health and stress resistance that locates the struggle between a girl and her world, not simply within the individual girl, and that holds the adults in girls' environments accountable for providing girls with experiences and opportunities for them to understand, to engage with, and to potentially transform what limits and harms them— so that they can develop strategies of "resistance for liberation" (Robinson & Ward, 1991).

Within health psychology, the concept of *hardiness* (Oullette [Kobasa], 1979, 1982; Ouellette, 1993, in press) describes the stance of an individual in relation to a stressful context. Using hardiness as a framework makes it possible for one to identify developmental experiences girls may need to resist the long-term harm of institutionalized racism and sexism. Within the large body of hardiness research with adults, the construct has been used, for example, to identify retrospectively and prospectively who falls ill under stressful life events (Kobasa, 1982); to predict successful adaptation of immigrants (including lower depression and less worry about finances; Kuo & Tsai, 1986); to explain successful aging (Magnani, 1990); to predict positive coping and adaptation of people with chronic illness (Okun, Zautra, & Robinson, 1988; Pollock, 1989) as well as in other situations in which one would expect the worst (for reviews of this literature, see, Funk, 1992; Orr & Westman, 1990; Ouellette, 1993; Younkin & Betz, 1996).

Consisting of three key components—*control, commitment,* and *challenge*—hardiness describes how people make sense of and respond to stresses in their lives. *Hardiness control* refers to the capability of making choices or courses of action in relation to stressful circumstances, the ability to understand and analyze stresses within a larger context, and a repertoire of positive coping skills. *Hardiness commitment* describes an individual's belief system, sense of purpose, connection to others, and recognition that there are resources for one's support. *Hardiness challenge* is a relationship to change in which one feels challenged and mobilized rather than defeated. People exhibiting hardiness challenge "are catalysts in their environment and are well practiced at responding to the unexpected" (Ouellette [Kobasa], 1979, p. 4). Such people know where to go for support and are cognitively flexible and persistent.

At adolescence, the stress and distress that girls experience can be understood as a loss of control in many arenas of their lives, a struggle to create an identity and a belief system to which they can wholeheartedly commit, and a sense of isolation within the challenges that face them. The protective potential that hardiness has demonstrated in adults has yet to be explored in adolescents. However, hardiness begins to define areas of knowledge, skills, and support that an individual can develop to resist and transform stresses. Through this perspective, relational and educational contexts in which girls find themselves can be assessed in terms of their capacities to facilitate hardiness, that is, to be a "hardiness zone." Thus, for adolescent girls to develop capacities to resist stresses that lead them toward negative risks and poor long-term life prospects, they need experiences in which they can exert control over more than their bodies, sexuality, or appearance; can connect to their own worth, to a positive belief system, and to others who will commit to them; and can experience support and encouragement to learn and persist in the face of struggles.

NOTES TOWARD HARDINESS ZONES

What would it mean for the significant adults in girls' lives to provide them with a relational hardiness zone—a context in which girls can experience greater control, commitment, and challenge? The recent research on girls' psychological and social development postulates that girls, rather than moving away from parental and other adult relationships, appear to respond to a developmental press for meaningful connectedness, especially with adult women—mothers, friends, teachers, and counselors—that could serve as a protective factor for them, especially as they navigate through adolescence (Apter, 1990; Brookins, n.d.; Brooks-Gunn & Petersen, 1983; Brooks-Gunn & Reiter, 1990; Brown & Gilligan, 1992; Debold et al., 1994; Gilligan, 1991; Gilligan, Lyons, & Hanmer, 1990; Orenstein, 1994; Taylor et al., 1995; Ward, 1996). Although there is a relative paucity of research on girls' relationships with their fathers, these relationships, too, offer important possibilities for support (Apter, 1993; Snarey, 1993; Way & Stauber, 1996). Other researchers (e.g., Coates, 1987) have examined the nature of social networks in relation to social competence during adolescence. Still others (Debold et al., 1994; Pipher, 1995) have argued that relationships beyond familial and parental ones often provide protective space for young girls moving through adolescence. Exploring the research on girls' relationships with significant adults in their lives, we ask what we can learn about hardiness zones from relationships that girls experience as positive.

Girls' relationships with their mothers are a critical arena for the development of hardiness. Given that girls' fundamental gender identity develops in relation to caretakers who are usually women—and, in fact, their mothers—relationships between mothers and daughters present powerful opportunities as hardiness zones in contexts in which self-development and cultural identity often become divided. Studies of poor adolescent mothers suggest that the achievement of the positive role of "mother" provides girls with deeper connections with mothers and older women and, often, motivation for further self-development (Taylor, 1989; Way, 1998). With the notable exception of Terri Apter's (1990) research on mother and daughter relationships among a range of socioeconomic strata in England and the United States, there is very little research that explores the positive aspects of these mother–daughter relationships (Surrey, n.d.), even though mothers are often considered by girls as a significant and an enduring source of support (Furman & Buhrmester, 1992; Gavin & Furman, 1996).

How can these relationships better support girls? Apter (1990) noted that mothers' culturally driven expectations of adolescent separation are the lens through which they interpret conflict and questions from their daughters. For the girls, she found, struggles in relationships were about fighting for a new way of relating, not a moving away. Apter found that girls wanted to be engaged in vibrant, searching, and challenging relationships—relationships in which they could experience control and commitment—but that mothers too often withdrew, teaching their daughters to back down in the face of challenges or conflict (see Debold et al., 1994).

Research suggests that of a variety of racial and ethnic groups of girls, African American girls hold their mothers and their relationships with their mothers in highest esteem (Joseph & Lewis, 1981). African American mothers thoughtfully balance the roles of parent and confidant in their relations with their daughters. These mothers strive for a balance achieved between pushing for achievement and pulling back, relative to the perceived harm that may come from racism (Brookins, 1998). Janie Victoria Ward (1996) observed African American mothers' strategies of "resistance-building truth-telling" in the service of "liberation." Such resistance for liberation not only "replaces negative critique with positive recognition" (Ward, 1996, p. 95) but also provides girls with a relational hardiness zone by preparing them for the sociopolitical environment in which they live and by providing them with the necessary tools to think critically about themselves, the world, and their place in it (Robinson & Ward, 1991).

Women teachers hold a possibility of providing relational hardiness zones for girls. This possibility is complicated by the women's own relationships to the systems of power that they represent as teachers. Entrusted with the nurturance and education of girls, Tova Hartman-Halbertal (1996) suggested that women teachers are "engaged in a kind of socio-cultural balancing" (p. 227) of themselves, their students, and their communities—struggling with the conflicts and contradictions among their roles and identities as women, as mentors and socializers, and as transmitters of patriarchal culture. Lyn Mikel Brown (1998) heard a group of White working-class girls allude to this sociocultural balancing in their descriptions of their women teachers. In spite of their intense anger at their teachers' ambivalences, what they seemed to want—what they longed for and seemed unable to attain—was a genuine closeness with their women teachers. They spoke fondly of those rare occasions when they felt "closer" to a teacher, when "it feels more like she's a person," when a teacher shows "she really cares about us," or when teachers "know how I'm feeling."

Like the African American mothers Ward (1996) alluded to, these White women teachers, particularly those with working-class roots, may see themselves as preparing the poor and working-class girls in their charge—albeit less consciously—for the harsh reality that lies ahead. Before teachers can do this preparation, however, they must understand the relational crises and systemic oppressions that girls face and must "validate the identities that their students have taken on as part of growing up" (McLeod, 1995, p. 263). And before they can do such validation, they must confront the "cross currents of desires and values and of traditions and loyalties" (Hartman-Halbertal, 1996, p. 232) that define the realities of their own lives and that, unexplored, seep into their work with girls (see Dorney, 1991).

Connections between girls and women teachers are complicated and difficult, particularly across class and cultural lines, in which women cannot fully read, understand, or identify with the girls in their charge. Such relationships, Lisa Delpit (1995) explained, demand "a very special kind of listening, listening that requires not only open eyes and ears, but also hearts and minds" (p. 46), a willingness to "put our beliefs on hold . . . to cease to exist as ourselves for a moment" (p. 46); it is, she insisted, "the only way to learn what it might feel like to be someone else and the only way to start a dialogue" (p. 46–47). Through such a relational stance, girls perceive connection and the commitment of adults in ways that open up possibilities for creating identities and making life choices that allow girls to hold their hearts and minds together.

Listening and, through listening, fostering meaningful participation in school and community life (rather than conformity and obedience) are means by which adults can create hardiness zones for girls and can promote collective action. Tantalizing evidence suggests that real involvement of young people in school and community programming has a very positive impact on their engagement with school and their health (see O'Connor, 1997). Linda Powell's (1994) creation of family group within an urban high school provided young people with a place to bring their questions about power and authority as well as their desire for connection with each other and their teachers. One result was an extraordinary improvement in retention rates. In a recent study of 25 school sites nationwide, girls who volunteered in their communities and who did not have sex education were less likely to become pregnant, to be suspended, or to fail school courses than girls who took a regular curriculum and had no community experience (Allen, Philliber, Herrling, & Kupermink, 1997). Speaking of girls' "hunger for an us" and their hope, fears, and excitement to "create their own homeplaces," Pastor et al. (1996) referred to the need for "schools and communities that engage young women (separately and with young men) in social critique and in activist experiences of social transformation" (p. 30). Listening is the critical precursor to collective action.

In many families, especially those of color, young women form strong relationships with aunts, uncles, and older cousins who serve as confidants, mentors, and prodders. Anecdotal data suggest that often these relationships offer benefits similar to healthy parental ones or, in some cases, subvert parent–daughter relations. Within African American communities, Patricia Hill Collins (1991) used the term *othermothers* to describe the women who are integral to the strength of caring communities by taking a real and persistent interest in the children of the community (Sampson, Raudenbush, & Earls, 1997; see Debold et al., 1994). In many instances, Geraldine Brookins (1998) noted, these othermothers helped the young women hold close to their aspirations while maintaining connections to their mothers. These othermothers have relationships with the girls' mothers that serve as bridges across generations and perspectives. They are part of both the mothers' communities and the daughters' hoped-for worlds, they are perceived as "being there" for the girls in ways mothers are not allowed, they are perceived as seeing the girls as "special," and they are respected and trusted by the mothers. "Othermothers" do not parachute in as mentors but are part of the physical and social community. Brown (1998), too, has heard of the many women in White working-class girls' daily lives who provide safe spaces for their feelings and thoughts, their questions, and their social critique—aunts, older sisters, family friends, and cousins. These women know them, love them, and teach them. Such relationships might foster effective use of social resources among young women, thus providing a relational hardiness zone through recognition that there are resources available for their support.

When young girls seek out relationships with nonparental adults who are within their immediate environment but are distanced enough, they often find women similar to, yet sufficiently distinct from, their mothers. In these relationships, they are able to form significant connections that offer fruitful developmental outcomes. Such evocative relationships, relationships in which girls' questions and women's ambivalences are brought to the surface, provide the scaffolding for public critique and political resistance. So many girls are hungry for such relationships and sites of possibility. These meaningful relationships, echoed in the urban girls she listened to, led Amy Sullivan (1996) to critique the traditional role of mentor—a "helping model ... which often assumes deficiencies in the adolescent" (p. 227) and locates knowledge and power in the adult—and to offer, instead, the role of "muse" and the possibility of "evocative relationships." Such relationships, Sullivan explained, are "distinguished by girls' ability to speak freely; by women's ability to listen to, understand, and validate girls' feelings and experience; and by women's willingness to share their own experience as well" (p. 246).

Girls' relationships with the "muses" in their lives suggest the importance of women who will listen with "open hearts and minds" (p. 46) and who will allow the experiences of girls who are different from them to "edge themselves into our consciousness" (Delpit, 1995, p. 47). Such relationships make room for girls' strong feelings and opinions, out of which come their social critique and a useful explication and interrogation of expectations, communicative patterns, rules, and norms of the culture of power. Without this explication—which depends on both the immediacy and expressed intensity of girls' feelings and an adult's willingness to remain in their presence and to be, in Adrienne Rich's (1979, p. 158) terms, "a witness in her defense"—girls are less likely to speak out or publicly respond to injustice or hurtful behavior in ways that are effective and constructive. In turn, they are likely to be less hardy.

Although girls learn about being female in the world from women, they often learn about the power relations between the sexes from the men in their lives. Perhaps not surprising, very little research exists on positive relationships between men—fathers, relatives, teachers, or mentors—and girls. Research not only points to the benefits of fathers' presence in girls' lives but also indicates that many girls do not feel close to their fathers and do not turn to them for help (Schonert-Reichl & Muller, 1996). Apter's (1993) study of White girls of diverse class backgrounds similarly found that the girls had little intimacy or even contact with their fathers—an experience with which their fathers disagreed. Way and Stauber (1996), however, found that a majority of the urban girls of color in their study had either warm or "hot" (i.e., angry) relationships with their fathers. Although we have little idea of what girls want or expect from their fathers or the men in their lives, the comfort men have with the rules of patriarchal cultures may provide girls with a perspective on, as well as experience with, negotiating male worlds. Indeed, fathers' involvement in their daughters' lives is positively associated with girls' work success, occupational competency, and sense of comfort in and mastery of the world around them (see Snarey, 1993).

The caring that girls want and find meaningful from adults is a caring that gives girls the opportunity for self-development through effective sociocultural critique. In a recent and provocative small study, Carla O'Connor (1997) identified knowledge of and engagement in collective liberation as a potentially critical factor for integrating educational ambition and social critique for low-income African American adolescents. She explored the biographies of six high-achieving, low-income urban African American high school students who were able to hold together both an aspiration and an articulation of the systemic forces of oppression. These young people explained how the language and strategies that Robinson and Ward (1991) call "resistance for liberation" were taught to them by their parents and families. In fact, the only distinguishing feature in their life stories was their familiarity with shared struggle and action. Learning such critical analysis through relationships provides girls with (a) greater hardiness control by giving them a way to understand their context such that choices and effective courses of action are more apparent, (b) greater hardiness commitment by providing girls with a sense of shared purpose and connection with others, and (c) greater hardiness challenge by demonstrating the positive benefit and importance of shared struggle.

For girls not to face, or to internalize, a divide between potential achievement and familial or cultural connection, they need to have adults who provide them with opportunities to develop a sense of purpose and to experience effective action that takes very seriously what they have experienced within systems of power and unequal resources. In *Urban Sanctuaries* (McLaughlin, Irby, & Langman, 1994), individuals known as "wizards" demonstrated commitment, respect for youth, and a belief that there was an untapped capacity to achieve in the youth with whom they worked. They are called wizards because of their perspicacity and their ability to capitalize on opportunity and healthy outcomes with youth vulnerable to the ravages of their ecological contexts (Brookins, Petersen, & Brooks, 1997). Researchers also know that girls can be important resources, especially when organizations capitalize on them as partners in developing programs and program goals. However, girls cannot act alone to move beyond their bodies as their only realm of power into a larger arena of possibility. They need adults, and the institutions that adults create and are part of, to join them.

Girls need safe spaces in schools, in neighborhoods, and within kinship networks as well as within families "where one can weave whole cloth from the fragments of social critique and sweet dreams" (Pastor et al., 1996, p. 15). The hardiness zones of which we speak are not precious spaces in which girls bond through suffering but spaces in which their personal experiences can be understood through systemic analysis and in which they can develop skills through being involved in making change within their communities. As Suzanne Ouellette has said, "If depression is linked to stressful life events, then you need to go in and change the situation in which those events are happening. . . . [Thus,] a sign for a positive outcome is girls' involvement in that intervention process" (quoted in Debold, 1995, p. 22). And adults need to take responsibility for creating those spaces and possibilities for change.

CONCLUSION

In this chapter, we have questioned psychology's emphasis on resilience and the notion of "one caring adult" as an insufficient framework to support girls' strengths. Resilience, in concept and measurement, is too individually based to describe the critical interaction between a girl and her environment that is the source of girls' struggles and stresses in adolescence. By measuring resilience in individuals and out of context, resilience appears internal to the girl and lacks a sense of agency, action, or transformation that is so critical for girls to move forward powerfully into the wider world of adulthood. Through psychologists' attention to girls as individuals, we allow ourselves to ignore the systemic oppressions that constrain their lives and sense of possibility.

Bonnie Leadbeater and Niobe Way (1996) asked us to remember that most poor adolescent girls do not fit media representations and stereotypes. Most girls move through adolescence without succumbing to depression, becoming a teen mother or a suicide statistic. Yet this is not an occasion for one to pat oneself on the back. By and large, as girls angrily tell us, they have been left to their own devices to negotiate the divide between their dreams and their commitments to others. In so doing, psychologists —as representatives of institutions that set the standards of development and achievement—force girls, particularly poor girls, to enact betrayal: Will they choose their own achievement or their connection with their cultural community and family?

The creation of community and critical education toward social change appears essential to develop hardiness zones that support the strengths of girls. Robert Blum (1997a), author of the national Add Health Study of 90,000 teens, has argued that programmatic interventions aimed at youth as individuals are wrongheaded and ineffective and that given the critical importance to young people (and girls, particularly) of family and community, support and intervention must be directed there (1997b). Sampson et al. (1997) have found that communities that are themselves hardiness zones in which there is control rather than chaos, commitment to neighbors rather than disengagment, and challenge rather than apathy provide young people with lives and contexts with less violence and substance abuse.

Finally, what would it mean for psychology and education, two key normalizing forces in the dominant culture, to become hardiness zones for girls? How could we give girls greater control within the ways that we conduct research or develop standards? What commitment are we willing to make to them that shows our support of their struggles? If we are serious about judging girls' health and resilience by the degree to which they live lives that separate them from their parents and communities, then will we join them, and their families and communities, in making a leap into the unknown?

REFERENCES

Allen, J. P., Philliber, S., Herrling, S., & Kupermink, G. P. (1997). Preventing teen pregnancy and academic failure: Experimental evaluation of a developmentally-based approach. *Child Development, 67*, 729–742.

American Association of University Women. (1991). *Shortchanging girls, shortchanging America.* Washington, DC: Author.

Apter, T. (1990). *Altered loves: Mothers and daughters during adolescence.* New York: St. Martin's Press.

Apter, T. (1993). Altered views: Father's closeness to teenage daughters. In R.

Josselson & A. Lieblich (Eds.), *The narrative study of lives* (pp. 163–190). London: Sage.

Bartelt, D. W. (1994). On resilience: Questions of validity. In M. C. Wang & E. W. Gordon (Eds.), *Educational resilience in inner-city America: Challenges and prospects* (pp. 97–108). Hillsdale, NJ: Erlbaum.

Blum, R. (1997, December). *Adolescent females: Vulnerabilities and risk reduction.* Paper presented at the meeting, The Culture of Girlhood: Implications for Teen Pregnancy, National Campaign to Prevent Teen Pregnancy, Washington, DC.

Brookins, G. K. (n.d.). *Rewriting the script: African American mothers and daughters.* Manuscript in preparation.

Brookins, G. K., Petersen, A. C., & Brooks, L. M. (1997). Youth and families in the inner city: Influencing positive outcomes. In H. J. Walberg, O. Reyes, & R. Weissberg (Eds.), *Children and youth: Interdisciplinary perspectives* (pp. 45–66). Thousand Oaks, CA: Sage.

Brooks-Gunn, J. (1991). How stressful is the transition to adolescence for girls? In M. E. Colten & S. Gore (Eds.), *Adolescent stress: Causes and consequences* (pp. 131–150). New York: Aldine de Gruyter.

Brooks-Gunn, J., & Petersen, A. C. (1983). *Girls at puberty.* New York: Plenum Press.

Brooks-Gunn, J., & Reiter, E. O. (1990). The role of pubertal processes. In S. S. Feldman & G. Elliott (Eds.), *At the threshold* (pp. 16–53). Cambridge, MA: Harvard University Press.

Brown, L. M. (1998). *Raising their voices: The politics of girls' anger.* Cambridge, MA: Harvard University Press.

Brown, L. M., & Gilligan, C. (1992). *Meeting at the crossroads.* Cambridge, MA: Harvard University Press.

Brumberg, J. J. (1997). *The body project.* New York: Random House.

Burton, L. M., Obeidallah, D. A., & Allison, K. (1996). Ethnographic insights on social context and adolescent development among inner-city African-American teens. In R. Jessor, A. Colby, & R. A. Shweder (Eds.), *Ethnography and human development: Context and meaning in social inquiry* (pp. 395–418). Chicago: University of Chicago Press.

Caspi, A., & Moffit, T. E. (1991). Individual differences are accentuated during periods of social change: The sample case of girls at puberty. *Journal of Personality and Social Psychology, 61,* 157–168.

Chen, P. Y. (1997). *Adolescent girls/lived fictions.* Unpublished manuscript, City University of New York.

Coates, D. L. (1987). Gender differences in the structure and support characteristics of Black adolescents' social networks. *Sex Roles, 17,* 667–687.

Cole, D. A. (1991). Adolescent suicide. In R. M. Lerner, A. C. Petersen, & J. Brooks-Gunn (Eds.), *Encyclopedia of adolescence* (Vol. 2, pp. 1113–1116). New York: Garland.

Collins, P. H. (1991). The meaning of motherhood in Black culture and Black mother–daughter relationships. In P. Bell-Scott (Eds.), *Double stitch: Black women write about mothers and daughters*. New York: Harper Perennial.

Colten, M. E., & Gore, S. (Eds.). (1991). *Adolescent stress*. New York: Aldine de Gruyter.

Cowen, E. L., & Work, W. C. (1988). Resilient children, psychological wellness, and primary prevention. *American Journal of Community Psychology, 16*, 591–607.

Debold, E. (1995). *Body politic: Transforming adolescent girls' health* (A report of the 1994 proceedings of the Healthy Girls/Healthy Women Research Roundtable). New York: Ms. Foundation for Women.

Debold, E., Wilson, M., & Malavé, I. (1994). *Mother daughter revolution: From good girls to great women*. New York: Bantam.

Delpit, L. (1995). *Other people's children: Cultural conflict in the classroom*. New York: New Press.

Dorney, J. (1991). *"Courage to act in a small way": Clues toward community and change among women teaching girls*. Unpublished doctoral dissertation, Harvard University, Cambridge, MA.

Erkut, S., Fields, J. P., Sing, R., & Marx, F. (1996). Diversity in girls' experiences: Feeling good about who you are. In B. J. R. Leadbeater & N. Way (Eds.), *Urban girls: Resisting stereotypes, creating identities* (pp. 53–64). New York: New York University Press.

Espin, O. M. (1997). *Latina realities*. Boulder, CO: Westview Press.

Fabian, L. J., & Thompson, J. K. (1989). Body image and eating disturbance in young females. *International Journal of Eating Disorders, 8*, 63–74.

Farber, E. A., & Egeland, B. (1989). Invulnerability among abused and neglected children. In E. J. Anthony & B. J. Cohler (Eds.), *The invulnerable child* (pp. 253–288). New York: Guilford Press.

Felner, R. D., Aber, M. S., Primavera, J., & Cauce, A. M. (1985). Adaptation and vulnerability in high-risk adolescents: An examination of environmental mediators. *American Journal of Community Psychology, 13*, 365–379.

Fine, M. (1991). *Framing dropouts: Notes on the politics of an urban public high school*. Albany: State University of New York Press.

Fordham, S. (1993). "Those loud Black girls": Women, silence, and gender "passing" in the academy. *Anthropology and Education Quarterly, 24, 1*, 3–32.

Fordham, S. (1996). *Blacked out: Dilemmas of race, ethnicity, and success at Capitol High*. Chicago: University of Chicago Press.

Fordham, S., & Ogbu, J. U. (1986). Black students' school success: Coping with the "burden of acting white." *Urban Review, 18*, 176–206.

Funk, S. C. (1992). Hardiness: A review of theory and research. *Health Psychology, 11*, 335–345.

Furman, W., & Buhrmester, D. (1992). Age and sex differences in perceptions of networks of personal relationships. *Child Development, 63*, 103–115.

Garmezy, N. (1985). Stress-resistant children: The search for protective factors. In J. E. Stevenson (Ed.), *Recent research in developmental psychopathology: Journal of Child Psychology and Psychiatry Book Supplement No. 4* (pp. 213–233). Oxford, England: Pergamon Press.

Garmezy, N. (1987). Stress, competence, and development: Continuities in the study of schizophrenic adults, children vulnerable to psychopathology, and the search for stress-resistant children. *American Journal of Orthopsychiatry, 57*, 159–174.

Gavin, L., & Furman, W. (1996). Adolescent girls' relationships with mothers and best friends. *Child Development, 67*, 375–386.

Gilligan, C. (1991). Women's psychological development: Implications for psychotherapy. *Women & Therapy, 11*(3–4), 5–31.

Gilligan, C. (1992). *In a different voice.* Cambridge, MA: Harvard University Press.

Gilligan, C., Lyons, N. P. , & Hanmer, T. J. (Eds.). (1990). *Making connections.* Cambridge, MA: Harvard University Press.

Gilligan, C., Taylor, J. M., Tolman, D., Sullivan, A. M., Pleasants, P., & Dorney, J. (July, 1992). *The relational world of adolescent girls considered to be at risk.* Boston: Boston Foundation.

Gjerde, P. F., Block, J., & Block, J. H. (1988). Depressive symptoms and personality during late adolescence: Gender differences in externalization–internalization of symptom expression. *Journal of Abnormal Psychology, 97*, 475–486.

Gore, S., & Colten, M. E. (1991). Gender, stress, and distress. In J. Eckenrode (Ed.), *The social context of coping* (pp. 139–163). New York: Plenum Press.

Harris, L. J., Blum, R. W., & Resnick, M. D. (1991). Teen females in Minnesota: A portrait of quiet disturbance. In C. Gilligan, A. Rogers, & D. Tolman (Eds.), *Women, girls and psychotherapy: Reframing resistance* (pp. 119–135). Binghampton, NY: Harrington Park Press.

Hartman-Halbertal, T. (1996). *Mothering in culture: Ambiguities in continuity.* Unpublished doctoral dissertation, Harvard University, Cambridge, MA.

Joseph, G., & Lewis, J. (1981). *Common differences: Conflicts in Black and White feminist perspectives.* Boston: South End Press.

Kessler, R. C., McGonagle, K. A., Zhao, S., Nelson, C. B., Hughes, M., Eshleman, M. A., Wittchen, H. U., & Kendler, K. S. (1994). Lifetime and 12-month prevalence of *DSM–III–R* psychiatric disorders in the United States: Results from the National Comorbidity Study. *Archives of General Psychiatry, 51*, 8–19.

Kuo, W. H., & Tsai, Y. (1986). Social networking, hardiness, and immigrant's mental health. *Journal of Health and Social Behavior, 27*, 133–149.

Leadbeater, B. R., & Way, N. (Eds.). (1996). *Urban girls.* New York: New York University Press.

Lee, S. (1996). *Unraveling the model minority stereotype: Listening to Asian American youth.* New York: Teachers College Press.

Luthar, S. S. (1991). Vulnerability and resilience: A study of high-risk adolescents. *Child Development*, *62*, 600–616.

Luthar, S. S., & Zigler, E. (1991). Vulnerability and competence: A review of research on resilience in childhood. *American Journal of Orthopsychiatry*, *61*, 6–22.

Maccoby, E. E. (1990). Gender and relationships: A developmental account. *American Psychologist*, *45*, 513–520.

Magnani, L. E. (1990). Hardiness, self-perceived health, and activity among independently functioning older adults. *Scholarly Inquiry for Nursing Practice: An International Journal*, *4*, 171–184.

Males, M. A. (1993). Schools, society, and "teen" pregnancy. *Phi Delta Kappan*, *74*, 566–568.

Males, M. A. (1994). Poverty, rape, adult/teen sex: Why "pregnancy prevention" programs don't work. *Phi Delta Kappan*, *75*, 407–410.

Masten, A. S. (1982). *Humor and creative thinking in stress-resistant children*. Unpublished doctoral dissertation, University of Minnesota Twin Cities Campus (Minneapolis).

Masten, A. S. (1994). Resilience in individual development: Successful adaptation despite risk and adversity. In M. C. Wang & E. W. Gordon (Eds.), *Educational resilience in inner-city America: Challenges and prospects* (pp. 3–25). Hillsdale, NJ: Erlbaum.

Masten, A. S., Garmezy, N., Tellegen, A., Pellegrini, D. S., Larkin, K., & Larsen, A. (1988). Competence and stress in school children: The moderating effects of individual and family qualities. *Journal of Child Psychology and Psychiatry and Allied Disciplines*, *29*, 745–764.

McLaughlin, M. W., Irby, M. A., & Langman, J. (1994). *Urban sanctuaries: Neighborhood organizations in the lives and futures of inner-city youth*. San Francisco: Jossey-Bass.

McLeod, J. (1995). *Ain't no makin' it*. Boulder, CO: Westview Press.

Millstein, S. G., & Litt, I. F. (1990). Adolescent health. In S. S. Feldman & G. R. Elliot (Eds.), *At the threshold* (pp. 431–456). Cambridge, MA: Harvard University Press.

Millstein, S. G., Petersen, A. C., & Nightingale, E. O. (Eds.). (1993). *Promoting the health of adolescents: New directions for the 21st century*. New York: Oxford University Press.

Minnesota Women's Fund. (1990). *Reflections of risk: Growing up female in Minnesota* (Report on the health and well-being of adolescent girls in Minnesota). Minneapolis, MN: Author.

Ms. Foundation for Women. (1993). *Programmed neglect: A survey of girls' programming in the United States*. New York: Author.

Musick, J. S. (1993). *Young, poor and pregnant*. New Haven, CT: Yale University Press.

Nolen-Hoeksema, S., & Girgus, J. S. (1994). The emergence of gender differences in depression during adolescence. *Psychological Bulletin*, *115*, 424–443.

O'Connor, C. (1997). Dispositions toward (collective) struggle and educational resilience in the inner-city: A case analysis of six African American high school students. *American Educational Research Journal, 34,* 593–629.

Ogbu, J. U. (1981). On origins of human competence: A cultural ecological perspective. *Child Development, 52,* 413–429.

Okun, M. A., Zautra, A. J., & Robinson, S. E. (1988). Hardiness and health among women with rheumatoid arthritis. *Personality and Individual Differences, 9,* 101–107.

Orenstein, P. (1994). *Schoolgirls.* New York: Doubleday.

Orr, E., & Westman, M. (1990). Does hardiness moderate stress, and how? A review. In M. Rosenbaum (Ed.), *Learned resourcefulness: On coping skills, self-control, and adaptive behavior* (pp. 64–94). New York: Springer.

[Oullette] Kobasa, S. (1979). Stressful life events, personality, and health: An inquiry into hardiness. *Journal of Personality and Social Psychology, 37,* 1–11.

[Oullette] Kobasa, S. (1982). The hardy personality: Toward a social psychology of stress and health. In J. Suls & G. Sanders (Eds.), *Social psychology of health and illness.* Hillsdale, NJ: Erlbaum.

Ouellette, S. (1993). Inquiries into hardiness. In L. Goldberger & S. Breznitz (Eds.), *Handbook of stress: Theoretical and clinical aspects* (2nd ed., pp. 77–100). New York: Free Press.

Ouellette, S. (in press). Personality's role in the protection and enhancement of health: Where the research has been, where it is stuck, how it might move.

Pastor, J. (1993). *Possible selves and academic achievement among inner-city students of color.* Unpublished master's thesis, City University of New York.

Pastor, J., McCormick, J., & Fine, M. (1996). Makin' homes: An urban girl thing. In B. R. Leadbeater & N. Way (Eds.), *Urban girls* (pp. 15–34). New York: New York University Press.

Petersen, A., & Craighead, W. (1986). Emotional and personality development in normal adolescents and young adults. In G. L. Klerman (Ed.), *Suicide and depression among adolescents and young adults* (pp. 19–52). Washington, DC: American Psychiatric Press.

Pipher, M. (1995). *Reviving Ophelia.* New York: Ballantine Books.

Pollock, S. E. (1989). The hardiness characteristic: A motivating factor in adaptation. *Advances in Nursing Science, 11,* 53–62.

Powell, L. (1994). Family group and social defenses. In M. Fine (Ed.), *Chartering urban school reform: Reflections on urban public high schools in the midst of change.* New York: Teachers College Press.

Reid, P. (1993). Poor women in psychological research: Shut up and shut out. *Psychology of Women Quarterly, 17,* 133–150.

Resnick, M. D., Bearman, P. E., Blum, R., Bauman, K. S., Harris, K. M., Jones, J., Tabor, J., Beuhring, T., Sieving, R., Shew, M., Ireland, M., Bearinger, L. H., & Udry, J. R. (1997). Protecting adolescents from harm: Findings from the National Longitudinal Study on Adolescent Health. *Journal of the American Medical Association, 278,* 823–831.

Resnick, M. D., Harris, L. J., & Blum, R. W. (1993). The impact of caring and connectedness on adolescent health and well being. *Pediatrics and Child Health, 29*(Suppl. 1), S3–9.

Rich, A. (1979). *On lies, secrets, and silence.* New York: Norton.

Rigsby, L. (1994). The Americanization of resilience: Deconstructing research practice. In M. C. Wang & E. W. Gordon (Eds.), *Educational resilience in inner-city America: Challenges and prospects* (pp. 85–94). Hillsdale, NJ: Erlbaum.

Robinson, T., & Ward, J. V. (1991). "A belief in self far greater than anyone's disbelief": Cultivating healthy resistance among African American female adolescents. In C. Gilligan, A. Rogers, & D. Tolman (Eds.), *Women, girls & psychotherapy: Reframing resistance* (pp. 87–103). Binghampton, NY: Harrington Park Press.

Russell, D. E. H. (1984). *Sexual exploitation.* Beverly Hills, CA: Sage.

Rutter, M. (1979). Protective factors in children's responses to stress and disadvantage. In M. W. Kent & J. E. Rolf (Eds.), *Primary prevention of psychopathology: Vol. 3. Social competence in children* (pp. 49–74). Hanover, NH: University Press of New England.

Sampson, R. J., Raudenbush, S. W., & Earls, F. (1997, August). Neighborhoods and violent crime: A multilevel study of collective efficacy. *Science, 277,* 918–924.

Schonert-Reichl, K., & Mullen, J. (1996). Correlates of help-seeking in adolescence. *Journal of Youth and Adolescence, 25,* 705–731.

Simmons, R. G., & Blyth, D. A. (1987). *Moving into adolescence: The impact of pubertal change on school context.* New York: Aldine de Gruyter.

Snarey, J. (1993). *How fathers care for the next generation.* Cambridge, MA: Harvard University Press.

Steiner-Adair, C. (1986). The body politic. *American Academy of Psychoanalysis, 14,* 95–114.

Story, M., Rosenwinkel, K., Himes, J., Resnick, M. D., Harris, L. J., & Blum, R. (1991). Demographic and risk factors associated with chronic dieting in adolescents. *American Journal of Diseases of Children, 145,* 994–998.

Sullivan, A. M. (1996). From mentor to muse: Recasting the role of women in relationship with urban adolescent girls. In B. R. Leadbeater & N. Way (Eds.), *Urban girls* (pp. 226–249). New York: New York University Press.

Surrey, J. (n.d.). *The mother–daughter relationship: Themes in psychotherapy* [Audiotape in progress]. Wellesley, MA: Wellesley College, Stone Center.

Taylor, J. M. (1989). *Development of self, moral voice, and the meaning of adolescent motherhood.* Unpublished doctoral dissertation, Harvard University Graduate School of Education.

Taylor, J. M., Gilligan, C., & Sullivan, A. M. (1995). *Between voice and silence: Women and girls, race and relationships.* Cambridge, MA: Harvard University Press.

Thompson, S. (1995). *Going all the way: Teenage girls' tales of sex, romance, and pregnancy.* New York: Hill & Wang.

Tolman, D. L. (1992). *Voicing the body: A psychological study of adolescent girls' sexual desire*. Unpublished doctoral dissertation, Harvard University Graduate School of Education, Cambridge, MA.

Ward, J. V. (1996). Raising resisters: The role of truth telling in the psychological development of African American girls. In B. R. Leadbeater & N. Way (Eds.), *Urban girls* (pp. 85–99). New York: New York University Press.

Way, N. (1998). *Everyday courage: The lives and stories of urban teenagers*. New York: New York University Press.

Way, N., & Stauber, H. (1996). Are "absent fathers" really absent? Urban adolescent girls speak out about their fathers. In B. R. Leadbeater & N. Way (Eds.), *Urban girls* (pp. 132–148). New York: New York University Press.

Weist, M. D., Freedman, A. H., Paskewitz, D. A., Proescher, E. J., & Flaherty, L. T. (1995). Urban youth under stress: Empirical identification of protective factors. *Journal of Youth and Adolescence, 24*, 705–721.

Werner, E., & Smith, R. S. (1982). *Vulnerable but invincible: A longitudinal study of resilient children and youth*. New York: McGraw-Hill.

Werner, E., & Smith, R. S. (1992). *Overcoming the odds: High risk children from birth to adulthood*. Ithaca, NY: Cornell University Press.

Weseen, S. (1998). *A critical review of resilience research: Issues of conceptualization, measurement and gender*. Manuscript in preparation, Ms. Foundation for Women, Healthy Girls/Healthy Women Collaborative Fund.

White, J. L., Moffitt, T. E., & Silva, P. A. (1989). A prospective replication of the protective effects of IQ in subjects at high risk for juvenile delinquency. *Journal of Consulting and Clinical Psychology, 57*, 719–724.

Wooley, S. C., & Wooley, O. W. (1980). Eating disorders, obesity and anorexia. In A. Brodsky & R. Hare-Mustin (Eds.), *Women and psychotherapy* (pp. 135–159). New York: Guilford Press.

Younkin, S. L., & Betz, N. E. (1996). Psychological hardiness: A reconceptualization and measurement. In T. W. Miller (Ed.), *Theory and assessment of stressful life events* (pp. 161–178). Madison, CT: International Universities Press.

9

THE OTHERS IN MY I: ADOLESCENT GIRLS' FRIENDSHIPS AND PEER RELATIONS

LYN MIKEL BROWN, NIOBE WAY, AND JULIA L. DUFF

Ana and Zoe are members of a panel of girls and young women asked to speak about their experiences in school.[1] The panelists, different ages and from a range of racial and cultural backgrounds, respond one by one to the questions posed to them by an adult woman facilitator. They sit on a raised platform behind a long linen-clothed table, facing a lecture hall full primarily of White women teachers. When the facilitator asks all six girls what they would most like to change about their schooling, these two 12-year-olds, the youngest girls participating, begin an impassioned exchange about their peer relations that breaks open a discussion that has, to this point, seemed somewhat formal and overrehearsed.

> *Ana:* I think what I would change would be, like, the quote, unquote "clique thing." Like, I mean, I'm Hispanic, you know, and like when I go to school I find that the guys more, like when they look at me,

We are grateful to Abby Wolfson, who helped us enormously with her careful search of the literature on girls' friendships and peer relations.
[1]This panel was held at Marymount College in Tarrytown, New York, in June 1994 and was part of a day-long exploration of girls' psychological development and education.

they go like, "Wow, she's Black, so let's put her into this section." And then when I start talking, it's like, "Oh, she's Hispanic, so we'll put her into this section." But the girls, they really don't care, you know, and it's like, they don't care; you're you. But the guys are like, "She's Spanish. She can fight, 'cause, you know, that's her background," you know. And I find that, like, the guys do that more often.

Zoe: Can I say something about the clique thing? OK, I think cliques happen *much* more in girls than in boys. I think cliques are so separating and demeaning for everybody, but I don't think that boys have cliques as much as girls, or maybe it's just that I don't notice it as much in boys as girls. But really, I think girls have the major clique on the mind, and I disagree that boys have it . . . I think boys have groups and the girls are really the cliques . . . it's like the Hispanics, the African Americans, the Whites. . . . I think, what the boys do, they don't really care as much about skin color—there are a lot of different cultural groups in my school—they don't really care as much about skin color in my school as the girls do. I really believe that.

The differences between Ana's and Zoe's experiences and interpretations of the problems associated with the peer groupings in their schools invite a range of questions associated with power, location, and relationships—questions about how race, ethnicity, and gender may be constructed and played out differently for them and their friends and about how their middle-class, relatively privileged upbringings affect their interactions with peers. Their responses also raise questions about how relationships with close friends might mitigate or enhance the negative consequences of stereotypes and cliques and about how the climate or context of their respective schools may affect their different relationships with girls and boys. What might the psychological literature on adolescent girls' friendships and peer relations offer by way of understanding the nature and significance of the girls' disagreement?

Research on adolescent friendship has shown that positive experiences of friendship and peer relations contribute considerably to cognitive, social, and moral development as well as to psychological adjustment and socioemotional health (Asher & Hymel, 1986; Crick, 1996; Goodyer, Wright, & Altham, 1989; Parker & Asher, 1987; Putallaz & Gottman, 1981; Savin-Williams & Berndt, 1990; Schonert-Reichl, 1995, 1996). Studies have indicated that friendships satisfy adolescents' desires for intimacy and greatly enhance their interpersonal skills, sensitivity, and understanding (Laursen, 1993; Selman, 1980; Shulman, 1993; Youniss, 1980; Youniss & Smollar, 1985). Adolescents who have difficulties finding and maintaining friends are more likely as adults to be unemployed, aggressive, or have poor mental health (Doll, 1996). Indeed, close friendships, considered by many social scientists to be the "most rewarding and satisfying of all human relationships" (Savin-Williams & Berndt, 1990, p. 277), are clearly important for the social and emotional health of all adolescents, regardless of ethnicity, race, or socioeconomic status (Clark, 1989).

This established, what can we really say about the issues raised by Ana and Zoe? At first glance, not very much. Over a decade ago, Donna Eder (1985) noted that "few studies have focused on female peer relations" during adolescence, and particularly few studies "focus on girls' relationships with other girls" (p. 154). This remains true today, at least in psychological research. Despite evidence that friendships are critically important for adolescents, psychologists know little about the intricacies, nuances, and contexts of girls' friendships and peer relations—little that would explain why Ana has a different experience and perception of her peers than does Zoe, much less how these differences might affect the girls' close friendships and their emerging subjectivities.

What we do know about girls' friendships and peer relations is based primarily on studies of gender differences. Although these studies provide important information, they offer us little understanding of the wide diversity in experiences and perceptions of friendships among girls. Nor have these studies addressed the important distinction girls make among types of friends and the nature and quality of these relationships. Furthermore, such studies are almost exclusively based on White, middle-class samples and thus do not provide insight into the experiences of girls of color or economically disadvantaged girls from various cultural and racial backgrounds. And although this research would seem to tell us much more about Zoe's experiences and understandings than about Ana's, the samples of White girls tend not to reflect Zoe's Jewish, urban, northeastern upbringing. Indeed, there has been scant attention to the ways in which class, culture, race, ethnicity, and sexual identity shape adolescent girls' friendships and peer groupings and even less attention to the ways in which racism, sexism, classism, and compulsory heterosexuality influence the environments in which girls' friendships are nurtured. There is, in addition, little research on the affective, as opposed to the purely cognitive, dimensions of adolescent friendships—a gap in the literature particularly troubling when one considers the importance of understanding and expressing feelings of pleasure, as well as hurt and betrayal, in adolescent girls' and women's descriptions of their significant relationships (Apter, 1990; Brown & Gilligan, 1992; Duff, 1996; Gilligan, 1982; Gilligan, Lyons, & Hanmer, 1990; Jordan, Kaplan, Miller, Stiver, & Surrey, 1991; Leadbeater & Way, 1996; Taylor, Gilligan, & Sullivan, 1995; Way, 1995, 1998).

Although we know little about how the contexts of girls' lives shape and give meaning to their friendships and peer relations, clearly relational, social, and cultural forces affect how adolescents understand themselves and how they relate to one another. In this chapter, after briefly addressing the definition and use of gender as a variable in psychological research, we review the psychological literature on girls' friendships and peer relations, paying particular attention to any such discussion of contextual forces. We then cast a wider interdisciplinary net, turning to current research in related fields such as sociology, anthropology, and education, with the hope of building a more inclusive and contextual picture of girls' friendships and interactions with their peers. Finally, we suggest a different theoretical grounding that takes seriously the complex developmental and social issues confronting contemporary adolescent girls and that considers the impact of power relations on girls' friendships, particularly with other girls.

PROBLEMATIZING GENDER

Although the psychological research has been slow to acknowledge the effects of race, ethnicity, social class, or sexual orientation on the quality and development of girls' friendships, it has addressed gender differences. Current research has shown repeatedly that adolescent girls spend more time with their friends than do boys (Wong & Csikszentmihalyi, 1991), have smaller groups of friends than do boys (Belle, 1989), expect and receive more kindness, loyalty, commitment, and empathic understanding from their best friendships than do boys (Clark & Bittle, 1992), and are more likely than adolescent boys to have open, intimate, self-disclosing relationships with their same-sex peers (Berndt, 1982; Caldwell & Peplau, 1982; Camarena, Sarigiani, & Petersen, 1990; Furman & Buhrmester, 1985; Parker & Asher, 1993; Reisman, 1990; Savin-Williams & Berndt, 1990). Yet, unasked questions remain: Why such differences? Which adolescent girls (and boys) are we talking about? What impact does social and material location, school or community context, have on such reported differences?

Much of the current research on gender differences in friendship formation, with some notable exceptions, relies on a decontextualized conception of gender that renders invisible its intricate relationship with other equally important social characteristics. Constructed as a binary variable, separated from the multiple contexts in which it is constructed, defined, and nurtured, gender becomes essentialized at the risk of "camouflaging all the complexities and contradictions among" girls and women (Fine, 1992, p. 15).

As we have already mentioned, not unlike the majority of research in developmental psychology (Jessor, 1993), studies of adolescent friendships have focused primarily on White, middle-class adolescents. In the case of adolescent girls' friendships, one might go so far as to say that the research has articulated, in the main, the qualities and characteristics of White middle- and working-class girls from the suburban Midwest. The few research projects, however, that have examined friendships among ethnically and socioeconomically diverse adolescents have suggested that generalizing the findings from studies of White adolescents to other cultural, ethnic, racial, and socioeconomic groups is problematic. For example, in their study of the quality of friendships among 240 predominantly lower-middle to middle-class Mexican American, African American, and European American sixth and ninth graders, Jones, Costin, and Ricard (1994) found that although the European American girls were more likely to reveal their personal thoughts and feelings to their friends than were the European American boys, these gender differences did not hold true for other groups. Similarly, in their study of friendships among 292 Black and White junior high school students, DuBois and Hirsch (1990) found that although the White girls reported more peer social support than did the White boys, there were no gender differences in peer social support among the Black students. Furthermore, the Black boys reported more frequent intimate conversations with best friends than did White boys, whereas no difference was found between Black and White girls. These studies call into question the monolithic and polarized construction of gendered identity and relationships that undergirds reports of sex differences in adolescent friendships; they also point to the importance of exploring the interrelationships among gender, class, and race and ethnicity.

RESEARCH ON ADOLESCENT GIRLS' FRIENDSHIPS AND PEER RELATIONS

With these qualifications in place, what does the extant research suggest about the ways adolescent girls experience and understand their friendships and peer relations? Intimacy, or the "ability to share one's thoughts and feelings with a friend" (Savin-Williams & Berndt, 1990, p. 278), is the central feature of adolescent girls' friendships; girls in early adolescence prefer intense dyadic relationships and appear to rely more heavily on their best friends than do boys (Furman & Buhrmester, 1985). Furthermore, girls' friendships become more intimate, self-disclosing, and stable over time, and gender differences in quality and stability become more apparent as adolescents grow older (Berndt, 1989; Berndt & Hoyle, 1985; Buhrmester & Furman, 1987; Crockett, Losoff, & Petersen, 1984; Epstein, 1986; Furman & Buhrmester, 1992; Hartup, 1996; Jones & Costin, 1995; Papini, Farmer, Clark, Micka, & Barnett, 1990; Sharabany, Gershoni, & Hofman, 1981; Youniss & Smollar, 1985). Adolescent girls also become increasingly concerned with the qualities of their friends, such as their beliefs and values, as they grow older, according to Youniss and Smollar. They are more likely than boys to have exclusive friendships and are less likely to make new friends when they already have intimate friendships (Savin-Williams & Berndt, 1990). Girls are also more likely than boys to pursue intimate friendships in spite of past experiences of betrayal (Way, 1996).

When researchers have ventured out of the White suburbs to explore the peer networks and friendships of ethnically and socioeconomically diverse teens, they have detected different patterns of friendships from those commonly found among White, middle-class adolescents (Cauce, 1986, 1987; Coates, 1987; DuBois & Hirsch, 1990; Duff, 1996; Gallagher & Busch-Rossnagal, 1991; Hamm, 1994; Jones et al., 1994; Way, 1996, 1998). In a 3-year longitudinal study of ethnically diverse urban poor and working-class adolescents, Way found that although girls appeared more likely than boys to have intimate same-sex friendships, boys and girls were equally likely to desire such friendships. Both the boys and the girls, however, also spoke increasingly about not trusting their same-sex peers as they went through high school. In their freshman year, 40% of the adolescents in Way's study spoke about not trusting their peers. By their junior year, however, 87% spoke about not trusting their peers. In addition, 75% of the boys and 33% of the girls spoke about not having any close friends as a consequence of not trusting their peers. Instead of becoming more intimate with their peers, these urban adolescents from low-income families, particularly the boys, became more isolated and alienated from their peers during their high school years. Duff's study of an ethnically and socioeconomically diverse group of urban adolescents suggests that although such adolescents may distrust their peers in general, they experience high levels of trust and respect in their relationships with best friends. Distinguishing peers or "associates" from those whom they consider "true" or "best" friends, the adolescents in this study point to the importance of acknowledging various types of adolescent friendships and differences in the nature and quality of these relationships. Duff also found that adolescents of color were more likely than White adolescents to include members of their immediate or extended families among their closest friends, a discovery that problematizes the usual equation of adolescent friendships with nonfamilial peer relations. Thus, what the psychological literature has taken for granted as "normal" adolescent development—a move away from parents and toward friends and peers—is interrupted by listening to ethnically diverse adolescent girls and boys from different socioeconomic backgrounds.

Research studies clearly indicate that the quality of adolescent friendships are affected in complex ways by social, cultural, and material location. DuBois and Hirsch (1990) found no differences in the frequency of White and Black girls' intimate conversations with their best friends. However, Gallagher and Busch-Rossnagal (1991) found in their study of relationships among 311 urban, low socioeconomic status (SES) and middle SES Black and White adolescent girls, that middle-class White and Black girls were more likely to self-disclose about beliefs and attitudes to their friends than were low SES Black or White girls. Exploring meanings of trust in close adolescent friendships, Duff (1996) found differences in how upper- and middle-class suburban White girls and poor and working-class urban girls of color described their closest friendships with other girls. She found, for example, that 95% of the White girls reported competition as an issue in their friendships, compared with 38% of girls of color. Seventy-six percent of the White girls reported incidents in which they felt "used" by a close friend, compared with 15% of girls of color. In addition, 81% of White girls reported jealousy as an issue in their close friendships with other girls, compared with 31% of the girls of color. These studies point to the importance of addressing the complex interrelationships among gender, class, race and ethnicity, and social context.

Indeed, social context affects adolescents' friendship patterns. Dubois and Hirsch (1990) found that Black adolescents are more likely than White adolescents to report having a large network of neighborhood friends and are almost twice as likely to report having a close other-race friend whom they saw frequently outside school. Clark and Ayers (1991) found that Black adolescents had more contact with their best friends outside of school, whereas White adolescent friends had more in-school contact. They concluded that for Black adolescents, school may not be as favorable a place for forming friendships as it may be for White youth, especially if the school is predominantly White.

Indeed, school climate has been singled out as having a significant effect on the social behaviors and interpersonal relationships of students (Doll, 1996; Epstein & Karweit, 1983; Haynes & Emmons, 1994; Rizzo, 1989). Epstein and Karweit noted that "[n]egative features in a school environment—ridicule, discrimination, low expectations, stereotypes, repressions, punishment, isolation—may increase the dissociative quality of the setting and affect the thought processes and social behavior of the students" (p. 60). Neighborhood climate, too, may have a profound effect on girls' friendships (Berg & Medrich, 1980; Brooks-Gunn, Duncan, Klebanov, & Sealand, 1993; Epstein, 1989; Furstenberg, 1994). Dubois and Hirsch (1990), for example, found that children who live in integrated neighborhoods rather than segregated ones are more likely to have interracial school friendships that extend to nonschool settings. Research evidence has repeatedly shown that friendships will be disrupted when opportunities to interact are limited (Berg & Medrich, 1980; Doll, 1996; Rizzo, 1989). Way (1998) suggested that racism and discrimination may influence both the quality and the characteristics of friendships by affecting where, when, and how often friends choose to spend time together.

POWER RELATIONS AND GIRLS' FRIENDSHIPS

Not only has the relatively small amount of research exploring the effects of ethnicity, race, social class, and social context on adolescent friendships significantly contributed to our understanding of girls' friendships, but the research focused exclusively on the nuances of adolescent girls' relationships has also added much to our knowledge of adolescent development. More specifically, such research has elucidated the effects of power relations on friendships and peer relations. In her exploration of girls' misogyny—of "girlfighting and girlfearing"—in a sample of 400 girls diverse with respect to race and ethnicity, class, sexual orientation, and geography, Thompson (1994) noted how common it is for girls to define themselves against other girls:

> Most teenage girls posit an "other girl" when they talk about social and sexual relations. Good girls treat other girls bad; bad girls derogate girls who have a different vice or more stigmatized identity: drugs instead of sex, lesbianism instead of promiscuity, bisexuality instead of lesbianism. Or, other girls are traitors to their gender—two-faces or backstabbers. You have to keep your eye on them all the time. Even those who embrace sexual freedom often take a righteous and divisive line. Their other girls are rigid prudes or teenage mothers. (p. 228)

Thompson found, among a smaller but significant number of teen mothers she interviewed who "posited *all* girls as 'other,'" a "story of splitting and attaching, distinguishing oneself from most 'other girls,' and simultaneously fixating the need for love on one particular boy or man." Such internal, psychological division, Thompson warned, has social and political implications. Among these girls, there was almost no expression of female solidarity; rather, it was not unusual to find an intense displaced anger: girls "hating girls, instead of boys or men, for injuries inflicted by boys or men" (Thompson, 1994, p. 245). Such "horizontal violence," Freire (1970/1992, pp. 48–49) argued, is tied intimately to the intrapsychic divisiveness brought on by identification with and internalization of the voices and categories of those in the dominant power positions.

Although Thompson's subsample of girls who posited all girls as other is unique, her larger discussion of "girlfighting" is important to consider. Researchers in psychology, sociology, and anthropology have, in fact, noted that it is not uncommon for girls to exhibit both direct and indirect aggression toward each other, and a number of studies explore bullying, fighting, ridicule, rejection, cliques, and stereotyping among and between adolescent girls (Brown & Gilligan, 1992; Eder, 1990, 1991, 1993; Merten, 1997; Miller, 1986). Yet, although psychological researchers may have noted these various aspects of girls' relationships with friends and peers (Savin-Williams & Berndt, 1990, p. 280), they have rarely attempted to explain the wider social and systemic forces that underlie, even nurture, such behaviors.

Early adolescence appears to be especially stressful on adolescent girls' friendships and peer relations, signified by a sharp increase in indirect aggression (Bjorkqvist, 1994) or what Grotpeter and Crick (1996) have called "relational aggression" (see also Jack, in press). Relational aggression, more typical of girls and more distressful to girls than to boys (Crick, 1995, 1996), is characterized by such behaviors as spreading rumors about a peer or threatening "withdrawal of affiliation for the purpose of controlling the behavior of others" (Rys & Bear, 1997, p. 89). Brown (1998) suggested that a rise in aggression may be connected to increased social control and regulation of girls' behaviors at early adolescence and is thus a function of girls' attempts to negotiate or to resist culturally inscribed and socially sanctioned notions of femininity that specify the normal, the typical, the desirable, and the good. Because open conflict and competition are taboo for adolescent girls, especially in school settings, girls who do not openly resist such norms find creative ways to disguise their disagreements and conflicts. They may hide or downplay their accomplishments, competitiveness, or desire for personal and social power by relying on social manipulation or more subtle relational forms of controlling others.

The ways in which girls respond to such heightened social control depends not only on context but also on their social and material locations. Listening to middle- and working-class White girls struggle with the tensions between local and dominant cultural constructions of femininity, Brown (1998) noted class-related differences in the girls' friendships. The working-class girls solidified their relationships with other girls in response to perceived threats and judgments from their teachers. The middle-class girls, negotiating the opposition between competition for individual success and solidarity with their friends, found it difficult to stay in touch with their thoughts and feelings, particularly "unfeminine" feelings such as anger, and struggled to remain in authentic and supportive relationships with one another (see also Brown & Gilligan, 1992). Debold (1996) further suggested that White middle-class girls' movement into and internalization of dominant cultural images and discourses of femininity is motivated, in large part, by the promise of security and safety offered to those who most closely resemble the ideal. Thus, vying for the attention of boys and worrying about fitting in and being liked by popular groups indicate, in part, middle-class girls' larger struggle with their place in the dominant culture and their relationship with those who have the authority to judge and protect and secure them a place in the hierarchy.

Girls' struggles, their capitulation or resistance to such social regulation, suggest an explanation for the emergence of cliques and exclusivity in girls' relationships as well as the role popularity and attractiveness play in the development and configuration of adolescent girls' peer groupings. If social acceptance is reserved for those who most closely approximate, in behavior and appearance, the dominant—White, middle-class, heterosexual, physically abled—cultural ideal of femininity, then girls may join with other girls in their desire for or rejection of this ideal as a worthy goal. Exclusive peer groups may be a way for more popular girls to secure their social position, whereas they may provide support for girls who privately or publicly resist such an avenue to success and acceptance.

Eder (1985) set out to understand "how changes in girls' relationships with other girls contribute to an increased concern with popularity and a decreased concern with achievement" as well as "why girls become increasingly other-directed and insecure during early adolescence" (p. 155). Adopting an ethnographic approach, Eder described an increasingly clear "hierarchical system of stable cliques" (Eder, p. 157) among White middle- and working-class girls from sixth to eighth grade. This system of social stratification hinged on girls' relative popularity—itself a deeply classed and cultured construct. Friendships with other girls were important avenues for status: Girls who were popular were either cheerleaders or friends of cheerleaders. Such popular girls also tended to be middle class, wore name-brand clothes, and were considered attractive.

Eder (1985) described a "cycle of popularity, in which feelings toward popular girls by unpopular girls moved from positive to negative, eventually making them some of the least liked individuals in the school" (p. 154). Although Eder described such intense dislike by other girls as an artifact of the friendship demands made on the popular girls—for example, demands to be supernice to everyone that they could not successfully meet—the popular girls' status seemed to benefit more, rather than less, from such increased negativity. Both popular girls and unpopular girls participated in the hierarchy—through self-imposed seating arrangements, stereotyping, and symbolic behaviors and strategies for avoiding body and eye contact. The growing dislike of the popular girls helped them maintain their distance from the unpopular girls and reified their position at the top of the hierarchy.

Evans and Eder (1993), however, described a "cycle of isolation" in White middle school girls who are highly visible "due to perceived deficiencies in the very areas of deepest normative concern: appearance, mental maturity, and gender identification" (p. 164). Once a student was viewed negatively in any one of these areas, other negative characteristics were assigned by classmates, most often in the form of "negative sexual labeling"—such as being called a "slut" or a "faggot" (Evans & Eder, p. 165). Their study moves responsibility for social isolation away from the individual behavior of those isolated by their peers and toward situational and environmental factors—most notably, school environments in which sexist and homophobic behavior goes unchecked and in which a high level of anxiety about social acceptance is created through "school policies and practices that promote social visibility and social hierarchy among students" (Evans & Eder, p. 168).

Merten (1997), exploring "the meaning of meanness" among a clique of popular girls dubbed "the dirty dozen" by their teachers, spoke to the complicated phenomena of popularity and isolation. Meanness, he explained, was an effective strategy for maintaining popularity for these junior high school girls. Girls who were not supernice or who did not satisfactorily meet an egalitarian norm of niceness risked losing their popularity by being called stuck-up, but girls who transformed the support and power of their popular position into meanness sidestepped such accusations or feelings of envy. Their "reputation for meanness acted as a deterrent to both competition *and* suggestions that one was stuck-up" (Merten, p. 188). A girl's effectiveness in using meanness to protect her popularity, however, depended on having high status in the group. Thus, in a social context in which open competition among girls was unacceptable, meanness became an effective "discourse about hierarchical position, popularity, and invulnerability" (Merten, p. 188).

Although Eder's and Merten's research allows social scientists a peek at the impact of dominant cultural norms of femininity on White girls' friendships, we know less about those who negotiate the disparate realities of their cultural and local community norms and discourses of femininity and those of the dominant culture. White middle-class girls' friendships and peer relationships may become threatened by the competitiveness, fraudulence, and disconnection necessary to reach the elite positions in their schools. By contrast, those who stand in a less central relationship to the dominant culture, whether because of social class, race and ethnicity, sexual orientation, or disability, may rely more on their close friendships and on group solidarity and support, particularly if they are openly critical of the status quo. Brown and Gilligan (1992) found that the girls who were located in the margins of their privileged predominantly White private girls' school, because of either race or class, although unlikely to be popular, were more likely to stay in touch with their thoughts and feelings and to have close, confiding friendships.

Eder (1990, 1991, 1993) and Schofield (1982) found that working-class White and Black adolescent girls experienced teasing as playful and collaborative and used strategies like ritual teasing and teasing about romantic and sexual behavior within their peer groups as a way to distance themselves from dominant cultural gender roles. In addition, the White working-class girls in Eder's studies, unlike the White middle-class girls, used teasing to support one another and to protect themselves from male ridicule (see also Hey, 1997). Competing for status did not appear to be as important to these working-class girls as it did to their middle-class counterparts. Ritual insulting or teasing was less about power struggles and competitiveness and more about socializing others into group behavior and norms, learning and practicing self-defense strategies, and also solidifying girls' group relationships, even dissolving or mitigating competition over boys. Negative feelings, such as anger and distrust, were directed at girls who did not comply with this group norm, and their expression reminded such girls of the consequences of disloyalty.

Indeed, loyalty and trust are of fundamental importance in adolescent girls' friendships and peer relations (Brown, 1998; Brown & Gilligan, 1992; Duff, 1996; Gilligan, 1986; Harris, 1994; Savin-Williams & Berndt, 1990; Taylor, Gilligan, & Sullivan, 1995; Ward, 1996; Way, 1996, 1998). Read against the backdrop of a dominant culture in which making it to the top of the hierarchy is valued, whereas competition, conflict, and strong feelings like anger are unacceptable for girls, adolescent girls' preoccupation with loyalty, and conversely, with betrayal or "backstabbing" behavior is perhaps understandable. There are severe consequences for not understanding or for responding inappropriately to the culture of power (Delpit, 1995; Deyhle & LeCompte, 1994; Fordham, 1993). Wilson (1991) found that Sioux Indian high school students attending an Anglo American school sought support from and gave solace to other Sioux students experiencing the trauma of racism, even when it meant skipping school or breaking other school rules. These acts of loyalty were critically important to the Indian students' psychological survival in school. Such a potentially treacherous social and political climate may also explain both why so many adolescent girls, White and of color, are concerned with finding friends they can trust and who can keep secrets and why girls are likely to have intimate and exclusive friendships and are reticent to bring new members into their small groups. Moreover, indications that girls at the edge of adolescence show a striking increase in self-disclosure with same-sex friends (Buhrmester & Furman, 1987) may suggest the powerful role friendships play in establishing security and forging a healthy defense against being hurt or treated badly, as girls begin to comprehend the wider culture and their place in it.

Although White working-class girls and girls of color from all socioeconomic backgrounds may seek each other out for support and may be more likely to openly critique and resist dominant cultural norms, the difficulties of negotiating the current social landscape can take a toll on their psyches and can affect their relationships. Way (1996) suggested that the high levels of distrust she heard from urban girls and boys of color "may directly and indirectly lie with the poverty, violence, and racism that shapes and pervades these adolescents' lives" (p. 187). Duff's (1996) research suggests that cultures that emphasize individualism, competition, and self-sufficiency may undermine trust in the context of girls' close friendships in ways they do not for middle-class White boys' friendships. Pastor, McCormick, and Fine (1996), drawing from in-depth interviews, group discussions, and participant observations of a small group of urban adolescent girls of color, found that although the girls developed a critical consciousness in response to the sexism, classism, and racism they endured, and although they were more likely than White, privileged girls "to assert themselves within White, often male-dominated institutions," they did not "seek each other out for collective action, which might address the inequities of which they are so critically conscious" (p. 17). Instead, they constructed "individualistic strategies" because there were "few experiences in their lives to prepare them to work collectively" (Pastor et al., p. 17). Indeed, Orenstein (1994), in her ethnography of girls in two junior high schools, documented the painful realities of individualistic strategies informed by race, ethnicity, class, and context. The most powerful moments of psychological healing and empowerment in her study were those in which, either inadvertently or by design, girls came together to talk about and address experiences of betrayal, unfairness, and hurt.

STRENGTHENING THE TIES THAT BIND

Friendships can be a source of both knowledge and great strength for adolescent girls. They can also be a source of struggle, hurt, and confusion, particularly as girls move into adolescence and begin to negotiate dominant cultural views of gender relations, femininity, appearance, and sexuality. If the quality of girls' friendships and peer relations is differentially affected by prevailing relational and systemic power asymmetries, it would seem important to directly engage girls in conversations about such issues and to encourage girls to name, to struggle with, and to critique such realities together in the contexts of their friendships and peer relationships.

Ana and Zoe, the 12-year-olds who introduced this chapter, began such a conversation in a most unlikely setting. Throughout the panel discussion, these two girls engaged one another and spoke to the issue of peer relations in their school, sometimes noticeably ignoring the preplanned script of their session to speak to each other rather than to the facilitator or the audience. After the formal discussion ended, the girls sought each other out and continued their conversation, a testament to both their passionate feelings about the issues raised and the ways their very different experiences and perceptions captivated their attention. Such openings are common for girls this age as they begin to negotiate the relationships among the particulars of their experiences, the values and norms of their communities, and the structures of the wider society.

Had they the opportunity to continue their exchange, Ana and Zoe may well have wondered not only why peer relations are formed along different fault lines in their schools but also what supports or encourages such patterns. They might wonder why cliques, if so "separating and demeaning for everybody," as Zoe protests, still exist and what they might offer to those who participate in them. They might consider how race and ethnicity, class, gender, sexual orientation, and differing abilities influence peer relations and friendships, and they may even come to an understanding of why they are concerned about quite different things. They may begin to wonder how their changing relationships with boys will affect their relationships with their girlfriends, or how expressions of closeness and intimacy with their girlfriends are hampered by strict codes of sexual and gender "normalcy" (Evans & Eder, 1993). Such questions may lead them to critique their respective middle schools and the ways such schools not only encourage normative behavior and expression but also affect their friendships and the dynamics of peer relations by institutionalizing a hierarchy of popularity and the ways their schools encourage feelings of isolation by privileging select extracurricular activities that allow only a few to feel successful (Eder & Kinney, 1995; Merten, 1997).

Such openly critical conversations among girls are extremely important and all too rarely encouraged. For middle-class White adolescent girls who accept radically individualized paths to success, and who often bury their strong feelings and thoughts, such conversations are a way to examine why they may feel, as Schonert-Reichl (1994) found, a diminished sense of their own uniqueness, omnipotence, and invulnerability; why they are more self-conscious of the ways they appear in public; and why they are more likely to be depressed than working-class White girls or girls of color. For girls of color and for White working-class girls, such conversations offer an opportunity to explore and to find support for their justified anger at injustice, to share their strategies for survival, and to develop constructive and effective responses.

Girls often valiantly struggle against and resist norms and expectations that move them away from their experiences and out of genuine relationship with each other, but such struggles may have uneven results. When out of relationship with other girls, they may blame themselves or lash out in ineffective, even dangerous ways. Group conversations hold particular promise when facilitated by an adult who can help girls translate and negotiate the culture of power—someone who can listen, stay with girls' critique, and also explore with girls their often contradictory feelings, their interactions with other girls and women, and their capitulation or resistance to social separations and internal divisions.

Within the field of psychology, adolescent friendships have usually been considered independent entities or associated with family relationships. They have not been examined in the context of school or neighborhood environments or with respect to current power relations in the United States. Yet adolescent girls live in a world that includes families, schools, neighborhoods, and communities, and these entities themselves embedded in a culture that remains socially, culturally, and racially stratified are likely to influence the nature, shape, quality, and characteristics of their friendships. It is important to encourage girls to explore the power dynamics at work in such contexts and to consider the effects these dynamics have on their understandings of themselves and their relationships with their friends and peers.

CONCLUSION

Reviewing the research on adolescent girls' friendships underscores the need to expand our knowledge of the relational worlds of diverse groups of girls and young women. This requires us to break down the current monoliths that undergird the research literature. There is, as evidenced in this volume, great diversity not only between but also within racial and ethnic groups, and the social category "White" is no exception (see, e.g., Fine, Weis, Powell, & Wong, 1997; Frankenberg, 1993). We suggest that adolescent girls from different socioeconomic classes and ethnicities, with different physical abilities, with different sexual identities, and from a range of environments and contexts be listened to in their own terms and within the layered complexity of their lived experiences. Only then can people begin to develop more explicit strategies and programs that encourage healthy, supportive, responsive relationships between and among girls, relationships that have the potential to break down destructive messages and to counter social realities that contribute to feelings of mistrust and alienation.

Finally, psychologists need to use the knowledge of such studies to develop new theories about adolescent friendships and peer relations. A useful theoretical conceptualization of adolescent girls' friendships will incorporate new research on girls' and young women's development. Studies from various disciplines suggest that early adolescence is not only a time of increased need and desire for intimacy with friends and peers but also a critically important developmental period for girls. How girls' friendships and peer relations might mitigate or exacerbate the psychological and social struggles of this period remains to be understood. Moreover, in any truly useful theoretical conceptualization of adolescent girls' friendships, one will consider the ways contextual and systemic factors influence the understanding, the definitions, the development, and the nurturance of relationships.

Finally, adolescent girls' creative relational strategies—the ways their interactions with each other and their inventive use of language help them transform, reappropriate, or resist dominant cultural expectations of femininity and detach from traditional gender roles—call into question the usual understanding of development and socialization as a predictable and consistent process (Brown, 1998; Eder, 1993; Walkerdine, 1990). Such strategies suggest that psychologists need to consider the uneven, contradictory aspects of the human psyche and the complicated negotiation of a variety of social and contextual forces. Only then can we tap the creative potential and transformative power of girls' relationships and appreciate the variety of meanings girls from different social and material locations give to their friendships and peer relations.

REFERENCES

Apter, T. (1990). *Altered loves: Mothers and daughters during adolescence*. New York: St. Martin's Press.

Asher, S. R., & Hymel, S. (1986). Coaching in social skills for children who lack friends in school. *Social Work in Education, 8*, 205–218.

Belle, D. (1989). *Children's social networks and social supports*. New York: Wiley.

Berg, M., & Medrich, E. A. (1980). Children in four neighborhoods: The physical environment and its effect on play and play patterns. *Environment and Behavior, 12*, 320–348.

Berndt, T. J. (1982). The features and effects of friendship in early adolescence. *Child Development, 53*, 1447–1460.

Berndt, T. J. (1989). Obtaining support from friends during childhood and adolescence. In D. Belle (Ed.), *Children's social networks and supports* (pp. 308–331). New York: Wiley.

Berndt, T. J., & Hoyle, S. G. (1985). Stability and change in childhood and adolescent friendships. *Developmental Psychology, 21*, 1007–1015.

Bjorkqvist, K. (1994). Sex differences in physical, verbal, and indirect aggression: A review of recent research. *Sex Roles, 30*, 177–188.

Brooks-Gunn, J., Duncan, G. J., Klebanov, P. K., & Sealand, N. (1993). Do neighborhoods influence child and adolescent development? *American Journal of Sociology, 99*, 353–395.

Brown, L. M. (1998). *Raising their voices: The politics of girls' anger*. Cambridge, MA: Harvard University Press.

Brown, L. M., & Gilligan, C. (1992). *Meeting at the crossroads: Women's psychology and girls' development*. Cambridge, MA: Harvard University Press.

Buhrmester, D., & Furman, W. (1987). The development of companionship and intimacy. *Child Development, 58*, 1101–1113.

Caldwell, M. A., & Peplau, L. A. (1982). Sex differences in same-sex friendships. *Sex Roles, 8*, 721–733.

Camarena, P. M., Sarigiani, P. A., & Petersen, A. C. (1990). Gender-specific pathways to intimacy in early adolescence. *Journal of Youth and Adolescence, 19*, 19–32.

Cauce, A. M. (1986). Social networks and social competence: Exploring the effects of early adolescent friendships. *American Journal of Community Psychology, 14*, 607–628.

Cauce, A. M. (1987). School and peer competence in early adolescence: A test of domain-specific self-perceived competence. *Developmental Psychology, 23*, 287–291.

Clark, M. L. (1989). Friendships and peer relations in Black adolescents. In R. Jones (Ed.), *Black adolescents* (pp. 175–204). Berkeley, CA: Cobb & Henry.

Clark, M. L., & Ayers, M. (1991). Friendship similarity during early adolescence: Gender and racial patterns. *Journal of Psychology, 126*, 393–405.

Clark, M. L., & Bittle, M. L. (1992). Friendship expectations and the evaluation of present friendships in middle childhood and early adolescence. *Child Study Journal, 22,* 115–135.

Coates, D. L. (1987). Gender differences in the structure and support characteristics of black adolescents' social networks. *Sex Roles, 17,* 667–687.

Crick, N. (1995). Relational aggression: The role of intent attributions, feelings of distress, and provocation type. *Development and Psychopathology, 7,* 313–322.

Crick, N. (1996). The role of overt aggression, relational aggression, and prosocial behavior in the prediction of children's future social adjustment. *Child Development, 67,* 2317–2327.

Crockett, L., Losoff, M., & Petersen, A. C. (1984). Perceptions of the peer group and friendship in early adolescence. *Journal of Early Adolescence, 4,* 155–181.

Debold, E. (1996). *Knowing bodies: Gender identity, cognitive development and embodiment in early childhood and early adolescence.* Unpublished doctoral dissertation, Harvard University.

Delpit, L. (1995). *Other people's children.* Cambridge, MA: Harvard University Press.

Deyhle, D., & LeCompte, M. (1994). Cultural differences in child development: Navajo adolescents in middle schools. *Theory Into Practice, 33,* 156–166.

Doll, B. (1996). Children without friends: Implications for practice and policy. *School Psychology Review, 25,* 165–183.

DuBois, D. L., & Hirsch, B. J. (1990). School and neighborhood friendship patterns of blacks and whites in early adolescence. *Child Development, 61,* 524–536.

Duff, J. L. (1996). *The best of friends: Exploring the moral domain of adolescent friendship.* Unpublished doctoral dissertation, Stanford University.

Eder, D. (1985). The cycle of popularity: Interpersonal relations among female adolescents. *Sociology of Education, 58,* 154–165.

Eder, D. (1990). Serious and playful disputes: Variation in conflict talk among female adolescents. In A. D. Grimshaw (Ed.), *Conflict talk: Sociolinguistic investigations of arguments in conversations* (pp. 67–84). Cambridge, England: Cambridge University Press.

Eder, D. (1991). The role of teasing in adolescent peer culture. *Sociological Studies of Child Development, 4,* 181–197.

Eder, D. (1993). "Go get ya a french!" Romantic and sexual teasing among adolescent girls. In D. Tannen (Ed.), *Gender and conversational interaction* (pp. 17–31). Oxford, England: Oxford University Press.

Eder, D., & Kinney, D. (1995). The effect of middle school extracurricular activities on adolescents' popularity and peer status. *Youth & Society, 26,* 298–324.

Epstein, J. (1986). Friendship selection: Developmental and environmental influences. In E. C. Mueller & C. R. Cooper (Eds.), *Process and outcome in peer relationships* (pp. 129–160). Orlando, FL: Academic Press.

Epstein, J. (1989). The selection of friends: Changes across the grades and in different school environments. In T. Berndt & G. Ladd (Eds.), *Peer relationships in child development* (pp. 158–187). New York: Wiley.

Epstein, J., & Karweit, N. (Eds.). (1983). *Friends in school: Patterns of selection and influence in secondary schools.* New York: Academic Press.

Evans, C., & Eder, D. (1993). "No exit": Processes of social isolation in the middle school. *Journal of Contemporary Ethnography, 22,* 139–170.

Fine, M. (1992). *Disruptive voices.* Albany: State University of New York Press.

Fine, M., Weis, L., Powell, L., & Wong, L. M. (Eds.). (1997). *Off white: Readings on race, power, and society.* New York: Routledge.

Fordham, S. (1993). "Those loud black girls": (Black) women, silence and gender "passing" in the academy. *Anthropology and Education Quarterly, 24,* 3–32.

Frankenberg, R. (1993). *The social construction of whiteness.* Minneapolis: University of Minnesota Press.

Freire, P. (1992). *Pedagogy of the oppressed.* New York: Continuum Publishing. (Original work published 1970)

Furman, W., & Buhrmester, D. (1985). Children's perceptions of the personal relationships in their social networks. *Developmental Psychology, 21,* 1016–1024.

Furman, W., & Buhrmester, D. (1992). Age and sex differences in perceptions of networks of personal relationships. *Child Development, 63,* 103–115.

Furstenberg, F. (1994, November). *The influence of neighborhoods on children's development: A theoretical perspective and a research agenda.* Paper presented at the Conference on Indicators of Children's Well-Being, Bethesda, MD.

Gallagher, C., & Busch-Rossnagal, N. A. (1991, March). *Self-disclosure and social support in the relationships of black and white female adolescents.* Poster session presented at the Society for Research on Child Development, Seattle, WA.

Gilligan, C. (1982). *In a different voice.* Cambridge, MA: Harvard University Press.

Gilligan, C. (1986). Exit-voice dilemmas in adolescent development. In A. Foxley, M. McPherson, & G. O'Donnell (Eds.), *Development, democracy, and the art of tresspassing: Essays in honor of Albert O. Hirschman* (pp. 283–300). Notre Dame, IN: University of Notre Dame Press.

Gilligan, C., Lyons, N. P., & Hanmer, T. J. (Eds.). (1990). *Making connections.* Cambridge, MA: Harvard University Press.

Goodyer, I. M., Wright, C., & Altham, P. M. (1989). Recent friendships in anxious and depressed school age children. *Psychological Medicine, 19,* 165–174.

Grotpeter, J., & Crick, N. (1996). Relational aggression, overt aggression, and friendship. *Child Development, 67,* 2328–2338.

Hamm, J. V. (1994, February). *Similarity in the face of diversity? African-American, Asian-American, European-American, and Hispanic-American adolescents' best friendships in ethnically diverse high schools.* Paper presented at the biennial meetings of the Society for Research on Adolescence, San Diego, CA.

Harris, M. G. (1994). Cholas, Mexican-American girls, and gangs. *Sex Roles, 30,* 289–301.

Hartup, W. (1996). The company they keep: Friendships and their developmental significance. *Child Development, 67,* 1–13.

Haynes, N., & Emmons, C. (1994, March). *The effects of school climate on adolescent adjustment.* Lecture given at the Developmental Psychology Luncheon Series, Yale University, Department of Psychology, New Haven, CT.

Hey, V. (1997). *The company she keeps: An ethnography of girls' friendships.* Philadelphia: Open University Press.

Jack, D. (in press). *Behind the mask: Destruction and creativity in women's aggression.* Cambridge, MA: Harvard University Press.

Jessor, R. (1993). Successful adolescent development among youth in high risk settings. *American Psychologist, 48,* 117–126.

Jones, D. C., & Costin, S. E. (1995). Friendship quality during preadolescence and adolescence: The contributions of relationship orientations, instrumentality, and expressivity. *Merrill-Palmer Quarterly, 41,* 517–535.

Jones, D. C., Costin, S. E., & Ricard, R. J. (1994, February). *Ethnic and sex differences in best friendship characteristics among African-American, Mexican-American, and European-American adolescents.* Poster session presented at the biennial meetings of the Society for Research on Adolescence, San Diego, CA.

Jordan, J., Kaplan, A. G., Miller, J. B., Stiver, I., & Surrey, J. (1991). *Women's growth in connection.* New York: Guilford Press.

Laursen, B. (Ed.). (1993). *New Directions for Child Development: Vol. 60. Close friendships in adolescence.* San Francisco: Jossey-Bass

Leadbeater, B. R., & Way, N. (1996). *Urban girls: Resisting stereotypes, creating identities.* New York: New York University Press.

Merten, D. (1997). The meaning of meanness: Popularity, competition, and conflict among junior high school girls. *Sociology of Education, 70,* 175–191.

Miller, P. (1986). Teasing as language socialization and verbal play in a white working-class community. In B. Schieffelin & E. Ochs (Eds.), *Language socialization across cultures* (pp. 199–212). Cambridge, England: Cambridge University Press.

Orenstein, P. (1994). *SchoolGirls.* New York: Doubleday.

Papini, D. R., Farmer, F. F., Clark, S. M., Micka, J. C., & Barnett, J. K. (1990). Early adolescent age and gender differences in patterns of emotional self-disclosure to parents and friends. *Adolescence, 25,* 959–976.

Parker, J., & Asher, S. R. (1987). Peer acceptance and later personal adjustment: Are low-accepted children "at risk"? *Psychological Bulletin, 102,* 357–369.

Parker, J., & Asher, S. R. (1993). Friendship and friendship quality in middle childhood: Links with peer group acceptance and feelings of loneliness and social dissatisfaction. *Developmental Psychology, 29,* 611–621.

Pastor, J., McCormick, J., & Fine, M. (1996). Makin' homes: An urban girl thing.

In B. Leadbeater & N. Way (Eds.), *Urban girls: Resisting stereotypes, creating identities* (pp. 15–34). New York: New York University Press.

Putallaz, M., & Gottman, J. (1981). An interactional model of children's entry into peer groups. *Child Development, 52,* 986–994.

Reisman, J. M. (1990). Intimacy in same-sex friendships. *Sex Roles, 23,* 65–82.

Rizzo, T. (1989). *Friendship development among children in school.* Norwood, NJ: Ablex.

Rys, G., & Bear, G. (1997). Relational aggression and peer relations: Gender and developmental issues. *Merrill-Palmer Quarterly, 43,* 87–106.

Savin-Williams, R. W., & Berndt, T. J. (1990). Friendship and peer relations. In S. S. Feldman & G. Elliot (Eds.), *At the threshold: The developing adolescent* (pp. 277–307). Cambridge, MA: Harvard University Press.

Schofield, J. (1982). *Black and White in school: Trust, tension, or tolerance?* New York: Praeger.

Schonert-Reichl, K. (1994). Gender differences in depressive symptomatology and egocentrism in adolescence. *Journal of Early Adolescence, 14,* 49–65.

Schonert-Reichl, K. (1995). The friendship and peer relations of adolescents with behavioral problems. *Exceptionality Education Canada, 5,* 55–80.

Schonert-Reichl, K. (1996, August). *Peer relationships and moral reasoning during early adolescence: The influence of peer status, social participation, and friendship quality.* Paper presented at the biennial meetings of the International Society for the Study of Behavioural Development, Quebec City, Quebec, Canada.

Selman, R. (1980). *The growth of interpersonal understanding.* London: Academic Press.

Sharabany, R., Gershoni, R., & Hofman, J. E. (1981). Girlfriend, boyfriend: Age and sex differences in intimate friendship. *Developmental Psychology, 17,* 800–808.

Shulman (1993). Close friends in early and middle adolescence: Typology and friendship reasoning. In B. Laursen (Ed.), *New Directions for Child Development: Vol. 60. Close friendships in adolescence* (pp. 55–71). San Francisco: Jossey-Bass.

Taylor, J. M., Gilligan, C., & Sullivan, A. (1995). *Between voice and silence: Women and girls, race and relationship.* Cambridge, MA: Harvard University Press.

Thompson, S. (1994). What friends are for: On girls' misogyny and romantic fusion. In J. Irvine (Ed.), *Sexual cultures and the construction of adolescent identities* (pp. 228–249). Philadelphia: Temple University Press.

Walkerdine, V. (1990). *Schoolgirl fictions.* London: Verso.

Ward, J. V. (1996). Raising resisters: The role of truth-telling in the psychological development of African-American girls. In B. Leadbeater & N. Way (Eds.), *Urban girls: Resisting stereotypes, creating identities* (pp. 85–99). New York: New York University Press.

Way, N. (1995). "Can't you see the courage, the strength that I have?" Listening to urban adolescent girls speak about their relationships. *Psychology of Women Quarterly, 19,* 107–128.

Way, N. (1996). Between experiences of betrayal and desire: Close friendships among urban adolescents. In B. Leadbeater & N. Way (Eds.), *Urban girls: Resisting stereotypes, creating identities* (pp. 173–192). New York: New York University Press.

Way, N. (1998). *Everyday courage: The lives and stories of urban teenagers.* New York: New York University Press.

Wilson, P. (1991). Trauma of Sioux Indian high school students. *Anthropology & Education Quarterly, 22,* 367–383.

Wong, M., & Csikszentmihalyi, M. (1991). Affiliation motivation and daily experience: Some issues on gender differences. *Journal of Personality and Social Psychology, 60,* 154–164.

Youniss, J. (1980). *Parent and peers in social development: A Sullivan–Piaget Perspective.* Chicago: University of Chicago Press.

Youniss, J., & Smollar, J. (1985). *Adolescent relations with mothers, fathers, and friends.* Chicago: University of Chicago Press.

10

FEMALE ADOLESCENT SEXUALITY IN RELATIONAL CONTEXT: BEYOND SEXUAL DECISION MAKING

DEBORAH L. TOLMAN

The timeworn adage that "boys want sex, girls want relationships" continues to hold sway in society and in the ways that adolescent sexuality is understood and researched. This division of sexuality from intimacy parses out desire for sex as normal for boys and desire for relationships as normal for girls. Given this cultural assumption, it is predictable that girls' sexual desire has only recently been acknowledged as a factor in girls' sexual decision making (Fine, 1988; Tolman, 1992, 1994a, 1994b, 1996). However, surprisingly little attention has been given to the relational dimensions of this domain of adolescent girls' lives until feminist psychologists began recently to challenge the gendered splitting of sexuality and intimacy.

In what has become a classic analysis of female adolescent sexuality, Michelle Fine (1988) identified a "missing discourse of desire" when she listened to urban Black and Latina public high school students and dropouts speak about their experiences with or questions about sexual desire or pleasure in school. Observing the ways that conflict erupted when adults resisted the students' knowledge about their own sexuality, Fine noted that "whether in a classroom, on the street, at work, or at home, the adolescent female's sexuality is negotiated by, for, and despite the young woman herself" (p. 35). Fine contrasted the complexity of how some of these girls could talk about the possibility of sexual subjectivity and the potential for sexual exploitation that they experienced in their relationships with young men with the pressure that adults applied to fit them into discourses of victimhood, morality, disease, and danger. When left to their own devices, girls' described the "braiding" of danger and desire in their sexual experiences and romantic relationships with boyfriends, with older men, or, for lesbian adolescents, with girlfriends, as well as the ways in which their relationships with mothers, teachers, friends, and male relatives shape their sexuality. Fine's observations in this ethnographic study of urban high school life led her to suggest that "public schooling may actually disable young women in their negotiations as sexual subjects. Trained through and into positions of passivity and victimization, young women are currently educated away from positions of sexual self interest" (p. 42).

Fine's work represents a critical departure from much of the literature on female adolescent sexuality, which focuses on problems or negative consequences associated with an individual girl's sexual behavior. Traditionally, the study of female adolescent sexuality has been more epidemiological than psychological, anchored in the demographics of who initiates sexual intercourse at what ages and who engages in what behaviors that lead to pregnancy and disease risk. For the most part, this body of research has assumed a kind of relational vacuum, in which sexual decision making is narrowly defined as an individual girl making good or bad decisions about sexual intercourse, meaning decisions that increase or diminish her risk of pregnancy and disease. The relational processes and consequences that shape, contextualize, and give meaning to girls' choices—that is, the relational contexts within and through which girls make decisions about sexual intercourse and experience other aspects of sexuality—have not been a focus of mainstream research on adolescent girls' sexuality development. This conception of girls' sexuality leaves out important relational questions, such as how girls' relationships with their own bodies, with specific people in their lives, and with the larger cultural ideals regulating "normal" and "moral" female identities shape their sexuality.

I begin this chapter with a brief examination of what the sexual decision-making literatures convey about how relationships factor into girls' sexuality development. I clarify how the theories, assumptions, and methods employed in these literatures make it difficult to move toward a multifaceted understanding of the relational contexts of girls' sexuality yet, at the same time, illustrate how important such an understanding is. I then turn to more recent feminist literature that focuses on adolescent girls' experiences of their sexuality. These studies represent a sea change in the conception of female adolescent sexuality, away from an individualistic approach and toward an understanding that girls' relationships are a central part of their developing sexuality.

SEXUAL DECISION-MAKING LITERATURE

Toward the Importance of Relationships for Girls' Sexuality

In the literature on sexual decision making, the relational context of girls' sexual decision making is understood primarily as (a) an individual girl's perceptions of the beliefs of various people in her life regarding behaviors that are associated with sexual intercourse or (b) the influence that people in a girl's life might exert that affect her decisions to engage in behaviors associated with sexual intercourse. These conceptions of relationship provide some information about the relational contexts of adolescent girls' sexual decision making. Because there is such a focus on sexual intercourse, other ways of expressing sexuality that are likely to be important in understanding the relational dimensions of adolescent sexuality are not framed or researched. This focus also yields studies about heterosexual decision making. There is a tendency to study girls primarily (Billy, Brewster, & Grady, 1994; East 1996; Lock & Vincent, 1995), even though sexual decisions, especially those that have negative consequences (pregnancy and disease), are partnered sexual events (Brooks-Gunn & Furstenberg, 1989; Brooks-Gunn & Paikoff, 1993). These studies often use samples of girls of color and of poor girls, adolescents who are considered most at risk for being "bad" sexual decision makers. Middle-class suburban girls or disabled girls, who are not considered at risk in part because their sexuality is less scrutinized or visible (Tolman, 1996), are thus not often the focus of such studies.

Brooks-Gunn and Furstenberg (1989) have suggested that in the conventional sexual decision-making literature, researchers have primarily investigated adolescent girls' sexual decision making as individual risk-taking behavior (i.e., Gibbons, Gerrard, & Boney-McCoy, 1995; Johnson & Green, 1993; Jorgensen & Sonstegard, 1984; Newcomb, Huba, & Bentler, 1986; Petersen, Leffert, & Graham, 1995; Pick & Andrade-Palos, 1995; St. Lawrence, Brasfield, Jefferson, Allyene & Shirley, 1994). The purpose of these studies is to identify who does and does not successfully avoid the negative consequences of unprotected sexual intercourse, that is, who makes "good" decisions (Cooper, Peirce, & Huselid, 1994; Di Blasio & Benda, 1992; Lock & Vincent, 1995; Pick & Andrade-Palos, 1995; Resnick & Blum, 1985; Warzak, Grow, Poler, & Walburn, 1995). These researchers used survey and other objective data to construct statistical models to predict which girls make what decisions under which conditions and to distinguish between groups of girls. Most distinguish girls who are "nonvirgins," that is, who have been labeled "sexually active" (those who have ever had sexual intercourse) from girls who have abstained from sexual intercourse. The use of these methods with large samples enables such distinctions to be made yet, at the same time, makes it difficult to articulate key features of the relational contexts of sexual decision making, such as how girls negotiate multiple relationships as they make their sexual decisions or how the relational meanings of such decisions affect girls' choices.

Two Psychology Traditions: Cognitive Decision Making and Behavioral Outcomes

Such research on risk taking in general, and girls' sexuality in particular, has come largely out of two traditions in psychology: (a) studying decisions as cognitive rather than embodied or relational processes and (b) focusing primarily on behavioral outcomes. As with the cognitive processes literature in general (Debold, 1996), the sexual decision-making literature is characterized by a construction of decision making as a rational, cognitive, and intentional process (i.e., Cervera, 1993; Gibbons et al., 1995; Norris & Ford, 1995; Reinecke, Schmidt, & Ajzen, 1996; Rosenthal, Hall, & Moore, 1992). These studies identify specific types of relationships within which adolescents might take risks, such as whether they use condoms with a new sexual partner (Reinecke et al., 1996) or with a known partner (Norris & Ford, 1995). The theory of planned behavior is a cognitive decision-making model often employed in such studies.[1] This theory postulates that a girl's attitudes toward a behavior, her perceptions of subjective norms (perceived social pressure, often conceived as perceptions of the beliefs of close friends, family, or other significant people in one's life), and her perceived behavioral control (one's beliefs about one's ability to enact one's intentions) predict intentions to engage in a behavior, such as contraceptive use or, more recently, condom use (Boldero, Moore, & Rosenthal, 1992; Breakwell, Millward, & Fife-Shaw, 1994; Doll & Ajzen, 1992).

This model provides very general information about the impact of girls' relational contexts on their sexual decision making, in that subjective norms reflect an individual girl's perceptions about the beliefs of those with whom she is in relationship, and perceived behavioral control reflects her perceptions about her ability to act within what is, by definition, a relational context. A focus on relationships in the study of heterosexual sexual

---

[1]The theory of planned behavior is an elaboration of the theory of reasoned action (Fishbein & Ajzen, 1975). This revision adds a component of perceived behavioral control to the original model of predicting behavior on the basis of intentions, which is determined by attitudes and perceptions of subjective norms; strong intentions are understood as predictive of actual behavior. Perceived behavioral control was added to account for the fact that intentions may be affected by one's ability to implement one's wishes in any given situation.

decision making highlights the realities of power differences associated with gender that may call into question or undermine a variable such as perceived behavioral control. The theory of planned behavior does not allow for the specific ways in which adolescent girls may be subtly or overtly denied the volition of their own wishes or intentions in their relationships with sexual partners, family, or others—through fear of violence or abuse —as well as the desire to please or to preserve a relationship for economic or social reasons. The protective psychological processes of denial and sublimation may be important factors in a girl's perception of her behavioral control in such a relational context (Ingham, Woodcock, & Stenner, 1992).

Kristen Luker's (1975) landmark study of contraceptive risk taking incorporates what proves to be a crucial gendered analysis usually overlooked in studies organized by the theory of planned behavior. Luker identified a girl's relationship with her partner as one aspect of risk for the older adolescent girls and young women in her study. Rather than focus on intentions or perceptions, Luker considered the process by which young women arrive at the decision not to contracept. Luker asserted that this process entails a series of "decision junctures" at which a woman assigns values to different aspects of her situation and, depending on the way that the decision juncture is negotiated, decides whether to contracept. Luker emphasized how being unsure of the state of the commitment of a woman's partner, whether married or not married, often leads to contraceptive risk taking in the hopes that one of the benefits of pregnancy will be a more explicit commitment. Philliber, Namerow, Kaye, and Kunkes (1986) found comparable patterns among younger adolescent girls.

Influence of Others

Research on sexual decision making also has focused on the influence of people with whom girls have relationships. A number of researchers have framed their investigations in terms of the negative effects parents, boyfriends, peers, and sisters can have on girls' sexual decisions and the outcomes of their behavior (Baumeister, Flores, & Marin, 1995; Duncan-Ricks, 1992; East, 1996; East & Felice 1992; East, Felice, & Morgan, 1993; Gerrard, Gibbons, & Boney-McCoy, 1993; Lock & Vincent, 1995; Morris, Warren, & Aral, 1993; Pick & Andrade-Palos, 1995; Smith, Udry, & Morris, 1985; Tucker, 1989). This formulation suggests that these relationships are potential threats to the likelihood that an individual girl will avoid the negative outcomes of pregnancy or disease. Such relationships are investigated as predictors of sexual intercourse, which is assumed to be a negative outcome in and of itself. For example, East et al. (1993) found that in a sample of 455 early adolescent girls from predominantly minority racial backgrounds, having sexually active girlfriends or sexually active or teen childbearing sisters was associated with permissive sexual attitudes, positive intentions of engaging in future sexual activity, and greater likelihood of being a nonvirgin. They equated these attitudes with an increased risk of adolescent pregnancy (see also East & Felice, 1992). The possibility that such relationships could lead to responsible sexual activity, which would be associated with a decreased risk of adolescent pregnancy, or that they might encourage openness to pleasurable sexual behaviors that do not invite pregnancy or other risk was not considered. Boyfriends are mostly absent in such studies of girls' sexual behavior; when they appear, they are positioned as coercive threats of harm or pregnancy, assumed to be motivated by uncontrollable urges, and thus need to be avoided or controlled by girls (Vicary, Klingaman, & Harkness, 1995; Zimmerman, Sprecher, Langer, & Holloway, 1995).

Such studies raise pressing questions about how these relationships generate negative outcomes as well as how such relationships might exert a positive influence on girls' sexual decision making. For instance, the question of whether a girl's relationships can inform her about relational risks associated with her sexuality development has not been investigated. Negative relational risks, such as the risk of being disappointed, hurt, or regretful about the choice to have sexual intercourse or to explore a range of sexual behaviors, could be explored. Positive relational possibilities associated with sexuality, such as intensified intimacy with a loved partner, the sense of well-being that can come from connection with oneself through one's body, or the ability to have agency and pleasure in relationships, have yet to be framed as research questions. By suggesting that boyfriends, peers, sisters, mothers, and others can influence girls' sexual behavior and decision making, these studies underscore the importance of girls' significant relationships in their experiences, choices, and understanding of their sexuality.

Much of the theoretical and educational literatures, and even the popular literature, have articulated concerns that girls are having sex to keep their boyfriends, to fit in with friends, to act out against parental authorities, or to relive the choices of poor role models, such as sisters or mothers who made "bad" choices. It is also possible that girls may have sex because they feel ready to explore their sexuality responsibly or to extend the intimacy of a relationship. The decision-making models that privilege cognitive processes and posit others primarily as negative influences provide a strikingly partial fit with what may be central to adolescent girls' sexual decision making.

The sexual decision-making literature is anchored by a concern with negative outcomes; therefore, girls' sexual decisions are constructed as inherently, and only, about risk. This literature raises the question of how the relational contexts of girls' experiences with their sexuality serve as possible sites of psychological resilience or hardiness in the face of either danger or pleasure. Recent research on adolescent girls' psychological development has shown how girls' understanding of themselves and their choices is grounded in their desire to maintain relationships, often positing a choice or a balance between authenticity and capitulation to conventional, oppressive norms of femininity to avoid conflict and disappointment (i.e., Brown & Gilligan, 1992; Debold, Wilson, & Malave, 1993; Taylor, Gilligan, & Sullivan, 1995). This research raises new questions about the relational dimensions of adolescent girls' sexuality: What are the meanings that girls confer on their relationships when they are making choices about sex and when they are exploring their sexuality in other ways? How do they understand the effect of their own feelings, choices, and actions on these relationships? In what ways is sexuality a source of strength for girls? I turn to feminist research on girls' sexuality, which begins with an analysis of the patriarchal context of girls' sexuality development and posits a more positive conception of girls' sexuality within which to ground a more comprehensive inquiry into its relational context.

BEYOND GOOD DECISIONS AND BAD INFLUENCES: FEMINIST RESEARCH ON FEMALE ADOLESCENT SEXUALITY

Recent research on girls' sexuality—conducted by feminist scholars from various disciplines, including sociology, education, journalism, and women's studies as well as psychology—contextualizes the study of girls' sexuality within a patriarchal analysis of gendered relationships. Rather than anchoring their inquiries in a focus on girls' sexual behavior defined as sexual intercourse, an artifact of an agenda that privileges the goal of diminishing adolescent pregnancies (Nathanson, 1991), these researchers frame adolescent girls' sexuality as an ongoing interplay of identity, body, psyche, and relationships. In their studies, the researchers attempt to understand how girls experience their developing sexuality to determine effective means for empowering girls to develop responsible sexual subjectivities. The focus of these researchers included understanding whether and how girls (a) make active and safe choices about sexual behaviors of all kinds and about the relationships within which they engage in these expressions of their sexuality, (b) develop a sense of entitlement to their own pleasure and desire and thus a sense of agency grounded in their own bodies, and (c) develop critical analyses of the often unequal power distribution that is typical within gendered relationships. These researchers share a belief that the "problem" of adolescent sexuality is not the province of individual girls; rather, it is a sociopolitical problem that is lived by individual girls. Thus, this body of literature begins with the study and analysis of the larger cultural contexts within which girls are becoming sexually mature individuals. The strength that these feminist researchers want to know about is primarily psychological: girls' sexual agency and their understanding that their sexuality at least includes their own subjectivity, rights, and pleasure.

This literature is unified not only by theory but also by method. In the feminist studies reported here, researchers primarily use qualitative methodologies, using in-depth interviews to gather narratives of girls' experiences of their own sexuality to learn what, from girls' own perspectives, is happening that may be disabling and empowering. Asking girls to tell their stories about their sexuality development, these researchers hear girls speak about how their own sexuality is enabled and constrained by social conventions, personal histories, and relational realities. That is, girls' relationships with their own bodies, their internalized beliefs about femininity that shape their identity formation processes and their relationships with others in their lives, emerge as central to girls' sexuality when researchers listen to girls tell their own stories about their experiences.

Because they focus on sexual intercourse only to the extent that girls themselves do, these researchers do not assume heterosexuality and include lesbian and bisexual girls explicitly in their studies. Research grounded in girls' descriptions and discussions of their experiences of sexuality has, in a sense, happened upon the centrality of relationships in the meaning that girls ascribe to their experiences with sexuality and thus elaborate how girls intertwine their sexuality and their relationships in the decisions they make. A limitation of this methodology is that there remain unanswered questions about the prevalence of these paradigms in general and specific populations of girls, as well as what specific variables may be associated with particular experiences of relationships. In the remainder of this chapter, I review some of the most informative studies within this body of scholarship. Much of this research has been conducted in Britain, perhaps because the shift in methods represented has been accepted more readily by the British academic psychology community. It is important to note that there are cultural differences between Britain and the United States, yet there are also similarities based on a shared heritage of a patriarchal, puritanical history, in which much of the analyses described here are rooted.

Relational Complexity in Girls' Sexuality: Strategies for Negotiating Safer Sex

The Women, Risk and AIDS Project (WRAP) collected accounts from 150 British young women, ages 16 to 21, from diverse cultural and class backgrounds about their heterosexual relationships. This collective of feminist sociologists explored girls' strategies for negotiating safer sex and identified obstacles to girls' abilities to make safer choices (Holland, Ramazanoglu, & Scott, 1990; Holland, Ramazanoglu, Scott, Sharpe, &

Thomson, 1992a, 1992b). They reported "overwhelming documentation" of inequalities of power in sexual relationships and encounters that are determined by boys' interests, needs, and desires. They also found "possibilities of negotiation in sexual relations" on the part of girls, which occur within a framework of social constraints, including (a) male pressure that can be as intense as male violence; (b) passive femininity; (c) girls' sense of responsibility for male sexuality; and (d) a "missing discourse of desire," as described by Michelle Fine (1988). Holland and her colleagues identified "femininity" as an "unsafe sexual strategy." They also found that sexual practice is neither consistent nor predictable for individual girls or for girls as a group. In a sense, young women have to be prepared to lose valued social relationships in order to assert control over their own sexuality. They are in a double bind because they need to take initiative in sexual situations, as well as to admit that they are being sexual, while they want to be conventionally feminine, which is by definition to be passive and sexually inexperienced (see also Woodhouse, 1982).

In particular, Holland and her colleagues (Holland et al., 1990; Holland et al., 1992a, 1992b) found that relationships not only were central for girls in their experiences of their sexuality but also defined the meaning of sexuality for girls. Holland et al. offer a counterintuitive analysis of how relationships function in girls' choices about sexual safety. The meanings that girls understand, which are conferred on relationships by the use of contraceptives and condoms, can create problems for them. The interplay between trust and risk emerged as key in girls' choices. Girls were concerned that asking a partner to use condoms would be seen by boys as a signal of distrust; a girl demonstrated her trust, love, and commitment by not asking her boyfriend to use a condom. At the same time, without intimacy, making such a request is difficult and potentially dangerous; such a request could be perceived by a boy as impugning negative qualities, and thus the threat of violence looms large. Overall, girls reported that it was difficult for them to make demands of boyfriends for their own needs and for their own safety. They also described lacking confidence about sexuality and reported a fear of being too knowledgeable and thus subject to being labeled a "slut" if they evidence sexual desires. Holland et al. concluded that girls may abandon safer sex in favor of a clear statement about the importance of a relationship.

Holland and her colleagues (Holland et al., 1992a) also found that a small group of young women in their study stood out from the rest of the sample by evidencing a sense of empowerment about their own sexuality. Specifically distinguishing between empowerment, which includes a sense of entitlement and rights to one's own pleasure and agency, and being simply more assertive in safer sex practices, they investigated different empowerment strategies that girls reported. They discovered three levels of empowerment: (a) intellectual, which consists of the knowledge, expectations, and intentions that girls bring to sexual experiences; (b) experiential, which is the level of girls' sexual practice; and (c) a transitional level, in which girls are empowered to exert control in some sexual contexts but not in others. More of the girls exhibited intellectual power than experiential power. Holland et al. found that, in practice, trying to take control and resist a passive model of female sexuality did not suffice for effective sexual empowerment; a recognition and challenge to male power was also required to enable girls to exert control and choice in their sexual experiences. In conclusion, Holland et al. identified women's conceptions of masculinity and femininity and broader social pressures, as well as men's behavior, as sources of challenge to a positive female sexuality.

Negotiating the Conventions of Romance

Having surveyed the larger sociocultural contexts within which girls are negotiating a developing sense of themselves as sexual within relational contexts, feminist studies begin with an analysis of how romance offers girls a structure for engaging with and interpreting their relationships and their own sexuality. In particular, Sharon Thompson (1984, 1995) has explored how the conventions of romance, which idealize male aggression, female passivity, an absence of female sexual desire, and the benefits of male protection, as well as fantasies about and the realities of pregnancy and reproduction, shape girls' experiences with sexuality.

Thompson conducted a large interview-based study with over 400 girls from diverse racial, ethnic, and class backgrounds, as well as from a spectrum of sexual orientations, from across the United States. She grouped these girls according to the "genre" or type of stories that they told about sex, romance, and pregnancy: "victims of love," popular narrators, successful girls, girls who became teen mothers, "hell year" narrators, lesbian narrators, and girls who actively sought out adult lovers as a route to sexual experience. Finally, she identified a relatively small group of girls whom she called "equality narrators," who engaged with but decentered romance such that they were able to maintain a strong sense of self. These girls kept their girlfriends and thus their ability to be part of collective analysis and action, did not divide girls into "good" and "bad" according to their sexual choices, and were willing to give up a relationship if they felt endangered.

In analyzing a White, working-class subset of this sample, Thompson (1990) reported that she heard two different stories of sexual initiation: One, told by 75% of this group of girls, revealed pain, boredom, coercion, and an absence of desire; the other group of girls, who she calls "pleasure narrators," included their own desire, agency, pleasure, and entitlement to protected sex in their stories of first sexual intercourse. She observed that this smaller group had mothers who spoke to them in positive ways about female sexuality, telling them about the pleasures and possibilities of masturbation, orgasm, a sense of connection to another person through sex, and the responsibilities that accompany such active sexuality. Thompson (1991) also described a second small group of pleasure narrators who were African American teen mothers. These girls articulated a sense of agency in their relationships with male lovers, marking a strong contrast with how young women who have more social privilege described dealing with boys. Thompson noted that "they portray themselves as strong women who take their pleasure and defend their body and their rights . . . [who] preserve a sense of power and freedom in the face of overwhelming circumstances" (1991, p. 22).

Thompson found that girls made meaning of their sexuality and their sexual experiences through the relationships in which they were involved. In particular, she identified how girls described love as a constitutive aspect of their experience of sexuality and found that girls who fell in love as a way of legitimating their sexual experience seemed more vulnerable to profound hurt and disappointment than girls who did not embrace an equation of love and sex. Other feminist researchers have noted how girls are encouraged to conflate love and desire under the terms of a patriarchal romance story (i.e., Lees, 1987) and how this way of dealing with a social system that disallows girls their desire can put them at risk psychologically and in relationships (Tolman & Higgins, 1996). Thompson also found that friends played an important role in how girls organized, learned about, and made sense of their sexual and relational experiences. They told about learning from their girlfriends, through observation and through discussion, both good and bad ways to manage relationships and to regulate their emotions and their sexuality—often an important aspect of maintaining much-desired relationships with boys.

Other feminist researchers have examined how girls describe the role of reputation and their social relationships in their experiences and negotiations of sexuality and their identities. Sue Lees (1987, 1996) collected narratives about school, friendship, marriage, and the future from one hundred 15- and 16-year-old British girls in the early 1980s. Unexpected was the pervasive and significant impact of sexuality and gender relations, which these girls revealed in talking about other realms of their relational and social lives. Lees observed the great extent to which feminine identity and social relationships rest on sexual reputation. She reported how the use of "slag" (the British form of "slut") is used as a form of social control over girls, regulating as well as interpreting their behavioral choices and "forc[ing] girls to submit to a very unfair set of gender relations" (Lees, 1987, p. 6). To avoid being called a slag, these girls accepted moral responsibility for male actions, including violence. In addition, the label "slag," which she noted is used ambiguously, reinforces racial as well as sexist stereotypes about women (Lees, 1993). The constant threat and fear of being ostracized by this label pressed girls to confuse sexual desire and love as a psychological and essentially practical defense against a negative identity and harmful social consequences, which then motivated them to enter or to stay in relationships with boys that were not, in fact, meaningful or even safe. In a more recent analysis, Jenny Kitzinger (1995) noted the persistence of these categories and their powerful organizing and regulatory effect on young British women's negotiations of their social relationships, as well as the impact on their psychic energy.

Sexual Identities: Negotiating Desire for Girls

Feminist researchers have also, to some degree, addressed girls' sexual identities. The taboo nature of homosexual desire in contemporary culture brings into strong relief the ways that sexuality is profoundly contextualized within a girl's relationships, not only with her sexual partner but also with her family, friends, community, school, and work. Mica Nava (1982) wrote about an ethnographic study of a 10-week project in Britain designed to support working-class girls' critical perspectives on gender roles, and her assessment of its lasting effects. As part of the project, a play was performed that addressed lesbian desire directly. She documented how the discussion that followed gave two adolescent girls an opportunity to tell their friends about their sexual identity and their friends a chance to lend their support to the lesbian girls, which included accompanying them to a lesbian club.

The lesbian girls were thus able to explore their sexuality safely, whereas the heterosexual girls had a chance to voice their contradictory observations and experiences about dealing with violence on the part of boys and men. After participating in the project, all of the girls described views that reflected an understanding of sexual identity as fluid and, when one of the lesbian girls was in an abusive relationship, an understanding that not all women are "good" and not all men are "bad." After interviewing the girls' mothers, their youth worker, and the girls themselves 2 years later, Nava (1982) concluded that as a result of the choices that both the heterosexual and the lesbian young women made regarding their behavior in public contexts, this short intervention had an indirect and permanent impact on the entire community's understanding and tolerance of lesbians.

Discourses of Desire

Michelle Fine's (1988) documentation of girls' "discourse of desire" in their conversations with her, teachers, and peers opened the question of how girls do, in fact, voice and experience desire. As I (Tolman, 1992) have observed, girls are able to speak in multiple ways about their sexuality:

in the acceptable discourses of the culture as a way of maintaining relationships and in ways that describe their experiences more accurately. In a study designed to understand how girls experienced their own sexual desire, I interviewed 30 urban and suburban juniors in high school (ages 15–18)[2] who described several different qualities of their relationship with their own bodies that were deeply contextualized by their relationships with boys, other girls, family, friends, their education, and cultural notions of female sexuality (Tolman, 1994a, 1994b, 1996; Tolman & Higgins, 1996). The majority of girls described their own desire in terms of a dilemma, contoured by how they could think of themselves and have others know them as good, acceptable, and normal girls and also acknowledge and act on their own sexual desire.

All of the girls in my study described an "erotic voice," that is, a clear knowledge of powerful sexual feelings in their bodies, which they observed often, though not exclusively, in the context of exploring sexuality in relationships with boys or other girls. Calling on Audre Lorde's (1984) use of the power of the erotic as the "yes within ourselves, our deepest cravings," (p. 34), I found that regardless of whether they lived in an urban or a suburban context, these girls' erotic voices reflected the intensity of their embodied experience (Tolman, 1994b). For instance, one girl said that she "knows" she is feeling desire when "my body says yes yes yes yes," whereas another said, "you just have this feeling, you just have to get rid of it." Yet another girl called desire "an overwhelming longing" and "a wicked urge," whereas still another said she is "extremely aware of every, every touch and everything" (p. 255). Girls' ability to speak of their embodied sexual feelings challenges the cultural convention of limiting girls' desire to a desire for relationships and suggests that one important relational process for girls may be determining how their physical and relational desires weave together.

I identified several different ways in which the girls to whom I listened related to their own sexual desire. Some girls described "silent bodies" or an absence of sexual feelings, despite experiences with sexual intercourse. Some girls were confused about whether they felt desire, and others described resisting their own feelings as a way to stay psychologically or socially safe. For instance, one young woman explained that feeling desire would put her educational goals at risk. Other girls described their exploration of sexual pleasure as intertwined with a developing knowledge of self in the context of trusting relationships with boyfriends who are not adversaries to be managed but partners with whom they sound out the contours of their embodied sexual connection (see also Bollerud, Christopherson, & Frank, 1989, for discussion of relationships with boyfriends as a context for attachment and partnered decision making).

---

[2]This large age span for a group of juniors in high school is due to the fact that many of the girls in the urban school were "old for grade," a common feature in urban school contexts.

Other girls in my study described a self-conscious choice to act on their own desire, voicing a critique of the double standard and unequal gender relations. Several of these girls who resisted the pressure to disconnect from their own desire also reported identifying and escaping experiences with sexual violence. As Paulina explained, a friend "wanted to have sexual intercourse and I didn't. I didn't have sex with him. He, he like pulled me over to the couch and I just kept on fighting. . . . I was just like begging him to like not to do anything and like, I really did not have like much choice. Because I had my hands behind me. And he just like kept on touching me, and I was like, just get off me. He goes, you know that you want to, and I said no I don't. Get off me, I hate you." (Tolman & Higgins, 1996, p. 220). In her interviews, Paulina claimed her sexual desire, described how it feels to have desire, and thus was able to know clearly when she was not having desire and, as in this situation, was being violated. In addition, she had a good grasp of the cultural double standard about desire for boys and girls—that "it's okay for a guy to have any feelings or anything, and the girl has to be this little virgin who is obedient to the men" (Tolman & Higgins, 1996, p. 219)—that she rejected.

In stark contrast to Paulina's narrative, another girl, Jenny, reported an incident that resonated with a description of date rape:

> "And then [her friend] asked me if I would have sex with him, and I said, well, I didn't think I, I mean I said I wanted to wait, 'cause I didn't want to. I mean I like him, but I don't *like* him so, and I mean he sorta pushed it on me, but it wasn't like I absolutely said no, don't. I . . . sort of let it happen to me and never like really said no, I don't want to do this. I mean I said no, but I never, I mean I never stopped him from doing anything. . . ." (Tolman & Higgins, 1996, p. 213).

Over the course of her interview, Jenny herself raised the possibility of rape yet, at the same time, doubted whether the male friend with whom she had sex could have raped her. Without access to knowing when she did feel desire, Jenny was also unable to identify its absence.

The context of possible sexual violence highlights the importance of a girl's ability to feel her own desire and to have it as a touchstone for interpreting her sexual experiences and for making sexual decisions. The context of a specific relationship can be crucial for the meanings that a girl ascribes to her feelings and behaviors as well as for her sense of the consequences that her decision can bring; in addition, the lack of a definitive decision, evidenced by girls in their frequent conclusion that "it just happened," may have important relational contours. Tracy Higgins and I concluded that there are both psychological strengths and legal consequences associated with a girl's ability to know and to voice her experience and sexual subjectivity.

In their narratives of desire, the majority of the girls in my study explained how they managed their desire to accommodate their relationships with boys, keeping their desire well disguised within acceptable feminine boundaries to avoid getting a bad reputation. The three bisexual and lesbian girls in this study located their desire as a source of danger and threat to their relationships with female friends, parents, and others (see also Nava, 1982). They also described how dealing with cultural norms of heterosexuality made it hard to stay connected with their desire for girls and to stay clear about their identity. Megan, who called herself bisexual, captured the pressure she felt to have a boyfriend: "Every teen magazine you look at is like, guy this, how to get a date, guys, guys, guys, guys, guys. So you're constantly faced with I have to have a boyfriend, I have to have a boyfriend, you know. . . . I've had that mentality for so long." (Tolman, 1994a, p. 334). Melissa, a self-named lesbian, described her awareness of how her sexual feelings for girls put her at risk of violence and threatened her friendships with heterosexual girls: "Well I'm really lucky that like nothing bad has happened or no one has gotten mad at me so far. . . . Whenever I start, I feel like I can't help looking at someone for more than a few seconds . . . I feel like I have to make myself not stare at them or something" (Tolman, 1994a, p. 336).

Dimensions of Desire: An Interplay of Qualitative and Quantitative Analyses

I heard a qualitative difference between urban and suburban girls' experiences of sexual desire: The urban girls I listened to voiced caution and fear of physical dangers and social consequences in their narratives, whereas the suburban girls described curiosity, inner conflict, and concern about how others think of them (Tolman, 1994a). Following up on this finding, Laura Szalacha and I (Tolman & Szalacha, 1999) conducted a quantitative analysis of the difference between the urban and suburban girls' experiences of sexual desire as expressed in their narratives and found a statistically significant difference between urban and suburban girls' associations with their own sexual desire: The urban girls were more likely to associate their desire with vulnerability, whereas the suburban girls were more likely to associate their desire with pleasure. In addition, we found an interaction between the girls' social location and reports of their sexual violence: Girls who were from the suburban setting and had not reported sexual violence were much more likely than any of the other girls to associate their own sexual feelings with pleasure. The suburban girls who had reported sexual violence and all of the urban girls were more likely to associate their sexual desire with vulnerability. A second qualitative analysis indicates that girls who have not been held hostage by environmental or personal exposures to violence voice an integration of their embodied and emotional feelings that is not audible among most of the other girls;

the exception is among the few girls who had experienced some form of violence but who also voiced a critique of patriarchal privileges associated with sexuality. These findings offer empirical support for a feminist theoretical and political position that claims sexual violence is a way of controlling women by pushing them out of relationship with themselves, their power, and their pleasure.

CONCLUSION

Sexuality is a profoundly relational aspect of human development and living. The centrality of relationships in girls' psychological development suggests the importance of relationships in girls' sexuality development, including girls' decisions about sexual behavior. The mainstream sexual decision-making literature suggests that girls' relationships are an important aspect of their sexuality. Feminist research begins to offer a nuanced understanding of the relational context of girls' sexuality development. This body of work suggests that to take girls' relational contexts seriously in our research demands a focus on the meanings of sexuality and sexual decisions and the processes by which girls develop their sexuality beyond their choice to have sexual intercourse.

REFERENCES

Baumeister, L. M., Flores, E., & Marin, B. V. (1995). Sex information given to Latina girls by parents. *Health Education Research: Theory and Practice, 10*, 233–239.

Billy, J. O. G., Brewster, K. L., & Grady, W. R. (1994). Contextual effects on the sexual behavior of adolescent women. *Journal of Marriage and the Family, 56*, 387–404.

Boldero, J., Moore, S. D., & Rosenthal, D. M. (1992). Intention, context, and safe sex: Australian adolescents' responses to AIDS. *Journal of Applied Social Psychology, 22*, 1374–1396.

Bollerud, K. H., Christopherson, S. B., & Frank, E. S. (1989). Girls' sexual choices: Looking for what is right. The intersection of sexual and moral development. In C. Gilligan, N. P. Lyons, & T. J. Hanmer (Eds.), *Making connections: The relational worlds of adolescent girls at Emma Willard School* (pp. 274–285). Cambridge, MA: Harvard University Press.

Breakwell, G. M., Millward, L. J., & Fife-Shaw, C. (1994). Commitment to "safer" sex as a predictor of condom use among 16–20 year olds. *Journal of Applied Social Psychology, 24*, 189–217.

Brooks-Gunn, J., & Furstenberg, F. F. (1989). Adolescent sexual behavior. *American Psychologist, 44*, 249–257.

Brooks-Gunn, J., & Paikoff, R. L. (1993). "Sex is a gamble, kissing is a game":

Adolescent sexuality and health promotion. In S. G. Millstein, A. C. Petersen, & E. O. Nightingale (Eds.), *Promoting the health of adolescents: New directions for the twenty-first century* (pp. 180–208). New York: Oxford University Press.

Brown, L. M., & Gilligan, C. (1992). *Meeting at the crossroads: Women's psychology and girls' development.* Cambridge, MA: Harvard University Press.

Cervera, N. J. (1993). Decision making for pregnant adolescents: Applying reasoned action theory to research and treatment. *Families in Society, 74,* 355–365.

Cooper, M. L., Peirce, R. S., & Huselid, R. (1994). Substance use and sexual risk taking among Black and White adolescents. *Health Psychology, 13,* 251–262.

Debold, E. (1996). *Knowing bodies: Gender identity, cognitive development and embodiment in early childhood and early adolescence.* Unpublished doctoral dissertation, Harvard University, Graduate School of Education.

Debold, E., Wilson, M., & Malave, I. (1993). *Mother daughter revolution.* New York: Addison-Wesley.

Di Blasio, F. A, & Benda, B. B. (1992). Gender differences in theories of adolescent sexual activity. *Sex Roles, 27,* 221–239.

Doll, J., & Ajzen, I. (1992). Accessibility and stability of predictors in the theory of planned behavior. *Journal of Personality and Social Psychology, 63,* 754–765.

Duncan-Ricks, E. N. (1992). Adolescent sexuality and peer pressure. *Child and Adolescent Social Work Journal, 9,* 319–327.

East, P. L. (1996). The younger sisters of childbearing adolescents: Their attitudes, expectations and behaviors. *Child Development, 67,* 267–282.

East, P. L., & Felice, M. E. (1992). Pregnancy risk among the younger sisters of pregnant and childbearing adolescents. *Developmental and Behavioral Pediatrics, 13,* 128–136.

East, P. L., Felice, M. E., & Morgan, M. C. (1993). Sisters' and girlfriends' sexual and childbearing behavior: Effects on early adolescent girls' sexual outcomes. *Journal of Marriage and the Family, 55,* 953–963.

Fine, M. (1988). Sexuality, schooling and adolescent females: The missing discourse of desire. *Harvard Educational Review, 58,* 29–53.

Fishbein, M., & Ajzen, I. (1975). *Belief, attitude, intention, and behavior: An introduction to theory and research.* Reading, MA: Addison-Wesley.

Gerrard, M., Gibbons, F. X., & Boney-McCoy, S. (1993). Emotional inhibition of effective contraception. *Anxiety, Stress and Coping, 6,* 73–88.

Gibbons, F. X., Gerrard, M., & Boney-McCoy, S. (1995). Prototype perception predicts (lack of) pregnancy prevention. *Personality and Social Psychology Bulletin, 21,* 85–93.

Holland, J., Ramazanoglu, C., & Scott, S. (1990). *Sex, risk, danger: AIDS education policy and young women's sexuality* (WRAP Paper 1). London: Tufnell Press.

Holland, J., Ramazanoglu, C., Scott, S., Sharpe, S., & Thomson, R. (1992a). Pressure, resistance, empowerment: Young women and the negotiation of safer sex. In P. Aggleton, P. Davies, & G. Hart (Eds.), *AIDS: Rights, risk and reason* (pp. 142–162). Washington, DC: Falmer Press.

Holland, J., Ramazanoglu, C., Scott, S., Sharpe, S., & Thomson, R. (1992b). Risk, power and the possibility of pleasure: Young women and safer sex. *AIDS Care, 4*, 273–283.

Ingham, R., Woodcock, A., & Stenner, K. (1992). The limitations of rational decision-making models as applied to young people's sexual behavior. In P. Aggleton, P. Davies, & G. Hart (Eds.), *AIDS: Rights, risk and reason* (pp. 163–173). Washington, DC: Falmer Press.

Johnson, S. A., & Green, V. (1993). Female adolescent contraceptive decision making and risk taking. *Adolescence, 28*, 81–96.

Jorgensen, S. R., & Sonstegard, J.S. (1984). Predicting adolescent sexual and contraceptive behavior: An application and test of the Fishbein model. *Journal of Marriage and the Family, 46*, 43–55.

Kitzinger, J. (1995). "I'm sexually active but I'm powerful": Young women negotiating sexual reputation. *Women's Studies International Forum, 18*, 187–196.

Lees, S. (1987). Sexual reputation, morality and the social control of girls: A British study. In Aspects of school culture and the social control of girls. *European University Institute Series, 87*(Serial No. 301), 1–20.

Lees, S. (1993). *Sugar and spice: Sexuality and adolescent girls.* London: Penguin Books.

Lees, S. (1996). *Losing out: Adolescent girls and sexuality.* London: Hutchinson.

Lock, S. E., & Vincent, M. L. (1995). Sexual decision-making among rural adolescent females. *Health Values, 19*, 47–58.

Lorde, A. (1984). *Sister outsider.* Freedom, CA: Crossing Press.

Luker, K. (1975). *Taking chances: Abortion and the decision not to contracept.* Berkeley: University of California Press.

Morris, L., Warren, C., & Aral, S. (1993). Measuring adolescent sexual behaviors and related health outcomes. *Public Health Reports, 108*(Suppl. 1), 31–35.

Nathanson, C. (1991). *Dangerous passage: The social control of sexuality in women's adolescence.* Philadelphia: Temple University Press.

Nava, M. (1982). "Everybody's views are just broadened": A girls project and some responses to lesbianism. *Feminist Review, 10*, 37–59.

Newcomb, M. D., Huba, G. J., & Bentler, P. M. (1986). Determinants of sexual and dating behaviors among adolescents. *Journal of Personality and Social Psychology, 50*, 428–438.

Norris, A., & Ford, K. (1995). Condom use by low-income African American and Hispanic youth with a well-known partner: Integrating the health belief model, theory of reasoned action and the construct accessibility model. *Journal of Applied Social Psychology, 25*, 1801–1830.

Petersen, A. C., Leffert, N., & Graham, B. (1995). Adolescent development and the emergence of sexuality. *Suicide and Life Threatening Behavior, 25*(Suppl.), 4–17.

Philliber, S., Namerow, P. B., Kaye, J. W., & Kunkes, C. H. (1986). Pregnancy risk taking among adolescents. *Journal of Adolescent Research, 1,* 463–481.

Pick, S., & Andrade-Palos, P. (1995). Impact of the family on the sex lives of adolescents. *Adolescence, 30,* 667–675.

Reinecke, J., Schmidt, P., & Ajzen, I. (1996). Application of the theory of planned behavior to adolescents' condom use: A panel study. *Journal of Applied Social Psychology, 269,* 749–772.

Resnick, M. D., & Blum, R. W. (1985). Developmental and personalogical correlates of adolescent sexual behavior and outcome. *International Journal of Adolescent Medicine and Health, 1,* 293–313.

Rosenthal, D. A., Hall, C., & Moore, S. M. (1992). AIDS, adolescents, and sexual risk taking: A test of the health belief model. *Australian Psychologist, 27,* 166–171.

Smith, E. A., Udry, J. R., & Morris, N. M. (1985). Pubertal development and friends: A biosocial explanation of adolescent sexual behavior. *Journal of Health and Social Behavior, 26,* 183–192.

St. Lawrence, J. S., Brasfield, T. L., Jefferson, K. W., Allyene, E., & Shirley, A. (1994). Social support as a factor in African-American adolescent's sexual risk behavior. *Journal of Adolescent Research, 9,* 292–310.

Taylor, J. M., Gilligan, C., & Sullivan, A. M. (1995). *Between voice and silence: Women and girls, race and relationship.* Cambridge, MA: Harvard University Press.

Thompson, S. (1984). Search for tomorrow: On feminism and the reconstruction of teen romance. In C. Vance (Ed.), *Pleasure and danger: Exploring female sexuality* (pp. 350–384). Boston: Routledge & Kegan Paul.

Thompson, S. (1990). Putting a big thing into a little hole: Teenage girls' accounts of sexual initiation. *Journal of Sex Research, 27,* 341–361.

Thompson, S. (1991). "Drastic entertainments": Teenage mothers' signifying narratives. In F. Ginsberg & A. Ising (Eds.), *Uncertain terms* (pp. 269–287). Boston: Beacon Press.

Thompson, S. (1995). *Going all the way: Teenage girls' tales of sex, romance and pregnancy.* New York: Farrar, Straus & Giroux.

Tolman, D. L. (1992). Adolescent girls, women and sexuality: Discerning dilemmas of desire. In C. Gilligan, A. Rogers, & D. Tolman (Eds.), *Women, girls and psychotherapy: Reframing resistance* (pp. 55–70). New York: Haworth Press.

Tolman, D. L. (1994a). Doing desire: Adolescent girls' struggles with/for sexuality. *Gender & Society, 8,* 324–342.

Tolman, D. L. (1994b). Daring to desire: Culture and the bodies of adolescent girls. In J. Irvine (Ed.), *Sexual cultures: Adolescent communities and the construction of identity* (pp. 250–284). Philadelphia: Temple University Press.

Tolman, D. L. (1996). Adolescent girls: Debunking the myth of the urban girl. In B. Ross-Leadbeater & N. Way (Eds.), *Urban girls: Resisting stereotypes, creating identities* (pp. 255–271). New York: New York University Press.

Tolman, D. L., & Higgins, T. E. (1996). How being a good girl can be bad for girls. In N. Bauer-Maglin & D. Perry (Eds.), *Bad girls/good girls* (pp. 205–225). New Brunswick, NJ: Rutgers University Press.

Tolman, D. L., & Szalacha, L. (1999). Dimensions of desire: Bridging qualitative and quantitative methods in a study of female adolescent sexuality. *Psychology of Women Quarterly, 23,* 9–41.

Tucker, S. K. (1989, Summer). Adolescent patterns of sexual communication about sexually related topics. *Adolescence, 24*(94), 269–278.

Vicary, J. R., Klingaman, L. R., & Harkness, W. L. (1995). Risk factors associated with date rape and sexual assault of adolescent girls. *Journal of Adolescence, 18,* 289–306.

Warzak, W. J., Grow, C. R., Poler, M. M., & Walburn, J. N. (1995). Enhancing refusal skills: Identifying contexts that place adolescents at risk for adolescent sexual activity. *Developmental and Behavioral Pediatrics, 16,* 98–100.

Woodhouse, A. (1982). Sexuality, femininity and fertility control. *Women's Studies International Forum, 5,* 1–15.

Zimmerman, R. S., Sprecher, S., Langer, L. M., & Holloway, C. D. (1995). Adolescents' perceived ability to say "no" to unwanted sex. *Journal of Adolescent Research, 10,* 383–399.

IV

COPING, NEGOTIATING, AND PROBLEM SOLVING IN COMMUNITY CONTEXTS

INTRODUCTION

DENISE M. DeZOLT

Adolescent girls find themselves involved in a myriad of settings that speak to, and sometimes ignore, their strengths and needs. In this section, we explore the worlds of adolescent girls in the context of community. Specifically, we consider the current research about their experiences and involvement in schools, community and religious systems, the health care community, and the juvenile justice system. Several major themes emerge across the three chapters.

First, it is clear from the review of research on adolescent girls that psychologists have much still to learn. Part of our current knowledge is limited by underrepresentation of studies that examine adolescent girls in general as well as those that have explicitly considered social class, race, and ethnicity as consequential variables in the research design. These same limitations may be applied to the types of intervention strategies and treatment approaches used with adolescent girls.

Despite these limitations, we found consistently across the three chapters that the development of adolescent girls' coping, negotiation, and problem-solving strategies was necessary for them to function optimally in these community contexts. Furthermore, we found that programs related to the enhancement of personal, social, and cultural competence that promoted coconstruction of norms facilitated the development of adolescent girls. We also saw the importance of having strong, supportive, and culturally relevant role models in promoting their development. Across the three chapters emerged the importance of responsive systems that collaborated with one another, were informed about strengths and needs of adolescent girls, and included their perspectives in design, implementation, and evaluation.

From a research and policy perspective, we found across all three chapters the need for further study of both efficacy and effectiveness of interventions. We saw the need for a systematic approach to research that involves young women who differ in age, race, ethnicity, and class in asking the research questions and in participating in the research agenda. In addition, our examination led us to see the need for interventions that are designed, implemented, and evaluated with participation of the major stakeholders, that is, the adolescent girls.

In chapter 11, "Adolescent Girls' Experiences in School and Community Settings," Denise M. DeZolt and Mary Henning-Stout examine adolescent girls as they encountered school, religious institutions, and community-based programs. Across settings, they discuss factors that support the development of adolescent girls as well as those that seem to interfere. Stories and narrative are used throughout to illustrate both the experiences of young women and the findings from the research literature. DeZolt and Henning-Stout examine gender equity, curricular concerns, differential socialization and treatment in schools by sex, lesbian and bisexual experiences, and patterns of sexual harassment in schools. For many adolescent girls, the school setting is both supportive and challenging. Next, they consider adolescent girls' involvement in community-based youth organizations. Such settings have the potential for promoting positive development across class, ethnicity, and race. In their discussion of the role of religiosity in adolescent girls' lives, DeZolt and Henning-Stout point to both the positive aspects, such as decision-making skills and contraception use, as well as the potential problem areas, such as the reinforcement of differential socialization and location of females in society. To illustrate the types of experiences and programs that enhance the development of adolescent girls, the authors next describe the Girls' Leadership Center, a project designed to enhance the leadership of adolescent girls. The project embodies many of the characteristics found to support girls' development, such as contextual relevance, participatory project development, community mentors, and community service. DeZolt and Henning-Stout then conclude with questions to consider in research and practice with adolescent girls.

From the perspective of the justice system, Michele Harway and Marsha Liss discuss primarily partner or dating violence and teen prostitution in chapter 12, "Dating Violence and Teen Prostitution: Adolescent Girls in the Justice System." The authors examine the prevalence data of these two aspects of adolescent girls' involvement in the juvenile justice system. They explore issues of ethnicity and point to the problematic disparities in representation across racial and ethnic groups that make it difficult to report an accurate view of the nature and extent of concern. From a theoretical perspective focusing on identity development, the authors examine the relationship between self-esteem and violence among adolescent girls involved in the justice system. In particular, they explore the role of voice in the context of relationships as well as notions of psychological dissociation and political resistance as forms for dealing with violence. As they conclude the chapter, Harway and Liss suggest intervention strategies that are participatory and involve adolescent girls, that are prevention focused, and that incorporate multiple systems' involvement. Finally, they conclude with recommendations for future research in the areas of prostitution and dating violence, including a closer examination of protective factors that increase resistance and reduce risk.

Denise M. Dougherty, in chapter 13, "Health Care for Adolescent Girls," examines adolescent girls' involvement in the health care system from a biopsychosocial perspective. From the backdrop of her description of the health care system in the United States, Dougherty stresses the unique aspects of adolescent girls as health care consumers in relation to their dependency status, epidemiological patterns, and developmental factors. In addition, she discusses limitations in research including efficacy and effectiveness data and the types of strategies that benefit adolescent girls. She further stresses the importance of hearing from these young women their perspectives concerning health care experiences and needs. Dougherty points out the full range of challenges faced by the health care system related to services to adolescents from guidance about health issues through appropriate diagnosis and treatment. In her examination of crosscutting issues, Dougherty focuses on the importance of participatory involvement of adolescent girls in their health care needs in conjunction with defining the role of care providers vis-à-vis adolescent girls' access to service and parental support or knowledge. Regarding health care research across diverse populations, Dougherty points out the limitations and proposes both an approach to research and a policy agenda that are responsive across gender, age, ethnicity, race, and class.

11

ADOLESCENT GIRLS' EXPERIENCES IN SCHOOL AND COMMUNITY SETTINGS

DENISE M. DeZOLT AND MARY HENNING-STOUT

In a middle school counselor's office, Anna reports being fondled in the hallway. The counselor tells her the halls are just too crowded and that none of the boys in that school would do such a thing anyway. Anna remembers that when she turned around in the hall and yelled, "Hey, stop that!" to the boys who were squeezing her breasts, they had looked at her with sad and confused faces and said, "We didn't do anything!" It doesn't take long for Anna to get the picture. Her version of reality doesn't hold up next to the reality that others are constructing. As psychologists, educators, counselors, and other concerned individuals endeavor to understand Anna's reality, several questions emerge. How is her experience similar to that of other adolescent girls in schools across race, ethnicity, culture, class, and sexual orientation? How are schools addressing issues of equity, harassment, and heterosexism? What factors seem to support the academic experiences of adolescent girls? What do community-based programs have to offer them? What support will they find in their religious institutions?

In an effort to address these questions, we approach our discussion of adolescent girls' interactions in the broader context of community from a

253

social constructivist perspective. In doing so, we hold the position that values, knowledge, and behavioral norms are coconstructed by individuals within multiple sociocultural contexts. Two common contexts for adolescent girls are schools and community-based programs. In this chapter, we first consider the experiences of adolescent girls in school settings. Specifically, we review the research related to (a) differential socialization of girls and boys, (b) gender equity in curricula, (c) single-sex schools, (d) issues of school harassment, and (e) the experiences of lesbian and bisexual students in schools. We also discuss factors that promote the academic success not only of girls but also of students in general. Next, we explore the research findings regarding community programs, including religious institutions, in which adolescent girls are embedded. Within these contexts, there are factors that support the developing skills of young women as well as other factors that promote gender stereotypes. Then, we describe the Girl's Leadership Center (GLC) at Lewis and Clark College, a project for, about, and with adolescent girls developed to facilitate responsive school and community collaboration to enhance girls' strengths and to address their needs. Through the GLC, women and adolescent girls from many walks of life meet together to support, to teach, and to learn from one another. Stories and narrative from our current research are shared throughout to provide a place for girls' voices and experiences as we discuss findings about them. We conclude our review with questions yet to be answered about the school- and community-based experiences of adolescent girls across race, class, culture, ethnicity, and sexual orientation.

NAVIGATING CLASSROOMS AND CORRIDORS

It's Wednesday afternoon in an alternative high school that serves immigrant and refugee students and others with behavioral concerns that interfere with their success in traditional academic settings. It's time for the class entitled "Race, Class, and Gender" to meet. The coteachers and three female and seven male students from a variety of social class, racial, and ethnic backgrounds constitute the class. Today they are discussing examples of race, class, and gender as they manifest themselves in our everyday world. Maria, Nadja, and Millicent sit together; the boys are scattered around the room. Tony, the first to volunteer, takes out a 20 dollar bill for discussion and says, "Yeah, look whose face is on this. It's some president." Mike, the coteacher, inquires about faces of people of color on American currency. A discussion ensues about the Anglocentric nature of American currency and its relationship to power. The students agree that there are only White faces on the money they use. Erin, the coteacher, asks what else they notice about this money. Then, in a certain and strong voice, Maria points out, "You don't see no faces of *women* on money."

"Yeah!" both Nadja and Millicent respond to support Maria's observation. Before they have an opportunity to continue, another male student interrupts, "If there's girls' faces on money it'd be on food stamps." His comment is greeted with laughter from the boys and silence from the girls. Marcus adds, "They're the ones on welfare, so why not put their picture on the food stamps." Despite the efforts of the teachers to capitalize on this teachable moment, the girls disengage from the discussion, and the boys continue with their examples. Ten minutes later, Maria attempts once again to explain her position. "Yeah, but what you say, that's not fair. Like, there's reasons we're on welfare, but I'm not. And men, they can be on welfare, too." Her comments are virtually ignored. The class has moved on to other issues. The story of three adolescent girls as they engage in a group discussion of symbols of power with their male counterparts illustrates and is related to several of the key research findings regarding adolescent girls' experiences in school settings. The vignette depicts situations that are consistent with findings from the American Association of University Women (AAUW; 1992) report and Myra and David Sadker's (1994) research. For example, Tony is the first to respond, and the first to be called on, to present his example of the day's topic. Consistent with the findings, the male student was quicker to respond, was called on first, and his comments were acknowledged. Young women are likely to censor or closely monitor their ideas. When Maria stated her ideas, she was laughed at and ignored, even in a course in which issues of gender were a central component. In this section, we discuss the findings of major research efforts on gender equity, single-sex schools, sexual harassment, and lesbian and bisexual experiences in schools.

Issues of Equity in Schools

From the moment children enter school, the female presence becomes apparent. For example, elementary schools are primarily staffed by female teachers and operate on rules, typically perceived as female oriented, such as manners, obedience, compliance, orderliness, and cleanliness. Although teachers view the perfect student as one who meets these criteria, girls who *do* tend to receive less attention. When given reinforcement for complying with these rules, girls are inadvertently encouraged to become even less assertive. Title IX of the Elementary and Secondary Education Act prohibits sex discrimination in education across areas such as athletics, admissions, financial aid, and physical and mental health. Despite this legislation and recent progress in gender equity in educational settings, one finds the needs of girls and young women in America's schools in general are not considered explicitly in recent education reform (AAUW, 1992; Sadker & Sadker, 1994) and goal setting (see National Education Goals, U.S. Department of Education, 1991).

The AAUW has assumed a leadership role in the examination of gender issues in the schools. Specifically, in *Shortchanging Girls, Shortchanging America*, (AAUW, 1991) and *The AAUW Report: How Schools Shortchange Girls* (AAUW, 1992), the AAUW provided troubling results regarding the major findings on the experiences of many girls in schools. Previous chapters have reviewed results of the AAUW (1991) large-scale study of self-esteem, career aspirations, educational experiences, and math and science interests of 3,000 girls and boys ages 9 to 15 years. Here, we consider another component of the AAUW effort. Specifically, we focus on two aspects of the AAUW 1992 report on the status of girls in America's schools, prepared by the Wellesley College Center for Research on Women (as commissioned by the AAUW). We first consider findings about several aspects of curriculum that influence the experiences of adolescent girls; next, we review the findings about girls' participation in extracurricular activities.

In the AAUW (1992) report, gender bias in both the latent and the manifest curricula was clearly evident. Research findings reported continued bias in current educational practices, perpetuating through the hidden curriculum the tacit assumptions of the roles of boys and girls. For example, boys received more teacher attention and were allotted more time to talk in class. Teachers, regardless of their sex or race, interacted more with boys, gave them feedback that was more precise and useful, and provided them with more feedback than girls received. Student–teacher interactions favored boys in accepting poor or even wrong answers, posing higher level questions, providing positive feedback, and responding to requests for help. Notably, educators were typically not sensitive to the presence or the potential impact of bias, although they were amenable to training to promote equity in the classrooms. With such training, classrooms typically became more equitable across gender lines.

When commonly used textbooks, materials, and activities were examined, findings revealed that in contrast to inclusive and affirmative elements of curriculum, in matters of gender equity, girls were often rendered as stereotypic, invisible, misrepresented, and marginalized. Examinations of patterns of course enrollment and achievement also revealed gender-differential course selection within tracking patterns, typically with boys in higher level or advanced courses, especially in math and science, or with boys and girls in gender-stereotypic vocational programs. Such patterns have implications for the career choices and opportunities for adolescent girls. In addition, adolescent girls receive clear messages about their relative unimportance, status, and power.

With regard to participation in extracurricular activities and sports, the AAUW (1992) study found that despite increases in adolescent girls' participation, most extracurricular activities were still male dominated across races. In addition, Latina, Asian, and Black girls were less participatory than White girls (for 8th graders), with Latinas having the least participation. There are exceptions to these findings. For example, Black and Asian adolescent girls were more or as likely to participate in science activities and media such as the yearbook or newspaper. These findings are particularly salient for two reasons. First, despite low participation of high-school-age Latinas, those who were involved in extracurricular activities were more likely to complete school and to pursue higher education. Second, by not participating, adolescent girls limited their potential involvement with mentors and role models and missed out on situations that could help them develop leadership and collaborative skills.

Other research has supported the AAUW (1992) findings. For example, in their examination of sexism in America's schools, Myra and David Sadker (1994) reported similar findings in their review of 20 years of research that have continuously demonstrated the differential treatment and experiences of girls and boys in school settings, mostly to the detriment of girls. Specifically, in high school years, many girls have continued to avoid courses that influence their future academic and career opportunities, such as math, science, and technology.

Given this disheartening research evidence, the AAUW has continued the effort to support girls in schools. To this end, the AAUW collaborates with educators, community coalitions, and business and industry to determine and understand those institutional climates and to support factors that enhance the likelihood of success for girls in school. In *Growing Smart: What's Working for Girls in Schools*, the AAUW (1995) provided a review of over 500 studies regarding those factors that facilitate girls' development in schools. Most recently, the AAUW (1996) report, *Girls in the Middle: Working to Succeed in School*, provided a qualitative analysis of middle school girls' experiences and specific factors that promote more equitable school climates. These efforts and those of other researchers (Eccles, 1989; Gilbert, 1996; Sadker & Sadker, 1994) regarding differential socialization in school settings have revealed several classroom environment and teacher factors that promote success for female students. Such factors included the use of inclusive (i.e., nonsexist, nonracist) materials and instructional techniques, lower levels of competitiveness, and higher levels of innovative learning in the classroom. Also, when girls were recognized as key players in their own lives and made connections with caring adults, they were more likely to meet with success. In addition, girls also benefited from liking the teacher and receiving high levels of teacher attention. The importance of a relationship emerged from these findings.

When adolescent girls talk about their experiences with teachers, they tell stories about their relationships (DeZolt, 1992, 1997) that include an interpersonal caring connection in the context of facilitating academic rigor. Genella, a high school senior, described her experience with teachers who recognized the relational aspect of teaching and the importance of holding students to high standards rather than "dumbing down" the curriculum.

> The teachers here, they just care about us. Like they don't just tell us what to do in class and forget about us. It's like we're real people with stuff going on in our lives. They make us work, too, real hard. But you want to because they believe we can do it, and we can. Not like in other schools I've been to where they think you're just stupid or something and give you worksheets and stuff.

These observations highlight the contradiction between what many girls need from their teachers and the roles and methods often required of teachers. Specifically, Genella articulated the concurrent nature of her relational and content–academic needs. In contrast, teachers find themselves faced with responsibilities as information transmitters, gatekeepers of resource acquisition, dispensers of rewards and punishments, and purveyors of competition. In addition, many teachers must use state-mandated curricula that fail to include the concerns of adolescent girls across social class, race, gender, sexual orientation, and ethnicity. For example, textbook editors are likely to be men (Apple, 1998; Apple & Christian-Smith, 1991), and state-selected textbooks tend to be written from a traditional White male point of view (Applebee, 1993; Sleeter & Grant, 1991). These same textbooks often perpetuate a socially constructed heterosexist and patriarchal paradigm—a paradigm that renders adolescent girls' needs and experiences invisible, misrepresented, or marginalized (AAUW, 1992; Sleeter & Grant, 1991). Furthermore, textbooks that do portray a more gender-sensitive orientation are likely to oversimplify the interplay of race, culture, and social class. Teachers also may be required to use standardized methods for teaching and for evaluating student performance. These methods often preclude the use of pedagogical and responsive assessment practices (Henning-Stout, 1994; Van Manen, 1994) that consider the contextual nature of learning and the learner. With these practices, students become active, informed participants in the their assessment and learning and are able to bring their lived experiences to the learning process. Such practices have been found to enhance the teacher–student relationship, a key element of learning for many young women.

Single-Sex Schools

With such emphasis on enhancing learning for adolescent girls, what happens for girls who attend single-sex schools? The literature on the benefits to girls of single-sex in contrast to coeducational schools is equivocal at best. Furthermore, it is difficult to draw consistent conclusions, given the variety of methodological differences in studies. For example, the range of samples (e.g., from small single private or Catholic schools to large national databases such as the National Educational Longitudinal Study [U.S. Department of Education, National Center for Education Statistics, 1995]), the degree of control for student preenrollment variables, and the variability in outcome measures (e.g., achievement, psychological variables, and behavior) contribute to this lack of clarity. In addition, comparisons of single-sex and coeducational schools often do not consider the socio-cultural contexts of students today, including an analysis of gender inclusiveness of curricula.

Single-sex schools appear to offer a variety of benefits to young women (AAUW, 1992; Bauch, 1988; Campbell & Evans, 1996; Lee & Bryk, 1986; Sadker & Sadker, 1994). For example, students in all-girl schools reported higher self-esteem, were likely to pursue math and science programs of study, and explored a variety of career options. These schools may provide for young women the type of learning environment that is responsive to their needs and is likely to facilitate their success. In contrast, other researchers (LePore & Warren, 1997; Marsh, 1989, 1991; Shmurak, 1998) concluded, at best, mixed, but not definitive, advantages for girls who attend single-sex schools when compared with their counterparts in coeducational schools. In a recent extensive review of the research on single-sex schools, the AAUW (1998) concluded that there is no clear evidence overall of the benefits of single-sex schools for girls. Furthermore, the report contended that quality education that includes academic rigor, small class size, and teaching practices inclusive of gender equity benefits students in general.

The future of single-sex schools appears to be uncertain, and new ventures meet with resistance. One can look at, for example, the recent situation in which a New York City inner-city public school offered an educational program for at-risk girls. Despite the support of parents, school officials, and the students, the future of this program is in jeopardy, as proponents of equity in education protest that boys have not been offered comparable services that are supported by public dollars.

Sexual Harassment in School Settings

The scene is a small alternative high school. Students are talking in small groups. The word is that two female students are reluctant to come to school because they have been sexually harassed by some male students. One of the boys poked a broken antenna between the girls' legs while he and the other boys made sexual comments to them. The girls expected this school to be a safe place for them. They expected that they would be able to come here to learn in an inclusive environment. Yet these expectations have been challenged and this, in turn, challenges the faculty and the student body. To address these and other sexual harassment concerns, the faculty decide to invite representatives of a local community agency to implement a sexual harassment program in the school. In addition, the faculty begin to work on a sexual harassment policy for the school.

Young heterosexual, lesbian, and bisexual women across the country are voicing their concerns about sexual harassment in a variety of settings as a barrier to their education and subsequent employment satisfaction. High school students in general, and female students in particular, are reporting a high degree of sexual harassment (AAUW, 1992, 1993; Lee, Croninger, Linn, & Chen, 1996; Orenstein, 1994; Sadker & Sadker, 1994; Shakeshaft et al., 1995; Stein, Marshall, & Tropp, 1993; "What's happening," 1992). For example, according to findings from the AAUW (1993) study of 1,632 eighth through 11th-grade girls and boys from 79 public high schools, the majority (81%) of girls and boys in Grades 8 to 11 (85% and 76%, respectively) have reported some form of sexual harassment. Acts included, but were not limited to, such behaviors as sexual looks and comments; touching, grabbing, and pinching; brushing up against a person in a sexual manner; mooning and flashing; being called gay, lesbian, queer, or faggot. Research findings suggest that experiences of harassment may vary with regard to levels (nature and extent of the harassment), status of the harassers (educator or peer), and gender. For example, high school girls compared with high school boys rated behaviors in scenarios involving sexual harassment as more harassing and more inappropriate (Loredo, Reid, & Deaux, 1995). According to the AAUW (1993), students reported being sexually harassed by peers, teachers, administrators, and other school-related personnel. In their analysis of data from the AAUW (1993) study, Lee et al. (1996) found that of 1,203 students, 44% reported having been harassed by a school staff member, with 16% indicating that they had been harassed by a teacher. It seems that for many students, and for female students in particular, schools are not safe places.

Of great concern are the academic, emotional, and behavioral sequelae of sexual harassment. For example, according to the AAUW report (1993), girls who had experienced harassment reported decreased desire to attend school or to speak in class, decreased grades, and difficulty paying attention. In addition, they were embarrassed, self-conscious, frightened, less confident, and expressed reservation about the possibility of a romantic relationship. In terms of behavioral concerns, girls tended to avoid their harassers, to avoid certain locations, and to change friendship and recreation patterns. These sequelae suggest that young women are not able to benefit from learning opportunities in their educational environments, in part because of sexual harassment. In addition, for many students who have been harassed, getting help to address their concerns has proved quite difficult (Lee et al., 1996). The two female students in the story that opened this section found it difficult to return to school. By their own admission, they were afraid and ashamed; however, they sought and received help. In a girl's leadership group that has been initiated in their school, the girls have begun to talk about their feelings and options regarding sexual harassment in the school.

In response to greater public awareness of harassment, there has been an increase in the number of junior high and high schools that have developed policies against gender-related harassment (Roscoe, Strouse, Goodwin, Taracks, & Henderson, 1994). School systems are implementing relevant curricula (Stein, 1995) that address harassment as a serious matter, concurrent with a focus on building a school community that supports more appropriate and inclusive behavior. Government initiatives have begun to provide incentive and support for addressing these concerns. For example, the federal government as part of the Safe Schools Act of 1994 provided funding and technical assistance to promote safety, security, and an atmosphere of inclusiveness in schools (Stephens, 1994). The success of sexual harassment programs in schools warrants further examination before one can make definitive statements about their impact on the lives of adolescent girls.

Lesbian and Bisexual Experiences in Schools

As a high school student, Anne was a founding member of a student organization developed to address sexual orientation issues on campus with the goals to inform, to educate, and to support one another. The organization received support from the school multicultural advisor, selected faculty, and the school counselor. Reflecting on the first year of the group, Anne comments, "People would walk in our meetings, but did not take us seriously." Despite a schoolwide campaign effort to support the rights of gay, lesbian, and bisexual youth in her school, Anne recognized that many students still didn't really understand the issues. "I had a poster [about sexual orientation acceptance] on my locker when some boys pointed to me and said 'you're a lesbian.'" In addition, there were homophobic slurs written on the walls in the boys restroom, and "You fag" comments were commonly heard on campus. Now, 1 year later, Anne is in college. Returning to visit her high school, she is excited about the progress she sees. "This year the school is open—girls holding hands in an open and nurturing environment. The support group is quite active. It was exciting to see that baby grow up."

Anne's story is one of hopefulness. She and her colleagues recognized a problem, obtained support from school personnel, developed a plan to address the problem, encountered additional challenges, and met with success. What remains in question is how reflective her experiences are of other youth in schools confronted with homophobia and heterosexism on a daily basis.

To examine the school experiences of lesbian, gay, and bisexual (LGB) youth, it is necessary to consider the limitations of the research in this area (Radkowsky & Siegel, 1997; Schneider, 1989). Specifically, it is unclear how representative the samples are in research about sexual orientation, given such factors as variability in age of coming out and the use of self-identified samples. It is not certain how these factors differentiate study participants from others who do not choose to participate in studies of sexual orientation. Further confounding research and subsequent explanations of the findings regarding LGB concerns is controversy about essentialist and social constructivist explanations that posit distinctly different points of view. In addition, there is concern that research findings regarding gay men may be generalized to lesbian and bisexual individuals without due consideration of the heterogeneity of these groups. Thus, as Celia Kitzinger (1987) observed, even gay affirmative research may contribute to the marginalization of lesbians. Finally, despite the emergence of a body of work on bisexuality (Firestein, 1996; Hutchins & Kaahumanu, 1991; Rust, 1995), the specific experiences of bisexual and transgendered adolescents are minimally understood.

Although little work exists on the specific experiences of lesbian and female bisexual adolescents across race and ethnicity, in one area the evidence is clear. Victimization of sexual minorities across settings and genders is on the increase (National Gay and Lesbian Task Force Policy Institute, 1993; Savin-Williams, 1994; Select Committee on Children, Youth, and Families, U.S. House of Representatives, 1989). In recent research, LGB youth reported a wide range of verbal and physical violence directed toward them in a variety of settings such as home, school, work, and the general community (Pilkington & D'Augelli, 1995). Young LGB respondents of color reported slightly less victimization, although this may be attributable to the difficulty in delineating victimization based on race from that based on sexual orientation. Respondents in general reported less victimization in the workplace and in the community at large, perhaps due in part to concealment of sexual orientation in these settings. Young lesbians reported loss of friendship and actual acts of abuse in school settings. Furthermore, school settings with demands for gender-stereotypic behaviors have been found to negatively affect lesbian identity formation in high school years (Waldner-Haugrud & Magruder, 1996).

Even with mandated inclusive curricula, there exists a consistent ignoring of sexual orientation in school curricula in general and in diversity curricula in particular. Rather, a heterosexist paradigm provides the foundation for much of the extant school curricula (Friend, 1993) and may unwittingly promote internalized homophobia. For example, lesbian and bisexual adolescents are faced repeatedly with texts that overtly or covertly recognize heterosexuality as normative and homosexuality as deviant. In addition, there is limited access to, or presence in, school libraries of literature portraying lesbian or bisexual main characters. School-related opportunities for exploring and discussing the coming-out process are often limited to LGB support groups, if such groups exist. Lesbian and bisexual teachers, who could serve as role models, also may be forced into this same silence for fear of job loss or recrimination from colleagues, administrators, or parents. Such systematic exclusion reinforces the closeted invisibility of lesbian and bisexual students. Efforts to address the concerns of LGB students have met with both success and controversy (Athanases, 1996; see also Unks, 1995, for elaboration).

In conclusion, we are faced with a legacy of inequity, harassment, and the violence of silence around homosexual concerns in school settings. Michelle Fine (1993), speaking more directly to sexuality in the curriculum (to include lesbian and bisexual issues), offered a direction to address issues of sexuality in the schools, "If we re-situate the adolescent woman in rich and empowering educational context, she develops a sense of self which is sexual as well as intellectual, social, and economic" (p. 90).

Summary of Strengths and Stresses in Schools

In our exploration of the experiences of adolescent girls in school settings, we found reasons for both pessimism and optimism. Girls continue to be marginalized in texts, differentially treated in classrooms, and sexually harassed in hallways and classrooms. For lesbian and bisexual adolescents, there is great concern about their experiences in schools, as they continue to be victims of sexual harassment and violence. Research on the interactions of gender with social class, race, ethnicity, sexual orientation, and myriad other school-related variables is very limited. Our understanding of girls' experiences is only beginning to emerge. Quite frequently, girls continue to question what they know. Yet, one sees that with equity awareness and training of school personnel, classrooms can become more gender fair. As more schools move toward violence prevention and creation of inclusive and safer campuses, perhaps people will see a greater reduction in the negative sequelae of harassment and violence.

FINDING SPACES AND PLACES IN COMMUNITY

Every day across the United States, millions of adolescents find themselves situated within a variety of community programs that provide them with opportunities for connection, skill building, physical challenges, and fun. Developmental and community psychology researchers (Bronfenbrenner, 1989) are cognizant of adolescents' needs for connection in their local neighborhoods, school settings, religious institutions, and community at large. Despite this knowledge, little empirical evidence exists to promote our understanding of the sense of community experienced by young people in general, and adolescent girls in particular. In this section, we discuss their connections to youth organizations and religious institutions.

Girls' Participation in Community Youth Organizations

Adolescent girls today have access to an array of community-based youth organizations, despite the smaller number of and the differential allocation of resources to those programs serving young women (Nicholson et al., 1992). When considering the role of such organizations in the lives of adolescent girls, it is important to remember that access to and function of social networks have been found to vary across social class and racial and ethnic lines (Stanton-Salazar, 1997). These factors have not been adequately addressed in current youth program research. With this caveat in mind, in this section, we discuss the research findings regarding variables associated with successful programs that have addressed the needs of girls.

The Carnegie Council on Adolescent Development (1992) studied a diverse sample of 11- to 15-year-old youth from at-risk communities' focus groups over a 2-year period. As participants met in focus groups to discuss time spent outside school hours, themes related to gender, types of participation, and support personnel and setting emerged. Specifically, the young people indicated a desire overall to participate in programs; however, there were differences by gender. For example, female respondents were more likely to be involved in religious groups and summer programs, whereas male adolescents preferred participation in team sports. The youth articulated the importance of adult role models in these settings and a preference for respectful and comfortable environments. The Carnegie Council recommended the collaboration of private and public sector efforts and attention to the hours that young people spend out of school. In their 5-year examination of 60 inner-city youth-serving organizations, Shirley Brice Heath and Milbrey McLaughlin (1993a, 1993b) found that many programs available for girls not only focused on heath care matters but also provided opportunities for sport and outdoor activities and skill building for team membership. Researchers in this area (Carnegie Council on Adolescent Development, 1992; Heath & McLaughlin, 1993a, 1993b, 1994; Nicholson et al., 1992) recommended that organizations established to meet the needs of adolescent girls should (a) provide positive, caring, and consistent adult role models of both sexes; (b) promote high yet realistic expectations in skill development; (c) promote the development of relation across class, gender, race, and ethnicity; (d) offer a range of experiences and topics that are of interest to girls, foster gender equity, or both; (e) encourage community involvement; and (f) involve the girls in settings in which they can be themselves, speak their truths, and find their own sources of power.

Religiosity in the Lives of Adolescent Girls

During the period of adolescence, in the journey of discovery, meaning making, and connection, it would seem that religious faith and institutions might play a role. In his examination of faith development, James Fowler (1981) proposed that adolescents seem to synthesize what they have been taught into a belief system that reflects their identity and connections to other people. In this synthetic–conventional stage of faith, they tend to conform to the religious values of significant others rather than to consider other religious ideologies. This aspect of faith looks more toward how one comes to a belief system and the content of that system. In a prior section of this book, the experience of morality and meaning making for adolescent girls was discussed. Here we present the role of religiosity (e.g., external expressions of faith including beliefs, ethical codes, and worship practices) as it supports adolescent girls.

What role does religiosity play in the lives of adolescent girls? Adolescent females, when compared with their male counterparts, are more actively religious (Dean & Yost, 1991; Donahue, 1995; Feldman, Fisher, Ransom, & Dimiceli, 1995; Miller & Hoffman, 1995; Ozorak, 1996). They participate in religious services and youth organizations and maintain their belief systems over longer periods of time. It seems also that such religiosity may have long-term benefits. For example, Feldman et al. (1995) found in their longitudinal work that female adult adjustment was predicted by their likelihood in adolescence to turn to religion and friends as means of coping. Not surprising, much of the literature in the area of religiosity and female adolescents focuses on factors related to girls' sexual behaviors, coping, social competence, self-esteem, and identity issues. For example, unmarried teen mothers' religious values have been found (a) to influence decision making related to choice to have and to keep the child (Farber, 1991) and (b) to be related to later first intercourse and use of contraception (Cooksey, Rindfuss, & Guilkey, 1996; Lock & Vincent, 1995). Maton and his colleagues (Maton et al., 1996) examined support systems of African American and Anglo American youth. They found that spiritual support was important, more so for pregnant African Americans than Anglo Americans. In addition, the researchers found a positive relationship between self-esteem and spiritual support for African American respondents. In fact, the authors indicate that their findings support a historical culture-based resource framework in explaining these findings. This is particularly salient, considering that in studies related to religiosity, several groups, including youth at risk and youth from various ethnic groups, are consistently underrepresented.

Despite evidence of the supportive nature of religiosity in the lives of some adolescent girls, the role of religion in reinforcing the differential socialization and location of women in society has concerned scholars.

Carol Rayburn (1992) spoke of these concerns, noting their perpetuation resides "within the very fiber of religious establishment." In their work, *The Feminine Face of God*, Sherry Anderson and Patricia Hopkins (1991) related the stories and themes that emerged from their interviews with over 100 women regarding their spiritual paths. Among the patterns in these women's stories was having a deep religious experience prior to adulthood, that is, encounters with the sacred in their childhood or adolescence. For those women who were provided spiritual support and understanding, this early experience of awareness remained with them through adulthood. In contrast, those who did not receive such support tended to become less vocal about their encounters. Valerie Chapman is a pastoral administrator in an inner-city catholic church. She is the mother of six, including four adolescent and young adult girls. Chapman's observations summarize the challenge religious communities face in supporting and not merely indoctrinating adolescent women.

> Participation in church-related activities is supposed to cultivate nice, obedient citizens. I speak primarily though not exclusively from a Christian perspective when I say that most churches do perpetuate this supposition, extolling their members to fear God by being honest, hard working, obedient, and chaste. Scripture is used in the process to legitimate the dominant reality. It is no surprise, then, that adolescent women hear the secondary role of women reinforced in their youth groups and other church settings.
>
> There are, however, other roles of religious activity, one of which is to be the prophetic voice, critiquing and correcting and encouraging liberation from the bonds that hold people captive, preventing the development of their full potential. This prophetic voice has been active in our own century in the labor movement, the civil rights movement, and the women's movement. In this context, scripture is used to legitimate activism leading to freedom for all people. It is the voice that young women need to hear so desperately today, and, I must add, it is not enough to bring women into the ministry if they merely perpetuate the same ideas as their male colleagues. Young women need to know that they are loved and accepted as they are and as they want to be. (V. Chapman, personal communication, May 12, 1997)

These women lead us to question how adolescent girls are likely to become empowered by the very institutions that reinforce the more traditional roles of women in religious settings and in society.

Summary of Strengths and Stresses in Community Settings

Adolescent girls have access to and participate in a range of community-based programs. Many of these programs support the development of personal and social competencies and foster physical behaviors. Studies of programs that meet the needs of girls indicate the importance of cultural and contextual relevance in terms of role models, program design, topics, developmental concerns, activities, and considerations of gender equity.

Yet these conclusions must be considered in the context of their limitations. Given the underrepresentation of various groups in research, the findings from religious programs are more likely to typify the experience of White middle-class young people. Variability of membership, participation, attendance, activities, and goals across and within youth clubs and religious programs potentially complicates researchers' making meaning from studies of youth involvement. In addition, a solid base of research on the community resources responsive to lesbian and bisexual adolescents must be developed to understand their specific strengths and stresses in community context.

Across all community youth programs, both secular and religious, the implications of gender must be more carefully examined. We need to understand both the impact of these programs on girls' competence and the ways in which they might perpetuate stereotypic socialization practices and location of girls as the disempowered. This understanding will best be examined in conjunction with other psychological theories of adolescent female development.

CONSTRUCTING BRIDGES BETWEEN SCHOOL AND COMMUNITY

In *Girls in the Middle: Working to Succeed in Schools* (AAUW, 1996), researchers found that some girls were able to build bridges or cross borders between and among groups, and with adults. In this section, we describe the Girls' Leadership Center (GLC) that facilitates responsive school and community collaboration to enhance adolescent girls' strengths and to address their needs. The GLC brings girls together to build bridges with one another and with the school and the community. From its inception, the GLC has embodied several of the principles found to be associated with successful program collaboration and for meeting girls' needs (AAUW, 1995; Ellis, 1990; Heath & McLaughlin, 1994). Specifically, the GLC supports girls' leadership groups that are flexible in structure, are situationally and culturally relevant to participants, and facilitate community connections. In addition, we incorporate several components related to successful programs. Specifically, we listen to the girls and involve them in the planning and the doing of the groups; we have facilitators who are caring, consistent, and competent mentors from the community. The girls have opportunities, as they construct them, to participate in community service.

Supporting Girls

Over the past few years, a group of women in Portland, Oregon, have been working to develop the GLC. With its emphasis on supporting girls, ages 8 to 18, of all ethnic backgrounds, economic classes, and religious affiliations, the GLC puts into action the concern spawned by increasing awareness of the challenges facing girls. The work of the center emerges from the interests and concerns of girls in their everyday lives and has three foci. First, girls' leadership groups are ongoing for girls and are facilitated by women from the neighborhood who engage the girls in exercising their abilities to both identify and assert their ideas and beliefs. Second, the GLC serves as a network center for the communication, collaboration, and formation of these organizations. Third, the center supports the development of research methods for reflecting the social and psychological phenomena of the emergence of leadership in girls.

In the process of forming leadership groups for girls, we sought to ensure representation of women and girls from a range of ethnic and socioeconomic communities. We knew from the research that much of what is known about adolescent girls is based on the experiences of White girls from middle- or upper-income backgrounds. We also knew from the limited research on the experiences of girls of color that there were both similarities and important distinctions. It was important to us to have leadership groups that were responsive to the needs of all girls. The group that initiated the entire project was begun in 1996 for Native American girls in a local middle school. It was facilitated by a Cheyenne woman and a woman who was raised as Anglo American but knows of her substantial Native American ancestry. The group dealt with the girls' experiences both as girls and as Native Americans. Because of shared ethnic identification with their facilitators and with one another, they were able to open doors to speaking of their lives that might otherwise have stayed closed. The Native American girls' group continued the following year as one of eight groups. In addition, there was a group for deaf girls; both facilitators were fluent in sign, one being a deaf woman. One group was sponsored by the Urban League. Most of the girls were African American, and their facilitators were both African American. In a local elementary school, a teacher and a counselor facilitated a mixed ethnicity group of 9- and 10-year-olds. Two teachers in an alternative high school for immigrant and refugee students were facilitating a group for young women there. Finally, three more groups of predominantly White girls, one for 9- to 11-year-olds and one for 14- to 16-year-olds, completed the collection of core groups.

Structured but Unscripted Groups

Our understanding of adolescence as a time when some girls step away from voicing their beliefs led to our seeking ways for providing girls with experiences that were affirming of their voiced beliefs and perceptions. Therefore, we have come to a concept of group life that we describe as structured but unscripted. Specifically, the group facilitators help the girls identify ways to open and close group meetings that can become group-specific rituals. The facilitators also help the girls identify ground rules for how they will be in relation with one another that are revised with each meeting so that they remain salient and continue to ensure safety for all participants. By maintaining the rituals, ground rules, and careful attention to overall safety available during the group time, the group facilitators provide the necessary structure for the leadership groups.

Beyond this fundamental structure, the girls themselves identify the foci of group activity—discussions, service projects, art projects, or whatever the girls view as meaningful. There is no curriculum and no script except for that arising from the beliefs, perceptions, experiences, interests, desires, and curiosities of the girls. Further structure might be needed and developed by the girls themselves. The facilitators may assert careful guidance that does not compromise the girls' initiative but helps to actualize their visions. The GLC groups, averaging eight girls, are ongoing and ideally remaining in place throughout their school years. Each group has two facilitators who stay with the group across years. A priority is for the groups to be community based. These last features are important for the meta-message that girls receive when they see their group facilitators in places other than the group.

It is our belief that the leadership these girls have rests firmly in their strong senses of who they are and what they know. Through their participation in these groups, girls experience shared and situational leadership. They come to understand firsthand the importance of the leadership each member brings to the group. They practice the leadership of women—leadership based on power with and power within. They observe around them the instability and harmfulness of power over.

WHAT MORE DO WE NEED TO KNOW AND HOW DO WE ASK?

Despite 25 years of school reform and an extensive history of women's rights, we have only minimally represented and responded to the needs of adolescent girls in schools and communities. Thus, what we summarize here is a mere beginning. In many ways, adolescent girls in general, and those who are poor or of color in particular, remain marginalized. Data on school variables document sustained inequities typically to the detriment of young women. Data also indicate increases in sexual harassment and in marginalization of lesbian and bisexual adolescents.

Yet, there are reasons for optimism. It seems that adolescent girls' access to and connections with institutional agents such as schools, community, and religion appear to be essential to their personal and social empowerment. Schools and communities constitute realms in which there is potential for sources of support. In fact, some school systems have begun to address issues of differential socialization and treatment of girls through curriculum reform and sexual harassment policy implementation. In addition to school-based support, affiliation with religious institutions may be helpful for some adolescent girls. Religious and other community systems may also provide sources of support and opportunity for adolescent girls and provide models for program design, implementation, and evaluation.

In school and community settings in which young women examine multiple perspectives and operate from their strengths, their skills develop for building bridges among themselves and across the multiple contexts in which they dwell. As they attend to and construct their own and one another's stories, they find the power to act with intention as leaders to transform their worlds.

Unanswered Questions

The relatively larger base of school-related research provides guidance for examining the questions of girls' experiences, interests, and concerns. Attention to the specific strengths and stresses of adolescent girls in the broader community is needed. The following questions may guide further exploration of adolescent girls in school and community connections.

- What formal and informal mechanisms facilitate adolescent girls' opportunities to be heard (about their experiences, wants, needs, expectations) in schools and communities?
- What barriers exist within these formal and informal mechanisms?
- What questions do we ask, and how do we listen, to the experiences of young women as they encounter the school, community, and religious institutions?
- How do we become more responsive to their expressed needs within the context of these institutions?
- What must be done in collaboration with, and on behalf of, young women to enhance already existing systems?
- What are the particular experiences of lesbian and female bisexual and transgendered adolescents in school and community settings?
- What issues do they share with their heterosexual peers, and which are different? How do we meet their needs?

- How do we work with adolescent girls in school and community settings over the long term as they construct norms and roles for themselves, as they find the source and strength of their own power?
- Across all of these questions, what are the ethnic, religious, ability, socioeconomic, and other contextual factors that we need to consider?

As professionals and adolescent girls encounter these questions and work toward resolution, we often find answers by looking in margins and fringes beyond our traditional theoretical and research paradigms. As Mary Catherine Bateson (1994) has suggested, "Openness to peripheral vision depends on rejecting such reductionism and rejecting it with the belief that questions of meaning have unitary answers" (p. 11). For psychologists, educators, and researchers, it will be important that we not restrict our lenses of inquiry nor our range of interpretation. Rather, we need to continue to be visionary in our efforts to understand and to work with adolescent girls.

REFERENCES

American Association of University Women. (1991). *Shortchanging girls, shortchanging America*. Washington, DC: American Association of University Women Educational Foundation.

American Association of University Women. (1992). *The AAUW report: How schools shortchange girls*. Washington, DC: American Association of University Women Educational Foundation.

American Association of University Women (1993). *Hostile hallways: AAUW survey on sexual harassment in American schools*. Washington, DC: American Association of University Women Educational Foundation.

American Association of University Women. (1995). *Growing smart: What's working for girls in school*. Washington, DC: American Association of University Women Educational Foundation.

American Association of University Women. (1996). *Girls in the middle: Working to succeed in school*. Washington, DC: American Association of University Women Educational Foundation.

American Association of University Women. (1998). *Separated by sex: A critical look at single-sex education for girls*. Washington, DC: American Association of University Women Educational Foundation.

Anderson, S. R., & Hopkins, P. (1991). *The feminine face of God*. New York: Bantam.

Apple, M. W. (1998). The culture and commerce of the textbook. In L. E. Beyer & M. W. Apple (Eds.), *The curriculum: Problems, politics, and possibilities* (2nd ed., pp. 157–176). New York: Routledge.

Apple, M. W., & Christian-Smith, L. K. (1991). The politics of the textbook. In M. W. White & L. K. Christian-Smith (Eds.), *The politics of the textbook* (pp. 1–21). New York: Routledge.

Applebee, A. N. (1993). *Literature in the secondary school: Studies of curriculum and instruction in the United States.* Urbana, IL: National Council of Teachers of English.

Athanases, S. Z. (1996). A gay-themed lesson in an ethnic literature curriculum: Tenth graders responses to "Dear Anita." *Harvard Educational Review, 66,* 231–256.

Bateson, M. C. (1994). *Peripheral visions: Learning along the way.* New York: HarperCollins.

Bauch, P. A. (1988). Differences among single-sex and coeducational high schools. *Momentum, 19,* 56–58.

Bronfenbrenner, U. (1989). Ecological systems theory. In R. Vasta (Ed.), *Six theories of child development: Revised formulations and current issues* (pp. 187–249). Greenwich, CT: JAI Press.

Campbell, K. T., & Evans, C. (1996). Gender issues in the classroom: A comparison of mathematics anxiety. *Education, 117,* 332–360.

Carnegie Council on Adolescent Development. (1992). *What young adolescents want and need from out-of-school programs.* Washington, DC: Author.

Cooksey, E. C., Rindfuss, R. R., & Guilkey, D. K. (1996). The initiation of adolescent sexual and contraceptive behavior during changing times. *Journal of Health and Social Behavior, 37,* 59–74.

Dean, K. C., & Yost, P. R. (1991). *A synthesis of the research on, and a descriptive overview of Protestant, Catholic, and Jewish religious youth groups in the United States.* Washington, DC: Carnegie Council on Adolescent Development.

DeZolt, D. M. (1992). *Themes, age, and gender differences in children's stories about caring.* Unpublished doctoral dissertation, Kent State University, Kent, OH.

DeZolt, D. M. (1997). *Doing school, gender, and relation: Adolescent girls' experiences in an alternative school.* Manuscript in preparation.

Donahue, M. J. (1995). Religion and the well-being of adolescents. *Journal of Social Issues, 51,* 145–160.

Eccles, J. S. (1989). Bringing young women to math and science. In M. Crawford & M. Gentry Entwisle (Eds.), *Gender and thought: Psychological perspectives* (pp. 36–58). New York: Springer-Verlag.

Ellis, J. (1990). *Formative research and teen SMART: Try, try again. Reports and papers in progress.* Newton, MA: Education Development Center.

Farber, N. B. (1991). The process of pregnancy resolution among adolescent mothers. *Adolescence, 26,* 697–716.

Feldman, S. S., Fisher, L., Ransom, D. C., & Dimiceli, S. (1995). Is "What is good for the goose good for the gander?": Sex differences in relations between adolescent coping and adult adaptation. *Journal of Research on Adolescence, 5,* 333–359.

Fine, M. (1993). Sexuality, schooling, and adolescent females: The missing discourse of desire. In L. Weis & M. Fine (Eds.), *Beyond silenced voices: Class, race, and gender in Unites States schools* (pp. 75–99). Albany: State University of New York Press.

Firestein, B. A. (Ed.). (1996). *Bisexuality: The psychology and politics of an invisible minority*. Thousand Oaks, CA: Sage.

Fowler, J. W. (1981). *Stages of faith: The psychology of human development and the quest for meaning*. New York: Harper & Row.

Friend, R. A. (1993). Choices, not closets: Heterosexism and homophobia in schools. In L. Weis & M. Fine (Eds.), *Beyond silenced voices: Class, race, and gender in Unites States schools* (pp. 209–235). Albany: State University of New York Press.

Gilbert, M. C. (1996). Attributional patterns and perceptions of math and science among fifth-grade through seventh-grade girls and boys. *Sex Roles, 35*, 489–506.

Heath, S. B., & McLaughlin, M. W. (1993a). Ethnicity and gender in theory and practice: The youth perspective. In S. B. Heath & M. W. McLaughlin (Eds.), *Identity and inner-city youth: Beyond ethnicity and gender* (pp. 13–35). New York: Teachers College.

Heath, S. B., & McLaughlin, M. W. (Eds.). (1993b). *Identity and inner-city youth: Beyond ethnicity and gender*. New York: Teachers College.

Heath, S. B., & McLaughlin, M. W. (1994). The best of both worlds: Connecting schools and community youth organizations for all-day, all-year learning. *Educational Administration Quarterly, 30*, 278–300.

Henning-Stout, M. (1994). *Responsive assessment: A new way of thinking about learning*. San Francisco: Jossey-Bass.

Hutchins, L., & Kaahumanu, L. (Eds.). (1991). *Bi any other name: Bisexual people speak out*. Boston: Alyson.

Kitzinger, C. (1987). *The social construction of lesbianism*. Newbury Park, CA: Sage.

Lee, V. E., & Bryk, A. S. (1986). Effects of single-sex secondary schools on student achievement and attitudes. *Journal of Educational Psychology, 78*, 381–395.

Lee, V. E., Croninger, R. G., Linn, E., & Chen, X. (1996). The culture of sexual harassment in secondary schools. *American Educational Research Journal, 33*, 383–417.

LePore, P. C., & Warren, J. R. (1997). A comparison of single-sex and coeducational Catholic secondary schooling: Evidence from the National Educational Longitudinal Study of 1988. *American Educational Research Journal, 34*, 485–511.

Lock, S. E., & Vincent, M. L. (1995). Sexual decision-making among rural adolescent females. *Health Values: The Journal of Health Behavior, Education, & Promotion, 19*, 47–58.

Loredo, C., Reid, A., & Deaux, K. (1995). Judgments and definitions of sexual harassment by high school students. *Sex Roles, 32*, 29–45.

Marsh, H. W. (1989). Effects of single-sex and coeducational high schools on achievement, attitudes, behaviors, and sex differences. *Journal of Educational Psychology, 81,* 70–85.

Marsh, H. W. (1991). Public, Catholic single-sex, and Catholic coeducational high schools: Their effects on achievement, affect, and behaviors. *American Journal of Education, 41,* 320–356.

Maton, K. I., Teti, M., Corns, K. M., Vieira-Baker, C. C., Lavine, J. R., Gouze, K. R., & Keating, D. P. (1996). Cultural specificity of support sources, correlates, and contexts: Three studies of African-American and Caucasian youth. *American Journal of Community Psychology, 24,* 551–588.

Miller, A. S., & Hoffman, J. P. (1995). Risk and religion: An explanation of gender differences in religiosity. *Journal for the Scientific Study of Religion, 34,* 63–75.

National Gay and Lesbian Task Force Policy Institute. (1993). *Anti-gay/lesbian violence, victimization, and defamation in 1992.* Washington, DC: Author.

Nicholson, H. J., Weiss, F. L., & Maschino, M. F. (1992). *Gender issues in youth development programs.* Washington, DC: Carnegie Council on Adolescent Development.

Orenstein, P. (1994). *Schoolgirls: Young women, self-esteem, and the confidence gap.* New York: Doubleday.

Ozorak, E. W. (1996). The power, but not the glory: How women empower themselves through religion. *Journal for the Scientific Study of Religion, 35,* 17–29.

Pilkington, N. W., & D'Augelli, A. R. (1995). Victimization of lesbian, gay, and bisexual youth in community settings. *Journal of Community Psychology, 23,* 34–56.

Radkowsky, M., & Siegel, L. J. (1997). The gay adolescent: Stressors, adaptations, and psychosocial interventions. *Clinical Psychology Review, 17,* 191–216.

Rayburn, C. (1992, August). *Morality, spirituality, religion, gender and stress: Unraveling the puzzles.* Paper presented at the 100th Annual Convention of the American Psychological Association, Washington, DC.

Roscoe, B., Strouse, J. S., Goodwin, M., Taracks, L., & Henderson, D. (1994). Sexual harassment: An educational program for middle school students. *Elementary School Guidance and Counseling, 29,* 110–120.

Ruch-Ross, H. S., Jones, E. D., & Musick, J. S. (1992). Comparing outcomes in a statewide program for adolescent mothers with outcomes in a national sample. *Family Planning Perspectives, 24,* 66–71, 96.

Rust, P. C. (1995). *Bisexuality and the challenge to lesbian politics: Sex, loyalty, and revolution.* New York: New York University Press.

Sadker, M., & Sadker, D. (1994). *Failing at fairness. How America's schools cheat girls.* New York: Scribner.

Savin-Williams, R. W. (1994). Verbal and physical abuse as stressors in the lives of lesbian, gay male, and bi-sexual youths: Associations with school problems, running away, substance abuse, prostitution, and suicide. *Journal of Consulting and Clinical Psychology, 62,* 261–269.

Schneider, M. (1989). Sappho was a right-on adolescent: Growing up lesbian. *Journal of Homosexuality, 17,* 111–130.

Select Committee on Children, Youth, and Families, U.S. House of Representatives. (1989). *Down these mean streets: Violence by and against America's children*. Washington, DC: U.S. Government Printing Office.

Shakeshaft, C., Barber, E., Hergenrother, M. A., Johnson, Y. M., Mandel, L. S., & Sawyer, J. (1995). Peer harassment in schools. *Journal for a Just and Caring Education, 1*, 30–44.

Shmurak, C. B. (1998). *Voices of hope: Adolescent girls at single sex and coeducational schools*. New York: Lang.

Sleeter, C. E., & Grant, C. A. (1991). Race, class, gender, and disability in current textbooks. In M. W. White & L. K. Christian-Smith (Eds.), *The politics of the textbook* (pp. 78–110). New York: Routledge.

Stanton-Salazar, R. D. (1997). A social capital framework for understanding the socialization of racial minority children and youths. *Harvard Educational Review, 67*, 1–40.

Stein, N. (1995). Sexual harassment in school: The public performance of gendered violence. *Harvard Educational Review, 65*, 145–162.

Stein, N., Marshall, N. L., & Tropp, L. R. (1993). *Secrets in public: Sexual harassment in our schools*. Wellesley, MA: Wellesley College, Center for Research on Women.

Stephens, R. D. (1994). Planning for safer and better schools: School violence prevention and intervention. *School Psychology Review, 23*, 204–215.

Unks, G. (Ed.) (1995). *The gay teen: Educational practice and theory for lesbian, gay, and bisexual adolescents*. New York: Routledge.

U.S. Department of Education. (1991). *America 2000: An education strategy*. Washington, DC: Author.

U.S. Department of Education, National Center for Education Statistics. (1995). *National Educational Longitudinal Study, 1988: Second follow-up (1992)* [ICPSR Document No. 6448]. Ann Arbor, MI: Interuniversity Consortium for Political and Social Research.

Van Manen, M. (1994). Pedagogy, virtue, and narrative identity in teaching. *Curriculum Inquiry, 24*, 135–170.

Waldner-Haugrud, L., & Magruder, B. (1996). Homosexual identity expression among lesbian and gay adolescents: An analysis of perceived structural associations. *Youth and Society, 27*, 313–333.

"What's happening to you?" (1992, September). *Seventeen Magazine, 51*, 165.

12

DATING VIOLENCE AND TEEN PROSTITUTION: ADOLESCENT GIRLS IN THE JUSTICE SYSTEM

MICHELE HARWAY AND MARSHA LISS

Whether as perpetrators of violence or as victims of violence, adolescents today are much more likely to come into contact with the legal/judicial system. Pipher (1994), in the popular best-seller *Reviving Ophelia*, contended that adolescent girls today experience more trauma than previous generations. This chapter considers adolescent girls' interface with the legal system. There are many situations that bring adolescent girls into contact with the legal system, both as victims and as offenders. As offenders they may be shoplifters, runaways, gang members, or thieves. They may exhibit violence toward others, use drugs, or become delinquents. They may be assaulted by gangs, by friends, or by partners or sexually exploited by family members, acquaintances, or strangers. We limit our discussion to partner–dating violence and teen prostitution because these two situations illustrate developmental crises with which adolescent girls struggle. Our analysis could be equally applied to an understanding of why and how

This chapter reflects the opinions of the authors only and not necessarily those of the Phillips Graduate Institute nor the U.S. Department of Justice.

adolescent girls find themselves involved in the long list of activities that may bring them into contact with the legal system.

In the sections that follow, we consider first the prevalence statistics of dating violence and prostitution among adolescent girls. Next, we discuss explanations for adolescent girls' involvement in dating violence and prostitution through the developmental lens of the self-in-relation theory. We conclude with suggestions for interventions and for future research.

PREVALENCE STATISTICS

Prior to describing the prevalence of dating violence and teen prostitution, it is important to consider the inherent limitations of these statistics. The manner in which prevalence statistics are reported is anything but consistent, and thus comparisons across age, gender, ethnicity, and forms of victimization are nearly impossible. Within a single group, diverse statistics are often cited for the same form of victimization. These disparities result from varied definitions of violence, differences in data collection techniques, and other methodological approaches. There is also virtually no information about adolescent girls as perpetrators of violence because the problem has been considered almost exclusively a problem of young men. With these limitations in mind, we consider what information is available about dating violence, date rape, and teen prostitution. We first present prevalence statistics for dating violence separately from those for date or acquaintance rape. These statistics are presented for the population of adolescent girls as a whole and, where available, broken out separately by younger and older adolescents and by ethnicity. We then consider the available figures for teen prostitution.

Dating Violence

Dating violence includes physical injuries, verbal assaults, and threats of violence in the context of a dating relationship. Dating violence has been reported to affect 10% of high school students (Roscoe & Callahan, 1985) and 22% of college students (Sorenson & Bowie, 1994). Jealousy and anger are the primary motives for dating violence, and most incidents occur when the partners have been dating each other steadily (Burke, Stets, & Pirog-Good,1989; Makepeace, 1986; Roscoe & Callahan, 1985). Young women are more likely than young men to indicate they were victims of severe physical dating violence (Gamache, 1991).

Few victims actually report dating violence and if they seek help, generally do so from their friends. Roscoe and Kelsey's (1986) study of dating violence indicates that 25% to 35% of victims and perpetrators consider the violence a sign of love. The victim reasons that her partner became violent because she denied him sex. Most violent young men say that they become violent with their dates to exert power over them or to intimidate them (Makepeace, 1986; Sorenson & Bowie, 1994).

There are a number of antecedent factors implicated in dating violence. Observing family violence is related to a fourfold increase in male adolescents' likelihood to assault their dates, a greater probability for male adolescents convicted of violent offenses (including rape) to repeat these crimes, and a one-third greater chance for female adolescents to be victims of date rape and other forms of assault by peers (Jaffe, Sudermann, & Reitzel, 1992). Dating violence can have serious consequences. For example, young women are three times more likely to report severe emotional trauma as a result of a violent episode in the dating context (Makepeace, 1986).

Date or Acquaintance Rape

Date or acquaintance rape is another form of dating violence. Adolescents are considered to be at higher risk for sexual assault than any other age group (Hall & Gloyer, 1985; Sorenson & Bowie, 1994). Thirty-seven percent of rape victims are between 11 and 17 years of age (Calhoun & Atkeson, 1991). Furthermore, it is estimated that 10% to 25% of young women 15 to 24 years old have been sexually assaulted or were the victims of attempted assaults (Ageton, 1983; Koss, 1988; Koss, Gidycz, & Wisniewski, 1987). Over half of the reported sexual assaults occurred in dating situations (Ageton, 1983, Koss, 1988), most likely in a vehicle or in the home of the victim or the assailant (Ageton, 1983).

Social factors may lead to the misinterpretation of the sexual cues implicated in cases of date rape. Muehlenhard (1988) studied young adults' attitudes toward date rape and how these related to their own dating habits. Respondents were presented with scenarios in which a sexual assault was committed. Respondents were most likely to justify rape and to perceive the partner as willing to engage in sexual intercourse in scenarios in which the victim initiated the date, went to the man's apartment, or allowed him to pay for the dating expenses. Young men and respondents with traditional attitudes about men's and women's roles were also more likely to justify rape than young women or those with less traditional attitudes. Jenkins and Dambrot (1987) found that sexually aggressive young men who believe in commonly held rape myths were less likely to view scenarios involving sexual assault as rape, blamed the victim more often, and saw her as "deserving it." Women who agreed with the rape myths had similar reactions. In a nationwide study, junior and senior high school students were asked to interpret what a young woman means when she says "no." Almost half of the students said that when the girl was affectionate and passionate, she was signaling that she was willing to continue the sexual activity even if she wanted to stop. There were no gender differences ("Teens believe," 1992). That date rape is a common phenomenon is supported by other findings of the same survey. Specifically, 31% of respondents said they knew someone who had been a victim of date rape, which is up from 24% in the preceding year's survey. Drinking alcohol was involved in almost all date rapes. In 45% of the rape cases, both members of the couple were said to be drinking; in 42% of cases, he alone was drinking; she alone was drinking in 13% of cases. More Hispanic students reported having been victims of date rape than any other ethnic group (25% of Latinos, 21% of Blacks, 13% of Whites, and 9% of Asians). In another study, 14% of girls surveyed reported being raped (Coles & Stokes, 1985). In half the cases, the assailant was a boyfriend or acquaintance. In explaining the high incidence of date or acquaintance rape, Katchadourian (1990) explained that by adolescence, young men accept the use of force with young women.

As with adult rape victims, adolescents are often unclear as to what constitutes rape when committed by a date or a friend. Consequently, most victims of date rape do not think the assault fits the definition of rape, so they do not report the rape to the police. Moreover, the victim may feel guilt or responsibility concerning her decision to be in the company of her attacker (and if she was drinking, she may experience additional guilt because of this). She may, as a result, interpret the occurrence as normal or deserved. In a random telephone survey of adolescent girls, in which 12% of whom reported having been raped or sexually assaulted, other reasons were given for not reporting, including fear of their parents' reactions to the rape and of their peers learning of the incident (Calhoun & Atkeson, 1991). Thus, the incidence of date rape is believed to be underreported, and the figures cited are likely to be underestimates of the actual occurrence.

The prevalence rates of date rape on college campuses are similar to those among high school students, ranging from 5% to 25% (Kilpatrick, Veronen, & Best, 1984; Koss, 1985; Russell, 1984). In a 1984 study, 15% of male college students admitted they had forced dates to have sexual intercourse despite their dates' protests (Rapaport & Burkhart, 1984). The number is increasing. The 1988 crime statistics included 266 reported rapes on college campuses; by 1991, there was a 46% increase to 388 cases (Federal Bureau of Investigation [FBI], 1989, 1992). This number is likely to substantially underreport actual on-campus rapes because only 58% of rape victims report the crime (Koss, 1988).

In a nationwide survey of sexual assaults on college campuses, 12% of the female respondents reported that young men had attempted to rape them, and another 15% had been raped (Koss et al., 1987). Although 75% of the male respondents reported that they did not force young women to have sex, 25% admitted to having engaged in some form of sexual assault, 3% indicated that they had tried to rape a date, and 4% had actually raped one or more dates. Self-reported incidence of sexual assault was higher at private colleges (14%) and major universities (17%) than in religiously affiliated schools (7%). There was a significant correlation between having been raped and the ethnic identity of both the victims and the assailants. Young White women comprised the largest number of victims but had a lower prevalence rate (16%) than young Native American women (40%); other ethnic groups were in the intermediate range. The average age of the rape victim was 18 years 6 months. Two thirds of the women did not report the rape, and the one third who did report indicated that the police were not supportive. The study found that 42% reported that they had sex with their assailant subsequent to the initial rape, but it was not clear whether this too was coerced. Forty percent reported that they believed that they were likely to be assaulted again. The self-reported assailants were 18 years 6 months, on average; they indicated that they forced the women to have sex with them in a house off campus or in a car. More than 60% reported they had raped their dates, and 74% had been drinking or using drugs when they attacked their victims. Rape usually followed heavy petting. Although they reported that the young women had not been clear about not wanting intercourse, the men acknowledged using force. Most of the men reported feeling proud during the rape, and 47% indicated they would likely engage in forced sex again.

Date rape has long-term effects on its victims, including the possibility of sexual dysfunction, flashbacks, a delayed stress reaction, and other symptoms of post-traumatic stress disorder (Sorensen & Bowie, 1994). A young woman may also have to deal with sexually transmitted diseases, pregnancy, and, in some groups, the social stigma of loss of virginity. In addition, women raped by someone they know may have more severe cognitive and psychological problems than women raped by strangers (Koss et al., 1994).

Ethnic Differences in Dating Violence

Examining data on dating violence by ethnicity presents several limitations. First, there is no consistent information about the prevalence of dating violence and date rape among adolescents from various ethnic groups. Comparisons across ethnic groups are difficult because of the disparities in presentation of the data and the absence of any information for some ethnic groups. Much of these data confound class, ethnic and racial identity, and urban or rural residence. Thus, interpretation of these data must be made cautiously.

African American Adolescents

When the ethnicity of victims of violence is considered, statistical figures suggest that most of the violence perpetrated against late adolescent and early adult African American girls and women is likely to originate with the boyfriend or the spouse (Harlow, 1991). Battering as antecedent to fatal partner abuse is more common among African Americans than among other ethnic groups (Koss et al., 1994; Stark, 1990). Cazenave and Straus (1979), controlling for race and socioeconomic status in a nationally representative sample, found that African Americans had lower rates of partner violence than Whites in the two highest income groups and the lowest income groups.

The effects of victimization are likely to be greater for African American girls and women. Thus, African American girls who experienced or witnessed violence were more likely than victims from other ethnic groups to exhibit emotional distress and behavioral problems (DuRant, Cadenhead, Pendergrast, Slavens, & Linder, 1994; Fitzpatrick, 1993; Miller, Handal, Gilner, & Cross, 1991). Although African American adolescents suffer more from their victimization, there is anecdotal evidence that they rarely seek psychological help or medical assistance. African American women who are raped are less likely than White women to disclose the rape until years later (64% in contrast to 36%; Wyatt, 1992). African American women who were raped were more likely than White women to offer explanations about their victimization that implicated the high-risk nature of their physical surroundings. They were also more likely to hold a general belief that African American women are at greatest risk for rape; these women may accept their vulnerability as inevitable. Abstracting from these data, we point out that African American adolescent girls may be at higher risk than others of the same age for dating violence and date rape.

Latino Adolescents

A whole different set of statistics is available for Latinos. The Uniform Crime Report (UCR; U.S. Department of Justice, 1991) indicates that nonstranger perpetration among 12- to 15-year-old Latinos is very high (50%); it is only slightly lower for 16- to 19-year-olds (38%). Victimization rates for Latinos 12 years or older for personal crimes of violence were higher than for Whites (37.3 vs. 28.8 per 1,000) and only slightly less than for African Americans (39.7 per 1,000). The figures are not available for female separately from male adolescents. Some other statistics indicate that Latinas experience higher rates of victimization by violence (25 per 1,000) compared with non-Latinas (21.9 per 1,000). These figures, by contrast, do not allow comparisons across age groups, and so it is unclear what is the exact incidence of acquaintance violence for adolescent Latino girls.

Latinas and non-Latinas have similar rates of experiencing completed and attempted rapes, but Latinas and Latinos had higher rates of victimization for violent crimes than male and female non-Latinos (30.3 and 49.9 per 1,000 vs. 25.5 and 44.7 per 1,000). Breakdowns are not available by age groups. National figures on the incidence of rape reported to police are highest for poor, inner-city, ethnic minority girls and women, with one exception: Latinas (Sorensen & Siegel, 1991). Lifetime prevalence of sexual assault among non-Latino Whites was 2.5 times that of Latinos. Contrasting with these figures were those reported as part of an earlier cited survey ("Teens Believe," 1992) in which more Latinas reported having been victims of date rape than any other ethnic group among high performing high school students. These disparities result from a discrepancy between incidence of reported date rape and numbers of overall rapes reported.

Asian and Pacific Islander Adolescents

No hard data are available on the extent of violence suffered by Asian or Pacific Islander female adolescents. There are anecdotal reports that suggest that many victims of date rape, dating violence, and stranger rape are of Asian extraction (Yoshihama, Parehk & Boyington, 1991). Chan (1987) conjectured that this results from the long-standing stereotyping and exploitation of Asian and Pacific Island women as sex objects in the United States and in Asian countries by U.S. soldiers and businessmen. As a result, these women are expected to be sexually available and to be victimized when they resist.

Ho (1990) indicated that domestic violence results from a history of women's oppression in Asian cultures, in which women are taught that they are to accept their fate and to suffer and persevere. Other information about spousal violence and dating violence is largely unknown, although a recent qualitative study of Korean immigrant women suggests that the incidence of spousal violence is quite high in this population (Kim, 1996).

Native American Adolescents

Data on violence in this ethnic group are not clear. A study of physical violence among Native American women in the 12 months preceding childbirth indicates that reported rates of battering are twice as high as for White women and 1.5 times as high as for African American women (U.S. Department of Health and Human Services, 1994).

Data regarding date rape are more readily available. Gruber, Di-Clemente, and Anderson (1994) reported that Native American male adolescents force sex on their partners more often than do White adolescents (10.6% vs. 4.6%) but less often than African American adolescents (11.7%). High percentages of physical and sexual abuse are reported by older female students in the 11th and 12th grades, with 25% reporting physical abuse and 20% sexual victimization; however, it is not clear who the assailant was (Blum, Harmon, Harris, Bergeisen, & Resnick, 1992; Blum, Harmon, Harris, Resnick, Stutelberg, & Robles, 1992). Kahn (1986) noted that Native Americans may be most vulnerable to violence perpetrated by an intimate, such as a spouse, a parent, another family member, a friend, or an acquaintance.

Alcohol abuse within the family may be a factor in the higher incidence of spouse abuse (Durst, 1991) and fatal violence among friends and acquaintances (Leyba, 1988). The same study showed a relationship between substance use and self-reported instances of violence perpetrated by Native American male adolescents (68%) and female adolescents (44%). These figures are higher than those reported for African American young men (51.6%), White young men (44%), African American young women (34.5%), and White young women (28.5%).

Teen Prostitution

The prevalence statistics for prostitution are extremely complex. This partly results from the revolving door of the legal system in prosecuting minors, the lack of parental presence in the environment, and the secluded nature of the underground environment in which these youths live and that keep this activity nearly invisible. The UCR indicated 2,116 arrests of female adolescents between 10 and 18 years for prostitution in 1989. Because adolescent prostitutes are often runaways, the 72,383 reported female runaways in that same year suggest that the incidence of teen prostitution may be considerably higher. Louie, Joe, Luu, and Tong (1991), studying adolescent runaways in San Francisco in 1990, found that 50 of 447 reported runaways were Asian, 56% of whom were girls ages 11 to 16. Most gave family problems as their reasons for running away. These young women were fed, clothed, and given spending money in return for participating in prostitution.

Early childhood sexual abuse and incest are common antecedent factors for teen prostitutes. The prevalence of child abuse is between 28.5% and 65% for female prostitutes (Seng, 1989). This early experience may condition these children to view sex as a means to communicate with and to receive love from adults. The token gifts that are given to an abused child by the perpetrator may mimic the transaction of sex for money. When they become prostitutes, they believe they will gain control of their sexual experience and their decision making vis-à-vis the client. Nonetheless, it is important to acknowledge that although intrafamilial sexual victimization is a frequent experience of underage prostitutes, many do not share this experience. Other factors related to teen prostitution include broken homes, foster homes, and absent parents, combined with inconsistent economic and emotional parental support, according to Seng. Truancy, poor academic performance, quitting school, running away, and drug abuse are commonly shared behavioral characteristics.

The majority of teen prostitutes are found in sheltered brothels or escort services. These settings provide more privacy from public scrutiny and diminished chances for detection and arrest (Rickel & Hendren, 1993). Teen prostitutes are often sold or traded by pimps through a cross-country circuit. Keeping them mobile and outside of their home state ensures that clients will not recognize them. Constant movement also breaks any ties a young girl may have to her community and makes the development of new bonds difficult. Prostitution may lead to other forms of exploitation, such as performing in pornographic films, blackmailing of clients, drug and alcohol abuse, theft, and violence. The introduction of teen prostitutes to alcohol and drugs minimizes their resistance during both the introduction and the apprenticeship phases. In addition, substance abuse creates a psychological and physiological dependence that enhances the pimps' control.

Female Adolescents as Offenders

The overlap between being a victim and being an offender is great with adolescent girls, especially where status offenses are concerned. When all classes of crimes are aggregated, crime is generally accomplished by male adolescents, although the increase in rates of engaging in criminal behavior is higher for female than for male juveniles (Butts, 1996). In 1995, girls under the age of 18 accounted for approximately one fourth of all crimes ("Female Offenders," 1996). From 1991 to 1995, there was a 34% increase in female adolescents arrested for violent crimes, a 17% increase in property offenses, a 56% increase in simple assaults, and a 33% increase in vandalism. Drug abuse convictions showed a 176% increase in offenses by female juveniles (Snyder, 1997).

Status offenses are defined as acts that are only considered violations because the individual involved is below the permissible or legal age for the behavior. Prominent among these is the status of being a runaway. The Juvenile Justice and Delinquency Act of 1974 was intended to decriminalize status offenses and deinstitutionalize juvenile offenders (National Research Council, Commission on Behavioral and Social Sciences and Education, Panel on High Risk Youth, 1993). From 1988 to 1995, arrests of female juveniles for running away from home ranged from 57% to 63% (Butts, 1996; Snyder, 1997; Snyder & Sickmund, 1995); another 30% of arrests for curfew and loitering violations were of female juveniles. Juvenile arrests for running away increased 17% from 1991 to 1995. Most runaways were 16 to 17 years old and came from broken homes, according to Snyder and Sickmund. The disposition of these cases is highly varied: Many juveniles are returned to their homes, and a few are sent to juvenile facilities; most are not arrested. Across status offenses, only 15% of female juveniles were formally charged, although they were involved in 42% of the cases, as Snyder and Sickmund indicated. Sherman (1998) noted that in a survey of girls committed to the Massachusetts Department of Youth Services, girls were confined for longer but for lesser offenses than boys.

From 1992 to 1995, 48% to 52% of arrests of female juveniles were for prostitution (Snyder, 1997; Snyder & Sickmund, 1995). Estimates of the numbers of juvenile female prostitutes range from 100,000 (Davidson & Loken, 1987) to 600,000 (Gibson-Ainyette, Templer, Brown & Veaco, 1988). A girl who was abused or neglected during childhood has a higher risk of violent behaviors in adolescence (Widom, 1994) as well as a higher rate of being a delinquent runaway (Janus, McCormack, Burgess, & Hartman, 1987). Female runaways became involved in prostitution, as a result of either solicitation by pimps or trading sex for food and shelter (Silbert & Pines, 1982). Even though the FBI UCR (1989, 1992) included the number of female juveniles arrested for prostitution, the UCR acknowledged that the number of juveniles arrested is a conservative estimate of the total (Rickel & Hendren, 1993).

Differential Handling of Male and Female Offenders

Differences in legal outcomes of male and female offenders have been attributed to paternalism in the courts. "'Paternalism' generally implies that women who behave in ways that are congruent with traditional female roles of purity and submission receive preferential or lenient treatment, whereas women who violate these standards do not receive this benefit and may be dealt with more severely than males committing the same offense" (Horowitz & Pottieger, 1991, p. 76). Studies indicate that more girls are found among status offenders and that these types of offenses are given harsher treatment than criminal offenses. Kashani, Daniel, Reid, and Sirinek (1984) reported that boys and girls are likely to be treated differently by the juvenile court system. The type of offenses for which they are brought to trial seems to be the major difference. Specifically, boys are most often sent to group homes for crimes against property and people, and girls are sent for status offenses and promiscuity. Rutter and Giller (1984) also reported that girls more often than boys are punished for sexual behavior and status offenses and receive harsher punishment for less serious offenses. Race also seems to affect the outcomes of juvenile courts (Visher, 1983; Zatz, 1987), with Whites being treated more leniently than ethnic minorities. Likewise, higher income families have more resources with which to attain a more favorable outcome for their adolescents or to divert the procedures away from court intervention altogether.

Horowitz and Pottieger (1991) conducted an empirical examination of the handling of seriously delinquent youths at the arrest, adjudication, and disposition stages. Controlling for a number of factors (criminal behavior level, seriousness of offense type, and juvenile record), Horowitz and Pottieger found a number of significant differences between the sexes in juvenile justice outcomes. The most salient differences occurred at the arrest stage. Female delinquent youths were more often arrested for prostitution than any other offense and were arrested more often for this than were their male counterparts. These outcomes suggest that young prostitutes were perceived not as youths in need of help but as dangerous elements.

Prostitution, more than any other offense, results in adjudication, perhaps because it more seriously violates gender norms. There were both gender and race differences at the disposition stage. White female repeat offenders received far more serious sentences than other types of repeat offenders. This suggests that society's moral outrage about prostitution is greater than its reactions to other criminal activities and supports the paternalism hypothesis advanced earlier.

Self-Esteem and Impact of Violence on Development in Adolescent Girls

Having described the prevalence of dating violence and teen prostitution, we now consider theoretical explanations for these phenomena and examine how adolescent girls' development and self-esteem are affected by these experiences. Adolescent girls who become involved with the legal system because of prostitution or dating violence share a similar trait. Many were sexually exploited (sometimes repeatedly) by those they trusted and with whom they shared a bond of friendship, if not love.

Recent conceptualizations of identity development suggest that the central issue for girls and women is balance in the development of the self and of intimate relationships. Our developmental analysis is predicated on our belief that dating violence and teen prostitution illustrate the struggle for self and voice in the context of intimate connection. Emergence from trauma may in fact lead to the development of survival mechanisms and competencies, allowing girls a voice while they struggle to maintain a self.

Erikson (1963) described identity (identity vs. role confusion) and intimacy (intimacy vs. isolation) as the developmental tasks of adolescence and early adulthood. Modifications to Erikson's theory involved women's development of identity. The Stone Center theorists (e.g., Surrey, 1985) described the core self as developing through a relational process and that young women, in particular, come to understand themselves through relating to another human being (self-in-relation). Chodorow (1978) noted that what adolescent girls had been experiencing up until adolescence and what the world soon demands of them is contradictory, a theme that Gilligan (1982) and Belenky, Clichy, Goldberger, and Tarule (1986) reprised in their notions of voice, self, and relationship with the larger society.

The family is seen as the context for identity development and interpersonal development. Contrary to the popular idea that adolescents need to leave the family and then come back, those who remain connected but are encouraged to individuate fare the best. For adolescent girls, the peer group is also a source of major connection both to understand the world they are moving into and to understand their own feelings by discussing them with their friends. They also learn trust and mutuality through their peer relationships. Date rape and violence represent major breaches of this just emerging sense of trust, and an adolescent girl's struggle with remaining in a relationship that has betrayed her and silenced her voice leads to the development of coping strategies—a major strength.

Dating Violence and the Struggle for Self and Voice

Much of the early literature on battering focused on understanding women who were battered (rather than on the batterer or on the act of violence itself). However, understanding why a man batters may ultimately provide the solution to this societal problem. Certainly, why he batters or rapes is an equally important question to ask about adolescents caught up in the pattern of date rape and violence and to help stop these repugnant behaviors. It may also be worthwhile to ask about the motivation of the young women who are the recipients of these unacceptable behaviors so that we might help them free themselves from these relationships. We conjecture that adolescent girls' youth and developmental vulnerability put them at greater risk for abusive behaviors, and the key to protecting them in such relationships is to understand what the appeal is.

The struggle for self and voice (while keeping relationships pivotal) as the core developmental task of adolescent girls provides the backdrop for our understanding of date rape and violence. Taylor, Gilligan, and Sullivan (1995) described the perfect girl as one "who is always nice and good, who never hurts other people's feelings, who either lacks or can control hunger and sexual desire, and who contains her feelings, especially anger" (p. 25). To be this "perfect" girl, adolescents must use what Gilligan referred to as *psychological dissociation*: "loss to the conscious self of knowledge or feelings that have become dangerous to know and feel" (Gilligan, 1991, as cited in Taylor, Gilligan, & Sullivan, 1995, p. 26). Psychological dissociation or resistance is contrasted to political resistance, in which girls challenge those social conventions that encourage them to lose their sense of self. Political resistance can be overt—speaking out or acting out against relationships or social conventions that silence women—or covert, overt compliance but dissimulation of actual feelings or knowledge. Covert political resistance may, over the long term, become a habit of acceptance of harmful societal conventions. Psychological dissociation, as described here, is also distinct from dissociative symptoms that are key features of several psychiatric diagnoses (*Diagnostic and Statistical Manual of Mental Disorders* [*DSM–IV*]; American Psychiatric Association, 1994).

There is evidence that women and girls who are caught in violent relationships alternate between psychological dissociation and political resistance. Adolescent girls, struggling with the process of individuation, are likely to have an even tougher time when a key figure in their life is a violent and controlling boyfriend. Girls and women who are involved with abusive men seldom want to leave the relationship. They simply want the abuse to stop and want their sometimes violent partner to return to the charming persona he presented during the honeymoon phase of their relationship (see Walker, 1979, for a description of the cycle of violence model). Much of the behavior of a woman living in a violent relationship is intended to minimize the violence and to extend the honeymoon. At first, stunned by a first violent episode, she may exhibit overt political resistance: for example, "You can't treat me this way. I'm not going to put up with this." Because this type of resistance is likely to yield more violence, she may then use other coping mechanisms, such as denial of the betrayal that such violence represents. She may also cope by attaching meanings to the violence (e.g., "He had a bad day at school, and when I nagged him about going out more often, he snapped."). While rationalizing his behavior, she may identify coping strategies (e.g., "I need to recognize when he is in a bad mood and avoid adding any stress."). At that stage, she is overtly complying while taking her own feelings of hurt and fear underground. Over the longer term, she may in fact accept that his behavior is appropriate and may entirely dissociate from her own feelings. Many writers about battered women (e.g., Follingstad, Neckerman, & Vormbrock, 1988) have described the psychological symptoms that battered women develop as the result of coping mechanisms that allow the woman to survive the battering relationship, but at psychological costs.

Why does the adolescent girl stay in a violent dating relationship? She wants intimacy and connection and is willing to sacrifice her own needs and voice to have it. What about dating violence that includes rape? Examining the prevalence statistics and associated studies reported above leads to the following conclusions:

1. A majority of sexual assaults against adolescent girls occur in dating relationships.
2. Almost half of those sexually assaulted subsequently had sex with the assailants.
3. A girl's sexual interest and responsiveness are given a bigger voice than her stated desire to stop and are seen as a green light to greater sexual involvement.
4. A girl's initial interest in the man's company may lead her to interpret an unwanted sexual act as normal or deserved, leading to date rape or prostitution.

5. Many girls experience more than one form of victimization in their communities or violent homes.

Therefore, the importance the young woman accords the relationship or the connectedness over her own needs and wishes is the key to understanding her involvement in date rape.

Teen Prostitution and Self and Voice

Although female prostitutes may first enter the legal system when arrested as offenders, for loitering, for soliciting, or for the status offense of running away, if one examines their histories, it is clear they had long been on paths of exploitation and victimization, with roots in their childhood. Transitioning from prostitution and victimization to a more traditional societally sanctioned life is a difficult developmental process and may be impossible for some.

Youth prostitution is not a new phenomenon. Throughout history youth were used in the commercial sex industry, with a strong negative correlation with social class (Downs & Hillje, 1993). In 1910, the United States enacted the Mann Act or White Slavery Act, prohibiting the transportation of women across state lines for prostitution. This statute has been amended and expanded to cover both sexes, special provisions regarding transportation of minors, and provisions prohibiting the luring and enticing of individuals to travel for purposes of prostitution (18 United States Code Sections 2421–2423). In addition to this federal law, each of the 50 states and the District of Columbia (National Center for the Prosecution of Child Abuse, 1994) prohibit juvenile prostitution. As with status offenses, laws prohibiting prostitution generally do not criminalize the minor's actions but, rather, those of the customer and the pimp. The age of the girl may, in fact, be a factor in increasing the penalty for both customer and pimp. There are also international conventions that decry the exploitation of women and children in the sex industry. With all these laws, why are there still circuits in which girls are trafficked for prostitution?

What then becomes of the youth? Why do youth enter prostitution? How are these youth defined as victims? Juvenile prostitutes can be characterized as offenders, victims, and sometimes as witnesses. At first glance, they are offenders, engaging in behaviors that are prohibited generally and even more so for their status. But they are also victims both at the moment of their actions of soliciting and sexual behavior and in their pasts. Aside from solicitations on the streets, prostitution can be a hidden activity existing in many communities, increasing the likelihood that the pimp and his girl will elude detection (Janus et al., 1987; Rickel & Hendren, 1993). Prostitution may occur on the street, through escort services, brothels, massage parlors, modeling studios, and related services. Some adolescent girls enter prostitution as a means of survival on the streets. There is a history of stories of girls leaving their small hometowns and getting off buses in faraway cities seeking a glamorous life. However, not all girls travel so far from home, and many begin their lives of bartering sex for food and shelter within their communities. Some prostitutes of all ages also trade sex for drugs. Other youth prostitutes are actually recruited by those who will exploit them. Those who prey on them are able to pick out the girls at a school or a mall who fit the pattern they seek. The recruiter serves as a seemingly caring adult, one who professes love and affection. The vulnerable adolescent perceives the adult as a stabilizing force to be relied on. Rickel and Hendren attributed the adolescent's willingness to follow the pimp partly as a means of controlling her life, partly to establish communication with an adult, and partly as evidence of her lack of self-esteem. The adolescent may be asserting herself in her rejection of the biological family and her adoption of the pimp as her guide.

Many girls in commercial prostitution come from broken homes or abusive homes (Campagna & Poffenberger, 1988). The lack of the family unit and its significance for attachment is critical in girls' willingness to be persuaded by the pimp to work for him by selling their bodies many times per night for money. They keep only a scant portion of the hundreds of dollars that cross their hands each evening. The pimp endears himself and develops their dependence on him; he will convince them that he was the only one who actually cared for them and that although he sold them repeatedly, he was still there. He fills a void, and thus the girls can rationalize much of their activities in the name of this commitment and attachment. Pimps will express affection and statements of love to girls who most likely have not heard such protestations from those around them. The affection may also come with violence. It is not uncommon for pimps to become angry and violent toward the girls for minor infractions of rules or for not bringing in sufficient money. Just as parents who harshly discipline children only to hug them, apologize, and express their love, the pimp may do the same after beating a girl, showing his bond to her.

School-related problems have been found to be associated with teen prostitution. It appears from the scant literature (Cohen, 1987; Janus et al., 1987) and from anecdotal reports (personal communications: S. Breault, 1996–1998; N. Hotaling, 1998; L. Lee, 1996–1997) that many of the girls have learning disabilities that interfere with their school performance and developmental tasks. The literature on learning disabilities indicates that the later the disability is diagnosed and supportive educational programs provided, the more the youth will have endured social and cognitive adjustment problems. Moreover, girls who suffer from the psychological aftereffects of abuse may also have learning difficulties. The pimp represents a path away from these problems and an apparent path toward something special for the girl.

The recruiter or exploiter will rarely work a girl in her hometown. If he can remove her from familiar people, she will have no resources to rely on, no one to call, and no one to turn to other than the exploiter and his friends. This isolation is another part of aligning the girl with the business, deepening her dependence on him (a parallel to the emotional dependence an abusive man develops in his partner). The greater the psychological distance between the hometown and the girl, the greater her psychological reliance on the exploiter. Pimps often move their girls from city to city. The pimp knows that the longer a girl stays in a community, the greater the chance that she will develop a connection with someone in the community, a customer, or another girl who will influence her to leave the pimp (Rickel & Hendren, 1993). The pimp may also exert other forms of control, including violence and threats; these threats may be aggression or loss of love.

Not surprising, pimps and customers often provide the adolescent prostitute with drugs or alcohol as an additional means of control. The substances may also bolster the girl's ability to engage in the repeated sexual acts as well as numb the realities of prostitution.

Most workers in the field acknowledge that youth prostitutes do not consciously choose to become prostitutes. Prostitution is a means of survival and not a career of choice. It is important to realize that the survival is a search not only for the necessities of food and shelter but also for a new self, a psychological survival, and escape (Barry, 1995).

Running away, as the first step toward prostitution, thus can be seen as a form of overt political resistance by an adolescent girl who is intent on expressing her voice in a family that she perceives is trying to prevent her moves toward independence. The original intent may in fact be a survival strategy, just as the coping mechanisms of battered women were strategies designed to survive dangerous relationships. Running away, and ultimately teen prostitution, can be seen as the results of a struggle between self and relationship that adolescent girls experience: "If girls know what they know and bring themselves into relationship, they will be in conflict with prevailing authorities. If girls do not know what they know and take themselves out of relationships they will be in trouble with themselves. The . . . difficult problem of relationship [is] how to stay connected with themselves and with others, how to keep in touch with themselves and with the world" (Gilligan, 1991, p. 43). It is through their attempts to maintain connection with others as well as with their own thoughts and feelings that girls may find themselves runaways and teen prostitutes. It is also through their desire to remain in relationship with their pimps that teen prostitutes remain.

Prostitutes operate within the arena of sexual behavior, in which teen girls are given the most confusing messages of all. They are supposed to deny sexual feelings and yet be attractive to men. Because of their youth and freshness, teen prostitutes are the most sought after, thereby commanding higher prices. Thus the teen prostitute holds a strange kind of power over others. This experience of being valued by others (the johns and the pimps) may serve to repair a self-esteem damaged by the normal adolescent struggles and a history of family dysfunction. Some teen prostitutes report feeling in control of their sexual experience and their decision making in regard to the client. Such control provides the girls with a voice in the context of a relationship, albeit a commercially transacted one laden with much judgment and shame by the larger society. Knowledge of their worth to the customers also gives them a voice with their pimps.

INTERVENTIONS

Interventions are needed for teen victims of both prostitution and dating violence. Victims of dating violence must receive immediate intervention to counteract the traumatic effects of experiencing a breach in trust by someone they know. Counseling services at high schools and colleges should be made more widely available to these young women to minimize immediate and long-term consequences. Programs emphasizing prevention, not just victimization prevention, are important. Some high schools have developed peer mediation programs to address violence among youths. Such programs could be enhanced to address the needs of survivors of dating violence. Teaching skills such as negotiation, interpersonal communication, anger management, problem solving, and coping strategies in schools would all be useful. Existing youth violence programs should also be expanded to include a focus on male-to-female violence. These programs must all include an awareness of different cultural norms around violence, especially in romantic relationships.

Additional programs that could benefit adolescents include education and role modeling for girls, emphasizing the relational context, and for boys, proactive socialization and programs that emphasize personal self-efficacy. Social educational campaigns would be of great benefit to encourage the active involvement of extended family and members of the surrounding community in the upbringing of individual youngsters. Programs for parents, teachers, and counselors on violence prevention and violence remediation would also be useful.

Outreach programs to assist youth in leaving prostitution have been developed in a few cities. Systematic evaluation of these efforts is needed. At what point should intervention be made? Should youth reach the juvenile justice system and be placed in a juvenile facility prior to being released to a program? Are residential or day programs most beneficial? How can such programs direct youths back to education and to skills and job training that could provide them with sufficient funds to establish independent living? Are programs for runaways who have not engaged in prostitution inappropriate settings for teen prostitutes (Whitcomb & De Vos, 1997)?

Another area of program development is the response to youth prostitution of the juvenile justice system itself (Whitcomb & De Vos, 1997). Sherman and colleagues (Sherman, in press), for instance, are exploring methods of addressing delinquency in general, especially status offenses and their handling by the justice system. Their approach incorporates many different service systems: health services, mental health and counseling, education, and vocational support. Other justice system approaches (L. Lee, personal communication, 1996–1997) are being explored for adolescent prostitutes that link child protection and social services with the justice system.

FUTURE RESEARCH

Research on both prostitution and dating violence is difficult to accomplish. Reporting rates of each are believed to be well below the actual prevalence. Potential differential variables distinguish those who report and those who keep their victimization hidden. The long-term effects on adolescent girls remain unknown.

Prevalence of prostitution has proved very difficult to determine. The Uniform Crime Report statistics are widely believed to be conservative estimates. Some researchers have extrapolated from the estimated numbers of runaways and the percentage of runaways in some studies admitting to commercial sexual activity (Davidson & Loken, 1987). Accurate prevalence statistics are important for community planning and services as well as for understanding this phenomenon itself. Likewise, existing data on dating violence and date rape suggest a vast underreporting of actual incidence. More valid data will lead to better efforts at prevention.

Although many researchers and policymakers surmise that there is a link between early sexual victimization and later adolescent prostitution (Browne & Finkelhor, 1986), there is little literature directly on this point. Anecdotal histories of youth engaged in prostitution and running away shed some light on these possibilities.

The protective factors cited by Widom (1994) of intelligence, temperament, cognitive appraisal, and a relationship with a significant person may well distinguish those girls who resist the temptations of exploiters or recruiters from those who succumb to the lures. Similarly, these protective factors may also be related to which survivors of relationship violence emerge relatively unscathed and which become symptomatic. Highlighting the possible adaptive functions of such factors might direct further development of programs to "inoculate" at-risk adolescent girls to resist the advances of pimps and to minimize the long-term consequences of relationship violence.

REFERENCES

Ageton, S. (1983). *Sexual assault among adolescents*. Lexington, MA: Heath.

American Psychiatric Association. (1994). *Diagnostic and statistical manual of mental disorders* (4th ed.). Washington, DC: Author.

Barry, K. (1995). *The prostitution of sexuality*. New York: New York University Press.

Belenky, M. F., Clichy, B., Goldberger, N. R., & Tarule, J. M. (1986). *Women's ways of knowing: The development of self, voice and mind*. New York: Basic Books.

Blum, R. W., Harmon, B., Harris, L. J., Bergeisen, L., & Resnick, M. D. (1992). American Indian-Alaska native youth health. *Journal of the American Medical Association, 267*, 1637–1644.

Blum, R., Harmon, B., Harris, L. J., Resnick, M. D., Stutelberg, K., & Robles, A. (1992). *The state of Native American youth health*. Minneapolis: University of Minnesota, Division of General Pediatrics and Adolescent Health.

Browne, A., & Finkelhor, D. (1986). Impact of sexual abuse: A review of the research. *Psychological Bulletin, 99*, 66–77.

Burke, P. J., Stets, J. E., & Pirog-Good, M. A. (1989). Gender identity, self-esteem and physical and sexual abuse in dating relationships. In M. A. Pirog-Good & J. E. Stets (Eds.), *Violence in dating relationships: Emerging social issues* (pp. 72–93). New York: Praeger.

Butts, J. A. (1996, July). *Offenders in juvenile court, 1993: Juvenile Justice Bulletin*. Washington, DC: U.S. Department of Justice, Office of Justice Programs, Office of Juvenile Justice and Delinquency Prevention.

Calhoun, K. S., & Atkeson, B. M. (1991). *Treatment of rape victims: Facilitating psychological adjustment*. New York: Pergamon Press.

Campagna, D. S., & Poffenberger, D. L. (1988). *The sexual trafficking in children*. Dover, MA: Auburn House.

Cazenave, N. A., & Straus, M. A. (1979). Race, class, network embededness and family violence: A search for potent support systems. *Journal of Comparative Family Studies, 10*, 280–300.

Chan, C. S. (1987). Asian-American women: Psychological responses to sexual exploitation and cultural stereotypes. *Asian American Psychological Association Journal, 12*, 11–15.

Chodorow, N. (1978). *The reproduction of mothering: Psychoanalysis and the sociology of gender*. Berkeley: University of California Press.

Cohen, M. (1987). *Identifying and combatting juvenile prostitution*. Washington, DC: National Association of Counties.

Coles, R., & Stokes, G. (1985). *Sex and the American teenager*. New York: Harper & Row.

Davidson, H. A., & Loken, G. A. (1987). *Child pornography and prostitution*. Arlington, VA: National Center for Missing and Exploited Children.

Downs, A. C., & Hillje, L. S. (1993). Historical and theoretical perspectives on adolescent sexuality: An overview. In T. P. Gullotta, G. R. Adams, & R.

Montemayer (Eds.), *Adolescent sexuality* (pp. 1–32). Newbury Park, CA: Sage.

DuRant, R. H., Cadenhead, C., Pendergrast, R. A., Slavens, G., & Linder, P. (1994). Factors associated with the use of violence among urban Black adolescents. *American Journal of Public Health, 84,* 612–617.

Durst, D. (1991). Conjugal violence: Changing attitudes in two northern native communities. *Community Mental Health Journal, 27,* 359–373.

Erikson, E. H. (1963). *Childhood and society.* New York: Norton.

Eron, L. D., Gentry, J. H., & Schlegel, P. (Eds.). (1994). *Reason to hope: A psychosocial perspective on violence and youth.* Washington, DC: American Psychological Association.

Federal Bureau of Investigation. (1989). *Uniform crime reports for the United States.* Washington, DC: U.S. Department of Justice.

Federal Bureau of Investigation. (1992). *Crime in the United States, 1991. Uniform crime reports.* Washington, DC: U.S. Department of Justice.

Female offenders in the juvenile justice system. (1996). (Report No. NCJ 160941). Washington, DC: U.S. Department of Justice, Office of Justice Programs, Office of Juvenile Justice and Delinquency Prevention.

Finkelhor, D., & Dziuba-Leatherman, J. (1994). Victimization of children. *American Psychologist, 49,* 173–183.

Fitzpatrick, K. M. (1993). Exposure to violence and presence of depression among low-income African American youth. *Journal of Consulting and Clinical Psychology, 61,* 528–531.

Follingstad, D. R., Neckerman, A. P., & Vormbrock, J. (1988). Reactions to victimization and coping strategies of battered women: The ties that bind. *Clinical Psychology Review, 8,* 373–390.

Gamache, D. (1991). Domination and control: The social context of dating violence. In B. Levy (Ed.), *Dating violence: Young women in danger* (pp. 69–83). Seattle, WA: Seal Press.

Gibson-Ainyette, I., Templer, D. I., Brown, R., & Veaco, L. (1988). Adolescent female prostitutes. *Archives of Sexual Behavior, 17,* 431–438.

Gidycz, C. A., & Koss, M. P. (1989). The impact of adolescent sexual victimization: Standardized measures of anxiety, depression, and behavioral deviancy. *Violence and Victims, 4,* 139–149.

Gilligan, C. (1982). *In a different voice: Psychological theory and women's development.* Cambridge, MA: Harvard University Press.

Gilligan, C. (1991). Women's psychological development: Implications for psychotherapy. *Women and Therapy, 11,* 531.

Gruber, E., DiClemente, R. J., & Anderson, M. (1994). Differences in risk-taking behavior among Native American, Black and White adolescents in a midwestern state [Abstract]. *Journal of Adolescent Health, 15,* 59.

Hall, E. R., & Gloyer, G. (1985). How adolescents perceive sexual assault services. *National Association of Social Workers, 10,* 120–128.

Harlow, C. (1991). *Female victims of violent crime* (Report No. NJC-126826). Washington, DC: U.S. Department of Justice, Office of Justice Programs, Bureau of Justice Statistics.

Ho, C. K. (1990). An analysis of domestic violence in Asian-American communities: A multicultural approach to counseling. In L. S. Brown & M. P. P. Root (Eds.), *Diversity and complexity in feminist therapy* (pp. 129–150). New York: Haworth Press.

Horowitz, R., & Pottieger A. E. (1991). Gender bias in juvenile justice handling of seriously crime-involved youths. *Journal of Research in Crime and Delinquency, 28,* 75–100.

Jaffe, P. G., Sudermann, M., & Reitzel, D. (1992). Working with children and adolescents to end the cycle of violence: A social learning approach to intervention and prevention programs. In R. DeV. Peters, R. J. McMahon, & V. L. Quinsey (Eds.), *Aggression and violence through the life span* (pp. 83–99). Newbury Park, CA.: Sage.

Janus, M., McCormack, A., Burgess, A. W., & Hartman, C. (1987). *Adolescent runaways: Causes and consequences.* New York: Lexington Books.

Jenkins, M. J., & Dambrot, F. H. (1987). The attribution of date rape: Observer's attitudes and sexual experiences and the dating situation. *Journal of Applied Social Psychology, 1,* 875–895.

Kahn, M. W. (1986). Psychosocial disorders of aboriginal populations in the United States and Australia. *Journal of Rural Community Psychology, 7,* 45–59.

Kashani, J. H., Daniel, A. E., Reid, J. C., & Sirinek, A. J. (1984). Comparison of delinquent boys and girls in group homes and factors associated with the outcome. *British Journal of Psychiatry, 144,* 156–160.

Katchadourian, H. (1990). Sexuality. In S. S. Feldman & G. R. Elliott (Eds.), *At the threshold: The developing adolescent* (pp. 330–351). Cambridge, MA: Harvard University Press.

Kilpatrick, D. G., Veronen, L. J., & Best, C. L. (1984). Factors predicting psychological distress among rape victims. In C. R. Figley (Ed.), *Trauma and its wake: The study and treatment of posttraumatic stress disorders* (pp. 113–141). New York: Brunner/Mazel.

Kim, T. H. (1996). Cultural aspects of marital violence in first generation immigrant Korean-American families. *Progress: Family Systems Research and Therapy, 5,* 127–138.

Koss, M. P. (1985). The hidden rape victim: Personality, attitudinal, and situational characteristics. *Psychology of Women Quarterly, 9,* 193–212.

Koss, M. P. (1988). Hidden rape: Sexual aggression and victimization in a national sample in higher education. In A. W. Burgess (Ed.), *Sexual assault* (Vol. II, pp. 3–25). New York: Garland.

Koss, M. P., Gidycz, C. A., & Wisniewski, N. (1987). The scope of rape: Incidence and prevalence of sexual aggression and victimization in a national sample of higher education students. *Journal of Consulting and Clinical Psychology, 55,* 162–170.

Koss, M. P., Goodman, L. A., Browne, A., Fitzgerald, L. F., Keita, G. P., & Russo, N. F. (1994). *No safe haven: Male violence against women at home, at work, and in the community.* Washington, DC: American Psychological Association.

Leyba, C. (1988). Homicides in Bernaillo County: 1978–1982. In J. Kraus, S. Sorenson, & P. Juarez (Eds.), *Research conference on violence and homicide in Hispanic communities* (pp. 101–118). Los Angeles: University of California Press.

Louie, L., Joe, K., Luu, M., & Tong, B. (1991, August). *Chinese American adolescent runaways.* Paper presented at the annual convention of the Asian American Psychological Association, San Francisco.

Makepeace, J. M. (1986). Gender differences in courtship violence victimization. *Family Relations, 32,* 101–109.

Miller, T. R., Handal, P. J., Gilner, F. H., & Cross, J. F. (1991). The relationship of abuse and witnessing violence on the Child Abuse Potential Inventory with Black adolescents. *Journal of Family Violence, 6,* 351–363.

Muehlenhard, C. L. (1988). Misinterpreting dating behavior and the risk of date rape. *Journal of Social and Clinical Psychology, 6,* 20–37.

National Center for the Prosecution of Child Abuse. (1994). *Child abuse crimes: Child prostitution.* Alexandria, VA: American Prosecutors Research Institute.

National Research Council, Commission on Behavioral and Social Sciences and Education, Panel on High-Risk Youth. (1993). *Losing generations: Adolescents in high-risk settings.* Washington, DC: National Academy Press.

Office of Technology Assessment. (1990). *Indian adolescent mental health* (Report No. OTA-H-446). Washington, DC: U.S. Government Printing Office.

Pipher, M. (1994). *Reviving Ophelia: Saving the selves of adolescent girls.* New York: Ballantine Books.

Quina, K., & Carlson, N. I. (1989). *Rape, incest and sexual harassment: A guide for helping others.* New York: Praeger.

Rapaport, K., & Burkhart, B. R. (1984). Personality and attitudinal characteristics of sexually coercive college males. *Journal of Abnormal Psychology, 93,* 216–221.

Rickel, A. U., & Hendren, M. C. (1993). Aberrant sexual experiences in adolescence. In T. P. Gullotta, G. R. Adams, & R. Montemayor (Eds.), *Adolescent sexuality* (pp. 141–159). Newbury Park, CA: Sage.

Roscoe, B., & Callahan, J. E. (1985). Adolescents' self report of violence in families and dating relations. *Adolescence, 20,* 545–553.

Roscoe, B., & Kelsey, T. (1986). Dating violence among high school students. *Psychology, 23,* 53–59.

Russell, D. E. H. (1984). *Sexual exploitation*. Beverly Hills, CA: Sage.

Rutter, M., & Giller, H. (1984). *Juvenile delinquency: Trends and perspectives*. New York: Guilford Press.

Seng, M. J. (1989). Child sexual abuse and adolescent prostitution: A comparative analysis. *Adolescence, 24*, 665–675.

Sherman, F. T. (1998, November). *Representative girls across systems: Multidisciplinary and cross-systems strategies*. Paper presented at the Juvenile Defender Leadership Summit, American Bar Association, Chicago.

Sherman, F. T. (in press). Leadership and lawyering: Learning new ways to see juvenile justice. In F. T. Sherman & W. Tobert (Eds.), *Transforming social inquiry, transforming social action: Creating communities of practice at the university and in the community*.

Silbert, M., & Pines, A. (1982). Entrance into prostitution. *Youth and Society, 13*, 471–500.

Sorensen, S., & Bowie, P. (1994). Vulnerable populations: Girls and young women. In L. Eron & J. Gentry (Eds.), *Violence and youth: Psychology's response. Vol. II. Papers of the American Psychological Association Commission on Violence and Youth*. Washington, DC: American Psychological Association.

Sorensen, S. B., & Siegel, J. M. (1991). Gender, ethnicity, and sexual assault: Findings from a Los Angeles study. *Journal of Social Issues, 48*, 93–104.

Snyder, H. N. (1997, February). *Juvenile arrest, 1995: Juvenile Justice Bulletin*. Washington, DC: U.S. Department of Justice, Office of Justice Programs, Office of Juvenile Justice and Delinquency Prevention.

Snyder, H. N., & Sickmund, M. (1995, August). *Juvenile offenders and victims: A national report*. Washington, DC: U.S. Department of Justice, Office of Justice Programs, Office of Juvenile Justice and Delinquency Prevention.

Stark, E. (1990). Rethinking homicide: Violence, race, and the politics of gender. *International Journal of Health Services, 20*, 3–26.

Surrey, J. (1985). *The self-in-relation: A theory of women's development* (Work in progress No. 13). Wellesley, MA.: The Stone Center Working Paper Series.

Taylor, J. M., Gilligan, C., & Sullivan, A. M. (1995). *Between voice and silence: Women and girls, race and relationship*. Cambridge, MA: Harvard University Press.

Teens believe "no" means "yes." (1992, November 25). *Manhattan Mercury*, p. C3.

U.S. Department of Health and Human Services. (1994). Physical violence during the 12 months preceding childbirth—Alaska, Maine, Oklahoma, and West Virginia, 1990–91. *Morbidity and Mortality Weekly Reports, 43*, 133–137.

U.S. Department of Justice. (1991). *Criminal victimization in the United States, 1990*. Washington, DC: Bureau of Justice Statistics.

Visher, C. (1983). Gender, police arrest decisions, and notions of chivalry. *Criminology, 21*, 5–28.

Walker, L. E. A. (1979). *The battered woman*. New York: Harper & Row.

Whitcomb, D., & De Vos, E. (1997). *Preliminary study of sexual trafficking of juveniles in the United States* (Rep. No. OJP-97-712-M). Washington, DC: US

Department of Justice, Office of Justice Programs, Office of Juvenile Justice and Delinquency Prevention.

Widom, C. S. (1994). Childhood victimization and adolescent problem behaviors. In R. D. Ketterlinus & M. E. Lamb (Eds.), *Adolescent problem behaviors* (pp. 127–164). Hillsdale, NJ: Erlbaum.

Wyatt, G. E. (1992). The sociocultural context of African-American and White American women's rape. *Journal of Social Issues, 48*, 77–91.

Yoshihama, M., Parehk, A. L., & Boyington, D. (1991). Dating violence in Asian/Pacific communities. In B. Levy (Ed.), *Dating violence: Young women in danger* (pp. 184–195). Seattle, WA: Seal Press.

Zatz, M. (1987). The changing forms of racial/ethnic bias in sentencing. *Journal of Research in Crime and Delinquency, 24*, 69–72.

13

HEALTH CARE FOR ADOLESCENT GIRLS

DENISE M. DOUGHERTY

This chapter focuses on health care in the United States as it affects adolescent girls. The chapter demonstrates that even though on many measures adolescent girls can be considered healthy relative to other populations, they are indeed affected by numerous health problems, they do use health services, and those health services can be improved. Health problems of adolescent girls range from common illnesses and injuries of childhood and adolescence (colds, flu, and sports and play-related injuries), to concerns about the changes accompanying puberty (e.g., breast development and menstruation), to living with chronic disorders (e.g., cancer) and disabilities (e.g., learning disabilities and cerebral palsy), to so-called behavioral or psychosocial problems (e.g., depression, suicide attempts, substance abuse, conduct disorder, violent victimization, and premature and unsafe sexuality). As is well accepted among adolescent health scholars, the model for thinking about adolescents, including ado-

Denise M. Doughtery, PhD, is the child health coordinator for the Agency for Health Care Policy and Research (in the U.S. Department of Health and Human Services). This chapter represents the views of Dr. Dougherty only and does not represent the views of the Agency for Health Care Policy or the U.S. Department of Health and Human Services.

lescent girls, should be biopsychosocial (Millstein, Petersen, & Nightingale, 1993).

Adolescent girls do use health services, and more than adolescent boys do, even for non-pregnancy-related health problems (Bernzweig, Takayama, Phibbs, Lewis, & Pantell, 1997).

However, adolescent girls' need for clinical health care services and the way they interact with the clinical system have received little attention among psychologists and health services researchers. This chapter hopes to remedy that situation. It provides an overview of the U.S. health care system (in which adolescent girls participate); an explanation for why research and services for adolescent girls must be different from these activities in adult populations, and suggestions for placing more emphasis on them; and a review of current health care challenges and opportunities for adolescent girls.

This chapter focuses on what psychologists and other researchers, providers, and policymakers do know about health care for adolescent girls—its problems, and its potential—and the implications for making improvements. The chapter argues the following:

1. Adolescent Girls Are Different: The Five Ds

Children and adolescents of both genders are different from many other health care "customers," and these differences have implications for the delivery of health care. First, depending on their age, cultural context, familial connections, type of problem, and geographic location, they are more or less dependent on parents or guardians. In many ways adolescent girls' health problems show different epidemiological patterns than those of other groups (e.g., younger children, adolescent boys, mature women, and elderly people). Compared with boys their age, they tend to use more health services (Shenkman et al., 1996). They also have different developmental patterns than other groups. Adolescent girls are, of course, different from each other: in health issues, ages, developmental state, ethnicity, family income level, and coping abilities (e.g., Kagawa-Singer, Katz, Taylor, & Vanderryn, 1996).

2. We Need More Efficacy and Effectiveness Information to Guide Changes in Health Care Delivery to Adolescent Girls

Psychologists and other health care researchers need to know more about the efficacy and effectiveness of services that could be or are being provided now to adolescent girls.[1] That is, we need to know what works,

---

[1]Efficacy is the probability of benefit to individuals in a defined population from a medical technology applied for a given medical problem under ideal conditions of use (e.g., in a well-done randomized clinical trial. Effectiveness is the degree to which medical interventions achieve health improvements in real practice setting (Gold, Schein, & Coupey, 1997).

for whom, and under what conditions. Prominent among the services for which more evidence is needed are mental health and substance abuse treatment services, including the talking therapies, psychopharmacotherapies, and milieu therapies (e.g., hospital stays, day treatment for drug abuse, and residential treatment centers). But the effectiveness of treatment for many other disorders for which adolescent girls are being treated is also unknown, including attention deficit hyperactivity disorder, genitourinary disorders (e.g., chronic and severe pain, endometriosis, ovarian cysts, and urinary infections), asthma, headaches, and acne. In addition to treatment effectiveness, it is essential to answer questions about current methods of screening and counseling for the following topics: development, reproductive health issues, mental health issues (including, but beyond, depression and suicide), violence (victimization and perpetration), and substance abuse (including alcohol, tobacco, and other drugs). We need to know what screening, early and minimal intervention (e.g., brief counseling by a primary care provider), and other clinical services work for which adolescent girls. Assessing the effectiveness or cost-effectiveness of services will not be an easy task.

In addition, health care researchers need to address the conditions under which clinical services are better than traditional public health strategies. We must begin to address the issue of what overall preventive strategies or combinations of strategies—traditional health care, alternative health care, and community-based public health strategies—work best, when, and why. (We need the why so that we understand general principles and are not continuously reinventing wheels under different names.) There are divisions between those who argue, for example, that community-based public health preventive approaches would be more effective than the provision of clinical services for adolescents. At another level, there are splits between those in favor of interventions in early childhood or immediately in preadolescence and those in favor of interventions in adolescence. All of these debates have important fiscal implications because resources for adolescent health will probably always be scarce. This chapter focuses on traditional health care (including mental health) services as they affect adolescent girls, but, as noted above, this is where relatively small amounts of resources go.

3. There Is a Relative Paucity of Researchers in Adolescent Health

To develop an evidence-based system of health care for adolescent girls, psychologists and other health care researchers need more researchers interested in adolescent health, particularly in adolescent girls' health. Because many of adolescent girls' health issues are biopsychosocial in nature, it would be good for more behavioral and social scientists and traditional medical researchers to work together.

4. There Is a Need to Do Effectiveness Research in a Wider Range of Real-World Settings

Psychologists and other health care researchers also need to conduct rigorous effectiveness research in the real-world settings in which adolescent girls receive care, such as the offices of all kinds of practitioners, school-based health centers (SBHCs), family planning and sexually transmitted disease (STD) clinics, emergency rooms, and hospitals. Otherwise, clinicians may have difficulty applying research findings to clinical practice (Greenhill et al., 1996; Hoagwood, Jensen, Petti, & Burns, 1996; Jensen, Hoagwood, & Petti, 1996). Conducting research in practice settings is an emerging area of interest and research (e.g., Kelleher et al., 1997), as is the use of new information technologies to create databases for adolescent health research.

5. Improved Monitoring and Reporting Is Needed

One drawback in trying to focus on the health care needs of adolescent girls is that few health and health services data are reported regularly on this population. Exceptions include data on drug use patterns and pregnancy. If researchers are to track progress (and problems), we need to do more effective routine monitoring and reporting of adolescent girls' health issues (physical and mental, self- and other reported) and the quality of health and health-related services. This monitoring and reporting will keep our eyes on where the problems lie and where we should focus research and health care priorities.

6. Adolescent Girls' Own Perspectives Should Be Taken Into Consideration

Gradually, researchers are beginning to realize that adolescents, including girls, are both capable of (Office of Technology Assessment [OTA], 1991c) and interested in commenting on health care issues of importance to them. The Commonwealth Fund (Louis Harris & Associates, 1997) recently released results of a survey of adolescent girls that included questions about their health care experiences, and Ginsburg, Slap, and their colleagues (Ginsburg et al., 1995) worked intensively with adolescents to ascertain what would make them feel more comfortable in health care settings. Currently, Paul Cleary and his colleagues in Boston are working to develop a version of the Consumer Assessment of Health Plans Survey suitable for adolescent self-reporting. This survey will enable adolescents and others to compare the services of different adolescent health care providers and health plans from the perspective of the adolescents themselves.

For the most part, however, information on adolescents of both genders relies on data from parents and providers.

7. The Health Care and Research Community Should Adopt a Future Orientation

Although reports on adolescent health are few, they tend to focus on the same rather limited set of issues. Both for the good of adolescent girls and as a smart research strategy, researchers, providers, and policymakers would do well to think creatively about not only the apparently perennial problems of adolescent girls but also the issues of the future. For many years, the adolescent health community has been addressing a few problems of long-standing or cyclical national concern (teen pregnancy, drug use, violence, and certain chronic illnesses and disabilities and their psychosocial sequelae). New technologies for preventing and treating these problems should be considered (Ellen & Irwin, 1996). In addition, it may be time for part of the adolescent health research community to begin to think ahead: What issues will adolescent girls and their communities face in the future? What alternative preventive strategies and health care delivery approaches (aside from SBHCs) might be effective? For example, U.S. adolescent girls have mothers who have suffered from breast cancer. With increasing evidence that breast cancer is genetically based (and other evidence that it tends to run in families) and the availability of genetic testing, what questions should adolescent girls be asking? How will providers answer their questions? What tests should which girls get? When should they get them?

THE U.S. HEALTH CARE SYSTEM: ESSENTIAL BACKGROUND FOR UNDERSTANDING THE HEALTH OF ADOLESCENT GIRLS

Despite a plethora of recommendations that could improve health care for adolescents, including adolescent girls, advances in policies and programs have been slow in coming (Brindis et al., 1998). Many factors could account for this slowness.

First, the U.S. health care system has been, in effect, a sickness care system that has been dominated by the medical professions whose main goals are to detect, to treat, and hopefully to cure disease. Although these goals may sometimes conflict with some needs of adolescent girls, they are consistent with patients' traditional primary interests in health care: to get better if they experience a health problem.

Second, ongoing concerns about reducing the costs of health care mean that people are unlikely to see much expansion of the types of problems and populations treated by the health care system. A recent exception was the passage of the new Title XXI of the Social Security Act, the State Child Health Insurance Program, and related relaxation of Medicaid rules (Public Law 105-33, the Balanced Budget Act of 1997; see Rosenbaum, Johnson, Sonosky, Markus, & DeGraw, 1998). Under this act, states can apply for federal matching funds to expand health insurance coverage to more categories of low-income uninsured children, can "presume" eligibility to enroll more children and adolescents in Medicaid, and can accelerate implementation of Medicaid for the so-called "Waxman" children—those born before September 30, 1983, that is, those who are now teens who might not have been covered.[2] It will be important to track states' responses to these federal provisions as they affect adolescent girls, but it is noteworthy that the expansion, amounting to $20.3 billion in federal spending over 5 years, was tied to Congress's ability to devise a balanced budget, meaning that the $20.3 billion will be taken from elsewhere in federal discretionary spending.

Third, especially relative to other U.S. populations (e.g., the elderly, high-risk infants, and middle-aged men and women who have heart attacks), adolescent girls as a whole are not perceived as being sick and in need of medical services.

Fourth, when adolescent girls are recognized by society at large as having problems (e.g., pregnancy or substance abuse), it is not clear that the remedies for those problems lie within the health *care* system. As much as the argument is made by some providers and policymakers that adolescents' problems should be considered the "new morbidities" (Haggerty, 1975) and should be dealt with, at least in part, by the health care system (e.g., Green, 1994; Elster & Kuznets, 1992), the predominant view still seems to be that many problems and solutions reside "outside" medical care—within the girls themselves (i.e., the "behavioral" problems), their parents, or, to some extent, their communities. In fact, the best avenues for maintaining and improving many facets of adolescent girls' health are not yet known.

Relatively little traditional health care is delivered to adolescents, and so adolescents don't cost much in health care expenditures. As a group, spending on personal health care services for individuals under age 18 represents 15% of total spending for personal health care services. (Spending for personal health care services represents that for clinical services only; it does not include health care costs for activities such as construction, research, public health, and most education.) Perhaps, as a result, very little research is conducted on the efficacy and effectiveness of care

---

[2] These children are called "Waxman" children after Congressman Henry A. Waxman of California, who was a leader in getting the original legislation passed that offered states the option of expanding Medicaid coverage to these children, Section 1902(r)(2) of the Social Security Act.

that is or could be delivered to adolescent girls.[3] In a self-fulfilling cycle, most health care spending, and thus most health care research funding, goes to problems that are either very costly to society in terms of health expenditures and lost productivity (e.g., heart disease and cancer), perceived to present a serious threat to public health (e.g., emerging infectious diseases), or potentially curable within the health care system (e.g., by surgery, pharmaceutical treatment, or some other means). In part, because little research demonstrates to what extent clinical services often encouraged for adolescents (e.g., anticipatory guidance, counseling, or screening for behavioral problems or disease) make a difference in terms of adolescent health (U.S. Preventive Services Task Force, 1996), and, in part, because many of the most common problems of adolescent girls contain some stigma or can be socially embarrassing—many providers hesitate to work with adolescent patients (including adolescent girls), parents may not be aware that adolescents may benefit from health care services, and many advocates for children may not focus on encouraging adolescent girls to seek health services. Thus, the Society for Adolescent Medicine (Rosen, Elster, Hedberg, & Paperny, n.d.) argued that health services for adolescents be not only accessible in the traditional sense, but also "visible" so that adolescents know the services are available. The advent and growth in the number of SBHCs has changed the picture of adolescent health care somewhat, but there are still only an estimated 1,000 SBHCs in the United States (Kott, 1996), and not all work predominantly with adolescents.

HEALTH CARE NOW: CHALLENGES FOR ADOLESCENT GIRLS

Shortcomings in Health Care for Adolescent Girls

At least since the early 1980s, small groups of adolescent health researchers have been examining health care services as delivered to adolescents and have been informing their colleagues of apparent problems (Cheng & Klein, 1995; OTA, 1991c). These apparent problems exist throughout the spectrum of clinical care, from health guidance to screening/assessment to diagnosis to treatment. These problems are referred to as "apparent" because there is sometimes a discrepancy between expert judgments of individuals and groups of providers and the published literature on effectiveness (e.g., see Elster, 1998; U.S. Preventive Services Task

---

[3]The traditional health system can, of course, treat the sexually transmitted diseases that adolescent girls sustain and can deliver the babies that adolescent girls deliver, but those occurrences are not really talked about in polite company; thus it may be difficult for adolescent girls to get access to care for even these standard problems. As for mental health and substance abuse problems, there is much suspicion that many of these are not real problems (in adolescents or in others) or that health care is not the best remedy for children and teens.

Force [USPSTF], 1996). In addition, some problems cut across problems and services, having to do with communications among providers, adolescents, and the parents of adolescents.

Screening/Assessment

Screenings are those preventive services in which either a test or a standardized examination procedure (USPSTF, 1996), or questions about girls' health history, which may or may not be standardized (Elster, 1998), are used to identify patients requiring special intervention. For example, the USPSTF recommended that adolescents of both sexes be screened with the following tests: height, weight, and assessment for problem drinking. In addition, the task force recommended that sexually active adolescent females be screened using a pap test, a chlamydia screen, and a blood test for rubella.[4] In their guidelines for adolescent preventive services (GAPS), the American Medical Association (AMA) recommends screening by test for a greater range of sexually transmitted diseases (STDs): gonorrhea, syphilis, and human papilloma virus. The USPSTF does not recommend screening except by objective test, but the GAPS recommends screening by history (i.e., physician inquiry) for eating disorders, sexual activity, alcohol and other drug use, tobacco use, abuse, school performance, depression, and risk for suicide (American Medical Association, 1997).

Blum and colleagues (Blum, Beuhring, Wunderlich, & Resnick, 1996) found that screening for 21 of the biomedical and sociobehavioral health risks listed in the GAPS was below recommended levels in the five practice sites they reviewed. Differences were found by site, with providers in private practice screening for fewer health risks, possibly because such providers believe that high-risk behaviors are less likely to occur among the predominantly middle- and upper-income adolescents in their practices (Barnett, 1996). There were no sex differences. Similarly, Millstein and colleagues (Millstein, Igra, & Gans, 1996) documented that only 40% of primary care physicians reported screening all of their adolescent patients for sexual activity. In another study, Franzgrote, Ellen, and colleagues (Franzgrote, Ellen, Millstein, & Irwin, 1997) found low rates of screening for adolescent smoking among primary care physicians. Herman-Giddens and colleagues (Herman-Giddens et al., 1997) reported that many providers may be using outdated age criteria to judge girls' pubertal status. Many providers fail to recognize adolescent substance abusers (OTA, 1991b). Kelleher and colleagues (Kelleher et al. 1997) recently reported that primary

---

[4]Rubella is generally a mild illness, but when contracted by pregnant women, it frequently causes serious complications, including miscarriage, abortion, stillbirth, and congenital rubella syndrome (CRS), which can manifest as hearing loss, developmental delay, growth retardation, or heart or vision defects (USPSTF, 1996). Documented vaccination history and routine vaccination against rubella are equally acceptable alternatives to testing for rubella, according to the USPSTF.

care providers (pediatricians, family physicians, and internal medicine specialists) were particularly unlikely to recognize the problems of adolescent girls (up to age 15) with psychosocial problems (identified by parents using a standardized instrument).

Diagnosis

Despite the fact that diagnostic errors are a leading cause of malpractice complaints (U.S. Department of Health and Human Services [USDHHS], Health Resources and Services Administration [HRSA], 1998), there has been little systematic study by medical researchers of what and why diagnostic errors occur, including among children and adolescents. A recent review of literature on selected conditions found reason to be concerned about how effective primary care providers are in diagnosing asthma in children and adolescents and about providers' screening for mental health problems in the same population.

Counseling

Counseling for adolescent girls comes in two forms: One is "anticipatory guidance" on problems common to adolescent girls, even though a particular girl may not show any evidence of a particular problem. A second is counseling to intervene in an identified problem. The first type of counseling is discussed below; the second type is discussed later, under *Treatment*.

Like most Americans (McGinnis & Foege, 1993), adolescent girls' present and future major health care problems are often the result of chronic and acute conditions related to individual behavior. An expectation of the preventive primary care visit for adolescents is that the teens will be counseled to maintain or to adopt health-enhancing behaviors and to drop risky behaviors. The GAPS recommends that "health guidance" be provided to adolescents on development, diet and physical activity, healthy lifestyles, and injury prevention. Guidance on "healthy lifestyles" includes counseling regarding sexual behavior and avoidance of tobacco, alcohol, and other drug use. In addition, the GAPS recommends that parents and guardians of adolescents receive health guidance on a variety of topics (e.g., normative adolescent development and parenting behaviors). The USPSTF's guidance recommendations are similar, except that they include use of smoke detectors, safe storage and removal of firearms, use of contraception, advice to floss, brush with fluoride toothpaste daily, and regular visits to dental care providers. Only some of these recommendations are based on factors other than evidence that clinician counseling can influence these behaviors. Both the GAPS and the USPSTF recommend abstinence counseling, but the USPSTF notes that the ability of clinician counseling to influence these behaviors is unproven.

Despite similarities among guidelines for health guidance for adolescents, studies commonly find that providers often fail to counsel adolescents to avoid high-risk behaviors (Louis Harris and Associates, 1997; Millstein et al., 1996; Schuster, Bell, Peterson, & Kanouse, 1996) or about health promotion activities. Only 25% of adolescent girls surveyed by the Commonwealth Fund reported that providers had discussed high-risk behaviors (e.g., sex, drinking, and smoking) with them. Millstein et al.'s study cited above reported that only 31% of providers reported educating all of their adolescent patients about STD/HIV transmission. Only 28% of physicians were found to counsel patients about emergency contraception methods during regular visits (Gold, Schein, & Coupey, 1997).

Physicians can fail to provide health guidance for many reasons, including the nature of their training, low reimbursement for counseling activities, insufficient time, lack of reminder systems, feelings of personal discomfort with sensitive topics (Fisher et al., 1996), perceptions that adolescents do not want to discuss sensitive topics, dislike of caring for adolescents (Klitsner, Borok, Neinstein, & MacKenzie, 1992), and lack of belief in the effectiveness of such interventions (Igra & Millstein, 1993; Steiner & Gest, 1996).

Treatment

When it comes to treatment, evidence of effectiveness is increasingly essential. In an article attempting to give advice to pediatricians on their roles in assisting teens to avoid the consequences of adolescent pregnancy, for example, a clinic director suggested that it is important for pediatricians who sees teens to have current knowledge about what birth control methods work best. Nonetheless, he was unable to provide much guidance on the state of contraception effectiveness to pediatricians because of the state of the science for this population. He noted, for example, that the intrauterine devices that his clinic had considerable success with in the 1960s and early 1970s were by 1993 contraindicated for teens; that the clinic's patient failure rate with oral contraceptives was 15% to 20% (which is consistent with available national averages; OTA, 1991b); and that depoprovera, another alternative, caused secondary amenorrhea after 6 to 12 months. Yet about half of adolescent girls age 15 and older are sexually active and at risk of pregnancy (Abma, Chandra, Mosher, Peterson, & Piccinino, 1997). In birth control and many other areas, lack of evidence leaves providers with no place to go.

Prescription drugs. Observers estimate that only 20% of prescription drugs currently being prescribed for children and adolescents up to age 18 have been tested in that population (Stapleton, 1997). Off-label use is common in pediatric care, prompting concern that some children may be at risk for adverse effects. To address this problem, the FDA has several activities under way to increase pediatric labeling (USDHHS, 1998).

Mental health treatments. Despite the lack of a national prevalence study of children and adolescents' mental health problems, a disturbing amount of evidence is mounting of the depth and breadth of depression and other disorders in adolescent girls (e.g., Novins, Beals, Shore, & Manson, 1996; Petersen et al., 1993). Resnick, Blum, Udry and their colleagues (Resnick et al., 1997) recently found that twice as many adolescent girls as adolescent boys reported having attempted suicide in a recent year. Safer, Zito, and Fine (1996) noted the rapid increase in the use of methylphenidate (Ritalin) for attention deficit hyperactivity disorder (ADHD) in Maryland girls between the 1980s and the mid 1990s. A conference sponsored by the National Institute of Mental Health (NIMH; part of the National Institutes of Health [NIH]) concluded that research is needed not only on sex differences related to ADHD but also on manifestations of ADHD in girls as such, with areas of focus including differences in life course, effects of hormones, effects of ADHD parenting on the next generation, response to and implications for the design of psychosocial treatment, effects of differential comorbidity, and possible interactions of sex and ethnicity (Arnold, 1996).

On the basis of evidence about violence-related behavior, conduct disorder (a *Diagnostic Statistical Manual of Mental Disorders*, 4th ed; [DSM–IV] disorder) is apparently on the rise among adolescent girls. In 1992, for example, more than 30% of the 12- to 21-year-old girls in a national survey reported that they had been in one or more physical fights (USDHHS, Public Health Service [PHS], Centers for Disease Control [CDC], National Center for Health Statistics [NCHS], 1997). In Massachusetts, 5% of female high school students in Massachusetts admitted to carrying weapons to school (DuRant, Kahn, Beckford, & Woods, 1997).

Despite the apparent increases in mental health problems among girls, researchers have provided little compelling evidence for the effectiveness of common or innovative treatments. Hoagwood, Jensen, Petti, and Burns (1996) found an appalling lack of research on the effectiveness in real-world settings of mental health treatments for children and adolescents (Hoagwood et al., 1996; Jensen et al., 1996; see also Bickman, 1996). Most of the research demonstrating efficacy of treatments had been conducted in university settings with atypical populations of children. Hoagwood and colleagues' findings are echoed by recent reviews on specific disorders and treatments in children and adolescents (including girls), such as early-onset depression, major depressive disorder, and depressive disorder; tricyclic antidepressants (Wilens et al., 1996); and anxiety (Bernstein, Brochardt, & Perwien, 1996). Kazdin (1997) noted that although there are many studies suggesting positive findings for psychotherapy in children and adolescents, specification of a systematic framework for the next generation of studies is needed for progress in this field to occur.

Substance use and abuse. Middle and early female adolescents' use of some substances—in particular, tobacco and alcohol—is now about on par with male use (Ellickson, McGuigan, Adams, Bell, & Hays, 1996). Recommended approaches to prevention and treatment in the health care system include one-on-one counseling by providers. Unfortunately, studies of smoking cessation in primary care have not shown evidence of effectiveness for adolescents. In 1996, smoking cessation guidelines for clinical practice, drawing from persuasive evidence of effectiveness of counseling and use of nicotine substitutes with adults, were published, and studies are under way to examine whether the same sorts of treatments work with adolescents.

The Substance Abuse and Mental Health Services Administration in the USDHHS acknowledges that adolescent addiction treatment outcome is a poorly studied area (Landry, 1997). Only a small number of controlled studies have addressed treatment outcomes for addicted adolescents, and most of the knowledge gained from such studies concerns nontreatment predictors of treatment success or failure. Although the conclusion drawn from the small number of available studies is that treatment is usually better than no treatment, research is particularly needed that would allow evaluations of the elements of treatment.

Chronic physical disorders. Links between chronic physical disorders and poor psychosocial functioning have long been reported, and the assumption has been that physical disorders lead to maladaptation emotionally and socially. Using a new comprehensive measure of adolescent health, Forrest and his colleagues (Forrest, Starfield, Riley, & Kang, 1997) found that compared with well teens, adolescents with asthma and recent wheezing had lower perceived well-being, more physical and emotional symptoms, greater limitations in activity, more comorbidities, and more negative behaviors that threaten social development. For many disorders, such as severe chronic disorders of congenital origin, this sequence of problems is undoubtedly true. For some disorders, however, recent research suggests that the causal directions may not be clear. An experimental study found that inducing positive or negative emotions influenced asthma symptoms in children, apparently by affecting involuntary responses in the cardiopulmonary system (Miller & Wood, 1997). Miller and Wood's finding suggests that emotional states may influence the course of asthma, a finding with intriguing clinical implications. However, providers need to be careful about attributing "psychiatric" causes to disorders with predominantly "physical causes." For example, asthma and panic disorder sometimes have similar signs and symptoms, but the treatment implications are vastly different (Schmaling & Bell, 1997). The tendency to conclude that "it's all in your head"—with a concomitant tendency to dismiss the problem as no longer the provider's responsibility—seems widespread among clinicians with female patients.

Providers should be aware that different disorders may have different psychosocial impacts. For example, young adults with a history of a certain form of epilepsy, particularly those without remission of their seizures, were found to have psychosocial outcomes that were considerably worse than those of young adults with juvenile rheumatoid arthritis (Wirrell et al., 1997). In research with adolescents with active or inactive epilepsy or asthma, girls with high seizure severity were found to be most at risk for quality-of-life problems (Austin, Huster, Dunn, & Risinger, 1996).

Finally, chronic physical illnesses can have comorbid physical consequences that can, in turn, have psychosocial consequences. For example, some girls with cystic fibrosis may experience significant delays in initiation of menses (Johannesson, Gottlieb, & Hjelte, 1997). Although puberty is a natural physical function, girls' perceptions that it is mistimed can have untoward emotional consequences (Hayward et al., 1997). Early puberty has been found to increase the risk of internalizing symptoms (e.g., low self-esteem and depressive mood) and possibly internalizing disorders (e.g., depression) in adolescent girls (Hayward et al., 1997).

Cross-Cutting Issues

Communication. Adolescents and providers often have different perceptions of what should be discussed in a health care visit (Cheng & Klein, 1995; OTA, 1991c; Steiner & Gest, 1996). Differences appear on topics of physical fitness, nutrition, growth, STDs, contraception, acne, fear of cancer, obesity, feelings of depression, lack of confidence, and violence. Some studies find that adolescents want to discuss the issues more than do the providers, and others find the opposite (Boekeloo, Schamus, Cheng, & Simmens, 1996), but most available studies have reported unsatisfactory communication between providers and adolescent patients (Schuster et al., 1996). Gender matching (matching female providers with female patients) has mixed evidence of desirability and effectiveness (e.g., Millstein et al., 1996; Wilson, Manoff, & Joffe, 1997). Adolescent fears that confidentiality will be breached have been found to be the leading reason why adolescents do not seek health care (Cheng & Klein, 1995; Ford, Millstein, Eyre, & Irwin, 1996); studies of providers find considerable variation in their adherence to confidentiality laws and professional ethical statements, and they often fail to disclose their policies on confidentiality to adolescent patients (Ford & Millstein, 1997).[5] Primary care providers are divided on

---

[5]Ford and Millstein (1997) accurately point out that adolescents cannot always be guaranteed confidentiality. Confidentiality assurances depend in large part on state laws and regulations, which vary considerably.

issues of abortion, just as are many adolescents and adults in the United States. Two fifths of pediatricians responding to a survey believed that abortion should be restricted for adolescents, and 7% believed adolescents should not have access to abortion under any circumstances (Fleming & O'Connor, 1993). Matching providers with patients in this area may be important.

The importance of a participatory patient–provider relationship to patient satisfaction, adherence to prescribed health regimens, and even health outcomes is supported by a growing number of researchers. Until very recently, however, little if any research was conducted with adolescents as patients. Differences between adolescents and providers about the nature of topics to be discussed, and concerns about cleanliness and confidentiality, may impede good communication, but adolescents have also expressed concern about other aspects of their interactions with health care providers. For example, focus groups that have explored adolescents' views on health care quality have elicited the following statements:

> "I don't like it when the doctor makes me feel like it's a 'chore' to see me." "[A good quality provider] gives you choices/options." "I'm eighteen. I don't want to be treated like a little baby." [6]

In a surprise finding in a study of adolescents, adolescents expressed most concern about the cleanliness of providers: Those providers who washed their hands in front of the adolescent patients were considered to be those least likely to transmit HIV infection (Ginsburg et al., 1995).

Parental role. Because most adolescent girls are still dependent on their parents financially and emotionally (e.g., Resnick et al., 1997), parents can be integral partners in the girls' health and health care. However, a number of other factors may interfere with parents' involvement in adolescent girls' health: adolescents' desire for privacy, fear of parents' reactions to certain health issues (e.g., contraception, pregnancy, or drug use), lack of parental knowledge, and parental fears. Finding the appropriate nexus among adolescent girls, health care providers, and parents can be difficult. Providers may rely too much or too little on parents to provide appropriate health care for their children and adolescents. For example, parental knowledge of a child's cholesterol value of 200 mg/dL or greater did not result in substantial further seeking of health care, as the screening program had expected (Nader et al., 1997). Fifty-nine percent of physicians reported evaluating children for cholesterol and reporting levels to parents; about half of the physicians reported repeating the cholesterol determination, a sign that parents did not follow up on the initial evaluation.

In another study suggesting the gaps among the primary participants providing children's health care, physician providers of child health care,

---

[6]Foundation for Accountability National Pediatric Prevention and Health Promotion Roundtable Meeting, Washington, DC (October 9, 1997).

62% of Massachusetts physicians responding to a survey stated that parents, the state, or the child's school should be responsible for seeing that children get access to Medicaid's Early and Periodic Screening Diagnosis and Treatment (EPSDT) services (Bauchner, Witzburg, & Jones, 1996). (EPSDT is intended to guarantee Medicaid-covered children ages 0 to 18 years important health services along the continuum from screening to treatment.) The investigators understandably questioned parents' ability to understand the benefits and services available to their children through the complex, and locally variable Medicaid programs.

Multiple and covarying problems. Some risk behaviors have been found to cluster (e.g., Donovan, Jessor, & Costa, 1993; Fortenberry, 1997; Osgood, 1991; Potthoff et al., 1998). For example, the use of many harmful substances covaries. Adolescent girls who are substance users are more likely than nonsubstance users to engage in violent behavior. Adolescent smoking has been found to correlate with marijuana use, binge drinking, and fighting (Escobedo, Reddy, & DuRant, 1997). Smoking is a (statistical) predictor of major depressive disorder and drug abuse or dependence, and vice versa (Brown, Lewinsohn, Seeley, & Wagner, 1996). For adolescent girls, the number of sexual partners (in a given time) has been associated with other potentially health-threatening behaviors such as aggression, drinking and drunkenness, marijuana use, disordered eating, lack of exercise, and failure to use seatbelts (Fortenberry, 1997). These clusterings raise different issues about health care delivery. Which is the primary, and which is the comorbid problem? Can successfully preventing one (e.g., premature sexuality or smoking) prevent other covarying behaviors? Can treatments be combined? If not, which problem gets treated first? Researchers suggest that health interventions designed to focus categorically on one risk dimension should focus on others as well, depending on the risk group's profile. In addition, research efforts need to focus on effective strategies for coping with social and psychological stressors (Potthoff et al., 1998).

Socioeconomic Factors

A recent report concluded that to understand the linkages between sociostructural inequalities and differences in health status, researchers and policymakers must consider gender. This report indicated that upper-middle-class girls reported the worst health status (according to General Health Perceptions scale of the Medical Outcomes Survey 36-Item Short Form Health Survey, SF-36). Their data suggested further that psychological well-being and self-reported physical health status mediate the effects of gender and the observed gender and social class interaction for general health perceptions. However, this study involved only a relatively small sample of 98 adolescent boys and girls of upper-middle and working classes, and so much remains to be learned about the interrelationships of social and economic factors with gender for adolescents (Guthrie, Caldwell, & Hunter, 1997).

Most of the data on normal adolescence are derived from studies of Caucasian middle-class girls, presenting a challenge to providers who desire to base interventions with non-White and poor girls on good normative data about their biopsychosocial development (Williams-Morris, 1996). When ethnic minority girls, especially African Americans, are the focus of a study, it is usually one related to premarital sexual behaviors and childbearing, leaving out a range of other behaviors. In addition, social class and ethnicity are often confounded. Thus, likely relationships between poverty and ethnicity, development, health problems, and service delivery are poorly understood (Kagawa-Singer et al., 1996).

Guthrie and her colleagues (Guthrie et al., 1997) provide a gender-specific framework for future work on health behavior of minority adolescent girls. The framework takes into account the influences of environment, social class, and ethnicity on gender socialization. Gender socialization is, in turn, seen as influencing adolescent girls' self-efficacy, which, in turn, influences mental health outcomes and health-related behaviors. The model could be easily expanded to involve key aspects of the design and provision of health care services.

HEALTH CARE FOR ADOLESCENT GIRLS: OPPORTUNITIES

Alternative Health Care Sites

In their study comparing five sites' adherence to recommendations for screening for biomedical and sociobehavioral health risks, Blum and colleagues (Blum et al., 1996) found greater provider adherence in the teen clinics than in a community family practice setting. In turn, the community family practice setting screened more extensively than the private family practice or private pediatric practice. School-based health centers continue to report a booming business among adolescents (Anglin, Naylor, & Kaplan, 1996), although some access barriers remain (Keyl, Hurtado, Barber, & Borton, 1996), including some pediatricians' lingering discomfort with the idea that an SBHC can be as good a "medical home" as a pediatrician's practice (Zanga, 1998). Some managed care organizations (e.g., HMOs) may be better at delivering some preventive services to adolescents (e.g., Millstein et al., 1996). A small, but perhaps growing trend, has been to marry managed care and SBHCs (Brindis & Sanghvi, 1997).

Adolescent Health Specialists

In the early 1990s, adolescent medicine was recognized as a subspecialty in the field of medicine. Although there remain concerns that an additional specialty could further fragment care for children, there is also evidence that adolescent health specialists do a better job serving the health care needs of adolescents (Franzgrote et al., 1997). Some psychologists have recently called for the field of clinical psychology to enhance its training for those who treat adolescents.

Other Training

Confidentiality can be a key issue for adolescents, yet many physicians feel inappropriately trained to deal with confidentiality. This situation may change in the future with the development of an ethics curriculum for pediatric residency programs. The proposed ethics curriculum includes a section on confidentiality and adolescents.

Focus on Customers and Quality of Care

Increased consumer activism is one of the latest results of recent changes in health care delivery and financing, and the power of consumers has not been overlooked by health care deliverers (Lewin Group, 1998). Adolescents, including adolescent girls, are beginning to be taken seriously in the design of health services (Burke & Liston, 1994; Jones, Hopkins, & Lester, 1997) and as judges of the quality of care. New instruments are being developed and tested that should help increase research and applications in outcomes and quality for adolescents, including adolescent girls (Forrest et al., 1997).

Policy Focus

Gradually, the health care needs of adolescents, including adolescent girls, are being recognized by policymakers. For example, May 8, 1997, was denoted Childhood Depression Awareness Day, and since October 1997, children have become a focus of the now-annual National Depression Screening Day. In 1996, the Secretary of the USDHHS announced a new initiative on "Girl Power" among young adolescent girls, and the department is also engaged in a National Strategy on Teen Pregnancy.

Research Policy Focus

The era of evidence-based health care has finally put a spotlight on the paucity of evidence for the effectiveness of many child and adolescent health services. New policies at the NIH and the Agency for Health Care Policy and Research, both USDHHS agencies that support research, should help to increase the proportion of drugs and other health technologies that are tested for their efficacy and effectiveness in children and adolescents before they are put on the market. In early 1997, both agencies announced their intentions to develop policies that would encourage the inclusion of children and adolescents in all extramural research applications, and both urged investigators to begin to include children or to address why children and adolescents should not participate in specific research projects. In March 1998, the NIH announced that all applicants must include children or adequately defend their exclusion from a protocol. These policies will require intensive work with major sectors of the child health research community (e.g., agency staff, researchers, Institutional Review Boards, researchers, and parents).

If these efforts bear fruit in the subfield of adolescent girls' health, they may make it more feasible for those who advocate particular clinical services and organizational arrangements to integrate evidence for effectiveness into their policy recommendations.

With increased policy attention to health care for children and adolescents, now is a good time for more researchers and providers to turn their attention to these populations. Although past research—only some of which has been reviewed in this chapter—provides a good knowledge base on many of the problems all adolescents face when they seek clinical services, we do not know enough about adolescent girls in particular. For example, adolescent girls are more likely than boys to use services such as family planning and STD clinics, hospitals, and SBHCs, but we know little about how care is delivered to girls in these settings and how it could be improved. In studies and surveillance, pregnant adolescent girls are generally grouped with female adults (e.g., 15- to 24-year-olds are grouped together). On the basis of what we do know, the time for exploring distinctions among boys and girls, and among girls and female adults, is here.

Also of critical importance is increased focus on intervention-based research (e.g., demonstrations with rigorous evaluations). In the mental health field, psychologists, other health care providers, and pharmaceutical companies can improve outcomes for adolescent girls by conducting rigorous research on what works for this population and by translating existing research into practice. As psychologists, we are perhaps most aware that gender, age, and developmental stage all create different psychological "settings" for health care services. We need to take heed of the evidence base pertaining to adolescent girls in our own clinical services (mental health providers and parts of integrated primary care teams) and be proactive by contributing such knowledge to other health care providers and researchers. Adolescent girls are different in many ways and so important that we cannot let them slip through the cracks of the health care provider and research systems.

REFERENCES

Abma, J. C., Chandra, A., Mosher, W., Peterson L., & Piccinino, L. (1997, May). Fertility, family planning, and women's health: New data from the 1995 National Survey of Family Growth. *Vital and Health Statistics Series 23*, No. 19. (DHHS Publ. No. PHS 97-1995). Hyattsville, MD: U.S. Department of Health and Human Services, Centers for Disease Control and Prevention, National Center for Health Statistics.

American Medical Association. (1997). *Preventive health services by age and procedure* [On-line]. Available: www.ama-assn.org

American Psychiatric Association. (1994). *Diagnostic and statistical manual of mental disorders* (4th ed.). Washington, DC: Author.

Anglin, T. M., Naylor, K. E., & Kaplan, D. W. (1996). Comprehensive school-based health care: High-school students' use of medical, mental health, and substance abuse services. *Pediatrics, 318–330.*

Arnold, L. E. (1996). Sex differences in ADHD: Conference summary. *Journal of Abnormal Child Psychology, 24,* 555–569.

Austin, J. K., Huster, G. A., Dunn, D. W., & Risinger, M. W. (1996). Adolescents with active or inactive epilepsy or asthma: A comparison of quality of life. *Epilepsia, 37,* 1228–1238.

Barnett, H. L. (1996). Annotation: Preventive screening for health risks among adolescents. *American Journal of Public Health, 86,* 1767–1772.

Bauchner, H., Witzburg, R., & Jones, C. (1996). Early and periodic screening diagnosis and treatment. *Archives of Pediatric and Adolescent Medicine, 150,* 1219–1220.

Bernstein, G. A., Brochardt, C. M., & Perwien, A. R. (1996). Anxiety disorders in children and adolescents: A review of the past ten years. *Journal of the American Academy of Child and Adolescent Psychiatry, 35,* 1110–1111.

Bernzweig, J., Takayama, J. I., Phibbs, C., Lewis, C., & Pantell, R. H. (1997). Gender differences in physician–patient communication: Evidence from pediatric visits. *Archives of Pediatric and Adolescent Medicine, 151,* 586–591.

Bickman, L. (1996). A continuum of care: More is not always better. *American Psychologist, 51,* 689–701.

Birmaher, B., Ryan, N. D., Williamson, D. E., Breant, D. A., & Kaufman, J. (1996). Childhood and adolescent depression: A review of the past 10 years. Part II. *Journal of the American Academy of Child and Adolescent Psychiatry, 35,* 1575–1583.

Blum, R. W., Beuhring, T., Wunderlich, M., & Resnick, M. D. (1996). Don't ask, they won't tell: The quality of adolescent health screening in five practice settings. *American Journal of Public Health, 86,* 1767–1771.

Boekeloo, B. O., Schamus, L. A., Cheng, T. L., & Simmens, S. J. (1996). Young adolescents' comfort with discussion about sexual problems with their physician. *Archives of Pediatric and Adolescent Medicine, 150,* 1146–1152.

Brindis, C. D., Ozer, E. M., Handley, M., Knopf, D. K., Millstein, S. G., & Irwin,

C. E. (1998). *Improving adolescent health: An analysis and synthesis of health policy recommendations: Full Report.* Rockville, MD: U.S. Department of Health and Human Services, Public Health Service, Health Resources and Services Administration, Maternal and Child Health Bureau, Office of Adolescent Health.

Brindis, C. D., & Sanghvi, R. V. (1997). School-based health clinics: Remaining viable in a changing health care delivery system. *Annual Review of Public Health, 18,* 567–587.

Brown, R. A., Lewinsohn, P. M., Seeley, J. R., & Wagner, E. F. (1996). Cigarette smoking, major depression, and other psychiatric disorders among adolescents. *Journal of the American Academy of Child and Adolescent Psychiatry, 35,* 1602–1610.

Burke, P. J., & Liston, W. J. (1994). Adolescent mothers' perceptions of social support and the impact of parenting on their lives. *Pediatric Nursing, 20,* 593–599.

Cheng, T. L., & Klein, J. D. (1995). The adolescent viewpoint: Implications for access and prevention. *Journal of the American Medical Association, 273,* 1957–1958.

Donovan, J. E., Jessor, R., & Costa, F. M. (1993). Structure of health-enhancing behavior in adolescence: A latent-variable approach. *Journal of Health and Social Behavior, 34,* 346–362.

DuRant, R. H., Treiber, F., Goodman, E., & Woods, E. R. (1996). Intentions to use violence among young adolescents. *Pediatrics, 98,* 1104–1108.

DuRant, R. H., Kahn, J., Beckford, P. H., & Woods, E. R. (1997). The association of weapon carrying and fighting on school property and other health risk and problem behaviors among high school students. *Archives of Pediatric and Adolescent Medicine, 151,* 360–366.

Ellen, J. M., & Irwin, C. E., Jr. (1996). Primary care management of adolescent sexual behavior. *Current Opinion in Pediatrics, 8,* 442–448.

Ellickson, P. L., McGuigan, K. A., Adams, V., Bell, R. M., & Hays, R. D. (1996). Teenagers and alcohol misuse in the United States: By any definition, it's a big problem. *Addiction, 91,* 1489–1503.

Elster, A. B. (1998). Comparison of recommendations for adolescent clinical preventive services developed by national organizations. *Archives of Pediatric and Adolescent Medicine, 152,* 193–198.

Elster, A. B., & Kuznets, N. J. (1992). *AMA Guidelines for Adolescent Preventive Services (GAPS): Recommendations and rationale.* Baltimore: Williams & Wilkins.

Escobedo, L. G., Reddy, M., & DuRant, R. H. (1997). Relationship between cigarette smoking and health risk and problem behaviors among U.S. adolescents. *Archives of Pediatric and Adolescent Medicine, 151,* 66–71.

Fisher, M., Golden, N. H., Bergeson, R., Bernstein, A., Saunders, D., Schneider, M., Seitz, M., & Seigel, W. (1996). Update on adolescent health care in pediatric practice. *Journal of Adolescent Health, 19,* 394–400.

Fleming, G. V., & O'Connor, K. G. (1993). Adolescent abortion: Views of the membership of the American Academy of Pediatrics. *Pediatrics, 91*, 561–565.

Ford, C. A., & Millstein, S. G. (1997). Delivery of confidentiality assurances to adolescents by primary care physicians. *Archives of Pediatric and Adolescent Medicine, 151*, 505–509.

Ford, C. A., Millstein, S. G., Eyre, S. L., & Irwin, C. E., Jr. (1996). Anticipatory guidance regarding sex: Views of virginal female adolescents. *Journal of Adolescent Health, 19*, 179–183.

Forrest, C. B., Starfield, B., Riley, A. W., & Kang, M. (1997). The impact of asthma on the health status of adolescents. *Pediatrics, 99*, e1.

Fortenberry, J. D. (1997). Public health brief: Health care seeking behaviors related to sexually transmitted diseases among adolescents. *American Journal of Public Health, 87*, 417–420.

Franzgrote, M., Ellen, J. M., Millstein, S. G., & Irwin, C. E., Jr. (1997). Screening for adolescent smoking among primary care physicians in California. *American Journal of Public Health, 8*, 1341–1345.

Ginsburg, K. R., Slap, G. B., Cnaan, A., Forke, C. M., Baisley, C. M., & Rouselle, D. M. (1995). Adolescents' perceptions of factors affecting their decisions to seek health care. *Journal of the American Medical Association, 273*, 1913–1918.

Gold, M. A., Schein, A., & Coupey, S. M. (1997). Emergency contraception: A national survey of adolescent health experts. *Family Planning Perspectives, 29*, 15–19, 24.

Goodman, E., Amick, B. C., Rezendes, M. O., Tarlov, A. R., Rogers, W. H., & Kagan, J. (1997). Influences of gender and social class on adolescents' perceptions of health. *Archives of Pediatric and Adolescent Medicine, 151*, 899–904.

Green, M. (Ed.). (1994). *Bright futures: Guidelines for health supervision of infants, children, and adolescents.* Arlington, VA: National Center for Education in Maternal and Child Health.

Greenhill, L. L., Abikoff, H. B., Arnold, E., Cantwell, D. P., Conners, C. K., & Elliott, G. (1996). Medication treatment strategies in the MTA study: Relevance to clinicians and researchers. *Journal of the American Academy of Child and Adolescent Psychiatry, 35*, 1304–1313.

Guthrie, B. J., Caldwell, H., & Hunter, A. G. (1997). Minority adolescent female health: Strategies for the next millennium. In D. K. Wilson, J. R. Rodrigue, & W. C. Taylor, (Eds.), *Health-promoting and health-compromising behaviors among minority adolescents* (pp. 153–171). Washington. DC: American Psychological Association.

Haggerty, R. J. (1975). The new morbidity. In R. J. Haggerty, K. J. Roghmann, & I. B. Pless (Eds.), *Child health and community* (pp. 94–110). New York: Wiley.

Halsey, L., Collin, M. F., & Anderson, C. L. (1996). Extremely low-birth-weight children and their peers: A comparison of school-age outcomes. *Archives of Pediatric and Adolescent Medicine, 150*, 790–794.

Hayward, C., Killen, J. D., Wilson, D. M., Hammer, L. D., Litt, I. F., & Kraemer,

H. C. (1997). Psychiatric risk associated with early puberty in adolescent girls. *Journal of the American Academy of Child and Adolescent Psychiatry, 36,* 255–262.

Herman-Giddens, M. E., Slora, E. J., Wasserman, R. C., Bourdony, C. J., Bhapkar, M. V., Koch, G. G., & Hasemeier, C. M. (1997). Secondary sexual characteristics and menses in young girls seen in office practice: A study from the pediatric research in office settings network. *Pediatrics, 99,* 505–512.

Hoagwood, K., Jensen, P. S., Petti, T., & Burns, B. J. (1996). Outcomes of mental health care for children and adolescents: I. A comprehensive conceptual model. *Journal of the American Academy of Child and Adolescent Psychiatry, 35,* 1055–1063.

Igra, V., & Millstein, S. G. (1993). Current status and approaches to improving preventive services for adolescents. *Journal of the American Medical Association, 269,* 1408–1412.

Jensen, P. S., Hoagwood, K., & Petti, T. (1996). Outcomes of mental health care for children and adolescents: II. Literature review and application of a comprehensive model. *Journal of the American Academy of Child and Adolescent Psychiatry, 35,* 1064–1077.

Johannesson, M., Gottlieb, C., & Hjelte, L. (1997). Delayed puberty in girls with cystic fibrosis despite good clinical status. *Pediatrics, 99,* 29–34.

Jones, S., Hopkins, S., & Lester C. (1997). Teenage sexual health through the eyes of the teenager: A study using focus groups. *Ambulatory Child Health, 3,* 3–11.

Kagawa-Singer, M., Katz, P. A., Taylor, D. A., & Vanderryn, J. H. M. (1996). *Health issues for minority adolescents.* Lincoln: University of Nebraska Press.

Kazdin, A. E. (1997). A model for developing effective treatments: Progression and interplay of theory, research, and practice. *Journal of Clinical Child Psychology, 26,* 114–129.

Kelleher, K. J., Childs, G. E., Wasserman, M. D., McInerney, T. K., Nutting, P. A., & Gardner, W. P. (1997). Insurance status and recognition of psychosocial problems: A report from the Pediatric Research in Office Settings and the Ambulatory Sentinel Practice Networks. *Archives of Pediatrics and Adolescent Medicine, 151,* 1109–1115.

Keyl, P. M., Hurtado, M. P., Barber, M. M., & Borton, J. (1996). School-based health centers: Students' access, knowledge, and use of services. *Archives of Pediatric and Adolescent Medicine, 150,* 175–180.

Klitsner, I. N., Borok, G. M., Neinstein, L., & MacKenzie, R. (1992). Adolescent health care in a large multispecialty prepaid group practice. Who provides it and how well are they doing? *Western Journal of Medicine, 156,* 628–632.

Kott, A. (1996). Health care and schools team up to help kids. *Advances: The Quarterly Newsletter of the Robert Wood Johnson Foundation*(3).

Landry, M. J. (1997, February). *Overview of addiction treatment effectiveness.* Rockville, MD: U.S. Department of Health and Human Services, Substance Abuse and Mental Health Services Administration.

Lewin Group. (1998). *Tracking the system: American health care, 1998*. Washington, DC: National Committee for Quality Health Care.

Lewinsohn, P. M., Seeley, J. R., Hibbard, J., Rohde, P., & Sack, W. H. (1996). Cross-sectional and prospective relationships between physical morbidity and depression in older adolescents. *Journal of the American Academy of Child and Adolescent Psychiatry, 35*, 1120–1129.

Louis Harris and Associates. (1997). *The Commonwealth Fund survey of the health of adolescent girls, 1997*. New York: Commonwealth Fund.

McGinnis, J. M., & Foege, W. H. (1993). Actual causes of death in the United States. *Journal of the American Medical Association, 270*, 2207–2212.

Meurer, J. R., Meurer, L. N., & Holloway, R. L. (1996, September). Clinical problems and counseling for single-parent families. *American Family Physicians, 54*, 864, 867–870.

Miller, B. D., & Wood, B. L. (1997). The influence of specific emotional states on automatic reactivity and pulmonary function in asthmatic children. *Journal of the American Academy of Child and Adolescent Psychiatry, 36*, 669–667.

Millstein, S. G., Igra, V., & Gans, J. (1996). Delivery of STD/HIV preventive services to adolescents by primary care physicians. *Journal of Adolescent Health, 19*, 249–257.

Millstein, S. G., Petersen, A. C., & Nightingale, E. O. (Eds.). (1993). *Promoting the health of adolescents: New directions for the twenty-first century*. New York: Oxford University Press.

Nader, P. R., Yang, M., Luepker, R. V., Parcel, G. S., Pirie, P., Feldman, H. A., Stone, E. J., & Webber, L. S. (1997). Parent and physician response to children's cholesterol values of 200 mg/dL or greater: The child and adolescent trial for cardiovascular health experiment. *Pediatrics, 99*(5), e5.

Novins, D. K., Beals, J., Shore, J. H., & Manson, S. M. (1996). Substance abuse treatment of American Indian adolescents: Comorbid symptomatology, gender differences, and treatment patterns. *Journal of the American Academy of Child and Adolescent Psychiatry, 35*, 1593–1601.

Office of Technology Assessment. (1991a). *Adolescent health—Volume 1*. Washington, DC: U.S. Government Printing Office.

Office of Technology Assessment. (1991b). *Adolescent health—Volume 2*. Washington, DC: U.S. Government Printing Office.

Office of Technology Assessment. (1991c). *Adolescent health—Volume 3*. Washington, DC: U.S. Government Printing Office.

Osgood, D. W. (1991). *Covariation among health-compromising behaviors in adolescents: A background paper for the adolescent health project of the U.S. Congress, Office of Technology Assessment* (Report No. PB91-154-377/AS). Springfield, VA: National Technical Information Service.

Ozer, E. M., Brindis, C. D., Millstein, S. G., Knopf, D. K., & Irwin, C. E., Jr. (1997). *America's adolescents: Are they healthy?* Rockville, MD: U.S. Department of Health and Human Services, Public Health Service, Health Resources and

Services Administration, Maternal and Child Health Bureau, Office of Adolescent Health.

Petersen, A. C., Compas, B. E., Brooks-Gunn, J., Stemmler, M., Ey, S., & Grant, K. E. (1993). Depression in adolescence. *American Psychologist, 48,* 155–168.

Potthoff, S. J., Bearinger, L. H., Skay, C. L., Cassuto, N., Blum, R. W., & Resnick, M. D. (1998). Dimensions of risk behaviors among American Indian youth. *Archives of Pediatric and Adolescent Medicine, 152,* 157–163.

Rauh, J. L. (1993). The pediatrician's role in assisting teenagers to avoid the consequences of adolescent pregnancy. *Pediatric Annals, 22,* 90–98.

Resnick, M. D., Bearman, P. S., Blum, R. W., Bauman, K. E., Harris, K. M., Jones, J., Tabor, J., Beuhring, T., Sieving, R. E., Shew, M., Ireland, M., Bearinger, L. H., & Udry, J. R. (1997). Protecting adolescents from harm: Findings from the National Longitudinal Study of Adolescent Health. *Journal of the American Medical Association, 278,* 823–832.

Rosen, D. S., Elster, A., Hedberg, V., & Paperny, D. (n.d.). *Clinical preventive services for adolescents: Position paper of society for adolescent medicine* [On-line]. Available: http://cortex.uchc.edu/~sam/samfinal/activities.

Rosenbaum, S., Johnson, K., Sonosky, C., Markus, A., & DeGraw, C. (1998). The children's hour: The state children's health program. *Health Affairs, 17*(1), 75–89.

Safer, D. J., Zito, J. M., & Fine, E. M. (1996). Increased methylphenidate usage for attention deficit disorder in the 1990s. *Pediatrics, 98,* 1084–1088.

Schmaling, K. B., & Bell, J. (1997). Asthma and panic disorder. *Archives of Family Medicine, 6,* 20–23.

Schuster, M. A., Bell, R. M., Peterson, L. P., & Kanouse, D. E. (1996). Communication between adolescents and physicians about sexual behavior and risk prevention. *Archives of Pediatric and Adolescent Medicine, 150,* 906–913.

Shenkman, E., Pendergast, J., Reiss, J., Waltern, E., Bucciarelli, R., & Freedman, S. (1996). The school enrollment-based health insurance program: Socioeconomic factors in enrollees' use of health services. *American Journal of Public Health, 86,* 1791–1793.

Spigelblatt, L., Laine-Ammara, G., Pless, I. B., & Guyver, A. (1994). The use of alternative medicine by children. *Pediatrics, 94,* 811–814.

Stapleton, S. (1997, June 2). Paving the way for pediatric drug trials [sidebar: Taking "their medicine?"]. *American Medical News, 40*(21), 3, 29.

Steiner, B. D., & Gest, K. L. (1996). Do adolescents want to hear preventive counseling messages in outpatient settings? *Journal of Family Practice, 43,* 375–381.

U.S. Department of Health and Human Services. (1998, November 27). *FDA acts to make drugs safer for children* [press release].

U.S. Department of Health and Human Services, Centers for Disease Control and Prevention. (1997, August 1). State- and sex-specific prevalence of selected characteristics—Behavioral Risk Factor Surveillance System, 1994 and 1995. *CDC Surveillance Summaries*, 46, No. SS-3.

U.S. Department of Health and Human Services, Health Resources and Services Administration. (1998). *National practitioner data bank* [On-line]. Available: www.hrsa.org.

U.S. Preventive Services Task Force. (1996). *Guide to clinical preventive services*. Baltimore: Williams & Wilkins.

Wilens, T. E., Biederman, J., Baldessarini, R. J., Geller, B., Schleifer, D., & Spencer, T. J. (1996). Cardiovascular effects of therapeutic doses of tricyclic antidepressants in children and adolescents. *Journal of the American Academy of Child and Adolescent Psychiatry*, 35, 1491–1501.

Williams-Morris, R. S. (1996). Racism and children's health: Issues in development. *Ethnicity and Disease*, 6, 69–82.

Wilson, M. D., Manoff, S., & Joffe, A. (1997). Residents' self-assessed skills in providing sexuality-related care to teenagers. *Archives of Pediatric and Adolescent Medicine*, 151, 418–422.

Wirrell, E. C., Camfield, C. S., Camfield, P. R., Dooley, J. M., Gordon, K. E., & Smith, B. (1997). Long-term psychosocial outcome in typical absence epilepsy. *Archives of Pediatric and Adolescent Medicine*, 151, 152–158.

Zanga, J. R. (1998, February). Insider's perspective reveals Academy's sphere of influence [letter]. *American Academy of Pediatrics News*, p. 8.

V

IMPLICATIONS AND FUTURE TRENDS

INTRODUCTION

MICHAEL C. ROBERTS

To this point in the book, the chapter authors have discussed the knowledge base and its limits in the major domains of adolescent girls' lives. They offer insights on what is known and what needs to be investigated to further this "new look" at adolescent girls. In this capstone section, the final three chapters link together the major components of psychology as an organized discipline in discussing the major issues in public policy, training and education, and clinical practice. The final chapter widens the view of the future for adolescent girls by discussing concrete ways in which psychologists and others can support their positive development.

Brian L. Wilcox, in his chapter, "Sexual Obsessions: Public Policy and Adolescent Girls" (chap. 14), offers a thought-provoking appraisal of public policy issues facing adolescent girls, their families, and those who work with them. He asserts that most of the policymaking dealing with adolescent girls has inordinately focused on sexual behavior. Included in his analysis are policies such as family planning services, sexuality education, promotion of sexual abstinence, limitations on autonomy of adolescent girls (parental notification in abortion access), and welfare reform. This chapter advances the view that a broader perspective is needed to develop reasonable social policies benefiting adolescent girls.

As noted by Wilcox, there have been a number of major policy reports dealing with some aspect of adolescents. All of the reports have documented that the fragmentation of policies, interests, and activities have ill served adolescents. For example, the National Commission on Children (1991) noted in its final report, *Beyond Rhetoric: A New American Agenda for Children and Families*, that the "United States does not have coherent national policy for children and families" (p. 61). As can be seen in this chapter, the few public policies concerned with adolescent girls are not only ill-planned but also often illogical in being divisive and contradictory.

Joanne E. Callan's chapter, "Education and Practice Issues Related to Adolescent Girls" (chap. 15), makes clear that training in psychology and the practice of psychology are reciprocally interrelated. She notes that competent practice relies on relevant and comprehensive education and training. Conversely, the content of training and the manner in which it is conducted are influenced to a large degree by those providing services for young people. These service providers need information on adolescent development and evaluations of "best practices" of interventions. Of course, training in psychology relevant to issues of adolescent girls goes beyond the application of psychological knowledge through practice. It is very important and necessary for professionals to have training in basic and applied research to produce the knowledge base about adolescent girls.

Callan notes that there are few adequately trained adolescent health care professionals, for practice and for research, across professional disciplines and that this is equally true in the field of psychology. Psychology should be oriented to training professionals in the provision of mental health and physical health promotion geared to the changing needs of adolescents, to the education of other disciplinary professionals (e.g., school and medical personnel) about the psychosocial issues and the unique developmental situations of adolescents, and to the development of scientists with the interest, expertise, and motivation to investigate adolescent issues and to evaluate programs to enhance development.

In her chapter, Callan articulates the position that clinical practice is influenced by social and cultural development, such as increased sexual freedom, changes in families and communities, and economic and occupational changes. She suggests that the types of psychological problems dictate both practice and training for such clinical applications. In the training realm, there are relatively few programs offering formal didactic and clinical experiences with children, adolescents, and families, more generally. Callan concludes that psychologist-educators need to take responsibility for a specialized curriculum leading to competence in providing services for adolescent girls, in particular.

In the culminating chapter of this book, "Enhancing the Development of Adolescent Girls," (chap. 16), Florence L. Denmark articulates the view that adolescence is a time of exploration, of freedom to learn and try new activities, and of growth in independence and self-awareness. This developmental period represents a period during which the adolescent girl forms a new unique identity. Denmark considers important research pointing to positive aspects of the future for adolescent girls. She presents a realistic, but hopeful future, and not necessarily an idealistic one. She notes that the social, economic, and technological changes reshaping the world facing adolescents in the future offer great possibilities for improvement. The adolescent girls, and those who seek to help them, need to have the vision to prepare for this unknown future.

In its final report *Great Transitions: Preparing Adolescents for the New Century*, the Carnegie Council on Adolescent Development (1995) concluded that the American institutions of family, schools, youth-serving social organizations, health care organizations, and the media "have fallen behind in their vital functions and must now be strengthened in their respective roles and linked in a mutually reinforcing system of support for adolescents" (p. 11). Although it is disheartening to see that the myriad of policies and programs often do not meet the needs of adolescent girls, there is always hope that new developments and "new looks" can produce positive change. For example, the creation of the federal Office of Adolescent Health in the Maternal and Child Health Bureau can help facilitate greater attention to this aspect of adolescents' lives. This office and its project partners (the American Medical Association, the American Bar Association, the National Association of Social Workers, the American Dietetics Association, and the American Psychological Association) can now give institutional recognition to the importance of doing something more organized in adolescent health. This recognition, in particular, will contribute greatly to an increased understanding of adolescent health issues and will help develop ways to improve intervention and prevention services to enhance adolescents' services and health, in particular.

Psychology has a great deal to contribute through its theoretical and applied conceptualizations, research methodology, service delivery systems and development, content knowledge base, and potentially large cadre of active and involved professionals. The American Psychological Association itself is a constituent member organization—the strength of having the organization involved in adolescent health initiatives comes from its 142,000 members involved in all aspects of science and professional activities. The membership interest divisions represent a resource to be garnered. Consequently, the initiatives to enhance the lives of adolescent girls can be successful if they draw from the potential richness of the professionals and their organizations. Other similar initiatives will be needed for other aspects of adolescents in general, and adolescent girls more specifically.

Developments involving public–private partnership, as well as federal and community initiatives, can generate more useful information and effective programs and interventions. Although a cohesive policy regarding adolescents, particularly for girls, is not likely in the near future, the issues are significant and are now getting the attention they deserve.

REFERENCES

Carnegie Council on Adolescent Development. (1995). *Great transitions: Preparing adolescents for a new century*. New York: Carnegie Corporation.

National Commission on Children. (1991). *Beyond rhetoric: A new American agenda for children and families*. Washington, DC: Author.

14

SEXUAL OBSESSIONS: PUBLIC POLICY AND ADOLESCENT GIRLS

BRIAN L. WILCOX

The United States lacks a coherent youth policy. That this is the case should not be surprising. Policy tools are relatively blunt means for achieving targeted change for segments of the population (Wilcox, 1993; Wilcox & O'Keeffe, 1990). Most policies are very broad in nature and are intended to have effects on broad segments of the populations. Further, coherence within a broad policy domain, such as "family policy" or "youth policy," is not to be expected within a policy system that has been described as being reactive, disjointed, and incremental by design. Nonetheless, it is surprising that so little policy activity has focused specifically on the psychological well-being, broadly conceived, of adolescents generally and adolescent girls specifically.

This is not to suggest that the concerns of adolescents and their well-being are being completely ignored in the policy arena. Indeed, there has been a recent upsurge in attention to issues related to the promotion of healthy adolescent development. This has occurred, in part, because in recent years, there has been a significant change in the ways in which health and health promotion are conceptualized (Millstein, Petersen, & Nightingale, 1993). The narrow medical conceptualization of adolescent

333

health, focusing as it has on deviations from health, has given way to a broader "biopsychosocial" model that defines health in terms of one's ability to fulfill important social roles and tasks and to reach one's potential in terms of both healthy development and quality of life.

The attention to adolescent health has manifested itself in a variety of other ways. In the past few years, a wide range of reports have appeared, addressing both the threats to adolescents' health and well-being and the opportunities presenting themselves during this developmental period to promote health and psychosocial competence. During this period, the government supported the development of a three-volume report on adolescent health (U.S. Congress Office of Technology Assessment, 1991a, 1991b, 1991c), an analysis of trends in adolescents' health status and services use (Irwin, Brindis, Brodt, Bennett, & Rodriquez, 1991), and a report from the National Commission on Children (1991) that addresses adolescent health among other topics. Outside of government, the National Research Council's Panel on High-Risk Youth released a report on the threats to health and well-being faced by youth in high-risk settings (National Research Council, 1993). A report titled "Code Blue: Uniting for a Healthier Youth," produced by the American Medical Association and the National Association of State Boards of Education, characterized the state of adolescent health as a state of emergency (National Commission on the Role of the School and the Community in Improving Adolescent Health, 1990). The Carnegie Corporation's Council on Adolescent Development sponsored a series of important reports addressing several aspects of adolescent health and well-being (Carnegie Corporation of New York, 1995; Hechinger, 1992; Millstein et al., 1993). Very recently, the National Academy of Sciences and the Institute of Medicine established a Forum on Adolescence to bring greater visibility to issues of importance to adolescents.

All of this activity speaks to the ferment around issues of adolescent health and development. Much of this attention grows out of an increasing recognition of the fact that adolescence is a period presenting great risks and opportunities. During this period, developmental needs such as intimacy, mastery, and autonomy come to the fore. Each need can be behaviorally expressed in ways that either promote health, psychological growth, and the transition to adult roles or pose serious dangers to health and future life chances. The various transformations—biological, psychological, and social—that take place during adolescence challenge not only the youth but also our families, schools, neighborhoods, communities, and health care settings. In some cases, our adolescents succeed marvelously, often in the face of considerable odds, whereas in other instances, adolescents fail to negotiate the obstacles before them.

Despite the range of activities described above that reflect public concern over the well-being of adolescents, the policy response has been muted at best. This is even more true when one considers the range of policies targeting adolescent girls in particular. Although issues of gender are raised in many of the reports previously cited, policymakers have only infrequently dealt with issues of unique concern to adolescent girls. It should come as little surprise that most of the policymaking action related to adolescent girls has focused on issues directly or tangentially related to their sexual behavior. The bulk of this chapter, then, focuses on policies designed to protect the sexual health or to control the sexual behavior of adolescent girls.

There are other policy areas within which the interests of adolescent girls are being addressed at some level. For example, there has been some, albeit limited, attention to the concerns of adolescent girls within the federal Office of Juvenile Justice and Delinquency Prevention (OJJDP). Studies and reports issued by the OJJDP have addressed issues such as the apparent increase in adolescent girls' involvement in gangs and the unique concerns of female offenders in the juvenile justice system. The Centers for Disease Control and Prevention have, in addition to their many programs related to adolescent sexual health, programs addressing violence involving adolescent girls. Within the U.S. Department of Health and Human Services (USDHHS), the Runaway and Homeless Youth program has sponsored initiatives on adolescent girls. Within the field of education policy, Title IX is opening new opportunities for adolescent girls' participation in sports, which has considerable implications for gender equity and the well-being of young women. At the legislative policy level, however, the action has focused on issues linked in some fashion to the sexual behavior of adolescent girls, especially in recent years.

ADOLESCENT GIRLS AND SEXUALITY-RELATED POLICIES

This chapter focuses on a number of these policy issues. They include (a) policies intended to prevent teen pregnancy through the provision of reproductive health services, (b) policies to provide children and youth with sexuality education, (c) policies to promote sexual abstinence among adolescents, (d) policies intended to limit adolescents' autonomy regarding reproductive health decisions, and (e) policies to create disincentives for teen pregnancy and childbearing.

Public concerns over adolescent sexual behavior, pregnancy, and childbearing, particularly nonmarital pregnancy and childbearing, can be traced to the American colonial period (D'Emilio & Freedman, 1988). The contemporary policy response to these issues, though, is linked to four primary factors. First, public attention to the issue of teen pregnancy was spurred in part by a highly publicized report by the Alan Guttmacher Institute (1976) that eloquently detailed the "epidemic" of adolescent pregnancy and was extensively cited by policymakers and the media. It is interesting to note that this report's publication came well after adolescent pregnancy rates had peaked and at a point when they were declining (Vinovskis, 1981, 1988). Second, it was widely believed that federal costs associated with adolescent pregnancy and childbearing grew significantly through the 1970s, around the same time that public support for welfare policies and welfare recipients began to wane (Garfinkel & McLanahan, 1986).[1] Third, with the legalization of abortion in the aftermath of *Roe v. Wade* (1973), the abortion rate for adolescents increased substantially, attracting the interest of antiabortion legislators. The increasing abortion rate had the effect of broadening policymakers' focus from the prevention of adolescent childbearing to the prevention of adolescent pregnancy (Luker, 1996). Finally, the most dramatic demographic trend in the 1970s, relative to adolescent girls, was that those adolescents bearing children increasingly chose to keep their children rather than put them up for adoption, and they were far less likely to marry prior to or shortly after the birth of a child. The real change that took place over the past two decades was not that adolescents bore more children; it was that adolescent mothers increasingly rejected marriage. This trend had the effect of making adolescent mothers more visible to the public. The combined set of factors seemed to spur policymakers into action. At the same time, the growing political strength of conservative groups shifted the political debate in ways that have made consensus policymaking nearly impossible in this arena.

Family Planning Services

Although federal legislators first passed legislation allowing family planning services to be covered under the Office of Economic Opportunity's "War on Poverty" programs in 1965, legislation that would come to have a meaningful impact on family planning for adolescent girls was passed 5 years later. In 1970, Congress passed and President Nixon signed the Family Planning Services and Population Research Act (1970), which, among other things, established Title X of the Public Health Services Act.[2] The Title X family planning program has helped establish a national net-

---

[1] It is widely believed now that many of the earlier estimates of the costs of adolescent childbearing for the federal government significantly overestimated those costs. Although the academic debate over the actual costs (federal and others) of adolescent childbearing remains vigorous and unsettled (cf. Grogger & Bronars, 1993; Hoffman, Foster, & Furstenberg, 1993; Hotz, McElroy, & Sanders, 1997; Maynard, 1997), nearly all observers agree that the economic costs remain significant. It is clear from the welfare reform debates that took place in 1995 and 1996 that policymakers certainly believe that the federal costs attributable to adolescent childbearing are unacceptably high.

[2] The Family Planning Services and Population Research Act of 1970 passed unanimously in the Senate and nearly so in the House. The strong bipartisan support reflected, in part, the fact that conservatives believed that public support for family planning services was warranted because such services could prevent the birth of children who might end up on public welfare. Liberals supported the bill because they believed poor women should have the same access to adequate reproductive health care as women with adequate financial resources. Just a decade later, this bipartisan support for Title X was a thing of the past, due largely to the emerging politics of abortion (Wilcox, Robbennolt, & O'Keeffe, 1998).

work of clinics devoted to the delivery of family planning and other reproductive health care services. The original Title X legislation did not specifically mention teens as targeted recipients for contraceptive and other reproductive health services, but neither did it preclude their participation. An early study of the program indicated that substantial numbers of adolescent girls used the Title X clinic services (Rosoff, 1973).

Contraceptive services for adolescents were first explicitly supported by Congress in 1972, when the Medicaid program was amended to require that all state Medicaid programs include family planning services to sexually active minors. Two years later, Congress specified that adolescents were to be served by the Title X program. As part of the 1977 and 1978 reauthorizations of the Title X program, Congress went further, indicating that Title X programs needed to invest more effort into reaching and serving adolescents. Adolescents were specifically identified as a target group in the amended statute.

This sequence of events was quite revolutionary. Only a decade earlier, some states were still banning the use of contraceptives by married women. A series of Supreme Court decisions changed this policy landscape. In *Griswold v. Connecticut* (1965), the Court concluded that the Constitution's due process clause protected married couples' right to private use of contraceptives. This "privacy right" was recognized as extending to unmarried adults by the Court in *Eisenstadt v. Baird* (1972), and, in a more limited fashion, to adolescents in *Carey v. Population Services International* (1977). The actions of Congress in extending Title X services explicitly to adolescents reflected, in part, an awareness of the changed legal context, but they also reflected the growing political consensus that preventing adolescent pregnancy and childbirth was fundamental to preventing future poverty.

The political consensus that led to overwhelming bipartisan support for the passage and funding of the Title X family planning program turned out to be relatively short lived. By 1981, following the election of President Reagan and a more conservative Congress, the political support for Title X began to diminish. Antiabortion legislators and their constituents were troubled by the fact that some Title X-funded clinics used their own funds to provide abortion services at the same sites in which Title X family planning services were offered. As abortion politics superseded poverty politics in Washington, funding for the Title X program declined from $151 million in 1980 to $51 million in 1994 (in 1980 dollars), a 65% decrease. This decrease was partially offset by the growth in Medicaid family planning expenditures, but total public contraceptive services expenditures still fell by 27% during this period (Alan Guttmacher Institute, 1997). In a more recent frontal assault on the integrity of the Title X program, Representative Bob Livingston (Republican-Louisiana) proposed that the program be eliminated and that the funds be transferred to two federal programs, the maternal and child health block grant and the community and migrant health centers program. This proposal, offered during debate on the 1995 bill reauthorizing the Title X program, would not have required that any of the transferred funds be spent on family planning services. The amendment was narrowly defeated, 221 to 207.[3]

Despite these attempts to limit the scope of the Title X program, it remains a key source of funding for contraceptive services for adolescent girls. Forrest and Samara (1996) estimated that publicly funded family planning services prevent approximately 386,000 adolescent pregnancies each year and, in doing so, prevent over 180,000 abortions by adolescents. Title X clinics also provide essential sexually transmitted disease testing and treatment. Very significantly, Title X clinics often serve as a means of linking low-income pregnant adolescents to early prenatal care. One recent study suggests that this linkage function is very effective in reducing low-birth-weight deliveries and infant and neonatal mortality (Meier & Mc-Farlane, 1994).

The effectiveness of the Title X program in serving adolescents is attributable to two key features of the program. First, the program largely eliminates financial barriers for adolescent girls in seeking reproductive health care services. Publicly financed contraceptive services allow many adolescents who lack both health insurance of any kind and adequate financial resources of their own to obtain preventive care. In examining the evidence to date, the Institute of Medicine's Committee on Unintended Pregnancy declared that for low-income women and adolescents who face major financial barriers to contraceptive services, Title X and Medicaid play a critical role in their well-being, and "it is essential that such public investment be maintained" (Brown & Eisenberg, 1995, p. 261). Second, the program provides adolescents with confidential access to reproductive health care. Confidentiality is widely regarded as integral to the Title X program's effectiveness in reaching sexually active adolescents (Donovan, 1992). Conservative lawmakers have on several occasions tried to limit the confidential nature of Title X services by requiring that clinics either notify parents of any girl under 18 years of age who received contraceptive services or actually obtain parental consent before such services might be provided. This issue is discussed in greater length below.

Sexuality Education

Although the federal government played a leadership role in the establishment of publicly supported family planning services for adolescent

---

[3]President Reagan also attempted to convert the Title X program into a state block grant program in 1981. His proposal would have drastically reduced the federal share of the funding for contraceptive services, and states would not have been required to fund any contraceptive services. Congress rejected the proposal. Additional proposals to convert Title X into a block grant or to redirect the funds to other federal programs have been offered in the House in 1997 but are unlikely to be acted on.

girls, it has not played a significant role in the development of sexuality education programs. This should come as no surprise to anyone familiar with education policy, as most areas of education policymaking fall under the jurisdiction of state and local governments. There are two exceptions to this general rule, related to curricula promoting sexual abstinence, but these issues will be discussed separately.[4]

Recent survey data indicate that most American adolescents receive some form of sexuality education that includes information on sex and contraceptive use. Ninety percent of 18- to 19-year-old women surveyed as part of the 1995 Survey of Family Growth indicated that they had received formal instruction on safe sex skills to prevent HIV and other sexually transmitted diseases, along with information on how to resist unwanted sexual advances (Abma, Chandra, Mosher, Peterson, & Piccinino, 1997). The same survey found a substantial increase in the percentage of adolescent girls who used contraception at first intercourse—76% in 1995, up from 64% in the late 1980s. Whether exposure to formal instruction is causally related to the trends in contraceptive practices of adolescent girls and their partners cannot be determined in this study. It may be that much of the formal instruction was delivered as part of an HIV/AIDS program rather than a more comprehensive sexuality education program.

The picture painted by a recent survey of state sexuality education policies and programs is somewhat less encouraging. Although most states have developed sex education curricula or curricula guidelines, the curricula and guidelines are often minimal and inadequate. Gambrell and Haffner (1993) found that fewer than a third of these materials included reference to any sexual behaviors other than abstinence. Discussions of sexual behaviors, when included, tended to focus on negative consequences of sexual activity. Potentially controversial topics, such as sexual orientation, abortion, masturbation, and shared sexual behavior, were rarely covered. Few states required those teaching sex education to have certification in a specific field or to receive training in sex education.

At both the state and the local level, sexuality education policy has proved to be a lightning rod. As Steiner (1981) has noted, policies touching on matters relating to sex and sexuality are divisive by nature because they tap fundamental differences in values that are not amenable to rational policy analysis. Although sex education has been a part of American public school education since the Progressive Era (Luker, 1996), the political consensus supporting it seemed to collapse in the early 1980s. Some opponents have argued that sex education is a matter best left to parents

---

[4]Sex (or sexuality) education programs are defined here as programs that address a comprehensive range of topics related to sexuality, including contraceptive use (cf. National Guidelines Task Force, 1991). The abstinence promotion programs funded by the federal government, by virtue of the fact that they preclude curricula containing comprehensive contraceptive information, are treated separately from sexuality education programs.

and religious institutions; others have gone beyond this viewpoint to argue that sex education actually contributes to early sexual activity and pregnancy. This last argument merits a closer examination because, unlike the first argument, it is open to empirical analysis.

Critics of comprehensive sex education base their claims that participation in sex education encourages early sexual activity primarily on one study that found a small (2%) increase in the probability that an adolescent experiencing sex education would have sexual intercourse (Marsiglio & Mott, 1986). Three comprehensive reviews of studies examining this issue, however, have concluded that the likelihood that an adolescent will become sexually active is not affected positively or negatively by participation in sex education (Grunseit & Kippax, 1993; Kirby, 1997; Kirby et al., 1994). The most recent of these reviews has stated the issue plainly: "sexuality and HIV education programs that include discussion of condoms and contraception do not increase sexual intercourse, either by hastening the onset of intercourse, increasing the frequency of intercourse, or increasing use of contraceptives" (Kirby, 1997, p. 31).

It remains the case, however, that there is no compelling evidence supporting the effectiveness of any given model of sexuality education with respect to altering sexual behaviors appreciably, though there have been individual programs that have demonstrated success in delaying the onset of sexual activity or increasing the use of contraceptives and safe sex techniques (Kirby, 1997). Many proponents of sexuality education argue, however, that sexuality education programs are not pregnancy prevention or STD/HIV prevention programs and should not be evaluated in terms of their effectiveness in reducing pregnancies or preventing disease but instead should be judged by criteria similar to those applied to other educational programs (cf. Haffner & Goldfarb, 1997). There is widespread agreement, however, that few high-quality evaluations of sexuality education programs exist.

Whereas most of the state policy activity related to sexuality education has focused on issues related to abstinence education (and thus will be discussed in the next section), local policymaking has addressed a wide variety of issues. In most instances, the policy actions being proposed would place new restrictions on how and to whom sexuality education is offered. The main policy debates taking place before local school boards and city councils address one or more of the following issues. First, there have been a number of attacks on sexuality education in elementary schools that have been predicated on the charge that early sexuality education is harmful to young children. These charges are often stated as being based on "psychological theory." A review of these claims found that they were typically based on a misconstrual of Freud's writings on the latency period and ignored that fact that Freud had written in support of early sexuality education (Limber, Wilcox, & Bartels, 1996). Second, a substantial number of communities have been struggling with the issue of separating sexuality education courses by gender. This is a complex issue, because although there may well be rational grounds for giving younger students the opportunity to discuss sexuality issues in same-gender groups, most of the efforts would keep the genders separated for all sexuality education sessions, and it would appear that the prime motivation behind these efforts is to make the administration of sexuality education so complicated that the support for such education is undermined (Mayer & Kantor, 1996). Third, the inclusion of sexual orientation issues in sexuality education curricula is one of the most contentious issues at the local community level. The issue has generated so much debate that Congress held a hearing in 1996 that was intended to determine whether sexuality education programs were "promoting homosexuality," although no policy proposals were offered. Finally, many opponents of sexuality education have advocated at the local level for "opt-in" policies that would require active parental consent for students to participate in sexuality education. The vast majority of communities, it should be noted, already have "opt-out" policies that allow parents to exclude their children from these courses. Although "opt-in" policies have been implemented in only a handful of communities and have not significantly reduced enrollments in sexuality education courses, these policies place a very heavy administrative burden on the schools, thereby increasing the cost of offering such courses (Mayer & Kantor, 1996).

Although gender issues have only played a tangential role in the battles over sexuality education in U.S. schools, the quality of sexuality education has clear implications for the well-being of American girls. In court cases in which issues relating to sexuality education have been contested, there have been several instances in which curricula have been challenged on the grounds that they promoted narrow, stereotyped portrayals of gender roles and sexual behavior (Mayer & Kantor, 1996). Numerous analyses of the state of sexuality education in the United States suggest that there are considerable grounds for concern (Fine, 1988; Gambrell & Haffner, 1993; Kirby, 1997; Luker, 1996).

Promoting Sexual Abstinence

Conservative politicians have repeatedly raised the concern that federal family planning services condone adolescent sexual activity by making contraceptives available to teens. In 1981, Senate conservatives led an effort resulting in the passage of the Adolescent Family Life Act (AFLA, Title XX of the Public Health Service Act). The AFLA was designed to continue support for programs for pregnant and parenting adolescents that were part of the Adolescent Health Services and Pregnancy Prevention and Care Act of 1978 (which AFLA replaced), but to fundamentally change the nature of prevention programs supported by the earlier legislation. The sponsors of the AFLA legislation argued that prevention efforts including information about contraceptive use sent a message to teens that sexual relations were acceptable or inevitable, thereby promoting sex outside of a monogamous marriage. As finally approved by Congress and signed by President Reagan, the AFLA restricted prevention activities to those that promoted sexual abstinence as the sole means of preventing pregnancy and exposure to sexually transmitted diseases (Mecklenburg & Thompson, 1983), prompting critics to dub it the "Chastity Act."

In the 16 years since the enactment of the AFLA, millions of dollars have been spent by the federal government to support what has been called "abstinence-only" sex education, a term used to differentiate these programs from sexuality education programs including components encouraging abstinence but not restricting content related to contraceptive methods, and so on. Although the federal government funding for these projects diminished substantially after 1992, many of the programs funded during the 1980s have been and continue to be implemented in communities around the country, despite the fact that very little information exists in the professional literature concerning the effectiveness of these programs (Kirby, 1997; Wilcox, 1997).

The advent of the Adolescent Family Life Program marked the beginning of a pitched battle, which has since taken on all the characteristics of a war, between supporters of abstinence-only approaches to sexuality education and supporters of comprehensive sexuality education. A recent report by the Sexuality Information and Education Council of the United States indicates that there are currently battles over this issue in communities in all 50 states (Mayer, 1997; see also Burlingame, 1997). Several states have mandated that all state-supported sexuality education programs promote abstinence as the sole means of reducing teen pregnancies and sexually transmitted diseases (Burlingame, 1997).

Federal support for such programs has recently increased dramatically. The Personal Responsibility and Work Opportunity Reconciliation Act of 1996, which was signed into law by President Clinton on August 22, 1996, contains a provision that will provide $50 million in annual matching grants to states for abstinence-only programs, beginning in 1998. All 50 states have applied for these funds. In addition, after years of decreasing funding for the AFLA abstinence-only program, Congress dramatically increased its funding in 1996.

There are two remarkable aspects to this policy action. First, Congress authorized $250 million to be spent on abstinence-only education programs over the next 5 years without requiring that any of these funds be directed to evaluation. After many in the reproductive health community protested this oversight, Congress allotted an additional $6 million for a national longitudinal evaluation of this program. These federal funds will be matched with state funds, bringing the total expenditures to approximately

EXHIBIT 14.1
Definition of Abstinence Education Included in the Personal Responsibility and Work Opportunity Reconciliation Act of 1996 (P.L. 104-193, Title IX, Sec. 912):

"The term 'abstinence education' means an educational or motivational program which—

A) has as its exclusive purpose, teaching the social, psychological, and health gains to be realized by abstaining from sexual activity;
B) teaches abstinence from sexual activity outside marriage as the expected standard for all school-age children;
C) teaches that abstinence from sexual activity is the only certain way to avoid out-of-wedlock pregnancy, sexually transmitted diseases, and other associated health problems;
D) teaches that a mutually faithful monogamous relationship in the context of marriage is the expected standard of human sexual activity;
E) teaches that sexual activity outside the context of marriage is likely to have harmful psychological and physical effects;
F) teaches that bearing children out-of-wedlock is likely to have harmful consequences for the child, the child's parents, and society;
G) teaches young people how to reject sexual advances and how alcohol and drug use increases vulnerability to sexual advances; and
H) teaches the importance of attaining self-sufficiency before engaging in sexual activity."

$500 million between 1998 and 2002. This is quite remarkable in light of the lack of evidence in support of the effectiveness of these types of programs.[5] Second, the legislation establishing the abstinence-only grant program is unusually specific in its definition of abstinence education (see Exhibit 14.1). The statute spells out a number of messages that must be included in supported curricula, including at least one indicating that non-marital sexual activity is psychologically and physically harmful, which is inconsistent with research findings. It is unusual for Congress to engage in the drafting of curricula guidelines. More typically, statutes give very general guidance that are then given greater specification by relevant federal agencies and then passed along for further interpretation and specification by those who will implement the program.

The growth of federal support for abstinence-only programs is all the more remarkable when the amount of funds dedicated to these programs is compared with the amount allocated for past federally supported adolescent pregnancy prevention efforts. Over the next 5 years, the federal government will spend more on abstinence education than it has on the Adolescent Health Services and Pregnancy Prevention and Care Act and the

---

[5]After numerous organizations and individuals raised concerns to the USDHHS over the lack of any evaluation component for the abstinence-only programs to be supported by federal funds, Congress approved $6 million ($3 million in fiscal year 1998 and $3 million in fiscal year 1999) as part of the balanced budget agreement for an evaluation effort to be managed by USDHHS.

Adolescent Family Life Act combined over the past 20 years. The value of this investment will not be known for some years, if at all. It is clear, however, that this investment of funds in abstinence-only education programs was precipitated largely by legislators' concerns regarding rates of sexual activity and nonmarital childbearing by adolescent girls (Haskins & Beran, 1996).

Limiting the Autonomy of Adolescent Girls

Adolescents' expanded access to both contraceptives and abortion services, which grew out of a series of legal and policy decisions in the early to mid 1970s, has brought about numerous efforts on the part of federal and state policymakers to limit the autonomy of adolescent girls with respect to access to contraception and abortion. These two issues will be addressed in turn.

As described earlier, the Title X family planning program requires that contraceptive services be made available to adolescents. The program regulations do not allow patient information to be released to anyone without the patient's consent. Despite the fact that the statute, as amended in 1981, states that family participation is to be encouraged with respect to a minor's decision to use contraceptives, conservatives have long been troubled by adolescents' ability to obtain contraceptives without parental consent or notification.

In 1982, the Reagan administration proposed new Title X regulations, predicated on the clause encouraging family involvement "to the extent practical," which would require that Title X clinics notify the parents or legal guardian of minors in writing within 10 days of providing them with a prescription for contraceptives. The administration argued that the Title X program had built a "Berlin Wall" between the adolescent and her family and that parents had a legitimate interest in protecting their children from the possible side effects of prescriptive medicines. During a hearing on the proposed regulations, dubbed the "Squeal Rule" by the press, the USDHHS Secretary Schweiker testified that he also believed that a notification requirement would not significantly deter adolescents from seeking contraceptives but might prevent some adolescents from becoming sexually active ("Proposed Regulations on Family Planning," 1982).

The proposed regulations were greeted with outrage by members of the family planning community (Kenney, Forrest, & Torres, 1982).[6] Citing research showing that over 20% of adolescent girls would stop coming to clinics if parental notification were required, whereas only 2% indicated that they would stop having sex (Torres & Eisman, 1980), opponents of

---

[6]It is interesting that the regulations were not embraced by many conservatives, who felt that a parental *notification* requirement did not go far enough. The conservative groups argued instead for a parental *consent* requirement (Kenney, Forrest, & Torres, 1982).

the regulations filed two suits against the USDHHS in federal court to block implementation of the regulations. The two suits claimed that the regulations were inconsistent with Congressional intent underlying the Title X program generally (to prevent adolescent pregnancy) and the family involvement portion of the legislation specifically. Opponents of the regulations noted that the administration did not argue for a parental notification requirement in the case of adolescents' use of clinic services for sexually transmitted diseases, suggesting that the regulations were clearly an attempt to limit adolescents' access to contraceptives rather than a means to facilitate family communication. Agreeing with the logic of the arguments stated by the opponents of the regulations, both courts issued permanent injunctions on March 2, 1983, the day the regulations would have gone into effect. The decisions were upheld in both appellate courts (*New York v. Heckler*, 1983; *Planned Parenthood Federation v. Heckler*, 1983). The Reagan administration declined to pursue the case further.

In the aftermath of the Reagan administration's failure to restrict adolescent girls' access to Title X contraceptive services through the regulatory process, several attempts have been made by members of Congress to limit the autonomy of minors in receiving confidential contraceptive services by amending the Title X statute to require parental notification or consent. For example, Representative William Dannemeyer (Republican-California) proposed an amendment to the 1984 Title X reauthorization legislation that mirrored the Reagan administration parental notification proposal. The amendment was defeated in committee, and despite support for the provision by Senator Orrin Hatch (Republican-Utah), chairman of the Senate authorizing committee, the provision was not included in the bill reported out of the House–Senate conference committee. In later years, as conservatives gained voting strength in the House, the Title X reauthorization bill was frequently held hostage by amendments of this type. Although no parental consent or notification provision for Title X has yet been approved, they continue to be offered and the votes for passage have grown closer.

In the years following the Supreme Court's decision in *Roe v. Wade* (1973), the rate of abortions among adolescents climbed (Donovan, 1992), a fact that precipitated action in many states to restrict adolescents' access to abortion services, typically involving the establishment of parental consent or notification requirements. The notification laws also frequently contained a 24- to 48-hour waiting period between parental notification and the provision of an abortion.

In response to suits arising from the wave of state laws designed to restrict minor girls' access to abortion services, the Supreme Court issued a number of decisions, beginning with *Bellotti v. Baird* (1979), that has over the past two decades framed the constraints on states' powers in this area. The Court has refrained from allowing states to give parents complete veto power over their minor daughters' abortion decisions. In *Bellotti v. Baird* (1979), the Court ruled that state consent laws must provide minors a confidential and expeditious alternative to parental consent in the form of a "judicial bypass" process, whereby minors can request judicial recognition and approval of their competence to make the decision to have an abortion or, in the case of immature minors, a judicial determination that the abortion is in their best interests. Later decisions affirmed the constitutionality of one-parent (*Ohio v. Akron Center for Reproductive Health*, 1990) and two-parent (*Hodgson v. Minnesota*, 1990) notification laws. The court also held that parental notification laws also necessitated a judicial bypass provision to pass constitutional muster (*City of Akron v. Akron Center for Reproductive Health*, 1983).

The laws restricting minors' access to abortion services are especially interesting when juxtaposed with other state laws affecting the decisions minors are allowed to make with regard to their health and reproductive health care as well as other important decisions affecting their lives. No states require parental consent or notification for minors to receive other reproductive health services, such as sexually transmitted disease care or contraceptive services.[7] Nearly all states have statutes allowing minors with drug or alcohol problems to obtain confidential treatment. Most states allow pregnant adolescents to obtain confidential prenatal care and obstetric services (National Youth Law Center, 1995). Forty states allow minors age 17 and under to drop out of school without their parents' permission, and 33 states explicitly allow minors to give up a child for adoption without their parents' knowledge or consent (Alan Guttmacher Institute, 1995). Most telling, even very young adolescents, who may be required in their state to obtain parental consent to have their ears pierced, are able to obtain obstetric services for the delivery of a child, a process widely regarded as riskier than early abortion.

These parental consent and notification laws have been built around the assumptions that adolescents lack the cognitive capacity to make reasonable, rational abortion decisions and that parental involvement in these decisions will benefit the adolescent. Similarly, both the courts and the state legislatures have frequently referred to the psychological vulnerability of adolescents consequent to having an abortion. Despite considerable evidence challenging these assumptions (Crosby & English, 1991; Gittler, Quigley-Rick, & Saks, 1990; Melton, 1986; O'Keeffe & Jones, 1990), state parental consent and notification laws have proliferated. Twenty-six states have consent or notification laws in place and enforced; a number of other states have passed such laws but have been blocked from enforcing them by the courts (National Youth Law Center, 1995).

---

[7]Utah prohibits the use of state funds for the provision of contraceptive services to unemancipated minors without parental consent.

It is still too early to determine the effect of these consent laws, but one study investigating the effects of parental involvement laws on adolescent abortions and births found that although abortion rates declined and birthrates stayed stable following the implementation of involvement laws, some evidence from a subset of the states studied suggests that these laws increase the likelihood that adolescents will travel to nearby states without parental involvement laws to seek abortion services. These laws also were shown to result in delays in receiving abortion services (Ellertson, 1997). Additional research is clearly needed to fully evaluate the effects of these policy changes.

Welfare Reform and Adolescent Fertility

The Personal Responsibility and Work Opportunity Reconciliation Act (1996) has fundamentally reshaped welfare policy in the United States. This legislation received its impetus from President Clinton's 1992 campaign promise to "end welfare as we know it" and from the efforts of conservative Republicans to both reduce federal social welfare spending and end the entitlement status of the major cash welfare program, Aid to Families With Dependent Children (AFDC).

One of the more remarkable aspects of the prolonged debate over this legislation was the degree to which discussions focused on adolescents and the fertility-related behavior of adolescent girls. If one simply looks at the relative attention paid to teens during the welfare debates, one might logically conclude that (a) teens make up a significant proportion of the welfare population, (b) teen births are on the increase, (c) teen nonmarital births make up the majority of nonmarital births, and (d) welfare benefits serve as a significant incentive for teens to bear out-of-wedlock children. None of these statements are supported by the data, however. Adolescents comprised only 7% of the AFDC population in 1995 (most of these being 18-year-olds); teen births have decreased (modestly) each of the last 5 years; adult women are responsible for the vast majority of nonmarital childbirths; and reviews of research on the so-called incentive effect of welfare on teen childbearing (i.e., the availability of welfare serves as an incentive for teens to bear children) do not generally support this hypothesis (Wilcox, Robbennolt, O'Keeffe, & Reddy, 1996). Although it is true that a significant number of AFDC recipients first became mothers as adolescents, the attention devoted to teens by policymakers was nevertheless more extensive than the numbers would warrant.

The new welfare law contains a number of provisions that are targeted to teens (Levin-Epstein, 1996). The underlying policy goal of most of these provisions was to discourage adolescent nonmarital childbearing. For example, to receive welfare block grant funds, all states are required to submit state plans that include two provisions related to teens. First, states must describe the special efforts they will make to reduce teen pregnancies. Second, states must show that they are directing attention to sex between "older" men and teen girls as part of a state statutory rape education program. Another provision provides up to five states with a financial bonus for reducing out-of-wedlock births ("illegitimacy" in the statute) as well as abortions for teens and nonteens.

Two important restrictions are placed on benefits to unmarried custodial minor teen parents (under age 18). First, these parents are required to live in an adult-supervised setting. Unless states decide an exception is warranted, they are not allowed to provide benefits to unmarried custodial minor parents not residing with an adult. Second, these same parents are required to stay enrolled in school to receive benefits.

States are given the option to develop "grandparent liability" policies that would allow them to collect child support from the parent or parents of a noncustodial, minor teen parent. The legislation encourages states to develop demonstration projects assessing the efficacy of such programs. States are also encouraged (but not required) to require noncustodial minor parents to participate in community work programs.

One provision in the act requires a series of reports and studies to be conducted. Two merit mentioning. First, the USDHHS is required to deliver a report to Congress assuring that at least 25% of U.S. communities have teen pregnancy prevention programs in place and outlining a national strategy for teen pregnancy prevention. Second, the USDHHS is required to report on the effect of various state welfare programs on teen pregnancies and nonmarital childbirths. The first report was completed in January 1997, with the USDHHS "certifying" that over 25% of communities already have teen pregnancy prevention programs in place and outlining a handful of ongoing and new activities as representing the "national plan." Congress provided no new funding for these activities.

"Prepregnancy" family planning services (i.e., not abortion services) may be, but are not required to be, supported by states with their block grant funds. Under the old AFDC program, family planning services were required to be made available to all recipients requesting them. In lieu of spending on family planning services, Congress created the previously described abstinence education program funded at $50 million per year for 5 years.

A final provision applies to all welfare recipients, but during Congressional debate teens were often the focal point: States have the option of denying additional cash payments to mothers who conceive and bear a child while already receiving welfare. This "family cap" provision has already been adopted by a number of states.

Many scholars addressed these policy proposals prior to the passage of welfare reform, often arguing that the new programs were likely to prove either ineffectual or harmful (Wilcox et al., 1996; "Welfare Reform and

Nonmarital Childbearing," 1995; "Welfare and Out-of-Wedlock Births: A Research Summary," 1994). One hopes that the role of researchers in the debate will be captured by the policy historians who will inevitably recount the events surrounding the passage of this landmark legislation.

WANTED: A BROADER PERSPECTIVE

If, as many observers argue, Americans have extremely ambivalent or conflicting feelings about human sexuality, this holds especially true for our attitudes regarding the emerging sexuality and sexual behavior of adolescent girls.[8] This chapter has reviewed five policy areas in which this ambivalence, which occasionally turns to outright hostility, is borne out. Family planning policies, originally designed to assist teens in preventing unwanted births, have been under attack since the early 1980s on the grounds that the availability of confidential contraceptive services encourages promiscuity and interferes with parents' ability to raise their daughters. Sexuality education, promoted as a means to help children and adolescents develop as healthy sexual persons, similarly has come under attack by policymakers, who have sought to limit curricula to discussions of diseases and other threats to adolescents. As one colleague of mine put it, these policymakers want to tell adolescents that sex is dirty, so they should save it for someone they love. Taking their concerns with adolescent girls' sexuality further, these policymakers have attempted to replace comprehensive sexuality education with abstinence-only programs and to construct a variety of barriers intended to limit adolescent girls' access to contraceptive services and abortion. According to one noted sexuality scholar, "the debate has stagnated for decades and is polarized around the question of whether it is best to do everything to suppress teenage sexual behavior or whether one should pragmatically accept the fact that the majority of young women and men will become sexually active in the second decade of their lives" (Ehrhardt, 1996, p. 1523).

Clearly, policymaking in the United States has embodied a primarily hostile approach to sexuality and sexual expression among the young, and this is particularly so for adolescent girls. Instead of pursuing policy mechanisms to enhance adolescents' sexual health, policymakers have attempted to restrict adolescents' access to information and services while scapegoating adolescents for high welfare costs. The failure of these policies is evi-

---

[8]Numerous writers have noted the imbalance of focus on adolescent girls' sexuality in public policy (Luker, 1996; Nathanson, 1991). However, as Nathanson (1991) noted, it is female sexuality, rather than sexuality per se, that is likely to generate the greatest concern among those shaping our laws. When males are considered, they are often characterized as sexual predators taking advantage of young girls (Males, 1995, 1996), and with the exception of child support and statutory rape laws, policymakers have given little attention to the role of males in policies linked to sexual behaviors.

dent in the persistently high rates of teen pregnancies (Alan Guttmacher Institute, 1994) and sexually transmitted diseases among adolescents (Eng & Butler, 1996).

Discussions of adolescent sexual health, in which issues of sexual feelings and competence are considered, are nonexistent in the policy arena. Lest social scientists become overly smug, it is also rare to find research that conceptualizes adolescent sex as anything other than "risk behavior" (Ehrhardt, 1996; Welsh, Rostosky, & Kawaguchi, in press). Adolescent sexual behavior is most typically portrayed as placing youth at risk for pregnancy, sexually transmitted diseases, and HIV infection. The narrow —and frequently moralistic—construction of adolescent sexuality in the research literature feeds public fears and helps breed a climate in which policies such as those described in this chapter come to appear as reasonable. Adolescent health researchers must broaden their research agendas to include the positive dimensions of adolescent sexuality if they wish to contribute to sound public policies.

REFERENCES

Abma, J. C., Chandra, A., Mosher, W. D., Peterson, L., & Piccinino, P. (1997, May). *Fertility, family planning, and women's health: New data from the 1995 National Survey of Family Growth* (Vital Health Statistics Series 23, No. 19). Hyattsville, MD: U.S. Department of Health and Human Services, Centers for Disease Control and Prevention, National Center for Health Statistics.

Alan Guttmacher Institute. (1976). *11 million teenagers: What can be done about the epidemic of adolescent pregnancies in the United States.* New York: Planned Parenthood Federation of America.

Alan Guttmacher Institute. (1994). *Sex and America's teenagers.* New York: Author.

Alan Guttmacher Institute. (1995). *Issues in brief: Lawmakers grapple with parents' role in teen access to reproductive health care* [On-line]. Available: http://206.215.210.5/pubs/ib6.html

Alan Guttmacher Institute. (1997). *Issues in brief: Title X and the U.S. family planning effort* [On-line]. Available: http://www.agi-usa.org/pubs/ib16/ib16.html

Bellotti v. Baird, 443 U.S. 622 (1979).

Brown, S. S., & Eisenberg, L. (Eds.). (1995). *The best intentions: Unintended pregnancy and the well-being of children and families.* Washington, DC: National Academy Press.

Burlingame, P. (1997). *Sex, lies, and politics: Abstinence-only curricula in California public schools.* Oakland, CA: Applied Research Center.

Carey v. Population Services International, 431 U.S. 678 (1977).

Carnegie Corporation of New York. (1995). *Great transitions: Preparing adolescents for a new century.* New York: Author.

City of Akron v. Akron Center for Reproductive Health, 450 U.S. 398 (1983).

Crosby, M. C., & English, A. (1991). Mandatory parental involvement/judicial bypass laws: Do they promote adolescents' health? *Journal of Adolescent Health, 12*, 143–161.

D'Emilio, J., & Freedman, E. (1988). *Intimate matters: A history of sexuality in America.* New York: Harper & Row.

Donovan, P. (1992). *Our daughters' decisions: The conflict in state law on abortion and other issues.* New York: Alan Guttmacher Institute.

Ehrhardt, A. A. (1996). Editorial: Our view of adolescent sexuality—A focus on risk behavior without the developmental context. *American Journal of Public Health, 86*, 1523–1525.

Eisenstadt v. Baird, 405 U.S. 438, 448 (1972).

Ellertson, C. (1997). Manditory parental involvement in minors' abortions: Effects of the laws in Minnesota, Missouri, and Indiana. *American Journal of Public Health, 87*, 1367–1374.

Eng, T. R., & Butler, W. T. (1996). *The hidden epidemic: Confronting sexually transmitted diseases.* Washington, DC: National Academy Press.

Fine, M. (1988). Sexuality, schooling, and adolescent females: The missing discourse of desire. *Harvard Educational Review, 58*, 29–53.

Forrest, J. D., & Samara, R. (1996). Impact of publicly funded contraceptive services on unintended pregnancies and implications for Medicaid. *Family Planning Perspectives, 28*, 188–195.

Gambrell, A. E., & Haffner, D. W. (1993). *Unfinished business: A SIECUS assessment of state sexuality education programs.* New York: Sexuality Information and Education Council of the United States.

Garfinkel, I., & McLanahan, S. S. (1986). *Single mothers and their children: A new American dilemma.* Washington, DC: Urban Institute Press.

Gittler, J., Quigley-Rick, M., & Saks, M. (1990). *Adolescent health care decision-making: The law and public policy.* Washington, DC: Carnegie Council on Adolescent Development.

Griswold v. Connecticut, 381 U.S. 479 (1965).

Grogger, J., & Bronars, S. (1993). The socioeconomic consequences of teenage childbearing using twins as a natural experiment. *Family Planning Perspectives, 25*, 156–161.

Grunseit, A., & Kippax, S. (1993). *Effects of sex education on young people's sexual behavior.* Geneva, Switzerland: Global Programme on AIDS, World Health Organization.

Haffner, D. W., & Goldfarb, E. S. (1997). But does it work? Improving evaluations of sexuality education. *SIECUS Report, 25*(6), 3–16.

Haskins, R., & Bevan, C. S. (1996). *Implementing the abstinence education provision of the welfare reform legislation.* Washington, DC: U.S. Congress, Committee on Ways and Means.

Hechinger, Fred M. (1992). *Fateful choices: Healthy youth for the 21st century.* New York: Carnegie Corporation of New York.

Hodgson v. Minnesota, 110 S. Ct. 2962 (1990).

Hoffman, S., Foster, M., & Furstenberg, F. F., Jr. (1993). Reevaluating the costs of teenage childbearing. *Demography, 30,* 1–13.

Hotz, V. J., McElroy, S., & Sanders, S. (1997). The impacts of teenage childbearing on the mothers and the consequences of those impacts for government. In R. A. Maynard (Ed.), *Kids having kids: Economic costs and social consequences of teen pregnancy* (pp. 55–94). Washington, DC: Urban Institute Press.

Irwin, C. E., Jr., Brindis, C. D., Brodt, S. E., Bennett, T. A., & Rodriquez, R. Q. (1991). *The health of America's youth: Current trends in health status and utilization of health services.* San Francisco: University of California Press.

Kenney, A., Forrest, J. D., & Torres, A. (1982). Storm over Washington: The parental notification proposal. *Family Planning Perspectives, 14,* 185–197.

Kirby, D. (1997). *No easy answers: Research findings on programs to reduce teen pregnancy.* Washington, DC: National Campaign to Prevent Teen Pregnancy.

Kirby, D., Short, L., Collins, J., Rugg, D., Kolbe, L., Howard, M., Miller, B., Sonenstein, F., & Zabin, L. S. (1994). School-based programs to reduce sexual risk behaviors: A review of effectiveness. *Public Health Reports, 109,* 339–359.

Levin-Epstein, J. (1996). *Teen parent provisions in the Personal Responsibility and Work Opportunity Reconciliation Act of 1996.* Washington, DC: Center on Law and Social Policy.

Limber, S. P., Wilcox, B. L., & Bartels, C. (1996, November). *The improper use of developmental theory and research to support abstinence-only sex education curricula.* Paper presented at the annual meeting of the American Public Health Association, New York.

Luker, K. (1996). *Dubious conception: The politics of teenage pregnancy.* Cambridge, MA: Harvard University Press.

Males, M. A. (1995, April). *Adult involvement in school-age fertility.* Paper presented at the meeting of the Population Association of America, San Francisco.

Males, M. A. (1996). *The scapegoat generation: America's war on adolescents.* Monroe, ME: Common Courage Press.

Marsiglio, W., & Mott, F. L. (1986). The impact of sex education on sexual activity, contraceptive use, and premarital pregnancy among American teenagers. *Family Planning Perspectives, 18,* 151–162.

Mayer, R. (1997). 1996–97 trends in opposition to comprehensive sexuality education in public schools in the United States. *SIECUS Report, 25*(6), 20–26.

Mayer, R., & Kantor, L. (1996). 1995–96 trends in opposition to comprehensive sexuality education in public schools in the United States. *SIECUS Report, 24*(6), 3–11.

Maynard, R. A. (1997). The costs of adolescent childbearing. In R. A. Maynard (Ed.), *Kids having kids: Economic costs and social consequences of teen pregnancy* (pp. 285–337). Washington, DC: Urban Institute Press.

Mecklenburg, M. E., & Thompson, P. G. (1983). The Adolescent Family Life Program as a prevenion measure. *Public Health Reports, 98,* 21–29.

Meier, K. J., & McFarlane, D. R. (1994). State family planning and abortion expenditures: Their effect on public health. *American Journal of Public Health*, *84*, 1468–1472.

Melton, G. B. (Ed.). (1986). *Adolescent abortion: Psychological and legal perspectives*. Lincoln: University of Nebraska Press.

Millstein, S. G., Petersen, A. C., & Nightingale, E. O. (1993). Adolescent health promotion: Rationale, goals, and objectives. In S. G. Millstein, A. C. Petersen, & E. O. Nightingale (Eds.), *Promoting the health of adolescents: New directions for the twenty-first century* (pp. 3–10). New York: Oxford University Press.

Nathanson, C. (1991). *Dangerous passage: The social control of women's sexuality in adolescence*. Philadelphia: Temple University Press.

National Commission on Children. (1991). *Beyond rhetoric: A new American agenda for children and families*. Washington, DC: Author.

National Commission on the Role of the School and the Community in Improving Adolescent Health. (1990). *Code blue: Uniting for healthier youth*. Chicago: American Medical Association.

National Guidelines Task Force. (1991). *Guidelines for comprehensive sexuality education, kindergarten–12th grade*. New York: Sexuality Information and Education Council of the United States.

National Research Council. (1993). *Losing generations: Adolescents in high-risk settings*. Washington, DC: National Academy Press.

National Youth Law Center. (1995). *State minor consent statutes: A summary*. Cincinnati, OH: Center for Continuation in Adolescent Health.

New York v. Heckler, 719 F.2d 1191 (1983).

Ohio v. Akron Center for Reproductive Health, 110 S. Ct. 2972 (1990).

O'Keeffe, J. E., & Jones, J. M. (1990, Fall). Easing restrictions on minors' abortion rights. *Issues in Science and Technology*, 74–80.

Personal Responsibility and Work Opportunity Reconciliation Act of 1996, Pub. L. No. 104–193.

Planned Parenthood Federation of America v. Heckler, 712 F.2d 650 (1983).

Proposed regulations on family planning: Hearing before the Subcommittee on Health and the Environment of the House Committee on Energy and Commerce, 97th Cong., 2d Sess. (1982) (testimony of Richard Schweiker).

Roe v. Wade, 410 U.S. 113 (1973).

Rosoff, J. (1973). The future of federal support for family planning services and population research. *Family Planning Perspectives*, *5*, 7–18.

Steiner, G. Y. (1981). *The futility of family policy*. Washington, DC: Brookings Institution Press.

Torres, A., & Eisman, S. (1980). Telling parents: Clinic policies and adolescents' use of family planning and abortion services. *Family Planning Perspectives*, *12*, 284–292.

U.S. Congress Office of Technology Assessment. (1991a). *Adolescent health—Vol-*

ume 1: Summary and policy options. Washington, DC: Government Printing Office.

U.S. Congress Office of Technology Assessment. (1991b). *Adolescent health—Volume 2: Background and the effectiveness of selected prevention and treatment services.* Washington, DC: Government Printing Office.

U.S. Congress Office of Technology Assessment. (1991c). *Adolescent health—Volume 3: Crosscutting issues in the delivery of related services.* Washington, DC: Government Printing Office.

Vinovskis, M. (1981, Summer). An "epidemic" of adolescent pregnancy? Some historical considerations. *Journal of Family History, 6,* 205–230.

Vinovskis, M. (1988). *An epidemic of adolescent pregnancy? Some historical and policy considerations.* New York: Oxford University Press.

Welfare and out-of-wedlock births: A research summary. (1994). Mimeo [letter signed by 77 social scientist poverty researchers]. Available from American Psychological Association Public Policy Office, 750 First St., NE, Washington, DC 20002.

Welfare reform and nonmarital childbearing: Hearings before the Subcommittee on Human Resources, of the House Committee on Ways and Means, 104th Cong., 1st Sess. (1995) (testimony of Rebecca M. Blank).

Welsh, D. P., Rostosky, S. S., & Kawaguchi, M. C. (in press). A normative perspective of adolescent girls' developing sexuality. In C. B. Travis & J. S. White (Eds.), *Sex, society and feminism: Psychological perspectives and women.* Washington, DC: American Psychological Association.

Wilcox, B. L. (1993). Deterring risky behavior: Policy perspectives on adolescent risk taking. In N. J. Bell & R. W. Bell (Eds.), *Adolescent risk taking* (pp. 148–164). Newbury Park, CA: Sage.

Wilcox, B. L. (1997, August). *Is abstinence-only sex education effective? An evaluation of the evaluations.* Paper presented at the meeting of the American Psychological Association, Chicago.

Wilcox, B. L., & O'Keeffe, J. E. (1990). Families, policy, and family support policies. *Prevention in Human Services, 9,* 109–126.

Wilcox, B. L., Robbennolt, J. K., & O'Keeffe, J. E. (1998). Federal abortion policy and politics: 1973–1996. In L. J. Beckman & S. M. Harvey (Eds.), *The new civil war: The psychology, culture, and politics of abortion* (pp. 3–24). Washington, DC: American Psychological Association.

Wilcox, B. L., Robbennolt, J. K., O'Keeffe, J. E., & Reddy, M. E. (1996). Teen nonmarital childbearing and welfare: The gap between research and political discourse. *Journal of Social Issues, 52,* 71–90.

15

PRACTICE AND EDUCATION ISSUES RELATED TO ADOLESCENT GIRLS

JOANNE E. CALLAN

Specific strengths and stressors of today's adolescent girls constitute the focus of this book, adding much-needed balance to the literature on adolescent girls, which too often has emphasized negative influences and experiences. The particular needs of adolescent girls have caught the attention of those living or working directly with them: parents, teachers, counselors, and clinicians, all of whom seek information on how to both protect and strengthen girls (e.g., see American Association of University Women, 1991). Psychology, as a discipline and as a profession, is in an excellent position to respond on both counts, using research, practice, teaching, and consulting expertise. Indeed, given this broad base of knowledge and understanding, psychologists have a responsibility to respond to the needs of adolescent girls. Specifically, they can support the acquisition and maintenance of girls' strengths and can address the many stressors and related problems adolescent girls face. Because competent practice relies on relevant and comprehensive education and training, psychologist-educators must offer training programs with specially designed curricula, covering courses as well as applied training, that address these special needs and problems.

Accordingly, this chapter focuses on practice and education issues in psychology as they relate to serving adolescent girls. Critical practice issues are presented first, with discussion of current psychosocial influences on girls' needs for support and intervention, including counseling and psychotherapy. Also presented are common psychological problems that today's adolescent girls experience, with discussion of their etiology and different treatment approaches, which psychologists and other clinicians must understand and address in their professional practices. The last section focuses on relevant training models and programs as well as specific learning activities currently offered, or not offered, by graduate programs in psychology.

CLINICAL PRACTICE WITH ADOLESCENT GIRLS

What is the essential nature of the world in which today's adolescent girls live and grow into adulthood? And what is the experience of adolescent girls in such a world? These are key matters for those who work to understand and support them. Unquestionably, practitioners in psychology and other mental health disciplines need to know more about the world of adolescent girls, what is working for them, and what is not. With the many gains women have made in the last 30 years or so, emanating from the Women's Movement in the 1960s and 1970s, one view is that girls in the 1990s have many more opportunities than ever before. Thus, women and girls are able to enjoy experiences previously either not open to them at all or extremely difficult to pursue. A corollary to this view is the idea that such progress means that today's adolescent girls not only should be experiencing fewer stressors and inhibitors but also should be exhibiting greater strength than their predecessors.

Many professionals most closely involved with adolescent girls differ with this perspective, however, asserting that progress related to gaining equal rights for women and girls has not created the open and supportive culture for adolescent girls that might have been anticipated. They point to multiple reasons for this outcome. Pipher (1995) suggested that sociocultural and family system problems are the culprits, noting as an example the negative impact of certain media images along with other cultural expectations and pressures. She observed that the media has great power in its essential emphasis more on ideals of physical appearance than on ideals of character; moreover, she described how girls seem to be experiencing an internal dilemma between being true to themselves and being true to others, one which leads, destructively, to their being false to themselves.

A related matter is the tension existing between the inherent need adolescent girls have for functioning within relationships and the lack of different, positive role models to guide them. Further, they lack precise rules and expectations as they consider the variety of roles now open to them, in contrast with more generally accepted expectations for girls in the past. It is paradoxical that as new directions and roles become accessible to adolescent girls, this wider array of opportunities actually complicates their basic need for attachment in relationships (see Brown & Gilligan, 1992; Cosse, 1992; Gilligan, 1982; Rubenstein, 1992). Even so, many professionals working with adolescent girls have identified positive developments that can enhance sense of self as well as personal relationships, thus contributing to overall strength. Brown and Gilligan (1992), for example, noted facilitating experiences that adolescent girls may enjoy with adult women when there is genuine openness and engagement with one another.

Generally, practitioners view adolescents as needing support from families, friends, teachers and other mentors, as well as from communities. All are seen as essential, but family support and sponsorship are viewed as particularly important to the development of healthy adolescent girls (Bloch, 1995; Orvin, 1995). In fact, Bloch (1995) identified the parent–adolescent relationship as essential, centering his entire theory of adolescent development on three basic issues: (a) the internal strivings within adolescents to complete development, (b) the need for parental sponsorship of those strivings, and (c) a wish to retain a positive relationship with parents. Even though the traditional family pattern of the past no longer exists to the same extent (Hernandez, 1988), adolescents require supportive and available parents or substitute figures who sponsor them, whatever the parental constellation is (Patterson, 1997).

From a broader, more ecological perspective, powerful and converging sociocultural forces present intrapersonal as well as interpersonal developmental crises for adolescent girls. These forces and potential crises can be strengthening, of course, if an adolescent girl has acquired sufficient ego strengths (e.g., such psychological functions as effective reality testing and impulse regulation and control; see Chethik, 1989) by the time she enters adolescence and if there is sufficient support of those strengths during her adolescence. At the same time, these crises can contribute to a rocky, painful adolescence or lead to serious, sometimes long-lasting, and even life-threatening problems. Rapid changes related to major social and cultural developments have contributed significantly to how these crises are experienced by adolescent girls. Because of the pervasive impact of these developments on many adolescent girls, it seems worthwhile to note a few here, thus providing a context in which practitioners can better understand what is working for adolescent girls, what is not, and how that is happening.

Social and Cultural Influences Affecting Clinical Practice

The following examples are among multiple social and cultural developments influencing girls, each contributing significantly to the nature of today's adolescent world and to the overall development and adjustment of adolescents. Coming together as a set of converging forces, as noted above, they have an impressive influence on adolescent girls.

Increased Sexual Freedom

With the availability and proper use of birth control measures, today's young women need not fear pregnancy as did their predecessors; yet, many sexually active teenage girls do not avail themselves of these measures and also do not practice safe sex, as reflected in the increase in sexually transmitted diseases (STDs; Carnegie Council on Adolescent Development, 1989).

Changes in the Family

Changes have occurred in family structure, such as the increase in divorce, variety of parenting patterns, number of households in which both parents work, and other changing family values and practices.

Community Life Changes

Social change and shifts in community life have led to the loss of traditional institutional and structural supports and involvement with them (e.g., churches), thus diminishing community support.

Economic and Workforce Changes

More women are in the workforce now than ever before, with up to 80% of all women working either full or part time. Other shifts include increased numbers of families with both parents and also adolescents working; welfare system changes, affecting poor families and especially single-mother families; and changes in job security with the increasingly common practice of corporate and industry downsizing (Cascio, 1995).

Increased Diversity

Although there are challenges related to understanding and accepting cultural and ethnic differences in communities across the country, enrichment also comes with such increasing diversity.

Heightened Violence and Unsafe Environments

Violent events and experiences negatively affect adolescent girls, creating fear and threats against individual freedoms and actual physical safety, as in unsafe schools and communities, and in some cases, from abuse and deprivation in girls' own homes.

Transportation and Portability Advances

Today, adolescent girls can get from place to place and can become involved in activities far from their homes with considerable ease. Although facilitating in many ways, such portability can mean less parental supervision, less community support, and greater freedom, understandably frightening parents about where and with whom their daughters may be.

Changing Health Care

Recent developments such as the loss of health insurance for many families and managed care restrictions increasingly limit some services needed by adolescent girls. Also, fragmented and inappropriate health and mental health services often available to adolescent girls interfere with the kind of integrated care they need (Holtzman, 1992).

Communication and Technology

In contrast with admonitions about negative media influences on adolescent girls (Pipher, 1995), advances in technology and communication are now available for them as sources of mass information and as readily accessible opportunities for enhanced learning and performance in various venues. Even so, especially given adolescent girls' need for relational learning and performance, one must use these advances wisely, as, for example, in assuring that computer programs of interest to adolescence girls are developed and made available to them.

Prevalence and Types of Psychological Problems

Prevalence

As a result of great social flux in the last few decades, many adolescents experience emotional distress and, therefore, need support or psychological intervention. In 1990, the report on general mental health disorders and problems, developed by the National Advisory Mental Health Council and produced by the National Institute of Mental Health, reported that a minimum of 12% of youth in the United States (i.e., about 7.5 million) suffer from some mental disorder, with an annual treatment cost at more than $1.5 billion. Only about one fifth of youth actually receive needed services, and many receiving treatment will not recover because their disorders are not sufficiently understood (e.g., schizophrenia or autism). Said differently, many youth receiving treatment will be "undertreated, overtreated, or treated ineffectively" (Roberts & Hinton-Nelson, 1996, p. 1). In a review of comorbid conditions (Nottelmann & Jensen, 1995), the prevalence of child and adolescent mental disorders based on the *Diagnostic and Statistical Manual of Mental Disorders* (3rd ed.,

DSM–III; American Psychiatric Association, 1980) criteria ranged from 5% to 26%, with a higher rate for adolescent girls, although larger studies indicated an even higher range of 17.6% to 22% (a higher rate for boys was reported in childhood). These numbers and costs are markedly greater when psychological intervention for adolescent adjustment problems is included.

In considering the prevalence of psychological problems among adolescent girls, it is important to note that adolescence is not viewed today as inevitably or inherently a period of psychopathology. Although a number of forces as well as developmental issues, as discussed herein, certainly have notable impact on adolescent girls, research as well as clinical data indicate that most teens will pass through adolescence with relatively few major problems (Hauser, Powers, & Noam, 1991; Offer & Offer, 1975). Nonetheless, in this chapter noting the range of emotional problems experienced by adolescent girls, from more minor ones of adjustment to the more pathological, it is relevant to emphasize the value of thorough assessment and appropriate intervention (Archer, Maruish, Imhof, & Piotrowski, 1991). Even for girls who may not suffer a serious emotional problem, counseling or therapy may be of critical benefit, and, moreover, the number of girls who clearly require mental health services is quite large. Accordingly, the profession must be prepared to provide competent services for them.

Types of Psychological Problems

Most professionals agree not only on which emotional problems, disorders, and symptoms occur most frequently but also on those reflecting the greatest distress among today's adolescent girls. In the current practices of psychologists and others involved in assessment and intervention with adolescent girls, there seem to be three primary areas of difficulty:

- Major adjustment and developmental problems—including personal identity and family issues, such as separation from parents and family, sexual identity issues, or concerns about one's sexual orientation and behaviors (these kinds of problems may exist along with more serious ones).
- Major psychological disorders—including the more serious problems such as schizophrenia, eating disorders, and mood disorders.
- Major psychosocially and culturally induced problems—including reactions to violence, drug use, and other abuse (all of which can lead to or have been associated with serious psychological problems).

Psychological problems of adolescent girls can be understood from a developmental perspective, with categories of mental health problems, as identified by Kessler (1988): internalizing disorders of conflicts, structural deficits and major object relations problems, and externalizing problems (see also Tuma & Russ, 1993).

Most clinicians see problematic behaviors and psychopathology in adolescent girls as derived from a combination of etiological factors including genetic, biological, and nonbiological–psychosocial influences (Colarusso, 1992; Willis & Walker, 1989). Rubenstein (1992) discussed several clinical issues that she sees as particularly important to adolescent girls: "birth control, body image, eating disorders, female friendships, male–female relationships, and mother–daughter relationships" (p. 17). Nottelmann and Jensen (1995), responding to accumulating evidence that cormorbidity in children and adolescents is pervasive, identified five prevalent child and adolescent disorders: conduct disorders, oppositional defiant disorders, attention deficit disorders, affective disorders (especially depression), and anxiety disorders. These authors reported that affective disorders and anxiety disorders, particularly overanxious disorders, were higher among adolescent girls than among boys.

Public Health Issues: Prevention and Other Responses From Psychology

Each year in this country, thousands of teen girls find themselves in psychological distress associated with problems so pervasive in our society that they have come to be known as public health issues. Several critical ones are noted here.

Sexual Behaviors

One of the most serious public health issues for adolescents—and particularly for adolescent girls—involves inappropriate or destructive sexual behaviors and their psychological as well as physical health ramifications. The high incidence of teen pregnancy is certainly one of our nation's most pressing problems. As reported by the Committee on School Health (1993), 1 million American teens become pregnant each year, 1 of 10 being girls between 15 and 19 years, with half of these 17 years and younger. Poverty and ethnicity are related to pregnancy rates. Not only do these pregnancies oftentimes result in economic as well as psychological difficulties for adolescent girls themselves, but they also lead frequently to situations of deprivation for their babies, because children are raising children.

A number of federal and state programs, as well as privately developed community programs, focus on the sexual behavior problems of adolescent girls; for example, there is high hope for success with interventions made available to teen mothers through the Early Head Start programs (Section 64A of the Head Start Act, as amended in 1995).

Another critical high-risk sexual behavior problem involves exposure to and contraction of STDs, including AIDS. As of January 1991, almost 20% of AIDs cases occurred in young people in their 20s, many infected as adolescents (Committee on School Health, 1993); this figure emphasizes the need for more programs addressing risky sexual behaviors (see Walker & Vaughan, 1993).

Psychologists are among practitioners who have skills for developing prevention programs that educate and support young women to engage in safe sex and to make decisions about pregnancy on the basis of physical, emotional, and economical readiness. In particular, those working in junior high and high schools and also in public health settings can support adolescent girls by developing prevention programs focused on safe and responsible sexual behaviors to deal with both pregnancy and STDs in adolescent girls. The Evaluation of the Self Center is described briefly by Durlak (1995) as one successful primary prevention program located near an inner-city junior high and high school.

Substance Use and Abuse

Use and abuse of drugs constitute another national public health issue for adolescent girls. Although reported to be declining in the 1970s and 1980s, abuse of some substances has actually increased among adolescents in the 1990s. There has been an upsurge in teen smoking (Winick, 1992), for example, and a parallel increase among adolescents in the smoking of marijuana, which is described by Johnson and Muffler (1992) as the most frequently used illicit drug in the United States. One dangerous outcome of marijuana use by adolescents, according to a Scripps Research Institute report (Graham, 1997), is that it may serve as a gateway drug, priming the brain for the use of harder drugs. In spite of these increases, treatment shifts and reductions in funding have occurred, so that most adolescent substance abuse treatment is occurring through outpatient interventions, short-term inpatient treatment, residential programs, partial hospitalization, and day treatment programs. Family therapy is viewed by many clinical practitioners as important, if not imperative, in the treatment of adolescent substance abuse (Craig, 1993; Selekman & Todd, 1991), a view supported by research on the effectiveness of family therapy in adolescent substance abuse treatment (Waldron, 1993).

Prevention programs seem to be particularly promising when they can be offered in the schools, reaching students through graduation or until dropout, or in other venues in which adolescents are (see Durlak, 1997). To be effective, however, programs must be offered early enough, frequently enough, long enough, and in ways that engage adolescent girls. Nirenberg (1983) described various skills used by psychologists in treating and managing addictive behaviors: social skills training, problem-solving skills, vocational skills, chemical treatment, aversive conditioning, and relaxation. To successfully treat adolescents abusing drugs, many clinicians use multimodal treatment approaches—for example, combining individual therapy, group therapy, family therapy, or specially developed programs (e.g., Alcoholics Anonymous, Narcotics Anonymous; see also Craig, 1993; Wexler, 1991) on either an inpatient or an outpatient basis, realizing that adolescent drug abuse is associated oftentimes with other psychological problems and disorders.

Interpersonal Violence

Another national public health issue affecting some adolescent girls is pervasive violence. Occurring in homes, schools, job settings, and on our streets, indeed, potentially almost everywhere, violence against girls is seen in verbal, physical, and sexual abuse. The National Institute of Mental Health (1985) study noted the lack of research on the sexual victimization of adolescents. Existing research indicates how negatively actual experiences as well as fears and intrusive thoughts interfere with an adolescent's ability to function in a healthy and productive manner (e.g., see Aber, 1989). Recent school-based prevention programs, emphasizing interventions with teachers, grade school children, early adolescents, and the enhancement of school and family attachments, reported reductions in boys' aggressive behaviors and in girls' self-destructive behaviors (Durlak, 1995).

Psychological Practices Supporting Adolescent Girls

Clinical practitioners in all settings are challenged to respond not only to the public health issues described above but also to the widest range of psychological problems among adolescent girls. The sheer range of problems is challenging, and the number of adolescents needing mental health treatment plus those who require support in their journey through "normal" adolescence is great.

GENERAL CLINICAL RESPONSES TO THE NEEDS AND PROBLEMS OF ADOLESCENT GIRLS

Although the problems of adolescent girls are described in somewhat different terms within various theories, what can be agreed on is not only how pervasive but also how complex they are. Clinical responses to these problems must take into account ethical and legal requirements as well as matters of theory, approach, and technique. The following comments focus on several key, but general, considerations for those working clinically with adolescent girls.

General Approaches and Special Issues in Clinical Work With Adolescent Girls

Aware that achieving successful interventions with adolescent girls can be difficult (e.g., because of the age-appropriate adolescent thrust toward separation–individuation), practitioners carefully seek to establish a workable treatment arrangement and positive therapeutic alliance with each girl they see. They give close attention to all relationships and systems with which an adolescent girl is associated. As noted above, most clinicians are very interested in the family or an alternative support system in which a girl lives. Not only do they need vital historical and situational information from parents but they also know how imperative it is that a young girl experiencing serious emotional problems have support and sponsorship as she pursues treatment. Indeed, for those girls whose families are so dysfunctional that they cannot be involved or in which there is no family, treatment outcome is enhanced when an alternate support system can be established for them.

Several special issues critical in clinical work with adolescent girls are those related to confidentiality, protection, age-appropriate identity, and cultural sensitivities. Because many adolescents are minors, for example, questions arise as to whom the commitment of confidentiality is made: to the adolescent girl or to her parents. Some authors take the position that confidentiality related to data gathered in therapy must be observed to protect the interest of the adolescent girl (DeKraai & Sales, 1991). Those seeking guidance on this matter, according to Morris and Nicholson (1993), may request information from state professional associations, state attorneys general, or executive officers of state licensing and certification boards. These authors noted greater problems, however, with respect to ethical issues related to interventions with adolescents (see also Gustafson & McNamara, 1996; Koocher, 1976, 1983; Taylor & Adelman, 1996). One area in which specific ethical questions may arise, for example, is in work with gay and lesbian adolescents, as when an adolescent girl has not informed her parents about her sexual identity or preference (e.g., Sobocinski, 1990). Similarly, sensitivity in regard to ethnic and sociocultural backgrounds must be exercised when working with adolescent girls (McClure & Teyber, 1996).

Assessment

When initially assessing the nature of presenting problems among adolescent girls, clinicians may use different approaches and somewhat different criteria to determine their nature and severity. A preliminary approach purported by many clinicians (e.g., Orvin, 1995) assesses three functional areas of an adolescent's life:

1. Relationships with the girl's family—that is, how well is a girl getting along with her family (or family substitute)?
2. Relationships with the girl's school and other work, because most adolescent girls are in school, which can be viewed as their primary "work" setting.
3. Relationships with friends. Does the girl have friends? How well is she getting along with them, and how fulfilling and constructive are these relationships?

A first step in determining the nature and extent of an adolescent girl's problems, when a psychological intervention is required, is to seek an evaluation. This step is so important that it deserves special emphasis. An evaluation may be only clinical in nature—that is, it may rely mostly, or altogether, on a clinical interview or interviews, which may or may not include a mental status examination, depending on the nature of the referral question. Many individual situations require more intensive assessment, however (e.g., the evaluation of conscious as well as unconscious functions), which typically involves psychological testing. Which specific psychological tests are used in the assessment of an adolescent girl depends on the particular nature of the presenting problem (Archer et al., 1991).

Clinical Intervention

Practitioners currently use a number of theories and modalities to meet the treatment needs of adolescent girls, ranging from short-term to more long-term intensive treatment arrangements. Initial referrals or contacts are usually followed by a clinical evaluation, and, when needed, a full psychological evaluation is conducted, as noted above. A next step involves a determination regarding diagnosis and appropriate treatment recommendations. It is critical, especially in these days of managed care, that these steps and also the specific goals of treatment be articulated clearly and their need documented, even though all vary with different practitioners. Robson (1994), for example, identified the larger goal of a therapeutic intervention with adolescents as facilitating development but pointed to the importance of "articulating specific component goals" (p. 126), such as establishing a working alliance, completing diagnostic evaluations, starting psychoactive drugs, and establishing contact with school personnel. Moreover, it is absolutely imperative that the nature of the problems and the treatment recommendations be made clear to an adolescent girl's parents or whoever is responsible for her care, including a written informed consent agreement.

Practitioners develop professional activities considerably around their respective theoretical orientations, usually on the basis of graduate or professional school education and then enhanced (although sometimes changed significantly) by postdoctoral study and subsequent continuing education and actual experience. Some psychologists working with adolescent girls base their work on a cognitive–behavioral approach (e.g., Beck, 1976; Hughes, 1993), whereas others work considerably from a rational–emotive approach (see Bernard & Joyce, 1993), from a client-centered/humanistic approach (see Ellinwood & Raskin, 1993), or from ecological approaches (see Morse, 1993). Still other practitioners follow a more psychodynamic or psychoanalytic approach to clinical work with adolescent girls, guided by psychoanalytic theories of human development and functioning, such as ego psychology, object relations, and self psychology (respectively, Bloch, 1995; Blos, 1962; Kohut, 1976; Kohut & Wolf, 1978; Mahler, Pine, & Bergman, 1975; Tyson & Tyson, 1991). Indeed, there are a number of different theories of development, personality, and psychopathology used by clinical practitioners, and, frequently, a combination of theories and techniques is used, depending on the particular needs of an individual adolescent girl (e.g., see Mark & Incorvaia, 1995).

Psychologists work with adolescents in a variety of professional settings. A summary of service delivery models is presented in an edited volume by Roberts (1996), covering a range of mental health services for children and adolescents. Programs designed to address problems within specific populations provide services in readily accessible venues: schools, clinics, hospitals, group homes, military bases, and foster homes, and also in one's home. One program, for example, is designed to support children and adolescents in foster homes; another to respond to mental health and substance abuse problems of military dependents; several work with families as well as with children and adolescents; and yet another provides services for children and adolescents with autism and communication problems.

A pediatric primary care program is also described (see also Schroeder & Gordon, 1991), representing a private pediatric practice as one model where psychologists affiliate with another professional group. Responding to the widest range of treatment needs for children and adolescents, from prevention programs via a range of community outreach activities and parent-child-adolescent support groups to individual and family assessment and intervention, the staff use a formal association supported by close geographical proximity with a pediatric practice group as an essential component of their work. Practitioners in independent and group private practice also may elect to develop affiliations with and accept referrals from area schools. Depending on the nature of a girl's problems, the interventions may include inpatient treatment, outpatient treatment, or both. They also consult with various other institutions and agencies providing services to adolescent girls, and they frequently negotiate a formal contractual arrangement to serve as a part-time staff member. Practitioners also collaborate with other professionals in both inpatient and outpatient work with adolescent girls. For example, a psychologist may serve as primary therapist for a teen with depression or with an eating disorder but arrange for a medical consultation and follow-up through collaboration with a local psychiatrist or other physician.

Although the treatment of major and more serious psychological problems and disorders of adolescent girls may be carried out on an outpatient basis, it may require inpatient treatment. A range of treatment approaches and strategies are available for inpatient intervention, with each treatment program having its own philosophy, on the basis of theoretical and intervention preferences (for a description of residential and inpatient treatment approaches for adolescents, see Lyman & Wilson, 1992). As one example, Wexler (1991) described the Program for Innovative Self-Management (PRISM) as a comprehensive inpatient treatment approach developed for teens with different diagnoses "to foster the essential building blocks of the adolescent sense of self: self-management, self-soothing, and self-esteem" (p. 3). Some inpatient and day-care programs for adolescent girls are designed to treat patients with a specific problem or diagnosis (e.g., eating disorders, anxiety disorders, and affective disorders). Masterson (1985), for example, advocated inpatient treatment for adolescent girls with borderline adjustments to control their behaviors while providing psychotherapeutic treatment (i.e., through a milieu therapy approach).

In the context of increasing focus on the psychological needs and problems of adolescent girls, a wide array of different treatment approaches and services have emerged in recent years; yet, there is an urgent need for greater understanding, more effective support of girls' strengths, and interventions to address their emotional distress and disorders. The complexity of the world in which today's adolescent girls live challenges psychology to devote its best efforts on their behalf in practice and in preparation for practice.

GRADUATE EDUCATION AND TRAINING IN PSYCHOLOGY ON ADOLESCENT GIRLS

An NIMH (1981) report decried the lack of training at the graduate professional level on adolescent psychology and adolescent development. Over 15 years later, with pressure for psychology's fullest response to the needs of adolescent girls, it is essential that graduate education and training respond with focus and vision. Following is a relevant question: What are graduate psychology programs doing to prepare competent, caring psychologists who can support the strengths and can respond to the needs of adolescent girls? Another relevant question is as follows: What else needs to be done? To address these questions, it is useful to understand how graduate education in psychology is offered, including not only various training models and different settings but also what is offered.

Training Models

Currently, graduate programs in psychology exist in several different institutional structures, offering education and training in a range of specialty or different substantive areas. Most are offered in traditional university settings, either (a) in psychology departments or other academic departments with close ties to psychology (e.g., education departments) or (b) within other professional schools, such as schools of medicine and schools of professional psychology (e.g., Rutgers University and Wright State University Schools of Professional Psychology). Since the 1970s, however, encouraged by the 1973 Vail Conference (Korman, 1976), a number of graduate programs in applied psychology with an emphasis on practitioner training have been established (most are clinical psychology programs, although some are counseling and school psychology programs). This development has been referred to as the professional school movement, with some programs existing as separate schools in university settings (alongside other professional schools, such as medicine, dentistry, and law, as noted just above), whereas some have been established as autonomous entities. A defining characteristic of these programs is that they are essentially applied programs whose major purpose is to educate and train students to be practitioners, although some which lead to the PhD emphasize research. In contrast, most university programs continue to design doctoral curricula with a major research emphasis based on a training model characterized as scientist–practitioner in focus. Typically, the research emphasis undertaken by a student is relevant to a specific specialty area (e.g., clinical, counseling, school, developmental, experimental [general], cognitive, or engineering psychology). Applied programs currently accredited by the American Psychological Association's Committee on Accreditation comprise, primarily, three specialty areas: clinical, counseling, and school psychology. In recent years, university graduate programs in other specialty areas have assumed a more applied nature (e.g., health, applied developmental, and applied cognitive psychology). Each of these programs is required to identify a philosophy of training undergirding a specific training model and to build its curriculum within the context of that model. The most recent revision of the accreditation guidelines (American Psychological Association, Committee on Accreditation, 1996) provides greater flexibility in allowing individual programs to develop special training models and curricula consistent with those models.

In applied graduate programs in universities and in professional schools, training models and curricula have been developed in what are sometimes referred to as subspecialty areas or emphasis areas. An example of one subspecialty is the clinical-child program, whose curriculum, including courses, practica, and internship training, focuses on children and adolescents. About a half dozen clinical-child programs, designed as separate entities, exist at this time—for example, at the University of Kansas, the University of North Carolina, the University of Washington, and the University of Minnesota (the last being integrated as a clinical program with the Institute of Child Development). Another type of doctoral program, one that can be characterized as a clinical psychology program with a child or child and adolescent concentration, is offered by departments within the following academic institutions (e.g., University of Alabama, University of Georgia, Louisiana State University, the University of Florida, the University of Miami, and the University of Virginia). Other graduate programs, a number of which are found in professional schools, offer a child emphasis or child and adolescent combination within general clinical, counseling, or school psychology programs. Graduate programs in developmental psychology also offer education and training that may reflect a life span approach or focus almost entirely on infant, child, or child and adolescent development.

State of Affairs: Education and Training Offerings Focused on Adolescent Girls

To gain more information about what training programs are doing with regard to adolescence, and girls in particular, researchers made inquiries by telephone and by e-mail correspondence to traditional programs and to professional schools. In absolute numbers, more responses were received from professional schools than from programs in universities. On the basis of all responses, including traditional and professional school programs, the most frequent single learning experience focusing on adolescent girls is the dissertation or doctoral project. The following conclusion can be drawn from this finding: Even when programs do not offer either required or elective courses—or when the number of such courses is limited to only a few or to narrow choices—individual faculty interests in adolescence are strong enough to support graduate student research and applied interests with adolescent girls and, in the case of doctoral projects, to support applied interests. Because of the limitations of the inquiries made in this initial effort, specific data on precise topics of current dissertations, doctoral projects, and numbers of those relating to adolescent girls that are in process will have to await another, more comprehensive survey.

Another way in which programs reported graduate training focused on adolescents, and specifically with adolescent girls, was through required applied experiences: practica and internships. One professional school program, for example, described a lock-step curriculum in which an internship experience with adolescents was required of all students, in addition to a developmental psychology course that included an emphasis on adolescents, both male and female. Another program, offered in a traditional university setting, reported an ongoing research project on adolescent girls, one that involves several faculty members as well as graduate students. Some psychology programs exist in universities and medical schools with established centers for studying and disseminating information about adolescents (e.g., the University of North Carolina). In reporting on the results of their survey on training in adolescent treatment, Rubenstein and Zager (1995) noted that although only 3% of the responding doctoral programs actually require students to work with adolescents, 24% of the postdoctoral and internship programs require work with adolescents, with another 24% offering optional training experiences.

More programs than not seemed to address education and training on adolescence through developmental psychology courses with a life span approach; yet, some programs, especially in the professional schools, offered either or both child and adolescent courses, either required or elective. None, however, reported courses focused only on adolescent girls, except in the context of psychology of women courses that often have a unit or subtopic on adolescent girls. Within individual graduate courses in clinical and counseling programs, the greatest number focusing on adolescents in general—and, including attention to adolescent girls—were identified as courses on adolescent development, adolescent adjustment and psychopathology, and adolescent psychotherapy—or a combination of these topics. Again, professional schools reported both more required and more elective courses in these areas, except in those traditional programs developed as clinical-child specialty programs. Particular methods or approaches used in the teaching of these courses emphasized case studies, which either were published and available to students for review and discussion or were case summaries prepared by faculty or by the students.

Although accredited internships as a group were not contacted in these inquiries, some information was received indirectly and anecdotally that deserves mention. Several program directors reported, for example, that the opportunities for learning about longer term treatment with adolescents—as well as with most mental health patients—had been sharply reduced. They also observed that a number of inpatient programs for adolescent girls had shifted to special service emphases (e.g., eating disorders, obesity, and drug abuse). Almost to a person, these educators and trainers wondered how future psychologists would learn about the widest spectrum of adolescent psychopathology and how they would develop competencies that would enable them to respond to the more serious adolescent disorders.

In summary, it must be noted regretfully that past arguments and current demands for education and training specifically focused on adolescent girls—or on adolescents in general—remain largely unheeded. As urgently as competent psychologists are needed to respond to provide services for adolescent girls, graduate programs in psychology are not responding sufficiently.

Following is a response to the second question from above, "What needs to be done?": Not only must more programs offer learning experiences that are responsive to these demands if they are to be met, but also psychologist-educators must take responsibility for designing and offering curricula that comprise the essential components leading to competency in providing services for adolescent girls. In short, comprehensive programs must be established, and, indeed, a training model has been developed recently by a group of psychologists for child and adolescent services (Roberts et al., 1998). They suggest the following:

> Training for the professional psychologist needs to be specialized to develop proper competence in conceptualization, tools, and implementation needed for child and family work. A downward extension of adult-oriented training is insufficient: A professional psychologist cannot competently function with child and family patients without having received specialized training to develop competence. (manuscript, pp. 21–22)

Further, the authors identify 11 integrated aspects of training as essential components for assuring competency in work with children and adolescents: life span developmental psychology; life span developmental psychopathology; child, adolescent, and family assessment methods; intervention strategies; research methods and systems evaluations; professional, ethical, and legal issues pertaining to children, adolescents, and families; issues of diversity; role of multiple disciplines and service delivery systems; prevention, family support, and health promotion; social issues affecting children, adolescents, and families; and specialized applied experiences in assessment, intervention, and consultation.

This comprehensive model offers promise for supporting the strengths and responding to the stressors of adolescent girls. It does so by guiding the education and training of psychologists specifically to advance competencies in providing services for adolescent girls. Applied programs responsible for educating and training future psychologists, as well as the individuals who are considering future work with adolescents girls, would do well to consider the pursuit of such a comprehensive curriculum.

REFERENCES

American Association of University Women (1991). *Shortchanging girls, shortchanging America.* Washington, DC: Author.

American Psychiatric Association. (1980). *Diagnostic and statistical manual of mental disorders* (3rd ed.). Washington, DC: Author.

American Psychological Association, Committee on Accreditation. (1996). *Guidelines and principles for accreditation of programs in professional psychology and accreditation operating procedures*. Washington, DC: Author.

Archer, R. P., Maruish, M., Imhof, E. A., & Piotrowski, C. (1991). Psychological test usage with adolescent clients: 1990 survey findings. *Professional Psychology: Research and Practice, 22,* 247–252.

Beck, A. (1976). *Cognitive therapy and the emotional disorders*. New York: International Universities Press.

Bernard, M. E., & Joyce, M. R. (1993). Rational-emotive therapy with children and adolescents. In T. R. Kratochwill & R. J. Morris, (Eds.), *Handbook of psychotherapy with children and adolescents* (pp. 221–246) Boston: Allyn & Bacon.

Bloch, H. S. (1995). *Adolescent development, psychopathology, and treatment*. Madison, CT: International Universities Press.

Blos, P. (1962). *On adolescence: A psychoanalytic interpretation*. New York: Free Press.

Brown, L. M., & Gilligan, C. (1992). *Meeting at the crossroads*. New York: Ballantine Books.

Carnegie Council on Adolescent Development. (1989). *Turning points: Preparing American youth for the 21st century*. New York: Author.

Cascio, W. F. (1995). Whither industrial and organizational psychology in a changing world of work? *American Psychologist, 50,* 928–939.

Chethik, M. (1989). *Techniques of child therapy: Psychodynamic strategies*. New York: Guilford Press.

Colarusso, C. A. (1992). *Child and adolescent development*. New York: Plenum.

Committee on School Health. (1993). *School health: Policy and practice* (5th ed.). Elk Grove Village, IL: American Academy of Pediatrics.

Cosse, W. J. (1992). Who's who and what's what? The effects of gender on development in adolescence. In B. R. Wainrib (Ed.), *Gender issues across the life cycle* (pp. 5–16). New York: Springer.

Craig, R. J. (1993). Contemporary trends in substance abuse. *Professional Psychology: Research and Practice, 24,* 182–189.

DeKraai, M. B., & Sales, B. D. (1991). Legal issues in the conduct of child therapy. *Journal of Consulting and Clinical Psychology, 59,* 853–860.

Durlak, J. A. (1997). Primary prevention programs in schools. *Advances in Clinical Child Psychology, 19,* 283–318.

Ellinwood, C. G., & Raskin, N. J. (1993). Client-centered/humanistic psychotherapy. In T. R. Kratochwill & R. J. Morris (Eds.), *Handbook of psychotherapy with children and adolescents* (pp. 258–287). Boston: Allyn & Bacon.

Gilligan, C. (1982). *In a different voice: Psychological theory and women's development*. Cambridge, MA: Harvard University Press.

Graham, D. (1997, June 27). Pot might prime the brain for harder drugs, study says. *San Diego Union*, p. A1.

Gustafson, K. E., & McNamara, J. R. (1996). Confidentiality with minor clients: Issues and guidelines for therapists. In D. N. Bersoff (Ed.), *Ethical conflicts in psychology* (pp. 193–197). Washington, DC: American Psychological Association.

Hauser, S., Powers, S., & Noam, G. (1991). *Adolescents and their families: Paths of ego development*. New York: Free Press.

Head Start Act, 42 U.S.C. §9801 *et seq.*

Hernandez, D. G. (1988). Demographic trends and the living arrangements of children. In E. M. Hetherington & J. D. Arasteh (Eds.), *Impact of divorce, single-parenting, and stepparenting on children* (pp. 3–22). Hillsdale, NJ: Erlbaum.

Holtzman, W. (1992). *School of the future*. Washington, DC: American Psychological Association.

Hughes, J. (1993). Behavior therapy. In T. R. Kratochwill & R. J. Morris (Eds.), *Handbook of psychotherapy with children and adolescents* (pp. 185–220). Boston: Allyn & Bacon.

Johnson, B. G., & Muffler, J. (1992). Sociocultural aspects of drug use and abuse in the 1990's. In J. H. Lowinson, P. Ruiz, R. B. Millman, & J. F. Langrod (Eds.), *Substance abuse: A comprehensive textbook* (2nd ed., pp. 118–137). Baltimore: Williams & Wilkins.

Kessler, J. (1988). *Psychopathology of childhood*. Englewood Cliffs, NJ: Prentice-Hall.

Kohut, H. (1976). *The analysis of the self*. New York: International Universities Press.

Kohut, H., & Wolf, E. (1978). The disorders of the self and their treatment: An outline. *International Journal of Psychoanalysis, 59,* 413–425.

Koocher, G. P. (1976). A bill of rights for children in psychotherapy. In G. P. Koocher (Ed.), *Children's rights and the mental health professions* (pp. 23–32). New York: Wiley.

Koocher, G. P. (1983). Competence to consent: Psychotherapy. In G. B. Melton, G. P. Koocher, & M. J. Saks (Eds.), *Children's competence to consent* (pp. 111–128). New York: Plenum.

Korman, M. (Ed.). (1976). *Levels and patterns of professional training*. Washington, DC: American Psychological Association.

Lyman, R. D., & Wilson, D. R. (1992). Residential and inpatient treatment of emotionally disturbed children and adolescents. In C. E. Walker & M. C. Roberts (Eds.), *Handbook of clinical child psychology* (2nd ed., pp. 829–843). New York: Wiley.

Mahler, M., Pine, F., & Bergman, A. (1975). *The psychological birth of the human infant*. New York: Basic Books

Mark, B. S., & Incorvaia, J. A. (1995). *The handbook of infant, child, and adolescent psychotherapy*. Northvale, NJ: Aronson.

Masterson, J. F. (1985). *Treatment of the borderline adolescent: A developmental approach*. New York: Brunner/Mazel.

McClure, F. H., & Teyber, E. (1996). *Child and adolescent therapy: A multicultural approach*. San Diego, CA: Harcourt Brace.

Morris, R. J., & Nicholson, J. (1993). The therapeutic relationship in child and adolescent psychotherapy: Research issues and trends. In T. R. Kratochwill & R. J. Morris (Eds.), *Handbook of psychotherapy with children and adolescents* (pp. 405–425). Boston: Allyn & Bacon.

Morse, W. C. (1993). Ecological approaches. In T. R. Kratochwill & R. J. Morris (Eds.), *Handbook of psychotherapy with children and adolescents* (pp. 320–355). Boston: Allyn & Bacon.

National Advisory Mental Health Council. (1990). *A report on general mental health disorders and problems*. Washington, DC: National Institute of Mental Health.

National Institute of Mental Health. (1981). *Professional training for competency with adolescents*. Washington, DC: Author.

National Institute of Mental Health. (1985). *Sexual victimization of adolescents*. Washington, DC: Author.

Nirenberg, J. D. (1983). Treatment of substance abuse. In C. E. Walker (Ed.), *A handbook of clinical psychology: II. Theory, research, and practice* (pp. 633–635). Homewood, Il: Dow Jones-Irwin.

Nottelmann, E. D., & Jensen, P. S. (1995). Comorbidity of disorders in children and adolescents: Developmental perspectives. In T. H. Ollendick & R. J. Prinz (Eds.), *Advances in clinical child psychology* (pp. 109–155). New York: Plenum.

Offer, D., & Offer, J. (1975). *From teenage to young manhood: A psychological study*. New York: Basic Books.

Orvin, G. H. (1995). *Understanding the adolescent*. Washington, DC: American Psychiatric Press.

Patterson, C. J. (1997). Children of lesbian and gay parents. In T. H. Ollendick & R. J. Prinz (Eds.), *Advances in clinical child psychology* (Vol. 19, pp. 235–282). New York: Plenum.

Pipher, M. (1995). *Reviving Ophelia: Saving the selves of our adolescent girls*. New York: Ballantine Books.

Roberts, M. C. (Ed.). (1996). *Model programs in child and family mental health*. Mahwah, NJ: Erlbaum.

Roberts, M. C., Carlson, C. I., Erickson, M. T., Friedman, R. M., La Greca, A. M., Lemanek, K. L., Russ, S. W., Schroeder, C. S., Vargas, L. A., & Wohlford, P. F. (1998). Training for child and adolescent services. *Professional Psychology: Research and Practice, 29*, 293–299.

Roberts, M. C., & Hinton-Nelson, M. (1996). Models for service delivery in child and family mental health. In M. C. Roberts (Ed.), *Model programs in child and family mental health* (pp. 1–21). Mahwah, NJ: Erlbaum.

Robson, K. S. (1994). *Manual of clinical child and adolescent psychiatry* (Rev. ed.). Washington, DC: American Psychiatric Press.

Rubenstein, A. (1992). Clinical issues in the treatment of adolescent girls. In B. R. Wainrib (Ed.), *Gender issues across the life cycle* (pp. 17–22). New York: Springer.

Rubenstein, A., & Zager, K. (1995). Training in adolescent treatment: Where is psychology? *Psychotherapy, 32,* 2–6.

Schroeder, C. S., & Gordon, B. N. (1991). *Assessment and treatment of childhood problems.* New York: Guilford Press.

Selekman, M. D., & Todd, T. C. (1991). *Assessment and treatment of childhood problems.* Needham, MA: Allyn & Bacon.

Sobocinski, M. R. (1990). Ethical principles in the counseling of gay and lesbian adolescents: Issues and autonomy, competence, and confidentiality. *Professional Psychology: Research and Practice, 21,* 240–247.

Taylor, L., & Adelman, H. S. (1996). Reframing the confidentiality dilemma to work in children's best interests. In D. N. Bersoff (Ed.), *Ethical conflicts in psychology* (pp. 198–201). Washington, DC: American Psychological Association.

Tuma, J. M., & Russ, S. W. (1993). Psychoanalytic psychotherapy with children. In T. R. Kratochwill & R. J. Morris (Eds.), *Handbook of psychotherapy with children and adolescents* (Vol. 19, pp. 131–161). Boston: Allyn & Bacon.

Tyson, P., & Tyson, R. L. (1991). *Psychoanalytic theories of development: An integration.* New Haven, CT: Yale University Press.

Waldron, H. N. (1993). Adolescent substance abuse and family therapy outcome. In T. R. Kratochwill & R. J. Morris (Eds.), *Handbook of psychotherapy with children and adolescents* (Vol. 19, pp. 199–234). Boston: Allyn & Bacon.

Walker, H. J., & Vaughan, R. D. (1993). AIDS risk reduction among a multiethnic sample of urban high school students. *Journal of the American Medical Association, 270,* 725–730.

Wexler, D. D. (1991). *The adolescent self: Strategies for self-management, self-soothing, and self-esteem in adolescents.* New York: Norton.

Willis, D. J., & Walker, C. E. (1989). Etiology. In T. H. Ollendick & M. Hersen (Eds.), *Handbook of child psychopathology* (2nd ed., pp. 29–52). New York: Plenum.

Winick, C. (1992). Substances of use and abuse and sexual behavior. In J. H. Lowinson, P. Ruiz, R. B. Millman, & J. F. Langrod (Eds.), *Substance abuse: A comprehensive textbook* (2nd ed., pp. 118–137). Baltimore: Williams & Wilkins.

16

ENHANCING THE DEVELOPMENT OF ADOLESCENT GIRLS

FLORENCE L. DENMARK

Adolescence represents a significant transition in a young woman's life. All too often, the media focus on the problems of adolescence. Depression, gangs, suicide, taking drugs, drinking alcohol, and teen pregnancies are reported as if they were a routine part of the teen years. It is true that adolescent girls are at a dangerous crossroads, facing the possibility of exploitation by their male peers as well as by adults as their sexuality emerges. Possible ramifications of this exploitation include exposure to HIV and other sexually transmitted diseases (STDs) as well as the danger of teen pregnancy. In addition, America's increasing immigrant population is introducing a subculture of adolescents with its own issues surrounding acculturation, bilingualism, and rifts with parents as the adolescents assimilate with greater success than their parents do.

Yet although adolescence represents an often difficult period in a young woman's life, for many teens, this is also a time of exploration, freedom to try new things, growing independence, and self-awareness. During this period, the adolescent girl begins to form her own unique identity.

In contrast to the preadolescent period when boys and girls appear relatively similar physically, the differences between females and males become more obvious in adolescence. Adolescents of both sexes experience a shift from a family-centered focus to a peer-centered focus. Friends become primary support figures (Furman & Buhrmester, 1992). In addition, gender-typed behaviors become more pronounced, a process referred to as *gender intensification* (Hill & Lynch, 1983). Female adolescents are beginning a process of self-definition as women and as young adults making their own way in the world.

Today's adolescents appear to be better off than past cohorts in many ways. Increased research and knowledge has provided society with a greater understanding of the adolescent experience. Adolescents frequently are depicted as the central characters in films, books, and songs, and their portrayal is a more open and honest one than in the past. Female adolescents, in particular, are growing up with various role models and goals, in contrast with earlier decades when women were depicted monolithically and one-dimensionally.

However, adolescent girls are confronted in today's age by society's mixed messages. They are urged to "have it all" in terms of marriage, family, and career, and express the desire to do so. By telling girls that they should pursue a career and actualize their potential to its full extent while simultaneously fulfilling all the roles of wife, mother, and nurturer, adults create an impossible conflict for adolescent girls (Kline & Short, 1991). Few role models or guidelines exist for these girls as to how to "have it all." Interventions with adolescent girls must address this unique predicament (Rubenstein, 1992), for it is an important factor of this transition.

Not all concerns of importance to adolescent girls are addressed in this chapter. Under the broad headings of the future in education, families, and leadership, issues will be considered where research points to positive aspects of the future that should be encouraged. These issues must be considered in the context of our era with its unique challenges of HIV/AIDS, economic recession, gangs and violence, increasing cultural pluralism, and teenage pregnancy. A realistic but hopeful future rather than an idealistic one will be presented.

ENHANCING EDUCATION

Although gender fairness and diversity in education are improving, schools have classically shortchanged female adolescents. Teachers have been found to treat boys and girls differentially in the classroom (Sadker & Sadker, 1985). Also, the learning atmospheres of most middle and junior high schools are more conducive to the success of male than that of female adolescents (Huston & Alvarez, 1990). These factors present probable culprits for girls' lower achievement expectations.

One answer *might* be single-sex education. Yet, despite some evidence that all-girls' schools are more beneficial to girls in terms of both academics and instilling self-confidence, the number of all-girls' schools is dropping dramatically (Mann, 1994). Even within the coeducational schools, however, interventions might be geared toward girls in terms of improving their self-esteem and achievement motivation. Mann recommended increasing assigned readings that focus on females and female experience, ensuring that science texts depict girls doing experiments as well as boys, and evaluating history texts for whether they tell the history of men exclusively or portray a complete history of an era with women playing critical roles. Despite the coeducational system in the public schools, it may be beneficial to girls to segregate the classes for math and science, according to Mann.

Despite the noted gender bias on the part of educators, it is surprising as well as reassuring to note that girls were found to have a higher academic self-concept (i.e., confidence in their academic abilities) in comparison with their male counterparts. Academic self-concept was also correlated with academic achievement in both genders, suggesting that those who view themselves as competent in school will perform successfully (Mboya, 1993). In addition, gifted girls were found to have a more positive view of their academic abilities than did gifted boys (Li, 1988). At least in the academic realm, some findings contraindicate the stereotype of adolescent girls as underconfident and overshadowed by their male peers. In fact, girls were found to be as ready as boys were to commit themselves to a career choice (Kelly & Colangelo, 1990).

White girls have been found to underestimate their performance capabilities, however, especially in math- and science-related areas. In contrast to male students, these female students do not view their math competence as highly, relative to other students, as one would predict, given their grades in math. White girls also tend to attribute success in math to effort and failure in math to ability, a more stable and enduring characteristic (Tapasak, 1990). Parental expectations were found to correlate significantly with their daughters' math performance, suggesting that educators should encourage girls to evaluate the role their parents' views played in shaping their mathematics self-concept. Parents might be advised to prevent their own successes or failures to influence their expectations for their daughters (Dickens & Cornell, 1993).

Attitude apparently plays a significant role in performance; girls with more positive attitudes toward math were found by various researchers to be more apt to enroll in and to succeed in mathematics courses (Yong, 1992). Things may be improving, because some researchers has found positive mathematics attitudes expressed by girls in general (Gwizdala & Steinback, 1990). Authors examining female math attitudes have cited articles prior to 1990 when establishing a lack of confidence on the part of adolescent girls, suggesting that stereotypes formed by outdated studies may be dictating much of present research. Newer studies and a fresh outlook are called for in this area.

Black female students, in contrast, do not appear to have stereotypic gender role expectations as far as mathematics being a "male" field, and their confidence in their skills seems to make them more apt to learn math (Yong, 1992). However, Black adolescent girls experience a unique challenge. According to Fordham (1993), these girls are compelled to conform to a universal gender ideal that is actually White and middle class, distancing themselves from the image of "those loud Black girls" (p. 22). Black girls who achieve academic success do so by assuming either a passive and silent persona or a male one. Success for a Black female is "far more disruptive of indigenous cultural conventions and practices than previously thought" (Fordham, 1993, p. 11). Black girls' underachieving peers, however, are rewarded with parental support and popularity (Fordham, 1993, p. 11). Those Black women who have overcome these cultural obstacles and have achieved status in the educational realm may be highly effective in counteracting this cultural tendency by serving as mentors and role models for Black female high school students.

Science

One area of much research concerns the processes taking place in elementary and secondary school that eventually lead to underrepresentation of girls in the sciences. Gender differences in science have been found to emerge as early as middle school, with boys being more likely than girls to find science interesting or to picture themselves using science or mathematics as adults. Ironically, most eighth-grade girls do not lag behind their male classmates in science test scores. However, they have less positive science attitudes and participate in fewer related extracurricular activities (Catsambis, 1995).

These differences are well-established by the time students reach their senior year of high school and have remained stable or have increased over the past several years, in contrast to gender differences in mathematics performance, which have decreased (American Association of University Women [AAUW], 1992). Ethnic variations exist, however. Asian American women and men both have high levels of achievement in the sciences and equal tendencies to pursue related careers (Campbell, 1991). This may be because girls in Asian cultures undergo a far more egalitarian education than do other American girls. In Asian culture, the connection between hard work, homework, and good teaching is emphasized with regard to achievement is, as opposed to beliefs about innate ability and math genes (Mann, 1994).

Black girls are also much more motivated to excel in science than are White girls (Atwater, Wiggins, & Gardner, 1995). This may coincide with the counterintuitive finding that as grade point average increases, African American girls prefer a competitive learning atmosphere to a co-operative one (Johnson & Engelhard, 1991). Academically inclined Black girls may respond well to the competitive atmosphere of a difficult science class, in contrast with White girls who may become intimidated. In general, however, although some minority students appear to be far more motivated than White students to excel in science, their scores are often lower (Cat-sambis, 1995).

These discrepancies must be examined. Because their test scores are not lower, White adolescent girls' lower achievement in science may be more a matter of encouragement or motivation than of ability (Catsambis, 1995). Some hypothesize that gender role stereotypes are at play here. Perceptions that scientists are emotionally removed, cold, precise, and introverted may force adolescent girls considering careers in science to choose "femininity" over a career they might find fulfilling (Frieze & Hanusa, 1984). This is particularly true of gifted adolescent girls, who may feel compelled to choose between their perceived obligation to develop their potential as talented individuals, on the one hand, and to be giving and selfless as young women, on the other hand (e.g., to marry and raise a family, placing their careers second to that of their husbands'; Kline & Short, 1991). This may explain a tendency on the part of gifted adolescent girls to self-deprecate their abilities (Fox & Tobin, 1988), which in turn may lead to their reluctance to choose careers that will actualize their potential (Yong, 1992). This might be remedied by sensitizing teachers in gifted programs to issues of their female students. These teachers should be urged to encourage their female students to actualize their potential and to provide the necessary support and nurturance for them to do so.

Female adolescents' needs may affect their responses to the style of science instruction; several girls report disliking instruction that isolates them, such as reading the textbook or taking notes while listening to lectures, as opposed to working in groups or having class discussions. Also, many girls felt that dissection was cruel (Baker & Leary, 1995). In a more practical vein, women may choose less technical occupations because of their expectations of multiple life roles (Arnold, 1992).

Educators should develop programs to foster a positive attitude toward science in adolescent girls. These programs can include activities such as dismantling and assembling machinery, caring for small animals, solving logic puzzles, working with tools, and experimenting with technological devices. Girls should be encouraged to test their hypotheses in user-friendly science labs with female instructors serving as mentors and role models.

Researchers suggest interventions that might inspire more female adolescents to pursue science careers. Baker and Leary (1995) suggest that the absence of such values as cooperation, working with people, and helping others in the training of women scientists may account for the low number of women in science. Science educators should address the female perspective as well as the male perspective. Catsambis (1995) felt that educational programs should focus on improving White girls' attitudes toward science and increasing their interest in related careers, while engaging minority students in more intensive coursework and activities to improve their test performance in this field. Yong (1992) recommended gender role restructuring that will stress science and math as neutral areas for both female and male students by way of counseling, discussions, simulations, role modeling, and rewarding scientific behaviors.

Sports

Physical fitness has ramifications for self-esteem, and prior research suggests that boys tend to have a more positive attitude toward their physical education classes than do girls (B. Jones, 1988). Some attribute this to the competitive nature of physical sports and suggest that girls have difficulty reconciling this with an emerging femininity (Sabo, 1985). Others suggest that sports are a patriarchal institution and considered a masculine domain (Chappel, 1989). In many societies, sports serve the function of proving boys' masculinity (Koivula, 1995). The media has enhanced a view of sports primarily as a masculine domain by allotting sportswomen only a limited amount of televised sports coverage time and treating them in a devaluing manner (Cohen, 1993). However, in the past year, support by the National Basketball Association (NBA) has generated more interest and television coverage of the Women's National Basketball Association (WNBA).

Boys also appear to have more self-confidence in their athletic abilities than do girls (Wersch, Trew, & Turner, 1990). In addition, a study examining the factors influencing boys and girls' decisions to elect physical education classes found that girls are more likely to be deterred from a gym class if they do not like the teacher (Luke & Sinclair, 1991). Girls' apparent need for relatedness seems to have a strong impact on this area, which has been implicated in self-concept. On a more positive note, however, girls' attitudes toward physical education seem to be improving, as is their confidence in this area and their ability to reconcile it with femininity (Hopwood & Carrington, 1994). Social biases favoring participation by women in more "feminine" sports over other athletic activities still exist to a degree, but seem to be diminishing over time (Pedersen & Kono, 1990).

Future changes to improve teen girls' situation might include more physical education in the schools, with a variety of options for exercise to appeal to girls' different preferences. The available athletic activities might focus on fitness and cooperativeness, making them more palatable to girls. In addition, Title IX, with its directive for equal sports scholarships for female and male athletes, is a major step in the right direction. Since its passage, more women have entered a broader variety of sports (Germone & Furst, 1991). One hopes that this will serve as an impetus to spur adolescent girls to pursue athletics more than in the past.

College-age men of varying ethnicity and religion in one study expressed positive attitudes toward their daughters' participation in all sports, including contact sports (Germone & Furst, 1991). Perhaps the evolution of American culture will see increasing popularity of father–daughter athletics. This, too, would facilitate the acceptability and desirability of sports among adolescent girls.

Diversity: Issues Confronting Minority Adolescent Girls

Culture plays a prominent role in the factors that make each adolescent girl's experience unique. This section focuses on various groups of adolescent girls with minority racial and ethnic backgrounds and selected issues pertaining to them.

Pressure to conform to the mainstream White male culture imposes a unique set of needs on Black and other minority adolescent girls. Young women of color are often compelled to engage in "gender passing," or suppressing their female, non-White identity characteristics to succeed in school (Fordham, 1993). In contrast, Black girls who have immigrated from the West Indies appear to have greater flexibility in forming their identities. They are able to claim a racial identity and maintain a position of solidarity with their racially similar peers while simultaneously being more bicultural than their male counterparts. The girls, unlike their male peers, do not see adopting certain specific American ideas as a challenge to their gender identity (Waters, 1996). Black adolescent girls might benefit from group work with their West Indian peers, with the latter serving as role models and encouraging the former to express themselves.

Hispanic American girls may have more difficulty than their non-Hispanic peers in asserting themselves. Authoritarian parenting, as opposed to authoritative, is more prevalent in this group. The emphasis on obedience and conformity in these homes, with its negative effects on autonomy and self-confidence, is at odds with American culture and with the school system in particular (Steinberg, Dornbusch, & Brown, 1992). One might view the issues of Hispanic adolescent girls as being the reverse of those of their Black counterparts: The former have a more submissive identity and suffer because of their difficulty asserting themselves, whereas the latter have a so-called "loud" and assertive identity that they are required to suppress in the interest of "gender passing" (Fordham, 1993). In addition, Hispanic adolescents were found to have language difficulties that pose a threat to acculturation, regardless of their nativity status (Vega, Khoury, Zimmerman, Gil, & Warheit, 1995). Research is needed to clarify the means by which the school system can help Hispanic female adolescents.

Asian female adolescents may also experience conflicts that are sourced in authoritarian families. One study found a high positive correlation among Asian teen girls between perceiving their parents as over-controlling and manifesting eating disorders. However, Asian female adolescents as a group express greater satisfaction with their bodies than do their Caucasian counterparts (Ahmad, Waller, & Verduyn, 1994). Family or individual therapy with Asian girls may be a means of reducing perceived parental protectiveness and thus reducing the conflict over control that appears to influence the development of eating disorders.

Multiracial adolescents are confronted with issues of physical appearance as the peer group and dating begins to gain importance. Boys, who usually take the initiative in the dating situation, may not view multiracial female adolescents as desirable because of their unusual and ambiguous appearance. Appearance is less important for multiracial boys, who can compensate with other appreciated qualities such as athletic ability, social status, or intelligence. For multiracial girls, however, self-worth may suffer greatly, as their appearance costs them dates. However, a multiracial status could have the positive effect of inspiring these girls to question the implicit social order (Comas-Diaz & Greene, 1994). These girls may be spurred to think more individualistically and develop self-worth independent of their social environment. In fact, studies of nonclinical mixed-race adolescents find that they are no worse off than their peers in terms of psychological well-being or popularity (Cauce et al., 1992).

Arab female adolescents who immigrate to the United States experience many cultural conflicts. As the parents of the adolescent experience racism, there is a tendency to retreat into a nostalgic recreation of their old life. This causes complications, as parents see their adolescent children acculturating within the rejected host culture. Arab culture emphasizes loyalty to the family over personal autonomy, a value that conflicts with contemporary Western society in general and particularly problematic at adolescence, a time of emerging autonomy. Culturally consistent behavior on the part of Arab parents would be viewed as highly intrusive and enmeshed by Western standards, especially once the child reaches adolescence (Timimi, 1995).

However, a pilot study of a few Soviet Jewish immigrant adolescent girls found the opposite effects for having a highly involved family. Although their family network might appear enmeshed by American standards, it served as a source of support and comfort for these girls. Although their background placed them at odds with the American cultural ideal of the autonomous adolescent, they were provided with necessary structure and boundaries that their American counterparts may have lacked. These girls were found to be well adjusted and equipped to surmount the very real difficulties of their immigrant status (Markowitz, 1994).

Adolescent Arab girls are also expected to behave carefully and to avoid giving the appearance of flirtatiousness. The sexes are highly segregated, and engaging in heterosexual social behavior for a girl or young woman risks alienation from the family. Western adolescent society, with its tremendous emphasis on dating and heterosexual encounters, very much conflicts with Arab culture. No easy answers exist for the cultural conflicts catalyzed by adolescence for Arab girls, but increased awareness on the part of therapists bodes well for assisting this population with their unique needs (Timimi, 1995).

Lesbian adolescents comprise a separate, often overlooked, minority culture. These girls encounter a great deal of prejudice in the form of "heterosexism," or denial, denigration, or stigmatizing of nonheterosexual behavior (Herek, 1992). They too are confronted with the challenge of conforming to a society that requires them to suppress vital aspects of their identity.

The good news is that increasing attention is being paid to diversity in our society. Having switched from the metaphor of the "melting pot" to that of "cultural pluralism," more and more minority groups are being acknowledged and being given opportunities to express themselves. On college campuses, student organizations for members of various minority groups sponsor events such as culture fairs that enhance the diversified atmosphere of the campus and create opportunities for interaction between the mainstream and minority cultures. It is hoped that the future will see more of these organizations and activities on the high school level so that gender and ethnic diversity may be appreciated. High school curricula might include an increased focus on women's and cultural studies.

Mentoring

Mentoring has become an increasingly popular intervention with adolescents (Freedman, 1993; Gambone, 1993). Mentoring, in general, describes "a process whereby an experienced individual transmits knowledge to a protégé" (Blechman, 1992, p. 161). Mentorship may be a formalized relationship through organizations such as Big Brother or Big Sister or a natural connection emerging from within the youth's support network (Klaw & Rhodes, 1995).

Traditionally, mentoring has been viewed as a one-on-one relationship between an older, more experienced adult and a younger protégé as a means of providing support and enhancing the transition from adolescence to adulthood (Philip & Hendry, 1996). A study of young teens found that mentoring actually takes several forms: classic mentoring, mentoring as a process undertaken by an individual or individuals with a group, friend-to-friend mentoring, peer group mentoring, and long-term relationship mentoring. The above definition describes classic mentoring, which was found to be more popular with young men. Female adolescents preferred the other forms of mentoring, as described below (Philip & Hendry, 1996).

Mentoring as a process undertaken by an individual or individuals with a group was demonstrated in a number of youth work settings. The mentoring role was concerned with dealing with the adolescents on their own terms rather than with having them conform to "adult" programs. The groups were often small and intimate, based around a loose network of friends. Rather than the mentor relationship being an exclusive one, the building of relationships with adults and with each other took place in a group setting. Group members described the relationship as different from those with other adults in being less authoritarian, more flexible and open to negotiation, and concerned with topics unlikely to be addressed in other contexts. Participants viewed youth workers as respecting youth culture and willing to meet on the teens' own territory. Central to this relationship was acknowledgment and acceptance of the group's identity and the existing network of friends. Individuals may choose to talk to the youth worker alone, and the group may meet to discuss an issue independently of the youth worker (Philip & Hendry, 1996).

Friend-to-friend mentoring was especially popular with young women, who cited close friends as supportive in times of trouble. Often these were not adults but peers who provided moral support, counseling, and advice. These relationships were described as reciprocal and highly intimate. Friends were preferred to adults because of the ability both to trust them with confidential information and to share anxieties (Philip & Hendry, 1996).

Peer groups themselves can provide a mentoring framework. Rather than providing one-on-one mentoring, the group itself identified appropriate forms of support and action. Female adolescents especially appreciated this form of mentoring as providing a reference point for maintaining reputations or supporting those damaged by accusations from peers or adults. This style of mentoring, in some cases, was a response to the inability of adults to grasp the realities of group members' lives. In these groups, adults were seen as hypocritical in their attitudes toward young people's actions and values. One issue of particular relevance to female group participants was that of having to manage an acceptable identity (Philip & Hendry, 1996).

Finally, long-term relationship mentoring was the form most closely related to classic mentoring. Adults such as aunts, former baby-sitters, or family friends whose connection with the youth had developed over time served as mentors. With this mentoring style, the adult was known to other family members but shared an exclusive relationship with the adolescent. This provided the mentor with the ability to serve as a mediator between the young person and the family when necessary. Mentors provided security, support, and sometimes challenges to the protégés but differed from classic mentors in that young people perceived them as deriving support for their own problems and concerns from the outset (Philip & Hendry, 1996).

For female adolescents, mentoring can serve many purposes. Mentors may be invaluable as a future intervention with adolescent girls, encouraging positive risk taking, appropriate choices, and self-development. They can guide adolescent girls through the challenges of growing up female and can encourage *bicultural competence* (Blechman, 1992), meaning the ability to be flexible with one's communication so as to function effectively within male or female culture.

With pregnant and parenting adolescents, mentoring can facilitate young mothers' educational and career development in addition to promoting psychosocial functioning (Klaw & Rhodes, 1995). Women's abovementioned need for connectedness with others may affect their career decisions (Baker & Leary, 1995; Eccles, 1986). Significantly more women than men reported viewing close relationships as a greater source of satisfaction than career development (Post-Kammer & Perrone, 1983). This may be why the use of female role models was found to successfully improve female students' attitudes toward science (Evans, Whigham, & Wang, 1995).

Types of Schools

Feminists' groundbreaking research has increased awareness of a female perspective. Schools such as the Emma Willard School in Troy, New York, have revamped their curricula in appreciation of girls' unique modes of operation and now encourage girls to "break the mold" rather than conform when voicing opinions (Gilligan, 1990). Teachers there appreciate, for example, the unique interests of girls when learning history. One teacher recounted an incident from his early days of teaching during which he taught about a deal struck between the Northern and Southern Democrats and Republicans. One girl raised her hand and asked what grounds the people involved had to trust each other. Although this question confused the teacher at first, because it did not fit in with the systems approach he was emphasizing, his colleagues later explained that rather than seeking to transcend time as the teacher was doing, the girl was interested in the particulars and the relationships between people. The Emma Willard School provides an atmosphere in which girls' interests in the subject matter are appreciated as a genuine desire to learn rather than being viewed as peripheral to the material (Gilligan, Lyons, & Hanmer, 1989).

Even schools that are not feminist in their agenda can educate girls to appreciate their female identity. For example, research has found that adolescent girls can resist negative messages through reading. Instead of traditionally read books like *The Scarlet Letter* by Nathaniel Hawthorne, which portrayed women as weak and lacking self-esteem according to adolescent girls who were interviewed, girls preferred comparable classics such as *Anne of Green Gables* by Lucy Maud Montgomery in which the female protagonist was brave, individualistic, and spoke her mind (Winter, 1996). Schools can include these books as well as more books by female authors on their syllabi.

ENHANCING FAMILIES AND CLOSE RELATIONSHIPS

For adolescent girls, early relationships—particularly those with their parents and caregivers—shape their awareness of themselves in ways that differ from their male counterparts. Early caregivers may go to great lengths to "protect" their daughters by restricting their play and exploratory behaviors, whereas boys may be encouraged to test the limits. Through both verbal and nonverbal communication, girls may be told that they are expected to be nice and accommodating, whereas their male counterparts may be encouraged to be individualistic and decisive, to take the lead in relationships.

These early communications significantly affect how adolescent girls experience themselves in later relationships with other girls and with adolescent boys. Research findings in this area generally suggest that girls who learned to define themselves according to strict gender roles may have more difficulty managing later relationships, whereas girls whose early relationships supported a more flexible definition of gender appear to approach relationships in a more confident manner.

We explore these issues in detail below, integrating recent research findings that address how adolescent girls understand their gender roles, how this understanding of gender relates to their self-concept, how they manage their emerging sexual and sensual selves, and how they communicate these understandings in relationships.

Gender Awareness

In a world in which standards have been set, women's emotional, social, and physical well-being may be jeopardized by rules that do not apply to them (Kline & Short, 1991). In general, female development during adolescence facilitates the growth of the self as an empathic being regarding others (Cosse, 1992). It is ironic that this unique aspect of young women's personality, which caused them to be viewed as meek, unimportant members of society in the past, actually motivates them to make valuable contributions. For example, adolescent girls are more likely to be involved in community service than are boys (Miller, 1994). Adolescent girls also have a more positive attitude toward religion and higher levels of belief (Levitt, 1995), which may suggest that their concern for human welfare is sourced in a spiritual perspective on life. Heightened sensitivity to gender differences in development is an optimistic outcome that bodes well for the future.

Girls in early adolescence begin to learn that their intense desire for affiliation is not valued in our male-dominated society (Chodorow, 1989; Gilligan, 1990). Thus, they are forced to choose between two modes of being—becoming autonomous and self-reliant (and appearing selfish), or remaining responsive to others (and being selfless). This conflict causes adolescent girls to develop self-doubt and reluctance as far as offering their opinions (Gilligan, 1990). This may explain why girls' self-perceived capabilities and confidence diminishes throughout the elementary and secondary school years (Kline & Short, 1991).

One way to address this would be to expose teen girls to assertiveness training and leadership training as well as women's consciousness raising. Programs might be developed to foster a "nurturing leadership" in adolescent girls. A different mode of leadership, using uniquely female characteristics, might be modeled and encouraged so that teen girls can both remain true to themselves and succeed in society.

For example, Girls Incorporated is an organization created specifically to address the needs of adolescent girls. Under the umbrella of Girls Incorporated, several programs exist that help girls eschew unhealthy risk-taking behavior and opt for positive outcomes. "Friendly PEERsuasion" is a two-part program that teaches girls assertiveness, decision making, and communication skills. In Part I, through games, group discussion, and role play, participants are educated about peer pressure and stress management. Part II has the newly trained girls planning activities for their younger counterparts in which they can serve as role models for dealing with challenges. Other programs encourage participating in physical activity, developing science and mathematics interest and skills, and preventing adolescent pregnancy (Girls Incorporated, 1998).

One important consideration is that of parent education. Parents must be made aware of the need for sensitivity to their female children. Their own upbringing may have taught them to put down or to ignore their daughters' individual issues. Parents can guide their daughters through their choices of what to emphasize and praise (i.e., praising academic achievement as opposed to popularity). Parents can also teach girls to set boundaries and to behave assertively with regard to boys and risk-taking situations in which peer pressure is at play (Mann, 1994). Parent effectiveness training and feminist child rearing may be the most salient interventions necessary to raise a healthy, confident generation of adolescent girls.

Girls should also be made aware of gender stereotypes depicted on television. Unreasonable standards of feminine perfection are portrayed both on classic shows like "Leave it to Beaver" and newer, popular shows like "Baywatch." In a 1995 survey of more than 2,000 children, more than half of the female participants felt that there were too few programs about girls their age and not enough shows about girls having adventures or women in challenging careers. In addition, girls were almost twice as likely as boys to say that they have dieted or exercised to look like a television character (Girls Incorporated, 1998).

Girls Re-Cast TV is a gender-focused media literacy curriculum for girls in which girls rewrite TV scripts, stage their own TV talk shows, and create their own public service announcements. They also meet with TV producers and executives, act as guest TV critics for local newspapers, and work with national news media to express their opinions. Girls Re-Cast TV is available through the World Wide Web and provides girls with opportunities to use their creativity to build awareness of media-perpetuated gender stereotyping (Girls Incorporated, 1998).

Sexuality

Adolescence's reputation as a troublesome period, if exaggerated, is not entirely undeserved. Adolescent girls and boys exhibit a tendency to engage in problem behavior, or "behavior which departs from familial or social standards and that poses some risk to the well-being of the individual or to society" (Maggs, Almeida, & Galambos, 1995, p. 344). Adolescents' sexual activity is particularly stigmatized. This behavior may stem from society's ambiguous messages regarding sexuality; although the media promotes sexuality's attractiveness, other authorities attempt to curb this behavior, or at least limit it. However, current research suggests that overt sexual behavior is on the wane as more and more adolescents choose to remain virgins (Ingrassia, 1994). Perhaps, contrary to popular belief, risk taking is becoming less popular among adolescents.

Sexual and other risk-taking behaviors among teens are mediated by several factors. Among Black, urban, adolescent girls, those who engage in sexual activity tend to come from families characterized by low maternal education and teen motherhood (Ensminger, 1990). Unfortunately, adolescent pregnancy does not appear to be decreasing among those of lower socioeconomic status, regardless of ethnicity, and seems to repeat itself in a vicious cycle. This underscores the need for more programs to prevent teenage pregnancy.

Although the negative aspects of engaging in risky activities are obvious, individuals working with adolescent girls cannot overlook findings that constructive outcomes from such behavior are possible as well. Specifically, adolescents who engaged in more frequent risk-taking activities were also more involved with a group of similarly-minded peers. (Maggs et al., 1995). Positive characteristics of risk-taking adolescents may include independent thinking, high energy and self-confidence, and feeling in control of their fate.

Although these adolescents may be stereotyped as "rebels without a cause," we must be sensitive to the adaptive role played by such behavior as well as the positive attributes it implies. After all, society's progress depends on those individuals who are willing to risk failure by trying new things. As therapists working with adolescent girls, psychologists must remain nonjudgmental (Rubenstein, 1992). In addition, interventions with female adolescents should focus on acceptable versus unacceptable modes of risk taking, providing an outlet for the adolescent drive to experiment while directing their energy in a constructive vein, and limiting the behaviors appropriately. One program begins with girls as young as 9 years old and follows them through the completion of high school, facilitating communication with other girls and with adults, assertiveness training, and educational and career planning (Girls Incorporated, 1998). Families can help by providing challenges and sanctioned activities.

Peers might serve as effective role models for risk-taking adolescents. For example, some teens are described as "resilient" (Winfield, 1991; in McMillan & Reed, 1994) because they have developed traits and coping mechanisms that enable them to succeed against all odds. Resiliency has been found to be a function of individual attributes and constructive use of time, school, and family, according to McMillan and Reed. Resilient students appear to find refuge in extracurricular events at school, hobbies, creative interests, sports, and the like. Perhaps as peer mediators and role models, resilient students can encourage at-risk teens to use such outlets and to model other effective coping strategies.

Friendships

Aspects of dating, friendship, and gender role ideology are a major focus for female identity development. Girls display higher identity exploration than do boys in the dating and friendship domains, which includes the formulation of personal values about involvement in relationships. Thus, female adolescents may have experienced more opportunities than male adolescents to hone their ideas about gender roles in relationships (Werrbach, Grotevant, & Cooper, 1990). This could be advantageous to girls if increased awareness of their expectations in a relationship leads to increased assertiveness about having these expectations fulfilled. In fact, adolescent girls have been found to experience more positive interpersonal relationships than do boys (Bracken & Crain, 1994; D. C. Jones & Costin, 1995), lending support to this notion. Girls report more positive friendships with their same-sex peers, according to Bracken and Crain; the support these friendships provide may mitigate some of the hurdles of adolescence for girls.

In terms of physical contact, adolescence may actually be easier for girls than for boys. When adolescents of both genders reported the frequency with which they had experienced positive and negative physical contact, girls reported more positive and less negative touch experience than boys. Perhaps this is because our culture condones different forms of touch experience for female than for male adolescents. Touch experience has ramifications for psychological well-being; girls who had perceived more frequent positive touch experiences were also less depressed, delinquent, and aggressive and expressed fewer somatic complaints (Pearce, Martin, & Wood, 1995). Adolescent girls may find support and comfort in positive touch experiences with their peers, whereas these affectionate displays might be frowned on for adolescent boys as a function of homophobia or male physical violence.

This differential condoning of positive touch for adolescent girls and boys is paralleled by findings that expressing sad feelings is viewed by adolescent boys as more acceptable for girls. Girls, in contrast, hold more positive views about men expressing feelings and emotions openly (Werrbach et al., 1990). Girls appear to feel more comfortable with flexible boundaries for the male gender role. However, they express less tolerance of women who behave in "unfeminine" ways, according to Werrbach et al. Through discussion, role play, and analysis or appropriate films and books, educators working with adolescent girls can address this double standard.

Self-Esteem

Self-esteem is clearly an important area to consider with adolescent girls. The rapid growth introduced by puberty often results in body consciousness on the part of adolescent girls, especially if they are maturing at a different rate than their peers. Early-maturing girls in particular are exposed to increased peer pressure to engage in heterosexual behaviors that they may not be prepared for psychologically. They are also at a disadvantage in terms of body image (Attie & Brooks-Gunn, 1989; Magnusson, Strattin, & Allen, 1985). Late-maturing girls, however, may feel inferior to their peers in terms of sophistication and attractiveness. All of these issues may affect adolescent girls' self-esteem and self-image. However, it is reassuring to note that most of the effects of puberty on body image and self-esteem are small and transient. Adolescent self-consciousness is common and rarely significantly affects global self-esteem, according to Attie and Brooks-Gunn.

Pubertal effects on self-esteem can be mediated by various factors. Adolescent girls who are involved in sports appear to have higher self-esteem (Butcher, 1989), healthier emotional expression, healthier emotional control, more androgynous characteristics (Covey & Feltz, 1991), better grades, and better social skills ("Girls Active in Sports," 1997; "Study Reveals," 1997). Ballet dancers, in particular, were found to have higher self-esteem, positive self-respect, and increased self-confidence (Kalliopuska, 1989).

Although girls may have a lower self-esteem than boys during adolescence, it is reassuring to note that this is not a function of gender role prescriptions. In fact, girls with positive attributes considered "feminine" (e.g., patience, loves children) were found to have high self-esteem, whereas both girls and boys with negative attributes considered "feminine" (e.g., dependent and timid) were found to have lower self-esteem. The latter attributes were endorsed equally by girls and boys, suggesting that they may not be gender related and that to label these traits "feminine" constitutes a misnomer (Pryor, 1994).

Harter (1990) suggests that intervention to improve self-esteem must address the causes of low self-esteem if it is to be effective. For example, White girls have been found to have lower expectations for achievement than do their male counterparts (Vollmer, 1984). Research also indicates that adolescents have the highest self-esteem when they are successful in areas they deem important (Harter, 1990). Therefore, encouraging adolescent girls to explore, to develop, and to take pride in their talents may be an appropriate means of increasing their self-esteem. Self-esteem may be especially improved if they can find a talent that is marketable; employment has been found to positively enhance adolescents' self-concept (Patton & Noller, 1990).

Black girls do not experience the same drop in self-esteem apparent in female adolescents who are White (Freiberg, 1991). Various studies have found that, unlike their White counterparts, Black girls' self-esteem is not significantly different from that of Black boys (see Mwamwenda, 1991) and is greater than that of White girls (Hare, 1985). They appear to be more confident in their academic abilities than are White girls or Black boys (Smith, 1982). Black female adolescents were also found to be more likely to graduate from high school and perceived themselves as having more job opportunities than their Black male counterparts. This appears to stem, at least in part, from Black boys' feeling more acutely aware of racial boundaries (Waters, 1996). Others attribute it to Black girls' increased ability, relative to Black boys, to suppress their racial identity characteristics to succeed in school (Fordham, 1993). The reasons for Black females' increased academic self-concept, relative to White females, are unclear, but more research might point to possibilities for interventions with White adolescent girls to raise their self-esteem. Group work with adolescent girls might integrate Black and White girls and focus on self-esteem issues, with the Black girls serving as models for their White counterparts.

Interventions with African American girls may address a separate issue. Black women, titled "Sapphires," are stereotyped as being shrewish.

One program, "Sapphires-in-Transition" (SIT), uses methods such as group counseling and peer evaluation to encourage awareness of socially appropriate behaviors in a culture controlled by neither Blacks nor women, practice of these behaviors when appropriate, and acknowledgment as well as esteem for Black standards and images of physical attractiveness (Young, 1994).

Two counselors, one Black and one White, designed structured developmental activities to address issues such as attire, attitudes, demeanor, grooming, poor academic performance, and negligible involvement in extracurricular activities. Daily observation was used in developing the program as a needs assessment tool. The daily observations highlighted areas of need such as developing positive self-concepts, building self-esteem, heightening consciousness of personal and career success opportunities for Black female adolescents who reflect societally appropriate behaviors, and learning and practicing appropriate behaviors. Program goals focused on participants' learning and executing specific behaviors of modulating voices, proper grooming, and assertive demeanor. This was accomplished through group counseling sessions, structured developmental activities, and procedural network support (Young, 1994).

The SIT group counseling involved counselor-facilitated group guidance, orientation, and group counseling, which included self-awareness and societal-awareness sessions held every day for two consecutive weeks. Participants received help in identifying their assets, strengths, and talents; becoming aware of the practical and aesthetic dimensions of developing and using their assets; learning to strengthen, to reverse, or to minimize their weaknesses; comprehending their traditional and transitional images and roles; acquiring knowledge of the accomplishments of Black women role models, past and present, to validate the achievements and the potential of Black female adolescents; and clarifying values, solving problems, making decisions, and setting goals regarding their future as successful students and adults. Developmental activities included workshops, seminars, and interest sessions on contemporary issues and relevant topics such as personal grooming, social skills, demeanor, poise, career and academic planning, job etiquette, voice modulation, assertive behavior, tact, college life, development of leadership, citizenship, marriage, and family. The SIT procedural support system included observation, positive reinforcement, and informal assessment. In addition, each SIT participant was observed by two peers of her choice, one Black and one White, who were instructed to provide feedback about behaviors and changes. This program was found to be successful in achieving all of its goals and can be applied to different populations (Young, 1994).

Kline and Short (1991) emphasized the need to "provide a major human-relations program for positive gender identity in young secondary-age females" (p. 121). They list the goals of the program as promoting body awareness, emotion awareness, stress management through positive self-encouragement, positive reinforcement of others, "I" messages, body language, reflective and active listening, problem solving, and helping and cooperation. Young women will be empowered through mastery of such assertive life skills, and this power will enable them to achieve what is in their own best interests as opposed to being manipulated by the desires of adults, their peers, or both. Ultimately, it is hoped that emotional resilience will be achieved. Programs sponsored by Girls Incorporated discussed earlier in this chapter provide examples of how this might be accomplished.

Communication

Self-disclosure may be defined as "an intentional and voluntary verbal utterance that conveys personal information to another within a specific social context" (Papini, Farmer, Clark, Micka, & Barnett, 1990, p. 960). *Emotional self-disclosure*, an important subdivision of general self-disclosure, is defined as "any intentional and voluntary verbal utterance which conveys information about the emotional state of the individual" (Papini et al., 1990, p. 960). Adolescents' willingness and ability to self-disclose facilitates psychosocial development. This ability was correlated with family warmth and feminine gender. Feminine willingness to self-disclose bodes well for adolescent girls because it enables them to make full use of the emotional support that best friends can provide, according to Papini et al. This vital ability enhances the viability of mentorship and group support networks as successful interventions for adolescent girls.

ADOLESCENT GIRLS AS FUTURE LEADERS

Career/Work: Dual Roles: Problems and Resolutions

Adolescent girls' educational and career aspirations have increased greatly in recent years, paralleling society's shift in gender roles. Their achievement orientation has been demonstrated to be on par with that of their male counterparts (Stevens, Puchtell, Ryu, & Mortimer, 1992). This finding has been replicated in Finnish, Israeli, and Australian cultures as well as in American culture (Nurmi, Poole, & Seginer, 1995). Yet, adolescent girls also anticipate greater concern with family roles than boys do, according to Stevens et al. This reflects findings that although adult women enjoy a more egalitarian role in the workplace, they are still relegated to traditional homemaking roles at home and receive little assistance from their husbands (Affleck, Morgan, & Hayes, 1989).

Gifted girls have classically experienced a particularly salient conflict between career development and traditionality. Although the gifted girl is expected to achieve high levels because of her intellectual talent, she may also fear the consequences of success in a society that considers success masculine. She is also challenged by the emphasis placed on the roles of wife and mother and may be expected to accomplish the formidable task of rising to the top of her profession while maintaining a successful home and family life. A vicious cycle is suggested in which bright girls and young women choose not to enroll in math or science courses, are relegated to careers with limited salary expectations and lower social status, and may even abandon their careers for marriage and family. As a result, the next generation lacks female role models for nontraditional careers and ends up following the path of the previous cohort. This appears to be changing, as gifted girls now report perceiving themselves equal to male peers in professional roles. This is less true of their attitudes toward male–female relationships (Bakken, Hershey, & Miller, 1990).

Researchers examining gender roles and career aspirations in female adolescents may be neglecting other factors affecting goal orientation. Religious beliefs play a role in determining young women's career choices, such that certain careers are automatically perceived as off limits because of conflicts with religious practices (e.g., modesty or Sabbath observance). These girls then choose among the careers afforded them that do not conflict with their religion, and it is here that gender roles and homemaking goals come into play (Rich & Golan, 1992).

Another factor that comes into play is the rate of employment for girls during adolescence. Employment rates for adolescent girls have increased markedly, and adolescent girls who work formally were found to express diminished interest in traditional family roles. The opposite effect was demonstrated for boys. Adolescent boys with high career aspirations anticipated high family involvement, whereas girls with high achievement orientations expected delayed marriage and briefer employment interruption because of children (Stevens et al., 1992), that is, less involvement with family.

Clearly, adolescent girls' achievement orientation is increasing and paralleling, if not surpassing, that of boys (Nurmi et al., 1995; Stevens et al., 1992). Although more egalitarian attitudes toward male–female relationships and on the home front are slower in coming, prospects for the future appear optimistic in this regard. Many of the educational interventions suggested in this chapter can help facilitate this improvement.

Solving World Problems With Feminine Strength

Although political activism has classically been considered a masculine domain, it is becoming an increasingly popular feminine domain. This is true even at the adolescent level, during which girls were found to be as interested as their male counterparts were in politics (Hahn, 1996;

Romer, 1990). In fact, girls in one study expressed stronger opinions about political issues than did boys, according to Hahn (1996).

Gender differences existed in the issues that interested adolescents. Girls were found to be more concerned with social issues such as abortion, welfare, or rape, whereas boys focused on patriotic issues like the military, world peace, and the United States' rivalry with other nations (Hahn, 1996). It is conceivable that the issues that interest women are less likely to be viewed as political and may get in the way of their considering a career in politics. Teachers can assist students by focusing on issues that interest them and connecting them to the political world. Encouraging girls to watch the news more might also help facilitate political interest, as girls were found to watch the news less than boys, according to Hahn.

Another issue of relevance to educators is that of addressing issues of women's involvement in history and politics, past and present. A content analysis of history texts found that efforts are being made to include women and minorities, but the tendency to create special sections about them rather than incorporate them into the text causes teachers to omit that material (Hahn, 1996). Texts that integrate women's issues and activism will demonstrate the significance of women to the political world. In addition, teachers should be trained to include supplemental information about women and politics in their curricula to emphasize the role young women can play in politics and to provide a more accurate portrayal of past and present history, according to Hahn.

Another factor that may affect women's political involvement is that of sex role identification. Masculine traits such as defending one's beliefs, independence, assertiveness, forcefulness, leadership, willingness to take risks, individualism, and competitiveness were found to correlate with political activism in both male and female adolescents. Female adolescents who were politically active also attributed feminine traits to themselves, but to a lesser extent than their nonpolitically active female peers (Romer, 1990). Clearly, although femininity can be incorporated into a political persona, traditionally masculine traits are a prerequisite for political activism.

Girls at the Emma Willard School described two modes of leadership derived from girls' ideas. The leader as interdependent derives goals and plans from listening to others, openness to new ideas, and using people's suggestions to develop a plan of action. Although she uses her own ideas as well, she mostly synthesizes those of others. Necessary interpersonal skills include listening to others, integrating ideas, and facilitating interactions. The leader makes the decision by taking into account all that people have said, considering individuals in their contexts, and testing her interpretation of the issues with those involved (Lyons, Saltenstall, & Hanmer, 1989).

In the autonomous-in-relation-to-others mode, goals come from the leader's own judgment. Although she will modify her ideas for others, she is the main idea generator. She requires the interpersonal skills to develop and to present her ideas and plans to others. Decisions are made by the leader herself, even if not everyone has been heard, to move things along (Lyons et al., 1989).

Lyons and her colleagues (Lyons et al., 1989) emphasized the importance of educating girls about power and leadership in a way that exposes them to the complexities involved without discouraging them. Schools should provide experiences and leadership models that exemplify both types of feminine leadership as well as traditionally masculine leadership. Perhaps the encouragement of interdependent feminine leadership as a viable mode will increase leadership possibilities for those girls with strongly feminine traits.

The increasing political interest for adolescent girls is a positive sign that bodes well for the future. The fact that girls and boys emphasize different political issues points to the possibility that women's concerns are being overlooked because the political arena is male dominated. The advent of women into politics is a step that can improve this situation, and encouragement must take place at the adolescent level. Although female representation in textbooks has increased greatly, more efforts can be made on the part of both publishers and teachers to incorporate more women into the curriculum. This, together with providing role models of and opportunities for feminine leadership, may encourage more adolescent girls to pursue political activism and consider it as a career.

CONCLUSION

In sum, the evidence points to society's lack of acknowledgment and respect for female development. Adolescent girls are learning that their needs for closeness and relatedness conflict with the competitive attitudes that drive success. Yet, they are expected to achieve in this society, in effect, being forced to choose between being true to themselves and realizing their goals.

Among the "visions for the future" that I suggest are educational interventions on both the macro (e.g., focusing more on girls as a group in the coeducational environment, more physical education, sensitizing teachers to female issues, providing assertiveness training and leadership training for girls) and micro (counseling teen girls both individually and in groups as to acceptable risk taking and women's consciousness raising) levels. Society must also focus on relationships as a source of both social support and influence for female adolescents. Girls may be socialized to have certain traits and aspirations. Through group work, psychologists can provide alternative social support for those adolescent girls who wish to "break the mold." Among the goals of this group work might be creating a sense of pride in who these adolescent girls are and nurturing leadership potential. Thus, we can attempt to transform the environment for adolescent girls and foster conditions that will foster their self-esteem.

With dramatic social, economic, and technological change reshaping the world, adolescents face an unknown future replete with possibilities for improvement. The world of information available to us through cyberspace can increase our knowledge and understanding and be a resource both for adolescents themselves and for those who are seeking to help them. New awareness of cultural differences may enable us to ease the experience of minority adolescents.

REFERENCES

Affleck, M., Morgan, C. S., & Hayes, M. (1989). The influence of gender role attitudes on life expectations of college students. *Youth and Society, 20,* 307–319.

Ahmad, S., Waller, G., & Verduyn, C. (1994). Eating attitudes among Asian schoolgirls: The role of perceived parental control. *International Journal of Eating Disorders, 15,* 91–97.

American Association of University Women. (1992). *How schools shortchange girls: A study of major findings of girls and education.* Washington, DC: Author.

Arnold, K. (1992, April). *The Illinois valedictorian project: Academically talented women ten years after high school graduation.* Paper presented at the annual meeting of the American Educational Research Association, San Francisco.

Attie, I., & Brooks-Gunn, J. (1989). The development of eating problems in adolescent girls: A longitudinal study. *Developmental Psychology, 25,* 70–79.

Atwater, M. M., Wiggins, J., & Gardner, C. M. (1995). A study of urban middle school students with high and low attitudes toward science. *Journal of Research in Science Teaching, 32,* 665–667.

Baker, D., & Leary, R. (1995). Letting girls speak out about science. *Journal of Research in Science Teaching, 32*(1), 3–27.

Bakken, L., Hershey, M., & Miller, P. (1990). Gifted adolescent females attitudes toward gender equality in educational and intergender relationships. *Roeper Review, 12,* 261–264.

Blechman, E. A. (1992). Mentors for high-risk minority youth: From effective communication to bicultural competence. *Journal of Clinical Child Psychology, 21,* 160–169.

Bracken, B. A., & Crain, R. M. (1994). Children and adolescents' interpersonal relations: Do age, race, and gender define normalcy? *Journal of Psychoeducational Assessment, 12,* 14–32.

Butcher, J. E. (1989). Adolescent girls' sex role development: Relationship with sports participation, self-esteem, and age at menarche. *Sex Roles, 20,* 575–593.

Campbell, J. R. (1991). The roots of gender inequity in technical areas. *Journal Research in Science Teaching, 28,* 251–264.

Catsambis, S. (1995). Gender, race, ethnicity, and science education in the middle grades. *Journal of Research in Science Teaching, 32,* 243–257.

Cauce, A. M., Hiraga, Y., Mason, C., Aguilar, T., Ordonez, N., & Gonzalez, N. (1992). Between a rock and a hard place. In M. P. Root (Ed.), *Racially mixed people in America* (pp. 207–222). Newbury Park, CA: Sage.

Chappel, R. (1989). Girls and participation in sport. *Bulletin of Physical Education, 25*(2), 25–28.

Chodorow, N. (1989). *Feminism and psychoanalytic theory.* New Haven, CT: Yale University Press.

Cohen, G. L. (1993). Media portrayal of the female athlete. In G. L. Cohen (Ed.), *Women in sport: Issues and controversies* (pp. 171–184). London: Sage.

Comas-Diaz, L., & Greene, B. (Eds.). (1994). *Women of color: Integrating ethnic and gender identities in psychotherapy.* New York: Guilford Press.

Cosse, W. J. (1992). Who's who and what's what? The effects of gender on development in adolescence. In B. Rubin Wainrib (Ed.), *Gender issues across the life cycle* (pp. 5–16). New York: Springer.

Covey, L. A., & Feltz, D. L. (1991). Physical activity and adolescent female psychological development. *Journal of Youth and Adolescence, 20,* 463–474.

Dickens, M. N., & Cornell, D. G. (1993). Parent influences on the mathematics self-concept of high ability adolescent girls. *Journal for the Education of the Gifted, 17*(1), 53–73.

Eccles, J. (1986). Gender roles and women's achievement. *Educational Researcher, 15,* 15–19.

Ensminger, M. E. (1990). Sexual activity and problem behaviors among Black, urban adolescents. *Child Development, 61,* 3032–3046.

Evans, M. A., Whigham, M., & Wang, M. C. (1995). The effect of a role model project upon the attitudes of ninth grade science students. *Journal of Research in Science Teaching, 32,* 195–204.

Fordham, S. (1993). "Those loud black girls": (Black) women, silence, and gender "passing" in the academy. *Anthropology and Education Quarterly, 24*(1), 3–32.

Fox, L. H., & Tobin, D. (1988). Broadening the career horizons for gifted girls. *Gifted Child Today, 11,* 9–13.

Freedman, M. (1993). *The kindness of strangers: Adult mentors, urban youth, and the new voluntarism.* New York: Jossey-Bass.

Freiberg, P. (1991). Self-esteem gender gap widens in adolescence. *APA Monitor, 22*(4), p. 29.

Frieze, I. H., & Hanusa, B. H. (1984). In M. W. Steinkamp & M. L. Machr (Eds.), *Advances in motivation and achievement: Women in science* (pp. 139–163). Greenwich, CT: JAI Press.

Furman, W., & Buhrmester, D. (1992). Age and sex differences in perceptions of networks of personal relationships. *Child Development, 63,* 103–115.

Gambone, M. A. (1993). *Strengthening programs for youth—promoting adolescent development in the JPTA system.* Philadelphia: Public/Private Ventures.

Germone, K. E., & Furst, D. M. (1991). Social acceptability of sport for young women. *Perceptual and Motor Skills, 73,* 323–326.

Gilligan, C. (1990). Teaching Shakespeare's sister. In C. Gilligan, N. Lyons, & T. Hanmer (Eds.), *Making connections: The relational worlds of adolescent girls at Emma Willard School* (pp. 6–29). Cambridge, MA: Harvard University Press.

Gilligan, C., Lyons, N. P., & Hanmer, T. (Eds.). (1989). *Making connections: The relational worlds of adolescent girls at Emma Willard School.* Cambridge, MA: Harvard University Press.

Girls active in sports do better in classroom. (1997, March 29). *New York Times,* p. L10.

Girls Incorporated. (1998). Available: http://www.girlsinc.org.

Gwizdala, J., & Steinback, M. C. (1990). High school females' mathematics attitudes: An interim report. *School Science and Mathematics, 90,* 215–222.

Hahn, C. L. (1996). Gender and political leaning. *Theory and Research in Social Education, 24*(1), 8–35.

Hare, B. R. (1985). Reexamining the achievement central tendency: Sex differences between race and race differences between sex. In H. P. McAdoo & J. L. McAdoo (Eds.), *Black children: Social, educational, and parental environments* (pp. 139–158). Beverly Hills, CA: Sage.

Harter, S. (1990). Self and identity development. In S. S. Feldman & G. R. Elliott (Eds.), *At the threshold: The developing adolescent* (pp. 352–387). Cambridge, MA: Harvard University Press.

Herek, G. M. (1992). Psychological heterosexism and antigay violence: The social psychology of bigotry and bashing. In E. S. Hetrick & K. T. Berril (Eds.), *Hate crimes: Confronting violence against lesbians and gay men* (pp. 89–101). Newbury Park, CA: Sage.

Hill, J. P., & Lynch, M. E. (1983). The intensification of gender-related role expectations during early adolescence. In J. Brooks-Gunn & A. C. Peterson (Eds.), *Girls at puberty: Biological and psychosocial perspectives* (pp. 201–228). New York: Plenum Press.

Hopwood, T., & Carrington, B. (1994). Physical education and femininity. *Educational Research, 36,* 237–246.

Huston, A. C., & Alvarez, M. (1990). The socialization context of gender-role development in early adolescence. In R. Montemayor, G. R. Adams, & T. P. Gulotta (Eds.), *From childhood to adolescence: A transitional period?* (pp. 156–179). Newbury Park, CA: Sage.

Ingrassia, M. (1994, October 17). Virgin cool. *Newsweek, 124,* 58–62, 64, 69.

Johnson, C., & Engelhard, G., Jr. (1991). Gender, academic achievement, and preferences for cooperative, competitive, and individualistic learning among African-American adolescents. *Journal of Psychology, 126,* 385–392.

Jones, B. (1988). Attitudes of school pupils to curriculum physical education. *British Journal of Physical Education: Research Supplement, 3*, 1–4.

Jones, D. C., & Costin, S. E. (1995). Friendship quality during preadolescence and adolescence: The contributions of relationship orientations, instrumentality, and expressivity. Merrill-Palmer Quarterly, *41*, 517–535.

Kalliopuska, M. (1989). Empathy, self-esteem, and creativity among junior ballet dancers. *Perceptual and Motor Skills, 69*, 1227–1234.

Kelly, K. R., & Colangelo, N. (1990). Effects of academic ability and gender on career development. *Journal for the Education of the Gifted, 13*, 168–175.

Klaw, E. L., & Rhodes, J. E. (1995). Mentor relationships and the career development of pregnant and parenting African-American teenagers. *Psychology of Women Quarterly, 19*, 551–562.

Kline, B. E., & Short, E. B. (1991). Changes in emotional resilience: Gifted adolescent females. *Roeper Review, 13*, 118–121.

Koivula, N. (1995). Ratings of gender appropriateness of sports participation: Effects of gender-based schematic processing. *Sex Roles, 33*, 543–557.

Levitt, M. (1995). Sexual identity and religious socialization. *British Journal of Sociology, 46*, 529–536.

Li, A. K. F. (1988). Self-perception and motivational orientation in gifted children. *Roeper Review, 10*, 175–180.

Luke, M. D., & Sinclair, G. D. (1991). Gender differences in adolescents' attitudes toward school physical education. *Journal of Teaching in Physical Education, 11*, 47–58.

Lyons, N. P., Saltenstall, J. F., & Hanmer, T. J. (1989). Competencies and visions: Emma Willard girls talk about being leaders. In C. Gilligan, N. P. Lyons, & T. J. Hanmer (Eds.), *Making connections: The relational worlds of adolescent girls at Emma Willard School* (pp. 183–214). Troy, NY: Emma Willard School.

Maggs, J. L., Almeida, D. M., & Galambos, N. L. (1995). Risky business: The paradoxical meaning of problem behavior for young adolescents. *Journal of Early Adolescence, 15*, 344–362.

Magnusson, D., Strattin, H., & Allen, V. L. (1985). Biological maturation and social development: A longitudinal study of some adjustment processes from mid-adolescence to adulthood. *Journal of Youth and Adolescence, 14*, 267–283.

Mann, J. (1994). *The difference: Growing up female in America.* New York: Warner Books.

Markowitz, F. (1994). Family dynamics and the teenage immigrant: Creating the self through the parents' image. *Adolescence, 29*(113), 151–161.

Mboya, M. M. (1993). Self-concept of academic ability: Relations with gender and academic achievement. *Perceptual and Motor Skills, 77*, 1131–1137.

McMillan, J. H., & Reed, D. F. (1994). At-risk students and resiliency: Factors contributing to academic success. In A. M. Meehan & E. Astor-Stetson (Eds.), *Adolescent psychology 97/98* (pp. 57–60). Guilford, CT: Dushkin.

Miller, F. (1994). Gender differences in adolescents' attitudes toward mandatory community service. *Journal of Adolescence, 17,* 381–393.

Mwamwenda, T. S. (1991). Sex differences in self-concept among African adolescents. *Perceptual and Motor Skills, 73,* 191–194.

Nurmi, J., Poole, M. E., & Seginer, R. (1995). Tracks and transitions—a comparison of adolescent future-oriented goals, explorations, and commitments in Australia, Israel, and Finland. *International Journal of Psychology, 30,* 355–375.

Papini, D. R., Farmer, F. F., Clark, S. M., Micka, J. C., & Barnett, J. K. (1990). Early adolescent age and gender differences in patterns of emotional self-disclosure to parents and friends. *Adolescence, 25,* 959–976.

Patton, W., & Noller, P. (1990). Adolescent self-concept: Effects of being employed, unemployed, or returning to school. *Australian Journal of Psychology, 42,* 247–259.

Pearce, C. M., Martin, G., & Wood, K. (1995). Significance of touch for perceptions of parenting and psychological adjustment among adolescents. *Journal of the American Academy of Child and Adolescent Psychiatry, 34,* 160–167.

Pedersen, D. M., & Kono, D. M. (1990). Perceived effects on femininity of the participation of women in sport. *Perceptual and Motor Skills, 71,* 783–792.

Philip, K., & Hendry, L. B. (1996). Young people and mentoring: Towards a topology. *Journal of Adolescence, 19,* 189–207.

Post-Kammer, P., & Perrone, P. A. (1983). Career perceptions of talented individuals: A follow-up study. *Vocational Guidance Quarterly, 31,* 203–211.

Pryor, J. (1994). Self-esteem and attitudes toward gender roles: Contributing factors in adolescents. *Australian Journal of Psychology, 46*(1), 48–52.

Rich, Y., & Golan, R. (1992). Career plans for male-dominated occupations among female seniors in religious and secular high schools. *Adolescence, 27*(105), 73–86.

Romer, N. (1990). Is political activism still a "masculine" endeavor? Gender comparisons among high school political activists. *Psychology of Women Quarterly, 14,* 229–243.

Rubenstein, A. (1992). Clinical issues in the treatment of adolescent girls. In B. R. Wainrib (Ed.), *Gender issues across the life cycle* (pp. 17–21). New York: Springer.

Sabo, D. (1985). Sport, patriarchy, and male identity: New questions about men and sport. *Arena Review, 9*(2), 1–30.

Sadker, M., & Sadker, D. (1985, March). Sexism in the schoolroom of the '80s. *Psychology Today, 19,* 54–57.

Smith, E. J. (1982). The black female adolescent: A review of the educational, career, and psychological literature. *Psychology of Women Quarterly, 6,* 261–288.

Steinberg, L., Dornbusch, S. M., & Brown, B. B. (1992). Ethnic differences in adolescent achievement: An ecological perspective. *American Psychologist, 47,* 723–729.

Stevens, C. J., Puchtell, L. A., Ryu, S., & Mortimer, J. T. (1992). Adolescent work and boys' and girls' orientation to the future. *Sociological Quarterly, 33,* 153–169.

Study reveals sports beneficial to women. (1997, March 28). *USA Today,* p. 6C.

Tapasak, R. C. (1990). Differences in expectancy–attribution patterns of cognitive components in male and female math performance. *Contemporary Educational Psychology, 15,* 284–298.

Timimi, S. B. (1995). Adolescence in immigrant Arab families. *Psychotherapy, 32*(1), 141–149.

Toufexis, A. (1990, Fall). Coming from a different place. *Time, 136,* 64–66.

Vega, W. A., Khoury, E. L., Zimmerman, R. S., Gil, A. G., & Warheit, G. J. (1995). Cultural conflicts and problem behaviors of Latino adolescents in home and school environments. *Journal of Community Psychology, 23,* 167–179.

Vollmer, E. (1984). Sex differences in personality and expectancy. *Sex Roles, 11,* 1121–1139.

Waters, M. C. (1996). The intersection of gender, race, and ethnicity in identity development of Caribbean American teens. In B. J. Ross Leadbeater & N. Way (Eds.), *Urban girls: Resisting stereotypes, creating identities* (pp. 65–81). New York: New York University Press.

Werrbach, G. B., Grotevant, H. D., & Cooper, C. R. (1990). Gender differences in adolescents' identity development in the domain of sex role concepts. *Sex Roles, 23,* 349–362.

Wersch, A. U., Trew, K., & Turner, I. (1990). Pupils' perceived physical competence and its implications for the new PE curriculum. *British Journal of Physical Education: Research Supplement, 7,* 1–5.

Winfield, L. A. (1991). Resilience, schooling, and development in African-American youth: A conceptual framework. *Education and Urban Society, 24,* 5–14.

Winter, B. (1996). Girls gain positive perceptions through reading [News release]. *Kansas State University News* [On-line]. Available E-mail: news@ksu.edu

Yong, F. L. (1992). Mathematics and science attitudes of African-American middle grade students identified as gifted: Gender and grade differences. *Roeper Review, 14,* 136–140.

Young, J. L. (1994). Sapphires-in-Transition: Enhancing personal development among Black female adolescents. *Journal of Multicultural Counseling and Development, 22,* 86–95.

APPENDIX:
A NEW LOOK AT
ADOLESCENT GIRLS:
STRENGTHS AND STRESSES

RESEARCH AGENDA

Edited by Michael C. Roberts,
assisted by Gabriele S. Clune

May 1999

American Psychological Association Task Force
on Adolescent Girls: Strengths and Stresses

CONTRIBUTORS

Bonnie Barber, PhD
Susan A. Basow, PhD
Geraldine Kearse Brookins, PhD
Lyn Mikel Brown, PhD
Fary M. Cachelin, PhD
Joanne E. Callan, PhD
Dorothy W. Cantor, PsyD
Jessica Henderson Daniel, PhD
Elizabeth Debold, PhD
Cynthia de las Fuentes, PhD
Florence L. Denmark, PhD
Denise M. DeZolt, PhD
Denise M. Dougherty, PhD
Julia L. Duff, PhD
Jacquelynne Eccles, PhD
Michele Harway, PhD

Mary Henning-Stout, PhD
Norine G. Johnson, PhD
Deborah Jozefowicz, PhD
Marsha Liss, PhD, JD
Oksana Malenchuk, PhD
Bonnie Y. Ohye, PhD
Michael C. Roberts, PhD
Lisa R. Rubin, PhD
Ruth H. Striegel-Moore, PhD
Deborah L. Tolman, PhD
Melba J. T. Vasquez, PhD
Niobe Way, PhD
Susan Weseen, PhD
Brian L.Wilcox, PhD
Judith Worell, PhD

APA TASK FORCE ON ADOLESCENT GIRLS: STRENGTHS AND STRESSES

Norine G. Johnson, PhD Co-Chair
Karen Zager, PhD Co-Chair
Lyn Mikel Brown, PhD
Dorothy W. Cantor, PsyD
Jessica Henderson Daniel, PhD

Denise M. DeZolt, PhD
Michael C. Roberts, PhD
Alice K. Rubenstein, EdD
Judith Worell, PhD

CONTENTS

INTRODUCTION

"How Do I Evolve From Confusion and Chaos to a Capable Strong Compassionate Woman?" Age 15

For a complex set of reasons, most of what is known about adolescent girls focuses on the problems they face. The fact that many adolescent girls are showing remarkable strength, resiliency, and "hardiness" during the stressful time of adolescence needs to be explored. Instead of focusing on the storm and stress of adolescence, a new understanding of adolescent girls that affirms their strength and resilience needs to be developed. Although the current day risks and stresses in the lives of adolescent girls must be understood, they should not be the defining factors in discussions of adolescent girls. There must be a focus on what is working for adolescent girls and why to assist adolescent girls in navigating these risks during their development.

To this end, the American Psychological Association's (APA's) Presidential Task Force on Adolescent Girls: Strengths and Stresses was created by Dorothy W. Cantor during her presidential year (1996). The task force's mission statement is as follows:

> The mission of the APA Presidential Task Force on Adolescent Girls: Strengths and Stresses is to integrate current knowledge regarding adolescent girls in order to focus on the strengths, challenges, and choices of adolescent girls today. The task force will also identify gaps and inconsistencies in research, education, practice, and public policy. In this endeavor, the task force is committed to the inclusion of the voices and lives of a range of adolescent girls in terms of age, racial and ethnic diversity, socioeconomic status, geographic area, and sexual orientation. The task force will work to raise public and professional consciousness in regard to adolescent girls with a particular focus on those who impact their lives including parents, educators, health care professionals, and policymakers. Through its activities, the task force will chart directions into the new frontiers of the next century through a critical examination of the policy issues, current knowledge, and research approaches to understanding adolescent girls.

The following work is excerpted from *Beyond Appearance: A New Look at Adolescent Girls*, a book written by psychologists across the country whose work focuses on adolescent girls, including psychologists serving on the APA task force on adolescent girls.

The authors set out to assemble and review the psychology and related research and literature for the past 10 years, with special attention to strengths, challenges, and choices within the contexts of girls' lives. Challenged to consider and move beyond an exploration of girls' psychological losses and to focus on those aspects of relationship and culture that support and engage girls—as well as girls' collective attempts to resist the negative impact of the media and other powerful, societal forces—the authors attempted to answer questions such as the following:

- What is important to help girls thrive during adolescence?
- Are there different positive influences at different developmental stages?
- What does the research say about girls with high self-esteem?
- Why is it important to include diversity in research?
- What are the roles of the educator, parent, psychologist, health care system, and policymakers in providing an environment that enriches the strengths adolescent girls bring to our society?

- How can adolescent girls best be prepared for the roles they will play in the future?
- How do adolescent girls influence the world around them?

In developing this book, the authors focused on several cross-cutting themes: strengths, development, ethnicity, class, risks, resilience, and research implications. To make the rich, diverse voices of actual girls in the United States heard above the statistics, questions from a research survey conducted by the task force on adolescent girls are included in this research agenda. A summary of the survey, "The State of the Hearts of Adolescent Girls," is found at the end of this research agenda.

The adolescent population in the United States is growing rapidly and will continue to grow into the next millennium. Approximately 18.5 million adolescent girls, ages 10 to 18 years, were living in the United States at the last census in 1990. The lives of these girls are complex, affected by their gender, race, ethnicity, class, differing abilities, and sexual orientation. Only by examining each of these complicated layers can the rich diversity of the lives of adolescent girls be understood.

GENDER

"Why Do Parents Treat Girls Differently Than Boys?" Age 14

Gender is a psychological and cultural term that refers to the meanings attached to being female or male in a particular culture. It is distinct from sex, which refers to the biological aspects of being female or male. Across the United States, expectations for gender roles vary according to culture, socioeconomic class, and sexual orientation. These expectations present a variety of pressures for adolescent girls as they develop into womanhood.

Between the ages of 8 and 11 years, girls tend to be androgynous. They view themselves as strong and confident and are not afraid to say what they think. However, as they cross over into adolescence, girls begin to experience pressure toward more rigid conceptions of gender roles; they become more concerned with how women are "supposed to behave" and with their physical and sexual attractiveness. Although research shows that self-esteem decreases for both sexes after elementary school, the drop is more dramatic for girls. Compared with boys of the same age, adolescent girls are more anxious and stressed, experience diminished academic achievement, suffer from increased depression and lower self esteem, experience more body dissatisfaction and distress over their looks, suffer from greater numbers of eating disorders, and attempt suicide more frequently.

And yet, across cultural groups, adolescent girls hold more flexible and liberal attitudes than boys about the rights and roles of women. White adolescent girls who hold traditional attitudes toward women's roles tend to have lower self-esteem than do girls who hold more liberal views.

Important sources of resistance to and liberation from negative cultural messages for adolescent girls include the following: a strong ethnic identity, close connections to family, learning positive messages about oneself, trusting oneself as a source of knowledge, speaking one's mind, participation in athletics, non-traditional sex typing, feminist ideas, and assertive female role models.

Research Agenda: Gender

- What factors contribute to resilience in adolescent girls who resist stereotyped and negative cultural messages about women?
- What factors support adolescent girls' formation of positive and optimistic perspectives on their developing womanhood and future roles?
- In what ways are adolescent expectations about gender roles influenced by racial and ethnic identities, socioeconomic status, religious values, health, and sexual orientation?

Across adolescent girls' group status (ethnic and racial, sexual orientation, socioeconomic, and religious), how do gender-related biological, psychological, and cultural factors interact during adolescence?

GENDER AND SELF-ESTEEM

"What Can I Do to Make Myself More Confident in Sports?" Age 17

Many aspects of girls' self-perceptions and mental health do not decline during adolescence; on most measures, the variations among girls are much larger than the differences between girls and boys. Girls' self-concepts of ability and self-esteem vary significantly across domains and ethnic groups. Competence beliefs for both girls and boys are related to the gender stereotyping of the activity. Girls have higher expectations of success than boys in their general academic abilities across domains and in their social skills, whereas boys are more confident about their math and sports abilities.

High school senior girls and boys are equally confident of their success in business and law and in their leadership, independence, intellectual, and computer skills. Girls and boys are equally invested in future careers, but girls place less emphasis on money and job status. Their career preferences show differences related to traditional gender expectations. Many adolescent girls still believe there is an inherent conflict between feminine goals and values and competitive achievement activities. This belief does limit their future opportunities. For many adolescent girls, sensitivity to failure limits their willingness to take risks for higher rewards or more demanding opportunities.

Declines in self-esteem during adolescence are not inevitable consequences of either pubertal or school changes. Both girls' and boys' self-esteem decreases during the high school years; but girls' self esteem tends to drop more over time. African American girls' self-esteem does not decrease over the high school years and tends to be higher than both White and African American boys.

It is important to note that these gendered patterns have been observed to decrease over time. Young women today are more likely to aspire to traditional male-stereotyped fields. In addition, young women today are much more involved in athletic activities than both their mothers and grandmothers.

Research Agenda: Gender and Self-Esteem

- What factors account for the cultural and ethnic differences in patterns of adolescent girls' self-esteem?
- How can adolescent girls be encouraged to resist traditional gender role expectations in considering academic pursuits and future careers?
- How can adolescent girls be encouraged to attribute their academic success to their ability as well as to their effort and hard work?

BODY IMAGE CONCERNS AND DISORDERED EATING

"Why Am I Always Concerned About How I Appear to People and How Much I Weigh?" Age 13

During adolescence, girls are challenged to come to terms with the physical changes of puberty, including considerable weight gain. As adolescent girls attempt to reconcile the reality of their bodies with the unrealistic and unattainable cultural demands for female thinness, large numbers of girls experience intense body image dissatisfaction. For a small group of girls, negative feelings about their bodies and their efforts to achieve or maintain thinness contribute to the development of disordered eating. This may include binge eating, restrictive dieting, or induced vomiting and over-eating, leading to more serious disorders such as anorexia or bulimia.

Research efforts have neglected the fact that disordered eating typically begins during early adolescence. A complex set of cultural, social, familial, personal, and biological factors contribute to the development of disordered eating. The negative impact of experiences that threaten a girl's healthy psychological development, such as physical or sexual abuse, increase her risk of disordered eating.

Although factors that protect adolescent girls from disordered eating have not been adequately researched, environments that enhance girls' self-esteem in general and body esteem specifically and that protect girls from risk factors such as physical and sexual abuse appear to increase resiliency against unhealthy eating patterns. In addition, certain cultural contexts and expectations that promote acceptance of a broad range of appearances provide support for individuality and healthy development and play an instrumental role in protecting adolescent girls from the development of eating and weight-related concerns.

Research Agenda: Body Concerns and Disordered Eating

- What factors help adolescent girls resist cultural messages that lead them to be dissatisfied with their bodies and their appearance to others?
- How can prevention and health promotion programs be developed that build personal resilience, interpersonal competence, and general self-valuing for adolescent girls?
- How can adolescent girls be assisted in defining themselves in positive terms, apart from their physical appearance?

ADOLESCENT GIRLS OF COLOR

"Why Do People Act Differently to People With a Different Skin Color?" Age 12

During the last few decades, the collective efforts of women psychologists and the feminist movement have established and legitimized the psychological study of women and girls, and have created an intellectual climate in which it is now commonplace to conceptualize gender as a social construction of enormous influence in individual psychology and female self-definition.

Within these movements, however, there has been a marginalization of women of color. One third of the 18.5 million girls between the ages of 10 and 18 living in the United States are Black, Hispanic, Asian/Pacific Islander, Native American, Eskimo, or Aleut. They remain virtually invisible in the psychological literature on adolescent girl development.

In examining recent research studies, the lack of data and information about the psychological development and lives in general of adolescent girls of color is of great concern. Major studies on adolescent development are flawed by the presence and absence of certain groups of girls of color, a lack of reliable data on the economic status of the households of some groups of adolescent girls of color, a failure to address the roles of race and gender, and a lack of information regarding the racial–ethnic identity of research participants.

Just as the notion that males and females differ in their development toward self-definition has become accepted, professionals and others who work with adolescent girls must move toward the fuller recognition of the contribution of race, ethnicity, culture, class, and sexual orientation to development in general and to the understanding of adolescents in particular.

Research Agenda: Adolescent Girls of Color

- What components of racial–ethnic culture are critical for the development of positive identities in girls of color? Do the components vary across racial–ethnic groups?
- What is the impact of economic status on the development of adolescent girls of color in terms of education, motivation, and behavior? Is the impact the same or different across racial–ethnic groups?
- Do race–ethnicity and social class have the same impact for adolescent girls and adolescent boys of color? Do the differences, if any, suggest different intervention strategies?
- What factors explain the drop in self-esteem in Black and Hispanic adolescent girls? What is the role of context in the examination of self-esteem for these two groups of girls?
- Do Asian American and American Indian girls experience changes in self-esteem during adolescence? What factors may contribute to this change, if any, within the subgroups of these two large "racial" categories?
- What are the direct and indirect effects of the oppressive and exploitative historical legacies on the identities, attitudes, and aspirations of adolescent girls of color?

IMMIGRANT ADOLESCENT GIRLS OF COLOR

"How Can I Not Change Myself Just to Fit in?" Age 15

For immigrant girls of color, their status as immigrants and the major changes they experience as a result of immigration further complicate and intensify the challenges they face as adolescent girls in American society. In addition to the newness of their physical surroundings, adolescent immigrant girls are psychologically at risk from a myriad of factors: loss and loneliness resulting from a lack of shared experiences with peers; strain and fatigue from their efforts to adapt and cope; feelings of rejection from a new culture that may affect self-esteem; confusion in terms of role expectations, values, and identity; and a sense of impotency from their inability to function as effectively in the new culture as in their home culture.

Although immigration presents challenges for people of all ages, adolescents face the particular challenge of having lost peers and a familiar culture that would have served and assisted them in their identity development. The stress brought about by their attempts to assimilate into a new culture can result in relatively more psychological and social problems, including disordered eating, lower self-esteem, and higher depression. Increased parent–child conflicts can result from the fact that children and adolescents learn the language of their new culture more quickly and often adapt to the new culture at a much faster rate than their parents. In many cases, their resulting emerging identities are at odds with the traditions and rituals of their native culture. Generational conflicts about sex roles, peer relations with the other sex, dating and marriage may occur within immigrant families. In addition, parental loss of power and the parent's inability to function as effectively in the new society may leave adolescents feeling unsafe and unable to rely on their parents for protection.

What then is working for these immigrant girls of color? What factors foster their ability to adapt to the particular changes brought about by immigration and their development as adolescent girls? Just as immigrant girls confront the same barriers as all racial and ethnic minorities, namely racism and discrimination, the solutions to their difficulties are very similar. In many cases, strong families able to convey warmth, affection, emotional support, and clear-cut, reasonable structure and limits are able to minimize the negative impact of the stress associated with immigration. Strong adherence to traditional family values, a strong commitment to a work ethic, and a high degree of involvement in the ethnic community can serve as protective factors for immigrant adolescent girls. Indeed, the most successful family strategy seems to be maintaining a close connection to the family's cultural roots and strong family relationships.

In addition, for some groups, English language proficiency has been shown to enhance self-esteem and to lower depression, thereby reducing stress levels associated with immigrant status. The availability of community resources and ethnic social support networks are also key factors in developing positive coping mechanisms for immigrant adolescents and their families.

Research Agenda: Immigrant Adolescent Girls of Color

- What is healthy functioning for immigrant adolescent girls of color? Is there any agreement between parents and other involved adults (e.g., school personnel?) Is this negotiable?
- What resilience factors, effective adaptation strategies, and coping mechanisms work for adolescent girls of color and their families?
- What are the particular psychological risks for adolescent girls of color, especially related to trauma?

AMERICAN-BORN ASIAN, AFRICAN, LATINA, AND AMERICAN INDIAN ADOLESCENT GIRLS

Why Can't People Just Put Prejudice Behind Them? Age 14

Very little research has been conducted on the unique lives of adolescent girls of color. Given the challenges and experiences of ethnic minorities in the United States, ethnic minority adolescent girls are differentially affected by the socialization process. An adolescent's ethnicity has intense influence on her development, as it effects her sense of belonging in a world that often determines inclusion and exclusion on the basis of skin color. For psychologists to understand these experiences, it is important for them to assess the interplay of what occurs within families and what occurs in the political, economic, social, and racial climates in which young girls are challenged.

Perhaps the most resilient factor common to all ethnic minority groups is identification with family and community. The bonding and sharing of values for families of people of color can provide strength and resources for adolescent girls of color. Strong, persistent families "inoculate" adolescent girls against the ravages of ethnic and gender discrimination. The degree to which families have incorporated the positive messages of their culture and heritage despite history of poor treatment is a predictor in the healthy development of an adolescent girl of color. Research must continue to focus on diversity and especially the intersection of gender and ethnicity.

RELATIONSHIPS WITH SIGNIFICANT ADULTS: CULTIVATING HARDINESS ZONES

"Do You Think Most Girls Today Will Have Good Futures?" Age 11

Although the research on resilience and protective factors suggests that connection to parents, significant adults, school and, perhaps, some greater sense of purpose or perspective fosters resilience or "odds-defying" behavior, it is often precisely a dilemma of connection, a forced choice between competing loyalties, that faces girls. Girls' struggles are rooted in systemic problems—such as poverty, racism, and sexism—that require a collective, rather than an individual, response. This suggests a need for a new concept of health and stress resistance that locates the struggle between the girl and her world, not within the individual girl, and that holds the adults in girls' environments accountable for providing girls with experiences and opportunities for them to understand, engage with, and potentially transform what limits and harms them.

Within health psychology, the concept of "hardiness" describes the stance of an individual in relation to a stressful context and, thus, points to developmental experiences girls may need to resist the long-term harm of institutionalized racism and sexism. Considering relationships with significant adults in girls' lives as potential "hardiness zones"—that is, spaces of real engagement and opportunities for girls to experience control, commitment, and challenge—one moves the focus from the individual girl to the network of relationships that create girls' social worlds and environments, allowing girls access to skills, relationships, and possibilities that enable them to experience power and meaning. Through this perspective, the relational and educational contexts, in both schools and other community organizations, in which girls find themselves can be assessed in terms of their capacity to facilitate hardiness.

Mothers, women teachers, and "othermothers" hold the possibility of providing relational hardiness zones for adolescent girls. Listening and fostering meaningful participation in school and community life, as well as providing the opportunity for self-development through effective sociocultural critique, are means by which adults can support the strengths of girls. Schools and communities that engage girls in social critique and in activist experiences appear to be particularly effective, as do adults who demonstrate commitment, respect for youth, and a willingness to involve them in making change within their communities.

Research Agenda: Relationships With Significant Adults

- What are the defining features of the individuals, institutions, and agencies that give rise to hardiness and strength in adolescent girls?

- What protective factors do "hardiness zones" offer adolescent girls? How can significant adults in girls' lives provide relational and environmental contexts that foster adolescent girls' strengths, support them in ways that are health promoting, and allow them to experience their potency in the world around them?
- How can adults help adolescent girls—particularly those who struggle with the effects of poverty, racism, homophobia, immigrant or refugee status—negotiate cultural conflicts and competing loyalties, especially in those cases in which they develop new possibilities and life choices different from their families and communities?
- What developmental and relational experiences do adolescent girls need to resist the long-term harm of institutionalized racism and sexism?
- What roles do "othermothers," such as aunts, grandmothers, adult friends, teachers, or community members, play in supporting adolescent girls and creating relational hardiness zones?
- What are the positive and protective aspects of mother–daughter relationships?
- What benefits and possibilities for support exist within girls' relationships with their fathers or other significant adult men in their lives?

FRIENDSHIPS AND PEER RELATIONSHIPS

"Why Is Popularity so Important to Most Girls?" Age 15

For psychologists to understand the way in which adolescent girls develop in relation to the world around them, it is important to examine adolescent girls' friendships. Close friendships, considered by many social scientists to be the "most rewarding and satisfying of all human relationships" are clearly important for the social and emotional health of all adolescents, regardless of ethnicity, race, or socioeconomic status.

What is known about girls' friendships and peer relations is based primarily on studies comparing girls with boys. Although these studies provide important information, they offer little understanding of the diversity of experiences and perceptions of friendships among girls, including the important distinction girls make among types of friends and the nature and quality of these relationships. There has also been little attention given to the ways in which class, culture, race, ethnicity, and sexual identity shape adolescent girls' friendships groupings and even less attention to the ways in which racism, sexism, classism, and homophobia influence the environments in which girls' friendships are nurtured.

Early adolescence appears to be especially stressful on adolescent girls' friendships and peer relations, signified by a sharp increase in indirect relational aggression. More typical of girls and more distressful to girls than to boys, relational aggression, characterized by such behaviors as spreading rumors or threatening withdrawal of affiliation, appears to emerge as girls' attempt to negotiate current power relations and affirm or resist conventional constructions of femininity. More research is needed to understand the nature and quality of this negotiation and the role popularity and attractiveness play in the development and configuration of adolescent girls' peer groupings.

Friendships can be a source of both knowledge and strength for adolescent girls. They can also be a source of struggle, hurt, and confusion, particularly as girls move into adolescence and begin to negotiate dominant cultural views of sexual relationships, femininity, and appearance. Directly engaging adolescent girls in conversations about such issues and encouraging them to explore together how current power relations are played out in the context of their relationships with other girls and women can provide support as well as opportunities to resist social separations.

Research Agenda: Friendships

- How do girls' friendships and peer relations mitigate or exacerbate the psychological and social struggles of adolescence? What possibilities for support and protective factors exist within girls' friendships?
- How does social location—that is, class, race, ethnicity, and sexual identity—affect the nature of adolescent girls' friendships and peer groupings and influence the forms and meanings of communication among girls, including the formation of cliques, aggressive behavior, bullying, and teasing?
- How do school environments and neighborhood contexts influence peer groupings and friendship patterns?
- How do changing relationships with boys affect relationships between girlfriends?
- How are expressions of closeness and intimacy between girls affected by conventional notions of femininity and codes of sexual and gender "normalcy"?

- What are the strengths and stresses of girls' friendships forged across lines of class and culture?

SEXUALITY AND SEXUAL DECISION MAKING

"Does the Woman Have the Right to Say No to a Man?" Age 12

Much of the literature on female adolescent sexuality focuses exclusively on the problems or negative consequences associated with individual girls' sexual behavior and narrowly defines sexual decision making as individual risk-taking behavior. Unfortunately, these studies often use samples of girls of color and poor girls, adolescents who are considered most at risk for being "bad" sexual decision makers; middle-class suburban girls or disabled girls, who are not considered at risk in part because their sexuality is less scrutinized or visible, are thus not often the focus of such studies. In addition, there exists a tendency to study girls primarily, even though sexual decisions, especially those that have negative consequences, are made by both partners.

In the United States, the timeworn adage that "boys want sex, girls want relationships" has permeated beliefs about adolescent sexuality. Only recently, as psychologists began to challenge these previous assumptions about male and female adolescent sexuality and intimacy, has girls' sexual desire been acknowledged as a factor in their sexual decision making.

Recent research attempts focus on understanding how adolescent girls experience their sexuality to determine effective means for empowering girls to develop responsible sexual subjectivities. Such research has generated new avenues for exploration, such as understanding if and how girls from different social and material locations negotiate the following:

- Make active and safe choices about sexual behaviors and about the relationships within which they engage in these expressions of their sexuality.
- Develop a sense of entitlement to their own pleasure and desire.
- Identify and learn to negotiate the often unequal power distribution typical of male–female relationships.

The centrality of relationships in girl's psychological development suggests the importance of relationships in girls' sexuality development, including girls' decisions about sexual behavior. Taking girls' relational contexts seriously in both research and practice demands a focus on the meanings of sexuality and sexual decisions and the processes by which girls develop their sexuality beyond their choice to have sexual intercourse.

Research Agenda: Sexuality and Sexual Decision Making

- How do adolescent girls experience and voice sexual desire?
- How do girls negotiate and make decisions about the dangers, responsibilities, and pleasures of sexual activity?
- How do girls' relationships with their own bodies, with specific people in their lives, and with the larger cultural ideals regulating "normal" and "moral" female sexual identities shape their sexuality?
- How do a girl's different relationships with peers, close friends, intimate partners, and significant adults in her life inform her about the development of her sexuality and about the pleasures and risks of sexual exploration and sexual intercourse?
- How do positive relational possibilities associated with sexuality and desire, such as intensified intimacy with a loved partner, the sense of well-being that can come from connection with oneself through one's body, or the ability to experience pleasure in sexual relationships affect adolescent girls' decisions to engage in sexual behavior?
- What effects do negative relational risks, such as being hurt, disappointed, or regretful about the choice to have sexual intercourse or to explore a range of sexual behaviors have on adolescent girls?
- How do White, middle-class suburban girls experience and express their sexuality?
- How do conventional notions of femininity and idealized relationships (i.e., compulsory heterosexuality or the traditional romance story) affect girls' sexual identities, sexual experiences, and expressions of desire?

SCHOOL AND COMMUNITY

"Today We Know the World for Adolescent Girls Is a Scary Place. Why Aren't Teachers Required to Gain a Certain Amount of Knowledge in This Area? Kids Spend A Lot of Time in School." Age 15

In an attempt to understand how to ensure success in schools for female students, the task force has identified several classroom environment and teacher factors:

- Students' liking the teacher.
- Teacher's use of inclusive (nonsexist and nonracist) materials.

- Teacher's paying attention to students.
- Girls' connecting with caring adults.
- Classrooms in which there are lower levels of competitiveness and higher levels of innovative learning. Teacher's use of gender-fair instructional techniques, especially those that support girls' participation and success.
- Teacher's recognition of girls as key players in their own lives.

For many students, and for female students in particular, schools are not safe places. A high degree of sexual harassment has been reported by female students in U.S. high schools. In recent research, lesbian, gay, and bisexual adolescents reported a wide range of verbal and physical violence directed toward them in a variety of settings, such as home, school, work, and the general community.

In response to greater public awareness of harassment, there has been an increase in the number of junior high and high schools that have developed policies against sexual harassment. In addition, some schools are implementing programs that address harassment as a serious matter, while focusing on building a school community that supports more appropriate and inclusive behavior. Government initiatives have begun to provide incentive and support for addressing sexual harassment concerns. Such initiatives are critically important and should continue.

Community Organizations

"How Can I Get People to Stop Looking at Me as Not Part of Their Group and as Not Important?" Age 13

Adolescent girls today have access to an array of community-based youth organizations, despite the fact that there are a smaller number of these programs serving young women than young men. Many of these programs aimed at young women provide support for personal development and the development of social skills and encourage physical activity. Research findings recommend that organizations established to meet the needs of adolescent girls should practice the following:

- Provide positive, caring, and consistent adult role models of both sexes.
- Promote high, yet realistic, expectations in skill development.
- Promote the development of relationships across class, gender, race, and ethnicity.
- Offer a range of experiences and topics that are of interest to girls and foster equality for girls.
- Encourage community involvement.
- Involve the girls in settings in which they can be themselves, speak their truths, and find their own sources of power.

Many of these factors have not been adequately addressed in current youth program research. Access to and the function of these community-based organizations have been found to vary across social class and racial and ethnic lines. In many studies, several groups, including at-risk youth, youth from various ethnic groups, and lesbian and bisexual adolescents, are consistently underrepresented.

Religious Organizations

Is God Someone I Should Believe in?" Age 16

Adolescent females, when compared with their male counterparts, are more actively religious. They participate in religious services and youth organizations and maintain their beliefs over longer periods of time. Such religiosity may have long-term benefits. Research has found that turning to religion and friends as a means of coping during adolescence is a significant indicator of healthy emotional development as a woman.

Not surprising, much of the literature in the area of religiosity and female adolescents focuses on factors related to girls' sexual behaviors, coping, social competence, self-esteem, and identity issues. Unmarried teen mothers' religious values have been found to influence decision-making related to the choice to have and keep a child, waiting to have first intercourse, and use of contraception. For African American girls, researchers have found a positive relationship between self-esteem and spiritual support.

Research Agenda: School and Community

- What formal and informal mechanisms facilitate adolescent girls' opportunities to be heard regarding their experiences, wants, needs, and expectations in schools and communities?
- What barriers exist within theses formal and informal mechanisms?
- How do we become more responsive to girls' expressed needs within the context of these institutions?
- What must be done in collaboration with, and on behalf of, young women to enhance already existing systems?
- What are the particular experiences of lesbian and female bisexual adolescents in school and community settings? What issues do they share with their heterosexual peers and which are different? How do we meet their needs? What are the experiences of lesbian and female bisexual adolescents across race and ethnicity? Which community resources are responsive to lesbian and bisexual adolescents?

- How do we work with adolescent girls in school and community settings over the long term as they construct norms and roles for themselves and as they find the source and strength of their own power?
- Across all of these questions, what are the ethnic, religious, ability, socioeconomic, and other contextual factors that need to be considered?
- How successful are sexual harassment programs in schools?
- How do access to and function of social networks in schools and communities vary across social class and racial and ethnic lines?
- What is the impact of community youth programs, both secular and religious, on girls' competence? Do these programs perpetuate stereotypic socialization practices?

DATING VIOLENCE

"Why Do Men Rape Girls?" Age 11

Pervasive violence is affecting adolescent girls everywhere. Occurring in homes, schools, job settings, and on the streets, violence against girls is seen in verbal, physical, and sexual abuse. Girls may be assaulted by gangs, by friends, or by romantic partners or sexually exploited by family members, acquaintances, or strangers.

Adolescents are considered to be at a higher risk for sexual assault than any other group. Over half of these reported sexual assaults occurred in dating situations. Dating violence includes physical injuries, verbal assaults, and threats of violence in the context of a dating relationship. Dating violence has been reported to affect 10% of high school students and 22% of college students.

It is believed that the incidence of date rape is underreported because most victims of date rape do not think the assault fits the definition of rape, so they do not report the rape to the police. Because of the dating situation, a girl may also feel guilt or responsibility for being in the company of the attacker and view the occurrence as normal or deserved. Other reasons girls give for not reporting date rape include fear of their parents' reactions to the rape and their peers' learning of the incident.

Dating violence has serious consequences. Young women are three times more likely to report severe emotional trauma when a violent episode occurs in a dating situation. Women raped by someone they know have more severe psychological problems than women raped by a stranger. Girls and women can suffer long-term effects from date rape, including sexual dysfunction, flashbacks, a delayed stress reaction, and other symptoms of post-traumatic stress disorder. A young woman may also have to deal with sexually transmitted diseases (STDs), pregnancy, and, in some groups, the social stigma of the loss of virginity.

Victims of dating violence must receive immediate intervention to counteract the traumatic effects of experiencing a breach in trust by someone they know. Counseling services at high schools and colleges should be made more widely available to these young women to minimize immediate and long-term consequences. Programs emphasizing prevention are extremely important. Teaching skills such as negotiation, interpersonal communication, anger management, problem solving, and coping strategies to girls and boys would be useful.

TEEN PROSTITUTION

"Why Do All the Cute Guys Date Sluts?" Age 14

Some adolescent girls enter prostitution as a means of survival on the streets. Some prostitutes trade sex for drugs. Other young prostitutes are actually recruited by those who will exploit them. Those who prey upon them are able to pick out the girls who fit the pattern of vulnerability they seek. When the histories of adolescent prostitutes are examined, it is clear that they had been on paths of exploitation and victimization with roots in their childhood. Running away and, ultimately, teen prostitution, can be seen as the result of a struggle that adolescent girls experience between themselves and others. It is through their attempt to maintain connection with others as well as with their own thoughts and feelings that girls may find themselves runaways and teen prostitutes.

Transitioning from prostitution to a more traditional socially acceptable life is a difficult developmental process. Outreach programs to assist young women in leaving prostitution have developed in a few cities, although there is no evaluation mechanism for these programs. A recent study cites intelligence, temperament, cognitive appraisal, and a relationship with a significant person as protective factors enabling at-risk girls to resist the temptations of exploiters.

Research Agenda: Interpersonal Violence and Teen Prostitution

- How prevalent is dating violence and date rape among adolescents from various ethnic groups?
- Why do male adolescents batter or rape?
- What is the motivation of young women who are the recipients of these behaviors?

- What is the connection between early sexual victimization and later adolescent prostitution?

HEALTH CARE FOR TEENS

"Can My Parents Find Out if I Go to Clinics for Information or Treatment?" Age 18

Although adolescent girls can be considered healthy relative to other populations, they are indeed affected by numerous health problems. Adolescent girls do use health services, however these health services need to be improved.

The health problems of adolescent girls range from common illnesses and injuries of childhood and adolescence (e.g., colds, flu, and sports and play-related injuries) to concerns about the changes accompanying puberty (e.g., breast development and menstruation) to living with chronic disorders (e.g., cancer) and disabilities (e.g., learning disabilities and cerebral palsy) to behavioral or psychosocial problems (e.g, depressions, suicide attempts, substance abuse, conduct disorder, violent victimization, and premature and unsafe sexuality).

Adolescents and providers often have different perceptions of what should be discussed in a health care visit. Most studies report unsatisfactory communication between providers and adolescent patients. Fear that confidentiality will be breached has been found to be the leading reason why adolescents do not seek health care. Training for providers of adolescent medical services must be improved. A growing body of research supports the idea that a communicative patient–provider relationship is essential for patient satisfaction, adherence to prescribed health regimens, and even health outcomes.

Parents can be integral partners in adolescent girls' health and health care. A number of factors that may interfere with the involvement of parents in adolescent girls' health issues must be addressed: adolescents' desire for privacy, fear of parents' reactions to certain health issues, and lack of parental knowledge and parental fears.

What additional changes need to occur for adolescent girls to fully use the resources within the American health care system? The Society for Adolescent Medicine argues that health services for adolescents need to be not only accessible in the traditional sense but also visible within the adolescent community as well, so that adolescents know which services are available to them and how to access these services. The advent and growth in the number of school-based health centers has positively changed the picture of adolescent health care somewhat, but there are still only an estimated 1,000 school-based health centers in the United States, and not all school-based health centers work predominantly with adolescents.

Research Agenda: Health Care

- To what extent do clinical services (i.e., anticipatory guidance, counseling, or screening for behavioral problems or disease) make a difference in terms of adolescent health?
- Which services that could be or are being provided now to adolescent girls are effective for which girls and under what conditions?
- Are current methods of screening and counseling for development, reproductive health issues, mental health issues (including, but beyond, depression and suicide), violence (victimization and perpetration), and substance abuse working for adolescent girls?
- What overall preventive strategies or combinations of strategies work best for adolescent girls—when and why?
- How effective is the health care received by adolescent girls in real world settings, such as offices of all kinds of practitioners, school-based health centers, family planning and STD clinics, and emergency rooms and hospitals?
- Which new technologies and techniques for prevention and treatment of current problems (e.g., teen pregnancy, drug use, violence, certain chronic illnesses, and disabilities) look promising for the future?
- How can research be developed that employs new models of thinking (i.e., an emphasis on health rather than pathology)?
- What is the importance of a participatory patient-provider relationship to patient satisfaction, adherence to prescribed health regimens, and health outcomes for adolescent patients?

PUBLIC POLICY AND ADOLESCENT SEXUALITY

"If a Teen Decides to Have Sex, What Should They Do About Their Parents? Should They Tell Them or What?" Age 15

It is interesting to note that most of the policymaking action that relates to adolescent girls has focused on issues directly or tangentially related to their sexual behavior. The focus has been on such policies as those intended (a) to provide reproductive health services and prevent teen pregnancy, (b) to provide children and youth with sexuality education, (c) to promote sexual abstinence among adolescents, (d) to limit adolescents' autonomy regarding reproductive health decisions, and (e) to create disincentives for teen pregnancy and childbearing. If, as many observers argue, Americans have extremely ambivalent or conflicting feelings about human sexuality, this holds especially true for attitudes regarding the emerging sexuality and sexual behavior of adolescent girls. Clearly, policymaking in the United States has embodied a primarily hostile approach to sexuality and sexual expression among the young, and this is particularly so for adolescent girls. Rather than attempt to restrict adolescent's access to information and services, policymakers should pursue policy mechanisms to enhance adolescents' sexual health. The failure of existing policies is evident in the persistently high rates of teen pregnancies and STDs among adolescents.

Reproductive Rights

"If You Have Your Tubes Tied, Can You Still Have a Baby if You Have Sex?"

In 1970, the Family Planning Services and Population Research Act, among other things, established Title X of the Public Health Services Act. The effectiveness of the Title X program in serving adolescents is attributable to two key features of the program. First, the program largely eliminates financial barriers for adolescent girls seeking reproductive health care services, including pregnancy prevention and testing for and treatment of STDs. Publicly financed contraceptive services allow many adolescents who lack both health insurance of any kind and adequate financial resources of their own to obtain preventive care. Second, the program provides adolescents with confidential access to reproductive health care. Confidentiality is widely regarded as integral to the Title X program's effectiveness in reaching sexually active adolescents.

Sexuality Education

"Why Are Parents So Uptight About the 'Sex Talks'" Age 18

Most American adolescents receive some form of sexuality education that includes information on sex and contraceptive use. Comprehensive reviews of studies examining the relationship between participation in sex education and early sexual activity conclude that the likelihood that an adolescent will become sexually active is not affected positively or negatively by participation in sex education. During the last 16 years, there have been major conflicts between supporters of abstinence-only approaches to sexuality education and supporters of comprehensive sexuality education. The growth of federal support for abstinence-only programs is remarkable when the amount of funds dedicated to these programs is compared with the amount allocated for past federally supported adolescent pregnancy prevention efforts. Over the next 5 years, the federal government will spend more on abstinence education that it has on adolescent health services and pregnancy prevention legislation over the past 20 years.

Abortion

"Can You Get an Abortion if You Are Pregnant Without Your Parents?"
Age 13

In the years following the Supreme Court's decision in Roe v. Wade (1973), the rate of abortions among adolescent girls climbed, a fact that precipitated the action in many states to restrict adolescents' access to abortion services, typically through the establishment of parental consent or parental notification requirements. Although parental consent and notification laws have been enacted, a number of Supreme Court decisions have refrained from allowing states to give parents complete veto power over their minor daughters' abortion decisions. Still, abortion remains the only reproductive health care service for which states require parental consent or notification. These parental consent and notification laws have been built around the assumptions that adolescents lack the ability to make reasonable, rational abortion decisions and that parental involvement in these decisions will benefit the adolescent. It is still too early to determine the effects of these consent laws, but one recent study suggests that these laws increase the likelihood that adolescents will travel to nearby states without parental involvement laws to seek abortion services.

Research Agenda: Sexuality and Sexual Decision Making

- How do adolescent girls experience and voice sexual desire?
- How do girls negotiate and make decisions about the dangers, responsibilities, and pleasures of sexual activity?
- How do girls' relationships with their own bodies, with specific people in their lives, and with the larger cultural ideals regulating "normal" and "moral" female sexual identities shape their sexuality?
- How does a girl's different relationships with peers, close friends, intimate partners, and significant adults in her life inform her about the development of her sexuality and about the pleasures and risks of sexual exploration and sexual intercourse?
- How do positive relational possibilities associated with sexuality and desire, such as intensified intimacy with a loved

partner, the sense of well-being that can come from connection with oneself through one's body, or the ability to experience pleasure in sexual relationships affect adolescent girls' decisions to engage in sexual behavior?

- What effects do negative relational risks, such as being hurt, disappointed, or regretful about the choice to have sexual intercourse or to explore a range of sexual behaviors have on adolescent girls?
- How do White middle-class suburban girls experience and express their sexuality?
- How do conventional notions of femininity and idealized relationships (i.e., compulsory heterosexuality or the traditional romance story) affect girls' sexual identities, sexual experiences, and expressions of desire?

PSYCHOLOGIST EDUCATION AND PRACTICE ISSUES

"When You Feel Like You Don't Know Which Way to Solve a Problem What Kinds of Steps Do You Take?" Age 16

For adolescent girls to thrive, they must be assisted in navigating the challenges that face them by mental health professionals who can both protect and strengthen them. Psychology, as a discipline and as a profession, is in an excellent position to respond on both counts, using research, practice, teaching, and consulting expertise. Indeed, given this broad base of knowledge and understanding, psychologists have a responsibility to respond to the needs of adolescent girls. Specifically, they can support the acquisition and maintenance of girls' strengths and can address the many stresses and related problems adolescent girls face. Because competent practice relies on relevant and comprehensive education and training, educators of psychologists must offer training programs with specially designed curricula, covering courses as well as applied training, that address these special needs and problems. The sheer range of problems is challenging, and the number of adolescents needing mental health treatment plus those who require some support in their journey through "normal" adolescence is large.

Each year in this country, thousands of teen girls find themselves in psychological distress associated with problems so pervasive in our society that they have come to be known as public health issues. The types of psychological problems reflecting the greatest distress among today's adolescent girls include the following:

- Major adjustment and developmental problems, including personal identity and family issues, such as separation from parents and family, sexual identity issues, or concerns about one's sexual orientation and behaviors. Major psychological disorders, such as schizophrenia, eating disorders and mood disorders.

- Major psychosocially and culturally induced problems, including reactions to violence, drug use, and other abuse.

These have psychological as well as physical health ramifications. To focus on the psychological needs and problems of adolescent girls, psychologists have developed a wide array of different treatment approaches and services that have emerged in recent years; yet, there is an urgent need for greater understanding and more effective support of girl's strengths and interventions to address their emotional distress and disorders. The complexity of the world in which today's adolescent girl lives challenges psychology to devote its best efforts in their behalf in practice and in preparation for practice.

What needs to be done? Past arguments and current demands for education and training specifically focused on adolescent girls or on adolescents in general remain largely unheeded. The value of thorough assessment and appropriate intervention must be emphasized. Mental health care professionals must be prepared to provide competent service for adolescent girls. Comprehensive programs must be established. The profession needs to guide the education and training of psychologists specifically to advance competencies in providing services for adolescent girls.

Research Agenda: Mental Health Care

- What are the psychological needs and problems of adolescent girls? How successful are current treatment approaches and services?
- How successful are current adolescent addiction treatments?
- How effective are mental health and substance abuse treatment services, including the talking therapies, psychopharmacotherapies, and milieu therapies?
- What are effective strategies for coping with social and psychological stressors?

VISION FOR THE FUTURE

"Will I Achieve My Dreams?" Age 12

As demonstrated by the content of this research agenda and the comprehensive volume *Beyond Appearance: A New Look at Adolescent Girls,* adolescence represents a significant transition in a young woman's life, a time of exploration with greater freedom to try new things, and a growing independence and increasing self-awareness. For many adolescents, this period poses some challenges and difficulties. Today's adolescents appear to be better off than past cohorts in many ways, yet they are not in other ways. Although not enough is known, increased research and knowledge has provided society with a greater understanding of the adolescent experience.

Adolescent girls today are faced with a unique predicament. Although progress related to gaining equal rights for women and girls has considerably broadened the range of choices girls have in living their lives, adolescent girls lack precise rules and expectations as they consider the variety of roles now open to them in contrast with more generally accepted expectations for girls in the past. Although these girls are expected to "have it all," few role models or guidelines exist. Interventions with adolescent girls must address this predicament, for it is an important factor of adolescent girls' transition.

Historically, American society has generally lacked an appreciation or respect for female development. With dramatic social, economic, and technological changes reshaping the world, adolescents shape an unknown future replete with possibilities for improvement. Any view of the future world of today's adolescent girls must be a realistic yet hopeful one, not necessarily idealistic. The social, economic, and technological changes reshaping the world offer great possibilities for improvement.

In the past and present, adolescent girls have learned that their needs for closeness and relatedness conflict with the competitive attitudes that drive success, yet they are expected to achieve in this society, in effect, being forced to choose between being true to themselves or realizing their goals. The increasing political interest for adolescent girls is a positive sign for the future. The advent of women into politics is a step that can improve their situation, and encouragement to do this must take place at the formative adolescent level.

The Carnegie Council on Adolescent Development concluded in its final report *Great Transitions: Preparing Adolescents for a New Century* that the American institutions of family, schools, youth-serving social organizations, and the media "have fallen behind in their vital functions and must now be strengthened in their respective roles and linked in a mutually reinforcing system of support for adolescents" (Carnegie Council on Adolescent Development, p. 11).[1] Although disheartening to see that the myriad of policies and programs often do not meet the needs of adolescent girls, there is always hope that new developments and new looks can produce

---

[1] Carnegie Council on Adolescent Development. (1995). *Great transitions: Preparing adolescents for a new century.* New York: Carnegie Corporation of New York.

positive change. Psychology has a great deal to contribute in fostering such change through its theoretical and applied conceptualizations, research methodology, service delivery system and development, content knowledge base, and potentially large cadre of active and involved professionals.

Research Agenda: Overall Questions

- How do race, ethnicity, culture, class, and sexual orientation affect the experiences of adolescent girls?
- What helps adolescent girls of different ethnicities, races, cultures, classes, and sexual orientations to build strengths during different developmental stages of adolescence?
- How can we develop relational and community "hardiness zones" for girls (i.e., places within kinship networks and families and in schools, churches, and neighborhoods where there are opportunities for control, commitment, and challenge)?
- What would adolescent girls of different ethnicities, races, cultures, classes, and sexual orientations define as strengths they would like to possess?

THE STATE OF THE HEARTS OF ADOLESCENT GIRLS

Currently in development, members of the APA Adolescent Girls Task Force: Strengths and Stresses are preparing a book for adolescent girls that seeks to stimulate relevant dialogue between and among them, their peers, their parents, and others who interact and work with them. Tentatively titled *The State of the Hearts of Adolescent Girls*, this book reflects what is on the minds of adolescent girls today through a series of questions to be used in a broad survey of adolescent girls.

The survey was given to a large sample of groups of adolescents in schools and community agencies. Each respondent was asked to indicate his or her gender and age. The survey asked the following question:

"If you had the chance to have a private and confidential conversation with an expert with a great deal of knowledge and understanding about the concerns of adolescent girls today what would you ask them? Please write down six questions about anything that is on your mind. Remember, do not put your name on the paper."

At its conclusion, the survey generated over 6,000 questions from and about adolescent girls. The survey responses are representative of White, Latin American, Black, Native American, and Asian populations. They represent adolescents from lower- to upper-class socioeconomic groups as well as urban, suburban, small town, and rural populations.

The survey responses are being used as a guide to formulate the questions that are on the minds of adolescent girls, their parents, and others who live and work with them. Once the questions were selected, they were forwarded to a panel of experts, each of whom provided a brief response to the question. The experts chosen for each of the questions were carefully selected for their expertise in the particular area. Particular attention was paid to ensure that the experts who responded to each of the questions reflect diversity of race and ethnic background. By providing several responses to each of the questions in the book, the editors sought to provide a catalyst for the consideration and understanding of multiple perspectives on the issues facing adolescent girls today.

AUTHOR INDEX

Numbers in italics refer to listings in the reference sections.

Barber, M. M., 316, *322*
Barnett, H. L., 308, *319*
Barnett, J. K., 209, *223*, 395, *403*
Barry, K., 292, *295*
Bartels, C., 340, *352*
Bartelt, D. W., 184, 185, *197*
Basow, S. A., 26, 32, *47*
Bateson, M. C., 267, *272*
Bauch, P. A., 259, *272*
Bauchner, H., 315, *319*
Bauh, J. L., *324*
Bauman, K. E., *18*, 202, *324*
Baumeister, L. M., 231, *242*
Baumeister, R. F., 98, *104*, 123, *126*
Bayer, B. M., 126, *128*
Beals, J., 311, *323*
Beaman, A. L., 86, *105*
Bear, G., 213, *224*
Beardslee, W. R., 93, *102*
Bearinger, L. H., *18*, 202, *324*
Bearman, P. S., *18*, 202, *324*
Beck, A., 366, *372*
Becker, J., 71, *78*
Beckford, P. H., 311, *320*
Beiser, M., 136, *146*
Belansky, E., 61, *79*
Belenky, M. F., 116, *126*, 287, *295*
Bell, J., 312, *324*
Bell, L. A., 55, 68, *78*
Bell, R. M., 310, 312, *320*, *324*
Belle, D., 208, *220*
Bem, S. L., 26, 29, 34, *47*
Bemak, F., 135, *146*
Benbow, C. P., 62, 66, *78*, *79*
Benda, B. B., 229, *243*
Bennett, T. A., 334, *352*
Bentler, P. M., 229, *244*
Beran, C. S., 344
Beren, S. E., 94, *102*
Berg, M., 211, *220*
Bergeisen, L., 283, *295*
Bergeson, R., *320*
Bergman, A., 366, *373*
Berk, L. E., 39, *47*
Berman, J. S., 156, *171*
Bernal, G., 155–157, *169*
Bernal, M. E., 160, *170*
Bernard, M. E., 366, *372*
Berndt, T. J., 206, 208, 209, 212, 216, *220*, *224*

Bernstein, A., 311, *320*
Bernstein, G. A., *319*
Bernzweig, J., 302, *319*
Best, C. L., 280, *297*
Betz, N. E., 55, 63, 78, 190, *204*
Beuhring, T., *18*, 308, *319*, *324*
Bevan, C. S., *351*
Bhapkar, M. V., *322*
Bickman, B., 311, *319*
Biederman, J., *325*
Billy, J. O. G., 229, *242*
Binion, V. J., 28, *47*
Birmaher, B., *319*
Bittle, M. L., 208, *221*
Bjorkqvist, K., 212, *220*
Black, L., 139, *147*, 158, 163, *169*
Blaine, B., 37, *47*
Blechman, E. A., 385, 387, *399*
Bloch, H. S., 357, 366, *372*
Block, J., 124, *127*, 186, *200*
Block, J. H., 186, *200*
Blos, P., 177, *179*, 366, *372*
Blum, R. W., *18*, 33, *47*, 86, *106*, 184, 189, *197*, 198, *200*, 202, 203, 229, 245, 283, 295, 308, 311, 316, *319*, *324*
Blumberg, R. L., 27, *47*
Blumenfeld, P. C., 80, *83*
Blyth, D. A., 54, 69–72, 74, 82, 187, *203*
Boehnlein, J., 136, *147*
Boekeloo, B. O., 313, *319*
Bohrnstedt, G., 71, *78*
Boldero, J., 230, *242*
Bollerud, K. H., 239, *242*
Bond, L., 92, *106*
Boney-McCoy, S., 229, 231, *243*
Borok, G. M., 310, *322*
Borton, J., 316, *322*
Bourdony, C. J., *322*
Bowen, R., 72, *80*
Bowie, P., 278, 279, 281, *299*
Boyd-Franklin, N., 158, 162, 165, *169*, *170*
Boyes, M. C., 124, *127*
Boyington, D., 283, *300*
Bracken, B. A., 391, *399*
Bradburn, I. S., 95, *104*
Bradshaw, C. K., 161, *169*

Brandt, H. R., *104*
Brasfield, T. L., 229, *245*
Breakwell, G. M., 230, *242*
Breant, D. A., *319*
Brewster, K. L., 229, *242*
Brindis, C. D., 305, 316, *319, 320, 323,*
        334, 352
Broadnax, S., 37, *47*
Brochardt, C. M., 311, *319*
Brodt, S. E., 334, *352*
Broken Nose, M. A., 160, *172*
Bronars, S., 336, *351*
Bronfenbrenner, U., 263, *272*
Brookins, G. K., 191–193, 196, *198*
Brooks, L. M., 196, *198*
Brooks-Gunn, J., 6, *17,* 33, *47,* 86, 87,
        99, *102, 104,* 106, 117, *127,*
        186, 187, 191, *198,* 211, *220,*
        229, *242, 323, 392, 399*
Brown, B. B., 383, *403*
Brown, J. A., 96, *102*
Brown, K. P., *50*
Brown, L. M., 29, 31, 42, *47,* 116, *127,*
        142, *147,* 182, 188, 189, 191,
        192, 194, *198,* 207, 212, 213,
        215, 216, 219, *220,* 233, *243,*
        357, *372*
Brown, L. S., 34, 38, *47*
Brown, R., 286, *296*
Brown, R. A., 315, *320*
Brown, S. S., 338, *350*
Browne, A., 294, *295, 298*
Bruch, H., 100, *102*
Brumberg, J. J., 92, *103,* 186, *198*
Bryk, A. S., 259, *273*
Bucciarelli, R., *324*
Buchanan, C. M., 71, 78, *80*
Buhrmester, D., 191, *199,* 208, 209, 216,
        220, 222, 378, 400
Burgess, A. W., 286, *297*
Burke, P. J., 278, *295,* 317, *320*
Burkhart, B. R., 280, *298*
Burlingame, P., 342, *350*
Burns, B. J., 304, 311
Burris, B. J., *322*
Burroughs, J., 97, *108*
Burton, J., *103*
Burton, L. M., 185, 189, *198*
Busch-Rossnagal, N. A., 210, *222*

Butcher, J. E., 43, 47, *392, 399*
Butler, W. T., 350, *351*
Button, E. J., 94, *103*
Butts, J. A., 285, *295*

Cabrugao, R., *148*
Cachelin, F. M., 95, *103*
Cadenhead, C., 282, *296*
Cain, L., 152, 167, *169*
Caldwell, H., 316, *321*
Caldwell, L. L., 43, *51*
Caldwell, M. A., 208, *220*
Calhoun, K. S., 279, 280, *295*
Callahan, J. E., 278, *298*
Camarena, P. M., 208, *220*
Camfield, C. S., *325*
Camfield, P. R., *325*
Campagna, D. S., 291, *295*
Campbell, J. R., 380, *400*
Campbell, K. T., 259, *272*
Cantwell, D. P., *321*
Carlson, C. I., *374*
Carlson, N. I., *298*
Carnegie Corporation of New York, 334,
        350
Carnegie Council on Adolescent Devel-
        opment, 264, *272,* 330, *332,*
        358, 372
Carr, S. J., *103*
Carrington, B., 382, *401*
Cascio, W. F., 358, *372*
Caspi, *187*
Cassuto, N., *324*
Castaneda, A., 161, *169*
Catsambis, S., 38, *47,* 380–382, *400*
Cauce, A. M., 160, *170,* 184, *199,* 210,
        220, 384, 400
Cauffman, E., 100, *103*
Cazenave, N. A., 282, *295*
Cervantes, R. C., 138, *149*
Cervera, N. J., 230, *243*
Chan, C. S., 164, *169,* 283, *295*
Chan, S., *148*
Chandler, M., 124, *127*
Chandra, A., 310, *319,* 339, *350*
Chapman, V., *266*
Chappel, R., 382, *400*
Chatoor, I., 97, *103*
Chavira, V., 37, *50*

D'Emilio, J., 335, *351*
Denham, S. A., 65, *81*
Denner, J., 28, *46*
De Vos, E., 294, *299*
Deyhle, D., 216, *221*
DeZolt, D. M., 257, *272*
Di Blasio, F. A., 229, *243*
Dickens, M. N., 379, *400*
DiClemente, R. J., 9, *17*, 283, *296*
Diggens, J., 94, *105*
Dimiceli, S., 265, *272*
Dines, G., 116, *127*
DiNicola, V. F., 139, *147*
Doll, B., 206, 211, *221*
Doll, H. A., *103*
Doll, J., 230, *243*
Dollinger, S. J., 124, 126, *127*, *128*
Donahue, M. J., 265, *272*
Donovan, J. E., 315, *320*
Donovan, P., 338, 345, *351*
Dooley, J. M., *325*
Dornbusch, S. M., 383, *403*
Dorney, J., 29, 45, 47, 193, *199*, *200*
Douglas, J. D., 61, *79*
Downs, A. C., 290, *295*
Dryfoos, J. G., 5, 8, *17*
DuBois, D. L., 209–211, *221*
Duff, J. L., 207, 210, 216, *221*
Dukes, R. L., 36, *48*, 124, *127*
Duncan, G. J., 6, *17*, 117, *127*, 211, *220*
Duncan-Ricks, E. N., 231, *243*
Dunn, D. W., 313, *319*
Dunteman, G. H., 68, *79*
DuRant, R. H., 282, *296*, 311, 315, *320*
Durlak, J. A., 362, 363, *372*
Durst, D., 284, *296*
Dweck, C. S., 60, 61, *79*
Dziuba-Leatherman, J., *296*

Eagly, A. H., 27, *48*
Earls, F., 193, *203*
Early, D. M., 61, *79*
Early-Zald, M. B., 98, *105*
East, P. L., 229, 231, 232, *243*
Eaves, L., *104*
Eccles, J. S., 12, *17*, 54–57, 59–62, 65–68, 70–72, 73, 74, 78-83, 257, *272*, 387, *400*

Eder, D., 207, 212, 214, 215, 218, 219, *221*, *222*
Edmonston, B., 145, *149*
Egan, J., 97, *103*
Egan, M. G., 135, *148*
Egeland, B., 185, *199*
Ehrhardt, A. A., 349, 350, *351*
Eisenberg, L., 338, *350*
Eisman, S., 344, *353*
Elder, G. H., Jr., 30, *48*, 138, *147*
Elkind, D., 72, *80*
Ellen, J. M., 305, 308, *320*, *321*
Ellertson, C., 347, *351*
Ellickson, P. L., 312, *320*
Ellinwood, C. G., 366, *372*
Elliott, G., *321*
Ellis, J., 267, *272*
Elster, A. B., 306, 307, 308, *320*, *324*
Ely, S., *106*
Emmons, C., 211, *223*
Eng, T. R., 350, *351*
Engelhard, G., Jr., 381, *401*
English, A., 346, *351*
Enright, A. B., 95, *108*
Ensminger, M. E., 390, *400*
Epstein, J., 209, 211, *221*, *222*
Erickson, M. T., *374*
Erikson, E. H., 11, *17*, 123, *127*, *287*, *296*
Erkut, S., 43, *48*, 94, *103*, 184, *199*
Eron, L. D., *296*
Escobedo, L. G., 315, *320*
Eshleman, M. A., *200*
Espin, O. M., 132, 133, 142, *147*, 188, *199*
Esquivel, G., 136, *148*
Evahn, C., 60, *82*
Evans, C., 214, 218, *222*, 259, *272*
Evans, M. A., 387, *400*
Ey, S., *323*
Eyre, S. L., 313, *321*

Fabian, L. J., 186, *199*
Fairburn, C. G., 95, 97–101, *103*, *107*, *108*
Fallon, P., 95, *105*
Faludi, S., 168, *170*

Guendelman, S., 142, *147*
Guilkey, D. K., 265, *272*
Gulerce, A., 126, *127*
Gullotta, T. P., 123, *126*
Gupta, O. K., 139, *147*
Gupta, S. O., 139, *147*
Guroff, J. J., *104*
Gustafson, K. E., 364, *373*
Gustavson, C. R., 94, *106*
Gustavson, J. C., 94, *106*
Guthrie, B. J., 316, *321*
Gutiérrez, L., 160, *170*
Guyver, A., *324*
Gwizdala, J., 379, *401*

Habenicht, M., *148*
Haffner, D. W., 339, 340, *341, 351*
Haggerty, R. J., 306, *321*
Hahn, C. L., 396, 397, *401*
Hall, C., 230, *245*
Hall, E. R., 279, *296*
Halpern, D. F., 152, 168, *170*
Halsey, L., *321*
Hamm, J. V., 210, *222*
Hammer, L. D., *104, 321*
Handal, P. J., 282, *298*
Handley, M., *319*
Hanmer, T. J., 191, 200, 207, 222, 387,
     397, 401, 402
Hansen, W. B., 9, *17*
Hanusa, B. H., 381, *400*
Harding, R. K., 135, *147*
Hare, B. R., 393, *401*
Hare-Mustin, R. T., 151, *170*
Haritos, C., 151–153, *171*
Harkness, W. L., 232, *246*
Harlow, C., 282, *297*
Harmon, B., 283, *295*
Harnisch, D. L., *72*
Harnish, D. L., *83*
Harold, R. D., 56, 57, 59, 61, 62, 65, 66,
     79, 80, 83
Harris, J. R., 13, *17*
Harris, K. M., 18, 202, *324*
Harris, L. J., 182, 184, 200, 202, 203,
     283, *295*
Harris, M. G., 216, *223*
Hart, D., 124, *128*
Harter, S., 56, 68, 70–72, *81, 393, 401*

Hartman, C., 286, *297*
Hartman-Halbertal, T., 192, *200*
Hartup, W., 209, *223*
Hasemeier, C. M., *322*
Haskins, R., 344, *351*
Hatfield, E., 86, *104*
Hauser, S., 360, *373*
Hawes, S. E., *17*
Hawk, D., 135, *147*
Hawley, D. R., 144, *148*
Haydel, F., *104*
Hayes, M., 395, *399*
Hayes-Bautista, D., 166, *170*
Haynes, N., 211, *223*
Hays, R. D., 312, *320*
Hayward, C., *104, 313, 321*
Healy, J. M., 131, *149, 153, 172*
Heath, A., *104*
Heath, S. B., 264, 267, *273*
Heatherton, T. F., 98, *104*
Hechinger, Fred M., 334, *351*
Hedberg, V., 307, *324*
Helmreich, R., 26, *51*
Helson, R., 31, *50*
Henderson, D., 261, *274*
Henderson, L., 158, *170*
Hendren, M. C., 285, 286, 290, 292, *298*
Hendry, L. B., 385–387, *403*
Henneberger, M., 44, *49*
Henning-Stout, M., 258, *273*
Herdt, G., 34, *49*
Herek, G. M., 385, *401*
Hergenrother, M. A., *275*
Herman, C. P., 100, *106*
Herman-Giddens, M. E., 308, *322*
Hernandez, D. G., 357, *373*
Hernandez, M., 140, *148*
Hernandez Jozefowicz, D. M., 38, *50*
Herrling, S., 193, *197*
Hershey, M., 396, *399*
Herzog, D. B., 95, *104*
Hesse-Biber, S., 93, *104*
Hey, V., 215, *223*
Heyle, A. M., 28, *49*
Hibbard, J., *322*
Higgins, E. T., 30, 46, 73, *81*
Higgins, T. E., 237, 239, 240, *245*
Hill, J. P., 29, 30, 32, 49, 61, 73, *81,*
     378, 401

Hill, K. T., 72, 81, 83
Hilliard, W., 44, 49
Hillje, L. S., 290, 295
Himes, J., 203
Hinderly, H. H., 127
Hines, P. M., 158, 165, 170
Hinton-Nelson, M., 359, 374
Hiraga, Y., 400
Hirsch, B. J., 209–211, 221
Hirschman, C., 138, 148
Hjelte, L., 313, 322
Ho, C. K., 283, 297
Hoagwood, K., 304, 311, 322
Hoek, H. W., 86, 104
Hoffman, J. M., 60, 82
Hoffman, J. P., 265, 274
Hoffman, L. W., 12, 17
Hoffman, S., 336, 352
Hofman, J. E., 209, 224
Holbrey, A., 94, 108
Holden, N. L., 98, 104
Holland, J., 234–236, 243, 244
Holland, N. E., 151–153, 171
Hollinger, C. L., 55, 81
Holloway, C. D., 232, 246
Holloway, R. L., 323
Holmes, R. A., 297
Holtzman, W., 359, 373
Homma-True, R., 28, 49
hooks, b., 40, 49, 116, 128
Hope, R. A., 103
Hopkins, P., 266, 271
Hopkins, S., 317, 322
Hopp, C., 38, 49
Hops, H., 86, 105
Hopwood, T., 382, 401
Horowitz, H. A., 90, 106
Horowitz, R., 286, 297
Horwood, L. J., 98, 103
Hotz, V. J., 336, 352
Howard, K. I., 5, 18
Howard, M., 352
Hoyle, S. G., 209, 220
Hsu, J., 96, 108
Hsu, L. G., 94, 104
Huba, G. J., 229, 244
Hudson, B., 177, 179
Hughes, J., 200, 366, 373
Humez, J. M., 116, 127

Hunter, A. G., 316, 321
Hurlbut, G., 156, 170
Hurtado, M. P., 316, 322
Hurtig, A. L., 30, 49
Huselid, R., 229, 243
Huster, G. A., 313, 319
Huston, A. C., 56, 59, 62, 81, 378, 401
Huston, T. L., 124, 128
Hutchins, L., 262, 273
Hyde, J. D., 17
Hyde, J. S., 38, 49
Hymel, S., 206, 220

Igra, V., 6, 10, 17, 308, 310, 322, 323
Imhof, E. A., 360, 372
Incorvaia, J. A., 366, 373
Ingham, R., 231, 244
Ingrassia, M., 390, 401
Irby, M. A., 196, 201
Ireland, M., 18, 202, 324
Irwin, C. E., Jr., 305, 308, 313, 319, 320,
    321, 323, 334, 352
Israel, A. C., 92, 93, 108

Jack, D., 213, 223
Jacklin, C., 116, 128
Jackson, S. A., 43, 49
Jacobs, C., 97, 108
Jacobs, J., 62, 80
Jaffe, P. G., 279, 297
James, A., 121, 128, 166, 171
James, W., 68, 81
Janus, M., 286, 290, 297
Jefferson, K. W., 229, 245
Jenkins, M. J., 279, 297
Jenkins, Y., 127
Jensen, L., 137, 138, 148
Jensen, P. S., 304, 311, 322, 359, 361,
    374
Jessor, R., 208, 223, 315, 320
Jimerson, D. C., 104
Joe, K., 284, 298
Joffe, A., 313, 325
Johannesson, M., 313, 322
Johnson, B. G., 362, 373
Johnson, C., 95, 108, 381, 401
Johnson, J., 108

Johnson, K., 306, 324
Johnson, L., 17
Johnson, N. G., 4, 17
Johnson, S. A., 229, 244
Johnson, Y. M., 275
Jones, B., 382, 401
Jones, C., 315, 319
Jones, D. C., 209, 210, 223, 391, 402
Jones, E. D., 274
Jones, J., 18, 202, 324
Jones, J. M., 346, 353
Jones, R., 103
Jones, S., 317, 322
Jordan, J., 116, 128, 207, 223
Jorgensen, S. R., 229, 244
Joseph, G., 192, 200
Joyce, M. R., 366, 372
Jozefowicz, D. M. H., 57, 62 64, 65, 67, 68, 79, 80, 81

Kaahumanu, L., 262, 273
Kaczala, C. M., 80
Kagan, J., 321
Kagan, S., 160, 170
Kagawa-Singer, M., 4, 17, 302, 316, 322
Kahn, J., 311, 320
Kahn, M. W., 283, 297
Kaiser Family Foundation and Children Now, 118, 122, 128
Kalikow, K., 108
Kalliopuska, M., 393, 402
Kamp, J., 99, 105
Kang, M., 312, 321
Kanouse, D. E., 310, 324
Kantor, L., 341, 352
Kaplan, A. G., 85, 104, 116, 128, 207, 223
Kaplan, A. S., 103
Kaplan, D. W., 316, 319
Karweit, N., 211, 222
Kashani, J. H., 286, 297
Kassett, J. A., 97, 104
Katchadourian, H., 280, 297
Katkovsky, W., 60, 78
Katz, P. A., 4, 17, 31, 49, 302, 322
Kaufman, J., 319
Kawaguchi, M. C., 350, 354
Kaye, J. W., 231, 245

Kaye, W. H., 97, 105
Kazdin, A. E., 311, 312, 322
Kazuba, D. M., 104
Kearney-Cooke, A., 97, 98, 104, 107
Keating, D. P., 274
Keita, G. P., 298
Kelleher, K. J., 304, 308, 322
Keller, M. B., 95, 104
Kelly, E., 151–153, 171
Kelly, K. R., 379, 402
Kelsey, T., 278, 298
Kendler, K. S., 92, 97, 98, 104, 108, 200
Kennedy, R. E., 88, 106
Kennedy, S., 103
Kenney, A., 344, 352
Kerlinger, F., 125, 128
Kerr, B. A., 55, 62, 81
Kessler, J., 361, 373
Kessler, R. C., 104, 186, 200
Keyl, P. M., 316, 322
Khoury, E. L., 140, 150, 383, 404
Killen, J. D., 101, 104, 321
Kilpatrick, D. G., 280, 297
Kim, T., II, 283, 297
Kimchi, J., 92, 95, 105
Kinney, D., 218, 221
Kinzie, J. D., 136, 147, 148
Kippax, S., 340, 351
Kirby, D., 340–342, 352
Kitayama, S., 21, 23
Kite, M. E., 28, 49
Kitzinger, C., 262, 273
Kitzinger, J., 238, 244
Klaw, E. L., 385, 387, 402
Klebanov, P. K., 211, 220
Kleiber, D. A., 43, 51
Klein, J. D., 307, 313, 320
Klentz, B., 86, 105
Kline, B. E., 378, 381, 388, 389, 394, 402
Klingaman, L. R., 232, 246
Klingenspor, B., 96, 105
Klitsner, I. N., 310, 322
Knight, G. P., 160, 170
Knopf, D. K., 319, 323
Kobak, R. R., 91, 105
Kobasa, S., 189, 190, 200
Koch, G. G., 322
Kohlberg, L., 29, 49

Kohut, H., 366, 373
Koivula, N., 382, 402
Kolbe, L., 352
Kono, D. M., 382, 403
Koocher, G. P., 364, 373
Kopala, M., 136, 138, 148
Korman, M., 368, 373
Koss, M. P., 279–282, 296–298
Kott, A., 307, 322
Kou, W. H., 190
Kraemer, H. C., 321
Kramer, H., 104
Kratzer, L., 60, 82
Kroll, J., 135, 136, 148
Kunkes, C. H., 231, 245
Kuo, W. H., 200
Kupermink, G. P., 193, 197
Kurian, G., 139, 148
Kuznets, N. J., 306, 320

LaBrecque, S. V., 44, 48
LaFromboise, T. D., 28, 49, 121, 128, 156, 157, 160, 166, 171
La Greca, A. M., 374
Laine-Ammara, G., 324
Lakoff, R. T., 86, 105
Lampert, C., 97, 108
Landrine, H., 28, 49, 128, 151, 152, 171
Landry, M. J., 312, 322
Langer, L. M., 232, 246
Langman, J., 196, 201
Larkin, K., 201
Larmer, B., 139, 148
Larsen, A., 201
Larson, R., 29, 50
Laursen, B., 206, 223
Lavine, J. R., 274
Lavori, P. W., 95, 104
Leadbeater, B. R., 185, 189, 196, 200, 207, 223
Leary, R., 381, 387, 399
LeCompte, M., 216, 221
Lee, C., 43, 47
Lee, D. D., 136, 148
Lee, E., 158, 161, 171
Lee, L., 294
Lee, S., 188, 200
Lee, V. E., 259, 260, 273
Lees, S., 237, 244

Leffert, N., 229, 244
Lemanek, K. L., 374
Leon, G. R., 98, 99, 105
Leonard-Spark, P. J., 137, 148
LePore, P. C., 259, 273
Lester, C., 317, 322
Levine, M. P., 87, 100, 106, 107
Levin-Epstein, J., 347, 352
Levinson, D., 31, 49
Levitt, M., 389, 402
Levy, G. D., 44, 50
Lewin Group, 317, 322
Lewinsohn, P. M., 86, 105, 315, 320, 322
Lewis, C., 302, 319
Lewis, J., 192, 200
Leyba, C., 284, 298
Li, A. K. F., 379, 402
Licht, B. G., 60, 61, 79
Liker, J. K., 138, 147
Lilienfeld, L. R., 97, 105
Lilly, M. W., 62, 82
Limber, S. P., 340, 352
Lin, E., 103
Linder, P., 282, 296
Linn, E., 260, 273
Liston, W. J., 317, 320
Litt, I. F., 104, 201, 321
Lock, A., 126, 127
Lock, S. E., 229, 231, 244, 265, 273
Locke, C., 136, 148
Loken, G. A., 286, 294, 295
Looney, J. G., 135, 147
Lord, S. E., 61, 71–74, 80, 81
Lorde, A., 116, 128, 239, 244
Loredo, C., 260, 273
Losoff, M., 209, 221
Louie, L., 284, 298
Louis Harris and Associates, 304, 310, 323
Lucas, A. R., 99, 105
Luepker, R. V., 323
Luhtanen, R., 37, 47
Luke, M. D., 382, 402
Luker, K., 231, 244, 336, 339, 341, 349, 352
Luthar, S. S., 182, 184, 185, 201

Luu, M., 284, 298
Ly, M., 148
Lyman, R. D., 367, 373
Lynch, M. E., 29, 30, 32, 49, 73, 81, 378, 401
Lynsky, M. T., 98, 103
Lyons, N. P., 191, 200, 207, 222, 387, 397, 398, 401, 402

Maccoby, E. E., 12, 17, 116, 128, 187, 201
Mac Iver, D., 56, 80, 83
MacKenzie, R., 310, 322
Mackenzie, T., 148
MacLean, C., 104
Macpherson, P., 43, 49
Maehr, M. L., 72, 83
Maggs, J. L., 390, 402
Magnani, L. E., 190, 201
Magnusson, D., 71, 82, 99, 107, 392, 402
Magruder, B., 262, 275
Mahler, M., 366, 373
Makepeace, J. M., 278, 279, 298
Malavé, I., 182, 199
Malave, I., 233, 243
Males, M. A., 187, 201, 349, 352
Mallon, G. P., 117, 128
Mandel, L. S., 275
Manley, J. J., 61, 81
Mann, J., 379, 380, 389, 402
Manoff, S., 313, 325
Manson, S. M., 311, 323
Mapelli, S. D., 86, 105
Maracek, J., 170
Marcus, H. R., 21, 23
Marcus, M., 87, 107
Marecek, J., 17, 151
Marin, B. V., 162, 172, 231, 242
Marin, G., 162, 172
Marino, M., 93, 104
Maritato, N., 117, 127
Mark, B. S., 366, 373
Markowitz, F., 384, 402
Markus, A., 306, 324
Marsh, H. W., 43, 49, 259, 273, 274
Marshall, N. L., 260, 275

Marsiglio, W., 340, 352
Martin, C. L., 61, 62, 82
Martin, G., 392, 403
Martinez, R., 36, 48, 124, 127
Maruish, M., 360, 372
Marx, F., 43, 48, 94, 103
Maschino, M. F., 274
Mason, C., 400
Masten, A. S., 92, 103, 184, 185, 201
Masterson, J. F., 367, 373
Maton, K. I., 265, 274
Matula, K. E., 124, 128
Maxwell, M. E., 104
Mayer, R., 341, 342, 352
Maynard, R. A., 336, 352
Mazur, A., 86, 105
Mboya, M. M., 379, 402
McBride Murray, V., 33, 49
McCall, R. B., 60, 82
McCarthy, K., 61, 81
McCloskey, L. A., 136, 138, 148
McClure, F. H., 364, 374
McCormack, A., 286, 297
McCormick, J., 45, 50, 189, 202, 216, 223
McDonald, D. L., 32, 50
McElroy, S., 336, 352
McFarlane, D. R., 338, 353
McGinn, P. V., 66, 82
McGinnis, J. M., 309, 323
McGoldrick, M., 131, 148, 153, 171
McGonagle, K. A., 200
McGuigan, K. A., 312, 320
McInerney, T. K., 322
McKinney, J. P., 32, 50
McLanahan, S. S., 336, 351
McLaughlin, M. W., 196, 201, 264, 267, 273
McLeod, J., 192, 201
McLoyd, V. C., 38, 50
McMillan, J. H., 391, 402
McNamara, J. R., 364, 373
Mecklenburg, M. E., 342, 352
Medrich, E. A., 211, 220
Meece, J. L., 57, 61, 80, 82
Meier, K. J., 338, 353
Melton, G. B., 346, 353
Melville, M. B., 157, 171
Menvielle, E., 97, 103

Nguyen, N. A., 161, *171*
Nguyen, T., *148*
Nicholson, H. J., 264, *274*
Nicholson, J., 364, *374*
Nightingale, E. O., *201*, 302, *323*, 333, *353*
Nirenberg, J. D., 362, *374*
Noam, G., 360, *373*
Nolen-Hoeksema, S., 32, *50*, 101, *105*, 186, *201*
Noller, P., 393, *403*
Nonas, C. A., 95, *108*
Normandin, D., 124, *128*
Norring, C. E. A., 95, *107*
Norris, A., 230, *244*
Norvell, N. K., 95, *104*
Nottelmann, E. D., 359, 361, *374*
Novins, D. K., 311, *323*
Nurmi, J., 395, 396, *403*
Nutting, P. A., *322*

Obarzanek, E., *106*
Obeidallah, D. A., 185, *198*
O'Brien, K. M., 55, *83*
O'Connor, C., 193, 195, *202*
O'Connor, K. G., 314, *320*
O'Connor, M. E., *103*
Oden, M. H., 66, *83*
O'Donnell, R., 97, *103*
Offer, D., 5, *18*, 203, 360, *374*
Offer, J., 360, *374*
Office of Technology Assessment, 298, 302, 304, 307, 308, 310, 313, *323*
Ogbu, J. U., 184, 188, *199*, *202*
Okazaki, S., 135, *147*
O'Keeffe, J. E., 333, 336, 346, 347, *353*, *354*
Okun, M. A., 190, *202*
Olmsted, M. P., 100, *103*
Orbach, S., 72, *82*
Ordonez, N., *400*
Orenstein, P., 69, *82*, 191, *202*, 217, *223*, 260, *274*
Orr, E., 190, *202*
Orvin, G. H., 357, 364, *374*
Osgood, D. W., 315, *323*
Osipow, S. H., 124, *129*
Ostrov, E., 5, *18*

Oswalt, W. H., 156, *171*
Otero-Sabogal, R., 162, *172*
Ouellette, S., 189, 190, *202*
Ozer, E., 28, *49*
Ozer, E. M., 319, *323*
Ozorak, E. W., 265, *274*

Padilla, A. M., 138, *149*, 155, *171*
Paget, W. B., 95, *103*
Paikoff, R. L., 87, *104*, 229, *242*
Pantell, R. H., 302, *319*
Paperny, D., 307, *324*
Papini, D. R., 209, *223*, 395, *403*
Parcel, G. S., *323*
Parehk, A. L., 283, *300*
Parker, J., 208, *223*
Parsons, J. E., 61, *82*
Paskewitz, D. A., 184, *204*
Pasternak, S. R., 66, *80*
Pastor, J., 45, *50*, 187–189, 193, 196, *202*, 216, 217, *223*
Patterson, C. J., 34, *50*, 357, *374*
Patton, W., 393, *403*
Paxton, S. J., 94, *105*
Pearce, C. M., 392, *403*
Pedersen, D. M., 382, *403*
Peirce, R. S., 229, *243*
Peiser, N. L., 66, *80*
Pellegrini, D. S., *201*
Pendergast, J., *324*
Pendergrast, R. A., 282, *296*
Peplau, L. A., 208, *220*
Perez-Stable, E. J., 162, *172*
Perrone, P. A., 387, *403*
Perry, C. L., 98, *105*
Perwien, A. R., 311, *319*
Peters, L., 95, *105*
Petersen, A. C., 30, 37, 48, *49*, 88, *106*, 187, 191, 196, 198, *201*, *202*, 208, 209, 220, 221, 229, *244*, 302, 311, *323*, 333, *353*
Peterson, L., 310, *319*, 339, *350*
Peterson, L. P., 310, *324*
Petrie, T. A., 94, *106*
Petti, T., 304, *322*
Peveler, R. C., *103*
Phibbs, C., 302, *319*
Philip, K., 385–387, *403*

Yee, D., 60, *80, 83*
Yeung, W., 6, *17*
Yew, W., 141, *150*
Yong, F. L., 379–382, *404*
Yoon, K. S., *80, 83*
Yoshihama, M., 283, *300*
Yoshikawa, H., 28, *46*
Yost, P. R., 265, *272*
Young, J. L., 394, *404*
Youniss, J., 124, *129*, 206, 209, *225*
Younkin, S. L., 190, *204*

Zabin, L. S., *352*

Zager, K., 370, *375*
Zahn-Waxler, C., 117, *129*
Zamur, A., 124, *128*
Zanga, J. R., 316, *325*
Zatz, M., 286, *300*
Zautra, A. J., 190, *202*
Zhao, S., *200*
Zhou, M., 134, 138, 143, *150*
Zigler, E., 182, 184, *201*
Zimmerman, R. S., 140, *150*, 232, *246*, 383, *404*
Zito, J. M., 311, *324*
Zucker, K. J., 34, *46*

SUBJECT INDEX

Bartelt, David, 184
Bateson, Mary Catherine, 271
Bellotti v. Baird, 345–346
Big Brothers/Big Sisters, 385
Bisexuality, 261–263
Black girls/adolescents. *See* African American girls/adolescents
Blum, Robert, 197
Body image
  and culture, 9–10, 85–86
  and eating disorders, 34–36, 86–88, 90, 96–98, 101
  and puberty, 86
  and self-esteem, 73
  and sexuality, 187
Brown, Lyn Mikel, 192
Bulimia nervosa, 76, 86

Cambodians, 135–136
Carey v. Population Services International, 337
Caring adults, relationships with, 183, 184, 191–196, 257–258
Carnegie Council on Adolescent Development, 264, 331, 334
Census data, 117–122
Centers for Disease Control and Prevention, 335
Chapman, Valerie, 266
Child Health Insurance Program, 306
Childhood and Beyond, 57
Childhood obesity, 99
Children, development of gender identity in, 29–31
Chronic physical disorders, 312–313
City of Akron v. Akron Center for Reproductive Health, 346
Cleary, Paul, 304
Clinical practice, 356–367. *See also* Health care
  and lack of role models, 356–357
  and lack of supportive culture, 356
  and prevalence of psychological problems, 359–360
  public health issues related to, 361–363
  social/cultural influences affecting, 357–359
  types of psychological problems addressed in, 360–361

and unique needs/problems of adolescent girls, 363–367
with victims of prostitution and dating violence, 293–294
Clinton, Hillary Rodham, 161
Cognitive-behavior therapy, 94
Cognitive development, gender and, 29
Collins, Patricia Hill, 193
Color, people of. *See* Ethnic/racial minority girls/adolescents; Immigrant adolescent girls of color
Committee on School Health, 361
Commonwealth Fund, 9, 304
Communication, 395
  and clinical practice, 359
  and health care, 313–314
Community, 183
  clinical practice and changes in, 358
  connection with, 188
  involvement in, 193
Community programs/organizations, 263–267, 269–271
  religion, 265–266
  schools, collaboration with, 267–269
  youth organizations, 264
Competence, self-perceptions of. *See* Self-concept(s)
Consumer Assessment of Health Plans Survey, 304
Contraceptive risk taking, 231
Contraceptives, 337
Coping skills, and eating disorders, 94–95
Counseling, 309–310
"Crossroads," adolescent, 31–32, 377
Cubans, 157
Cultural identity, 12, 142–144
Culture
  and gender roles/stereotypes, 26–28
  and physical attractiveness, 85–86
Cystic fibrosis, 313

Date rape, 279–281
Dating, 32–33
Dating violence, 278–284
  antecedent factors in, 279
  ethnic differences in, 281–284
  interventions for victims of, 293–294
  prevalence of, 278–281
  rape, date/acquaintance, 279–281
  scope of, 278

and struggle for self and voice, 288–
290
Decision making, sexual, 229–233
Delpit, Lisa, 193
Depression, 9, 32, 99, 140, 186, 311, 315
Desire, sexual, 238–242
Development, 6
effect of violence on, 287–288
of gender identity, 29–32
and identity formation, 11
problems in, 360
*Diagnostic and Statistical Manual of Mental
Disorders (DSM)*, 86, 311, 359–
360
Discrimination, 140
Disidentification, 68–69
Diversity, 6–7, 358, 383–385
Dryfoos, Joy, 5–6, 8
DSM. *See Diagnostic and Statistical Manual
of Mental Disorders*

Early Head Start, 361
Eating Attitudes Test (EAT), 35
Eating disorders, 9–10, 76, 86–102, 188
and body image, 86–88, 90, 96–98,
101
and childhood obesity, 99
familial context of, 92, 97–98
and intelligence, 93
model of risk and protective factors for
development of, 88–91
and perfectionism, 100
and personal characteristics, 93–95,
98–100
resilience against, 91–95
and self-esteem, 94–95
and social class, 92
social context of, 95
sociocultural context of, 95–96
and timing of menarche, 99–100
Education. *See also* Academic motivation/
performance; Schools
parent, 389
sexuality, 338–341
single-sex, 378–379
Eisenstadt v. Baird, 337
Elementary and Secondary Education
Act, 255
Emma Willard School, 397–398
Emotional intelligence, 93
Emotional self-disclosure, 395

Erikson, Erik, 11, 287
Erotic voice, 239
Ethnic identity, 12
Ethnicity, 6
Ethnic/racial minority girls/adolescents,
151–169. *See also specific groups,
e.g.:* African American girls/ado-
lescents
achievement motivation among, 38
census data on, 117–122
and family/community, 159–163
and feminism, 116
gender/racial identity of, 163–167
and gender stereotypes, 27–29
and historical legacy, 155–159
identity development in, 122–125
immigrant. *See* Immigrant adolescent
girls of color
and psychology's role, 126
self-esteem in, 36–37, 70–77, 152, 164
socialization of, 40–45
unique challenges facing, 154–155

Family, 11–12
clinical practice and changes in, 358
connection with, 188, 193–195
and development, 287–288
and eating disorders, 92, 97–98
of immigrant adolescent girls of color,
139–140, 144–145
Family planning services, 336–338
Family Planning Services and Population
Research Act, 336
Fathers, 195
The Feminine Mystique (Betty Friedan),
115
Feminism, 7, 44–45
adolescent sexuality, research on, 233–
242
waves of, 115–116
Filipinos, 141, 159
Fine, Michelle, 184, 185, 227–228, 238
Fordham, Signithia, 184–185, 188
Freud, Anna, 8
Friedan, Betty, 115
Friendly PEERsuasion, 389
Friendships and peer relations, 12–13,
205–219, 391–392
and gender differences, 207–209
girls' experience and understanding of,
209

Identity, gender. *See* Gender identity
Identity development, 11
  in ethnic/racial minority girls, 122–125
  in immigrant adolescent girls of color, 141–142
IHS (Indian Health Service), 166
Immigrant adolescent girls of color, 131–146
  acculturation of, 138–139
  cultural identity of, 142–144
  and escape from violence, 135–136
  and family, 139–140, 144–145
  identity development in, 141–142
  language fluency of, 137, 141
  and motives for immigration, 134–135
  and parent–child relationships, 139
  socioeconomic status of, 137–138
  and sociopolitical climate of 1990s, 145–146
  special challenges facing, 132–133
  statistics on, 133–134
Indian Health Service (IHS), 166
Individual agency, 185–186
Intelligence, and eating disorders, 93
Interpersonal violence, 363

Jamaicans, 139
Japanese, 159
Juvenile Justice and Delinquency Act of 1974, 285

Kasinga, Fauziya, 134–135
Khmer Rouge, 135
Kitzinger, Jenny, 238
Kohlberg, L., 29
Koreans, 159

Lakota, 166
Language fluency (of immigrant adolescent girls), 137, 141
Latina girls/adolescents, 157, 160–162, 164, 166, 167
  body image in, 36
  census data on, 119–120, 122
  dating violence among, 282–283
  immigrants, 133–134, 139–140
  and school, 185
  self-esteem in, 36, 152

socialization of, 42
unique challenges facing, 383
Leadbeater, Bonnie, 196
Leaders, adolescent girls as future, 395–398
Lees, Sue, 237
Legal system, 277–278
Lesbians and lesbianism, 34, 86, 238, 261–263, 385
Livingston, Bob, 337–338
Locus of control, 59–61
Luker, Kristen, 231

Machismo, 28
MAGIC. *See* Maryland Adolescent Growth in Context
Malcriado, 161
Manifest destiny, 155–156
Mann Act, 290
Marginalization, 111
Marianismo, 28, 164
Maryland Adolescent Growth in Context (MAGIC), 57, 70, 73, 74
Masculine skills, 74–75
Masten, Anne, 184
Math competence, self-perceptions of, 57–59, 379–380
Medicaid, 315, 337
Medical Outcomes Survey 36-Item Short Form Health Survey, 315–316
Men, positive relationships with, 195
Menarche, timing of, 99–100
Mental health, 311–312, 360–361. *See also* Clinical practice
Mentoring, 385–387
Michigan Study of Adolescent Life Transitions (MSALT), 56–57, 63, 66, 69–71, 74, 75
Middle class, 18n2
Minorities. *See* Ethnic/racial minority girls/adolescents
Mothers, relationships with, 191–192
Ms. Foundation Research Roundtable, 184
MSALT. *See* Michigan Study of Adolescent Life Transitions
Musick, Judith, 188

National Academy of Sciences, 145

National Basketball Association (NBA), 382
National Depression Screening Day, 317
National Educational Longitudinal Study, 38
National Longitudinal Study on Adolescent Health, 5, 8, 11–12
National Organization for Women, 44
National Strategy on Teen Pregnancy, 317
Native American girls/adolescents, 166, 268
    acculturative challenges facing, 156–157
    census data on, 120–122
    dating violence among, 283–284
    and family, 160
    friendships/peer relationships among, 216
    and gender stereotypes, 28
Nava, Mica, 238
NBA (National Basketball Association), 382
Nixon, Richard, 336

Obesity, childhood, 99
Occupational ability, self-perceptions of, 63–65
O'Connor, Carla, 195
Offenders, female adolescents as, 285–287
Office of Juvenile Justice and Delinquency Prevention, 335
Ogbu, John, 184–185
Ohio v. Akron Center for Reproductive Health, 346
Othermothers, 193–194
Ouellette, Suzanne, 196

Parent education, 389
Parents/parenting
    and adolescent health care, 314–315
    and eating disorders, 97–98
    of immigrant adolescent girls of color, 132–133, 139–140
Pastor, Jennifer, 188
Paternalism (of court system), 286
Peer relations. See Friendships and peer relations

Perfectionism, 100
Personal Responsibility and Work Opportunity Reconciliation Act of 1996, 342–343
Person orientation, 68
Physical attractiveness, 85–86
Physical disorders, chronic, 312–313
Physical education, 382–383
Pipher, Mary, 8, 53, 161, 277, 356
Popularity, 214
Post-traumatic stress disorder (PSTD), 136
Pot, Pol, 135
Poverty, 6–7, 137–138, 316
Power relations, 211–217
Pratt, Richard H., 156
Pregnancy, teen, 33, 182, 187, 313–314, 317, 335–336
Prescription drugs, 310–311
PRISM (Program for Innovative Self-Management), 367
Problem behaviors, traditional focus on, 4
Program for Innovative Self-Management (PRISM), 367
Prostitution, teen, 284–285
PSTD (post-traumatic stress disorder), 136
Psychohistorical analysis, 155
Psychological disorders, 360–361
Psychology, 355. See also Clinical practice
    and feminism, 116
    graduate education/training in adolescent, 367–371
    transformative role of, 125–126
Puberty, 32, 85, 99–100, 313, 392–393
Public health, 361–363
Public Health Services Act, 336
Public policy, 333–335. See also Sexuality-related policies
Puerto Ricans, 157
Race, 6, 12. See also Ethnic/racial minority girls/adolescents
Racial socialization, 41
Rayburn, Carol, 266
Reagan administration, 344–345
Reid, Pamela T., 184
Relationships. See Caring adults, relationships with; Friendships and peer relations; Sexuality, female adolescent
Religiosity, 265–266

ABOUT THE EDITORS

Norine G. Johnson, PhD, is a member of the American Psychological Association (APA) Board of Directors and is the past president of the Division of the Psychology of Women. She is cochair of the APA's Presidential Task Force on Adolescent Girls. Dr. Johnson has a full-time independent practice in Quincy, Massachusetts, and specializes in adolescent girls' and women's issues. She is a clinical assistant professor in the Boston University Medical School, Department of Neurology. She is coeditor with Judith Worell of the volume, *Shaping the Future of Feminist Psychology: Education, Research, and Practice.* Dr. Johnson received her doctorate in clinical psychology from Wayne State University and did her postdoctoral work in the 2-year Program for Mental Health Planners/Administrators sponsored by Harvard Medical School.

Michael C. Roberts, PhD, ABPP, graduated from Purdue University in clinical psychology with a specialization in clinical child psychology, after completing his clinical internship at Oklahoma Children's Hospital. Dr. Roberts has served as editor for the *Journal of Pediatric Psychology and Children's Health Care.* He is the current editor of *Children's Services: Social Policy, Research, and Practice.* Dr. Roberts has served as president of the Society of Pediatric Psychology and of the Section on Clinical Child Psychology of the American Psychological Association (APA). Recently, he chaired the APA Committee on Children, Youth, and Families and now is the liaison between the APA and the American Academy of Pediatrics. His professional and research interests include topics in services for children and families in mental and physical health care, and public policy.

Judith Worell, PhD, is a professor of child clinical psychology in the Department of Educational and Counseling Psychology at the University of

Kentucky, where she teaches courses on social development, gender development, and counseling women. She is the author or coauthor of six prior books, is a member of numerous journal editorial and consulting boards, and was the editor of *Psychology of Women Quarterly* from 1989 to 1995. Dr. Worell has conducted research on feminist identity development and process and outcomes of feminist therapy and is a past president of the American Psychological Association Division of the Psychology of Women.